T0299363

NOTE ON THE AUTHOR

John Maynard Keynes was born in Cambridge in 1883, son of John Neville Keynes, later registrary of the university; his mother was one of the earliest women students. Educated at Eton and King's, he passed into the Civil Service in 1906, working for over two years in the India Office. He returned to Cambridge in 1908, became a Fellow of King's in 1909 and remained so until his death.

His first entry into public affairs came with his membership of the Royal Commission on Indian Finance and Currency of 1913. Soon after the outbreak of war in 1914 he was called to the Treasury. Over the next four years his ability and his immense capacity for work took him to the top. By 1919 he was principal Treasury representative at the Peace Conference at Versailles. His passionate disagreement with decisions regarding reparations led to his resignation and the writing of *The Economic Consequences of the Peace*. From then on, Keynes was a national figure, in the centre of every economic argument and the author of countless 'Keynes plans' to solve one problem after another.

In 1936 he published the most provocative book written by any economist of his generation. *The General Theory*, as it is known to all economists, cut through all the Gordian knots of pre-Keynesian discussion of the trade cycle and propounded a new approach to the determination of the level of economic activity, the problems of employment and unemployment, the causes of inflation, the strategies of budgetary policy. Argument about the book continued until his death in 1946 and still continues today.

THE COLLECTED WRITINGS OF
JOHN MAYNARD KEYNES

Managing Editors:
Professor Austin Robinson and Professor Donald Moggridge

John Maynard Keynes (1883–1946) was without doubt one of the most influential thinkers of the twentieth century. His work revolutionised the theory
and practice of modern economics. It has had a profound impact on the
way economics is taught and written, and on economic policy, around the
world. *The Collected Writings of John Maynard Keynes*, published in full in
electronic and paperback format for the first time, makes available in thirty
volumes all of Keynes's published books and articles. This includes writings
from his time in the India Office and Treasury, correspondence in which he
developed his ideas in discussion with fellow economists and correspondence
relating to public affairs. Arguments about Keynes's work have continued
long beyond his lifetime, but his ideas remain central to any understanding of
modern economics, and a point of departure from which each new generation
of economists draws inspiration.

This volume brings together Keynes's attempts to influence public opinion
and policy concerning primarily British affairs between 1922 and 1929. During this period, his major concerns were Britain's attempt to return to the
gold standard and its consequences, industrial policy (especially in the cotton textile industry) and unemployment policy, although he became briefly
involved in many other subjects. Most of the volume consists of Keynes's
journalism for the period, but it also contains his previously unpublished
evidence to official committees, anonymous contributions to the *Nation and
Athenaeum*, and related correspondence.

At a meeting of the Liberal Industrial Inquiry, 1927.

Sir Herbert Samuel, Walter Layton, David Lloyd George,
Hubert Henderson and J.M.K.

THE COLLECTED WRITINGS OF
JOHN MAYNARD KEYNES

VOLUME XIX

ACTIVITIES 1922–1929

THE RETURN TO GOLD AND
INDUSTRIAL POLICY

EDITED BY

DONALD MOGGRIDGE

CAMBRIDGE UNIVERSITY PRESS

FOR THE

ROYAL ECONOMIC SOCIETY

CAMBRIDGE
UNIVERSITY PRESS

University Printing House, Cambridge CB2 8BS, United Kingdom

One Liberty Plaza, 20th Floor, New York, NY 10006, USA

477 Williamstown Road, Port Melbourne, VIC 3207, Australia

4843/24, 2nd Floor, Ansari Road, Daryaganj, Delhi - 110002, India

79 Anson Road, #06-04/06, Singapore 079906

Cambridge University Press is part of the University of Cambridge.

It furthers the University's mission by disseminating knowledge in the pursuit of education, learning and research at the highest international levels of excellence.

www.cambridge.org
Information on this title: www.cambridge.org/9781107618015

© The Royal Economic Society 1981, 2013

Published for the Royal Economic Society throughout the world by Cambridge University Press

This edition published 2013
3rd printing 2013

A catalogue record for this publication is available from the British Library

ISBN 978-1-107-61801-5 Paperback

CONTENTS

GENERAL INTRODUCTION

This new standard edition of *The Collected Writings of John Maynard Keynes* forms the memorial to him of the Royal Economic Society. He devoted a very large share of his busy life to the Society. In 1911, at the age of twenty-eight, he became editor of the *Economic Journal* in succession to Edgeworth: two years later he was made secretary as well. He held these offices without intermittence until almost the end of his life. Edgeworth, it is true, returned to help him with the editorship from 1919 to 1925; Macgregor took Edgeworth's place until 1934, when Austin Robinson succeeded him and continued to assist Keynes down to 1945. But through all these years Keynes himself carried the major responsibility and made the principal decisions about the articles that were to appear in the *Economic Journal*, without any break save for one or two issues when he was seriously ill in 1937. It was only a few months before his death at Easter 1946 that he was elected president and handed over his editorship to Roy Harrod and the secretaryship to Austin Robinson.

In his dual capacity of editor and secretary Keynes played a major part in framing the policies of the Royal Economic Society. It was very largely due to him that some of the major publishing activities of the Society—Sraffa's edition of Ricardo, Stark's edition of the economic writings of Bentham, and Guillebaud's edition of Marshall, as well as a number of earlier publications in the 1930s—were initiated.

When Keynes died in 1946 it was natural that the Royal Economic Society should wish to commemorate him. It was perhaps equally natural that the Society chose to commemorate him by producing an edition of his collected works. Keynes himself had always taken a joy in fine printing, and the Society, with the help of Messrs Macmillan as publishers and the Cambridge University Press as printers, has been anxious to give Keynes's writings a permanent form that is worthy of him.

The present edition will publish as much as is possible of his work in the field of economics. It will not include any private and personal correspondence or publish many letters in the possession of his family. The edition is concerned, that is to say, with Keynes as an economist.

Keynes's writings fall into five broad categories. First there are the books which he wrote and published as books. Second there are collections of articles and pamphlets which he himself made during his lifetime (*Essays in Persuasion* and *Essays in Biography*). Third, there is a very considerable volume of published but uncollected writings—articles written for newspapers, letters to newspapers, articles in journals that have not been included in his two volumes of collections, and various pamphlets. Fourth, there are a few hitherto unpublished writings. Fifth, there is correspondence with economists and concerned with economics of public affairs. It is the intention of this series to publish almost completely the whole of the first four categories listed above. The only exceptions are a few syndicated articles where Keynes wrote almost the same material for publication in different newspapers or in different countries, with minor and unimportant variations. In these cases, this series will publish one only of the variations, choosing the most interesting.

The publication of Keynes's economic correspondence must inevitably be selective. In the day of the typewriter and the filing cabinet and particularly in the case of so active and busy a man, to publish every scrap of paper that he may have dictated about some unimportant or ephemeral matter is impossible. We are aiming to collect and publish as much as possible, however, of the correspondence in which Keynes developed his own ideas in argument with his fellow economists, as well as the more significant correspondence at times when Keynes was in the middle of public affairs.

Apart from his published books, the main sources available to those preparing this series have been two. First, Keynes in his will made Richard Kahn his executor and responsible for his economic papers. They have been placed in the Marshall Library of the University of Cambridge and have been available for this edition. Until 1914 Keynes did not have a secretary and his earliest papers are in the main limited to drafts of important letters that he made in his own handwriting and retained. At that stage most of the correspondence that we possess is represented by what he received rather than by what he wrote. During the war years of 1914–18 and 1940–6 Keynes was serving in the Treasury. With the opening in 1968 of the records under the thirty-year rule, the papers that he wrote then and between the wars have become available. From 1919 onwards, throughout the rest of his life, Keynes had the help of a secretary—for many years Mrs Stephens. Thus for the last twenty-five years of his working life we have in most cases the carbon copies of his own letters as well as the originals of the letters he received.

There were, of course, occasions during this period on which Keynes wrote himself in his own handwriting. In some of these cases, with the help of his correspondents, we have been able to collect the whole of both sides of some important interchanges, and we have been anxious, in justice to both correspondents, to see that both sides of the correspondence are published in full.

The second main source of information has been a group of scrapbooks kept over a very long period of years by Keynes's mother, Florence Keynes, wife of Neville Keynes. From 1919 onwards these scrapbooks contain almost the whole of Maynard Keynes's more ephemeral writing, his letters to newspapers and a great deal of material which enables one to see not only what he wrote but the reaction of others to his writing. Without these very carefully kept scrapbooks the task of any editor or biographer of Keynes would have been immensely more difficult.

The plan of the edition, as at present intended, is this. It will total thirty volumes. Of these the first eight are Keynes's published books from *Indian Currency and Finance*, in 1913, to the *General Theory* in 1936, with the addition of his *Treatise on Probability*. There next follow, as vols. IX and X, *Essays in Persuasion* and *Essays in Biography*, representing Keynes's own collections of articles. *Essays in Persuasion* differs from the original printing in two respects: it contains the full texts of the articles or pamphlets included in it and not (as in the original printing) abbreviated versions of these articles, and it also contains one or two later articles which are of exactly the same character as those included by Keynes in his original collection. In *Essays in Biography* there have been added a number of biographical studies that Keynes wrote both before and after 1933.

There will follow two volumes, XI–XII, of economic articles and correspondence and a further two volumes, already published, XIII–XIV, covering the development of his thinking as he moved towards the *General Theory*. There are included in these volumes such part of Keynes's economic correspondence as is closely associated with the articles that are printed in them. A supplement to these volumes, XXIX, prints some further material relating to the same issues, which has since been discovered.

The remaining fourteen volumes deal with Keynes's *Activities* during the years from the beginning of his public life in 1905 until his death. In each of the periods into which we divide this material, the volume concerned publishes his more ephemeral writings, all of it hitherto uncollected, his correspondence relating to these activities, and such other material and correspondence as is necessary to the understanding of Keynes's activities. These volumes are edited by Elizabeth Johnson and Donald Moggridge, and it has been their task to trace and interpret Keynes's activities sufficiently to make the material fully intelligible to a later generation. Elizabeth Johnson has been responsible for vols. XV–XVIII, covering Keynes's earlier years and his activities down to the end of World War I reparations and reconstruction. Donald Moggridge is responsible for all the remaining volumes recording Keynes's other activities from 1922 until his death in 1946.

The record of Keynes's activities during World War II is now complete with the publication of volumes XXV–XXVII. It thus remains to fill the gap between 1922 and 1939 with three volumes of which this is the first; to print certain of Keynes's published articles and the correspondence relating to them which have not appeared elsewhere in this edition, and to publish a volume of his social, political and literary writings.

Those responsible for this edition have been: Lord Kahn, both as Lord Keynes's executor and as a long and intimate friend of Lord Keynes, able to help in the interpreting of much that would be otherwise misunderstood; the late Sir Roy Harrod as the author of his biography; Austin Robinson as Keynes's co-editor on the *Economic Journal* and successor as Secretary of the Royal Economic Society. Austin Robinson has acted throughout as Managing Editor; Donald Moggridge is now associated with him as Joint Managing Editor.

In the early stages of the work Elizabeth Johnson was assisted by Jane Thistlethwaite, and by Mrs McDonald, who was originally responsible for the systematic ordering of the files of the Keynes papers. Judith Masterman for many years worked with Mrs Johnson on the papers. More recently Susan Wilsher, Margaret Butler and Leonora Woollam have continued the secretarial work. Barbara Lowe has been responsible for the indexing. Since 1977 Judith Allen has been responsible for much of the day-to-day management of the edition as well as seeing the volumes through the press.

EDITORIAL NOTE

In this and subsequent volumes, in general all of Keynes's own writings are printed in large type. All introductory matter and all writings by others than Keynes are printed in smaller type. The only exception to this general rule is that occasional short quotations from a letter from Keynes to his parents or to a friend, used in introductory passages to clarify a situation, are treated as introductory material and printed in the smaller type.

Most of Keynes's letters included in this and other volumes are reprinted from the carbon copies remaining among his papers. In most cases he added his initials to the carbon. We have no means of knowing in most circumstances whether the top copy sent to the recipient carried a more formal signature.

Most of Keynes's journalism appeared under his own name. However, in the case of *The Nation and Athenaeum* of which he was Chairman, Keynes wrote more than he signed. In determining what unsigned material was Keynes's we have used two sources of information: the incomplete run of marked copies of the magazine that survive in the Keynes Papers[1] and the two special scrapbooks of *Nation* articles which he asked his mother to keep and for which he provided the necessary information as regards unsigned articles. Naturally the two sources overlap on some occasions, as do other fragments surviving in the Keynes Papers, thus giving us more confidence about particular items.[2]

Keynes's own footnotes, as well as those of his correspondents,

[1] *The Nation*'s complete set of marked copies was destroyed during the Blitz.
[2] Sir Roy Harrod was thus mistaken when he suggested that Keynes, with one exception, 'contributed nothing to the paper which was not signed or initialled' (*The Life of John Maynard Keynes*, p. 337).

are indicated by asterisks or other symbols to distinguish them from the editorial footnotes indicated by numbers.

Crown copyright material appears with the permission of the Controller of Her Majesty's Stationery Office. The Social Sciences and Humanities Research Council of Canada provided financial support.

The Editor wishes to thank Gary Dobinson for assistance with the proofs.

Chapter 1

FINANCE AND INVESTMENT, 1922–1923

Although domestic events and policies absorbed some of Keynes's attention during 1920–2, international affairs, most notably the working out of the peace treaties and post-war reconstruction, absorbed most of the time and energy he devoted to public affairs. From late 1922 onwards, however, the focus of his interests began to shift more towards Britain and her problems.

An indication of this shift in focus came with the fall of Lloyd George's Coalition Government, in the midst of talk of an election campaign, following the meeting of Conservative members of Parliament at the Carlton Club on 19 October 1922, and Bonar Law's succession as Prime Minister. Two days after Law assumed office, Keynes spoke to the 95 Club, a Liberal society, in Manchester.

Notes for a speech at the 95 Club, Manchester, 25 October 1922

I believe in the depth and reality of the great traditional divisions between parties,—that they depend on deep principles which are forever reappearing in changing circumstances.

I therefore welcome it with profound relief that the confusions which perhaps inevitably followed the suspension of political controversy during the war have been brought suddenly to an end; and that Liberals can again stand together as Liberals determined to make prevail sooner or later the principles of wise government.

But eight years have passed since we were in this position. Other preoccupations have overwhelmed us. We need therefore a greater intellectual effort than usual to get our principles clearly embodied in a programme. And when Liberals meet together on such an occasion as this, we shall spend our time best in discussing together what this programme ought to be.

We must begin with the national finance, the consolidation of which is the necessary condition of progress in most other directions.

I venture to lay down this proposition—that the field of possible economies is comparatively narrow.

A large part of our expenditure—service of debt, pensions— honourable and unalterable commitments.

A further part are social services which it would be wasteful to curtail. I am afraid that we must agree that all further expensive schemes of social improvement, even though they may be productive in the long run, must be postponed. But we must be equally obstinate in keeping those we have.

Beyond this there may be waste arising from mismanagement. Economies in this direction not significant in relation to the budget.

There only remain two categories of large expenditure, armaments and commitments abroad.

I think we have got to go for these two items bald-headed.

B[onar] L[aw]'s administration will do its best but not bald-headed.

We must have a change of policy so drastic that it may even involve some risks.

Beginning with overseas commitments

    Evacuation of Palestine and Mesopotamia with possible exception of Basra

    Appeal to Dominions to take up more fully their share of policing the Empire

    Reduction of the Army even to a point incompatible with our exerting agreed influence in Europe.

There is no better way of ensuring peace than by assuming it. We can only save ourselves by assuming that for 15 years we are not going to be involved in a war by land, even if the assumption is doubtful and needs courage. If no one is afraid of us, I do not think that there is anyone of whom *we* need be afraid.

We must take the lead in disarmament and not make it conditional on the action of others.

If we have a happy and prosperous people at home, we should always be equal to a great emergency if it ever arises again. This is the best form of preparedness and if, as I believe it is, it is incompatible with the other forms of preparedness, this is the one to be followed.

There are no important economies to be made except in this direction. We must therefore attack these with courage and the utmost determination. So much for expenditure. (Does Mr McK.[enna] feel confident that the conservative administration will do this?) What about revenue?

It would be very nice to reduce the income tax—too high for social expediency. But very rash at present to promise reduction of any taxes at all.

Are there any new taxes which ought to be put on. What about protective import duties?

I have not the slightest doubt that B[onar] L[aw]'s administration will introduce protection sooner or later. Mr Law himself won his spurs on this subject. He is still an ardent and convinced protectionist. He has selected as his C[hancellor] of [the] E[xchequer] the parent of the Safeguarding of Industries Bill.[1] He will find it hard to balance his budget. Partly on pretext of revenue etc.

You in Manchester all know what a disastrous and deceptive prescription this would be for making both ends meet.

Nevertheless the danger is great—a wave of protective sentiment passing over Europe.

Yet every scrap of experience which accumulates emphasizes the blindness and disastrous folly of this policy. We in this country must not only hold high the banner of unfettered trade here. But everywhere where we can exert our influence in Europe we must cast it on the side of freedom.

Formerly free trade was a desirable aid to increased wealth. It has now become a necessary and essential defence against a crushing poverty. Unless we direct our resources into the directions where they are most productive, we shall not be able to gain a living at all.

There is one other tax which deserves mention. The capital

[1] Stanley Baldwin.

levy. Two years ago I was in favour. The collapse of values since that date has changed the situation. But circumstances may still arise from which the capital levy will be the right way out.

The circumstances for which a levy is reserved are easily indicated.

The working part of the population owes the burden of old obligations—proportion of the fruits of their toil.

If this proportion becomes unbearably high there are two remedies—one deliberate, the other undeliberate. The capital levy and depreciation of the currency.

All the continental belligerents have chosen the second alternative—Germany, France.

It is possible that we here can avoid both. But it would not be prudent to rely on this until we find by trying what economies are possible.

Even here I think there would be not much harm in a modest dose of depreciation. I believe that we should be in a better equilibrium all round if prices rose to 2 or $2\frac{1}{2}$ times pre-war. This would go a long way towards balancing the budget. But if we could not balance our budget at this level, I should prefer a capital levy, which I believe to be perfectly feasible technically (as a Manchester man Mr Sydney Arnold[2] has shown more clearly than anyone), to further depreciation.

In short I do not think that a capital levy is practical politics at present but it is not inconceivable that we may be forced to fall back on it.

My financial policy for Liberalism is therefore

(1) Drastic economies on fighting and foreign services

(2) Uncompromising free trade

(3) No promises of any reduction in taxation until the Budget has been balanced including provision for sinking funds

(4) The preservation of our existing social expenditure, especially on health and education, but no new expensive projects just at present.

[2] The reference is to S. Arnold, 'A Capital Levy: The Problems of Realisation and Valuation', *Economic Journal*, June 1918.

I believe that the Liberal Party is the only party in the state which can achieve this programme.

I do not agree with McKenna that Bonar is the one man who can do it because

(1) His economies will not be firm enough

(2) He will be led into protection

(3) If he attacks the social services he will cause a dangerous reaction.

On the other hand the Labour Party though they may make the economies and may be freetraders are likely to neutralise these virtues by premature reductions of taxation and premature social programmes

Webb's article

A word or two about Foreign Policy

Our course is plain—a sincere, open and generous policy with which we persevere. Peace, Freedom and Reconstruction. Seeking for ourselves no direct advantages. It may now be much too late to preserve Europe from past catastrophes. The moral defection of Mr L.G. at the last election and during the Peace Conference, when he more or less consciously sinned against the light, have made him an architect of almost irreparable ruin.

We can only do our best. I am not confident but I am not pessimistic. Anyway the only possible hope lies in an attempt to settle things on their merits, to tell the truth and not to talk cant and humbug to please anyone.

I do not think that any party except ours combines the wisdom and the experience with freedom from recent entanglements necessary to carry this policy to success.

One further point. In the present situation of the Liberal Party the personality of Mr L.G. has an inevitable importance. At the moment apparently he is up for auction willing to heed any party or section from Limehouse to Belgravia who makes him a good offer. At this auction I hope we shall not be bidders.

But so far as our programme is concerned does it not exhibit a policy on which all rank-and-file Liberals can combine? And is it not a policy which none but Liberals can hope to carry to success?

The next day Keynes spoke to the Manchester Luncheon Club on 'Is the Nineteenth Century Over?'. No notes for this speech survive.

Bonar Law obtained a dissolution of Parliament on 25 October, and called the general election for 15 November. Keynes was out of the country for most of the election campaign, acting as an unofficial adviser to the German Government.[3]

On the night of the election, with Sir Charles Addis a director of the Bank of England in the chair, Keynes delivered the first of four lectures to the Institute of Bankers. The lectures, which were followed by an examination for those attending, were private and, as a result, not extensively reported. A stenographer's transcript, corrected by Keynes, survives. These lectures provide a useful transition from Keynes's German preoccupations to domestic matters.

Lecture to the Institute of Bankers, 15 November 1922

MR KEYNES: Ladies and gentlemen, Sir Charles Addis, I owe you all a sincere apology for not appearing last week. I tried up to the last moment to be here, but I was unavoidably detained. But perhaps there have been two advantages from that. In the first place, you and I have the pleasure of having with us now Sir Charles Addis on his first public appearance, I think, since his recovery. In the second place, my visit to Berlin will, I hope, enable me to illustrate some of the economic theories which I shall put before you from some very recent events.

A great number of years ago now Professor Irving Fisher wrote his book, which was called *Appreciation and Interest* [1896]. He first emphasised what other economists had noted but had not emphasised, namely, the important distinction between the real rate of interest and the money rate of interest. If prices are going up or going down there is a distinction between the two. If a man lends for a year at 5 per cent £100,

---

[3] See *JMK*, vol. XVIII, pp. 61–3.

which is worth one hundred units of goods, and if at the end of the year that sum of money is worth one hundred and ten units of goods, he gets at the end of the year not one hundred and five but one hundred and fifteen units of goods, because he receives back the hundred units of money plus the five units of money interest; so that, while the money rate of interest is five per cent the real or commodity rate of interest is fifteen per cent. Correspondingly, when prices are rising so that the money is worth a smaller amount of commodities, at the end of the period you may have a real rate of interest which is much lower than the money rate of interest. If the £100 were worth ninety units of commodities at the end of the period instead of one hundred or one hundred and ten, as in the first example, then he would receive back at the end of the period about ninety-five units, so that the one hundred and five units of money would buy ninety-five units of commodities. Therefore, while the money rate of interest would still be five per cent, the real rate of interest would now be minus five per cent. A man who had simply kept the commodities or had bought the commodities at the beginning of the period and had held them, would be in a better position than the man who had lent out the money at five per cent because the rate of depreciation in the value of the money itself had been going on at a greater rate than was represented by the interest. Professor Fisher brought that fundamental truth to the front, and he illustrated it in connection with dear and cheap money in relation to rising and falling prices. When it is generally supposed that prices are going to rise, a much higher money rate of interest is required in order to make it the real rate of interest at a given level. Suppose that it is generally expected that prices may rise anything up to ten per cent in the period in question. If that is anticipated, clearly a higher money rate of interest will be required in order to compensate the lender for the fact that he will be repaid in a currency of smaller value than that in which he lent in the first instance. Businessmen do not look at it in that way; but they look at it in a way which comes to the same thing, because if they feel that prices are going to go up rather than down they are much more willing to buy commodities ahead and, therefore, much more prepared to pay a stiffish rate of interest for the money which they must borrow in order to enable them to do so. When a boom is in full swing and is expected to continue, businessmen think it imprudent to put off buying and, therefore, they are not deterred by the high rate of interest. That is because they believe, although they do not put it that way, that though the money rate of interest is high, the real rate of interest is not high. Correspondingly, when you have a depression in full swing, the unwillingness of people to buy, because they think that if they hold off they will get goods at a lower price, makes them particularly unwilling to borrow money in any case in which they can postpone purchase; so that when you have a depression and falling prices are anticipated there is a tendency for money to be cheap, so the dearness or cheapness of money in the boom and in the depression are attempts to keep the real rate of interest more stable than it would be if we had the same money rate of interest, whether prices were going up or were going down.

It very seldom happens that the fluctuations of the money rate of interest are nearly large enough to keep the thing stable. That is partly because people do not act sufficiently consciously in the matter, and also because, when people have a general impression that prices are going to rise or fall, they do not know it for certain and, therefore, they are not prepared to pay the same rate of interest that they would pay if they knew for certain that prices were going up. Thus you find in general that when prices are rising there is a tendency for money to be dear, but not dear enough to counteract the actual rise of prices that takes place.

That is a piece of what is now fairly familiar theory. I found in Berlin a very startling example of its operation in practice. In Germany prices have now continued to rise for so long and with such violence that, rightly or wrongly (very likely rightly,

8

but that does not matter), the impression in everybody's mind is that they will continue to rise. Nobody has confidence in the future of the mark. Therefore everyone wishes to buy at once, and nobody wishes to put off buying. They are willing to pay what in ordinary times would be fantastic rates of interest. On all past dates in the recent history of the mark, the real rate of interest in Germany has been negative, to a very great extent; that is to say, anybody who can borrow marks and turn them into assets would at the end of any given period find that the appreciation in the value of the assets in terms of marks was far greater than the interest he had to pay for borrowing those marks. It has been good business for many months now to borrow marks and turn them into assets. Everybody is at the game. The consequence is that now the rate of interest has risen to fantastic heights with extremely interesting reactions on business enterprise of all kinds.

When I was in Berlin a week ago, what you might call the gilt-edged rate of interest for short loans was about twenty-two per cent; that is to say, the Deutsche Bank or institutions of that kind making advances to a favoured customer, on absolutely perfect collateral, would charge about twenty-two per cent. That worked out as follows: two per cent above bank rate (bank rate at that date was eight per cent: it was altered to ten per cent a day or two ago) plus a commission of one per cent a month. That is the gilt-edged rate. I daresay that today it is two per cent higher, because the Reichsbank has raised its rate to ten per cent. It is two per cent above bank rate, plus the commission of one per cent a month. Anybody who can borrow at twenty-two per cent feels extremely pleased. As a matter of fact, demands for credit at that rate are rationed. You must not only bring perfect collateral, and you must not only be a favoured customer, but you must make out a very strong case why you must have the money before your bank will lend it you, even at that rate. The open market rate for stock exchange transactions, or for anything speculative, or for dealings in exchange was from sixty

9

to one hundred per cent per annum. In particular, anybody who had mark balances, anybody who had cash marks and was prepared to sell them for foreign exchange spot and buy them back three months forward so that he ran no exchange risk, could earn interest for that three months—and I think that he can today—at the rate of about one hundred per cent per annum. Anybody who has mark assets, anybody who has cash marks can utilise cash marks to earn interest at the rate of about one hundred per cent per annum today, by dealing spot and forward, over the exchanges. But people are not particularly willing to embark on such transactions, because the general impression is that it is much better business to sell your marks for foreign *valuta* than to buy them back three months forward. People prefer the speculation of the exchanges to the certainty of one hundred per cent per annum, that is, to the certainty of twenty-five per cent over three months. It shows the extent to which the demoralisation of opinion in the matter has now proceeded.

Professor Cassel and Mr Hawtrey and other authorities have held that the solution for a great many monetary troubles and for the maladjustment of the market consists in raising the rate of discount, the bank rate. In ordinary circumstances I agree with them that the world under-estimates the power of that instrument for bringing about a better adjustment. In such circumstances as exist in Germany that instrument has lost its power, because the lack of confidence in the money is such that people will pay these enormous rates of interest and will not be deterred. Consequently, that particular method is virtually ineffective. The scarcity of money which results from the situation, the dearness of money, is bound obviously sooner or later to have the most far-reaching effects on industry. The position has been getting more acute for some months past, but since about last August it has become really important. The ordinary manufacturing concern in Germany is now suffering acutely, not only from the higher rates of money which it has to pay, but from the inability to get funds at all to finance the productive process during the period of production. In the ordinary way a given firm can, of course, get money from its bank for that purpose. The firm is chiefly influenced by whether it sees good business. There are now cases in Germany in which a factory sees good business, that is to say, that at the prices it has to pay it anticipates that it can sell its products, after it has manufactured them, at a profit; but it cannot obtain from its bank enough credit during the productive process to finance the purchase of the raw materials and the payment of wages. I heard of many firms that were going at something less than full time, even half-time in some cases, not because business was not profitable, not because they could not sell their goods at a profit when they had manufactured them, but simply because they could not get from their banker, even at fancy rates, enough cash to enable them to buy their raw material and pay wages during the time that must elapse before their goods were ready for sale. That sort of thing is bound to happen when you get money rising to these heights. Money is bound to be at very high rates as long as the present state of lack of confidence continues to prevail. It may be—and I think that it is very likely the case—that people are now not doing it; but people always do what it has been profitable to do during the previous six months—they look back and not forward—and as everyone who has borrowed marks has done very well for a considerable time past now, that is the popular way of conducting one's affairs, and a high rate of interest, as I have explained is not as deterrent as one might have expected. That is one side of the situation.

I will now deal with more or less the same phenomenon from a slightly different angle of approach. I daresay that many of you are familiar, using Mr Fisher's name again, with his method of stating the quantity theory. There is an alternative method, not so well known, which is more illuminating, I think. I think that it is set forth in detail only by Professor Pigou. This theory puts the quantity theory thus. In ordinary circumstances it is convenient for private persons and businesses to keep a certain proportion of their total resources in the form of claims to legal tender—in the form of money, if you like, but I take rather a wider thing than [that to be] money—which will, of course, include bank deposits. If, therefore, you measure the community's resources in terms of something other than money, say in wheat, it suits the community for the purposes of convenience and the rest of it that a certain proportion, k, of their total resources should be kept in the form of titles to legal tender, that is to say, money, bank deposits and the like. That is obviously a true thing. Claims to legal tender, the amount of claims for legal tender, depend on a certain proportion of the scale of everybody's turnover and the resources of the community in general. It will fluctuate as the habits of the community fluctuate; but in a given set of habits a certain proportion of the community's resources will be kept in the form of titles to legal tender. If the number of titles to legal tender is M and the value of each unit is P, then the total value is PM, so that you have PM equal to kR. The number of claims to legal tender multiplied by the value of each claim is equal to the proportion of their resources that it suits the community to keep in the form of titles to legal tender. That is absolutely indisputable, although it may not take you very far until you have further analysed the several items. In pre-war days it was usual to concentrate on these two elements in the equation. It was assumed that the community's resources either changed slowly or were constant. It was assumed that the proportion that it suited the community to keep in the form of titles to legal tender always was a comparatively stationary thing, that if you doubled M you halved P, that PM was equal to something that did not change rapidly or in the ordinary way; so if you double the number of units of currency you halve their value, P being their value and M their number. That is the ordinary crude quantity theory. That, of course, is only the case if the other elements in the equation remain unchanged. It is only true that doubling M halves P if kR is remaining constant. The depreciation of the currencies of Central Europe began by the increase of M. The value of P began to fall because M was multiplied so largely. But we have now got to a different stage of the proceedings. People who have kept their resources in the form of titles to legal tender have come out of it so badly that they are beginning materially to alter their habits and to try to protect themselves from their losses by keeping a smaller and smaller proportion of their resources in the form of money. The great trouble in Germany now is not that M is getting so very big, though that is getting big, too, but that k is getting so very small. People are keeping a smaller and smaller proportion of their resources in money. Nobody keeps a bank balance which is going to be worth half its real value at the end of a month. Equally, people keep very little money in their pockets; so that the value of each unit of money has been falling much more than in proportion to the increase in M because that little factor k has been falling.

The depreciation of the German money could not now be cured merely by reducing the units of legal tender; it could not be cured merely by reducing M. You have to get k back to something like normal, and the extent to which people have economised in the proportion of their resources which they keep in the form of money has been something phenomenal. It is rather difficult to use figures because in the present state of the market one's figures change every day by something very material. A week ago—and I do not think that it is very different now—the value of all the notes in circulation in Germany was about one-tenth of the gold value of the pre-war German circulation; so that, though the Reichsbank has so enormously multiplied its note issue, the value of the mark has fallen ten times as fast as would be justified merely by the multiplication of the number of units of currency. Since pre-war days the territory of Germany has been reduced by about ten per cent and the scale of operations of business in Germany has also been, to a certain extent, diminished. On the other hand, gold prices, world prices, have risen fifty per cent, so I think that one can very roughly set off one of those things against the other and say that if Germany was pursuing its normal pre-war habits in the matter of the proportion of its resources which it kept in the form of money, it would require ten times as much currency at the present value of each unit as it is actually using today. That is what one means when one says that the value of the currency is a matter of confidence. The phrase is very often used very loosely. Politicians very often will tell you that it is a matter of confidence when it is really a matter of the value of M. After M has been multiplied to a certain extent there is a further reaction. k begins to fall, apart from alterations in M. That is what one scientifically means by the failure of confidence. In Germany, in order to get things straight, you have to do more than control M. You have to prevent the undue increase of M; but the main thing you have to do is to increase k. If you increased k and did not increase M, prices would have to rise a good deal further, or rather prices would have to fall a good deal, because the amount of currency would not go round if k was increased; so, unless you seek a great deflation in Germany, unless you are anxious for a very great deflation, you must allow, I think, a certain further increase in the units of currency, provided you have first of all set some definite limit to that. You must not let M increase indefinitely. If you are going to increase k by creating confidence, you must simultaneously be prepared to increase M a little. Otherwise P would have to fall to so great an extent—I think that I might have it the wrong way round, but you can easily keep me right: one always does that in lecturing—would have to increase to such an extent that you would have all the usual ill effects of deflation.

In present circumstances the attempts to economise the use of money and to do without money have reached lengths that are highly inconvenient to everybody concerned. Banks have not nearly enough cash in their tills and customers have not nearly enough deposits. Nobody has enough change. The economising of the use of money has gone to an extent which is extraordinarily inconvenient. The moment there was any revival of confidence the amount of money which people would want to have would rapidly increase. I daresay that in pre-war days people were unduly extravagant because they had more of their resources in the form of titles to legal tender than was, in fact, wise. Now they have gone very far in the other direction in Germany. There is not nearly enough money, and great practical inconveniences result. People cannot give change for ridiculously small sums of money. It happens that banks have to refuse in a most extraordinary manner on Saturday claims from their customers for cash to pay wages. When I was in Hamburg in August there was one Saturday there when the branch of the Reichsbank actually advised all the leading banks of Hamburg not to cash any cheque for a greater number of marks than at that time represented a pound. You had firms employing hundreds of men, coming for money to pay weekly wages and being told that they could not have cash for a cheque for more than a pound, simply because the banks had not enough money in their tills, and the Reichsbank branch had not enough money in its till to feed the other banks. Therefore, I say the situation is a very artificial one. A very small revival of confidence would immensely increase the amount of money which was wanted in circulation.

To a certain extent those people who economise in this way do without money at all, but in certain important respects they use foreign money. No doubt, one of the reasons why they can get along with one-tenth of the gold value of the money they used to have is the fact that for a considerable number of purposes foreign money and foreign deposits are now employed.

In that connection I would emphasise one point. There is now what everybody is very familiar with, namely, the flight from the mark. Money hoarded was speculatively employed in the hope of making profit arising from the fall in the value of the mark or, perhaps, to get out of the reach of the German tax collector, who was impelled by the Allied demands to require a great deal. There is the flight from the mark. In Germany now there is a considerable use of foreign currency. It is by no means in the full sense of the words a flight from the mark. It is merely the act of an ordinary prudent person. For example, I heard of such a case as this. A man had saved enough marks to build a house. He had been intending to do that, and he was told by his friends and by his banker and everybody—and he acted upon their advice—that the moment he let the contract to build the house he must forthwith sell his marks for dollars, because, if he did not do that, the depreciation of the mark during the period when the house was being built would mean that his marks might be utterly insufficient to pay the builder's bill. The builder, of course, would not give him a firm contract. It depended upon wages and upon the cost of materials and so forth. He was told that he ran the risk that, perhaps, the marks would fall to such an extent that they would pay only one-tenth part of his bill and that, in order to be quite sure that he really could pay for the house during the period the house was being built, he must hold his assets in the form of dollars and then, when the bills came along, he would sell the dollars and would pay the builder with the proceeds, which, in terms of marks, would have risen in proportion to the depreciation of the mark, if it had taken place in the meantime. If, on the other hand, the mark had remained stable or had appreciated, provided prices responded, he would be no loser. It was simply the act of a cautious man.

The position has now been reached that people who keep money as reserve against contingencies or against their commitments for short periods will not keep it in the form of marks any longer. It would be foolish and dangerous and rash to do so. There is, therefore, a considerable demand for foreign currency merely as a means of holding money safe for a short period. If a German has accumulated some marks for the purpose and is going abroad on business, he does not turn his marks into foreign currency as he requires it in the way that an English traveller turns his money into foreign currency as he requires it. The moment he decides to go abroad he turns the whole thing into foreign currency in order that his plans may not be completely deranged by an alteration in the value of the mark in the meantime. That is, obviously, a legitimate and sensible thing to do, and that you cannot complain of. It is a way of protecting yourself. As the result of that, the German balance of payments is burdened at the present time by the fact that people have to have foreign money to bank in. Over and above the flight from the mark strictly speaking, they have to have foreign money in which to keep their bank reserves, in which they keep the kind of money which persons in England would put on deposit with their bankers for three or six months against a commitment which was falling due at the end of that period.

There is one point of detail which it is worthwhile to introduce at this point. Many persons who have bought foreign currency, partly perhaps for security, partly in a speculative spirit, now see very big profits. Other persons who have not bought foreign currency have bought ordinary shares in order to get out of money and to be in assets. That is being very widely done in Germany. These ordinary shares have now risen, in terms of marks, to dizzy heights. Some of the shares are quoted at a thousand times what their price was a few months ago. Many such persons might be content with their profit. They might say, 'The thing has gone on a very long way. It will not go on for ever. Now, perhaps, is the moment to turn round. I will bring my foreign assets back to Germany. I will sell my dollars and pay off my banker', or 'I will get my assets in some other shape than in ordinary shares.' But there is a law in Germany now which stands very much in the way of that. Owing to the fall in the value of the mark since the law was passed, practically everybody in Germany who is not starving pays income tax at the maximum rate, because any income that is above starvation point in terms of marks is so much above what it was when the law was passed that everybody is liable for the maximum rate of income tax. According to this law, realised profits on stock exchange transactions or from dealings in foreign exchange are liable to income tax. Unrealised profits, book profits, are not so liable. Therefore the man does not pay any income tax as long as he keeps his shares or keeps his foreign exchange. If he sells them he at once has to hand over to the tax collector sixty per cent of his profit. Therefore, he has to take a very decidedly bearish view of the situation before he is prepared to sell at the cost of handing over sixty per cent to the tax collector. The effect of that tax is to prevent people from realising. That, obviously, works out in the absurdest way when the tax is so very heavy. It means that the more any security rises in price the less willing people are to sell because the bigger the sacrifice they have to make to the tax collector. On the other hand, if a security begins to fall in price everybody wants to sell it and everybody wants to have a realised loss which they can set off in their income tax returns against income or against profits. So whenever a security falls in price it becomes an extremely popular thing to unload. You have, therefore, the situation that the more prices fall the more people sell, and the more they rise the less they sell. Therefore a thing can go on rising to an absurd height.

I ought to say with regard to this income tax matter that the Germans are not yet suffering as they will suffer if no change is made from this crushing tax. Income tax in Germany, as in all other countries, is necessarily collected a little in arrear. If you are paying sixty per cent of your last year's income in today's marks, you can clear it off by selling a handkerchief; so actually at the moment the income tax paid by the Germans is not at all burdensome. But supposing that the tax went on as it is now, if the mark does not depreciate further, then, when next year the tax collector comes round and tries to collect sixty per cent of this year's income in a mark of the same value or of a high value, the burden will be a crushing one because, as I say, the maximum income is now such a very small income that everybody who is not starving has to pay it. No doubt, there will have to be some modification of the income tax, and, no doubt, when the modification comes, we shall say, 'The Germans, as usual, are evading their proper liabilities and evading the taxation that ought to be imposed upon them.' The worst of the existing situation is that you are always at one extreme or the other. At present the Germans are getting off income tax; but it is quite hopeless: you cannot prevent it. You cannot levy a tax of £10 in the pound on your last year's income, and unless you levy a tax of £10 in the pound you are bound to get very little if the tax is paid up in the mark at its present value. It is quite hopeless to budget and collect your taxes in terms of a unit which fluctuates in value to such an extraordinary extent as the mark does at present. It means that direct taxation becomes hopeless because it is either totally inadequate, as it is at this moment, or hopelessly oppressive, as it will be next year if the present situation is stabilised.

One part of the German income tax which they are getting in which is proving of the utmost utility to them is the tax on wages. Part of the income tax in Germany now takes the form of a ten per cent tax on wages, which is deducted at the source by every employer every week, and as wages rise roughly in proportion to the depreciation of the mark, the yield of this tax keeps up pretty well, even in actual value. The best part of the return to direct taxation in Germany is really not income tax proper in our sense of the word, but it is this weekly tax on wages which is responding very well to the successive depreciations of the mark.

There is one other point of detail which illustrates the extraordinary anomaly of the situation. As I have just stated, many Germans and many German firms, partly out of prudence and partly out of a speculative spirit, own foreign assets. One would have supposed that if a man in Germany wanted to borrow marks the very best security that he could offer to his bank would be sterling in London—that he would offer to transfer sterling in London to his banker and borrow against it. That is precisely the form of borrowing which it is most difficult to do in Germany. Big firms will go to their bankers and ask for loans and will be quoted a most prohibitive rate, the reason for that being that the Reichsbank for two reasons discriminates against that class of operations. The Reichsbank has got it into its head, and it is half right, that if it allowed loans of that kind it would mean that there was absolutely no limit to the extent to which speculators could bear the mark because they would have, say £1,000 in sterling, and if they then borrowed marks against that sterling and then at once sold those marks they would then have some more sterling, and then again, no doubt, with appropriate margins, they could borrow some more on it, and the only way of stopping bear speculation in the mark is to have money tight. Therefore, if you take off the stopper at all and allow people to borrow against foreign assets and to speculate against the mark, you make it easier for that class of persons to borrow more money. Therefore you must not do it. You are driven to the absurd situation that you stifle industry, you prevent your factories from having enough money to carry on, for fear that if money could be procured your speculator would procure it and proceed at once to be a bear of the mark. That is, obviously, an absurd situation; but it is not quite easy to see what the cure for it is.

There is also a second reason which obviously ought to be cured. In the old days the Reichsbank had to keep, against its note issue, a reserve of one third in the form of gold. At the outbreak of the War a new decree was passed, making the Treasury bills of the Empire the equivalent of gold for the purposes of the note issue. That is the existing situation; so that the Reichsbank can, as you all know, issue notes to an unlimited extent on the security of Treasury bills. It cannot issue notes against any other sort of security. It is not permissible for the Reichsbank to issue notes against a bank balance in London. One would have supposed that the Reichsbank would have wished to have as many of its notes as possible represented by foreign balances of good currency, but that is precisely what is not permitted to it. The Reichsbank is not allowed to issue its notes except against worthless Treasury bills; so if the Reichsbank was to accept foreign balances as collateral they could not in any sense be made a legitimate, lawful backing for its notes.

One of the technical points that one would have to secure in any new system would, I am sure, be to facilitate the accumulation by the Reichsbank of foreign balances on gold exchange standard principles and the issue of notes against them. The Reichsbank is deterred from any change in the existing situation for the reasons I have just mentioned. At present with the existing lack of confidence they do not want to have loans against foreign assets because that might possibly facilitate bear speculation, although I am inclined myself to think that that is a short-sighted point of view.

One point in conclusion before I leave this section of my subject. I pointed out the total inadequacy of the amount of currency in circulation as compared with pre-war times, and I measured that by the figure of one-tenth. As a matter of fact, the scarcity is not quite so great as that in practice for a reason which I have not mentioned, namely, that that figure is arrived at by taking the gold value of the currency, whereas internal prices in Germany have not by any means adjusted themselves to the fall in the external value of the mark; so that money goes a great deal further in Germany in proportion to its gold value than it does here. I tried to obtain statistics, but matters were moving so fast that it was impossible to do so. Also commodities fall into three classes. Commodities which can be imported, which must be imported, respond very rapidly indeed to alterations in the gold value of the mark. Imported goods rise very nearly as fast as the exchange falls. Also, articles which can be exported, against which the export regulations are not severe, rise very quickly. In fact, small articles which tourists and persons of that kind can remove in their pockets or trunks have now risen to very great heights indeed. I should think that they are probably dearer than they are in London. I should anticipate that before long there will be a very brisk import trade into Germany of such things as watches, for example. Every foreigner who goes to Germany thinks that such a thing as a watch is going to be very cheap just in proportion to his lunch. He sees that his lunch costs him fourpence, and so he thinks that a watch will be extraordinarily cheap, and, as nobody knows what the right price of a watch is unless he is a watchmaker, he is apt to think that it is good business to buy two or three watches and put them in his waistcoat pocket and take them home. So articles of that kind rise in price very smartly indeed. I should think that they are above the world price, and you may anticipate a heavy import into Germany, just as, at an earlier date, there was a heavy import into Vienna of printed books and oriental carpets and other such bargains, which rose to such heights in Vienna that it paid to send them there from London. Those classes of goods rise rapidly. At the other end of the scale come a great many forms of services. There the rise is very much slower. Then there are also articles of food in regard to which there is a considerable amount of control and which are not allowed to be exported. They rise very much more slowly. There is an important class of articles in between which rise partly because they use raw material imported from abroad, but which do not rise to the full extent because they are still able to make use of cheap labour. I think that one's tendency from living in Berlin is to under-estimate the extent of the adjustment. I should have said, going about the streets, lunching in restaurants, taking taxis and so forth, that money went about five times as far in Berlin as in London; but I think that the adjustment is a great deal nearer than that. If you are doing that kind of thing, you are largely eating food and employing services. They are two of the things that have not risen proportionately. I should suppose that prices really are, perhaps, one third of what they ought to be if things were completely adjusted, whereas particular classes of things are not above one fifth. I was in Berlin immediately after a very big fall of the mark, and every week things were rising extremely fast. For the purpose of tips, for example, or anything of that kind, a penny went a very, very long way indeed. The cheapness of food at the present moment is very striking to any foreigner. That is one reason why the country is able to get along with one tenth of the gold value of the currency which was used before the War. It is, perhaps, really more like a third or a quarter, if you allow for the fact that prices are not completely adjusted. If prices were adjusted the people would require more currency even with their present habits of economising the mark.

That is enough for today. I propose to continue next week with various facts relating to the present situation in Germany, and then in later lectures I shall go on to other topics.

Lecture to the Institute of Bankers, 22 November 1922

MR KEYNES: Ladies and gentlemen, in the last lecture I was concerned with certain features of the situation in Germany today. I go on this time to an examination of the possible remedies that might be employed in Germany, and the conditions under which those remedies could be applied if people were willing to make those conditions exist.

In the minds of the German authorities two of the greatest obstacles to any plan of stabilisation are the budget and the balance of trade. At the present moment both of those are adverse. The budget is unbalanced and there is an adverse trade deficit. In many authoritative circles the view is held that there must be a more favourable situation in both those respects before it is any good to attempt to stabilise. It was held that, even if the Allies were to be accommodating about reparations and were to agree to a moratorium, it would be extremely rash for the Reichsbank to employ its gold in a scheme of stabilisation until the unfavourable symptoms of the unbalanced budget and of the adverse balance of trade showed signs of curing themselves or of being cured. Personally, I am not satisfied that that view is correct. It is certain that in the long run the mark could not be stabilised unless in the long run the budget was balanced and the balance of trade was not excessively adverse. That is perfectly true. You could not maintain stabilisation unless those conditions were fulfilled. Nevertheless, I think it can be argued that, speaking in order of time and thinking of provisional measures, stabilisation has to come first and that you will not balance either the budget or the trade account until you have, first of all, given things a chance of settling down by a measure of stabilisation. You must use your resources to stabilise for the moment and then, during the transitional period, you must try to get things straight, and then, if you do get things straight during that period, your stabilisation will be a lasting one. But to think that the budget or the balance of trade are going to put themselves right with the mark as it is at present is, I believe, much more optimistic than the alternative view which I have been advocating.

First of all, taking the budget in a little more detail, I think that I mentioned last week that in the case of the income tax you necessarily assess a man on his income at a date somewhat prior to the date of collection. The only exception to that is the tax on wages which can be collected weekly at source. The income tax on earnings of the type on which income tax falls in this country must be collected to a certain extent in arrear. The period on which you are assessing must be complete before you can hope to collect the money. If the unit of legal tender is depreciating as fast as is now the case in Germany, you are inevitably always collecting your tax in a worse currency than that in which you levied it and at which you have assessed, so that by no ingenuity that I can see can you hope to get a full return, the return which you ought to get, from direct taxation. You must first stabilise in order to be able to collect your revenue in the same unit as that in which you are assessing.

It is equally so in the case of state services. You cannot very well put up prices beforehand. The Government cannot presume that the mark is going to fall, and, therefore, inevitably all changes in postage, railway fares, and so forth are bound to be in arrear. I do not think that it need be as much in arrear as is, in fact, the case in Germany now. The costs of public services such as the Post Office, or railway travelling, or the telegraph are ludicrously low. When I was in Germany in August—I think that it might have been even cheaper when I was there in November—I sent a telegram of about twenty words inside Germany for a halfpenny. That was a degree of maladjustment that did not exist in prices outside Government control. Nevertheless, bureaucratic establishments cannot possibly keep pace with rapid fluctuations and, therefore, the revenue from state services will always tend to be inadequate. For these reasons, and also because of the general disturbance and destruction of real income which takes place with an unstabilised mark, it will, I think, be immensely easier for the budget to be balanced when you have stabilised than as a preliminary to stabilising. The German Treasury officials seem to think that, apart from the extraordinary charges under the Peace Treaty, there was no particular reason why they should not balance their budget with a stabilised mark, and, indeed, I cannot see any reason why they should not. It might mean that they must have public services on rather a niggardly scale; but the problem is a soluble one; whereas, when your money is falling all the time, it is very nearly an insoluble one.

There is one other illustration which I might have given a little earlier, but it left my mind for the moment. Germany has no longer a bread subsidy which she had for a considerable time after the Armistice; but she still imports wheat under the auspices of the state. There is still a department that imports wheat, and that department has lost money lately over its deals in wheat, so that indirectly there has been a subsidy, an unintentional subsidy, due to the fact that they were not raising the price of their commodity in terms of marks as fast as the mark was falling. There is another illustration of the way in which you are almost bound to make losses on state trading in such conditions.

I say, therefore, that stabilisation must come first. If you wait until the budget is balanced you will have to wait for ever, unless in the meantime you have attempted stabilisation.

However, that point did not weigh so heavily with the authorities in Germany as did the other point, namely, the balance of trade. It is commonly believed that the balance of trade is heavily adverse, and the view is therefore held that if the Reichsbank was to use some of its gold—it need not use, perhaps, more than say half, which would be twenty-five millions sterling—such a sum would be engulfed in no time by the adverse balance of trade, and that it would be futile to throw in a part of the last reserve so long as the conditions continue to exist in which that could be absorbed in a very brief period.

I examined a great many figures in order to see what the adverse balance of trade was. Through no fault of the German Government, I think it is almost impossible at the present time to prepare reliable figures. The returns of imports and exports are made in terms of paper marks. Those paper marks have to be converted into gold marks at some rate of exchange. The method of the statistical office is certainly crude, because it was found half-way through my stay in Berlin that the rate of exchange as applied to exports was a month different in time from the rate of exchange as applied to imports. For example, for the October trade figure they had converted the exports at the figure—I forget which way round it was, but that does not matter—of the average rate of November, and they had converted the imports at the average rate of October and, as the mark had fluctuated one hundred per cent or two hundred per cent in the interval, it was clear that all the conclusions drawn were perfectly worthless. But even if they converted them both at the same month they were still nearly as worthless, first of all because the fluctuations within the month were so big, and also because there was no sort of guarantee that the exchange would have been provided in the month and at the rate prevailing when the goods crossed the frontier. The actual marks may have been converted into foreign *valuta*, either at an earlier date or at a later date. In the ordinary way, of course, that does not involve a very big error if the fluctuations of the exchange over a period of three months are not portentous; but with the sort of fluctuations which have been going on in the last three months, when there have been periods when the mark has been one eighth of what it had been worth as short a time ago as three months previously, you can clearly get no clue worth anything at all as to what the real adverse balance is from the published trade figures. Further, owing to the numerous regulations that exist governing exports and also governing imports, one may be pretty sure that there will be a fair percentage of erroneous declarations and a fair percentage of complete evasions. A very considerable value of goods must be carried out of the country in tourists' luggage which probably escapes declaration almost wholly. Therefore, I am not prepared to believe, merely on the basis of the figures of the statistical office, that the adverse trade balance is as big as the German Government represented it to be.

According to their representations, there is an adverse trade balance at the present time of something between two and a half and four milliards of gold marks a year, say from one hundred and fifty millions sterling to two hundred millions sterling. They represented that they had an adverse balance of imports over exports to that extent.

Then, in addition to that, there are, of course, the payments under the Treaty and the coal deliveries, which amounted to a quite appreciable figure in the course of last year. Including payments under the Clearing, that is to say, pre-war debts, and the value of deliveries and the value of cash paid to the Reparations Commission, I think that probably something like sixty million sterling has been paid during the year. Then in addition, it is alleged—I do not know with what truth—that there has been some flight of capital from Germany, which, of course, throws a burden on the exchange. Personally, I doubt whether there has been any appreciable additional flight of capital during the past year. I think that some people have had to bring their capital back through lack of funds and other persons may have exported money; but I doubt whether German balances abroad have very much increased. However, the ordinary popular view is that they have increased. Therefore, on the debit side of her balance-sheet, Germany has had somehow or other to look after the adverse balance of exports and imports payments under the Treaty and the flight of capital. On that side of the account she has also had to meet a certain amount of interest on her foreign indebtedness. On the other side of the account there are the receipts from tourists, which, though not large, is not an entirely negligible item, and the purchase of marks and mark assets by foreigners. While at various dates in the past the purchase of marks and of mark assets by foreigners has, of course, reached a big figure, though not, I think, a figure so large as the figure generally mentioned, it is to me quite unthinkable that the purchase of marks and mark assets by foreigners during the past year can possibly have reached a total sufficient to balance the account on the hypothesis that the statistics given us were correct.

On the debit side, the net debit, on the hypothesis which I have stated, would amount to something like from two hundred millions to two hundred and fifty millions sterling. We will be modest and we will take the sum of two hundred millions sterling. I think that it cannot be argued seriously that, during the current year, foreigners have bought marks and mark assets to the extent of two hundred and fifty millions sterling. That would represent in terms of marks, at the rate of exchange which ruled during the past year, a quite impossible quantity of marks. One cannot do it exactly because the value of the mark has

28

fluctuated so much that you would have to decide in exactly which month or even on which day the transactions had taken place; but if you take a rough shot at the thing I do not think that you would be far out in saying that if foreigners have really bought marks and mark assets to as large an amount as that, they would have had to buy practically all the ordinary shares quoted on the German stock exchanges, all the mark notes circulating in Germany and all the deposits in all the banks, which we know, in fact, is not the case. The actual additional sum purchased by foreigners must be a very much smaller sum than that. I, therefore, draw the conclusion that if Germany was relieved of the Peace Treaty payments, which, as I say, have come to something like sixty millions sterling during the past year, she should not be very far from balancing her accounts.

People will not understand that somehow or other trade balances every day, that for every buyer of exchange there must be a seller of exchange, that the total balance of payments is always level at every moment and, consequently, there never is in the strict sense of the words an uncovered balance. It may be that the balance has to be covered by a bank having an open position or by a speculator stepping in temporarily (that may be the case: it is the case from day to day), but the uncovered margin of that sort which the financial world is prepared to carry is not very large. It is much too risky for them. Therefore, you are thrown back for any important sum on the more long-period speculator, not merely on the person who carries over from day to day to deal with the adverse balance in the evening. If you get it firmly in your head that somehow or other the balance of payments is always covered every day, that it is as impossible for there to be an uncovered balance as it is for a man to pay out money that he has not got—if once you understand that, you will, I think, dismiss from your mind the idea which is popular in regard to a great many European countries that there is somehow a permanent adverse balance that is not covered at all in any way and that you have to get rid of that. The truth

29

is that the exchange has to fall until somehow or other the thing is balanced, until the country in question has either cancelled certain purchases, or speculators or investors or somebody or other have been tempted by the rate of exchange which is quoted. Once having got that clear, I think you will cease to be as pessimistic as the Germans are themselves as to the possibility of their balancing the budget if they were granted a moratorium. If they were relieved of payments under the Peace Treaty they would be that much better off as compared with the past year, and that sum would be sufficient, I should have thought, to make the difference. I agree with the view that as long as they have to make important indeterminate reparation payments, payments under the Treaty and other payments of the kind, it may be right to argue that stabilisation is impossible and that any resources which might be used for that purpose will be poured unavailingly into the sea. But once there is a moratorium, and once Germany is relieved of those payments, then I see no impossibility in the case.

That is on the statistical side; but I rely even more on a more theoretical argument which it is very difficult to make appeal to the minds of practical people. That is that once you have a sound currency regulated on sound lines it cannot become depreciated by what is called the adverse balance of trade, and it acts as a corrective to the adverse balance of trade and prevents an unduly adverse balance of trade from existing. In pre-war days Turkey had practically no paper circulating. She had only gold and silver. Nobody could maintain that, because Turkey was an impoverished and ill-governed country and liable, therefore, to an adverse balance of trade, her money must therefore become depreciated. When Turkey was importing too much some of her gold and silver would flow out in payment therefore, and before more than a very small amount had flowed, various corrective forces would be brought into operation and the thing would tend to get straight. So, provided that the German Government was in the position to have a currency, the amount of which could not be increased at will, you might leave the balance of trade to look after itself. Once you have really established a situation in which, by having balanced your budget and having got a certain amount of reserve resources, you are confident that you will not have to increase the volume of your currency, you need not bother any more at all about the balance of trade. It will be impossible for you to make certain payments if more money is demanded of you than you have got; but there will not be some subtle trade influence which you cannot control making the adverse balance and depreciating your currency, because as soon as the thing begins to work, as soon as the imports are beyond what the country can afford, a corrective is brought into play, tending to bring you back into equilibrium. Whereas, under the present state of affairs that corrective is not brought about in the orthodox and correct way; it is brought about by the exchange falling to such a point that people cannot afford to buy at all.

If trade must balance every day there are two ways in which it could happen. You may have your population not having enough money to make the purchases, or you may have the money they have got falling in value to such an extent that it will not cover the purchases. In both cases the ultimate result is the same. When you have a depreciating currency a country is prevented automatically from importing more than it can pay for by the fact that the money it has got is falling in value all the time. If you have an orthodox currency of a proper limited kind which has a stable basis in terms of foreign *valuta*, then the country is prevented from importing too much by the fact that it has begun to buy more than it can afford. So the idea that when you have established sound arrangements they can be upset by the ordinary movements of trade as distinct from sudden demands on the Government by a foreign authority is really a bogey which plays a very large part in responsible German mentality at the present time—(certainly one of the things which fill them with timidity is the statistics which they have collected)—that they have this enormous uncovered balance, and there is an inability to see the theoretical arguments why that is not so formidable as it looks. You find responsible bankers in Berlin at the present time solemnly assuring you that the situation in Germany is such that, even if she were let off reparations entirely and permanently, she would have to have a foreign loan each year in order to enable her to balance her accounts and that she must live at the expense of other people permanently. Of course, that is an absurdity. It is only seen to be an absurdity, I think, if you get firmly into your heads this point that I keep on repeating that, somehow or other, the balance of payments is equal every day, and that therefore she is somehow or other paying her way at this moment, and that if she gets an appreciable relief from her present situation she is to that extent definitely on the plus side.

So much for the two great obstacles. I am assuming, by the way—it is hardly worth mentioning—that a moratorium is required. As long as you demand from Germany resources which she does not possess and insist on her Government attempting to sell paper in order to fail in obtaining the resources, you can do nothing. That is obvious. Without the moratorium you have no basis for discussion of any kind, and I have not heard any rational argument to the contrary or any person whose opinion was worth anything asserting it with any backing to his assertion. But having put that out of the way, let me say that I do not agree with those who hold that the budget and the balance of trade remain insuperable obstacles. Having got to that point, that a stabilised mark is not necessarily impracticable once a moratorium is granted, what are the methods that you would employ?

For the transitional period you must plainly have some reserve resources. I have said that you must first stabilise and then trust to your budget and trade to get balanced, and then that will enable you to make your stabilisation permanent. But during the preliminary period you must be prepared to support your scheme by paying out foreign reserves if required. You must, therefore, have some sort of original nest-egg. A great matter of controversy is how that nest-egg should be provided. For my part, I do not think that a very large nest-egg would be required if the scheme was properly managed. Owing to the extreme dearness and shortness of money which I mentioned in my last lecture, as soon as people believed that there was any chance of stabilisation holding good, money would tend to flow towards Germany rather than to flow out, and it is unlikely that she would have to find any large amounts of resources in the earlier period. The danger would be a considerable number of months later. I think that the first effect of a stabilisation scheme might actually be that the Reichsbank would gain gold rather than lose it. There are not enough people who have marks that they can spare, that they have not an immediate urgent demand for, for them to be able to throw them at you to any important extent. The gold in the Reichsbank now amounts to several times the value of the note issue, so at the present rate of exchange the Reichsbank could buy up all the notes there are and still have a large amount of gold left. There is not really, therefore, any danger of a very appreciable drain in the first instance. The risk would be nine months or a year later in the event of the attempts to balance the budget failing and inflation continuing so that you were always issuing more notes available for redemption. But I think that you would have to take the risk that in the period of a year's grace, say, you would manage to balance your budget. If by bad management or by misfortune it turned out to be impossible to balance in that period, then the drain on your resources might come nine months or a year later, or a little longer. You would not run a very big risk in the first nine months. I believe, therefore, that the technical position is such that you could do it with a comparatively small amount of gold, and I think that the Reichsbank's gold would be probably adequate for the purpose, even though there was no question of using anything like the whole of it. The Reichsbank has fifty millions of gold sterling. If half of that was used as a pool, if that was combined with a prolonged moratorium and a firm policy, I believe it ought to be sufficient to put things straight, and I think that it would be reasonable, if Germany was granted a moratorium, to require of her that she should make a sincere effort to use her gold for that purpose. I should doubt if there is any case in history of a currency having gone to such a complete smash as the mark has while it had a gold reserve and while it was covered by gold at the prevailing rate of exchange to the extent of several times its value. It is a most extraordinary situation and one which can only exist on the hypothesis that the existing inflation will not merely persist but will increase a great deal. If there was a moratorium and if a good attempt was made to balance the budget there is no reason in the world why the assumption that a great deal more inflation will take place should be justified, and as soon as it ceases to be justified the gold reserve of the Reichsbank is fully adequate to sustain the value of the notes.

However, in Berlin a different view is widely held. The Reichsbank, like all Continental banks, believes that gold is not kept in reserve to be used on any occasion whatever. They are rather inclined to the view that the correct theory of a gold reserve is that you only make it available when you are absolutely certain that it will not be required. That view is not only held by the Reichsbank. It is traditionally held by all Continental state banks. The opposite view has been traditionally held for more than a hundred years past now in England. One of the great foundations, I believe, of our financial security has been this simple point of the correct theory about the gold reserve. We have very often had to use it, but not to a great extent; but the fact that we were prepared to use it has been of the utmost importance. There was one episode during the War which is not generally known and of which the details have never been published, in which, in my opinion, we only saved our position and enabled ourselves to keep our credit by the fact

34

that we were prepared to throw in our gold [*JMK*, vol. XXII, pp. 10–11.] As it turned out, we did not have to use all of it, but there was a moment when we had to decide whether, if the pinch came, we were going to use our gold or were going to hang on to it. The fact that we were willing to use the gold carried us through. That doctrine is the traditional English doctrine established as a result of many arguments and much pamphleteering and so forth a hundred years ago. Although it has had its occasional opponents, it has sunk deep into the tradition of the City of London that there are circumstances, not ordinary circumstances, when you do bring your final reserves into play. But the tendency on the Continent is never to bring them into play, but when things have gone completely to smash perhaps to fritter them away under force of circumstances. The doctrine stands very much in the way of any stabilisation notions now.

There is also another reason. What corresponds to 'the City' in Berlin suffers from the illusion that even in present conditions they have a real prospect of getting a foreign loan. Their minds have been on that subject ever since the Armistice. I was the responsible official during the Armistice negotiations in reference to the question how the food which was going to Germany was to be paid for [*JMK*, vol. XVI, pp. 391–404.] It was then a question of their using part of their gold or part of their own resources. We spent all our time trying to persuade the Germans that in the months of January and February, 1919, it was not possible to raise a loan on their behalf either in the City of London or in New York. They were very reluctant to believe it. At every date since then they have had that same illusion, and they are extremely unwilling to use their own gold so long as they think that people here will put up money for them. It is not quite a certainty, and they would much rather have the funds supplied here. As I say, I think that that is a complete illusion. There, again, it is useless to suppose that you can borrow money before your credit is re-established; but when Germany, if she ever is, is stabilised and when her credit is restored to a certain extent, ordinary loan operations might possibly be feasible. The notion that the foreigner is going to lend to you before your stabilisation and that he is going to take the risk of your stabilisation breaking down seems to me to be quite preposterous and to be a piece of extremely bad psychology.

As you will have observed from the replies of the German Government to the Reparations Commission, they still make their plans contingent upon foreign assistance. If they put forward a good plan, they ought, I think, to have all the co-operation possible of international financiers. I think that moral aid ought to be given to them and convenient overdraft facilities against their own gold and so forth, and even, perhaps, small overdraft arrangements in addition. All that might be useful and might have a great effect on the psychology; but the notion that at this stage in the affair you are going to make your stabilisation scheme mainly dependent on foreign capital seems to me to be very wide of the mark. The worst of the present situation is that the talking of so much outrageous nonsense on our side has provoked a situation in which no sense is talked on either side. You find almost as much outrageous nonsense talked in Berlin in one direction as you hear in Paris and London in the other. Therefore, while I have been spending the last half-hour explaining why I think stabilisation to be technically a feasible proposition, and I see no reason except human wills why the thing should not be put straight, I do not have any very optimistic hopes because the psychological situation does not seem to be one which will enable the technical solution to be put into operation.

Assuming that point, I pass on to the next stage of my argument. Assuming that Germany was granted a moratorium, supposing that we were sensible on our side and supposing that she was prepared to use her own resources with what aid we could give her—because I hope that we should be able to give her some practical assistance if she was prepared to use her own resources in a genuine attempt to put things straight—what, in those conditions, would be the right technical plan? Two plans were discussed in Berlin, one of which was incorporated in the report of four of the foreigners called in, and the other of which is in the report of the other three. I do not think that the readers of the newspapers have got quite clear what the essential difference between the reports by the two bodies of experts really was.

The four experts held that the only chance of success was stabilisation: that is to say, that you should fix some rate as appropriate, the rate being selected with reference to the degree of adjustment in existence at the moment when the change was introduced—say, at the present moment, something like fifteen thousand marks to the pound sterling, though it may be quite a different rate months hence—and, having fixed it, to have some official body which was prepared to buy and sell foreign *valuta* at that rate. We held that you should abolish all exchange regulations whatsoever and that you should have absolutely free and unfettered dealings, and that there should be a buying and selling rate for foreign *valuta* which might be, say, one or two per cent apart, corresponding to the gold parity, as it were, but that at those fixed rates the official body would be prepared both to buy and sell unlimited quantities of marks. That would knock out any hopes from speculation, and therefore you would be back on the genuine demands of the country both ways, but you would be protected by the fact that there is at present a shortage of money in Germany so that you could not possibly have an undue amount of marks thrown at you. You would rather have people who would want to take advantage of the very high rate of interest prevailing in Germany to buy marks from you than to sell marks to you. We would combine that with a prolonged period of dear money in order that the present incentive to remit money to Germany rather than otherwise, apart from the fear of loss of money on the exchange, should continue to operate. We would have absolute fixity, we would have an absolute

37

abolition of exchange regulations, and we would have dear money. We would also rather put away from our minds the idea of a subsequent improvement in the mark. I think that a long period of deflation would be a very disastrous thing and might bring German industry almost to a standstill. Possibly in the early part of the period for a short time your rate might be a little tentative; but the idea that some people have that you might start, say, at fifteen thousand marks to the pound sterling and then improve the rate by easy stages till it was ten times as valuable and had got down to fifteen hundred marks to the pound sterling seems to me to be a disastrous idea because, with the constantly falling prices in Germany, you would have constant struggles over wages, you would have the whole industry of the country thrown into disorder and you would have all the trouble that we have had during our industrial crises worse tenfold. No modern industrial community could stand the prospect of official recognition that the legal tender was going to appreciate in the course of the next few years by one thousand per cent, which is what that scheme would amount to.

One recognises, of course, that if the mark was raised in value it would be a pleasing thing to foreign speculators, and it would also restore persons inside Germany who had been cheated of their savings by what has happened; but it does not seem to me to be a practicable thing. It is not feasible that the holdings of foreign speculators should be appreciated in that way, and, as regards the people inside Germany who have suffered so much by that, that is a thing that is done and cannot at this date be remedied. The suggestion was a fixed rate, free dealing, and no intention of altering the rate except possibly that it might be a little tentative at the very beginning of the period.

We added one technical point, which is important, and to which I should like to call your attention; that is, that the official body which was in control of the exchange should not only deal spot but should also deal in forward exchange; that is to say, at appropriate rates it would always sell you marks spot and buy those marks back from you forward one month or three months.

That would mean that a German who had foreign assets which he would like to employ for the time being in Germany but did not dare remove altogether from the form of foreign assets because he was not certain that the stabilisation scheme would last, would be perfectly protected. He could then replenish his resources in Germany by handing over his foreign *valuta* spot against marks. He would receive marks in Germany, and he woud have a forward contract that three months later he could have the foreign *valuta* back again at an appropriate rate, and the difference between the spot and forward rates would have to be corresponding to the rate of discount inside Germany. In effect it would be a way by which the Reichsbank or the official body controlling the exchange could borrow foreign *valuta*. I believe they might receive a considerable amount in that way, which would have the effect of putting in the hands of the official exchange body the foreign floating resources of Germany. At present you may have Germans with foreign resources which they would like to use temporarily in Berlin, particularly when money is as tight there as it is now, and they simply dare not because they cannot. If they sell their foreign *valuta* spot they cannot at present buy it back again forward at any reasonable rate.

As I explained in my last lecture, the reason for that state of affairs is that the present position is said to be a check on speculation. Perhaps it is; but it has these various other bad consequences. Once you have stabilised things I can see no objection to developing a free foreign market in exchange. That would enable the Reichsbank to collect temporarily loans of foreign *valuta* which would not be drawn upon probably all at one time. That would concentrate Germany's resources and would enable additional currency that must be put into circulation to be put into circulation against the security of foreign currency instead of Treasury bills. That is a little extra to the scheme, so to speak, but it is not an unimportant part of it technically.

The other three experts took a different view. They held that at present, even in the event of a moratorium, the whole situation is too precarious for it to be safe for the Reichsbank or for the body controlling exchange to guarantee any fixed rate. Their notion was, therefore, that the Reichsbank would form a foreign reserve, partly by means of its own gold and partly by a loan from foreign capitalists, and that that reserve would be used for intervening on the exchange market whenever the mark looked particularly weak, and whenever you suspected that there was a bear campaign going on you would raid the bears by buying marks heavily and so give them a good fright. You would get a corresponding appreciation of the mark in the next day or two, and you would do that always trying to raise the mark to a higher level, gradually supporting it at a rather better level than you had supported it at the previous month. I think that is technically an entirely hopeless plan, if I may say so. It seems to me that if you do not fix the thing, you will preserve the whole of the existing state of uncertainty, and it is quite likely that you would dribble your resources away without having got anything like stabilisation because you would not have knocked out speculation. You would rather have encouraged it, although speculators would, no doubt, have to have in their minds the possibility of these counter raids by the Reichsbank. They would probably become quite as clever at it as the operators of the Reichsbank, and, I should think, would very likely so arrange their operations that the Reichsbank dealings would be in their favour rather than against them. Secondly, if there was the idea that the policy of the Reichsbank was steadily to raise the value of the mark over a period, for the reasons I have already given, you would tend to bring business to a standstill. If the scheme was unsuccessful you would dribble away your resources. If it was successful you would have all the evils of deflation in Germany on a pronounced scale, and you would very soon reach a point when your labour troubles became of an extraordinarily severe character. It seems to me that in the matter of stabilisation you have to go the whole way or not at all. It may be that the conditions for a courageous policy do not exist; but there is no middle course really between leaving things as they are and fixing them. Merely intervening irregularly and throwing some resources in, without any real fixed policy, is exactly what you are at and is the way to throw money away. I should have thought that the whole history of the spasmodic interventions of foreign bourses in support of particular exchanges showed that that policy never succeeded.

The persistence of these two schools of opinion shows the practical difficulties of the case. I believe that our plan is much the safer, that you would run far less risk if you fixed your rate and tried to make your rate believed in; but the other party hold that it is a much rasher policy and that theirs is a much safer one, because if at any moment you saw that your policy was being a failure and was not working, you would withdraw your support, you would keep the rest of your gold unused, and therefore you would not have committed yourselves to anything, and so you could draw back. But the very fact that you had not committed yourselves to anything would be what had ruined the scheme. It would be known that the support might be withdrawn at any moment, and if the Reichsbank was losing gold it would lose heart also and, almost directly, there would not be any real strength in the market at all. That half-hearted kind of policy is not the real one for such circumstances as these.

I have now given you two divergencies. One is whether the Reichsbank gold by itself would be sufficient or whether there must be a foreign loan. The next point is: Are you going to stabilise exchange or are you going to support it? There is a third policy which I think everybody will admit to be a *pis aller* (I do not myself fancy it), but which on theoretical grounds is not open to particular objection. That is the idea of having a parallel currency to the existing one; not of attempting to fix the existing mark at any particular level but of introducing a new unit, say a gold mark, and providing that the new currency issued should be the gold mark and that the gold mark should be redeemable for gold. By that means you would also make both the gold mark and the paper mark legal tender. You would allow people to fix their contracts in either and to pay in either at the official rate. So you would then have these two currencies, the gold currency and the paper currency, with a fluctuating rate between them. You would fix that rate from time to time by a legal notice in conformity more or less with the market rates prevailing at the time, and the official rate fixed would be one at which you could discharge in one currency obligations incurred in the other.

One can easily see that there are certain advantages in that scheme. To begin with, it would provide German merchants with one of their great *desiderata*—namely, a sound money of account. Everybody could keep their balance-sheets in terms of the gold mark. It would also provide Germans who must have money which would be of permanent value as reserves, with something other than foreign currency which they can use for that purpose. Such persons could acquire gold marks and the new gold marks—which would be a paper document, of course—would serve the purpose that foreign currency has to serve now; so that Germany could reduce her requirements of foreign currency. It would meet those two points: a good money of account, and a good store of value. But so long as the paper mark fluctuated in terms of the gold mark, one of the great problems would be left unsolved, namely, the existence of a stable unit in which taxation could be collected. People would still have their taxes fixed in paper marks or, at any rate, they might have their incomes in them, and unless the paper mark was a completely exploded thing, as long as it existed side by side with the gold mark, you would have instability in your budget, and I do not think that you would have gained by any means all the advantages, whereas it might be just as difficult to keep up the value of your new gold mark as it would be to keep up the value of the entire currency. Assuming that no more paper marks were issued, in the other things you would be able to be successful. The present gold value of the existing paper marks is not a thing that need alarm anybody. Therefore if you feel strong enough to lay it down that all future issues shall be of a gold mark which you will keep at a stable value, you may as well, I think, go the whole hog and not go in for this *pis aller* which solves part of the problem, but by no means the whole of it.

That is the essence of the case as it now stands. I explained to you the chief facts of the German situation in my first lecture and in this lecture I have tried to analyse the possible cures that have been put forward in different quarters, the arguments as they appear to me for and against, and the psychological atmosphere which, I fear, makes the carrying out of any of them a little improbable at the moment.

Lecture to the Institute of Bankers, 29 November 1922

MR J. M. KEYNES: Ladies and Gentlemen: I propose to give this lecture on the subject of devaluation. You probably all of you know what that means. It may possibly be safer if I were to repeat that it is concerned with stabilising the value of certain legal tender monies somewhere near their present value in terms of gold, in place of attempting to restore them to their pre-war value in terms of gold. That is to say, of accepting existing facts and fixing the level to which they are now adjusted permanently rather than attempting to go back.

For the purposes of the devaluation argument currencies fall into three groups. The first group are the very bad currencies such as the mark and others about which it is not really a matter of dispute. People may be in favour of raising them above their present level, but no-one proposes that those currencies can be restored to their pre-existing value.

Then there is another group of currencies of which our own is a leading example, which I will deal with towards the end of my lecture, in which the divergence from the pre-war parity is not very considerable, so that there can be very little doubt that

43

they could be restored to par if it is thought wise and expedient to do so.

In between comes a very important class of which the franc and the lira are the most important examples, where the depreciation certainly exceeds 20 per cent and is very often a good deal bigger than that, but where it is not as fantastic to propose you should restore them to the pre-war level as in the case of the mark.

I shall devote the first part of my lecture to these intermediate currencies, and I shall return at the end of the lecture to the rather special case of sterling.

About eight months ago I published an article [*JMK*, vol. XVII, pp. 355–69] about devaluation in which I went so far as to propose some actual details of a scheme which at that time I thought could be put into operation. That was just before the Genoa Conference. This subject was considered very carefully by the Financial Commission at Genoa, and the Conference reported decidedly in favour of stabilisation at the existing level rather than at the pre-war level in the case of all currencies which were seriously depreciated. I do not think it is very easy to find any reasoned statement of the arguments on the other side. There is a good deal of dispute about currencies in the position of sterling, but amongst accredited authorities there is not very much divergence as regards the franc and lira. One might have supposed, therefore, that I was not wasting my time, though I might have been putting forward a bad scheme in principle, so to speak in proposing actual details. But what has happened since that time has convinced me that nevertheless I was, and that although the opponents of stabilising somewhere near the existing level are not free from that argument nevertheless the other side has by no means won over universal opinion, and that we still have to do a great deal of enunciating the fundamental facts of the case before it is worth while going into the details of an actual scheme.

I want therefore with your approval to run through the

fundamental simple facts of the situation, which I think ought to be universally recognised and ought to govern all discussions on the subject. Although the Genoa Conference declared in favour of devaluation unanimously I think the representatives of France, Italy and Belgium, in approving the principle, stated at the same time that they wholly repudiated it as regards its application to their own individual countries. Those gentlemen may have been guided by political rather than intellectual considerations, but that they should have thought it desirable to deny what their intellect had just approved is a measure of the difficulty which still exists in putting these things into force. Genoa approved it in principle, but all the countries most affected repudiated it in particular.

One argument which weighs so much with many people, which has to be dealt with first of all, is the argument of justice. It is thought that it would be a grave injustice not to put back these monies to their pre-war parity. Some injustice is always wrought by economic changes. That one has to admit. But to regard the weight of gold as the measure of justice rather than the purchasing power of the currencies is, I think, a very technical form of justice, and yet no-one suggests in the United States, for example, that it is an act of injustice not to restore the dollar to its pre-war purchasing power.

Quite apart from that, justice means presumably that you must put back people who have entered into contracts into the position which they had reason to anticipate they would be in when they entered into those contracts. If all contracts expressed in terms of money had been entered into prior to the War there might be a strong case on those lines, but the actual fact is that the vast majority of the contracts have been entered into much more recently. In particular war loans, which form a very important category, were contracted to a very great extent since the Armistice in terms of the depreciated money. So that you would be giving a large uncovenanted bonus to the lenders if you were to restore the value of the franc and lira to their pre-war value. In the case of the United States Irving Fisher has roughly calculated that contracts in terms of money are on the average about a year old, so that if you put the value of money back to a very different value from what it has now with reference to a period eight years ago you are almost certainly doing more injustice than you are doing justice if you are considering the relative position of creditors and debtors who are the parties to the money contracts now in existence. There might be a case on this head for a certain restoration, but the longer the depreciation lasts the weaker the case is. More and more contracts will have been entered into at the depreciated rate, and more and more of the holders even of those contracts which have a history back to pre-war times will have changed hands [*sic*] in the interval.

I think therefore there is a great deal of misapprehension first of all in making the criterion of justice a quantity of gold rather than a quantity of purchasing power, and secondly in supposing that the contracts which would be affected by any change mainly relate to a pre-war epoch. I therefore argue that that particular reason for making great sacrifices in order to get back, while it has some force has not so much force as some people think it has.

That is the argument of justice. The next argument is the argument of possibility. When the question of possibility is considered it is common to look to the existing rates of exchange and to the balance of trade, and to criteria of that kind. That is a mistake, I think, when one is considering a long period problem of this kind. From the long period point of view I say that a different criterion is the one that settles the matter. The long-period obstacle to any possible improvement, for example of the franc, is the burden of the internal debt. You can always restore the currency to any value you like if you want to, if you think it worth while and adopt a sufficiently stringent policy to do it, provided that it does not increase the claims of the bond-holders beyond what is tolerable. If it does, the Government is certain to be forced to inflate again, and the work will be undone.

In the case of France and Italy, I shall deal with France in detail as an illustration. The policy of internal finance which has been followed has brought up the burden of the internal debt to a point which already makes it nearly impossible for their budgets to balance. If you were to restore the franc and the lira to their pre-war parity you would make the problem quite hopeless. In the case of France you would rather more than double the present burden of the internal debt; in the case of Italy you would approximately multiply it by four.

Now what does this burden of the internal debt amount to? It is not a question of economy and extravagance. Questions of economy and extravagance can always be dealt with in the last resort. It is a question of the distribution of the national wealth between different classes. The burden of the national debt is the measure of what the active earning part of the community have to hand over to the *rentier* or bond-holding class. No community ancient or modern will tolerate more than a certain proportion. You will never induce the active earning taxpayer to surrender more than a certain proportion to the inactive bond-holding *rentier* class, and the general principles of contract have all through history had to moderate themselves and to yield to that grand principle of expediency that you cannot increase the claim of the bond-holder, of the inactive person, beyond a certain extent, and those persons who would press a contract to its extremity and say that justice in the matter of contract must be done at all costs are the people who are really the greatest enemies of the sanctity of contract, because policies of that kind are what bring the whole thing into complete disrepute and eventually bring down the entire structure. The whole thing if you are dealing, not with individuals, but with nations and with epochs, has to be handled with moderation and with reason, and it is utterly impossible to compel the active part of the community to hand over an undue proportion to the bond-holding class.

Therefore I say that the long-period criterion is this: Will the improvement in the value of the currency so much increase the burden of the internal debt as to make the proportion that is so to be handed over an intolerable one?

If it is intolerable there are only three solutions open. The first solution is repudiation, which as regards internal debt in Western Europe I think we can neglect at present. The second way out is a capital levy which, when the necessary circumstances arise, seems to be much the justest and wisest instrument, because you can make the burden fall in the right place. But the capital levy, as we have seen in the recent election, is a thing difficult to explain or to understand, and the terrifying ignorance of the real arguments on either side shown in the columns of the Press shows that it is an expedient which a modern community will very likely reject even when the conditions for applying it exist. I do not want to be taken to imply by this that I am in favour of a capital levy in this country at this moment. I am not. I think you ought to have a capital levy only when it is clear that the proportion of taxation which has to be handed over to the bond-holder is more than the country can support, and that premise has not yet been demonstrated beyond controversy in this country. But most of the arguments raised against a capital levy seem to me to be a little childish in character, and not to go at all to the root of the matter.

I throw that out rather in parenthesis, but the controversy with regard to the matter has I think brought home to everybody how very difficult it will be to bring in a capital levy even when it is the right thing. Therefore I strongly suspect that the continental countries, who indubitably ought to have a capital levy, will probably not do so but will follow the line of least resistance, and the line of least resistance is to let your money depreciate. You can always have a capital levy that way; you can always allow the unit in which your money debts are expressed to fall in value. In Austria, in Russia and in Germany they have already had a capital levy of 100 per cent. In France they have already had a capital levy of 50 per cent; and in Italy of about 75 per cent; and other countries in varying degrees. Experience shows that the population will quietly accept enormous de-predations by this instrument when they would throw out of power any Government that attempted to take one tenth of the amount from them by juster and more scientific methods.

The great objection to the method of depreciation as compared with the capital levy is that it falls entirely upon persons whose wealth is in the form of claims to legal tender, to money, who are generally, amongst the capitalists, the poorer capitalists. It is entirely ungraduated; it falls on small savings just as hardly as on big ones; and incidentally it benefits the capitalist *entrepreneur* class, because those persons who borrow money and possess assets, which is the case with the *entrepreneur* capitalist class, benefit by depreciation. So that by that means you make a capital levy which falls mainly on small savings and on moderate savings. At any rate it treats them just as hardly as it treats the richer man, and it may actually enrich the ordinary *entrepreneur* capitalist. The small savers who have most to lose from depreciation are precisely the sort of conservative people who would be most alarmed by the capital levy, so that they would probably oppose it. On the other hand, the *entrepreneur* capitalist class would obviously prefer depreciation which does not hit them very much and may actually enrich them. The combination of those two forces will generally bring it about that a country will prefer the unjust, inequitable, disastrous method of depreciation rather than the more scientific one of a capital levy.

For those reasons I think that if the countries cannot balance their budget at the present level they will probably have a bit more depreciation until they can, rather than have a capital levy. But anyhow, it is utterly impracticable for them to go back.

The advocate of stabilisation somewhere near the present level takes a middle course. He says we accept the *fait accompli*. It is quite out of the question for budgetary reasons to go back on our steps, and also it would create a great deal of injustice and a great deal of harm to trade. We must accept the depreciation that exists, but let us at any rate make an effort to avoid further depreciation. That will be immensely facilitated by fixing it if we can somewhere near the present level. But he has to admit that those forces which make it impossible to go back may also make it inevitable that there shall be further depreciation.

Let me illustrate that by reference to the particular example of France. The internal debt of France amounts at the moment to about 250 milliards of paper francs. That is excluding all external debt including what she owes her allies. The further borrowing already definitely in sight and more or less provided for will, including reconstruction loans which the Government has guaranteed, bring the aggregate internal debt by the end of 1923 to somewhere about 300 milliards of francs. The service of that debt will be about 18 milliards of francs, that is to say at 6 per cent. That I think allows a certain amount for statutory sinking fund, for while the recent debt has been raised at 6 per cent, some part of the debt has been raised at lower rates. I am not quite sure how much that sinking fund allows for, but I think I am not far wrong in saying that including the statutory sinking fund the service of that debt will be somewhere about 18 milliards of francs. That figure happens to be the budget estimate of the ordinary revenue from all sources for the year 1923. So that by the end of 1923 the service of the internal debt will absorb 100 per cent of the revenue. That is rather optimistic, because it is assuming that all external debts are cancelled; and it is also assuming what certainly will not be the case, that after the end of 1923 France will be in a position to assume that the burden of the external budget, that is to say pensions and further expenditure for reconstruction will have vanished. But still, take it at that. Within a short period the service of the debt will absorb the whole of the revenue. As the necessary expenditure of the Government is probably 10 or 11 milliards at least, that means that even at the present level of the franc the Government will have to increase the yield of taxation by something like 60 per cent in order to make both ends meet, and if the franc was materially to improve in its value in terms of commodities the amount which the Government would have to take from the taxpayer in terms of commodities in order to satisfy the claims of the *rentiers* would become something fantastic, something quite beyond the taxpaying capacity of France.

Therefore I say in the long run that is the fundamental reason why the franc cannot possibly return to parity, and I go further and say that the difficulty of balancing the budget even now will prove a strong temptation to France to pursue a policy of further depreciation.

This figure I think is an interesting one. If the franc was to fall to 100 to the £ sterling it would be possible to balance the French budget by taking very little more in terms of commodities from the taxpayer than is taken now. The French will have to come to some compromise between increasing taxation and diminishing ordinary expenditure and reducing what they owe their *rentiers* by means of a further depreciation, and I have not the smallest doubt that the French Government will consider that course, as they have hitherto, as far more conservative, far more orthodox, far more in the interests of the class of small savers than they would a justly constructed capital levy.

Those figures I give in detail because they are particularly striking, but something very similar, or at any rate if not quite similar in degree the same in kind is also true of other countries. On the one hand, therefore, when M. Picard, speaking for the Government of France at Genoa, said it was the policy of the French Government to restore the franc to par he was talking rubbish.

The reasons I have given are reasons why the critics of devaluation from the point of view of improvement cannot maintain their case. But of course there is another class of critic who have much more reason on their side, who must be met, namely those who say that the chief European currencies are so very likely to go much worse that it would be a foolhardy thing to try and fix them at their present level, and that the time has not yet come at which there is any real hope of balancing. I think there is a great deal of force in that criticism. I think it is very likely that the governments are not strong enough to enforce a policy of stabilisation, but I think it ought to be possible, if the will is there and if the thing was understood, to stabilise at a rate not very much worse than the present. I think it is very unlikely that it will happen, but one has in these cases to preach an ideal policy rather than to dilate on what is going to happen, and if their affairs were conducted with wisdom I do not think it ought to be impossible to stabilise at some rate not very much worse than the existing levels of the exchange.

Why am I so anxious to stabilise? It is obvious that it would be foolish to try and improve the value of the currencies, but what is the overwhelming argument for fixing them? The argument that is much the most important in my mind is one which is fairly familiar, but I think it is under-emphasised. It is this. Even though a country may be in adjustment with other countries in respect of its balance of trade and so forth over a year as a whole, it does not follow that it is perfectly balanced every day. It is well known that industrial countries which buy large amounts of agricultural products find it convenient to make the bulk of their purchases, or at any rate a larger proportion than normal of their purchases, rather early in the crop year. That was very familiar in pre-war days. Even when the balance is level for the year as a whole, the industrial countries are in debt to the agricultural countries in the autumn and winter, and they get level with them again in the spring and summer. If you want to have just the quantity and just the quality of the leading crops you do well to buy them rather early in the year. That is an ordinary practice of trade which has not been abandoned even in post-war times. That was recognised in the pre-war financial world, and one of the most important functions of international banking used to be to adjust this temporary balance between two seasons of the year, and very admirable machinery has been devised by means of which that function was carried out at very small cost to trade. When the banker knew that there were gold points, so that his loss on the exchange was limited, he was willing to move floating balances between London and New York, for example, for a very moderate commission. A little higher rate of discount in the temporarily debtor country so that his money earned a little more there than it could in the other country, together with a slight exchange turn due to movement between the gold points, was enough to remunerate him. He was content with a normal banker's commission, the reason for that being that his losses were definitely limited, and his profit was more or less calculable beforehand. He did not have to be rewarded for taking a risk, because he was not taking an appreciable amount of risk.

That worked extremely well, but what happens now? The autumn pressure comes along just as usual, but now the banker is not content or able to move his balances for small turns, as he could formerly, because he now has no guarantee at all as to the rate at which he will be able to bring his money back again later in the year. He may have a very strong opinion as to the course of the exchange, but the transaction is no longer a calculable one. He is bearing a risk, and owing to what has happened in recent years he estimates the risk as a very big one. And even apart from the fact that he has to be remunerated for risk, it ceases to be quite a banker's business. A banker, even though he thinks the risk is actuarily rewarded by the prospective profit, cannot afford to run risks of that kind on a big scale. Consequently this business that used to be a proper banker's business for a small term has become a speculator's business. The balancing of the account in the autumn, quite apart from the account for the year as a whole, has to be looked after in part by the suppliers of speculative finance. In order to attract the suppliers of speculative finance there has to be a very large movement. They will not come in and support the market until the exchange has moved to a figure which in their judgment gives them good prospects of profit when the next easy season comes round. Moreover, as speculative finance of that kind is discouraged by other banking institutions, and by state banks and so forth, it is generally in short supply. The amount of speculative finance going is barely enough to look after the autumn trend in its pre-war dimensions. Where a banker would not at all mind in the old days remitting millions to and from New York, hundreds of thousands are now as much risk as even very big people care to look to. So that, partly from the shortage of people who are in a position to look after that kind of business, and partly because they, estimating the risk to be a large one, do not operate until they see a big profit, you may have a very large seasonal fluctuation of the exchange even though the thing is in perfect adjustment over the year as a whole. You will not get a steady exchange until you have a 'pegged' exchange, because, until you have that, every little up and down is bound to have a disproportionate effect on the exchange, because the adjustment has to be effected by persons who are speculating rather than by persons who are conducting banking.

It is no good therefore to think, as some people do, that you must first of all wait for the exchanges to be stable, and after you have seen them stable for a year or two you will then fix them. They never will be stable until you have fixed them; you have to act first. And it is extremely important to do so in the case of any country for which it is practicable, because this seasonal fluctuation and the big rewards which have to be paid to speculative finance are a very heavy burden on trade. It means partly that those merchants who make their purchases according to the pre-war rule in the autumn have to finance them at a very unfavourable rate of exchange as compared with the average exchange of the year, and also to a certain extent it means that merchants deterred by the bad exchange rates that are offered them in the autumn postpone a part of their purchases to a season of the year in which they hope the exchange will be better, but one which may be far less convenient and efficient from the point of view of the transaction of their business. Nothing but harm therefore results from these big seasonal swings.

That is known in a general way, but I wonder how many people realise the extent to which the fluctuations of sterling and of francs and lire during the last three years have been seasonal rather than progressive. In the year 1919 when the exchanges were unpegged because the inter-allied arrangement for finance came to an end, there was a very heavy fall in francs and lire and sterling of a non-seasonal kind. All through the early part and the middle of 1919 they were falling for that reason and for non-seasonal reasons. There has also been this year an improvement in sterling which is of a non-seasonal character, and it may be for the reasons that I have just given relating to the internal debt that at some future date there may be a non-seasonal decline of some of the continental exchanges. But although those facts are true—two of them are true, and one of them possible—nevertheless the bulk of the movements between the autumn of 1919 and the autumn of this year have been seasonal and not progressive.

I will put on the blackboard, if I may, a rather striking table. It is a table of percentage of dollar parity. The figures I shall put down represent the percent of dollar par that each currency reached at various dates, and I will give the lowest and higher for each season. For this purpose a season has to run from, say, August to August, rather than the calendar year, but I have not taken any exact period. Taking 1919–20, and beginning with sterling, the lowest percentage of dollar par that sterling touched was 69, and the highest was 82. In the following year 1920–21, the lowest percentage of dollar par reached by sterling was 69, and the highest was 82. In 1921–22, the lowest reached was 73, and the highest 93. In 1922–23, only half of which season is over, the £ sterling has fallen below 90.

Now here of course there is an improvement which is independent of seasons, but it is remarkable how steady the lowest figures are, and how steady the highest figures are, and how very big the fluctuations between the lowest and the highest are. It looks to me from that as though the fluctuations between the lowest and the highest were mainly seasonal, but you have to fall down to that point before the speculator would come in to look after the seasonal adverse balance. The difference between the two sets of figures is some measure of the enormous burden thrown on trade.

It looks from that table as though, supposing we had decided as long ago as 1919–20 that we would stabilise the £ sterling say at 75 per cent of its pre-war parity, we could probably have kept sterling pegged without any disturbance to trade through the whole of this period, and I believe it would have been a very much wiser policy to have done so.

Sterling is a fairly impressive case, but the franc and lira are in a way, I think, even more impressive. We realise that the movement of sterling has been mainly seasonal, but the extent to which it is true of the franc and lira is equally striking.

Let us take the franc. In 1919–20 the lowest point of the franc was 31, and the highest point was 44. In the next year the lowest was 30, and the highest 45. In the following year the lowest was 37, and the highest 47. This year so far the lowest has been 34.

I think that this is an extraordinarily striking table. There has not been any clear movement of the franc either up or down if you take the highest figures in each year, and the lowest figures in each year. But there is an enormous divergence between the highest and lowest figures. So that the man who imported his goods in the autumn and covered his exchange has had to pay a tremendous fine for the convenience of importing then rather than later in the year, and the people who have eventually accommodated him in the exchange have reaped an enormous profit. Surely it would have been much better all through this period to have stabilised the franc at some intermediate figure. Although for the reasons I have given I am not very optimistic for the future, I think it looks from this as though it would have been practicable for the Bank of France to have taken a figure such as 40 and to have kept the franc pegged at 40 all through that period. They would have lost reserves at certain seasons, but they would have gained them at others, and they would have added enormously to the prosperity of the country.

The lira, which is my last example, is almost the most striking of all. The lowest point reached by the lira in the first year was 22, and the highest was 32. In the next year the lowest was 18, and the highest 29. In the following year the lowest was 20, and the highest 27. And in this year the lowest has been 20 so far.

One sees from that [that] the lowest points of the lira in terms of the dollar have been 22, 18, 20 and 20, while the highest points have been 32, 29 and 27. But whereas the lowest points are steady, and whereas the highest points are steady, the fluctuation between the lowest and the highest has been as much as 50 per cent, and has never been less than 35 per cent. That shows that the violent movement of the lira has not been a progressive movement, but it has been a seasonal movement.

Therefore I argue that if you are thinking of the hindrances to trade, it is the seasonal point which one must largely attend to. And I also draw this conclusion: that so long as the exchanges are not stabilised by policy they will never come to an equilibrium of themselves. You may get smaller oscillations than these. Suppose this sort of thing went on year after year people would learn by experience, and no doubt the oscillations would not be nearly so large. Speculators would come in a little sooner, and importers would make even greater efforts to spread their importations more evenly over the year. But even so, I should think there would always be a very substantial difference between the busy season and the slack season so long as nobody knows at what level these currencies are going to settle down.

While people talk as they do at present there is, quite apart from underlying facts, an enormous risk in the matter. You have all the official authorities threatening to bring back the franc and the lira to par, so that any operations on the one side are very dangerous. On the other hand, you have the condition of internal finance which I have just been talking about, which indicates that they might possibly go a great deal worse. So that nobody knows with certainty, or even with probability, whether they are going to be a great deal better or very much worse. Therefore you must have a very wide fluctuation before people will come in purely from motives of self-interest to balance the day to day fluctuations and the month to month fluctuations as distinct from the annual fluctuations.

Signor Mussolini has lately threatened, I am told, to bring back the lira to 50. It is such an awful threat that I should think the Italians will do almost anything rather than accede to it. But would Signor Mussolini have said that if he had understood what he was saying? Suppose he put it like this: I propose to halve wages, double the burden of the national debt and reduce by 50 per cent the prices which Sicilians will obtain for the export of oranges and lemons. If he put his policy in that form, it would not have been as popular. But that is what his policy amounted to.

When you have those kinds of remarks being made on one side, and the hopeless state of the internal debt on the other side, naturally you have a complete uncertainty of mind which can only be cured by the government adopting a deliberate policy and saying we are going to do all in our power to prevent further depreciation, and we are not going to be so crazy as to try to perform an impossible task and restore our currency to par. When they do that you may be in sight of getting rid of this enormous hindrance and expense to trade by these vast seasonal fluctuations.

There has been one country—I should like to point the moral from this—which was unusually in a position to adopt a course of wisdom. That is Czecho-Slovakia. Early in this year Czecho-Slovakia found herself with a budget that was not very far from balancing, with, comparatively, a freedom from the internal debt that oppresses France and Italy and other countries. Her credit was good. She raised quite important loans in London and in New York. Nobody would have blamed her for fixing the Czech crown at the level which then prevailed. It had been ruined by no fault of her own, and was an inheritance from the Hapsburg Empire. At that time the Czech crown was worth about one twelfth of its pre-war parity. Czecho-Slovakia was in a splendid position for stabilising. She had the foreign resources to make a reserve fund, and there was no internal reason why the thing should not have been perfectly successful. In the light of what has actually happened it is clear she could have stabilised with complete success. What did she do? She has used the funds that she raised on the New York and London markets to buy Czech crowns over the exchange, and gradually to raise her exchange until the Czech crown is now worth double what it was in the spring. The consequence of that has been to throw out of gear the whole of her industries. She has had very severe unemployment, and a crisis through the greater part of her industries. She now finds herself a year later with her foreign resources partially depleted, with her crown worth one sixth of its pre-war parity instead of one twelfth, and still completely unstabilised, blown about by the breath of the seasons and the wind of politics. Could anything have been more foolish.

How long is it to go on? Is Czecho-Slovakia going to go on having industrial crises until she has raised her currency to six times its value? It is no easier for her to stabilise now than it was six months ago; indeed it is more difficult because her resources in foreign currency are no longer quite intact. What good has she done by deflating the value of legal tender? Apart from the satisfaction and pride in getting back to pre-war parity, it is very little better to have it at one sixth than to have it at one twelfth. The whole thing, as far as I can see, has been entirely purposeless, and it has been the result of deliberate policy. M. Alois Razin the Finance Minister, has dogmatic views on this subject. He is one of the leading bankers, and unfortunately he has had the opportunity of putting his tenets into practice. There has been a strong opposition, but he has overcome it. I should like to have it explained to me what good of any sort or kind he has done his country by this revolution in the value of legal tender money?

The modern capitalist world is even less suited in my opinion for violent fluctuations in the value of money upwards than it is for violent fluctuations in the value of money downwards. Either form of action is very ill advised, and ought never to be undertaken on purpose. I give that example partly as illustrating the disadvantages of following a false doctrine, but also as showing the state of opinion at the moment. When you do get a country which could stabilise, it immediately follows this vain and empty project of improving the value of its currency up to an undetermined point.

I have left over two questions which I must deal with. I should like to deal in a little more detail with the effect of a deflationary policy on industry, and I should also like to deal with the rather peculiar case of our own country and with the relation of sterling to the dollar. But if you will excuse me, I will not embark on that part of the argument today but will postpone it till next week, when the lecture, as Mr Steele [the chairman] has said, will be given on Tuesday instead of Wednesday.

Lecture to the Institute of Bankers, 5 December 1922

MR J. M. KEYNES: In my last lecture I discussed some of the general principles governing the proposals for devaluation, and I went into some particular details relating to France and to Czecho-Slovakia, but I made no comment as regards this country. In this lecture I propose to repair that omission. I have kept this country till the last because it raises rather separate questions from other countries, I think. To begin with, the problem of restoring sterling parity is a perfectly possible problem. There is no reason why we should not put sterling back to its pre-war parity if we wish to. So that one of the strongest arguments which I mentioned in the case of foreign countries, that any attempt was bound to be futile in the end, does not hold good in our case. There are also, owing to our past history, and owing to our position as an international financial centre, some rather specially strong, if sentimental reasons, if you like, for returning to the old parity. I recognise the force of those arguments. In the course of the wars of Napoleon, sterling suffered a depreciation just as it did in the course of the late war; but after many years, by a persistent effort, we succeeded in returning to par. It would naturally be a matter of great pride to this country if, after even the worst war of the twentieth century, we were again able to return to our previous undisturbed parity. These matters cannot be neglected in any monetary affairs where confidence, security, and all that, are of very real weight. So that not only is it possible for us to return to par, but there are special reasons both of self-interest and of pride why we should wish to do so. If it is our policy, and I believe it is, that we should return to par, then certainly it is to our interest that we should do so as rapidly as possible. The transitional period of uncertainty is undesirable, and if sterling is going to par with the dollar, the sooner it gets there, in my judgment, the better for all of us; and it looks now as if it were quite conceivable—whether it will stay there or not—that sterling may touch par at no very remote date. Nevertheless, while we have pursued this policy, and while it looks as though we shall pursue it with a considerable measure of success, I still think that the policy of restoring sterling to par was a mistake. In spite of the arguments which I have mentioned, and to which I give full weight, I think we should have been better advised if in the course of the last two years—perhaps two years ago—we had stabilised, say, somewhere between four dollars and four and a half dollars to the £ sterling. What I want to go into in detail are the reasons why it seems to me that we should have been more prudent to have adopted a policy of stabilisation which, at the level to which I think experience points, would have been possible at any time in the course of the last two years.

My first argument why that would have been a wise course brings me back to one argument I emphasised very much in my last lecture, namely, the burden of the national debt. In the case of France, as I pointed out, the burden of the internal debt is an overwhelming reason why the restoration of the franc to par is impossible; but it is also an argument which must not be neglected in the case of sterling. We are in danger of being the only country which will have a very heavy internal debt in relation to its resources. The countries of which the money has become depreciated have been relieved, as I explained in my last lecture, of a very large part of their burden. In the United States, while the nominal figure is considerable, in relation to the wealth of the country, it is no serious burden. We, however, will have to govern our tax system for a long time to come by reference to the tremendous burden of debt, and that, I think, may hinder the prosperity of our industry in relation to the prosperity of other countries which are not similarly burdened. I think the policy of bringing sterling to par renders it decidedly less likely that we shall be able to do without a capital levy. You will remember how in my last lecture I put the capital levy and currency devaluation as to a considerable extent alternatives. I think there is a slight prospect that we may be able to come to an equilibrium without a capital levy. But if sterling goes to its old par and is kept there, unless gold prices rise—of course, a fall in the value of gold might see us out—it will make very much more probable the necessity of a capital levy. I will illustrate that by some very rough figures. Suppose we put the burden of the debt, which is fixed in the terms of legal tender, at somewhere about £350,000,000 a year. I am not sure how exactly accurate that is, but it is a round figure. Suppose, after making what economies we can at the present level of prices, we are able to reduce the other expenditure to about £500,000,000, so that we are spending £850,000,000 altogether. Well, that will be an extremely heavy burden on the country. It is quite likely that we shall not be able to get below that at the present level of prices. If the value of gold falls and prices rise, the yield of taxation, generally speaking, will respond sooner or later. This part of the expenditure will also probably respond and increase proportionately sooner or later, but the other part will remain fixed; so that the real burden of the debt will be diminishing. The argument is equally true if you are comparing stabilisation, say, at four dollars to the £ sterling, with stabilisation at the old parity. If that is the situation with sterling at par, if we had stabilised at four dollars to the £ sterling, then you may suppose that that figure would have remained the same, that the expenditure would have risen, say, 20 per cent, to £600,000,000, and the revenue, which I am assuming just balances that, would also, without any increased real burden to the people, have risen 20 per cent to £1,025,000,000; so that we should have a surplus of £75,000,000 for the reduction of taxation. That margin of £75,000,000 is again the amount which you might hope to save by a moderate capital levy scheme. The schemes that I have seen drawn up which are not very oppressive, and which allow for hard cases, I think can be made to yield something of the order of an annual equivalent of £75,000,000 to £100,000,000 sterling. So that if a capital levy of that sort is brought in, it would make just about the same relief to the Budget in the long run as we should have obtained by fixing sterling at four instead of at the old par. Taken in conjunction with various other factors, I believe it would be a far less disturbing thing to have done to have a fixed sterling at four, rather than to have the burden of internal debt which is very near the limit. As I said in my last lecture, I do not know yet whether it is above what we can support without a capital levy or not—I think only time can show—but everybody will agree that it is very near the margin. I think those people suffer from a certain confusion of mind who simultaneously hold we must indubitably restore sterling to par, in all circumstances we must respect contract, and in no circumstances must we have a capital levy. If you lay down those things as *a priori* absolute principles, you will land yourselves, or you may land yourselves in an *impasse*—you will produce a situation which you cannot possibly solve on those principles, and you will have to give way to persons of other ideas who may solve them, on principles not moderately opposed to your own, but radically opposed to your own. The right way of preserving stability is not by *a priori* principles of that sort, but by considering the whole matter coolly and intellectually. That is my first reason for thinking it would be more prudent to have stabilised sterling at an early stage.

The next argument is of a more fleeting kind, and of the disadvantages of which we have already borne the greater part of the brunt. The depressing influence of a prospective fall of prices in relation to world prices on trade, hardly needs to be pointed out. Sterling is now about 7 per cent below its parity. Well, if it is going to its parity, that means that English prices, sterling prices, must drag 7 per cent behind American prices. If American prices remain steady then English prices must fall 7 per cent. If American prices rise a further 7 per cent, then English prices need not, in fact must not follow them. In the meantime, nobody quite knows what will happen, and you have a continuance of the depressing influence we have had in the last eighteen months, and a further prospective possible fall in prices. In the first place, that reacts on trade in many more ways than one easily realises at first sight. The Manchester merchants are complaining very much that the price of cotton goods is too dear. Well, in the terms of sterling, the prices of cotton goods are not very dear. They are a great deal cheaper than they have been for a good many years. The real trouble is that the silver exchange is so adverse to the silver-using countries. I take one instance in one particular kind of country. What makes Manchester goods dear in China is not their sterling price, but their sterling price taken in connection with the present value of silver. As silver has a world value, every time you raise the value of sterling, you put down the sterling price of silver. Every time that the sterling goes nearer to par, it makes it more difficult for China to buy our cotton goods, until China has shaken down to the new level of prices. All this has a fleeting influence. Once you have reached your equilibrium it is all over. But we have already had about eighteen months of it, and the prospect of another six months of it is, I think, a very serious damper on trade. My own view is that, apart from the depressing influence of the actual and prospective rise of sterling, and apart from the European situation, which I take very seriously, apart from those two influences, trade is straining at the leash, and will easily have a very fine revival. The European situation may develop at an early date, of course—I am not speaking of that today—but the other influence, the course of sterling, is one which has been under the control of our financiers, as European policy has not been; and I think the policy they have actually adopted, although I understand the honourable motives which have prompted it, has certainly prolonged the trade depression. It may have been worth it—I do not say it was not—but it is a very important argument on the other side if I am right in thinking that the slowness of the revival of trade in this country as compared with what is now going on in America, is due to an important extent to the course of the sterling exchange. The tremendous fillip that trade has had in America through the rise of prices has hardly been reflected here. The rise of prices in America has been counterbalanced here in the improvement in the rate of sterling, so that things are left here very nearly as they were. That is hindering our merchants, I think, partly because trade will never go ahead until people are certain they have touched bottom. They will never be certain that they have touched bottom until they see them going up a little; so that I am in favour of a moderate rise in prices as the only way of getting out of the present period of depression, and I think the improvement of sterling towards par is a hampering influence on that. Indeed, it is obvious it must be. In that connection, in connection with a rise of prices being necessary, the more I study statistics the more convinced I am that we shall not be in equilibrium until wholesale prices have risen from 15 to 20 per cent. The business of forcing down certain levels of wages, and so forth, into equilibrium is almost hopeless, or it will take a long time. The continuance of unemployment is to an important extent due to the fact that we have got the level of wages, particularly the level of wages of the unskilled, out of gear with everything else. The only way in which they will get into gear will be by an increase in the level of prices. Some figures have been lately published which are very striking in showing just how we are out of gear. At the moment you may say, broadly speaking, that food and the cost of living generally is somewhere about 60 per cent above pre-war. It is also interesting that this year we have been paying for our imports generally about 60 per cent above the pre-war price. On the other hand, the average level of wages is about 80 per cent above pre-war. That is the level of weekly wages. The level of unskilled labour is very materially more than that, the level of skilled labour rather less; and it averages out at 180. The skilled labourer is being paid by no means too much, rather to the contrary; but one of the things that has happened is that the old margin between skilled and unskilled labour has largely disappeared, and the unskilled labourer is now being overpaid in relation to the cost of living, and in relation to what the skilled labourer is getting. At any rate, the thing averages out at somewhere about 180, or more. I am putting it rather low at 180, because I think in that index number some of the more highly paid unskilled labourers have not been taken full account of. That is weekly earnings; but owing to the reduced hours of working, the wages that were paid per hour are probably double pre-war, that is to say, 200. 200 is the remuneration of labour compared with pre-war 100 per cent of work done; but food and raw materials are only 160. The effect of that 200 means that we are actually having to charge for our exports a materially higher price that we are having to pay for our imports. Our exports generally during this year have been sold at a price double the pre-war price exactly corresponding to the wages. High wages are compelling us to ask double for our exports when the world level of prices as measured by what we must pay for our imports, is only about 60 per cent up. It is clear that that is not a situation which can go on permanently. People will not pay us for our exports at so discrepant a price from what goods generally are worth in the world; and we see the fruits of high prices in the diminishing volume of our exports, and in our complete incapacity to employ the whole body of labour. I do not mean that that is the whole reason—I think there are many reasons why we are unable to employ all the available workmen—but I think one important reason is that we are attempting the impossible task of raising their remuneration something like 20 per cent more than is justified by the prices they have to pay for their food and living, and what we generally have to pay for our imports. I do not see much prospect of bringing that 200 up to 160, but I think there is a very real likelihood of the 160, that is to say, the general level of prices, rising to 200. Every hindrance in the way of that puts off the day when we shall be in equilibrium, and when we can employ our population.

The business of raising the value of sterling 20 per cent has put off the moment of equilibrium from anything from six months to two years, so we have had to pay a very high price for the sentimental satisfaction to our pride in the prolongation of the industrial depression, and in the immense volume of unemployment which we have had, and still have, and are likely to continue to have, I think, until the basic statistics of our economic life have got into some better equilibrium than they are at the present.

But there is also a third reason which ought not to be neglected, and that is this. Sterling still fluctuates, and even if sterling reaches par in the course of the next spring season, it is uncertain, to my mind, whether it can be kept there during the autumn pressure. We have already suffered for two or three years the immense expense of the autumn seasonal fluctuation which I expounded in my last lecture; and it is not at all unlikely that we may have to suffer that for at least one year more. Measured in money, I believe that the expense to trade and efficiency of the uncorrected seasonal swing is enormous; whereas though we could have probably stabilised with complete success at a lower value, it is uncertain how soon we shall be able to stabilise at par.

Even though the upward swing of this spring takes sterling to par without any difficulty or effort on our part, there is no guarantee that it will stay there. So that the present policy, apart from the first two arguments, puts off for an unduly long period the moment when we can get back to complete stability of the exchanges. One particular reason for doubting whether we can keep it there is the still unsolved question of the payment of the interest that we owe to America. I should like to say a few words about that, because it is quite impossible to come to a conclusion as to how easy it is to maintain sterling at par until one has thought a little about the payment of the interest to America which we have not yet discharged on the basis of a full year's payments. I confess that I am a little alarmed at the light-hearted way in which some authorities talk about the supposed ease with which we can discharge that liability. I quite agree that if we are called upon to pay it we must pay; but I think it is a great mistake to pretend that it would be an easy thing to pay, or that it will not create very great disturbance to all parties concerned. We have to think out a great deal more carefully than we have what the exact course of events is likely to be. If we are to pay the debt within the limits of the present Act of the American Congress, that is to say, interest plus sufficient sinking fund to discharge the debt in 25 years, that will cost something between sixty to seventy millions sterling annually, according to the rate of exchange. I think at the par exchange, it will be a little over sixty millions sterling, or at $4.40 it would be about seventy millions sterling. That is an enormous sum, 300,000,000 dollars, to be found over the exchange every year. When Mr McKenna was speaking in America he pointed out quite correctly that it must be within the capacity of this country to pay that sum, if it was already lending a more than equivalent sum to foreign borrowers. Our annual investments abroad, even now, on their diminished post-war scale, probably amount to not less than £70,000,000. That is a reason for supposing we can pay that sum of money. I quite agree with that; but we have to follow out the causal train a little more carefully. Supposing the American investor would step straight into our shoes, and would take over precisely the same loans that we otherwise would have taken over from the same borrowers on the same terms, then the payment of this £70,000,000 a year can be arranged with the least possible disturbance. There would be no particular reason why the dollar exchange should be affected, and no particular reason why the balance of exports and imports need be interfered with. They would merely hold in their safes documents from foreign debtors which otherwise we should hold in ours. But it will not happen automatically. When we announce that we are going to pay 300,000,000 dollars a year to America, nothing will automatically happen to make Americans step into our shoes as lenders. At present the foreign borrowers come to London because the terms they can get in London are more satisfactory to them in some cases—not always, and then they go to New York—than the terms they can get in New York. They do not come here for any other reason. At any rate, they would not go to New York instead of coming here until New York is offering them more attractive terms than London is offering them. Something will have to happen, therefore, which will make the New York market more attractive to borrowers than London to the extent of 300,000,000 dollars a year. If the American investor is very nearly primed for this class of investment, if he is only just hanging off because he would like another quarter per cent, or something of the kind; if he just cannot quite compete with the terms London can offer to India or to Australia, or whoever it is, if that is the case, then a comparatively small amount of pressure of dear money in London might make borrowers go to New York instead. But I am not sure that that is the case. One of the difficulties is not the rate of money, but the fact that New York is more inclined than we are to insist on tying up the loans with contracts. If the loan is tied up with conditions as to who gets the contracts, then the substitution of America as the lender will not help us to pay the debt, because other factors in the balance of trade will also be altered. It is only a loan on the same conditions as we make the loan which will help us to pay the debt. That is one reason. The other reason is that it is very doubtful whether the American investor for a very long time to come is going to take the attitude towards foreign investment that we in this country traditionally have taken. In the first place, in a great undeveloped country of that kind, there are immensely more opportunities for investment at home. Secondly, in a country like America, the average investor necessarily knows far less about the outside world from an investment point of view than a country like this, where such an enormous number of business men have direct connection with international trade, and are in a position to know of their own knowledge a good deal about the relative credit of foreign borrowers. Thirdly, there is another influence which I think is rather alarming. America has in fact lent on a very large scale during the last two or three years, and if you look through the list of what she has lent I think that any London issuing house would think she has lent a good deal rather injudiciously. The Americans have taken up a great many loans that the best issuing houses in London have been inclined to turn down. It is not at all outside possibility that a good many of those loans which America has made lately will not turn out very well for her. If that is the case, there will be a very considerable reaction against lending abroad. The combination of that with other factors I have mentioned may make a very great reaction against lending abroad, so that the American investor will only be willing to step into the shoes of the London investor on very different terms from those which the London investor has been prepared to take.

Suppose we start paying 300,000,000 dollars a year to America, as I say, nothing will automatically happen to stop the foreign borrower from coming to London, and send him to New York instead. In order to preserve our exchange under the burden of the payment of 300,000,000 dollars, we shall have to take steps to induce or to drive the foreign borrower to go to New York. There are various ways in which we could do that. The Bank of England might exert its influence and take a very stiff line against the admission of any foreign borrowers to London at all. It probably would be within the power of the Bank of England to exert very great influence in that direction. That is one way. But while we may prevent the foreign borrower from coming to London, we could not ensure that he would be entertained in New York, and if the class of foreign loans which we have been making are not made at all, that may have very serious reactions on foreign trade generally. That will not leave things exactly as they are. It will not mean that our exporting industries can go on exactly as they have done if the countries which are in the habit, for reasons of development, of being large borrowers, are cut off from the market altogether. If America steps into our shoes, well and good, but if they are merely cut off from London by the attempt of England to preserve the London market from a charge which is incompatible with our paying the American debt, then the situation is in all respects different.

Another method would be to keep money in London for a long period very dear—decidedly dearer than in New York. We might have a policy which we intended to maintain over years of keeping money, say, effectively two per cent higher in London than in New York, in order to make sure that the price which we should have to charge for loans for foreign borrowers would be very much higher than they could probably get accommodated with in New York. There would be a great objection to that on our part. People do not like very dear money going on for years. They would point out quite justly that, while it might be effective for the particular purpose, it would also hinder our own industry enormously that they should have to pay a rate for money which was not justified on its merits, but which was merely a deterrent rate to keep foreign borrowers away. If, on the other hand, you try to meet them by attempting, as was the case at one time during the War, to have a different rate for foreign money from what you have for home money, I think you are landed into all kinds of interference with the freedom of finance which is the essence of the success of London. During the War it was necessary to do it, and during the war there were so many interferences with freedom that one more did not very greatly matter; but a continuing policy of interference, not merely for months, but for years, I believe would be extraordinarily injurious to the position of London, and to its whole finances. For all these reasons, therefore, I think that the Bank of England, the Treasury, and the City generally, will have their work cut out to make sure that borrowers to the tune of 300,000,000 dollars per annum, who would naturally come to London, shall not come to London but shall visit New York instead, and be favourably entertained there. Unless that can be arranged, there will be enormous difficulties in our paying the interest on this loan. We could not do it merely by an alteration of exports and imports without undergoing a significant change in our level of life, and in fact no one really thinks we could do that. The source from which we are supposed to be going to pay it is the source which I am mentioning, namely, that fund which we are now investing abroad will be transferred to America instead of to the pockets of people who would otherwise borrow from us. Nobody looks to any other source. But the business of diverting that source from the channels into which it naturally flows into the channels into which it would have to flow in the future, is going to be extraordinarily difficult and anxious, and it is not likely that we shall discover quite the right way to do it possibly for a few years to come. We shall make experiments, but we shall have a new problem of extreme difficulty which our financial genius may enable us to solve sooner or later, but which will not be easy.

During the transitional period, before we have solved how to get that adjustment brought about, it will be very difficult to stabilise sterling for good at the old par—in fact, it will be difficult to stabilise it anywhere, and it will probably be more difficult to stabilise at a high level than at a lower level which gives us a certain margin in hand. Unless, therefore, there is a distinctly satisfactory solution in our favour of the American debt question, the whole future is very full of anxiety, and trade will be very liable to be burdened for a considerable time to come with the expense, inconvenience, and uncertainty of the big seasonal fluctuation, which, for the reasons I gave in my last lecture, is bound to take place till you have sterling pegged again. Unless you have sterling pegged, there is no possible way of avoiding the seasonal fluctuation, though as time goes on, it may keep within rather narrower limits than has been the case in the past.

All this I am saying tonight is a little complicated, and it is not very clear-cut; but it is these things which have to be in the mind of the banker when he is deciding what his policy is towards the levelling of sterling and all these linked-up questions of the repayment of the debt and so forth. I am not satisfied, from the discussions which I have heard, and from the discussions which I have seen in print, that all these considerations have been taken fully into account. The thing has been done a little blindly. People have said, 'Of course we must go back to par, and we can do it, and honour requires it', and so forth. But we have put a bandage round our eyes and just plunged blindly in that direction. If it was absolutely required by honour,

I agree we ought to do it; but for the reasons which I quoted from Professor Irving Fisher in an earlier lecture, that is not really the case—we are under no such obligation. In fact, in so far from injuring creditors by having sterling below par, we are helping foreign debtors. A great many countries owe us money in terms of sterling. The more we raise sterling in the terms of value, the more they owe us. That is one of the subtle advantages we get, but, so far as the outside world goes, they owe us much more sterling than we owe them. It is quite untrue, therefore, to suppose that we are cheating the rest of the world in any sense by fixing legal tender at a new value. Legal tender has constantly been fixed at new values in history. We have a long history, but even after the wars of Napoleon a change was made. Our standard is the only one which has existed for a hundred years. There is no other standard in Europe which has lasted for fifty years, and all the precedents are in favour of change. The worst of it is they generally take place, not judiciously, not moderately, but under the pressure of events, immoderately and injudiciously, and very often with a considerable flavour of dishonesty. It is worth mentioning again, if there is any question of justice, surely it is a stable purchasing power you have to give to people rather than a stable quantity of metal. However, I see the point of view of those who hold the opposite opinion, only I say those who hold the opposite opinion must not take it light-heartedly. Those who think that for reasons that they regard as overwhelming we must fix it at par must face, which I do not think they do, the cost of that. They must not do it without facing the cost. Just as I agree with those who say that we must pay America what they call upon us to pay, also we must not say that light-heartedly, or without thinking a very great deal about what the consequences are going to be. It is so easy to get a good reputation by saying, 'Of course we shall pay', without going into any detail about it. That is not, in fact, the way we shall pay. We shall only pay if we go into full details and arrange our policy in all particulars so as to bring about the result to which we have committed ourselves.

That completes what I have to say about devaluation in this country. I just have one word in conclusion on a small theoretical point which I think is a little interesting; that is the difference in the method of adjustment of a currency to the outside world when the exchanges are pegged and when they are unpegged. Under present conditions, as soon as we import too much or export too little, the exchanges move against us; and when the exchanges move very rapidly the price of every article is changed—the price of imports and exports is changed almost forthwith. In Germany now when the exchange falls, prices adjust themselves not completely, but very rapidly so that as soon as the country is buying too much, prices rise very rapidly, and the reaction sets in—it economises and it purchases less. So that the unpegged exchange has one curious advantage which people overlook—it puts the brake on very rapidly. If, on the other hand, you have a pegged exchange, then if you are purchasing more than you can afford, there is a tendency for gold to flow out in payment of the adverse balance. The effect of the outflow of gold is to make money dearer by slow stages which are familiar to people. That reacts on trade. It makes trade curtail itself rather, and gradually, by a very slow causal process, forces home prices down, until the home price is no longer attractive to the importer because it is falling below the outside price, and the country then economises in its consumption. But it is a very long and slow process. You do not get adjustment anything like as fast as you do with the unpegged exchange; consequently the pegged exchange is very hard to operate except in rather stable conditions, because the method by which correction comes into play is such a very slow one. That is one of the very deep reasons why in unstable conditions you almost invariably do have an unpegged exchange. The advantage of the pegged exchange is that as the method is a slow one a mere seasonal or temporary deficit does not produce an excessive result. If it is a seasonal or temporary deficit, the method of correcting this, long before parity, which operates under the pegged exchange, has had time to work itself out, so that things are left undisturbed; whereas, the unpegged exchange is sensitive, not only to influences to which it ought to be sensitive, namely, when the country has been buying too much, but it is sensitive to mere fleeting influences, mere news in the newspapers, or the mere season of the year, and so on; so that you have home prices bobbing about for reasons which are not permanent causes at all. The unpegged exchange is so sensitive that it is valuable for certain purposes, but it is far too sensitive for other purposes; yet one has to admit that the pegged exchange is so slow in its operation that it is dangerous for a country to adopt until it is sure that the basic conditions are fairly sound: then, as a correction to the seasonal movement, it is essential. That is an argument which is rather of the opposite tenor to most of what I have been saying in these lectures, but it is of sufficient interest and importance, and has enough relevance on the other side of the case for it to be right that I should mention it in conclusion.

Keynes sent a copy of the transcript of his lecture of 5 December to Stanley Baldwin, the Chancellor of the Exchequer.[4] He met Baldwin on 18 December.

During the remainder of 1922 and early 1923, Keynes returned to international matters. However, he also began work on what was to become *A Tract on Monetary Reform* (*JMK*, vol. IV). On 15 January 1923 he reported on his progress to his publisher.

To MAURICE MACMILLAN, *15 January 1923*

Dear Mr Macmillan,

I am preparing for early publication, I hope in March, a short volume entitled 'Essays on Money and the Exchanges'. I enclose a provisional Table of Contents.[5] I estimate that the length ought not to run to more than 40,000 to 50,000 words.

---

[4] See *JMK*, vol. XVIII, pp. 99, 101–2.
[5] This has not survived in Keynes's own papers.

76

I am proposing to make use in this volume of the material of articles which I have contributed during the past year to the *Manchester Guardian* Special Supplements on *Reconstruction in Europe*, of which I have been the Editor. But the volume will be a continuous one, by no means a mere reprint of articles. I am discarding a good deal of what I printed in the articles, on the other hand adding a good deal of new matter, and, generally speaking, modifying and re-arranging the whole so as to weld it into a continuous story.

I should be grateful if your firm would publish this volume on the same terms as you have agreed to for my other recent publications. I think the format might be the same as my last volume, *A Revision of the Treaty*, on which I estimate my matter would run from 160 to 200 pages. I am in a position to send more than half the copy to the printer forthwith, and as I should like him to get on with the proof sheets without delay, I should propose to send this to you for transmission to Messrs Clark (if they are to print the volume) as soon as I hear from you that you are willing to undertake publication.

The book will differ from my other recent volumes in that it will be suitable for use as a textbook in universities, and as it contains a considerable amount of new matter adapted either for advanced or relatively elementary work I think it might have a considerable vogue as time goes on for this purpose. This means that the sales are likely to be spread over a long period, and not so much concentrated as was the case with my pamphleteering works. I should also hope, however, for a considerable immediate circulation in financial circles, and should propose to print a first edition of 5,000 copies.

As regards the American rights, I am writing to Messrs Harcourt, Brace & Co., who have published my two volumes on the Peace Treaty.

Yours sincerely,

[copy initialled] J.M.K.

On 31 January, during his speech as Chairman of the National Mutual Life Assurance Society, Keynes returned to domestic affairs.

From a speech to the Annual Meeting of the National Mutual, 31 January 1923

My own view is that the strong tendency towards the revival of trade and confidence in this country, which has already begun, will need facts, and not merely fears, to hold it back. Many favourable conditions are now developing, and although the growth of confidence about the level of prices has been necessarily retarded here, as compared with the United States, so long as the rise of the sterling exchange has continued to depress sterling prices in relation to dollar prices, the end of this movement must come sooner or later. Whether political developments are good or bad, I expect a rise, rather than a fall, of prices, which, however, is not necessarily the same thing at all as general prosperity. The number of men in employment is now about the same as before the War, which is something to set against the depressing facts that no work is at present available for the substantial increase in the employable population since 1913, and that those who are employed are probably producing on the average about 10 per cent less than formerly for approximately the same real wage. Without great improvements in the technique and intelligence of trade and industry, it looks doubtful whether, on these terms, we shall be able to employ the whole employable population except at the very top of the periodic booms. The above estimate is in conformity with the indications of several other groups of statistics that the general turnover of trade is now on the average somewhere round about 10 per cent below the *pre-war level.*

Keynes's comment was picked up by several newspapers and by Ramsay MacDonald, the leader of the Opposition in the House of Commons, during the debate following the King's Speech; Keynes then clarified his views.

FINANCE AND INVESTMENT, 1922–1923

To the Editor of The Times, *14 February 1923*

Sir,

A statement which I made as chairman of the National Mutual Assurance Society about the capacity of this country to find work for the whole employable population has been so widely quoted in a form slightly but materially different from that in which I made it, notably by Mr Ramsay MacDonald in the course of the debate on the Address, that I beg leave to explain myself.

I estimated, speaking broadly, that the working classes were receiving approximately the same real wage as before the War for an output (largely due to a diminution of working hours), perhaps 10 per cent less, and then went on to say that I doubted 'whether *on these terms* we shall be able to employ the whole employable population except at the very top of the periodic booms *without great improvements in the technique and intelligence of trade and industry*'.

The words which I have italicised have been generally omitted by those who have quoted me. But they are important. I limited myself to doubting whether the present standards of working-class conditions of life were compatible with the provision of full and continuous employment, failing more economical production by some means or another.

Nevertheless, even though we may still hope to get relief from the progress of science, the accumulation of capital, and more good will and skill, in their respective functions, from workmen and from employers; yet, if the young men entering on their working life continue to exceed in number the old men completing theirs by 100,000 to 250,000 every year, sooner or later knowledge, saving, industry, and skill may be outpaced, and the standard of life decline. I meant to suggest, therefore, that the problem of unemployment is already, in part, a problem of population.

Your obedient servant,

J. M. KEYNES

Except for an article 'Some Aspects of Commodity Markets' (*JMK.*, vol. XII) and a reply to a criticism of the National Mutual's investment policy (*JMK.*, vol. XII), Keynes then remained out of public print until control of *The Nation and Athenaeum* passed in May to the group of Liberals of which he was chairman. Thereafter, he was a regular contributor to that journal, both in longer articles, initially dealing with international affairs, and in a weekly contribution under the general title 'Finance and Investment', often with a more informative sub-title.

From The Nation and Athenaeum, *5 May 1923*

THE RISE IN GILT-EDGED SECURITIES

The prolonged rise in long-dated Government stocks from their low point at the end of 1920 has profoundly modified the rate of interest obtainable. If we take Funding Loan as representing the general movement (Funding Loan, Conversion Loan, and Local Loans Stock all yield nearly the same rate of interest), the interest yield (allowing for redemption) has been as follows:—

	£ s.		£ s.
Jan. 1, 1920	5 8	Jan. 1, 1922	5 6
April 1	5 18	April 1	4 15
July 1	5 18	July 1	4 12
Oct. 1	6 0	Oct. 1	4 16
Jan. 1, 1921	6 2	Jan. 1, 1923	4 14
April 1	5 15	April 1	4 9
July 1	5 14	May 1	4 6
Oct. 1	5 12		

Deducting income tax at 4s. 6d. in the £, the net yield to the investor on these stocks has now fallen as low as £3 7s. per cent, which is within a few shillings of the corresponding net yield on Consols in 1914. That is to say, the return to new savings has practically gone back to its pre-war figure. This seems rather remarkable having regard to the vastly increased supply of Government securities, the shortage of available capital for (e.g.) housing and many other desirable enterprises, and (according to the general belief) the diminished volume of saving. Thus a question arises of the greatest possible interest and importance to every banker and insurance company, and even to most trustees and average investors: Is the movement of recent months an indication of permanent tendency and of a return under peace conditions to a low yield on new savings? Or is it, in part at any rate, merely a phase of the business depression out of which we are just emerging and a consequence of low Bank rate, which is certainly not going to last for ever.

It is very much the fashion just at present to give the first answer. The conventional advice to trustees and others is that the rate of interest may be expected to fall further and that they will do well, therefore, to get into long-dated securities. Yet we cannot help thinking that this may be just the contrary of what is wise. To begin with, the conventional advice is often wrong, because of the natural tendency, in the absence of a reasoned opinion, to believe that what has been happening lately is going on happening for the future; whereas, in truth, every rise in Conversion Loan makes a further rise not more, but less, likely. When, three years ago, long-dated securities were falling in price and beginning to look attractive, that was just the moment when the conventional advisers put it about that short war bonds were the only safe investment.

But there are deeper reasons than this for thinking that the present prices of long-dated securities may be connected with the present phase of the business cycle, and may weaken when, in due course, this phase gives place to the next. We have now had cheap money and low rates of interest on bank deposits for a long enough time to affect the slow-moving mind of the general public. Money rates fell by half during 1921, but bank deposits were undiminished. During 1922, while money became still cheaper, deposits began to diminish steadily. For nine months now, ever since last July, the banks have paid only 1 per cent upon deposits. And at last, this spring, bank deposits have experienced a really sharp fall—£100,000,000 in two months. Probably part of this money has been paid over to the Government in taxes and has enabled the Treasury to redeem debt, and part has flowed into the investment market. A movement on this scale cannot continue long, and, when Bank rate rises again, the deposit account may recover its popularity with the public and will certainly be needed by the banks to finance trade.

If and when trade and business activity revive (and they show many signs of recovery), a direct influence will be felt on the price of long-dated securities. At present stocks of goods of all kinds are low and average prices have not risen materially. Thus firms which are financially strong are not yet in need of all their resources and have temporarily invested many millions in the gilt-edged market. So far the reduction of bankers' deposits has been mainly met by a reduction of the banks' holdings of Treasury bills, which are now only half what they were at the beginning of 1922. Consequently, when their customers again require an expansion of advances, it may be necessary for the banks to sell investments to provide the funds.

To a material extent, therefore, the present strength of the gilt-edged market is due to the ease of the money market and the low Bank rate. Thus it depends for its continuance on a continuance of these conditions. Is such a continuance likely? When we look at what is happening in America it hardly seems so. Conditions in America have been of late about six months ahead of conditions here. Experience there is not encouraging to holders of long-dated securities. In New York gilt-edged securities touched their highest prices last September. Since then they have depreciated about 8 per cent. During the same period similar securities in London have appreciated 9 per cent. Thus within six months relative bond prices in the two centres have changed by 17 per cent. A big volume of buying of bonds by London in New York has been the inevitable result—a factor which may largely explain the fall of the dollar–sterling exchange so early in the year (from 4.72 touched in February to 4.63 this week).

The same situation is apparent in the bill market (sixty to ninety day bills). Last September the average New York rate for these maturities was 4 per cent and the London rate about $2\frac{1}{2}$ per cent—already a dangerous difference in favour of New York. At the present time the New York rate has risen to 5 per cent; that is to say, a difference of $1\frac{1}{2}$ per cent per annum has widened to 3 per cent within the last six months. New York is anxiously watching lest the intense business activity there should flare up into a boom, and the tendency of money with them is upwards rather than downwards. Thus the London position is highly unstable. The sterling exchange is already showing great sensitiveness, and it is unlikely that we can get through the usual autumn pressure with such a disparity of discount rates between London and New York.

The general upshot is that—at present prices, at the present season of the year, at the present phase in the credit cycle, with present conditions in New York—Conversion Loan, Funding Loan, and the like are a highly speculative proposition, unsuitable for timid investors, and especially unsuitable for businesses which will want their money liquid if trade and prices revive.

From The Nation and Athenaeum, *12 May 1923*

FURTHER REFLECTIONS ON GILT-EDGED SECURITIES

Several comments in the City columns of the Press on the contents of this page last week include, amongst much complete or partial agreement, some friendly criticisms. The City Editor of *The Times* points out that the reduction in the supply of Treasury bills may have played a considerable part by driving the banks into longer-dated securities. If this is the case, the effect has probably been produced rather by the banks' customers transferring deposits, against which the banks had held Treasury bills, into long-dated securities than by direct purchase of such securities on the part of the banks themselves. Between January, 1921, and the present time, the banks' deposits have fallen by about £200,000,000. During the same period the banks' advances fell by £100,000,000, and their discounts by £113,000,000. Thus the amount of the reduction of their bill-holdings was almost wholly required to meet the falling off in the excess of deposits over advances.

Moreover, the banks, so far from increasing their investments in recent months, have largely diminished them. Between August, 1921, and August, 1922, the banks' investments were rising, but since last August they have fallen by more than £60,000,000. The complete figures are worth giving in detail:—

Nine clearing banks (£000,000s)

	Deposits	Advances	Excess of deposits
Jan. 1921	1810	845	965
Jan. 1922	1826	752	1074
July 1922	1730	721	1009
October 1922	1686	724	962
Jan. 1923	1693	726	967
March 1923	1596	742	854
April 1923	1606	744	862

Thus the banks have for investment £212,000,000 less than at the beginning of 1922, the other side of which is shown by the following figures:—

	Discounts	Investments	Total
Jan. 1921	362	317	679
Jan. 1922	440	333	773
July 1922	335	386	721
Oct. 1922	309	370	679
Jan. 1923	320	358	678
March 1923	250	333	583
April 1923	249	327	576

Thus whilst since the beginning of the year the public have been taking their money off deposit for investment, the banks have been busy turning their investments out. The public have been buying what the banks have been selling.

In arguing along these lines, however, one is liable to overlook that the Government can only pay off Treasury bills out of the receipts of taxation or new bond issues. Thus the deposits lost by the banks, in excess of the amount used to pay off the banks' own advances and to buy investments which the banks are selling, must have been spent, directly or indirectly, either in paying taxes or in buying the new bond issues, leaving nothing over to compete for pre-existing bond issues. The word 'deflation' used in this connection is perplexingly ambiguous. If the gradual replacement of Treasury bills by Treasury bonds and other longer-dated Government issues is called deflation, Mr McKenna has constantly proclaimed, from his vantage post of knowledge, that this policy has actually retarded the rise in the gilt-edged market. On the other hand, one must accept the argument of *The Times* that the reduction in the supply of Treasury bills has been a factor in keeping money cheap, which in turn is largely responsible for the strength of the gilt-edged market.

Perhaps a complicated situation can be summed up like this: a relatively small excess of demand over supply for long-dated British Government securities, due to the lack of competing uses for money has been able with the assistance of favourable sentiment and the unattractive yields on short-dated securities, to drive up their price. But if this is right, the tendency may be rapidly reversed as soon as competing uses for money revive and the yield on short-dated securities improves. In short, we get back to the same conclusion as before, that the prices of long-dated securities will find it hard to stand up against a revival of enterprise and a higher Bank rate.

It must be admitted that this argument leaves open one contingency, in the event of which long-dated securities may

85

continue to rise in price, namely, a prolonged period of stagnation and lack of confidence such as was experienced in the 1890s. If loans for foreign governments and home industrials are both distrusted, the rate of interest obtainable on British Government securities may remain artificially low.

These broad movements are hard to analyse correctly. More simple-minded correspondents ask—if they are not to buy Conversion Loan and the like, what *ought* they to buy? On the assumption that they are limited to trustee securities, there is really only one answer—5 per cent National War Bonds, due in 1927 and 1928. These investments, allowing for a small loss on redemption (they stand at about $106\frac{5}{8}$ and will be paid off at 105), yield a shade more than Conversion and Funding Loan, namely, about $4\frac{3}{8}$ per cent. They have only shared very slightly in the recent rise, and should not fall much even if the gilt-edged market has a set-back. Incidentally, they have the advantage of a continuing option of convertibility into 5 per cent War Loan (at the rate of £$105\frac{1}{4}$ War Loan for each £100 War Bond); an option which costs next to nothing at present prices, since with War Loan at 101, the amount of War Loan into which £100 War Bond is convertible is worth £$106\frac{3}{8}$. Thus in order to prefer Conversion Loan and the like to these War Bonds, it is necessary to be fairly confident that there will not be a revival of trade between now and 1927 sufficient to bring Conversion Loan *at any time* materially below its present level. Many authorities believe that Conversion Loan is on an uninterrupted progress to a 4 per cent basis, which would mean a price of $87\frac{1}{2}$ as compared with the present price of nearly 81. It would be rash to deny the possibility of this. But Conversion Loan will be poised between two opposing sets of influences, and might just as well fall by $6\frac{1}{2}$ points as rise by that amount.

Those investors for whom stability of money income over a large number of years to come is of paramount importance can properly ignore these arguments. But there are just as many for whom stability of capital value is important. Amongst these, firms holding more money than they can use in the business for the time being must certainly be included; and for them War Bonds seem clearly the right alternative.

All readers of *The Nation* who hold 5 per cent National War Bonds (3rd series) due September, 1923, ought to do something about it immediately. Owing to these bonds having an option of conversion into 5 per cent War Loan, they stand at present at an artificial price. This option, however, must be exercised at latest within a fortnight of June 1st next. Holders should, therefore, either sell and deliver their bonds before the option right expires, or exercise the option themselves. Otherwise they will incur a certain loss of about $4\frac{1}{2}$ per cent. The present price of the bonds is $106\frac{5}{8}$ *plus* accrued interest. On September 1st next they will be paid off at 102. It is an unusual pleasure to be able to give a piece of financial advice which will almost certainly benefit some reader of *The Nation* and will quite certainly be right!

From The Nation and Athenaeum, *19 May 1923*

THE FOREIGN EXCHANGES AND THE SEASONS

The dollar-sterling exchange merely compares the value of the dollar and of the pound. The value of the dollar is what it will buy in the United States. The value of the pound is what it will buy in England. Therefore the rate of exchange depends on the level of prices in America compared with the level of prices here. That, in a nutshell, is the modern theory of exchanges, which perplexes nine-tenths of the world under the honorific designation of purchasing-power-parity.

In theory and even in practice there are some refinements to mention. But if we are comparing one year with another they are comparatively unimportant. Ever since the Armistice the theory has *worked* on the whole amazingly. If you draw curves of the actual rates of exchange between the United States, England, France, and Italy, and then another set of curves showing the ratios of the price levels in these countries, you find that the two are seldom far apart and always tend together again after every divergence. For example, between the United States and England the actual rate of exchange and the ratio of the price levels in the two countries have been within 1 per cent of one another in September–November, 1919; March–April, 1920; April, 1921; September 1921; January–June, 1921; and February, 1923. If, however, we are comparing, not one year with another, but one week with another, or one month with another, there are two other influences which are very important.

The first is *speculation*. A country's exchange is more sensitive than its price level to what the world thinks is going to happen but has not happened yet. Speculators may sell or buy a country's money because they *anticipate* that it is going to fall or rise in value. But this influence obviously cannot last very long. Speculators can only cause the exchange to rise or fall at an earlier date than it would have done otherwise. For they have to reverse their transaction in due course, buying back or selling out as the case may be; so that, whether the thing which they anticipated has happened or not, their influence washes out sooner or later. Generally sooner rather than later, because the mass of speculators take short views and lose heart very quickly if there is any delay in what they anticipated. The various Reparation Conferences of recent years have caused the most ridiculous fluctuations in the franc exchange, but the lasting influence of the speculation to which they have given rise has been absolutely *nil*. Most people vastly exaggerate the effect of speculation on the course of exchange. Its momentary effect is often so sensational that we forget what a fleeting affair it is—worth three months hence about as much as a leader in today's *Daily Mail*. It is only really important on the very rare occasions on which it precipitates a panic—that is to say, imitative action on a large scale by numbers of people who are not speculators at all, but are just terror stricken.

The other is the *season* of the year. This influence is as much under-estimated by the public as that of speculation is exaggerated. Sensible speculators ought to observe a close season for shooting at the franc just as much as at other high-flying birds. Economical tourists will find it, as a quite general rule, decidedly cheaper to travel in France and Italy in the summer and autumn than in the spring—quite apart from the fact that these countries are always much colder at Easter than is generally supposed. If France had walked into the Ruhr in July instead of in January, the franc exchange might have told quite a different tale.

Why is this? It is mainly due to the revolution of the earth round the sun. Western Europe buys from the rest of the Northern Hemisphere the fruitful produce which the soil yields in the late summer and autumn. If her merchants are to get what they want on the best terms and of the right quality they must buy a considerable proportion just after harvest, when the agriculturalist is selling it. Somewhat earlier than this—some time between June and August—they begin to make their financial preparations. Simultaneously, America tends to call in her floating balances from abroad to help her in financing the crop movements. Thus in the summer and autumn Europe owes America money which she can only pay off gradually over the average of the year. This has always been so—before the War just as much as now. But when the exchanges were fixed within narrow limits, by virtue of the convertibility of the various national currencies into gold, international finance found on easy terms the credit required to tide over the seasonal difficulty. But now, when no one can say for certain what sterling, francs or lire are going to be worth in terms of dollars six months hence, it is not worth anyone's while to run the risk of supplying it except for an expectation of considerable profit; which expectation can only be provided by the European currencies, which are being pressed for sale, falling to a price decidedly below what, on balance is thought to be the probable price six months hence. Recently these expectations have been, on the whole, pretty well realised in practice, and international finance has pocketed its reward for the risk it has run. Perhaps this favourable experience may lead to its being prepared to do the business a bit cheaper this year, which would mean a less violent seasonal depression of the Western European exchanges. But the volume of risk-carrying required is so large, and the effect of affairs like the Ruhr is so upsetting and makes the calculation of risk so precarious, that we may possibly see this summer a fairly sharp movement of the usual kind. If the Ruhr business were to be settled, that, of course, might make a considerable difference; and short-range speculators may make themselves felt for a moment whenever the rumours in the newspaper suggest that something is in the air.

In 1919 the European exchanges fell heavily as a result of the Inter-Allied credits coming to an end. In 1922 there was a definite recovery of sterling, and this year there has been a definite deterioration of the franc for obvious reasons. But the following table shows how largely recurrent the movements have been:—

Percentage of dollar parity

Aug.–July	Sterling		Francs		Lire	
	Lowest	Highest	Lowest	Highest	Lowest	Highest
1919–20	69	88	31	66	22	56
1920–21	69	82	30	45	18	29
1921–22	73	92	37	48	20	28
1922–23*	90	97	29	41	20	27

* August–May.

During the past three years, francs and lire have been at their best in April and May, and at their worst between October and December. Sterling has not been quite so punctual in its movements, the best point of the year falling somewhere between March and June, and the worst between August and November. It will be seen that we are just approaching what has been hitherto the turning point of the year, and it will be interesting to watch what happens.

From The Nation and Athenaeum, *26 May 1923*

FINANCE AND INVESTMENT

Investors have short memories, and it is not easy to remember just what proportion the recent slight slump in industrial securities bears to the previous rise. For such a comparison the index number of twenty representative industrial ordinary stocks, published weekly by *The Economic Review*, is very useful. It tells the following story:—

1919	Jan. 1	148	1922	Oct. 14	114
	Nov. 1	173		Dec. 30	119
1920	Mar. 1	187	1923	Feb. 3	122
	July 1	149		Mar. 3	129
	Dec. 1	130		April 7	130
1921	Oct. 20	91		April 28	138
	Dec. 31	100		May 11	133
1922	April 1	103		May 18	132
	July 15	112			

In the past week there has been a further fall of about one point. Thus the reaction has merely obliterated the big improvement between April 7th and April 28th, and has lost very little of the progressive improvement of nearly 50 per cent since the low point of October, 1921. The latter also shows how very far off we still are from the boom conditions of 1920. We are not yet back at the level prevailing immediately after the Armistice.

The reaction in the United States began a little earlier,—in the middle of March; and has progressed rather further. Indeed, the downward movement on the London Stock Exchange has not been by any means an isolated phenomenon. Staple commodities, of which the price is sensitive,—copper, tin, rubber, cotton, jute and linseed, for example—have suffered at the same time quite a substantial fall. Memories of the slump are still so vivid that markets are unduly nervous, and everyone is on the look-out to avoid losses like those of 1920-21. The Ruhr situation is also extremely damaging to confidence. Nevertheless, the underlying conditions do not seem to be compatible with any serious set-back. Money is cheap and stocks of many commodities are in short supply. The business world is borrowing too little rather than too much. A renewal in due course of the upward movement is therefore the more probable alternative.

We are reaching the season of the year when the first forecasts of the harvest prospects begin to appear. In India a large crop has been just gathered. The Argentine crop harvested at the beginning of the year has also been large,—20 per cent better than last year. The Australian crop, however,—though this is not a big factor in the situation—was only moderate. The prospects in North America, to judge from the acreage and the condition of the winter-sown wheat, are fairly good, but are not unlikely to show some decrease on last year, when the Canadian crop realised a record figure. The most striking and fortunate feature is the unusually good promise of the European crops. In France the acreage has been increased by 10 per cent, and the condition is very good. In Italy the acreage is only slightly better, but the condition is brilliant. Throughout Germany, Austria, Hungary, and Jugo-Slavia the prospects are satisfactory to good. It is too early to say much about Russia. But there is more land under wheat than a year ago, and the outlook is promising. M. Krassin has published an article forecasting a considerable export surplus next autumn. The only important exception to these favourable conditions is in Roumania, where there is a serious reduction in acreage, mainly due to a huge falling off in Transylvania, and it does not appear at present as though there would be much surplus this year for export. Our own crops are rather backward. There was not enough frost in the winter and too much cold lately. But whilst British farmers can never be cheerful, they need never despair. Anything can happen.

From The Nation and Athenaeum, *2 June 1923*

TRUSTEE INVESTMENTS—HOME, COLONIAL, AND INDIAN

A note of caution was sounded in this column a few weeks ago [above, p. 86] about the merits of long-dated British Government stocks, such as Conversion Loan, as compared with short-dated stocks, such as National War Bonds. We pointed out that the latter offered less risk to any investor for whom stability of capital value was an important consideration. Nevertheless, if we are comparing not British Government stocks amongst themselves, but British Government stocks with other trustee investments, there are strong arguments for sticking to our own home securities. It is generally a good rule for an investor, having settled on the class of security he prefers—long-dated, or short-dated bonds, trustee investments or foreign government bonds, or bank shares, or oil shares, or investment trusts, or industrials, debentures, preference or ordinary, whatever it may be—to buy only the best within that category. The extra yield obtainable on the second-best seldom compensates adequately for the increased risk and diminished marketability. This is not less true in the gilt-edged than in other markets.

The extra yield obtainable just now on Indian and colonial stocks is too small to justify the investor in preferring them to home stocks. It is not prudent for those who take long views to overlook either the precarious element in the Indian situation or the great weight of foreign debt accumulating in Australia in proportion to population. The slump in India stocks some little time ago may have been overdone; but the subsequent recovery has left no adequate margin to cover contingencies. And on Australian and other colonial stocks the extra yield is so trifling as to do little more than compensate for their inferior marketability. The following comparisons exhibit the present situation, all the yields being calculated to allow approximately for accrued interest and for loss or profit on redemption:—

Long-dated stocks

	Price	Yield £. s. d.		
3½% Conversion Loan (after 1961)	80½	4	7	6
4% New South Wales (1942–62)	91	4	10	0
4% New Zealand (1943–63)	92½	4	8	0
4% Victoria (1940–60)	91¼	4	9	0
4% South Africa (1943–63)	91	4	9	0
3½% India Stock (after 1931)	71½	4	19	0

For the period between the dates given in brackets there is an *option* to the borrowing governments to redeem which they are free to exercise if it benefits themselves, and not to exercise if it would benefit the investor. Thus, in the case of the colonial stocks this option *against* the investor for a period of twenty years outweighs the advantage of definite redemption some forty years hence. Surely Conversion Loan is far preferable to any of these alternatives amongst long-dated stocks. Or if a somewhat higher yield is required, Bank of England stock yields, on the assumption of a continuance of half-yearly 6 per cent dividends, which the Governor's speech at the last Court seemed decidedly to encourage, about £4 15s. 6d. If a slight element of uncertainty is not disliked, is not Bank stock to be very much preferred to India Stock at the present level of prices?

94

Intermediate stocks

	Price	Yield £ s. d.
5% War Loan (1929–47)	101⅛	4 15 6
5% Victoria (1932–42)	101½	4 17 6
5% New South Wales (1932–40)	102⅝	4 16 6
5% South Australia (1932–42)	102¾	4 16 0

Here again the British Government security seems the cheaper at the price, even allowing for the extra three years' run on the colonial stocks before the option to redeem operates. It is not worth while to leave the straightforward course of home Government stocks for a shilling or two per cent.

Stocks redeemable within ten years

	Price	Yield £ s. d.
5% National War Bonds (1929)	106¼	4 10 6
5¼% Treasury Bonds (1930)	105	4 13 0
4% New Zealand (1929)	95¼	4 16 0
5¾% New South Wales (1922–32)	101	5 15 0
5½% India (1932)	103½	5 5 6

For these maturities the extra yield on Indian and colonial stocks is much more adequate. For example, 15s. per cent extra is obtainable on the comparable Indian security, as against 10s. per cent extra on the long-dated stocks. Moreover, the risk attaching to India stocks is more likely to eventuate after 1932 than before that date; so that there are some attractions in a ten-year Indian security yielding five guineas per cent. Nevertheless, in this, as in the other categories, there is not really enough inducement to tempt the ordinary investor outside his home Government stocks.

The prices at which new colonial and Indian loans have been

floated during the past month indicate, however, that the ordinary investor *is* tempted. New Zealand has just borrowed £4,000,000 at £4 12s. 7d.; and India £20,000,000 at £5 4s. 4d. The New Zealand loan stands at a trifling discount, and the other at a premium. Part of the explanation is probably to be found in the preference of many investors for new issues which can be purchased by filling up a form cut out of the newspapers without the interposition of banks or brokers. Immense numbers of small investors have no regular broker, and do not know the address of one. This big gap in our investment system is difficult to fill, yet requires some remedy. The brokerless investor may be reminded, however, that for any family which has not yet acquired its full quota Savings Certificates are still by far the biggest bargains in the gilt-edged market.

The 6 per cent cumulative income stock of the New Town Trust, redeemable at 110 not before 1933 or after 1945, of which the prospectus has been published in *The Nation and Athenæum* (May 19th), and which is still open for subscription, makes it appeal not to the ordinary investor, but to those anxious to support Garden City developments. The company has been formed to work in association with Welwyn Garden City Ltd., which has already secured substantial success. The board of directors receive no remuneration. The Trust holds £20,000 shares and debentures of the Welwyn Garden City Company, and its purpose is the general development of the new Garden City, particularly in connection with the farming of the permanent rural belt through an agricultural guild. £34,082 of the income stock has been already issued, and also £12,771 of ordinary capital. This stock has speculative features without offering speculative rewards; but investment in it will assist an interesting social experiment.

Keynes used his 'Finance and Investment' columns of 9 and 16 June for comments on the situation in Germany and the League of Nations loan to

Austria.[6] He then took a break from *The Nation* to work on his *Tract on Monetary Reform* [*JMK*, vol. IV], only returning to its columns on 7 July.

From The Nation and Athenaeum, *7 July 1923*

IS CREDIT ABUNDANT?—THE GRAND TRUNK RAILWAY

In spite of a low Bank rate, it is doubtful whether credit is really abundant, or adequate to carry on the business that offers at the present level of prices. Indeed, there is some indication that a secret process of deflation—surely to be regretted with trade as discouraged and unemployment as high as they are now—still continues. The most fundamental figure of our banking system is that of the 'other deposits' at the Bank of England, because these furnish the basis upon which the other banks, by an almost unvarying rule, build up their advances and their deposits. The banks lend in the form of advances to their customers between 40 and 50 per cent of their deposits, and they keep a trifle over 11 per cent of their deposits in cash and at the Bank of England. Unless they are armed with deposits at the Bank of England, their hands are tied, however cheap money may look, and however eager borrowers may be. Now the outstanding fact is that the 'other deposits' at the Bank of England, which averaged £128,000,000 in the first quarter of last year, £118,000,000 in the second quarter, and £112,000,000 in the third and fourth quarters, have been steady for the past five months at an average of £108,000,000. £20,000,000 off the other deposits may not look big; but it means that the banks must bring down their deposits by £180,000,000 and their advances by £90,000,000. These reductions have been fully realised; although the banks have been able latterly to keep their advances about steady by severely reducing their investments and bill holdings. The figures show that it cannot be easy for the banks to find resources for additional loans. It is impossible to say precisely why the 'other deposits' of the Bank of England have fallen, because the

---

[6] See *JMK*, vol. XVIII, pp. 161–5, 176–9.

Bank works in secret and does not explain itself. But whether it is deliberate or accidental, this deflation of at least 10 per cent can have done no good, and must share with political developments in Europe the responsibility for the weakening of the trade revival and the severe continuing unemployment.

The settlement of the claims of the United States for the payment of the expenses of its army of occupation, amounting to about £50,000,000, has been scarcely noticed in the English Press. According to the *New Republic* the sum due is to be paid in twelve annual instalments;—for four years the United States is to receive a quarter of the cash paid by Germany after the costs of the Allied armies of occupation have been met, and after four years the American claim will be a first charge on the cash receipts. After the expiry of four years the arrears are to carry interest.

Only now is there a Bill before the German Reichstag releasing trustees from the obligation to invest in fixed-interest bearing securities. The result of this obligation, intended presumably to secure safety, has been the total loss of all trust funds. The result of compelling any class of persons to invest solely in titles to legal-tender money is, sooner or later, in almost any country—to judge from past history—to deprive that class of a large part of their fortunes. Indeed, modern legislation governing trustee investments could be regarded, if we take a long view, as a provision to secure the gradual disappearance of inheritances and to avoid the foundation of perpetual fortunes.

Not that other types of investment are immune from disaster. The history of the Grand Trunk of Canada is a lesson against investing in public utilities abroad. It is within the power of any government, by means of suitable legislation, to render valueless an investment in a public utility; and if the proprietors are

98

absentee, the temptation to do so is considerable. In this particular case, however, the argument that the property is in fact altogether valueless has not completely convinced anyone outside Canada. There are two particular weaknesses in it which are worth pointing out. The incompetence of the late management is adduced as a reason for the worthlessness of the property. But this fact, precisely because it accounts for the absence of profits in the past, is, inasmuch as it is *remediable*, a bull point for the future. The worse the railway has been managed hitherto, the more hope for it in better hands. The other point is of a different kind. The arbitrators who judged the property to have no value seem to have believed that this result followed if, on the evidence, it was highly improbable that it would ever pay a dividend. This is not sound reasoning. Even if the odds were ten to one against a dividend being paid, still the property is not valueless; for a one-tenth chance of a dividend is worth something. No one could say, considering the future possibilities of increased population and prosperity in Canada, that the odds are more than a hundred to one against the first preference shares ever earning a dividend. But if not, then these shares have *some* value. The case of the Canadian Government must be based entirely on the argument that the liabilities of the Grand Trunk to the debenture holders of the Grand Trunk Pacific exceed the value of the Grand Trunk itself, and on the argument that it is within the power of the Canadian Government to render any railway valueless by its freight-rate legislation. It must not be forgotten, however, that the stockholders accepted arbitration, and naturally have no redress merely because the result of the arbitration is arguable. Apart from questions of equity, the attitude of Canada might be of doubtful prudence, —unless the country is prepared to be relatively independent in future of the type of foreign investor whose feelings and pockets are now suffering outrage,—if experience did not show abundantly how short memories are.

The path of the average investor is a miserable one. There is no financial reform more needed than a new and better organisation for taking reasonable care of ordinary savings.

On 5 July 1923, in the light of sterling's weakness on the foreign exchanges, the Bank of England raised Bank rate from 3 to 4 per cent. Keynes did not comment on the change at the first opportunity, *The Nation* for 7 July, but he turned to the issue the next week.

From The Nation and Athenaeum, *14 July 1923*

BANK RATE AT FOUR PER CENT

The raising of the Bank rate to 4 per cent is one of the most misguided movements of that indicator which have ever occurred. Trade is discouraged and declining; prices are falling slightly; employment is very bad; and the political situation is such as to damp down enterprise and hold everyone back from entering into new business. It is a moment when the business world requires every scrap of stimulus and encouragement which can be given it. There is *no necessary* reason why disturbances on the Continent need cause a million or two of Englishmen to stand idle. The present state of affairs is due quite as much, indeed much more, to depression in home trade than to loss of business with Europe. Our job is to do our best to free ourselves from the psychological reactions of foreign politics, which are found, in any case, to produce very considerable evils here also, and resolutely to keep our own business going as best we can. This is the moment which the Bank of England chooses deliberately to add one more discouragement, one more warning sign to anyone who contemplates new business that he had better wait a bit and keep his hands in his pockets, even if it means that his workmen must keep their hands in their pockets, too.

What is the explanation? It is not the practice of the Bank of England to give explanations. But there is not much doubt that the explanation is to be found in the fall of the dollar exchange (not at all unusual at this time of year) of about 2 per cent. That is to say, the Bank of England think it more important to raise the dollar exchange a few points than to encourage flagging trade. They do this under the influence of the Report of the Cunliffe Committee, a document written several months before the Armistice, necessarily without any knowledge of all the extraordinary post-war developments, and not containing a single reference to stability of prices and employment. The revision of this Report in the light of subsequent events is becoming a matter of first-rate political importance.

If the rise of the dollar were due to a rise in British prices, that is, to the depreciation of sterling, an increase in the Bank rate would be an appropriate remedy. But this is not the case. Many influences are at work,—a tendency of dollar prices to fall, the relative rates of interest here and in New York, the usual seasonal pressure, and political unrest. In so far as the fall of dollar prices is responsible, the dollar-sterling exchange *ought* to fall if, as Mr Baldwin said last week, we want to keep British prices stable. In so far as temporary transfers of funds are in question, by speculators on political prospects, or to meet seasonal requirements, the matter will cure itself sooner or later, and ought to be remedied, if the movement is severe enough to call for remedy, by the Bank's shipping gold or by the Treasury's postponing its purchases of dollars to meet interest on the debt. We are left, therefore, with the difference between the rates of interest in London and New York as the sole justification.

This difference is certainly *one* factor in the fall of the exchange. In this column, more than two months ago, [above, p. 83] we were amongst the first to point out the probable effect of the disparity on the dollar exchange. When the exchange is fixed within narrow limits, as it was before the War, relative interest rates are of paramount importance of determining the volume of short-period remittances,—a fact upon which the pre-war theory of Bank rate was largely based. When the exchange is not far off parity, as was the case earlier this year, this influence is still important. But with every movement of the exchange downwards its effect is diminished; and, as we have seen on several occasions in the recent past, a comparatively moderate fall in the exchange is sufficient to weaken the connection between the London and New York short-loan markets. That this must be so is made plain by straightforward arithmetic. If interest rates are raised 1 per cent per annum, the borrower for three months pays an additional $\frac{1}{4}$ per cent. At the present rate of exchange this is a little more than one American cent in the £ sterling; more exactly, the effect of the increased interest rate to the borrower would be counterbalanced by a movement of the exchange from $4\cdot57\frac{1}{4}$ to $4\cdot56$ between the date of borrowing and the date of repayment. A fluctuation of this amount is often experienced in a single day; a movement of ten times this amount has occurred in the past three months, and may very likely occur, one way or the other, in the next three months. Thus a trifling movement in the exchange would wipe out the advantage or disadvantage of paying 1 per cent per annum less or more for loans. The alleged American borrowing in London cannot be a pure interest transaction, but must be mainly an exchange speculation, either outright or in anticipation of the proceeds of sterling trade bills normally negotiated by American banks later in the year.

The effect on the exchange of raising the Bank rate at the present time is, in fact, limited to two influences. In so far as it is taken to indicate a determined policy on the part of the Bank of England to hold up the dollar exchange, it may have a temporary effect by inducing short-period speculators against sterling to close their positions. If such action is worth while—which is always doubtful, because the effect of such speculation cancels out over quite a short period—the same result can be achieved, without a bad effect on home trade, by shipping, or threatening to ship, gold, with the idea of buying it back again when the reaction comes.

The remaining influence, which is the only real and lasting one, brings us back to where we started. The paramount significance of an increase in the Bank rate must lie in its effect on sterling prices. Its real influence depends upon its leading to some curtailment of credit and some fall of sterling prices. It cannot be right to raise the Bank rate in present-day conditions,—which differ vitally from pre-war conditions, in that our currency is inconvertible,—*unless we deliberately desire to bring about a curtailment of credit, and to arrest a rising tendency or to produce a falling tendency in sterling prices.* This is not the case. The day before Bank rate was raised the Prime Minister and Chancellor of the Exchequer had rightly committed himself [*sic*] to the contrary. The Bank of England, acting under the influence of a narrow and obsolete doctrine, has made a grave mistake.

Keynes's article was the subject of extensive critical comment elsewhere in the Press. He dealt with his critics in the next issue of *The Nation*.

From The Nation and Athenaeum, *21 July 1923*

BANK RATE AND STABILITY OF PRICES—
A REPLY TO CRITICS

The articles in *The Nation and Athenaeum* on this subject have been widely quoted and have succeeded in creating a lively and useful controversy. Even the *Daily Mail* has done us the honour of a leading article entitled 'The New Suicide Club', the main point of which is that the dollar exchange should be as high as possible, because in that case the burden of the American debt will be as low as possible—a point to which we will return in a later issue. The *Manchester Guardian* heads its comments 'An Inflationist View'—a charge which anti-inflationists can, I suppose hardly expect to escape. If a low Bank rate helps trade, why, the *Manchester Guardian* asks, should not the present writer 'go farther and advocate a 1 per cent Bank rate and Government inflation to assist in providing credit for industry? Where exactly does he propose to draw the line?' He draws it at inflation. Why not? Rising prices stimulate trade unhealthily; falling prices depress trade injuriously. If prices had continued to rise sharply, as was the tendency earlier in the year, an increase in the Bank rate would have been perfectly right. A policy of price stability is the very opposite of a policy of permanently cheap money. During the last boom the present writer preached vehemently in favour of very dear money, months before the Bank of England acted. But when employment is very bad, enterprise disheartened, and prices with a falling tendency, *that* is not the moment to raise the Bank rate.

Some of our gentler critics, notably *The Economist*, agree with us in our general contention, but point out that a 4 per cent Bank rate is really a very mild measure, since the rates at which most bank advances are made do not follow Bank rate downwards below 4 per cent, and are therefore unaffected by the recent increase (although they would feel the full effect of a further rise to 5 per cent). There is much force in this argument. In so far as raising the Bank rate has no consequences, it will do no harm. A four per cent Bank rate is not nearly so injurious as a five per cent rate. If the recent movement is not to be regarded as an indication of a policy which may soon require five per cent for its maintenance, but is, so to speak, a casual act, it need not, we agree, be taken too seriously. Nevertheless, even a four per cent rate does have consequences—psychological reactions which cause enterprise to hesitate, dearer rates for trade bills, and marked discouragement to new issues, all of which depress trade.

One apologist for the Bank—the City Editor of the *Morning Post*—has discovered a reason for its action which had not occurred to us, namely 'enormous speculative positions' in gilt-edged stocks.* The object of the Bank, according to this

---

* He did not support us, however, when, more than two months ago, we suggested in this column that long-dated Government securities might be standing rather too high.

authority, was to make these speculators unload, this step being required because they were absorbing funds 'required for trade purposes'. 'Enormous benefit,' the argument goes on, 'has accrued to speculators in gilt-edged stocks, who have been able to borrow money on such terms as to secure very large profits arising both out of appreciation in capital value and the difference between the interest payable on the stock purchased and the rate of interest paid to the bankers.' Earlier in the year, bull speculation in this market was certainly very profitable; but the argument overlooks the fact that for two months before the Bank rate was raised, these bulls, in so far as they exist, had been steadily losing money. Moreover, it is cruel for those who have been predicting week by week that Conversion Loan was going to rise many points further, to turn round in this way on those who have taken their advice. If the object of the Bank was really to bring about a slump in the gilt-edged market, it has scored a modest success. It is possible, however, to agree that there has been a great deal of unwise investment of temporary funds in long-dated securities, especially by the financially stronger of our industrial concerns, without thinking it worth while to raise the Bank rate merely to force these holders out.†

Many of our contemporaries, however, have shared our views in greater or less degree—*The Spectator*, *The Saturday Review*, *The Investors' Chronicle*, *The Economist* (on essentials), the *Westminster Gazette* (with an admirably clear argument), for example; the weight of opinion making it clear that, whilst a four per cent Bank rate may, by itself, have only limited consequences, the policy behind it will, if it is persisted in at the cost of a further rise, provoke a widespread hostile criticism. Indeed, so long as unemployment is a matter of general political importance, it is impossible that Bank rate should be regarded, as it used to be, as the secret *peculium* of the Pope and Cardinals of the City.

† *The Economist* goes further than the *Morning Post* and thinks that the object of the Bank was to bring about speculative liquidation of all types of securities, and to shake markets generally—rather a savage procedure in view of the fact that these markets had been drooping and shaky for some little time.

The criticism of *The Nation*'s articles set forth in the City columns of *The Times* was perhaps the most interesting of all, because of the divided mind between the old school and the new, very representative of the state of mind of the City generally, which these comments show. *The Times* begins by agreeing that the object of monetary policy is to keep the price level stable,— which is our main point. In the next paragraph it perceives that this might mean abandoning the gold standard, a step which would be 'too complicated and hazardous'. It continues that 'the official policy is to restore the old gold parity'; that 'the penal monetary measures' which such a policy might require are objectionable; and that 'that, at any rate, is no part of our present monetary policy,'—which finally boxes the compass. *The Times* account of the matter might seem comical, if it were not such an accurate reflection of the actual state of affairs. It used to be our policy to restore the gold standard. It has become our policy to keep prices stable. We have taken on the new doctrine, without, as yet, discarding the old, and when they are incompatible we are torn between the two. Fortunately, we cannot but feel, reading its comments carefully, that *The Times*, like *The Economist*, is really with us on the main issue. We attacked the grandmother of Threadneedle Street, which was very improper, and we must expect a slight peppering. But *The Times*, like nearly everyone else, shrinks from the practical measures which the old doctrine would require from true believers.

The next week saw him turn to another comment by the City Editor of *The Times*.

FINANCE AND INVESTMENT, 1922–1923

From The Nation and Athenaeum, *28 July 1923*

THE MEASURE OF DEFLATION—AN INQUIRY INTO INDEX NUMBERS

The City Editor of *The Times* writes:—' As prices have remained stable within the past eighteen months, it is difficult to appreciate the force of many arguments employed by those who are avowedly in favour of stabilisation.' This statement is nearly true if we take, for example, the Board of Trade index of wholesale prices as our measure of stability. But this is not the whole story. The following figures show that the raising of the Bank rate is only one more step in a policy of deflation which has been silently but steadily pursued for some time,—a policy which is partly responsible for the failure of trade and employment in this country to keep pace with the revival in the United States during the first half of this year. The following attempt at a rough statistical estimate indicates that the actual deflation of purchasing power during the past eighteen months has amounted to about 10 per cent.

	(1) Bank of England private deposits*	(2) Aggregate note issue*	(3) Average of (1) and (2)*	(4) Clearing bank deposits†
1922				
1st Quarter	100	100	100	100
2nd Quarter	92	99	96	97
3rd Quarter	88	98	93	94
4th Quarter	88	96	92	94
1923				
1st Quarter	91	93	92	92
2nd Quarter	84	95	90	90

* Average of middle of each month.
† Average of end of each month.

The Bank of England's private deposits and the note issue comprise between them the available 'cash', upon the basis of which credit can be created. The clearing banks' deposits are the measure of the credit actually created. There is, as there should be, a fairly close agreement between the two, justifying 10 per cent as the best available estimate of the amount by which purchasing power has been deflated.

What has been happening to prices in the meantime? The index numbers of wholesale prices have only fallen slightly. But, as stated above, these figures do not give a complete account of the situation. The cost of food (and the cost of living generally), and also the level of wages, both of which have an effect on the demand for purchasing power out of proportion to the weight given them in index numbers of wholesale prices, have fallen much more sharply:—

	Board of Trade wholesale prices	Food prices	Wages
1922			
1st Quarter	100	100	100
2nd Quarter	99	100	94
3rd Quarter	97	95	88
4th Quarter	96	92	83
1923			
1st Quarter	98	90	82
2nd Quarter	99	87	82

The cost-of-living index number has moved practically with food prices.

The effective demand for purchasing power depends partly on the volume of trade and partly on the level of prices and wages. The above figures indicate that the latter, so far from being stable, have fallen probably as much as 10 per cent— perhaps more. If this is correct the volume of trade must have increased somewhat,—a conclusion which is also in accordance with the direct evidence of the employment figures and other data. The volume of employment, for example, has risen nearly 5 per cent, whilst other tests, such as output of coal, iron and steel, shipbuilding commenced, and tonnage of goods entering and leaving British ports yield much higher figures of improvement. On the whole, if we are to risk a generalisation, it might be fairly accurate to say that during the past eighteen months, purchasing power has been deflated 10 per cent, the effective level of prices and wages has fallen 10 per cent, and the activity of trade and employment throughout the country has increased by 5 per cent or more.

This represents a gallant effort on the part of business, in face of a falling price level and curtailed credit. But it has seemed latterly, with the added discouragement of the European situation that the struggle is too severe. The above figures indicate that the Bank of England has succeeded in restricting credit to such an extent that no further increase of business activity is possible without a further fall in the level of prices and wages, —a process which necessarily discourages new business, so long as it is going on.

We have had, during the period under review, the rare combination of a falling price level and expanding business, —both of them are indicative that an expansion of credit is required. Nevertheless the Bank of England has been using its secret and enormous powers to *contract* credit by no less an amount than 10 per cent. No one, least of all the writer of this page, will deny the evil influence on trade of the Ruhr occupation. But this is an *extra* reason for not discouraging trade in other ways. If the Labour Party are interested in remediable causes of unemployment, they would do well to cast their eyes more frequently and searchingly than they have done hitherto in the direction of monetary policy.

We should like to support most strongly the recommendation of an admirable article by Dr E. C. Snow in *The Manchester Guardian Commercial* that there should be an authoritative inquiry into the methods of compilation of index numbers. Some of those which are most widely quoted are open to serious criticism, if not for all purposes, at least for many of those to which they are in fact applied. The method of compilation ought to depend upon the precise purpose for which the index number is to be used to an extent which is seldom understood. Two recent events reinforce his argument. The dockers' strike was partly due to lack of confidence in the official cost-of-living index number. The Board of Trade index number of the wholesale cost of food rose from 147 in May to 153 in June; whilst the *Statist* (Sauerbeck) index number, also of the wholesale cost of food, fell from 163 in May to 154 in June. If one of the two most familiar index numbers rises 9 points and the other falls 9 points during the same month for the same limited category of articles, what is one to say? In 1887 the British Association appointed a Committee of Inquiry into the subject, the report of which remained for many years the leading authority. Perhaps the subject is better suited for inquiry by learned bodies than by the Government. Should not the British Association, the Royal Statistical Society, and the Royal Economic Society be urged to appoint a Joint Committee of Investigation?

Keynes's comments of 28 July brought further comment from the City Editor of *The Times* to which Keynes felt bound to reply.

To the Editor of The Times, *1 August 1923*

Sir,

I thank you for the comments you make in your City Notes of today on some observations of mine in *The Nation and Athenaeum* about the course of prices and of deflation. We can agree without difficulty about two facts:—

(1) For the past three months prices have shown a marked tendency to fall. Your own index number of wholesale prices published today gives April 164·8, May 162·5, June 158·8, and July 155·6—a sharp and decided movement. If we consider a longer period—namely, eighteen months, and take account not only of wholesale prices, but also of cost of living and of wages,

which are of high importance in determining the effective demand for purchasing power, we find that a movement downwards rather than upwards (which I estimate at around 10 per cent) is characteristic of the whole period, in spite of the fact that wholesale prices of materials made a determined attempt to rise between September, 1922, and April, 1923—a spurt which they have been unable to maintain in the face of other conditions.

(2) The basis of credit, and the actual creation of credit have both been deflated about 10 per cent over the same period of eighteen months.

When we come to the connexion between these two facts and the question how far fact (2) is controllable, I admit that no one can dogmatise. Nevertheless, I am supported by expert opinion in the belief that over a period of months the connexion between the two facts is very close indeed, and also that it lies in the power of the Bank of England, and the Treasury, within wide limits, to determine in the long run how much credit is created. If the Bank of England had pursued a different policy, I believe that prices would stand at a different level. Indeed, this is a third fact about which the contending parties can agree; for the policy of the Cunliffe Committee assumes that the authorities have the power in the long run to fix the price level, just as much as the policy of price stabilisation assumes it.

There is also a fourth fact, equally undeniable, of great practical importance just at this moment—namely, that in recent weeks prices in the United States have been falling even more sharply than here. This fall is more significant than the index numbers indicate, since it has affected especially certain commodities—namely, wheat, cotton, sugar, and oil, of which the real importance is far greater than that assigned to them in most index numbers.

The reason why this last fact matters so much is that it brings to a head a divergence between two policies which was previously latent. So long as dollar prices were rising, the policy of improving the dollar–sterling exchange was compatible with the policy of keeping sterling prices reasonably steady. We have most of us been expecting that there would be a slight tendency towards inflation in the United States, which would help to lift the sterling exchange. This tendency may indeed reassert itself before long, if the sky clears, in which case, all will be well, but for the time being it is reversed.

The question which matters in this controversy, the answer to which we want to know and are surely entitled to know, is whether it is the policy of the Bank of England to protect the sterling exchange, even at the risk of causing sterling prices to fall. The oracles are dumb. When the Pythian Prophetess makes signs in terms of Bank rate, she allows her votaries to breathe ambiguous interpretations of her meaning. We may differ legitimately as to the right policy for this country in difficult and unprecedented circumstances. But we have a right to know what the official policy in fact is. The Federation of British Industries can fairly claim a clear answer to their question, presented to the Prime Minister in a moderate and cogently argued memorandum, whether or not the official policy of the Bank of England is the same as that lately acknowledged by the Prime Minister—namely, to promote confidence in the price level. For my part I believe that confidence in the price level is the biggest practical help which the official world can give to the business world; and that the lack of this confidence is a considerable cause, and probably the only remedial one, of present unemployment. If the Prime Minister were able to announce that he had consulted the Governor of the Bank of England and that the two of them were determined to do all in their power to promote and preserve confidence in the existing level of sterling prices (letting the dollar exchange go hang, if necessary), great good would result. Failing this, I hope that the Federation of British Industries will call to their assistance the Federation of Trade Unions and push the controversy home.

Yours, &c.,

J. M. KEYNES

After the issue of 28 July, Keynes's signed contributions to Finance and Investment ceased on a regular basis, although unsigned contributions appeared from time to time. Keynes continued to deal with the issues he had raised in these columns in other places.

On 8 August Keynes contributed a paper at the Cambridge meetings of the Liberal Summer School. It appeared in full in *The Nation* of 11 August.

From The Nation and Athenaeum, *11 August 1923*

CURRENCY POLICY AND UNEMPLOYMENT

It may be inevitable that the average real wages of labour cannot, with the resources of nature, of invention, and of industry at our command, be raised to so high a figure as we should like. But the absurdity of labour being from time to time totally unemployed, in spite of everyone wanting more goods, can only be due to a muddle, which should be remediable if we could think and act clearly.

The most serious charge which can be brought against the system of private enterprise in business and of capitalistic investment as it exists to-day, is that it has failed, so far, to deal with this muddle. As time goes on things seem to get worse rather than better.

Indeed, Socialists might, I think, have pushed home this charge more powerfully than they have, inasmuch as the main part of the explanation of this muddle is deeply rooted in the peculiarities of the *existing* economic organisation of society. I shall not attempt in this paper to cover the ground, and I must not be supposed to ignore other factors in the total situation, if, in what follows, I concentrate exclusively on one particular aspect of the problem.

With the development of international trade, involving great distances between the place of original production and the place of final consumption, with the increased complication of the technical processes of manufacture, and with the seasons governing the date of supply of farm products, there must be a considerable interval of time between the dates when effort is expended and the date when the commodity finally yields up its usefulness. During this interval the business world is entering into liabilities in terms of *money*—borrowing money and paying out in money for wages and other expenses of production—in the expectation of recouping this outlay by disposing of the product for *money* at a later date. That is to say, the business world as a whole must *always* be in a position where it stands to gain by a rise of price and to lose by a fall of price. Whether it likes it or not, the technique of production under a régime of money-contract forces the business world always to carry a big speculative position; and if they are reluctant to carry this position, the productive process must be brought to a standstill. The argument is not affected by the fact that there is some degree of specialisation of function within the business world, the professional speculator coming to the assistance of the producer proper by taking over from him a part of his risk.

Now it follows from this, not merely that price changes profit some people and injure others, but that a *general expectation* of falling prices may inhibit the productive process altogether. For if prices are expected to fall, not enough people can be found who are willing to carry a speculative 'bull' position, and this means that lengthy productive processes involving a money outlay cannot be undertaken,—whence unemployment.

If prices fluctuate in a manner which cannot be, or at least is not, foreseen, some groups in the community will lose and some will gain. This often occurred before the War, and it was bad enough, particularly because falls of price were often foreseen to a certain extent, such foresight bearing its inevitable fruits in unemployment.

A deliberate policy of deflation, however, greatly aggravates the situation. In so far as the business world believe that those responsible for currency policy really intend to carry out a declared policy of deflation, they are bound to feel some lack of confidence in the existing price level, in which case they will naturally draw in their horns to a certain extent with the result of diminishing employment. For this reason a modern industrial community organised on lines of individualistic capitalism simply cannot stand a declared policy of deflation. The business world, it is true, can save its pocket to a certain extent by refraining from new enterprises for the time being. But it can only do this at the expense of passing on to the rest of the community a heavy burden of unemployment and of unemployment doles.

I attribute the bad state of business and of employment more to a lack of confidence in the price level than to any other factor. This lack of confidence is certainly due, in its turn, to a number of different causes,—the political situation in Europe, recent memories of the slump of 1920–21, the fact that the price level is still much higher than it used to be in pre-war days, as well as to a policy of deflation. But none of these things *need* cause prices to fall, and the best way of remedying unemployment would be for those responsible to declare that they would do all they could by means of currency policy to avoid a fall of prices and to promote the confidence of the business world in the existing level of prices.

Let me amplify this point a little. At the present moment the situation in the Ruhr is rightly blamed for the falling off of trade as compared with the revival which was apparent in the spring. How does this happen? To a slight extent directly by cutting off Central European markets; but the purchasing power of Central Europe was very feeble even in the spring, and very feeble also during the boom of 1920–21. The main influence of the Ruhr is felt through its effect on *other* markets, which are induced to withhold their purchases because events in the Ruhr upset their confidence in the price level. Purchasers of tin-plates in Australia, of cotton goods in Asia, or jute products in South America, and so on, are afraid that, if they place their orders now, events in the Ruhr may lead to a fall in their price by the time they are delivered. If they felt confident that the price would not fall, they would not hesitate to buy. They put off their purchases, not because they lack purchasing power, but because their demand is capable of postponement and may, they think, be satisfied at a lower price later on. It is these postponements which are at the root of remediable unemployment.

Now there is no necessary reason in the world why political catastrophes should cause prices to fall. Indeed, in the long run, they generally tend to make prices to [sic] rise because of their inflationary effect on governmental finance. Why should the impoverishment of the world cause *more* goods to be obtainable for gold or for legal tender money? No reason at all. Sooner or later a rising tendency of prices will spring up again, Ruhr or no Ruhr, partly because postponed demands cannot go on being postponed indefinitely; partly because catastrophes tend to diminish the supply of goods and to increase, rather than to diminish, the supply of money. For this reason I am not so pessimistic as the President of the Board of Trade about the prospects of employment in the long run.

For the past eighteen months the authorities have been deflating; for the past six months political anxiety has been acute. Naturally, orders are postponed; inevitably there is unemployment. Some fanatics think that deflation is morally so admirable, that unemployment is a price worth paying for it. But to deny that deflation tends to increase unemployment is profoundly to misunderstand the working of our industrial system.

During recent months employment in a great part of the world has been moderate to good; in another part deplorable. The latter consists without exception of the countries in which deflation has been taking place, namely Great Britain, Sweden, Holland, and Czecho-Slovakia.

I argue, therefore, in the first place, that our existing industrial system is singularly ill-adapted to a policy of deliberate deflation, and that unemployment to-day is due to a very considerable extent not to the absence of markets or to the impoverishment of customers, but to a lack of confidence, arising out of many causes, in the existing level of prices.

I argue, further, that this lack of confidence is in some measure remediable by a resolute policy on the part of the Treasury and the Bank of England. At any rate these authorities can refrain from deliberately aggravating the situation, and should not continue to act, as they have been acting hitherto, on the deflationary recommendations of the Cunliffe Committee.

These observations have been directed, rather more than I intended when I began, to the immediate situation. But they illustrate a fundamental principle which I recommend to this assembly as likely to be of first-rate political importance in the near future. Modern individualistic society, organised on lines of capitalistic industry, cannot support a violently fluctuating standard of value, whether the movement is upwards or downwards. Its arrangements presume and absolutely require a reasonably stable standard. Unless we can give it such a standard, this society will be stricken with a mortal disease and will not survive. I have dwelt in this paper on the evils of deflation because these are with us now. But the evils of inflation, which were visited on us three years ago, although they are different in kind, are not less in degree. We can do with neither.

For these grave causes we must free ourselves from the deep distrust which exists against allowing the value of the currency to be the subject of *voluntary decision*. Only by wisely regulating the creation of currency and credit along new lines, can we protect society against the attacks and criticisms of Socialist and Communist innovators.

On the scientific side economists are as united about the theory of the matter as they are about free trade. The argument is not more intricate than that which underlies tariff controversies.

In reading a forecast of the autumn campaign of our leaders of which unemployment is to be the chief subject, I was disappointed to see no reference whatever to the regulation of credit, which, for good or for evil, must have a vast influence.

I hope that the forecast was incomplete. Nineteenth-century Liberalism was greatly concerned with the establishment of certain economic principles, which were, a hundred years ago, highly controversial, novel, and intellectually difficult. These found their chief embodiment in the doctrine of free trade. This battle has been nearly won, though vigilance is still required. I venture to propound this evening a newer doctrine of hardly less importance. I believe that the reform of the standard of value is, within the economic sphere, the question of greatest urgency now before us. It is a problem which Liberalism is by its traditions well adapted to attack. We cannot live for ever on fragments of our pre-war policies.

An editorial in *The Spectator* two months later under the title 'Deflation Means Unemployment' asked for Keynes's comments. A week later that newspaper printed his reply.

To the Editor of The Spectator, *22 October 1923*

Sir,

You ask me whether I am in agreement with your article 'Deflation Means Unemployment'. I agree most heartily, and I think that there are two steps, neither of them impracticable or dangerous, which ought to be pressed on the Government as immediately urgent: (1) The present Treasury Minute limiting the fiduciary issue of currency notes to the actual maximum of the preceding year should be amended before the end of this year. (2) A definite statement should be made, binding both the Treasury and the Bank of England, that these authorities attach more importance to the maintenance and stability of the price level than to the improvement of the dollar exchange, and that their policy will be deliberately directed to the former object rather than to the latter.

I am, sir, &c.,

J. M. KEYNES

Chapter 2

POPULATION, PROTECTION AND UNEMPLOYMENT

On 18 September 1923 at the meetings of the British Association for the Advancement of Science in Liverpool, Sir William Beveridge, the president of the Economics Section, delivered an address entitled 'Population and Unemployment' In the course of his remarks he addressed himself to Keynes's *Economic Consequences of the Peace* (*JMK*, vol. II), especially his remarks on the terms of trade between bread and manufactures (pp. 5–6, 13–15, 161). On 22 September, under the title 'Malthusian Moonshine' the editor of *The New Statesman* welcomed Sir William's remarks. Keynes replied in the next issue.

To the Editor of The New Statesman, *25 September 1923*

Sir,

Since you refer to a criticism by Sir W. Beveridge, in his address to the British Association on 'Population and Unemployment', of a statement made by me some time ago relating to the course of the relative values of agricultural produce and manufactured articles between 1900 and 1910, may I say that Sir William's figures do not confute my statement, because they give little or no weight to the prices of manufactured articles? My rejoinder furnishing the evidence on which I was relying will be published in *The Economic Journal* for December next, together with the full text of Sir William's address.

Yours, etc.,

J. M. KEYNES

Keynes turned to another aspect of Beveridge's address in the columns of *The Nation*.

From The Nation and Athenaeum, *6 October 1923*

POPULATION AND UNEMPLOYMENT

Sir William Beveridge's interesting address, under this title, before the British Association has revived discussion on a matter which, whatever way it touches our hopes or our prejudices, must surely trouble the thoughts of anyone who concerns himself with political or social purpose. Sir William, in common with many other people, dislikes the idea of birth control; but, like the good economist he is, he remains on the broad issue a sound Malthusian. 'Nothing that I have said', he finally concludes, 'discredits the fundamental principle of Malthus, reinforced as it can be by the teachings of modern science.' His main themes were, first, that we must not be too ready to argue from unemployment to over-population, instancing the excellence of employment in Germany today, 'a nation which assuredly should be suffering from over-population if any nation is'; and, secondly, that an *obiter dictum* of mine in *The Economic Consequences of the Peace* about the state of affairs in 1900–1910 was unjustifiably pessimistic.

I will deal elsewhere with the criticism personal to myself. My main point in the brief passage taken by Sir W. Beveridge as his text was that the pre-war balance in Europe between population and the means of life was, for various reasons, already precarious; and from this I do not think that he seriously dissents. But I also threw out the suggestion that the turning-point in the strongly favourable developments of the latter half of the nineteenth century may have come about the year 1900. The suggestion is one which it is not easy either to refute or to establish, and the exact date is a matter of historical interest, and not one of decisive importance in relation to the present state of the world. But, in any case, Sir William Beveridge's statistics do not touch me, inasmuch as my suggestion related to the 'equation of exchange' between the manufactured products of the Old World and the raw produce of the New, an indication to which his particular figures, since they nearly all deal with raw produce, are not relevant. I shall discuss this statistical point, giving the evidence on which my statement was based, in the December issue of *The Economic Journal*, where those interested will also have the advantage of reading the full text of Sir William Beveridge's address.

Let us, however, turn to Sir William's first point, namely, the relation of unemployment to over-population. I agree with him that it would be rash to argue straight from one to the other. Unemployment is a phenomenon of maladjustment, and the maladjustment may be due to causes which have nothing to do with population;—as, for example, the maladjustment due to a transition, through deflation of purchasing power, from a higher to a lower price level, or that due to the necessity of changing over from supplying one type of outside market to supplying another because of a sudden change in the relative wealth and requirements of the rest of the world. Each of these influences is probably responsible for an important part of the existing unemployment in Great Britain.

But, on the other hand, unemployment may be a symptom of a maladjustment very closely connected with population— namely, that which results from an attempt on the part of organised labour, or of the community as a whole, to maintain real wages at a higher level than the underlying economic conditions are able to support. The most alarming aspect of the prolongation and the intensity of the existing unemployment is the possibility that transitory influences may not wholly explain it, and that deep causes may be operating which interfere with our continuing ability to maintain in these islands an expanding population at an improving standard of life. The doubt is a dreadful one. Our social aims and objects flow from the opposite assumption, and are rendered futile by its negation. What is the use or the purpose of all our strivings if they are to be neutralised or defeated by the mere growth of numbers? Malthus's Devil is a terrible devil because he undermines our faith in the real value of our social purposes, just as much now as when Malthus loosed him against the amiable dreams of Godwin. The *prima facie* case for doubting our ability to provide during the present generation for growing numbers at an improving standard, and for seeing some corroboration of this doubt in the present state of our labour market and of our staple industries, is so serious that it is frivolous to think we can dismiss it by mentioning that unemployment is not *necessarily* due to over-population and by pointing to the disastrous example of Germany, where the nation's submission, under the overwhelming pressure of events, to a drastic lowering of their standard of life and the impairment of their capital resources has put away this particular symptom for the time being.

No statistics can be decisive on such a matter unless they extend over a period long enough to eliminate other influences,— which means that their final answer may be too late to determine policy. But it is useful to keep ourselves reminded from time to time of one or two simple and well-known figures. In 1851 the population of Great Britain was about 21,000,000; in 1902, 37,000,000; and in 1921, 43,000,000. Thus, the population which is growing old is the remnant of a population not much more than half the size of the population which is growing up. Several conclusions follow from this.

(1) Although the birth rate is materially lower than it was half a century ago, nevertheless the absolute number of daily births in Great Britain today is nearly double the number of deaths.

(2) The fact that the average age of the population is less than it would be in a stationary population means that the proportion of old people of pensionable age, which the community will have to support as time goes on, will tend to increase to a figure not far short of double what it is at present.

(3) Most important of all, the supply of adult labourers will continue to increase sharply for a generation to come, irrespective

of the contemporary birth rate, because the number of boys now growing up to working age will greatly exceed year by year that of the old men dying or reaching pensionable age. In round numbers the male population between twenty and sixty-five years of age is now between 14,000,000 and 15,000,000. In the course of the next twenty years the boys (already born) entering these age limits will exceed by between 4,000,000 and 5,000,000 the old men passing out. That is to say, we shall have to find, within this short period, employment, equipment, and houses for 25–30 per cent more working-class families than at present; and the net productivity of these additional hands will have to support a larger proportion of old people, and, if the present birth rate continues, as large a proportion of children. Now that this surplus already exists, emigration may be a palliative. As a continuing policy, however, emigration is a ruinous expedient for an old country, as is obvious when one considers that, if the males are shipped abroad, a corresponding number of females must be sent also, and that the cost per head of rearing and educating a child up to working age is a heavy charge for which the country will get no return of productivity if the youth then emigrates.

(4) Very few of our staple export industries are operating above their pre-war level of ten years ago, and some of them, notably textiles, are seriously below it. Most of these industries are well satisfied if they see a prospect ahead even of their former level of activity in normal times. Their difficulties are increased in some cases by the fact that the American demand for certain essential raw materials has risen more than the total supply, and that America is able to pay a higher price than we can. We cannot rely, unless the material conditions of the rest of the world greatly improve, on finding markets for a much larger quantity of goods at as good a net return to ourselves. With Europe's present prospects, and with the growing tendency of the New World to keep its advantages to itself, we are not entitled to rely on so great an advance in our own opportunities.

These *prima facie* grounds, for fear and hesitation, and for straining our minds to find a way out, are not disposed of by the fact that many improvements are conceivable, other than restriction, which would postpone or alleviate the problem. Sir William Beveridge concluded his address, after admitting and emphasising the dangers of our economic situation, by urging that the cure was to be found not in birth control, but in peace and world trade resuming their sway. He might have mentioned many other desirable things which would put off the evil day,—a greater accumulation of capital, the swifter progress of science, a raising of the acquired and inborn endowments of the average man, more commonsense, intelligence and public spirit.

But it is not safe to leave the question of numbers unregulated, in the mere hope that we may be rescued by one of these conceivable, but as yet unrealised, improvements. And even if we do realise them, is it not discouraging that they should only operate to compensate an increase of numbers, when they might, if there had been no increase, have availed to improve the lot of the average man?

Is not a country over-populated when its standards are lower than they would be if its numbers were less? In that case the question of what numbers are desirable arises long before starvation sets in, and even before the level of life begins to fall. Perhaps we have already sacrificed too much to population. For is not the improvement in the average conditions of life during the past century very small in comparison with the extraordinary material progress of that period? Does it not seem that the greater part of man's achievements are already swallowed up in the support of mere numbers?

It is easy to understand the distaste provoked by particular methods, and the fear inspired by any proposal to modify the *laissez-faire* of nature, and to bring the workings of a fundamental instinct under social control. But it is strange to be untroubled or to deny the existence of the problem for our generation.

Keynes's final, published comment on Beveridge appeared in *The Economic Journal* immediately following the text of the latter's address.

From The Economic Journal, *December 1923*

A REPLY TO SIR WILLIAM BEVERIDGE

I

It is flattering but a little severe to be taken up through a Presidential address on the strength of an *obiter dictum* of a few sentences. (The subject is a large one and an author may have more to say in support of his general attitude to it than can be well expressed in a single page of a book on another topic.) But worse still when even that paragraph is mis-handled.

My main convictions relate to the present state of affairs— whether Great Britain and Europe can continue to support an increasing population on an improving standard of life now that the precarious equilibrium which existed before the War* has been fatally disturbed. Incidentally I expressed a doubt whether the state of affairs by which 'up to about 1900 a unit of labour applied to industry yielded year by year a purchasing power over an increasing quantity of food' may not perhaps have been already reversed about that date.

It is always difficult to trace, through the oscillations which obscure the long-period trend, the precise moment when a diminishing rate of improvement passes over into an actual loss of ground. But Sir W. Beveridge's paper makes me no clearer than I was as to whether I was rash to express the doubt in question; for the statistics which he quotes have no direct bearing on my remarks.

I was concerned with the ratio of real interchange between the manufactured products offered by the Old World, and the food and raw materials supplied by the New. I thought I saw a tendency of this ratio to alter, with the result that Europe was

---

* My phrases about this are those first quoted above by Sir W. Beveridge on p. 452.

having to offer more of her own goods in exchange for important agricultural produce. I made no fresh study of this question when I wrote *The Economic Consequences of the Peace*, but was merely repeating a view which I had expressed in *The Economic Journal* 1912 (vol. XXII, p. 630) [*JMK*, vol. XI], based on some figures given there and on the more comprehensive calculations set forth in Professor Bowley's well-known memorandum published in *The Economic Journal* in 1903 (vol. XIII, p. 628). It will be useful to repeat here the salient figures.

Professor Bowley's object was to make a table year by year, for the United Kingdom and for Germany, of 'the quantity of exports (the kind supposed unchanged) that were given for a uniform quantity of imports.' His results for the United Kingdom were as follows:

Volume of exports given for a uniform quantity of imports

1873	100	1883	118	1893	105
1874	103	1884	115	1894	102
1875	107	1885	114	1895	102
1876	110	1886	113	1896	102
1877	118	1887	111	1897	102
1878	114	1888	113	1898	103
1879	116	1889	112	1899	99
1880	119	1890	104	1900	94
1881	123	1891	105	1901	95
1882	118	1892	106	1902	100

This is *prima facie* evidence that our position, after deteriorating from 1873 to 1881, improved uninterruptedly from 1881 to 1900.

In my memorandum of 1912 (*loc. cit.*) I was reviewing the corresponding figures of the Board of Trade for the years 1900–1911 (Cd. 6314), which were as follows-*

1900	94	1906	99
1901	96	1907	98
1902	99	1908	98
1903	101	1909	103
1904	100	1910	104
1905	101	1911	101

* To render the series continuous with Professor Bowley's I have modified the base year.

This long series of figures seemed to indicate that a period of continuous improvement covering two decades had culminated about 1900 and had been brought to an end about that time.

The above figures compare all exports with all imports. For the full justification of my remark, however, it would be better to compare exported manufactures with imported foodstuffs. The result, the general character of which is much the same as before, is as follows:

Volume of manufactured exports given for a uniform quantity of food imports†

1881	132	1891	106	1901	95
1882	130	1892	112	1902	100
1883	128	1893	112	1903	100
1884	120	1894	107	1904	96
1885	114	1895	104	1905	99
1886	117	1896	106	1906	92
1887	116	1897	110	1907	92
1888	114	1898	111	1908	98
1889	116	1899	105	1909	104
1890	107	1900	93	1910	100

† Professor Bowley's tables for 1881 to 1902 distinguish 'Imported Food and Tobacco', 'Exported Textile Manufactures' and 'Exported Metal Products'. I take the first of these categories as representing imported food, and the mean of the other two as representing manufactured exports. The Board of Trade tables for 1900–1911 deal separately with their usual categories of 'Articles of Food, Drink and Tobacco', and 'Articles Wholly or Mainly Manufactured'.

Here also we have a progressive improvement culminating in 1900, with no further improvement after that date and some signs of deterioration. Incidentally it is interesting to notice how decidedly the boom of 1906–7 turned the ratio of real interchange in our favour, and how equally decidedly the depression of 1908–9 turned it against us. Since, however, we are concerned here with the long-period trend, the total result of the table can be best summarised as follows:

Volume of manufactured exports given for a uniform quantity of food imports

1881	132	1900	93
Decade ending 1890	119	Decade ending 1910	98
Decade ending 1900	107	1911	98

A table of this kind by itself cannot, of course, be regarded as conclusive. But some of the possible sources of error are not probable. For example, the prices of imported raw materials during the period under review suggest that, if these were eliminated from the prices of manufactures so as to give the net return to home manufacture, the force of the above table, whilst not much changed, would be increased rather than diminished.

Now from 1881 to 1900 there was certainly a great improvement in manufacturing technique. Thus not only did a unit of manufacture purchase more food, but it cost less labour. Not only so; as we shall see below, whilst we were producing at less real cost and selling at a better real price, we were also marketing a growing volume of goods. It was this fortunate combination of circumstances which made it possible for us to support a rapidly increasing number of workers at a somewhat improving standard of life. Between that time and the outbreak of war the situation may have been helped by some further improvement in manufacturing technique; and the volume of our trade was still increasing; but the other factor—the purchasing power of our manufactures—had ceased to help and seems from the above *data* to have begun to turn adverse. We were no longer able to sell more goods at a better price.

I claim, therefore, that the best evidence available supports the contention briefly stated by me in *The Economic Consequences of the Peace*. I was there speaking of the industrial countries of Western Europe, and suggested that, whereas 'up to 1900 a unit of labour applied to industry yielded year by year a purchasing power over an increasing quantity of food, it is possible that about the year 1900 this process began to reverse'.

What evidence does Sir W. Beveridge produce to confute this? His facts fall into two groups. The first show that Europe as a whole produced 3 per cent more wheat per head in 1910 than in 1900. His second show that the price of wheat rose less than that of other raw materials. Why he imagines that either of these facts confute my statement I cannot say. Let us consider them in turn.

Take his figures of wheat production. Two tables are given, one of which includes and the other excludes Russia and Poland. The first decade shows some increase in the production of food grains per head in the decade 1900–1910 and no figures available for 1910–20; the second shows a small decrease in the production of wheat and barley per head in the decade 1900–1910, compensated by an increase of rye and maize (which are not important articles of human food in this country) and a huge reduction all round in 1910–1920. I have the following observations to make:

(1) It is not obvious that his own table for 'Western and Central Europe', taken at its face value, namely:

	1880	1890	1900	1910	1920
Yield of wheat (bushels per head)	3·93	3·97	4·16	4·13	3·10

confutes my suggestion that the year 1900 marked a turning-point. Indeed it might be held by some to confirm it.

(2) He has, however, included in 'Western and Central Europe' the agricultural countries of South-Eastern Europe—Roumania, Hungary, Jugo-Slavia and Bulgaria. The inclusion of these countries vitiates an argument concerned with the situation of the industrial communities of Western Europe. 'More surprising still', Sir W. Beveridge concludes this passage, 'everyone but four (Belgium, France, Holland and the United Kingdom) shows an increase of wheat per head of total population in the decade (1900–1910).' But are not these four (together with Germany) precisely the countries we were talking about?

(3) Even if his facts were correct, they are not relevant to my contention about the ratio of real exchange between agriculture and industry; and, anyhow, it would be rash to treat them as an indication of progress without examining the attendant circumstances. If, for example, the wheat grown in Great Britain per head were at the present stage in our economic

development to show a considerable increase, it might well indicate a serious deterioration in our prosperity; for it might mean that as a result of hostile tariffs or other causes we were no longer able to obtain food on favourable terms in exchange for our manufactured exports and were being driven, as a last resort, to grow an increased quantity of food for ourselves.

Take next Sir W. Beveridge's tables of prices. Since these relate almost wholly to raw materials, and mainly to imported raw materials, I do not know what relevance he thinks that they possess to my statement about the relative values of imported food and exported manufactures. He seems half aware that they are irrelevant, and goes on to give other reasons for supposing *a priori* that, *if* his figures had related to exported manufactures, they would have supported his conclusion. But he seems to have clean forgotten the existence of the Board of Trade estimates, published year by year, of the very thing under discussion,—although the figures must, of course, be familiar to him in other connections.

II

Since Sir W. Beveridge's criticisms have caused me to recur to the subject of my inquiries of 1912, it may be of interest that I should now bring these inquiries up to date.

The Board of Trade continued to publish comparable figures for the years up to 1916 (though 1913 was the last year to be dealt with in a comprehensive white paper). For the years 1917 and 1918 the conditions under which our foreign trade was carried on rendered comparisons impossible, and no returns were compiled. Since 1919 the figures have been published quarterly in the *Board of Trade Journal.** Reducing these official figures to the same form as in the table given above (p. 127), we have the following result:

---

* Up to and including 1922 the figures have been calculated in respect of 1913 as the base year. In 1923 the Board of Trade has returned to its pre-war (and preferable) technique of the 'chain-method' by which each year is calculated by reference to the immediately preceding year.

Volume of manufactured exports given for a uniform quantity of food imports

1912	102	1915	118	1918	—	1921	72
1913	97	1916	118	1919	91	1922	77
1914	105	1917	—	1920	82	1923	80
						(for 9 months)	

It appears, therefore, that up to the outbreak of War, and also during the War years, the state of affairs, which dates from about 1900, was maintained, the table, repeated in terms of ten-year averages,* being as follows:

Volume of manufactured exports given for a uniform quantity of food imports

Decade ending	1890	119	Decade ending	1899	108	Decade ending	1908	97
	1891	117		1900	107		1909	97
	1892	115		1901	105		1910	98
	1893	113		1902	104		1911	98
	1894	112		1903	103		1912	98
	1895	111		1904	102		1913	98
	1896	110		1905	101		1914	99
	1897	109		1906	100		1915	100
	1898	109		1907	98		1916	101

This table shows that the uninterrupted improvement, which had been proceeding at a steady rate for a quarter of a century up to the decade (ending 1907–8) of which the middle year is 1903, came to an end at about that date.

In the light of this more extended table, my former generalisation should be modified by placing the turning-point at 1903 rather than at 1900 (the figures of the period 1899–1903 being much upset for purposes of comparison by the South African War and by the boom and the subsequent depression within that period), and by emphasising more decidedly the cessation of improvement and less decidedly the extent of the actual deterioration between that date and the outbreak of war.

* Ten-year averages are successful on the whole in eliminating the very disturbing influences on these tables of the periodic booms and depressions.

What is the situation as regards the post-war years? They show that my original generalisation was open to the criticism that by dealing solely with the *ratio* of real exchange without reference to the *volume* of trade it might be misleading. The figures quoted above for the pre-war years, taken by themselves, indicate, paradoxically, a vast improvement, even if we allow for a disturbance of the figures, as on previous occasions, by the boom of 1920* in proportion to the magnitude of the boom. A closer examination, however, shows that the improvement in real price has only been obtained at the expense of a disastrous falling off in volume. My generalisation would have been more accurately stated:—'We are no longer able to sell a growing volume of manufactured goods (or a volume increasing in proportion to population) at a better real price in terms of food.'

The figures of the volume of trade for earlier years can be found in Professor Bowley's memorandum (*loc. cit.*). Those for the years since 1900 (omitting the war years) are as follows in percentages of the volume in 1900:

	Total net imports	Food imports	Total British exports	Manufactured exports
1900	100·0	100·0	100·0	100·0
1901	102·1	102·4	101·0	100·8
1902	105·3	103·2	107·2	107·1
1903	106·2	106·9	110·1	109·8
1904	107·4	107·5	112·5	111·4
1905	108·4	104·3	123·6	123·6
1906	111·6	108·0	132·9	131·5
1907	113·1	107·5	143·6	140·9
1908	108·9	106·3	132·2	127·1
1909	111·9	105·2	137·8	131·7
1910	114·1	105·3	150·3	145·7
1911	117·6	108·7	155·7	150·8
1912	126·6	109·3	164·3	158·7
1913	131·2	115·6	170·8	164·6
1919	118·1	110·6	93·8	92·8
1920	115·5	99·8	121·1	125·9
1921	96·4	104·7	85·1	83·6
1922	113·5	114·6	117·7	109·5
1923 (9 months)	127·3	130·8	132·3	121·4

* These tables show that with great regularity this country obtains a better *real* price than usual for its manufactured exports during a boom. To this extent the greater prosperity of industrial countries during a boom seems to be at the expense of the agricultural countries.

Broadly speaking, the volume of our manufactured exports has gone back to what it was about twenty years previously. Meanwhile the volume of our food imports has maintained a steady increase to a figure about 15 per cent above what it was twenty years ago, roughly corresponding to the increase of population.

Thus the improved prices of our manufactured exports, measured in terms of food imports, has compensated to a considerable extent, but by no means completely for the falling off in volume. Off-setting the one thing against the other, our manufactured exports are now buying *in the aggregate* about 12 per cent less foodstuffs than before the War.*

Looked at another way, since the War we have been asking for our exports (in round figures) a real price (i.e. in terms of food imports) 20 per cent higher than before the War and have been selling 30 per cent less in quantity. In the slump year 1921 we were asking a real price 35 per cent higher than in 1913 and were selling in volume 50 per cent less.

These figures suggest interesting reflections as to the elasticity of the world's demand for our manufactures in terms of foodstuffs. It looks on the face of it as though we are asking too much for our exports, and will have to ask less if we are to sell enough to pay for our necessary imports. But the post-war conditions of world markets are so materially different from pre-war conditions, that we cannot safely infer from the above figures by how much we shall have to lower our (real) prices for what we produce in order to find an outlet for a sufficient quantity of goods. We are bound to hope—and have reasonable grounds to hope—that the demand for our goods is elastic, i.e. that if we lower our (real) price the demand will increase *more* than in proportion. But I see no grounds for the expectation that

---

* Triennial averages (e.g. 1912 = averages of 1911, 1912, 1913) of amount of food imports purchased by the aggregate of our manufactured exports (1912 = 100):

Pre-war		Post-war	
1910	89	1920	77
1911	95	1921	86
1912	100	1922	85

we can obtain a (real) price a great deal higher (which we are asking at present) than the pre-war price for the pre-war volume of sales.

The following is an illustration of the way in which equilibrium might be restored. Food prices (in terms of money) might rise 20 per cent, money wages might rise 10 per cent, other manufacturing costs might be reduced (with a larger output and more efficiency) sufficiently to compensate the rise of money wages thus leaving the money-price of manufactures unchanged;* our real price for manufactured exports would then have returned to its pre-war level and this might encourage a sufficient increase in their volume to absorb an important proportion of our unemployed. But it must be observed that in this illustration the result would have been achieved at the cost of a reduction in real wages.

Arguments and figures such as I have been dealing with here can never do more than suggest conclusions,—they cannot prove them. But they do certainly suggest—in the absence of other indications to the contrary—that we could maintain a higher standard of life if we had fewer to employ and to feed, and that the more we have to force the volume of our trade (especially in existing conditions) the worse terms do we get. Numbers are already, if this is true, inimical to standards of life.

One more table of the ratio of real interchange, looked at this time from the standpoint of the New World, is worth giving. The Federal Reserve Board of the United States has published during the past year a monthly table of the price index of different classes of commodities as follows [see table, p. 135]:

This table shows that of the three classes of goods produced and consumed within the United States—raw materials, producers' goods and consumers' goods—the increase of price since

---

* I have neglected throughout the cost of the imported raw materials entering with our manufactured goods, because, so far as I can judge, their price has risen less than the price of the manufactured goods; so that if accurate account had been taken of this factor, my argument would not have been weakened. But this matter deserves a more exact examination than I have been able to give it in this article.

	Goods produced	Goods imported	Goods exported	Raw materials	Producers' goods	Con-sumers' goods	All com-modities
				(1913 = 100)			
1922							
July	162	128	165	177	143	163	165
Oct.	161	135	163	179	150	156	165
1923							
Jan.	162	139	180	182	150	156	165
April	173	156	186	181	169	158	170
May	170	155	179	176	167	158	167
June	167	148	182	171	164	157	164
July	163	141	170	163	160	155	159
Aug.	163	137	166	162	158	157	159
Sept.	167	145	176	167	160	162	163

1913 has been greatest in raw materials, although the disparity has been diminishing lately. But the big divergence is between the price changes in imported goods and those in exported goods. In order to pay for a given volume of imports the United States does not have to export, it seems, more than 80–85 per cent of what it had to export before the War. In other words, the ratio of real interchange has moved some 15 per cent in favour of the United States and against the rest of the world.*

I do not wish at the present stage to draw any certain conclusions from the figures set forth in this section. But the indications are not optimistic. Sir W. Beveridge and I do not disagree about the disturbing possibilities of the present state of affairs.

III

Finally, I must emphasise strongly, what is perhaps obvious,— that conclusions as to the actual or impending over-population of the older countries do not stand or fall with the particular point of detail here discussed. This is only one item in a vast field of evidence and argument. I complain, therefore, that Sir

---

* If we compare goods imported with goods produced, the change amounts to 10 per cent, which might be the safer figure to take.

W. Beveridge should convey the impression that his criticisms, even if they were better founded than they are, would dispose of Malthus's Devil. Sir W. Beveridge seems to speak with two voices. It is on grounds which are flimsy and inadequate to the magnitude and significance of the subject (if he intends them to apply to the whole great issue) that he asserts: 'Mr Keynes's fears seem not merely unnecessary but baseless.' Yet the outside world has not heard with the same distinctness the other voice, which says later on: 'The last thing I wish is to over-emphasise points of disagreement with Mr Keynes...Nothing that I have said discredits the fundamental principle of Malthus, reinforced as it can be by the teachings of modern science.'

I offer Sir W. Beveridge the following few samples from the collections of the press-cutting agency, to show what the outside world thinks that he has said:

The Guardian. 'At the British Association Sir William Beveridge effectively laid the bogey and convinced most of us that there are no grounds for Malthusian pessimism.'

The Month. 'The bogey of an overcrowded earth, first raised by the short-sighted Malthus, and eagerly exploited by eugenists as a means of overcoming the abhorrence with which all decent people regard abuse of the marriage function, was effectively laid by the Director of the London School of Economics...We hope that our Government will follow, however belatedly, the example of France and America in making such publications (relating to contraceptives) a criminal offence.'

The New Age. 'No; we really shall not be able to take Malthus seriously until we see people starving with money in their pockets...There is only one famine to fear; and that is a money famine.'

Daily Mail. 'Sir William said there was no ground for Malthusian pessimism. Enormous areas of the world fit for cultivation were not yet cultivated, and in other areas only the surface has been scratched.'

Liverpool Post. 'It is surely obvious that the great and deplorable mass of unemployment in the country at present has no direct connection with the number of the inhabitants.'

Mr C. F. G. Masterman (in numerous organs of the provincial press): 'Sir William Beveridge, by the substitution of scientific investigation for theory, has blown into pieces the assertion that England is over-populated, or that Europe is over-populated, or that population is growing in excess of the development of food supply, or that the present unemployment in this country is in any way due to over-population.'

New Statesman. 'There is no evidence whatever of which we are aware, or which Mr Keynes or any other Malthusian has yet produced, to show that those limits (to the number of human beings who can find means of sustaining life) are being approached or are even likely to be approached for centuries to come...Economic and statistical science offer no ground whatever for what Sir William calls "Malthusian pessimism",....Sir William Beveridge's demonstration that the "over-population" bogey is moonshine is a most valuable and timely piece of work.'

Sir William Beveridge has given to ignorance and prejudice the shelter of his name. Can I not with these cuttings make him a little uneasy?

On reading Keynes's comments in the *Economic Journal*, Beveridge continued the discussion in correspondence.

From SIR WILLIAM BEVERIDGE, *1 January 1924*

My dear Keynes,

I have been looking at your reply and export and import prices and have got some rather remarkable results.

The first is that you only get your turning point about 1900 by switching (illegitimately) from Bowley's figures for textiles and metal products to the Board of Trade figures for exported manufactures as a whole. If you carried on with Bowley's figures and calculated in the way in which he has in fact calculated them, the uninterrupted decline would continue, the average for the decade 1913 being 93 as compared with the 98 with which you end.

The second result is that the uninterrupted decline itself from 1891 onwards is largely if not wholly bogus. It is there because Bowley in calculating the average price of exported metal products has (illegitimately) treated 'iron and steel manufactures' as a single group instead of breaking it up into its component parts (pig iron, hoops and sheets, wire, railway material, tinplates, etc.). These components vary very much in price and also in the proportion which they form of the whole. By breaking up this group one gets (on the basis of 1902 = 100) a price in 1881 for metal products of 105 instead of 90 as given by Bowley in the *Economic Journal*. And so one gets for the same year 124 instead of 132 as the quantity of textile and metal exports required to be given for a uniform quantity of food imports. The apparent improvement in our trading ratio is largely due to the increasing proportion of our iron and steel trade which consists of more finished instead of less finished products.

A third result is that the German figures for exported manufactures and imports of food show no trend at all.

I hope to send the draft of my next article to you but have been delayed by certain further discoveries. I think you will find that there is really nothing whatever to be made of import and export prices, and that my own address in the section on England gives you much better evidence for pessimism than anything else does.

Yours ever,

W. H. BEVERIDGE

The next month he sent Keynes a proof of a reply he proposed to make to Keynes in *Economica* for February 1924 under the title 'Mr Keynes' Evidence for Overpopulation'. He asked Keynes for any comments or criticisms he might wish to make. Keynes replied ten days later.

To SIR WILLIAM BEVERIDGE, *16 February 1924*

Dear Beveridge,

Many thanks for the proof. The discussion falls into two quite different sections: (1) the purely statistical question as to the right method of compiling a table of the relative cost of manufactured exports and imported food and the inferences which can justifiably be drawn from this table; and (2) the position of this particular piece of statistical evidence in my general argument about population.

As regards (1) there are several things that I could say. In particular, I am disappointed that you did not carry my figures for manufactured exports as a whole back to the earlier years instead of bringing Bowley's corrected figures forward. Since you do not criticise my post-1900 figures, that would have seemed the obvious thing to do. In this section of your paper, however, I have no complaint to make of any misrepresentation.

(2) On the other hand, as regards the general relation of all this to my main argument, let me summarise my objections as follows:—

(a) You imply in the third paragraph and elsewhere that I have set forth my case on this subject and pronounced definite conclusions in print. This is not so. I have never, so far as I can remember, printed in my a life a single word on the subject of population, with the exception of three pages in *The Economic Consequences of the Peace* and an introductory article of a few pages to other peoples' work, of a purely general character.* I have a definite opinion on these matters of course, and have expressed it in conversation; I also have, I believe, a body of arguments with which to support these conclusions. But you are mistaken in supposing that all these things are published to the world and open to criticism. Take, for instance, your reference to my advocacy of birth control. I rather doubt if I have ever used the word in print.† I have certainly never presented any arguments whatever in favour of it. It is flattering to be treated as the leading exponent of all these things on the strength of having written three sentences about them; but it inevitably leads to misrepresentation if these three sentences are treated as though they represented a three-volume exposition of all the author's arguments.

(b) The question whether what I wrote in *The Economic Consequences of the Peace* related to Europe as a whole or only to Western Europe seems to me, in your paper, a muddle. Some parts of the argument related to the one and some parts to the

---

* *Plus* what I have written since your B.A. address.
† I expect I have really, but I can't recall it.

other. Why not? In fact, one of the most definite statements in the book about population related to Russia. But when I was using the particular argument about manufactured exports buying less food it is obvious that this could only apply to the industrial countries, since for the agricultural countries it would work, if anything, the other way. Surely there is nothing illogical in maintaining both that Russia and that Great Britain were over-populated, but the precise statistical evidence of the statement in the one case would not be identical with the evidence of it in the other, the conditions of the two countries being quite different. There is no shift in my position on this matter.

(c) This is part of the general suggestion in the first part of your paper and elsewhere that the statistical point discussed under (1) is the whole or an essential part of my argument. For instance, the paragraph at the bottom of the fourth slip is, in my opinion, a serious misrepresentation. Take again the tenth paragraph on the first slip, where you say 'Had I realised that they were the basis of Mr Keynes's statements I should of course have discussed them'. The figures about export and import prices were not the whole basis of my statement about population. But they obviously were bound to be the basis of my statements about the relative values of exports and imports; and it still seems to be strange that you should not have realised that statements about the relative values of exports and imports would naturally be based upon statistics of export and import prices. Having now made this discovery you appear to rush to the conclusion that statistics of export and import prices are also the sole basis of everything I have to say about population in general.

(d) The point, however, where there seems to me to be the greatest misunderstanding of what I said in *The Economic Consequences of the Peace* can be illustrated by the first sentence of your second paragraph. I was not arguing in *The Economic Consequences of the Peace* that there had been an actual fall in the standard of life in Europe before the war.* Indeed this was notoriously not the case. Practically all your arguments, being directed to prove that there was no such fall in the standard of living, are therefore quite irrelevant to my position, since the point was never denied. The misunderstanding seems to arise in two ways. First, you seem to think that no country can be said to be over-populated until its standards of living are actually falling, from which, for example, it would follow that a country which was already at the lowest standard which could support life could never be over-populated. My definition of over-population would be totally different from this. The other source of misunderstanding seems to be that you do not remember that the gist of my argument in *The Economic Consequences of the Peace* related to the *precariousness* of the situation, that it was full of elements of instability, that many factors which had operated favourably in the preceding years could not, quite apart from the war, be relied upon to continue as favourable, etc., etc.† Thus you assume that my definition of over-population depends upon a lowering of the standards of life; you twist my statements as to the precariousness of the existing standards into a statement as to their absolute decline; and then, because no such absolute decline actually took place, which I was prepared to admit from the outset, you consider that you have disposed of my argument. If you will read again Chap. II of *The Economic Consequences*, you will find that it is quite different from the picture given in your latest article.

Well! I have set out fully, and not in the sort of way in which I should print anything, my reaction to your proof. But I do not know what to do about it. I could have wished you had confined your reply to the statistical question where, whatever differences of opinion or of inference there may be, there can be no question of misrepresentation. I feel that a continuance

* E.g. on p. 8 [*JMK*, vol. II, p. 5] the sentence immediately following the one which is the basis of your criticism runs as follows:—'But the tendency of cereals to rise in real cost was balanced by other improvements'.
† See, for example, my summary on p. 22 [*JMK*, vol. II, p. 16].

of this controversy on fierce lines tends to make the public and our pupils believe that we differ on the essential matters far more seriously that we really do?

Yours ever,

[copy not signed or initialled]

Beveridge replied almost a month later.

From SIR WILLIAM BEVERIDGE, *14 March 1924*

Dear Keynes,

I send you herewith a reprint of my *Economica* article. Your letter came when my final proof had already gone in, and I have since been too busy with University Grants Committee and other matters to go further into the question. Would you care, however, to develop your letter in a reply for the next number of *Economica*? We would be delighted, of course, to have it.

But I certainly contemplate myself abandoning the paths of historical controversy for consideration of the practical and present problem.

Yours sincerely,

W. H. BEVERIDGE

Keynes did not pursue the matter further.

One sidelight of Keynes's controversy with Beveridge was a letter from C. R. Fay, a contemporary of Keynes's at King's College, Cambridge who was then Professor of Economics at the University of Toronto.

From C. R. FAY, *27 March 1924*

Dear Malthus,

For more than a century you have been worrying about it and all the while the answer was in Shakespeare's *Tempest*, Act II, Sc. 1.

Gonzalo.   Had I plantation of this isle, my lord—

        . . .

        All things in common nature should produce
        Without sweat or endeavour. . .

                nature should bring forth
        Of its own kind, all foison, all abundance,
        To feed my innocent people.

Sebastian.   No marrying 'mong his subjects?
Antonio.   None, man; *all idle; whores and knaves.*

In other words leave the wheat crop alone. Concentrate on human beings. 10 years of Labour government will turn the unskilled labourers into idle knaves. 10 years of life in factories and on the street will turn the females into the social equivalent of whores, i.e. copulators without issue.

It was you and your school who from 1798 onwards exalted work and childbearing into virtues and so disturbed nature's balance.

But you will say, I have always opposed population. No, you have encouraged it. If men work, women will labour. If men are idle, women will be idle too. Paris knows this, Paris lives up to it. But Paris is frightened, because London and Berlin and the Pope will not follow suit. So [?] in your next Summer School, men & women in equal numbers: take as your subject all play and no work, & see that the women understand their part in it: and 'thus by contraries execute all things'

No charge for this instruction.

Yrs

C. R. FAY

Meanwhile, on 25 October 1923, Stanley Baldwin, who had become Prime Minister when Bonar Law resigned owing to throat cancer the previous May, announced that he could only fight unemployment if he had a free hand to introduce protection. As Bonar Law had sworn off protection during the 1922 election, Baldwin's policy change involved another general election and he called one for 6 December. Keynes took some part in the campaign, speaking for the Liberals at Blackburn and Barrow on 4 and 5 December. He also contributed to the discussion of the election issues in *The Nation*, first of all with an unsigned leader on 17 November and then with a two-part article on free trade.

From The Nation and Athenaeum, *17 November 1923*

THE LIBERAL PARTY

The historic Liberal Party has been reunited this week, in the only conditions in which reunion can be sincere or desirable,— identical opinions and identical antagonisms on immediate issues of the first degree of importance.

143

The questions of to-day are not the same as those of a generation ago. It has taken a little time for the distinctions of temperament and ideal, corresponding to what we call 'party', deep, unchangeable and permanent though they are in the characters of Englishmen, to sort themselves out. Foreign policy and economic policy, each presenting in detail mainly new problems, are what matter now. Though the details are new, nevertheless the general lines, along which the Liberal and Conservative temperaments would try to solve them, have been predetermined. After a period of doubt, this is plain at last. For a short time it seemed as though the real differences between, for example, Mr Baldwin and Mr Asquith, were shadowy and indistinct. Party strife was half-hearted. The ideal of carrying on the King's Government by the best men, regardless of party, had a momentary plausibility. But the after-war twilight has suddenly cleared. We find ourselves, overnight, standing shoulder to shoulder in the old ranks.

Two pairs of speeches, lately delivered, illuminate the gulf. In the realm of foreign policy, Lord Birkenhead's Rectorial Address and General Smuts broadcasted oration disclose the opposite assumptions upon which the Tory and the Liberal Ministers of Foreign Affairs build their diplomacy,—the appeal to national force, which leads, the Liberal thinks, to universal suicide, and the organisation of international opinion, which leads, the Tory thinks, to the decay of national prestige. In the realm of economic policy, the speeches of Mr Baldwin at Manchester and of Mr Asquith at Dewsbury typify, on the one hand, the exaltation of a sort of mystical stupidity, with which the Tory, generally sentimentalising himself on these occasions as the 'plain, business man', likes to present his nostrums for the cure of economic facts; and, on the other, the intellectual answer, which the Liberal, whether he always succeeds or not, tries to give to an intellectual problem. Liberalism to-day must make us soft-hearted to foreign affairs and hard-headed to economic facts. Tories have shown themselves lately hard where we are soft, and soft where we are hard.

All Liberals of both wings must feel an exhilaration of spirit and a heightening of excitement. The party struggle is not an ignoble instrument for the advancement of human affairs. Old associates have joined their ranks again under their old leaders, by general admission the most famous and experienced body of statesmen in the world, with clear issues before them and with great hopes of winning much ground. Coalition has failed; and Toryism has failed. We too would like to try our hand at mitigating the moral and economic disorders of the stricken modern world.

We have not mentioned Labour. Does this invalidate our argument? We think not. An underlying current of weakness in the inner life of the Labour Party is obvious to any observer. It is possible that they may have some electoral success. But in power and in action, there is no likelihood of their accomplishing in the near future any part of their programme which is peculiar to themselves. Labour cannot accomplish anything at present which is not on Liberal rather than on Labour lines, and is not carried through with Liberal support,—not least because the best of their ability is drawn from good friends of our own who in the twilight temporarily strayed away. The Labour Party is no more a 'party', in the sense in which we have used this good old word, than super-taxpayers are. It includes every discrepancy of temperament from the highest Toryism to the wildest spirit of destruction, from the driest intellectualism to a degree of mystical stupidity which would satisfy the standards of Mr Baldwin. Let no man vote Tory to keep Labour out when his true preference is for the Liberal. In the short run it will be Liberal strength which will be most potent to check Labour excesses; and in the long run nothing but Liberal weakness can cause the eventual reaction from Toryism to play into the hands of extremists.

The precise form which Liberal reunion has taken is marked, in our opinion, by the wisdom which has characterised throughout Mr Asquith's handling of this problem. The two wings of the party retain their separate organisations, but they are to collaborate without reserve and without distinction of name. The joint action of the Conservative and the Liberal Unionist parties in old days, though in that case the separate designations were retained for many years, provides an instructive precedent. By this arrangement, the rank and file of Liberals in the constituencies can come together and fight for a common programme,—which has been the crying need; whilst the personal questions—which have been the difficulty—are left, deprived, for the moment, of their power to do harm, to the assuagements of time and the test of experience.

We predict that the coming election will be distinguished from the other elections since the war by a general return to political allegiances and a strict party vote. If it were not for the complications of three-cornered contests and the absence of an alternative vote, this election would probably indicate with considerable accuracy the relative strength to-day of the three great parties. For ten years before the War the Liberal vote dominated the country. Many, as yet incalculable, elements have been added since then. It is probable, nevertheless, that a return to 'party' will benefit Liberalism more than either of its rivals, and may achieve that moderate improvement of relative position which will be sufficient to make the Liberal Party a deciding power in the state. It is only necessary that Conservatives should lose forty seats on balance and that Liberals should win forty seats, for the Liberal Party to attain a relative strength in the new House of Commons, which, in combination with its middle position, would render it the only party capable—with support from the moderates of both the other parties—of carrying on the government of the country.

Liberal workers have, therefore, something to work for. Let them enter the brief fight with hope and with courage, determined if they can to restore Liberalism to its rightful task in this moderate and magnanimous country of finding a *via media* to peace abroad and contentment at home. It is on them that has now fallen the mantle of tranquility which won the last election.

From The Nation and Athenaeum, *24 November and 1 December 1923*

FREE TRADE

I

Before we examine Mr Baldwin's contention that new facts have changed the significance of old proposals, let us remind ourselves of some principles which have certainly not changed.

Free trade is based on two fundamental truths which, stated with their due qualifications, no one can dispute who is capable of understanding the meaning of the words:—

I. It is better to employ our capital and our labour in trades where we are relatively more efficient than other people are, and to exchange the products of these trades for goods in the production of which we are relatively less efficient.

Every sane man pursues this principle in his private life. He concentrates his energies on those employments where his efficiency is greatest in comparison with other people's; and leaves to others what they can do better than he can.

There are four, and only four, recognised types of exception to this principle, which apply equally to nations and to individuals:—

1. If, for non-economic reasons, a particular trade, or the conditions in which it is carried on, are degrading or unpleasant, or if, on the other hand, they are peculiarly desirable, we may recognise such facts by prohibitions and by encouragements. Such cases are certainly not to be found amongst manufactured imports or exports as a class. Many believe, however, that the encouragement of agriculture comes under this head.

2. If a particular article or service is of such a kind that it is not safe for nations or individuals to leave themselves entirely dependent on the services of outsiders, this is a reason for insisting that we should retain at least the capacity for providing it at home. This is the case of 'key industries'. It is already covered by existing legislation. The main objection to such

147

legislation is that, under cover of it, protectionists are apt to slip in articles which do not really satisfy the conditions.

3. Where relative inefficiency is due to a remediable lack of practice or of education on the part of our own industries, it may be worth while to spend something on gaining the necessary experience. This is the case of 'infant industries'. Here again the objection is that protectionists are apt to father on it elderly or unpromising 'infants'. It can hardly occur in an old industrial country, such as England, except in an industry based on a new invention. I do not know any important case of this, except possibly that of the motor industry,—which is already heavily protected.

4. Where, for special reasons, the cheapness of the imported goods does not look like being permanent, yet may bankrupt and destroy our own organisation so long as it lasts, temporary measures may be justified. This is the case of 'dumping' and of imports from countries of depreciating currency. Generally speaking, the occasions for action under this head are not so common as may appear at first. We have to weigh the direct benefit of getting the goods cheap against the indirect injury done to our organisation. It is not true, at present, that we are suffering seriously under this head; and in so far as it can be proved that we are suffering in particular cases, this is already provided for by existing legislation.

II. The second great principle is that there can be no disadvantage in receiving useful objects from abroad. If we have to pay at once, we can only pay with the export of goods and services, and the exchange would not take place (subject to the necessary exceptions just stated) unless there was an advantage in it. Every export, which is not paid for by an import, represents a decrease in the capital available within the country.

Thus an artificial interference with imports must *either* interfere with exports *or* involve an artificial stimulation to capital to leave the country. Now, if we are to interfere at all with the natural course of trade, surely it should be with the object of keeping capital at home, not of driving it abroad. With our shortage of housing and the need of factories and equipment to render efficient our growing supply of labour, we need to keep more capital at home, and so to arrange matters that our surplus resources are occupied in increasing our own equipment for future production and for the shelter of our own population. There is already, in my opinion, too much encouragement to the export of our capital. With our diminished savings and our increasing needs, we are not in the position in which we used to be for sending out goods to the rest of the world and getting back, for the time being, nothing whatever in return.

Our imports are our income. To put obstacles in their way is to be as crazy as a business man would be who tried to prevent his customers and his debtors from paying their bills.

Neither of these principles is in the least affected by whether or not foreign countries impose tariffs.

There is a third argument for free trade, but one far less absolute and more relative to changing circumstances than the first two,—namely, the principle of *laissez-faire*. This is never a final argument. The old view, that the self-interest of individuals, operating without interference, will always produce the best results, is not true. As knowledge increases and the arts of government improve, the public good requires many checks on the unregulated acts of individual traders. Nevertheless, in a case like this, where lobbying, expense, waste of time, and friction of all kinds will endlessly ensue, we require, to justify the change, not the momentary caprice of a minister who is short of material for a speech at a party gathering, but solid and certain advantages to the state, carefully thought out and clearly explained.

The above arguments are directed against import duties of which the object is to keep out foreign goods. This is Mr Baldwin's main object. It is these arguments, therefore, which are relevant to his proposals. Since, however, protectionists rapidly shift to other ground than that from which the argument is driving them, it will be safer to complete our rapid survey of the whole field.

There are three principal objects, other than the prevention of imports, for which import duties have been proposed at various times:—

1. The favouring of imports from some sources of supply rather than others, namely *preference*.

2. The annoyance of foreign countries, in the hope that they will offer you some concession to abate the nuisance, namely *retaliation*.

3. The exploitation of a position of monopoly or partial monopoly, in order, by restricting the volume of trade, to get a more favourable ratio of exchange, namely, *making the foreigner pay*.

In each of these cases it is a question of where the *balance* of advantage lies. There is nothing whatever new about them. They have been argued out, up and down the country, hundreds of times. I need only point out that the last of them is peculiarly inapplicable to our present circumstances. The imposition of an import or export duty with this object in view is equivalent to a combination of producers to extract from their customers a price higher than the competitive price. Such action is very imprudent unless those who take it feel confident as to the strength of their monopoly position and as to the inability of their customers to go elsewhere. It is not aimed at expanding the volume of trade; but the contrary. It is an attempt to get better terms from foreigners by contracting the volume of trade. Such an attempt would be exceptionally ill-advised at a time when we are already losing trade by charging too high.

The complication of the free trade issue has generally arisen in the past from the fact that, whilst protectionists have really wanted protection for its own fallacious sake, they have generally advanced under a thick smoke-screen of the exceptional cases,—agriculture and race-virility, key industries, infant industries, dumping, preference, retaliation, and making the foreigner pay. It is always more difficult to prove in a few words that certain possible advantages are unlikely or infrequent, than to meet the straight case—where there is and can be no advantage at all. This time, however, the air is clearer. There is no talk of food taxes. The only important industry—the motor industry—which could by the wildest stretch be called an infant, has a heavy duty already. Key industries and dumping are covered by the Safeguarding of Industries Act. Preference is already accorded almost to the full extent that is possible without food taxes. 'Making the foreigner pay' is a preposterous idea just now for the reasons given above. There remains retaliation available for an occasional mention. But the worst of this cry is its utter inconsistency with the main cry of providing permanent employment. For it is of the essence of retaliation that the duties are put on with the idea of taking them off again, soon and suddenly, when they have served their purpose. It is obvious that no expansion of home industry could be started under the precarious and deceptive shelter of retaliatory duties.

The truth is that since the war we have been experimenting (unwisely, in my opinion) with all the more plausible cases for protection, and already have quite a formidable array of trade obstacles. It has been reserved, therefore, for Mr Baldwin, the last and most foolish protagonist of this old play, to plunge headlong into pure error of the $2+2 = 5$ variety.

For if there is one thing that protection can *not* do, it is to cure unemployment. It is the central idea of protection *to contract trade*,—for the advancement of various ulterior objects which may or may not be wise. The characteristic of protection—admitted, I should have thought, by friend and foe alike—is that it is an attempt to trade on better terms or on nationally more advantageous lines at the expense of doing less business. The free trader has always been the expansionist,—the man who is accused of exchanging with the foreigner too cheap or sacrificing the character of the business, merely for the sake of carrying on a *large* trade. Whoever, before Mr Baldwin, dared to assert that putting obstacles in the way of trade would *increase its volume?*

There are some arguments for protection, based upon its securing possible but improbable advantages, to which there is no simple answer. But the claim to cure unemployment involves the protectionist fallacy in its grossest and crudest form.

Protection must mean—to this there is no exception—an attempt to limit the volume of trade; it must mean charging the foreigner more (more, measured in terms of goods demanded against goods supplied) at the expense of doing less trade with him. And in so far as the keeping out of an import does not involve a corresponding restriction of export, it must drive some capital out of the country.

Our problem is to find expanding markets and an increased capital equipment for a growing industrial population. A proposal to solve this by contracting markets and encouraging the export of capital is an imposition on the credulity of the country, which would be impossible if we had more than a fortnight to expose it.

II

What are Mr Baldwin's 'new facts' to justify his departure from old wisdom? It is difficult to extract anything clear from the nebulous orations of himself and his lieutenants. They have made no attempt to meet the *general* argument for free trade, the familiar outlines of which I repeated last week. But even if we abandon the processes of reason in favour of superficial appearances, the protectionists' campaign has been infertile. The cupboards of their minds are bare. The so-called 'new facts' boil down to one thing—the severity of the present unemployment.

One cannot attempt the cure of unemployment without first endeavouring to understand its causes. I should have thought that it was admittedly due to four main influences, and that the only matter of doubt was the relative importance of each of them.

We have serious unemployment to-day, first because we have had an unusually violent up-and-down of trade from the trough of which we are only just beginning to emerge. We suffered a violent inflation of credit followed by the inevitable reaction and aggravated in its later stages by an official policy of deflation. There are now many indications that we have seen the worst of this. Unemployment, though still very serious, is diminishing. The trade union unemployment figures are lower now than they have been for two and a half years. Organised short time in the cotton trade has been abandoned this week, and the prospective troubles of that industry are due to the shortage of the raw material rather than to a lack of demand for their goods. The iron and steel industries are definitely reviving, the output of steel being already a good deal larger than before the war. The production of coal is at a high level. Even shipbuilding—with the settlement of the boilermakers' dispute—is showing signs of life. I venture to predict that the unemployment due to the periodic trade depression will have largely disappeared before any protectionist measures can take effect. But apart from this, in what way could a tariff obviate the world-wide phenomenon of a trade depression? The United States suffered as severe a fluctuation of employment in spite of its tariff wall.

The second reason—who disputes it?—is the present state of Europe,—as much by its indirect as by its direct reactions. How will a tariff help this? Is a series of tariff wars going to help the world to settle down to stable economic conditions? It is not true that Europe is flooding us with goods. If we take France and Germany as typical of the two extremes in Europe to-day, the results are surprising. Allowing for the change in prices, the volume of our trade with these countries during the first six months of this year compared with the first six months of 1914 has been as follows:—

	Imports from France	Exports to France	Imports from Germany	Exports to Germany
1914	100	100	100	100
1923	74	130	25	65

The French tariff does not seem to have helped France much; nor the depreciated exchange, Germany. Free-trade England has been much more successful in selling her goods to these countries than they have been in selling to us.

The third reason is the high cost of our manufactures. Measured, not in money, but in terms of the amount of manufactured goods which we are offering in return for a unit of food imports, we are charging 20 per cent higher than before the war; and—not unnaturally perhaps—we are selling 30 per cent less in quantity. These high charges are due to a variety of causes. Some of them are being remedied,—this year is better than last year, and last year was better than the year before. But clearly a tariff must make matters worse; for it must, on the average, raise charges.

The fourth reason is the increase of population. We have more mouths to feed, and more hands to occupy in productive tasks. Readers of *The Nation and Athenæum* may know that I regard this with anxiety. But it is clear that this factor can be compensated in no other way than by expanding our international markets so as to sell more goods to pay for the needed imports. How can a tariff help this? By placing obstacles in the way of trade and increasing costs, it must hinder, not help, the expansion of our foreign markets.

Thus a tariff will not remedy any of the main causes of unemployment. Why does Mr Baldwin think that it will? I believe, as I wrote last week, that it is because he is a victim of the protectionist fallacy in its crudest form. If we keep out an imported article, he argues, which it is not impossible to make at home, some Englishman, now unemployed, will be employed on making it. *Voila tout*,—Mr Baldwin sees no further than that.

Does he suppose that we now get that import for nothing? If it has crossed his mind that we probably pay for it by an export, is it his idea that for the future we should make a present of that export to the foreigner? I have found no indication that Mr Baldwin and his friends* have advanced a step beyond this elementary folly when they prescribe a tariff to cure unemployment.

If protectionists merely mean that under their system men will have to sweat and labour more, I grant their case. By cutting off imports we might increase the aggregate of work; but we should be diminishing the aggregate of wages. The protectionist has to prove not merely that he has made work, but that he has increased the national income. Imports are receipts; and exports are payments. How, as a nation, can we expect to better ourselves by diminishing our receipts? Is there anything that a tariff could do, which an earthquake could not do better?

Let us pass from the general arguments to the immediate statistics. Our 'manufactured' imports, as classified by the Board of Trade, include many items, such as lead, copper, tin, oil, leather, &c., which for practical purposes are raw materials. Excluding these, we are importing manufactured goods to the value of about £130 millions a year,—a much smaller volume than before the War. Much of the value of these goods, however, comes from the raw materials which they contain and which we could not produce ourselves. For example, the largest single item is silk goods. Many other goods are specialities which we do not make here at all. Other important classes, e.g., motor-cars are taxed already. The industrial labour which would be required if we excluded all goods which we could make ourselves at a reasonable price would not be worth above £30 to £35 millions a year at the outside. Much of this labour would have to be highly skilled and highly specialised, and could not be

---

* See (e.g.) Mr Amery's 'reply' to Sir W. Beveridge in Wednesday's *Times*, where Mr Amery's argument clearly contemplates cutting down our imports by £100,000,000 and leaving our exports as they are. Mr Amery offers to the public in that letter, not new facts or plausible exceptional cases of a difficult balance of advantages, but just nonsense.

drawn from the ranks of the present unemployed. A more detailed analysis, showing that the vast bulk of our unemployed are in industries where there is no competition from manufactured imports, has been given in *The Times* (November 27th) in a most valuable communication from Sir William Beveridge. 'It is almost inconceivable', he concludes, 'that any committee of impartial and competent inquirers, who, as a preliminary to dealing with unemployment in this country to-day, looked at the facts of unemployment, would give a second thought to protection of the home market as a serious contribution to their task.'

But this is not the end. Mr Baldwin has made promises to agriculture, to Empire cotton-growing, and to consumers of tea and sugar, which will cost £25,000,000 to £30,000,000 to fulfil,—promises for which he proposes to pay out of duties on those manufactured goods which continue to come in. If the tariff is levied on classes of goods which we now import to the value of about £130 millions, the tariff would have to average 20 per cent all round to yield the required revenue, even if *no* goods whatever were kept out. Mr Baldwin has not given any indication how high a tariff he contemplates. Let us assume a tariff *averaging* 40 to 50 per cent *ad valorem* all round; he could then get the revenue he requires, if about half the goods were kept out. But obviously, taxation on this scale would change the direction of consumption; people would do without the taxed goods and buy more of the untaxed imports. Nor could our export industries be unaffected by the colossal rise which would ensue in the price of many goods. No one would believe in the permanence of a tariff on this scale, whilst a severe dislocation of industry must be the first result. The proposal to cure the present unemployment by a tariff on manufactured goods, which will also bring in a revenue of £25 millions, is a gigantic fraud, comparable in its intrinsic absurdity to the fraud of the 1918 Election about Germany paying for all.

The results of the election saw a decisive rejection of protection. The Conservatives, while still the largest party in the House of Commons with 258 members, lost their majority, while the Liberals elected 158 members and Labour 191. Baldwin did not resign until he met the new House and was defeated in the debate on the Speech from the Throne. Labour took office on 23 January 1924.

Chapter 3

MONETARY REFORM AND UNEMPLOYMENT

Keynes's *Tract on Monetary Reform* (*JMK*, vol. IV) was published on 11 December 1923. Keynes took advantage of its publication and a winter series of lectures at the National Liberal Club organised by the Liberal Summer School to discuss 'Currency Policy and Social Reform' on 13 December. He gave the same lecture in Edinburgh the next evening to the Young Scots Society.

Notes for a speech at the National Liberal Club, 13 December 1923

I have so big a subject today that I cannot hope to cover it. It falls naturally into two parts.

> The importance of controlling currency and credit policy in the social interest.

> The technical methods to be employed

I propose this evening to concentrate on the first of these topics. I am not addressing an audience solely of experts.

Technical matters of some complexity are more easily apprehended in writing and [than?] by word of mouth. And I have the better excuse for adopting this course in that I have just published a book where my proposals are set forth in detail.

To begin with a few words about what should be the attitude of Liberalism towards social policy.

We are traditionally the party of *laissez-faire*.

But just as the economists led the party into this policy, so I hope they may lead them out again.

It is not true that individuals acting separately in their own economic interest always produce the best results.

It is obvious that an individualist society left to itself does not work well or even tolerably.

Here I agree with Labour.

I differ from them not in the desirability of state action in the common interest, but as to the forms which such interference should take. Their proposals are out of date and contrary to human nature.

But it is not safe or right just to leave things alone.

It is our duty to think out wise controls and workable interferences.

Now there is no part of our economic system which works so badly as our monetary and credit arrangements; none where the results of bad working are so disastrous socially; and none where it is easier to propose a scientific solution.

In the City of London there is a widespread belief that the pre-war system was as nearly perfect as the frailty of human nature permits, and that we need nothing but to return to it in every particle. This is a superstition which, if it did not exist, one would have deemed incredible.

Two kinds of changes in the value of money

(1) long period

(2) credit cycle

During 19th century gold moderately good in (1) but not very good, necessarily a failure in (2)

In 20th century a failure in both.

In last ten years a dreadful and disastrous failure in both and for reasons I will give no grounds for expecting good behaviour in future.

Why do changes matter?

Under a regime of money-control

Expectations are based on stability

The investor lends in terms of money

The entrepreneur incurs liabilities in terms of money

If money fluctuates, expectations are upset and the harmony between individual interest and social interest is destroyed

If prices go up investment is discouraged and enterprise discredited

If prices go down enterprise is brought to a standstill

(Example in full)

The triple evils of modern society
> Vast enrichment of individuals out of proportion to any services rendered
> Disappointment of expectation and difficulty of laying plans ahead—i.e. the precariousness of our economic system
> Unemployment   Strikes

All these mainly due to instability of standard of value.

The more troublous the times, the worse does a *laissez-faire* system work. I believe that the times are likely to remain troublous for a generation and that the magnification of the evils of monetary instability which we have suffered in the past 5 years are likely to continue unless we do something about it.

Arguments against gold standard

1st long period
> Accidents of 19th century won't be repeated
> No longer in circulation
> No longer in general use
> No longer a natural but already a managed standard
> Gold standard is now a dollar standard

Much as I admire the Americans, when *laissez-faire* takes the form of agreeing to do whatever the Americans do, I am a little terrified.

2nd short period
> Progress of scientific investigation since the War
> Hawtrey, Harvard Cambridge everywhere

One of the biggest jumps forward ever achieved in economic science

Although widely bruited, not yet taken in detail outside limited scientific circles.

Ups and downs of trade long existing back to 18th century

Various theories   Sun spots   Colds in the head

Now recognised as mainly monetary

The diagnosis almost complete

Now even if gold was stable over long periods, it cannot deal with short periods

For the cure for short period fluctuations depends on being able rapidly to expand or contract the volume of money.

The Bank of England since the war has always done exactly the opposite of what the latest science recommends. I conclude from this that their opposition comes, not from mere obstinacy or conservatism, but from their not yet understanding the point. I am, therefore, optimistic about the future.

What is the alternative to gold?

Our existing system but worked self-consciously and for a wise, deliberate purpose.

Here lies our golden opportunity,

Practically no legislation required

The object so to regulate the supply of Bradburies and of bank credit that their volume in terms of goods will be reasonably steady; i.e. that the index number of prices will never move far from a fixed point.

The methods essentially the same as with a gold standard. Under a gold standard we do not actually use gold as lega tender, but we try so to regulate the supply of legal tender that it has a fixed value in gold. Under my system our object is that it shall have a fixed value in goods.

A stable measuring rod

Contract requires it just as much as in weight

A sound money as great a step forward as when in the 32nd millennium B.C. Dungi conceived stability of weight

Since I am speaking under political auspices, I must mention the question often asked me

Can it be made a subject of platform controversy? I doubt it except in the most general terms if you mean platform meetings at a general election. But that is true of most serious, scientific reforms in our complicated economic life

Truth is complex.

But in study circles of serious Liberals such as this—certainly.

If I can persuade the younger generation of the City and the younger generations of Liberal politicians that what I am saying is wise and sensible, it will prevail.

The arguments are new and sufficiently complicated.

But I should like to warn the gentlemen of the City and of High Finance that if they do not listen in time to the voice of reason their days may be numbered. I speak to this great City as Jonah spoke to Nineveh that great city. I prophesy that unless they embrace Wisdom in good time, the system upon which they live will work so very ill that they will be overwhelmed by irresistible things which they hate much more than the mild and limited remedies offered them now.

The publication of the *Tract* brought several letters of comment. The first came from Cecil Lubbock, the Deputy Governor of the Bank of England.

From CECIL LUBBOCK, *12 December 1923*

Dear Keynes,

(I write to you this familiarly because we did meet the other day—at the Pol. Economy Club—and, chiefly, because we are both old K.S.'s,[1] though not of the same election.)

I am very grateful to you for sending me a copy of your book, which I began last night, and shall study carefully. Whatever my 'reaction' will be when I reach the end, I shall learn much from it.

We should all be grateful to you (1) for writing on economics in a style which 'an educated man' (as Broadbent would say) can read with pleasure and (2) for having your books printed in a type and got up in a style which makes them pleasant to deal with.

Believe me,

Sincerely yours

CECIL LUBBOCK

A week later, he heard from Alfred Marshall.

From ALFRED MARSHALL, *19 December 1923*

My dear Keynes,

Many thanks for your fascinating *Monetary Reform*. I have several times as much 'half-baked' work on hand, as I can hope to bring out of the oven: but I have been unable to keep my eyes off it. As years go on it seems to

[1]   King's Scholars at Eton.

162

become even clearer that there ought to be an international currency; and that the—in itself foolish—superstition that gold is the 'natural' representation of value has done excellent service. I have appointed myself amateur currency-mediciner; but I cannot give myself even a tolerably good testimonial in that capacity. And I am soon to go away: but, if I have opportunity, I shall ask all new-comers to the celestial regions whether you have succeeded in finding a remedy for currency-maladies.

Yours ever,

A.M.

Another note came from Sir Charles Addis.

From SIR CHARLES ADDIS, *21 December 1923*

Dear Keynes,

I had ordered a copy of your book but am glad to have one from the author. Many thanks.

I find myself in agreement with nearly all of it, I think, except the conclusion. A managed currency may come some day, but I do not believe we are ripe for it yet. It would be ill to work except in an atmosphere of confidence and belief which at present is non-existent.

Believe me,
Yours sincerely
C. S. ADDIS

A final note came from Sir Basil Blackett, then Finance Member for the Viceroy's Council in India.

From SIR BASIL BLACKETT, *31 December 1923*

My dear Keynes,

I received yesterday from Montagu Norman a copy of your *Tract on Monetary Reform*, and read it through with immense interest. I think in chapter II you have brought out clearly for the first time what inflation is as a method of taxation. I at any rate feel I was much clearer about it than before after reading your book. In chapter V, though I agree with your self-criticism that you have compressed the argument unduly (p. 185) [*JMK*, vol. IV, p. 146], you have, I think, described the system actually in operation in England today very well. I do not think I agree with your proposals for the future. They seem to me to be further outside the realm of practical politics than I should have expected from you, though I am very likely wrong. I agree rather with Hawtrey. Indeed, I would go no further than Hawtrey in demanding a return to the gold standard as a preliminary to an attempt to stabilise the value of gold.

I send you another copy of a speech I made on December 4th; I believe I already sent you one. It is remarkable, I think, how closely our minds have been travelling in the same sort of direction. You will see that at the time you were writing your book I was anticipating your recommendation on page 156 [*JMK*, vol. IV, pp. 127–8] to defend the Government of India on the ground of the advantages of stable internal prices. I seem to have used almost your phrases on more than one occasion.

I have just completed a year here, and am starting again with a new Budget. But for the extraordinary uncertainty about the attitude of the Swarajists in the new Assembly, I should say that things are looking up financially for India. Something depends on what happens at home. I fear Baldwin seems to have made a bad mis-calculation.

With best wishes for 1924,

Yours sincerely,

BASIL P. BLACKETT

Keynes returned to the subject matter of the *Tract* in the new year with an article in *The Nation*.

From The Nation and Athenaeum, *2 February 1924*

GOLD IN 1923

Recent discussions about the future of gold lend special interest to Messrs Samuel Montagu & Co.'s annual bullion letter. Almost the whole of the world's output of gold is absorbed by India and the United States. 'In neither country', Messrs Montagu point out, 'is the gold put into circulation as currency. In the former it is regarded as a precious metal bearing a ratio towards rupees differing from that set up by the Imperial Government. In the latter, it is interned in the reserve of the Federal Banks, and its accumulation watched with anxious care, lest it should operate to the prejudice of prices and trade. In other words, the United States is suffering to some extent from the trouble that afflicted King Midas.'

The output of gold in the British Empire and the rest of the world respectively (taken at £4 4s. 11¾d. per fine oz.) has been distributed as follows:—

| | (000s omitted) | | | |
| | 1923 (est.) | 1922 | 1921 | 1920 |
	£	£	£	£
Transvaal	38,800	29,800	34,500	34,700
Canada	5,000	5,200	3,900	3,300
Australasia	3,300	3,700	4,200	4,700
Rhodesia	2,700	2,800	2,500	2,300
India	1,800	1,800	2,000	2,100
West Africa	900	900	900	1,000
British Empire total	52,500	44,200	48,000	48,100
Rest of the world	20,000	19,800	20,000	21,200
World's total	72,500	64,000	68,000	69,300

The stock of gold now held in the United Kingdom is:—

	£
Bank of England	126,000,000
Currency note reserve	27,000,000
Total	£153,000,000

The rest of the British Empire holds a visible stock of £105,000,000, distributed as follows:—

	£
Australia	24,800,000
New Zealand	7,900,000
Canada	38,200,000
South Africa	11,000,000
India	22,300,000
Straits Settlements	800,000
	£105,000,000

The United States, on the other hand, now holds more than three times as much gold as the whole of the British Empire, namely, £784,000,000, made up of:—

| U.S. Treasury | £145,500,000 |
| Federal Reserve Banks | £638,500,000 |

During 1923 gold imports into the U.S. have proceeded at a rate of some $25,000,000 (*net*) monthly. Not a dollar of this was wanted, and the gold reserves of the Federal Reserve System have now reached the unprecedented figure of 80 per cent of their note issue and deposits combined. Thus it has cost the United States during the past year about £100,000,000 to maintain gold at a purely artificial value (made up of about £30,000,000 interest on idle reserves and £70,000,000 for fresh redundant gold imported). Yet if the United States were to close their mints to the reception of further gold, everything would go on exactly as before, except that an additional £70,000,000 of capital reserves would become available during the year for use in other forms. It cannot be reasonable to suppose that this sort of thing will continue indefinitely. For example, it will take less than three years at the present rate—assuming that inflation is successfully avoided—for the gold of the Federal Reserve Banks to reach 100 per cent of their liabilities. What will they do then? They must close their mints to gold, or suffer an involuntary inflation.

If, under the pressure of such circumstances, the United States were to close their mints to the reception of imported gold—which could be done without upsetting any American interest and without interfering with the convertibility of American legal-tender money into gold—the producers of gold elsewhere would probably have to accept the Bank of England price for the bulk of their output. In this case sterling would immediately recover its full gold value whilst remaining at a discount on the dollar. And unless we were prepared to step into America's shoes and waste our money on bottling up gold (which we certainly could not afford), we also should be faced with the alternative of closing our mints to gold or suffering an involuntary inflation.

These ideas may be based on an extreme hypothesis. But they illustrate how precarious the future of gold now is, and what a cataract of superstition must cloud the eyes of those who think it reasonable to assume as a matter of course that the future value of gold in these altered conditions will be governed by just the same sort of considerations as before the War.

Some say that the large interest of the British Empire in gold-mining, as shown in the above figures, is a reason why we should strain ourselves to maintain the value of gold. If we are to abandon arguments about the general social advantages of a sound currency for calculations of this kind, it is worth pointing out that our debt to America is fixed in gold, that the annual burden of this is several times as large as our annual profits from gold-mining, and that every fall in the value of gold lightens this burden.

It would be rash to prophesy the future of an object to which the human race has been so anciently attached as gold. But the situation is peculiar. Only twice before have we had a state of affairs comparable with that produced by the dissipation, through the War, of the temple hoards (i.e., bank reserves) of Europe;—once when Alexander pillaged the bank reserves (i.e., temple hoards) of Persia, again when Spain pillaged those of Mexico and Peru. On each occasion there followed a catastrophic fall in the value of the sacred metal. If we are to judge the present situation by experience, we must cover a longer range of history than the City quotes; if we are to judge it by the light of reason, we must let our minds be bold.

Currency reform has two objects: to remedy the credit cycle and to mitigate unemployment and all the evils of uncertainty; and to link the monetary standard to what matters, namely, the value of staple articles of consumption, instead of to an object of oriental splendour, it is true, and one to which Egyptian and Chaldæan Bank Directors attributed magical properties, but not otherwise useful in itself and precarious in its future prospects. The time may come when currency reformers will appear plainly, not as suspects of inflation, but as the only safeguard against it.

The next week, acting under the guise of 'a French Correspondent'.[2] Keynes turned to another subject.

From The Nation and Athenaeum, *9 February 1924*

THE FRENCH PRESS AND RUSSIA

(*From a French Correspondent*)

L'Humanité, the chief organ of the French Socialist Party, has recently published, under the sweeping and sensational title of 'L'abominable vénalité de la Presse Française', a series of documents, which it states to be drawn from the secret archives of the Russian Government, demonstrating that from 1897 and particularly during the Russo-Japanese War (1904–5), right up to the Revolution of 1917, the Imperial Russian Government controlled a substantial number of the leading Paris newspapers, dictated their attitude on foreign policy, and supplied them with considerable sums. The fact that most of the papers attacked have taken so little action against the Socialist organ, seems to indicate that the documents published are authentic.

The Russian Minister of Finance had a representative in Paris, M. Raffalovich, with considerable sums at his disposal to use as he liked. It was he who handled the funds for the French press. He did not pay out anything himself, but only through the Syndicate of Bankers or through the Banque de Paris et des Pays-Bas, and on the advice of the head of the Stock Exchange, M. de Verneuil. Doubtless he feared to what dimensions its demands might reach, if the Press got wind officially of the fact that the Russian Government thought it important enough to vote it a large appropriation.

[2] Keynes had been in Monte Carlo for a holiday after Christmas.

Leaving aside the year 1897, when the first distributions were made, let us come at once to the years 1904–5, the time of the Russo-Japanese War and the Moscow riots. Raffalovich then forced the Parisian press to conceal the news of the Russian disasters in the field and the revolutionary troubles at home. On August 30th, 1904, he wrote to M. Kokovtzev, Minister of Finance, with the object of establishing his appropriation on the basis of the current year. 'For the first ten months,' he wrote, 'the abominable venality of the French press will have absorbed (over and above the advertising of the loan of 800 millions) a sum of 600 thousand francs, of which the banks have put up half. . . This payment is made to maintain Russian prestige, and to soften the systematic attacks made upon the Russian Government in general, though it cannot prevent them. If, in course of time, we wanted to get anything into the papers, we should have to take advantage of circumstances which had given us some influence over them.'

On March 1st, 1905, he further outlined his plan. 'It is necessary, according to Verneuil, that we should put great pressure on the political section of the newspapers to publish, along with the telegrams, editorial notes calculated to reassure the public about the solvency of Russia and the improbability of revolutionary success. He reckons the expense at between two and three millions for the year. It seems a lot; in February, 1904, it took 1,200,000 francs.'

This programme was carried out. One can guess to what extent the French public was kept informed about the real position of affairs in the country of her ally. M. Raffalovich effected these payments either in the form of financial advertisements, or bogus subscriptions, or even by private cheques slipped from hand to hand.

It would be tedious to set out here the names of all the papers which, according to the published documents, were effectively subsidised by the Russian Government, and the amount of the sums which they received. But among the papers with large circulations, Raffalovich shows that *Le Petit Parisien*, *Le Petit Journal*, *La Liberté*, *Le Figaro*, and *Le Temps*, cashed the largest subsidies. *Le Matin* also figures on the list with considerable sums. But it claims to be able to justify the sums it has received by authentic advertisements, not that that signifies that its attitude was uninfluenced by such lucrative contracts.

It may be interesting by way of example to read the following lines from Raffalovich's pen. They show how cleverly the representative of the Russian Finance Minister checked the attacks on his own Government, and indicate the degree to which the news in the most serious and representative organs was independent. The *Temps*, in spite of the 100,000 francs it had received in 1905 from the Banking Syndicate, had published a gloomy report upon the state of Russian finance, at the time of the issue of the loan. Raffalovich writes, on March 9th, 1905, that he has sent 1,000 francs 'to Hebrard, the editor of the *Temps*, to influence him'. On July 2nd of the same year he is more precise: 'Having found it essential to put an end to the veiled attacks of the *Temps*, I have given orders to bring about an arrangement, which has been carried out, in return for another 3,000 francs.'

The *Temps* went on receiving money from Russia for a long time. In the middle of the War, when the Empire was tottering, it undertook to publish special numbers on Russia. A contract on this subject was agreed upon in Petersburg in January, 1916, between the Imperial Minister of Finance and M. Charles Rivet, the Russian correspondent of the *Temps*.

The following are its two essential clauses:—

'The Russian Minister of Finance has complete liberty to settle the text of the Russian numbers, which will be published under his sole control. He can therefore dispose as he likes of the whole or part of the 5,000 lines or the equivalent space in each number.'

'. . . The Finance Minister gives M. Charles Rivet an annual subsidy of 150,000 francs.'

That is only one example. The list of cheques sent by Raffalovich to be distributed to the French press, which M. Souvarine publishes, is a long one. It amounts to several millions. Even so, these sums did not suffice to attach the press securely. As soon as the distributions ceased the papers started on new campaigns, doubtless to induce renewed outpourings. From 1906 to 1912 the subsidies decreased. M. Iswolski was able to write to M. Sazonov, Foreign Minister, on October 10th, 1912:—

'From then (1906) until now there has not been one copeck spent on the French press, and that has undoubtedly resulted in the press campaigns against us of 1908 and 1910.'

In 1912 the largesse was resumed.

What aggravates these acts of corruption—if the documents are authentic—is that the French Government knew about them, encouraged them, and on occasion directed them. In 1905 Rouvier consulted Raffalovich. In 1912, in the letter which we have already quoted, Iswolski was able to write: 'From my conversation with M. Poincaré I feel sure that he is ready to give his co-operation in this matter, and to show us the most suitable lines along which to spread out the subsidies.'

On February 14th, 1913, he added, still writing to M. Sazonov:—

'In my letter of October 10th/23rd last I told you the cogent reasons in favour of our financial deal with the French press. In the course of my conversation with the ex-President of the Council, M. Poincaré, now President of the Republic, I was convinced that he shares my opinion on this matter. Furthermore, M. Poincaré has expressed a wish that nothing should be done unknown to him, and that the distribution of the sums should be effected in co-operation with the French Government and through M. Lenoir.'

On June 4th, 1914, M. Kokovtzev, instructed by Raffalovich, wrote to M. Sazonov the following lines, which indicate the attitude of the Government of the Republic:—

'M. Klotz [he was then Minister for the Interior] insists upon the necessity now of disbursing large amounts to the Press because of the possibility of a campaign against the new military law, and also because of the general embarrassment of the French Government.'

One hesitates to speak of the action of a Minister who relies on the funds of a foreign Government to 'influence' the press of his own country in favour of the Government to which he himself belongs. Neither M. Poincaré nor M. Klotz has given an explanation in Parliament of the value, authenticity, and bearing of these documents

Thus, with the consent and support of the French Government, a foreign power was able by the vilest methods to suborn the greater part of the Paris press. The enslaved papers—assuming the correctness of the revelations in *L'Humanité*—encouraged the French public to subscribe to Russian loans which were often described as *formidable escroquerie*. They hid from France the advancing decay of the Empire to which she had bound her fate. They defended, for purely selfish interests, a policy which, by its ambitious designs, often inspired solely by dynastic sentiment, helped to create the atmosphere of trouble and ill-will which rendered the conflagration of 1914 inevitable. But this corruption, injected by a foreign Government, did not prevent the so-called patriotic newspapers from denouncing as traitors, as 'in the foreigner's pay', those statesmen and politicians who dared to face the danger and tell the truth at the peril of their lives.

A nation pays dear for such things. Who knows what part such systematic poison, extending over many years, may have played in preparing the way for the War? However this may be, the unhappy French investors who were deceived by these methods have totally lost a sum approaching one thousand million pounds sterling—probably more than one-half of the total savings of the country during the period in question.

A week later, however, he was back on the subject of gold.

From The Nation and Athenaeum, *16 February 1924*

THE PROSPECTS OF GOLD

In an interesting letter, which was published in *The Nation and Athenaeum* last week, commenting on my article 'Gold in 1923', Sir Henry Strakosch [a South African banker and member of the Financial Committee of the League of Nations] writes as follows:—

'America has so far refused—for reasons of her own—to accept from her foreign debtors payment either in goods, services, or securities. She has accepted gold from them, and in doing so has secured a free option to acquire goods, services, and securities in exchange for the gold whenever it happens to suit her.'

This passage, which is representative of a widely held opinion, can serve as my text in a further attempt to make clear why I differ from it.

I hold that gold flows to America because America offers in return for it a greater value in commodities than the gold is worth to the rest of the world. As none know better than Sir Henry Strakosch, gold is freely offered for sale in London every week; America is open to buy unlimited quantities of it at an almost fixed price in terms of goods (since, as Sir Henry points out, her price level has remained admirably stable for two and a half years); whilst the amount which the rest of the world wants on these terms falls far short of the current output. So long as these conditions continue, nothing on earth can prevent gold from flowing to the United States. She does not refuse to accept payment in other forms. She merely rates this particular form of payment at a higher value than the rest of the world does, with the result that it is profitable for the rest of the world to pay in this form rather than in any other.

It is not true, therefore, that she 'has secured a free option to acquire goods, services, and securities in exchange for the gold whenever it happens to suit her', if this means 'getting as much goods for the gold as she originally gave for it'. She can only get rid of the gold by selling it at a sacrifice,—that is to say by lowering its price in terms of goods.

This she can do in two ways only:—

1. By inflation, thus raising the dollar prices of goods and, which is the same thing, lowering the commodity price of gold in the United States; or

2. By closing her mints to the reception of further gold, thus allowing a fall in the value of gold without involving a corresponding fall in the value of the dollar.

As regards the first way, one trembles to think how much inflation would be required to enable her to get rid of an important proportion of her gold;—something so terrific, I should say, that this expedient may be ruled out of practical politics. Quite likely she will inflate; but not enough, I should anticipate, to lose any large quantity of her gold. Probably, therefore, she is stuck for all eternity with what she has already got, unless she is prepared to clear it at a great sacrifice. Thus her choice really lies between a continuance of the present state of affairs with gold steadily flowing in, more in some years, less in others, and occasionally perhaps a small outflow, and closing her mints as above. I suggested in my original article that in course of time the United States might tire of carrying the ever-growing weight of the golden calf, with its vast and vain expense.*

A third way out could only come through the rest of the world *raising* its relative valuation of gold. Some people think that a general restoration of the gold standard might bring this about. I agree that such might be the case to a certain extent. But even in this event the rest of the world would not want much more

* Sir H. Strakosch ignores, in his calculation of the cost to America, the burden of accepting additional gold. His figures represent, not what the gold standard costs America now, but what it would cost them if they were to take my advice and close their mints to new gold.

gold than it has already, or relieve the United States more than slightly. The more solvent countries of Europe, e.g., Great Britain, France, Sweden, Spain, and Holland, already have enough gold to run a gold standard, if the other conditions were present necessary for the restoration of such a standard; whilst the less solvent, e.g., Germany, Russia, Hungary, could not afford for many years to accumulate large stocks of barren metal.

It is commonly believed that the United States could relieve herself of her redundant gold if her investors would become more willing to lend abroad and to purchase foreign investments. This is a delusion,—unless the new foreign loans were of a purely inflationary character. If Americans were to invest their savings abroad instead of at home, there is no reason why this should cause any drain of gold out of America, any more than in the case of other countries which have invested abroad. If foreign investment always involved a drain of gold, it would have to be confined to gold-producing countries. A drain of gold would only follow if America's foreign loans did not represent real savings and involved an internal inflation; which brings us back to where we started, namely, that America can only get rid of this gold by depreciating the dollar through inflation.

The United States have, in fact, embarked on a vast valorisation scheme for the commodity gold, just like other valorisation schemes, e.g., that of Brazil for the commodity coffee;—but with much less prospect of the world demand overtaking the world supply. The value of gold depends upon the United States being willing to continue this valorisation scheme year after year, regardless of cost. It is for this reason, amongst others, that I declare the future prospects of gold to be precarious; particularly the prospects of gold mined outside the United States. The United States has no sufficient interest in spending £50,000,000 or more each year to absorb the redundant world supplies of a commodity she does not want. For a time she may continue,—partly because 'metallist' superstitions cloud men's eyes where the sacred metal is concerned, partly from the argument of 'protecting' the value of the existing stock, the usual argument when top-heavy valorisation schemes are getting too expensive; but, surely, not for ever.

There is a further question, just touched on in my previous article, which Sir Henry Strakosch and also Mr Coutts raised last week in their letters to the Editor,—namely, the effect of a fall in the commodity value of gold on the position of creditor countries. I do not think that currency policy ought to be determined, one way or the other, by such considerations; for the point arises with every change in the price level, whatever the cause or the direction of the change may be. But I agree with these correspondents that, when the calculation is made, there are several items to be reckoned on both sides of the account. Nevertheless, this question does not arise, except where foreign loans have been expressly contracted in terms of gold. The United States, it is true, both owes and is owed certain sums in gold. It is not the case with Great Britain. Our loans are in terms of sterling, not of gold; and during the ten years which have elapsed since we were on a gold standard, no suggestion to the contrary has ever arisen. If, indeed, we were proposing to raise the commodity value of sterling, our creditors might have a grievance in equity; but this is not the intention. If the commodity value of sterling were to be stabilised near the present level, our debtors would still be repaying us in a currency much less valuable than that in which the debt was originally contracted; and since they pay us in goods and services, this is what matters to them. If, however, it were thought necessary, for this or any other reason, to protect the value of gold by artificial means, it would be much cheaper to buy up the South African mines in order to close them down, rather than to buy their output year by year in order to bury it. The United States could buy all the mines in Africa and cement them down securely for about twice the sum which they now expend in a single year in purchasing and burying their output. I recommend this programme to the devotees of the gold standard.

On 23 February Keynes began what was to become his series of comments on the annual speeches of the chairmen of the London clearing banks.[3] Three weeks later, he turned his attention to the French financial situation.

From The Nation and Athenaeum, *15 March 1924*

THE FRANC

The expected has occurred; and it has occurred so precisely as it was expected that we are almost surprised. The watched pot has boiled. We can, after all, repeat:—

> *Raro antecedentum scelestum*
> *Deseruit pede Pœna claudo.*

But what, everyone now asks, will happen next? In a confused situation one must cling to first principles. The value of the franc will be determined, first, by the quantity, present and prospective, of the francs in circulation; and, second, by the amount of purchasing power which it suits the public to hold in that shape. The former of these two elements depends on the loan and budgetary policies of the French Treasury; the latter (in present conditions) mainly on the trust or distrust which the public feel in the prospects of the value of the franc.

With the franc between 100 and 120 to the £ sterling, the control of the former does not appear to the outside observer to be unduly difficult. When the internal price level has adjusted itself to this figure, the yield of many of the existing taxes in terms of paper francs will naturally be increased. On the other hand, the biggest item of expenditure, namely, the service of the internal debt, will remain the same as before. Thus, even apart from additional taxation, the mere movement of the exchange has in itself a tendency to restore the budget towards equilibrium, provided always that public faith is maintained in the prospects of the national currency. It is in this second factor, therefore, that the crux of the situation lies,—namely the attitude of the

[3] It appears in *JMK*, vol. IX, pp. 188–92.

French public towards their own currency. I emphasise the fact that the matter lies in the hands of Frenchmen themselves, not in those of any foreign persons. For the amount of francs owned by foreigners is probably not very great,—not much more than what is still left in their hands as the remnant of disappointed 'bull' operations; whilst the obstacles are insuperable to 'bear' sales by foreigners of francs, which they do not possess, on a really large scale. On the other hand, the volume of franc notes and franc bills and other short-dated investments held in France itself is enormous,—far beyond the minimum required for the convenient transaction of business. If Frenchmen get it into their heads (as, each in their turn, Russians, Austrians, and Germans have done) that their national legal-tender money and titles to legal tender represent a depreciating asset, then there is no limit to the fall in the value of the franc. For, in this event, they will diminish their holdings of such assets; they will keep fewer Bank of France notes in their pocket-books and in their safes, will liquidate their *Bons de Trésor* and will sell their *Rentes*. No law or regulation will avail to restrain them. Moreover, the process will be cumulative; for each successive liquidation of franc assets and their transference into 'real values', by provoking a further fall, will seem to justify the prescience of those who fled first from the franc, and will thus prepare the way for a second outbreak of distrust.

In this case the fall of the franc will not be prevented even by a reformed budget or a favourable surplus of trade. For it would be necessary for the Government to absorb the redundant bank notes and franc bonds and bills, which the public no longer cared to hold,—a task unavoidably beyond the Government's power. We have the experience of many countries to demonstrate that unbalanced budgets are the initial cause of a collapse, but that the real *dégringolade* only comes when the confidence of the general public is so far undermined that they begin to contract their holdings of the legal-tender money.

The central task of the French Government at this moment

is, therefore, to preserve confidence in the franc in the minds of the widest circles of the French public. For it is the failure of this internal confidence, not speculation by foreigners (though foreigners and Frenchmen too may take advantage of a collapsing currency to win great gains), which would prove their undoing.

Now, if they go the right way about it, there is nothing impossible in the task of restoring and maintaining confidence. The examples of Russia, Austria, and Germany are not a just parallel. Those who foresee the future of the franc in the light of such previous experiences may make a big mistake. For in those countries the problem of balancing the budget was, during the earlier phases, a virtual impossibility. The initial impulse towards collapse was, therefore, also a continuing impulse. This is not so in France. There is no impossibility in achieving a fiscal equilibrium, provided that reconstruction expenditure is reasonably postponed. I applaud the efforts of M. Poincaré and the French Treasury in this direction. But this is not enough by itself. It is also necessary to restore public confidence; and in this sphere of action every step taken by M. de Lasteyrie has been away from wisdom.

For upon what foundations does the credit of a currency rest? They are much the same as with a bank. A bank can only attract and retain the deposits of its clients so long as these clients possess a complete confidence in their freedom to withdraw their deposits for exchange into other assets, if they have a mind to do so. As long as this liberty is beyond doubt, it will not be exercised;—the deposits will rest and grow. But if it is once called in question, they shrink and disappear. So is it with a currency. Men hold a part of their resources in money, because they believe it to be more readily and freely interchangeable, than any alternative hoard, into whatsoever object of value they may select hereafter. If this belief proves false, they will not hold money and nothing can make them do so.

Now the prime object of most of M. de Lasteyrie's regulations is to restrict the liberty of holders of francs to exchange them at their discretion into other forms of value. So far, therefore, from protecting the franc and restoring its credit, they are directly calculated to shatter confidence and to destroy its credit. A sufficient number of regulations would destroy the value, precisely because they would destroy the utility, of any currency in the world. As soon as there is a doubt as to whether francs (or *Bons de Trésor*) are a truly liquid asset, these instruments cease to serve the purpose for which they are held, and holders hasten to dispose of them before the doubt is resolved into a certainty and yet further obstacles can have been placed in the way. Just as a man draws out his deposits at the bank, whether he needs the money or not, as soon as he has reason to believe that he may not be free to do so later on; so the general public and the financial world alike withdraw their resources from a currency, if they fear a limitation on their subsequent freedom of withdrawal.

What course then should the French Treasury now take in face of the dangers surrounding them? It is soon said. First, the Government must so strengthen its fiscal position that its power to control the volume of the currency is beyond doubt,—the necessity of which is at last accepted. Secondly—and especially during the interval which must needs elapse before the first category of measures can be brought into full operation—the Government must restore such complete confidence in the liberty of the franc that no one will think it worth while to enter by way of precaution into sales of francs not immediately urgent,—the equal necessity of which seems to be overlooked.

To achieve this latter object nothing more is required than a reversal of the recent policy of restrictions on dealing, of the useless hoarding of gold, of a relatively low bank rate, and of secrecy about the actual position of the Treasury and the Bank of France. The chief measures which are necessary can be summarised under three heads:—

(1) All limitations on the use of francs to purchase foreign currencies, foreign bonds, or goods, whether for immediate or for deferred delivery, should be wholly repealed.

(2) The discount rate of the Bank of France should be raised to a high figure, probably not less than 10 per cent in present circumstances (though it might not be necessary to maintain such a high rate for any length of time), so as to counteract anticipations, well or ill founded, as to the possible depreciation of the franc. In view of the high rate of interest now obtainable on French Government securities (let alone the rates on forward exchange) the present rate of discount does not correspond to the facts of the situation and is calculated to stimulate over-borrowing. Possibly some increase of the Bank of France's rate may have been effected by the time these lines are in print.

(3) A considerable sum, drawn from the still ample gold reserve of the Bank of France, should be made the basis of a foreign credit, either by outright sale or by borrowing against it, to be available for use without stint in supporting the exchange near the present level and restoring confidence during the interval before fiscal reforms can produce their full effect. An advance of a hundred million dollars from Messrs J. P. Morgan has actually been arranged on these lines since the above was written.

I warrant that these simple well-tried measures, in combination with political moderation and with the drastic economies and taxes without which no other measures can finally avail, would have a marvellous efficacy. After a few weeks of this medicine and with a benevolent reception by M. Poincaré (or his successor) of the forthcoming Experts' Reports,[4] the franc might be as steady as a rock. But if, on the other hand, distrust in the franc is countered by the methods of the Holy Inquisition, if Frenchmen prefer the concealed capital levy of inflation to other forms of taxation, if France remains the trouble-peace of Europe—then the franc may follow the course of other once-noble tokens.

[4] In December 1923 two committees of experts were appointed under the auspices of the Reparations Commission to enquire into the possibilities of (1) the restoration of Germany's financial stability, and (2) the expropriation of German capital abroad. For Keynes's view of the work of these committees, which reported on 19 April, see *JMK*, vol. XVIII, pp. 235–46.

From 25 to 27 March the League of Nations Union held a conference in London on Unemployment in its National and International Aspects. Amongst those who took part were Edwin Cannan, T. E. Gregory, H. D. Henderson, Keynes and Barbara Wootton. Keynes addressed the conference on the first day as part of a panel dealing with financial factors.

From Unemployment in its National and International Aspects[5]

MR J. M. KEYNES'S SPEECH

Mr J. M. Keynes, C.B. (author of *The Economic Consequences of the Peace*, etc.) said:

I think it may assist clearness in this discussion if we try to disentangle several distinct issues that have arisen out of the speeches of the two preceding speakers. There is, first of all, the question: Is the financial factor a big one in causing unemployment? The second question (assuming that the first is answered in the affirmative) is: Are our bankers of such feeble intellect that they are incapable of applying up-to-date remedies, with the result that up-to-date remedies are not worth discussing? The third question is: Are the up-to-date remedies really efficacious? Professor Cannan, I think, denied all those three things in part. I should like to take them in order.

First of all, is the financial factor an important one in causing unemployment? It was not quite clear what Professor Cannan's answer to that was. He told us that the financial factor was not the sole factor. That is agreed. But I did not hear any other argument as to its not being an important factor.

According to Professor Cannan, there were two other very significant factors at the present time: first, that owing to the interruption of the war labour was often in the wrong place, that labour was arranged to produce a different category of articles from that which was required. That is certainly so. If, for example, in England now there were 50,000 fewer men in the

---

[5] International Labour Office, *Studies and Reports*, series C (Unemployment), no. 9 (Geneva, 1924).

engineering, iron and steel industries and 50,000 more men in the building industries there would probably be less unemployment. The second cause he gave was that with better unemployed pay there is not quite the same pressure that there used to be on the individual unemployed man to secure employment. Well, the point may be approaching when those two causes are beginning to be responsible for a large part of the residuum. The unemployment figures which, a little time back, were of the order of 12 per cent have now fallen, I think, to 7 or 8 per cent, and may easily fall in the near future towards 5 per cent; and when we reach 5 per cent it may be correct to argue that the other causes to which Professor Cannan called attention are largely responsible.

I would add a third possible cause, and that is that wages may be maintained by the power of trade unions at a higher level than the export trades can support, with the result that at that level of wages all the men cannot be employed. Those three causes: the fact that in some industries wages may be too high, that in other industries there may be more labour than can be absorbed and the labour ought to go to other industries where they are short of labour, and the fact of better unemployed pay compared with old days—those causes may be the predominant ones when we have got unemployment down to 4 or 5 per cent, and in that case they may be a very significant factor now.

But Professor Cannan has not only to maintain that; he has to maintain that they were a very predominant factor a year ago or more when our unemployment figures were 12 per cent. The worst of the slump, in my opinion, is nearly over. The great damage done on this particular occasion by the financial factor is working towards its conclusion, as is always the case. When you are near the end of a slump, when you are even perhaps at the beginning of the new boom, the financial factor has ceased to be an important one for unemployment. I should think that it still plays a part, though a very much less important part, than it did when the unemployment figures were 12 per cent.

I do not believe that it is possible to make a plausible case for supposing that when unemployment was 12 per cent, such factors as were mentioned by Professor Cannan were predominant ones, and it is quite sufficient for the purposes of this discussion that at certain phases of the credit cycle the unemployment should be largely caused by the monetary factor, because what we want to deal with is the cause of unemployment which makes these very bad unemployment figures. When we have got unemployment down to 4 or 5 per cent, then there are other causes which also have to be tackled by other methods, but, if you have the financial factor responsible for the difference (say) between 5 and 12 per cent, then it is an enormous cause of immense poverty, immense suffering, and it is a matter which it is well worth bending our energies to get rid of.

I daresay that Professor Cannan would not deny that, when unemployment was 12 per cent, the financial factor was important; and if he agrees that the financial factor was important at that point, or that it was important in the depressions following pre-war times, then we agree that the consideration of the means of curing the financial factor is one of the chief things to which those people interested in getting rid of unemployment have to pay attention.

Operation of the financial factor

The precise way in which the financial factor operates is, of course, a big question which one cannot deal with fully in the course of a single afternoon's discussion. Mr Henderson dwelt on a great many sides of it. I should like just to mention in passing one aspect which perhaps he did not stress so much as I should. That is, quite apart from the positive action of the banks, the effect on the business world of an *anticipation* that prices are going to go up or down.

The business world has to provide for the considerable period which elapses between beginning the process of production and the consumer getting the goods and paying for them. In different industries that interval of time varies, but in many industries it is not less than six months from the beginning to the end of the process, and, where long distances are concerned, it is very often a great deal more. All through that time the entrepreneur is engaged in paying out money for wages, and in other ways, which he will recoup when, at the end of the process, he sells his article for money. All his normal calculations as to rate of profit and correct level of wages and so forth are based on the assumption that money is going to be worth more or less the same at the end of the period that it is at the beginning. If it is worth a very different amount, then such sound calculations are thrown out. If it is worth a great deal less—that is to say, if prices have risen—the entrepreneur receives a very large unexpected, uncalculated bonus; if, on the other hand, money has risen in value and prices have fallen, he suffers a very large loss. It therefore is an important part of his business to try to predict which of these two things is going to happen, and if he anticipates that prices are going to fall it is very often (not always, but very often) the case that the only way in which he can protect himself from this very large loss, for which he cannot make any adequate provision in his normal profits, is by reducing his scale of operations and more or less going out of business.

Thus you get a situation in which the individual employer has an interest in acting in a way opposite to the public interest. So far as the community as a whole is concerned, the thing is as broad as it is long. If the article in question is worth a given amount of effort to produce to the community, if the amount of effort that it is worth to the community is the same at the beginning of the process as at the end, it is in the interest of the community that it should be made; but it does not follow that it is in the interest of the employer, because of this calculation of money which comes in. It is only worth his while if the calculations that he makes about the value of money are borne out.

Therefore I should say that one of the principal ways in which the financial factor operates is to cause, rightly or wrongly, an expectation in the minds of individual persons that prices are going to move in a certain direction; and if the business world as a whole is widely of the opinion that prices are going to fall, then there will be numerous individuals who can only protect themselves from loss by throwing their employees out of work, although the things those employees would make if they were in work are necessary and useful and desirable, at that cost of effort, to the community as a whole.

So the method of curing that would be to prevent, so far as one could, that there should be any reason why business men should expect that prices are going to fall. If you have a paper deflation, if the government announces that prices are going to fall, then, of course, the thing being almost a certainty, you have unemployment at its worst; but without that being the case circumstances may arise—often have arisen in the past—in which the business world has valid reasons for expecting a fall of prices, and the way of handling that must be to have a new method of regulation so that it would be a very rare thing—if possible, a thing that never happened—that there would be any valid reasons why the business world as a whole should entertain the expectation of falling prices.

Mental capacity of bankers

That is all I am going to say about the question whether the financial factor causes unemployment. I think myself that it is a thing absolutely outside argument: it is certain that it does. The next question is: Are our bankers intellectually so feeble that they are incapable of applying the up-to-date remedies? Dr Cannan expressed the opinion that they were. I do not agree with him. I think that those bankers who would be responsible for this class of control are perfectly capable of carrying it out.

But let us consider the alternative. Let us imagine Professor

Cannan's answer to the people of this country. Suppose it is true that the financial factor is the cause of unemployment, suppose it is true that there is an up-to-date remedy which, if intelligently applied, would cure that unemployment. Professor Cannan is going to the people of this country and he is going to say: 'You have those unemployed, and the reason why is because bankers are intellectually feeble, and as it is necessary that bankers should be intellectually feeble you will always have unemployed and there is no more to be said about it.' That does not seem to me a situation in which the public are likely to acquiesce. If it is true that the bankers are incapable of exercising this kind of control, obviously they must be replaced by other persons and there can be no question that that is the attitude which the community would rapidly take.

But I think there is one great mistake about this. There are two kinds of banking: there is the kind of banking undertaken by the ordinary banker as the public thinks of him, who deals with his customers, whose main business is to see that his customers are solvent and suitable to lend money to, and who directs the deposits of the community into the most advantageous channels. That is a business in itself, a business which bankers, I think, carry on in this country with great efficiency. But there is also this totally different problem of national policy in the matter of the aggregate of credit as a whole, as distinct from the particular individuals who obtain it.

A wholly different question requires different training and different gifts, and that the bankers who are largely occupied in the first task should not always be the most suitable persons for carrying out the second is no more surprising than that stockbrokers should not be the most suitable for insurance brokers. It is not more surprising and not more discreditable to them than that the persons who canvass for the Prudential should not be the right persons for managing the investment policy of the Prudential Insurance Company. But as a matter of fact it is of no great importance, because no one would propose to hand over this sort of control to the particular individuals who are mainly engaged in that kind of banking.

As Mr Henderson pointed out, this is a matter which should be in the hands of the Bank of England and of the central authorities generally. Exactly what division of functions there would be between the Bank of England and the Treasury, one could talk about for a long time. The matter would be in the hands of the central authorities, and they would have totally different tasks in front of them from those the ordinary individual banker has had. For a very long time past the kind of tasks that the Governors of the Bank of England have had to carry out have required gifts of quite a different kind from those which were needed from the ordinary joint-stock banker, and I do not think there is the slightest reason for supposing that the talent of the country available for work of that kind is in any way short of what it ought to be. I think that the intellectual ability which has controlled the policy of the Bank of England over past years has been extraordinary. New ideas have lately grown up as to what the aim of their policy ought to be. That is one thing. But the success with which they have in the past carried out the daily technique of quite as difficult a problem namely, the maintenance of the gold standard in conditions where gold is not the primary medium of circulation, is quite enough encouragement. At any rate, I do not think that we could seriously be stopped from using this particular cure for unemployment for such reasons as Professor Cannan suggested under that heading.

Dual method of credit control

I come to the third heading, which is much the most difficult and most important. Are these new-fangled remedies adequate to solve the problem? That seems to me the real serious subject of discussion. It is extraordinarily difficult to demonstrate that any new remedy which has never been tried on an important scale will be effective. One will never have a final answer to this question until one has tried. In the case of any new proposal all one can do is to show that there are some theoretical reasons for thinking it might be effective, and then, if the importance of the occasion justifies it (which it would in this case), to make the experiment and see how successfully it can be carried out.

I think that Professor Cannan expressed scepticism on this head, partly because he has not appreciated—or, at any rate, did not mention—the nature of the method that we propose to employ. He seemed to think that the sole method of effecting this would be by movements of the Bank rate very much as they used to move prior to the War, and to argue quite plausibly that the extra expense of paying a high rate for money for a short period would not be a very important element entering into the calculations of business men.

But why does he suppose that that is the only method which would be employed? It is one of the methods, but I personally have come more and more to the view that the more powerful method—certainly the weapon upon which one would have to depend in the last resort—would be variations in the volume of deposits in the Bank of England available to joint-stock banks as the basis of their working credit. For all practical purposes joint-stock banks leave their cash in the strict sense and their deposits at the Bank of England. They then use those almost in accordance with rules of thumb for building up a superstructure.

Now, there are two ways in which the amount of credit they offer can be reduced, partly by raising the price—that is the method of the Bank rate—and partly by diminishing the supply or increasing it, as the case may be; that is to say, by varying the amount of the deposits of the bankers at the Bank of England. That is a matter which is just as much under the control of the Bank of England as the Bank rate is, because by buying or selling Conversion Loan or any other security they can reduce the bankers' balances or increase them within considerable limits at will, and I believe the limits are quite big enough to produce a drastic effect, so that the actual technique of the business would be by expanding and curtailing the basis of credit quite as much as by raising or lowering the price of credit.

The psychological factor

But I should depend almost more upon the third factor, namely, the psychological factor. Suppose the business world believed that this policy was going to be put through with determination, so that when there was a tendency for prices to rise all the forces of the financial world would be brought to bear to prevent them rising further, then the kind of expectation of which I have spoken would never arise strongly enough to make them go out of business and reduce the extent of employment to the degree they do now.

It is not the actual rise or fall or prices that causes unemployment, although the actual rise and fall of prices causes profits and losses to business men. What chiefly causes unemployment is the anticipation of falling prices. If, therefore, this policy can be put strongly into force, so that the business world knows that when prices have risen more than a certain amount every possible measure will be taken to prevent them rising further, that will very much diminish the expectation of falling prices which they would otherwise entertain. It may not abolish it altogether. In the early days they will not feel as much confidence as they will later on, so in the early days you may have to allow yourself a little more oscillation than you have to have later on, and have to act rather more ruthlessly than you would wish to as a permanency. But if you can by success on some critical occasion convince the business world as to the efficacy of your weapons, if you use them to the full, the psychological effect will be that on future occasions it will probably be quite unnecessary to use anything like such drastic methods as you had to use on the first occasion or two.

If both those weapons were used, I must say I cannot understand a doubt as to their producing some effect. Again, one is up against the kind of argument which Mr Henderson foreshadowed. Of course, the thing will not be absolutely successful; therefore it is no use at all. That is the kind of argument one is constantly having to deal with. It will be quite sufficient to justify the attempt at the experiment if it would produce some results, if action of this kind would diminish the expectation of falling prices and damp down the extent of the oscillation. Enthusiastic individuals, or those who have more faith in these theories, may entertain exaggerated hopes, may think they will cure it entirely; but it is not necessary for the general public to go all the way with you to agree that the experiment is well worth trying. Though very partially success-ful, it would still have done a great deal of good and no harm whatever.

A case for experiment

If one is making only that limited claim for it, I find it very difficult to doubt the efficacy of the weapon in the hands of the Bank of England. Of course, those persons who dispute altogether the relation between the volume of purchasing power and the level of prices will be impressed no more by this argument than by any other rational argument on the subject of money. But those who agree on the fundamentals of monetary theory with Professor Cannan and myself—I do not think we differ in the slightest on that—can hardly doubt, I should have thought, that contracting and expanding the ultimate volume of purchasing power on which credit is based must have its effect on prices and on the expectation of rising and falling prices; and, if that is the case, you have a sufficient *prima facie* argument for trying this great experiment.

It happens that, at the moment, we can try it without jeopardising anything else. We are not on a gold standard basis;

we are not likely to be in the very near future. The policy of deflation has been abandoned, and we therefore have an extraordinary opportunity of trying the experiment of the new policy without doing any harm to anyone.

I would like to say, in conclusion, that I think the situation may arise in which possibly Professor Cannan and I will be happily agreed once more as to practical politics. There is an extraordinary tendency in the world to think that if you are in favour of dear money at one time you must always be in favour of it, and if you are in favour of cheap money at one time you must always be in favour of cheap money. Many people are congenital deflationists and many others congenital inflationists. In many circles it is considered almost as indecent to be sometimes in favour of a high Bank rate and sometimes a low Bank rate as to be sometimes a Conservative and sometimes a Liberal. Just as every little boy and girl is supposed to be born into the world either Liberal or Conservative, there are supposed to be born dear-money children and cheap-money children, and any oscillation between those two tendencies is very incorrect.

That is all rubbish. Any sensible person is in favour of dear money in certain circumstances and cheap money in other circumstances. When one is in favour of dear money one is considered highly respectable amongst the congenital deflationists and a great obstructionist of the progress of industry amongst the congenital inflationists; and the other way round when one is in favour of cheap money one becomes highly disreputable in the minds of the congenital deflationists and one gets a lot of unmerited sympathy from the congenital inflationists.

I was in favour of dear money before the break of the boom in 1920, and got into a good deal of trouble for wanting a 7 per cent Bank rate at what was called an inappropriate date. When the whole thing had broken and we had the depression, cheap money seemed to me to be an absolute *desideratum*. I then became a disreputable person in the eyes of Professor Cannan and his friends. I believe that not many months will elapse before I shall be in favour of dear money again. In the ordinary course the present slump will come to its final conclusion, and, just as on previous occasions, a boom will begin; so that we may be able to make our first experiment with the new policy, not in checking the slump, which will bring one to discredit with Professor Cannan, but in checking the boom, which will bring one to credit with him.

If, therefore, by the date at which one could hope that some of these ideas may be beginning to fructify, the slump is thoroughly over and the boom beginning, we shall make our first experiment in the form of putting on dear money at a very early date compared with previous occasions and avoiding the impending boom of 1925 or 1926; and that may, at any rate for the moment, unite with the reformers that respectable body of persons who think that what one really requires is always falling prices rather than stable prices.

So I look forward to an opportunity in the near future of making a little test as to the efficacy of the new ideas. I stress the fact that they are new ideas because I think very few economists held quite the view on this subject ten years ago that they hold now. An enormous amount of work has been done, an enormous amount of thinking and investigation of details. I believe that a great leap forward has been made, economists have really discovered something thoroughly useful for once, and if they have the chance of experimenting with these ideas in circumstances in which, even in the eyes of Professor Cannan, they can do no harm, we may make a great step forward in the solution of the problem which this Conference is to discuss.

On 5 April Keynes returned to the columns of *The Nation* to provide an anonymous leader on recent financial dealings in the newspaper world.

From The Nation and Athenaeum, *5 April 1924*

NEWSPAPER FINANCE

We had occasion six months ago to comment on the finance of the Rothermere Newspaper Trust. This week the Messrs Berry (whose principal newspaper properties are *The Financial Times*, *The Graphic*, and *The Sunday Times*) have gone one better. Last Monday's issue of £4,750,000 8 per cent preference shares of the Allied Newspapers Ltd. has carried to its extreme point the policy of utilising a boom period and the powers of giant advertising to unload on the public the financial risk and burden of one of the most speculative of industries, whilst retaining for the inner ring the surplus profits, if any, together with complete control of the newspapers, in return for next to nothing.

Let us start with the bare facts. Last autumn the Daily Mail Trust purchased the Hulton Press at a net cost of £4,750,000 (after allowing for the proceeds of certain portions of it which were disposed of immediately). These same properties, *minus* the valuable London properties *The Daily Sketch* and *The Illustrated Sunday Herald*, are now sold by them for £5,500,000 in cash and debentures. Thus the Daily Mail Trust has secured an immediate profit of £750,000 *plus The Daily Sketch* and *The Illustrated Sunday Herald* for nothing. The subscribers to the Daily Mail Trust debentures do not touch much of this, although it was they who found the money for the original deal; nevertheless they are to have half their holdings repaid at 10 per cent premium, so that they have no reason to complain that another party has been found to carry the baby.

Unless Sir Edward Hulton, who may be presumed to have understood his own papers, sold outrageously too low, it appears on the face of it that the new purchasers have bought outrageously too high. But this is not the end of the deal. The new purchasers are in the first instance the Sunday Times Ltd, but this company immediately resells to a new company, the Allied Newspapers

Ltd, which has been floated for the purpose, the above properties *plus The Sunday Times* at a price equal to that paid to the Daily Mail Trust *plus* £400,000 in cash and £2,000,000 in ordinary shares. Since the Sunday Times Ltd distributes £510,000 of these ordinary shares to the underwriters of the new issue, the sale price of *The Sunday Times* appears to be £400,000 in cash and £1,490,000 in ordinary shares. The present capital of the Sunday Times Ltd is £67,257 in ordinary shares, all owned by the Messrs Berry, and £30,000 in preference shares. Thus the Messrs Berry obtain in cash what looks like a full price for *The Sunday Times*, and get in addition ordinary shares in the new company, which may be worth much or nothing, but give them in either case effective control of the newspapers. (The preference shareholders do not vote, in normal circumstances, unless their dividends are in arrear, and even then will have to organise themselves energetically to outvote the holders of the ordinary shares. The principal officials have five-year contracts.) The public are asked to put up a sum which a reasonable person might estimate to be not less than the full value of the properties, whilst surrendering to the promoters the right to surplus profits and the control of the papers.

What security have the public for the due payment of their dividends? We notice at the outset that, whereas the Daily Mail Trust offered 7 per cent *debentures*, the new Company offers 8 per cent *preference* shares, with £1,500,000 debentures in front of them, and ordinary shares, which are wholly water, behind them. Next, the published figures disclose the fact that in no year prior to 1922 were the profits of the joint concerns sufficient to pay the preference dividend in full. In 1920 there was a net loss, explained by the high price of paper. On the average of the four years 1918–1921 the surplus profits, after meeting debenture charges, were equivalent to an average of less than $3\frac{1}{2}$ per cent on the preference shares now issued. The capitalisation is entirely based, therefore, on the results of the two years 1922 and 1923, on the basis of which the preference dividend is covered rather less than twice. The interest is cumulative, but there appears to be no provision for building up a fund for the equalisation of dividends in poor years. If the present boom in the profits of big newspaper syndicates continues two or three years longer, the large temporary surplus can be drained away out of the business into the pockets of the ordinary shareholders.

How is the public induced to swallow this prodigious proposition? The answer to this question is not the least interesting part of the business. There have been several recent issues, of which the expenses have been out of all reason. But here again the Messrs Berry go one better. The expenses of the issue are estimated at £150,000 for preliminary expenses, of which stamp duty presumably accounts for £82,500, *plus* £354,000 in cash and £510,000 in ordinary shares as underwriting commission and expenses of the offer for sale. Thus the mere flotation, exclusive of stamp duty, and apart from promotion profits, costs more than £400,000 in cash and £500,000 in shares. This must constitute a record! Evidently the risk that the public would not bite was reckoned high. But enormous commissions to the financial world and enormous advertising expenditure in the newspaper world can go a long way towards silencing criticism. The fear, lest the hand might this time have been overplayed, proved baseless. The public oversubscribed the issue within a few hours. As *The Financial Times* put it next morning, 'investment was not deterred by slightly prattling criticism'. Apart from *The Daily Mirror*'s headline *Lists Open for Golden Chance*, most of the daily papers refrained from good words and quoted the prospectus without comment, the City Editor of *The Times* and *The Daily Herald* being almost alone, amongst the leading organs, in outspoken criticism. The names of the Westminster Bank, Lloyd's Bank, and Barclay's Bank appear on the prospectus, and not all of the public are aware that the name of a bank on a prospectus means nothing as to the merits of the issue.

The episode is now over. The money of the public is engaged, and we must hope for the best. But we can draw the moral from this and other recent experiences that the power of large-scale advertising in securing the savings of the public is altogether excessive. It means, first of all, that very large issues of capital have an undue advantage over moderate issues which cannot support the expense of an intensive campaign in newspapers and through outside brokers. It means also that a company which squanders a fifth or a tenth of its capital in getting floated is more likely to secure capital than one which does not, yet is, by precisely that amount, a worse investment. The source of the trouble probably lies in the fact that savings, very substantial in the aggregate, accumulate in the hands of investors who are not in touch with regular stockbrokers, and find it much easier to invest in response to appeals advertised in the press than in any other way. It is impossible to prevent offers for sale at an unduly high price. But an addition to our company law, prohibiting expenditure on underwriting and issue expenses in excess of a prescribed percentage of the capital on offer, might check a growing abuse. We cannot afford to allow the direction of the savings of the public by advertisement into inferior channels.

No one in the City seems to think it his duty to protect the public, when these episodes occur. Yet it is low standards in such matters, not Socialism or Bolshevism, which are the real enemy of the system for which the City stands.

Also on 5 April, Keynes resumed his contributions to the *Nation*'s Finance and Investment column, this time anonymously. His columns echoed many of his current and forthcoming concerns.

From The Nation and Athenaeum, *5 April 1924*

TRUSTEE SECURITIES—WAR LOAN CONVERSION—
FOREIGN ISSUES

The *Investors' Chronicle and Money Market Review* published last week the following useful table showing the yields at current prices on Home Railway prior charges, as well as the surplus profits in excess of the amount required to meet each of these charges:—

	Price	Yield £ s. d.	Annual interest requirements £	Surplus over interest 1923 £
Great Western				
2¼% debentures	52	4 17 3 ⎫		
4% debentures	83	4 17 0 ⎪		
4¼% debentures	88¼	4 16 9 ⎬	1,463,931	6,207,324
4½% debentures	92¼	4 19 9 ⎪		
5% debentures	103¼	4 17 0 ⎭		
5% rent charge stock (cum.)	101½	4 19 0	385,412	5,821,912
5% cons. gtd. stock (cum.)	99½	5 0 6	1,190,827	4,631,085
5% cons. preference	98¼	5 1 6	1,387,738	3,243,347
London and North-Eastern				
3% debentures	61	4 19 3 ⎫		
4% debentures	81	4 19 9 ⎬	3,608,798	9,427,206
4% first guaranteed (cum.)	79	5 1 3	1,244,469	8,182,737
4% second guaranteed (cum.)	78	5 2 6	1,107,777	7,074,960
4% first preference (non-cum.)	77xd.	5 4 0	1,928,752	5,146,208
4% second pref. (non-cum.)	76xd.	5 5 3	2,641,306	2,504,902
5% preferred ord. (non-cum.)	82xd.	6 2 0	2,117,673	384,510
London, Midland and Scottish				
4% debentures	82	4 18 0	4,071,643	14,557,379
4% guaranteed stock (cum.)	80	5 0 0	1,627,716	12,929,663
4% preference	78	5 2 6	4,858,850	8,070,813
4% 1923 preference	77	5 4 0	1,605,359	6,465,454
Southern				
4% debentures	81	4 19 6	1,520,701	4,516,100
5% guaranteed pref. (cum.)	98¼xd.	5 1 6	254,328	4,261,772
5% preference (non–cum.)	97½xd.	5 3 0	2,080,660	2,181,112
5% preferred ord.	82xd.	6 2 0	1,376,554	804,558

With the exception of the two preferred ordinary stocks given in this table, all the above have the status of trustee securities.

In view of the provisions of the Railways Act, 1921, any of these is a very well-secured investment. The debentures and guaranteed stocks, in any case, are beyond criticism, yet yield a better income (particularly the guaranteed stocks) than long-dated British Government securities. A minor consideration to be borne in mind is the fact that a transfer duty of 1 per cent is payable by the purchaser, a burden from which Government securities are exempt. Nevertheless, several of these stocks seem decidedly superior to Funding Loan or Conversion Loan or Local Loans for the trustee investor who attaches primary importance to the permanent yield; whilst for those who are prepared to be a little less secure in order to get a little more income, the preferred ordinary stocks offer an admirable 6 per cent investment.

Next week we hope, in response to numerous requests, to offer in this column some general advice to investors in trustee securities. Will readers who are interested kindly keep the above table at hand for purposes of reference and comparison?

The Treasury have offered to exchange £103 of 4½ per cent [Conversion] Loan (1940–44) for £100 of 5 per cent War Loan (1929–47) up to an aggregate of £200,000,000, which is about one-tenth of the outstanding War Loan. The proposal is a curious one, and seems scarcely worth while, because it does not seem to offer any palpable advantage to either party. The investor accepts a reduction of income from £5 to £4 12s. 8d. (or £4 14. 8d. allowing for the £3 profit on ultimate redemption), in return for a moderate extension of time before the Government has an option to redeem the Loan. The Treasury saves £730,000 in annual interest, or about £600,000 after allowing for income tax; pays the Stock Exchange up to £500,000 in brokerage if they persuade their clients to make the exchange; and adds £6,000,000 to the capital of the national debt. They also surrender their option to redeem between 1929 and 1940; while the date when they are *bound* to redeem is brought nearer by three years. It is not clear how the transaction helps the Treasury, or why any investor should make the exchange. Probably the Treasury consider that it is worth making sure of even a slight reduction in the effective interest on part of the War Loan, as what remains is more than it would be easy to convert, should the rate of interest fall substantially between 1929 and 1940. Perhaps it is the first of a series of transactions.

We welcome the outspoken disapproval by the City Editor of *The Times* of the flotation in London of the City of Amsterdam sterling loan for £2½ millions. The interest is 5½ per cent, and the issue price 96½; so that the return is about £5 14s. per £100 subscribed. The credit of the City of Amsterdam stands high; and *The Times* does not criticise the loan from the standpoint of the individual investor, though it may perhaps be questioned whether, in view of the kaleidoscopic changes which history shows can take place in fifty years, the credit of any foreign municipality can be good enough to justify such a low rate for a loan which is not repayable till 1974. But how does the matter stand from the national standpoint? The object of the issue is to 'consolidate expenditure' already incurred in acquiring and preparing land for building purposes. It stands, therefore, as *The Times* points out, on a different footing from 'loans for sound, reproductive enterprises, the spending of which will directly and immediately assist British trade'. It is true that in the long run any foreign investment must be translated into exports; but this may take a very long time to happen; and the channel through which it happens, it is well to observe, is the depression of the British exchange. When, a few months ago, the prospect of a Labour Government terrified a foolish section of the British public into putting their money into foreign securities, the City rang with denunciations of such unpatriotic behaviour. But it makes not the slightest difference to the effects whether a man purchases an existing foreign security out of panic or subscribes with a feeling of virtue to a new issue like the City of Amsterdam loan.

Sir James Wilson has recently prepared an interesting table showing the gold value of various national currencies in March of each of the last three years:—

Gold value of paper currency as a percentage of the corresponding gold coin

Country	In March 1922	In March 1923	On 17 March 1924
United States	100	100	100
Sweden	97·5	99·3	98·4
Canada	97·0	98·0	96·8
Holland	94·3	98·2	92·0
Switzerland	100·9	96·3	89·6
Great Britain	90·0	96·5	88·0
Japan	95·5	97·2	86·0
Argentine	88·8	87·6	80·0
Spain	94·2	80·2	65·2
Denmark	78·7	71·6	57·6
Norway	65·7	67·8	50·4
France	46·7	32·7	25·6
Italy	26·6	25·2	22·1
Belgium	43·8	28·4	21·1
Austria	0·075	0·007	0·007

This table must be a signal disappointment to those who have taken the view that the world is steadily returning towards the restoration of its former gold parities. It will be seen that practically every country in the world is further away from its nominal gold parity this year than it was at the same date last year; and further that most of them are also further away than they were two years ago. Great Britain in particular has made no progress on balance towards a return to the old pre-war parity during the past two years.

A welcome feature of the Annual Report of the Prudential Assurance Company is the further decrease which they record in the expense ratio in their industrial branch. The expenses have fallen steadily from just over 40 per cent of the total premiums in 1920 to just under 30 per cent in 1923; and the Prudential have accordingly been able to issue a new prospectus offering higher benefits to the assured.

Keynes's comments in the Finance and Investment column on the City of Amsterdam issue brought criticism from *The Economist*. To this Keynes replied.

To the Editor of The Economist, *14 April 1924*

Sir,

May I ask a question about your article, 'Discrimination in Lending'? You seem to suggest that the consequences of the flotation in London of a loan like the recent Amsterdam loan are in some way different from the nervous movement of British investors into American securities alleged to have occurred last autumn. Do I misunderstand you? If not, what is the difference?

Did you welcome the so-called 'flight from the pound' last autumn on the ground that it would stimulate our export trade? If not, should you not have done so on the principles you now enunciate?

Personally, I think that there is a good deal of muddle in circulation about the supposed advantages of the prevalent type of foreign investment, and I believe that the City Editor of *The Times* was more nearly right than you allow.

Yours faithfully,
J. M. KEYNES

In the next issue of the *Nation*, Keynes provided more advice to investors.

From The Nation and Athenaeum, *12 April 1924*

ADVICE TO TRUSTEE INVESTORS

Every man must choose for himself the *class* of investment that he wants. And, having settled that matter, he will do well always to buy what appears the *best* of that class, even at the cost of some diminution of income. Advice comes in most usefully in helping him to judge which is the best in the class he has decided to favour. We will endeavour this week to give our readers some assistance of this kind in the field of gilt-edged investments.

There is, first of all, the choice between long-dated securities, where the investor is certain of the *same* money income for many years; short-dated securities, where the investor is certain of the return of his capital in full at an early date; and optionally redeemable securities, where the investor is liable to be paid off either soon or late at the option of the borrower. The following are typical long-dated securities. For the sake of clear summary the interest yields (which allow for accrued interest included in the price and for loss or profit on redemption) are given in groups, which are accurate for the individual securities within 1s. Detailed particulars of the railway securities were given in last week's *Nation and Athenaeum*:—

	Net interest yield £ s. d.		
Funding Loan ⎫ Conversion Loan ⎬ Local Loans ⎭	4	10	0
L.C.C. 2½%, 3%, and 3½% stocks	4	13	0
South Africa 4% (1943–63)	4	13	6
Nigeria 4% (1963)	4	15	6
Bank of England stock	4	17	0
G.W.R. ⎫ L. and N.E.R. ⎬ Debentures L.M. and S. ⎪ Southern Railway ⎭	4	16	0
Ditto Guaranteed stocks	4	18	0
Ditto First Preference stocks (non. cum.)	5	0	0
India 3% and 3½% stocks	5	7	0

We think that the investor in this class would do best to take the middle of the list and to leave both extremities alone. In the case of the railway preference stocks and the Government of India stocks, the investor is giving away too much in respect of absolute security for the sake of the extra yield. On the other hand, Bank stock and the railway debenture and guaranteed stocks are as good as any man can ask for security, and it scarcely seems worth while to sacrifice $\frac{1}{4}$ to $\frac{3}{8}$ per cent per annum in income for the sake of the extra gilt of British Government and London County Council stocks. The colonial stocks mentioned above appear to be preposterously over-valued. South Africa 4 per cent stands at nearly the same price as Funding Loan 4 per cent. Nigeria stock (which has no British Government guarantee) yields about the same as London and North-Eastern Railway debentures. It seems strange that there should be investors who prefer the former.

The typical short-dated securities are:—

	Net interest yield		
	£	s.	d.
5% National War Bonds due 1927	4	6	0
5% National War Bonds due 1928	4	8	0
5% National War Bonds due 1929	4	8	0
War Loan 3½% due 1928	4	10	0
Exchequer Bonds due 1930	4	11	0
Metropolitan 3½% due 1929	4	13	0
India 5½% due 1932	5	8	6
Queensland 5½% (1926–1929)	5	11	6

It may be presumed that the investor in this class *either* attaches importance to being able to realise his holding without material risk of capital depreciation within the next three or four years, *or* believes (as well he may) that the combined effects of trade revival, housing schemes and the like, high income tax, and diminished savings are likely to raise the rate of interest (and, which is the same thing, diminish the price of long-dated securities) in the near future, thus giving him better opportunities than exist now of exchanging into a permement investment. Such an investor had better avoid half measures, and plump for National War Bonds due 1927; for a small difference in interest yield is of far less importance in a short-dated than in a long-dated security, and should not divert him from his main purpose. Next after this, the 3½ per cent War Loan (1928) and the 3½ per cent

Metropolitan stock (1929) have substantial attractions. For those who are not afraid of possible developments in India, the $5\frac{1}{2}$ percent 1932 stock is much preferable to the long-dated Government of India securities.

The intermediate securities, where the borrowing authority has a considerable latitude as to the exact date of redemption, are as follows. The pair of dates, given in brackets after each security, indicate the period within which the borrower can exercise his option to redeem,—he can redeem at any time after the first date, but not later than the last date. The net interest yields are worked out on the hypothesis least favourable to the investor.

	Net interest yield		
	£	s.	d.
5% War Loan (1929–47)	4	16	0
5% South Africa (1933–43)	4	18	6
5% Australia (1935–45)	4	19	0
5% Victoria (1932–42)	5	0	0
5% Southern Rhodesia (1934–49)	5	0	0

In this class there can be little doubt as to which is to be preferred. Our own War Loan is surely better than any of the Colonial stocks. The additional income obtainable from the latter is negligible, and the additional period before the right to redeem comes into force is very short. It is remarkable that Southern Rhodesia—a place in the middle of Africa with a few thousand white inhabitants and less than a million black ones—can place an unguaranteed loan on terms not very different from those of our own War Loan. One of the surest pieces of advice which can be given to trustees at the present time is to avoid colonial stocks, the prices of which are far nearer to those of our own Government and other home gilt-edged securities than the permanent facts of the situation are likely to warrant.

The exchange from 5 per cent War Loan into the new $4\frac{1}{2}$ per cent stock (1940–1944), which has just been offered by the

Treasury, supplies a stock which is neither long nor short, giving a net interest yield (at present prices) of about £4 13s. We dealt with this offer in last week's *Nation and Athenaeum*. Compared with other stocks, it does not seem to offer to the investor any particular attractions, and we prefer the 5 per cent War Loan.

There remains one other British Government security, not yet mentioned, which is the best of all for those investors who have not already secured their quota,—namely, National Savings Certificates. A certificate (of the third issue, which is now current) costs 16s. At the end of the first year 3d. interest is added, and thereafter interest is added at the rate of 3d. for each complete period of four months up to the end of the tenth year, when a bonus of 1s. is given, making a total of 20s. after six years, and 24s. after ten years. The interest and bonus are free of income tax, and no mention of these certificates need be made in any income tax return. No individual may hold (in general) more than 500 certificates; but, since the certificates can be registered in the names of children, a family man can secure altogether a substantial holding. The rate of interest works out, if the bonds are held for the full ten years, at nearly £4 3s. per cent free of tax, equivalent to about £5 7s. per cent subject to deduction of tax.

On 14 April 1924 the Royal Economic Society held its annual meeting. After concluding its business meeting, the Society held a discussion on monetary reform with Sir Charles Addis, Edwin Cannan, R. G. Hawtrey and Keynes as speakers. Keynes's comments ran as follows.

From The Economic Journal, *June 1924*

Mr Hawtrey has defined for us very clearly the issues to be discussed. First of all there is the problem whether we want monetary reform at all or whether we want to get back to something as near as possible to the pre-war system. Secondly, there is the question what precise device we should adopt, if we want reform, in order to bring it into operation. I will begin with the first problem.

Mr Hawtrey has emphasised what is perhaps the main difference between the attitude of a good many economists now and their pre-war attitude, namely, their greater confidence as to the connection between monetary causes, the credit cycle, and unemployment. Mr Hawtrey himself has been a great pioneer in the exploration of that subject. I myself believe that there is no longer any reason to doubt the connection. Professor Cannan referred to an equation which I published recently in the form $n = pk$, where n is the volume of money, p the level of prices and k the quantity of goods for which it suits the public to have purchasing power in the form of money. The view used to be that k was not subject to rapid fluctuations. It would move up and down over long periods, but over short periods it did not change very much. Therefore if you kept the quantity of currency stable you probably kept prices reasonably stable. It was argued from this, that, as you would not have in any one year any very big change in the volume of money, therefore you could not have in any one year any big change in prices, so that though gold might move up or down slowly over a long period of years, a fair measure of stability would be secured over short periods. It is true that this was not in fact borne out, because booms and depressions occurred in pre-war days just as much as since; but the tendency was to explain these by particular causes. Many economists now take a different view from that. They think that k, and accordingly the quantity of real purchasing power required, is itself capable of sharp fluctuations, and in fact that it is the leading characteristic of booms and depressions that there should be a variation in the magnitude of k, so that it is this variation which makes those price fluctuations that occur even when there is no marked change in the total volume of money. That being so, attention is naturally transferred to a certain extent from the mere volume of money to this other element. We no longer believe that prices can be kept as steady as they might be simply by securing a constant volume of money, and we hold, rather, that we can only keep prices steady by varying the quantity of money to balance changes in k. If the public, for some one or another cause, decide on the average to keep more purchasing power than before, prices must fall to counterbalance this, and the tendency of prices to fall may produce a situation likely to provoke unemployment. That theory in a clear form is essentially new; and if it is correct it opens up enormous opportunities for far-reaching social reforms.

If we really have the power to control in some measure credit cycles which cause unemployment and other social disturbances experienced in the past, surely it is our duty to follow up this line of thought to the utmost, to make experiments and to see whether by a control of the monetary machine we cannot cure one of the greatest and most dangerous social evils of the economic system. We feel that those who oppose monetary reform ought to make it clear how far they agree with us on that diagnosis. If we have even a half-chance of getting rid by monetary reform of the evils of the credit cycle, I should have thought most people would have agreed that it was worth while, and that it is no good for Professor Cannan to talk about a barbarous age if his object in speaking thus is to keep it barbarous. We certainly live in a barbarous age, but our object should be to emerge from it, and if there is a new weapon forged for that purpose we have no right to overlook it. It is not so much a change in the whole theory of our view of the credit cycle, as the increased clearness with which we now see the various steps, that is the reason why the minds of some of us have changed since pre-war days.

But there is another reason also for change which has arisen out of events connected with the War. Can we rely on gold to give in future even that amount of stability that it has given in the past? Formerly there was a great deal of gold in circulation in people's pockets. Many countries were rich enough and sufficiently inclined to hoard resources to keep a considerable amount in gold in banks and elsewhere. Any given country might suffer sudden changes in that respect, but it was not likely that in a short period of time there would be a simultaneous change of any magnitude in a number of different countries. As a result of the War, however, there is now extremely little gold in circulation in the world; in most countries none whatever. It is unlikely that gold will return into circulation both because of the expense and because of the change of habits. It is also much more difficult than it used to be for some countries to hold large amounts of gold in banks or to increase their holdings. A great stimulus has been given to all those methods of economising the use of gold, which have been gradually developing as a result of the growth of the credit system. We may even tend now to be up against the ultimate truth that a perfectly conducted gold standard does not require any gold at all, or practically none. Suppose those who manage the credit policies of banks were to acquire sufficient skill in the management of international adjustments, no actual gold would be required at all; and while we are still very far from that position, we are probably already in the position in which the necessary quantity of gold for the maintenance of the existing price level is far [and] away less than the volume of gold in the world, and the difference between the two is getting larger every day. This redundance of gold pressing upon the world is a phenomenon which someone has to look after, and the problem of preventing that redundance from causing sudden changes in its value is much more acute than it was.

Those of us who are in favour of monetary reform support it, therefore, for two main reasons: first, because we believe that we ought to do all we can in any reasonable way in the direction of the social aims already referred to; secondly, for fear that gold left to itself may prove a much less safe standard of value than in former times. I do not believe that there is sufficient weight on the other side to outweigh those two considerations. There are, of course, two sides to every argument, and it is generally a question of weighing advantages. It is not that there are no advantages on the other side, but rather that a return to our pre-war system does not offer sufficient advantage to outweigh the factors I have emphasised.

We come next to a further most interesting question. Assuming that we want to reform our currency, what is the right way to do it? There is a certain difference of opinion between Mr Hawtrey and myself, though I should be perfectly ready to accept his system it it turned out to be practicable. Mr Hawtrey wants to placate a good deal of feeling that exists in the world by pretending that he keeps [a] gold standard, whereas in fact he establishes a commodity standard. He proposes to erect a façade of gold and then to regulate its value on the same principles as would be adopted by those who aim at the stabilisation of general prices. In monetary affairs there is a great deal to be said in favour of placating prejudice. I do not underate any of those advantages. And Mr Hawtrey may be right, that this is the best way to do it. But I should like to point out two important disadvantages in his plan. First of all, there is the question who is going to bear the expense of maintaining the value of gold. On his system there would still be mined, I suppose, about as much gold as is mined now. There is also the problem of existing stocks. At present the United States is bearing the expense of that, both in maintaining stocks and in absorbing new supplies. Mr Hawtrey's system would mean a very difficult debate on the question how expenses should be shared in the future, and presumably we in this country would have to bear some reasonable proportion of them. We should have to consider, therefore, how many millions a year it was worth wasting in order to maintain this façade. We should also be embarking on a system which would become more and more artificial and indefensible as time went on, and would, therefore, be inevitably unstable in the long run. It would be too absurd to go on indefinitely mining gold out of the earth with great labour, in order that certain countries should bury it again after having met the expenses of mining. Sooner or later the world would see that no sufficient advantages accrued from it, and everyone would seek to escape from the burden of spending a certain number of millions a year in maintaining the value of gold.

It is, perhaps, a more fundamental objection against this proposal that it involves very far-reaching agreements between a number of central banks. Mr Hawtrey and I have both had a certain experience of international conferences, but they seem to have left him more optimistic than they have left me. My feeling is that for some years to come we shall never secure a binding agreement of that kind. Putting all other countries on one side, I think it would not be easy even for the Bank of England and the Federal Reserve Board of the United States to arrive at any binding agreement. It would be very difficult to decide how, when there was a difference of opinion, the matter was to be settled. Moreover, I believe that any such agreement would weaken the hands of the Federal Reserve Board in the United States. There is difficulty enough in any case in pursuing a sound policy, and if the Board was open to the suggestion that they were not acting solely in American interests but at the dictation of the Bank of England, they would be in a much weaker position than they are in now, when no one can possibly accuse them of being governed by any other motive than American interests. I should prefer, therefore, that we should enter into no binding agreement as to the relation between the British standard of value and the American standard of value, but rather than each country separately should aim at stability, and in addition co-operate by the exchange of information and in all other possible ways. If this co-operation were to be successful, then we should also have a policy of a stable dollar exchange, and we and the United States between us could probably manage the rest of the world. It would require no international conference or binding agreement of any kind, and we could gradually improve our methods as experience showed us the way. The only disadvantage it could have might be, that, since we should not accept gold into our mints here unless we wanted it, America herself would probably get tired of the burden of absorbing the world's gold, and that she too would close her mints to gold, with the result that the value of gold itself would fall. Nevertheless it would be better, I think, to face the opposition of the gold-mining interests rather than to embark upon the very costly and difficult path of trying to stabilise the value of gold itself by means of a binding agreement between ourselves and the United States.

In conclusion, let me turn to the matter of immediate policy which Mr Hawtrey also dealt with. What ought we to do at once? I suggest, as he also suggested, there is room at the moment for a considerable measure of agreement even if we differ for the future. I am afraid there is no room for agreement between us and Sir Charles Addis, if Sir Charles insists on immediate deflation. On that matter the Government, I think, are in a contradictory position, both this and the previous Governments, when they state that their object is to get back to a gold standard as soon as possible, yet also at times admit in public, as Mr Baldwin did, that the policy of deflation has been definitely reversed. The Government think it wise to placate Sir Charles Addis by stating that their intention is to return to the gold standard. But fortunately they are not so foolish as to take any active steps in that direction. They have, in fact, no clear policy, but so far as they have one at all they seem to aim at some measure of stability for the present and, as Mr Hawtrey suggested, have postponed making up their minds any further, until they see what happens to exchange [rates], hoping that the natural course of events will bring sterling to its parity with gold without any degree of deflation. I agree that this expectation may very well be realised, that a further fall of prices in America is not very likely, being indeed wholly unnecessary from any point of view, and that sooner or later the Federal Reserve Board is likely to be overwhelmed by the incoming tides of gold, with the result that a sufficient depreciation of the dollar will take place to bring our own exchange to par—though that this may require a depreciation in the value of the dollar amounting to more than 10 per cent is also likely, since prices here, in the event of this policy being adopted, would follow dollar prices to a certain extent. Thus it is certainly quite possible that we shall return to our former parity of exchange without resorting to deflation. I should like to point out, however, that the policy of waiting for that to happen and thereafter depending on the Federal Reserve Board to prevent any further depreciation of the dollar seems to assume that the Federal Reserve Board is going to be overwhelmed to precisely that degree which it pleases us should occur, and that when that has happened they are not going to be overwhelmed a scrap further, but are going to retain their price level at just that figure which happens to suit us at the present time. A nice balance is assumed between skill and want of skill on the part of the Federal Reserve Board. This policy requires that the Federal Reserve Board should lose control of their own situation and should then begin again to exercise skill just at the time that *our* policy requires that they should. I am not confident that this is a coincidence we can rely upon.

At any rate, let us suppose that this is the position, that the Government is disinclined to take any further steps towards deflation, and also that the underlying facts of the situation may quite likely bring sterling back to par. What is our right course? Well, we have a golden opportunity for making on an adequate scale precisely the experiment that I want. Why should we not aim for the present at keeping our own price level steady and, in order to please other parties, postpone any final decision until our exchange has reached parity. The arguments of all the speakers seem to me really to imply that at one stage or another the price level *is* under our control. No one wants to diminish the value of our money. If, then, we do not want to increase the value of our money, which would mean deflation, why should we not spend the next few years in keeping prices steady, and seeing if we can do it, meanwhile learning, perhaps, how to do it without exciting prejudice? If after having done this successfully for a few years we reached our old parity, I myself would have a great deal of confidence that the success of the method would justify its continuance, that after having kept prices steady without the use of gold for some appreciable time, we should be rather loth to abandon it and to follow a tide of involuntary inflation by linking ourselves once more to gold, which by hypothesis would have just been depreciating substantially. I believe that currency reformers will experience much less prejudice and hostility when it is a question of letting sterling go above its old gold value rather than of keeping sterling below it. I believe many people in the City of London have much more feeling about the return to parity than they have about sticking there, when it is once attained and not going above it. For instance, Sweden, it has been reported, in the last week or two has decided upon a new policy of convertibility by which the krone will not be allowed to fall below the old gold parity, but with no provision, however, to prevent its rising above it. This is a return to the gold standard in its most harmless form. To undertake that the value of the currency shall not fall below its old parity, whilst allowing the value of the currency to rise above it, is quite possibly the most practicable solution. It would be sound policy in the United States at this moment to maintain convertibility, but at the same time to close the mints to further foreign gold. A plan of maintaining convertibility into gold at a fixed ratio, but of not accepting further gold into the mints when gold is redundant and depreciating, may prove the right compromise between old and new wisdom. If we return to the old gold parity, I would prefer that compromise to the plan which Mr Hawtrey suggests. I do not suggest that his would not be an improvement, if it came into operation, on what we have had in the past. But the practical difficulties operating against it are far greater than those operating against the alternatives which I myself prefer.

MONETARY REFORM AND UNEMPLOYMENT

Keynes also continued to make anonymous contributions to 'Finance and Investment'.

From The Nation and Athenaeum, *3 May 1924*

THE BUDGET—THE DISTRIBUTION OF THE NATIONAL DEBT

'I am not appalled by the total figures,' said Mr Philip Snowden in 1910, discussing a budget which threatened to approach what was then widely regarded as the appalling figure of £200 millions. 'I hope to live to see the time when the Chancellor of the Exchequer will stand at that box and propose a budget of 300 or 400 millions.' Fate, as the fable tells us, takes a grim pleasure in fulfilling our wishes in an unexpected way. Mr Snowden has lived to 'stand at that box' himself, and propose a budget which for the first time in the last ten years falls just short of 800 millions. He comes not to increase but to remit taxation—to remit, indeed, a sum which would have sufficed to abolish the income tax three times over in Mr Gladstone's day. The audacious critic of orthodox financial traditions, who saw no advantage in reducing debt, now devotes long passages to emphasising its 'vital and first-class importance'. The chief bogey-man of the City has succeeded in delighting it more than any other Chancellor in recent years. In this there is some change in Mr Snowden himself; there is still more in the financial situation.

The chief doubt raised by the Budget is whether Mr Snowden is justified, from the standpoint of sound finance, in remitting so much taxation. He estimates his surplus, on the basis of existing taxes, at £38 millions, while he puts the revenue he will lose from the tax reductions at £34 millions, and at £48 millions when they have produced their full effect. Thus in the present year he keeps only £4 millions in hand to meet the further expenditure which Parliament is almost certain to sanction. The removal of the Old Age Pensions thrift disqualification, which the Government have undertaken to deal with, would alone (in a full year) swallow up this sum several times

215

over. Mr Snowden, indeed, does not profess to hope that his £4 millions will be enough; he relies on further administrative savings to avert a deficit in the present year. But all the administrative economies which it is reasonable to expect will be required in subsequent years to meet the additional £14 millions loss from the tax reductions. On the other hand, it is of the essence of housing schemes, of a reversal of educational engines, and the like that they entail an expenditure which is modest at first but grows rapidly. Thus Mr Snowden is confronting himself or his successor next year with the strong probability of a heavy deficit. This probability is not likely to be confuted this time by an unexpected buoyancy in the revenue returns; for Mr Snowden has made a sanguine (though we do not think too sanguine) allowance for this factor in the estimates.

The Economist published recently a very interesting calculation of the distribution of the National Debt among the various categories of holders. The calculation may be roughly summarised as follows:—

	£ millions
External debt to U.S. and other Governments	1,100
Held by banks (including Bank of England and savings banks)	1,140
Held by insurance companies	350
Held by railway companies	80
Treasury bills held by bill-brokers and others not included above	300
Held by other companies, colleges, hospitals, trade unions, trusts &c.,and by persons abroad	1,550
Held by savings bank depositors	240
Held by other private persons	2,350
Held by the Government itself (Treasury note reserve. &c.)	310

Some of these estimates relate to market values, and would need to be increased to represent the nominal value of the debt so held. Perhaps the most striking feature of the calculation is the comparatively small proportion of the debt held by private persons. This suggests strongly that the idea that a capital levy designed to raise £3,000 millions, and confined, of course, to private individuals, could be paid mainly by handing over Government securities, is a delusion.

The preference shares of the Allied Newspapers Ltd, upon the terms of offer of which we have already commented, now stand at a discount of about 1s. per £1 share. It is stated that there were over 30,000 applications, which were met in full up to seventy-five shares, so that nearly half the issue was spread in this way over a vast number of small holders. Since the Daily Mail Trust shareholders received 80 per cent of their application and most other applicants 60 per cent, it is clear that the *average* amount of the subscriptions was not much more than £200. It is the small and ignorant investor who has been reached by giant advertisement.

The German Government have lately prepared some striking figures of the reduction of domestic consumption in 1922–23 as compared with 1913:—

	Date	Amounts (kg per head)	Date	Amounts (kg per head)	Decrease per cent
Wheat and spelt	1913–14	95·8	1922–23	47·6	50·3
Rye	1913–14	153·1	1922–23	91·9	40·0
Potatoes	1913–14	700·2	1922–23	573·2	18·1
Meat	1913	40·26	1922	24·98	38·0
Coffee	1913	2·44	1922–23	0·59	75·8
Rice	1913	7·23	1922–23	4·25	41·2
Cotton	1913	2·49	1922–23	1·64	34·1

The enormous percentage reduction of the consumption of staple articles of food per head is a striking and irrefutable testimony to the reduction in the standard of life of the great bulk of the population. Few countries have exhibited such contrasting extremes as Germany at the present day. The effect of the inflation of the currency has been to transfer millions of pounds' worth of wealth from the many to the few, with the result that whilst the country as a whole and the vast majority of individuals have been frightfully impoverished, there is at the same time a large class of those who have been newly enriched on a prodigious scale and are in a position to live in as much luxury as the wealthy classes of any part of Europe.

The new edition of the *Stock Exchange Official Intelligence* has been reduced in price from £4 to £3, although, as usual, the size has been somewhat increased, and now runs to about 2,000 pages quarto. At this price it is a very good investment for anyone who takes an active interest in his Stock Exchange securities. The special chapters for the year deal with municipal, Indian, and colonial finance, with company law in 1923 and with the Railways Act, 1921. But the real value of the volume lies, of course, in its exhaustive précis of every single Stock Exchange security, all the essential facts about the board, accounts, dividends, capital, recent prices, &c., being given in the most convenient possible form. Many more private investors ought to have this volume than has been the case hitherto, and the reduction in price shows that the Committee of the Stock Exchange, under whose authority the volume is issued, want to encourage such purchases.

On 12 April, in the columns of *The Nation*, Lloyd George stated that he viewed Britain's immediate economic future with grave misgivings and suggested that the most urgent task facing her industrial and political leaders was improving production. During the weeks that followed discussion continued in the columns of the *Nation*, with contributors such as Sir William Beveridge, A. L. Bowley, Norman Angell, Walter Layton and Lord Wier, before Keynes added his views.

MONETARY REFORM AND UNEMPLOYMENT

From The Nation and Athenaeum, *24 May 1924*

DOES EMPLOYMENT NEED A DRASTIC REMEDY?

The discussion on this subject in the columns of *The Nation* has not lacked a few optimists. Nevertheless most of those who have taken part share in some degree the misgivings which Mr Lloyd George voiced in opening the debate. If a country, with no new advantages of raw materials or competitive power, with a larger population, produces less and lives better, it seems probable that its poise may be unstable, and that something more drastic is needed than merely hoping for the best. But what? It is in the lameness of the answers to this question—we must all admit—that *The Nation* discussion has proved weak.

What is the magnitude of the problem? The number of unemployed adult males is now about 770,000, after having been 1,200,000 at the beginning of 1923, and 1,450,000 at the beginning of 1922. If the figures be analysed we find a great concentration of unemployment in the shipbuilding and engineering industries (i.e., nearly four times the percentage elsewhere). Outside these industries, unemployment amongst adult males does not now much exceed 4 per cent of the employable population. The following is a rash guess at the composition of the total:—

1. Normal unemployed (i.e., brief intervals of unemployment between jobs, &c.)	200,000
2. Unemployables from age, disablement, temperament, &c.	100,000
3. Excess of labour supply in engineering and associated industries	150,000
4. Excess of labour supply in other industries	320,000
	770,000

It seems very optimistic to assume, with Mr Layton, that the figures in the third and fourth groups will cure themselves if we merely sit by smiling and avoid gross errors of policy. No one has a firmer belief than I in the relation between unemployment and monetary policy, and when, two years ago, the figures were nearly double what they are now, this disastrous situation was, I am sure, largely attributable to the slump provoked by a misguided inflation and prolonged by a misguided deflation. But the evil effects of these policies have been working themselves out. Perhaps this cause is not yet eliminated entirely,—but a monetary policy which aimed at reducing the unemployed by more than (say) a further 100,000, would run dangerously near another inflation. On the other hand, the settlement of Europe, if it takes place, and the resuscitation of German export trade will not be an unmixed blessing to our own export industries. To what favourable influences, then, do the optimists look? I do not know.

I agree, therefore, with Mr Lloyd George, Mr Baldwin, and Mr Sidney Webb, that there is no place or time here for *laissez-faire*. Furthermore, we must look for succour to the principle that *prosperity is cumulative*. We have stuck in a rut. We need an impulse, a jolt, an acceleration.

Unluckily this good principle has often got into bad hands. It is the grain of truth behind the false promises and hopes of protectionists and inflationists alike. They see the initial impact of their policies on the lumbering car of state, and assess justly the social value of an impulse, yet slip backwards through overlooking remoter adjustments and indirect results.

But this is not a good reason for doing nothing. There may be stimulating medicines which are wholesome. There are many examples of cumulative prosperity, both in recent and in earlier experience. British prosperity in the nineteenth century owed very much to the railway boom in its first half, beginning at home and extending abroad, and to the immense building activity of its latter half. In the past five years the rebuilding of the devastated areas has, independently of its inflationary features, given a stimulus to French enterprise which has much enriched the nation. The boom in motors and in building, combined, no doubt, with many favourable attendant circumstances, has carried the United States to an unprecedented standard of high living. Is there no tonic draught for us to give us courage and confidence to be active?

Business is weighed down by timidity. It lacks conviction that anything good will continue for long. It watches anxiously for the signs of retrogression; and, as soon as the army wavers, individuals bolt. No one is ready to plant seeds which only a long summer can bring to fruit.

Yet some of the causes of our unemployment are of such a kind that this halting, wavering mood is fatal. Part of it is due to the immobility of labour as between industries; part to the fault of trade unions; and part to a disparity of wages between what are called the sheltered and the unsheltered industries. But we cannot cure these ills by forcing labour into new directions by the pressure of starvation, or by breaking the power for evil, and perhaps for good also, of the trade unions, or by reducing wages in the sheltered industries to the level of the unsheltered. From these thoughts the mind must be averted, for from such directions help will not come. Rather we must seek to submerge the rocks in a rising sea,—not forcing labour out of what is depressed, but attracting it into what is prosperous; not crushing the blind strength of organised labour, but relieving its fears; not abating wages where they are high, but raising them where they are low. And there is no way in the world of achieving these better alternatives but by confidence and courage in those who set enterprise in motion.

Is there not a chance that we can best achieve this by recreating the mood and the conditions in which great works of construction, requiring large capital outlays, can again be set on foot? Current savings are already available on a sufficient scale—savings which from lack of an outlet at home, are now drifting abroad to destinations from which we as a society shall gain the least possible advantage. Private enterprise unaided

221

cannot stop this flow. The policy of preventing public utilities from yielding more than a modest private profit has gone so far that it is no longer worth the while of private enterprise to run a risk in a field where the gain is limited and the loss unlimited. We are in danger, therefore, of interfering with private initiative, yet substituting nothing for it. The advances under the Trade Facilities Act, begun for a temporary emergency and on a small scale, point the way, perhaps, to a new method of administering an important part of the savings of the public. The next developments of politico-economic evolution may be found in co-operation between private initiative and the public exchequer. The true socialism of the future will emerge, I think, from an endless variety of experiments directed towards discovering the respective appropriate spheres of the individual and of the social, and the terms of fruitful alliance between these sister instincts.

In the light of such reflections, we can indicate the next steps. The Chancellor of the Exchequer should devote his sinking fund and his surplus resources, not to redeeming old debt with the result of driving the national savings to find a foreign outlet, but to replacing unproductive debt by productive debt. The Treasury should not shrink from promoting expenditure up to (say) £100,000,000 a year on the construction of capital works at home, enlisting in various ways the aid of private genius, temperament, and skill.

It is for the technicians of building, engineering, and transport to tell us in what directions the most fruitful new improvements are awaiting us. But three fields of construction are already known to everyone in a general way. It should not be beyond the technical accomplishments of our engineers to devise a national scheme for the mass production of houses which would supplement the normal activities of the building industry and make up in five or ten years the deficiency with which the latter has proved unable to deal. The adaptation of road-building to the needs of motor transport must plainly be undertaken some day, whether in detail Sir W. Acworth or Lord Montagu is in the right. The development of economical means for the transmission of electrical power is in its infancy in this country. Unaided private enterprise is not capable of dealing with any of these projects, even when their technical soundness is beyond doubt.

I look, then, for the ultimate cure of unemployment, and for the stimulus which shall initiate a cumulative prosperity, to monetary reform—which will remove fear—and to the diversion of national savings from relatively barren foreign investment into state-encouraged constructive enterprises at home—which will inspire confidence. That part of our recent unemployment, which is not attributable to an ill-controlled credit cycle, has been largely due to the slump in our constructional industries. By conducting the national wealth into capital developments at home, we may restore the balance of our economy. Let us experiment with boldness on such lines,—even though some of the schemes may turn out to be failures, which is very likely.

Keynes's article brought a comment from the City Editor of *The Times* on 26 May which doubted whether there would be anything to gain by adopting Keynes's suggestions which, he suggested, relied on raiding the sinking fund and other surplus resources of the Treasury.

To the Editor of The Times, *28 May 1924*

Sir,

I thank you for your comments on my article in last Saturday's *Nation*, with much of which I agree, but must ask leave to correct a misunderstanding about my attitude towards the sinking fund. The sinking fund consists in raising by taxation a substantial surplus over current expenditure and applying this surplus to the reduction of the War debt. I agree with yourself in strongly supporting this policy. It would be disastrous to abandon it. I regret that the wording of my article should have left this open to doubt. My concern was with a different matter—namely, with the investment of the liquid capital accruing from this policy. Perhaps I can make my point clear in five sentences:—

1. The application of £50,000,000 to £100,000,000 a year to the redemption of War debt throws this amount of funds on the market seeking investment in a similar type of security.

2. Private enterprise at home is not providing an outlet for these amounts *plus* new savings on anywhere near adequate scale.

3. Consequently they find an outlet in foreign and colonial government loans, most of which do little directly to stimulate British industry and can only operate by depreciating our exchanges: I cannot agree with you that 'we have very few loans of this type'.

4. Rent Restriction Acts, the control of profits and charges of public utility undertakings, and the fear of further developments in the same direction have deprived private enterprise of sufficient incentive to embark on new schemes of construction involving great expenditures. If steam locomotion were to be discovered today I much doubt if unaided private enterprise would build railways in England.

5. The Trade Facilities Act, as administered hitherto, having been a comparative failure, we must make new experiments to stimulate capital investment at home.

I am strongly opposed to encouraging non-economic projects, by subsidies or otherwise. But, for good or for evil, in present-day conditions *laissez-faire* can no longer be relied on to furnish economic projects with the capital they need. We are drifting into financing port improvements, housing, electrical developments, &c., abroad at low rates of interest, while forgetting similar projects at home. Yet it is not true that there is nothing at home which wants doing.

The only reasonable object of a sinking fund is to reduce the dead-weight debt. This can be achieved just as effectively by converting it into productive capital at home as by paying it off and offering no alternative investment.

Yours, &c.,

J. M. KEYNES

On 7 June, Keynes returned to the columns of *The Nation* to answer other critics.

From The Nation and Athenaeum, *7 June 1924*

A DRASTIC REMEDY FOR UNEMPLOYMENT:
REPLY TO CRITICS

The main purpose of my article in *The Nation* of May 24th was to ask whether it might not be in the national interest that the State should intervene to direct a larger part of our savings into capital enterprises at home. In the course of it I rashly mentioned the sinking fund, and thereby pressed with careless finger one of those irrelevant buttons which stud the public brain, and released the reaction—'We should regard it as a retrograde step if the Chancellor were to raid the sinking funds.' Half the comment which the article evoked has been directed against my supposed impiety in this matter. I apologise for misleading many readers, and will try again to make my argument clear.

The maintenance of a sinking fund means raising a surplus on revenue account and devoting this surplus to the reduction of the dead-weight debt. With a heavy public debt and reduced private savings, I agree unreservedly that a substantial sinking fund is a cardinal point of policy. My heresy consists in proposing not to abolish (or raid) the sinking fund, but to use it. The sinking fund releases liquid resources for capital purposes,—that is its whole object. Do my critics want to apply these resources to consumptive expenditure? No! Then they want to apply them to productive, capital expenditure? Yes!

225

Then let them join with me to discuss how we can do this to the greatest social advantage.

The problem on a big scale is new. Before the War the proceeds of the sinking fund were a trifling proportion of the national savings. Recently, ranging from £40,000,000 to £100,000,000 a year, they have dominated the investment market. We have extracted these sums from the taxpayers, and using them to pay off debt, we have thrown an equal amount on the capital market seeking an outlet of a similar kind. It is dangerous to do this on so great a scale without giving a thought to the supply of alternative investments.

At first Local Loans, home municipals, and industrial debentures partly filled the bill. But with the advent of deflation, the Geddes Axe, and industrial depression, the supply has dried up.* The lack of supply of home investments involving new capital expenditure has now been acute for at least two years. During the past six months it has almost reached vanishing point. I estimate that, omitting issues which are merely conversions, or re-sales of existing enterprises, the total investments offered to the public to provide for new capital expenditure at home during the whole of the last half-year (which covers the busiest season) is in the neighbourhood of no more than £10,000,000. This includes issues under the Trade Facilities Act. Taken together with the acute depression in the engineering and metallurgical industries, such facts deserve consideration as a contributory cause of unemployment.

Meanwhile, the long rate of interest has fallen by about 1 per cent—to the delight of the Treasury (who, let me add in parenthesis, are in danger of desiring to keep the country depressed until 1929 in order to have the rate of interest low for their conversions). The rate of interest on foreign bonds is established ¾ to 1 per cent below the rate in New York for similar bonds. London has become—to the pride of many—the

* In 1921–22 Local Loans advances amounted to £50,500,000; in 1923–24 to £6,500,000. (See interesting figures relating to this and connected matters in *The Times*, June 2nd.)

principal, indeed almost the exclusive, international loan market, ready to lend to approved borrowers much cheaper than anyone else will lend. No other country in the world pursues this policy. So far from the United States exporting capital, the official figures for 1923 show that in that year, as the net result of all items on capital account, they actually imported capital.

In my opinion there are many reasons for thinking that our present rate of foreign investment is excessive and undesirable. We are lending too cheaply resources we can ill spare. Our traditional, conventional attitude towards foreign investment demands reconsideration;—it is high time to give it a bad name and call it 'the flight of capital'. But I must limit myself here to the single aspect which is relevant to the special problem of unemployment.

Some foreign investments lead directly to the placing of orders in this country which would not be so placed otherwise. Whether or not they are desirable on general grounds, such investments do no harm to employment. As a rule, however, this is not the case. A foreign loan does not, any more than a demand for reparations, automatically create a corresponding flow of exports. Let us take a particular example. Last week New South Wales borrowed in the London market £5,500,000 new money 'for railways, tramways, harbours, rivers and bridges, water supply, irrigation, sewerage, and other purposes'. A part of this may pay for orders placed here arising out of these undertakings. Probably the greater portion will not be used thus, but in paying labour on the spot, and importing supplies from elsewhere; that is to say, the resources will be transferred to Australia in roundabout ways. Sooner or later, the matter must be adjusted by increased British exports or diminished British imports. But this can only come about through the medium of a depreciation of the sterling exchange. Our exchanges have to depreciate so as to stimulate our export industries at the expense of our 'sheltered' non-export industries, and so redress the balance between the two. If the world demand for our exports at the present price level is inelastic, a considerable depreciation may be necessary to do the trick. Moreover, there may be violent resistances to the process of adjustment. The fall of the exchange tends to raise the 'cost of living', and the 'sheltered' industries may struggle to avoid the reduction of real wages which this entails. Our economic structure is far from elastic, and much time may elapse and indirect loss result from the strains set up and the breakages incurred. Meanwhile, resources may lie idle and labour be out of employment.

The old principle of *laissez-faire* was to ignore these strains and to assume that capital and labour were fluid; it also assumed that, if investors choose to send their money abroad at 5 per cent, this must mean that there is nothing at home worth doing at 5 per cent. Fifty years ago this may have been a closer approximation to the truth than it is now. With the existing rigidity of the trade-union organisation of labour, with the undue preference which the City organisation of new issues and the Trustee Acts afford to overseas investment, and with the caution which for many reasons, some good and some bad, now oppresses the undertaking of new capital investment at home, it does not work.

Can I now carry my critics with me this far,—that, if in the last six months, instead of £10,000,000 capital issues for new home developments and £50,000,000 for new developments abroad, the figures had been the other way round, this would have been a change for the better, and favourable to employment? Surely they cannot maintain that England is a finished job, and that there is nothing in it worth doing on a 5 per cent basis. Then let them agree with me in wishing, if we could manage it, to stimulate investment at home.

In considering how to do this, we are brought to my heresy—if it is a heresy. I bring in the State; I abandon *laissez-faire*,—not enthusiastically, not from contempt of that good old doctrine, but because, whether we like it or not, the conditions for its success have disappeared. It was a double doctrine,—it entrusted the public weal to private enterprise *unchecked* and *unaided*. Private enterprise is no longer unchecked,—it is checked and threatened in many different ways. There is no going back on this. The forces which press us may be blind, but they exist and are strong. And if private enterprise is not unchecked, we cannot leave it unaided.

For these reasons I claim to be nearer than Mr Brand to the realities and possibilities of the modern world in repeating that the next developments of politico-economic evolution will emerge from new experiments directed towards determining the appropriate spheres of individual and of governmental action. And proceeding to particulars, I suggest that the state encouragement of new capital undertakings, by employing the best technical advice to lay the foundations of great schemes, and by lending the credit and the guarantee of the Treasury to finance them more boldly than hitherto, is becoming an inevitable policy. There is no sphere where private initiative is so lacking—for quite intelligible reasons—as in the conception and execution of very costly projects which may be expected to yield from 5 to 6 per cent. The Trade Facilities Act continues to depend on private initiative, and only such projects are helped by it as private enterprise is already inclined to plan and to back. Mr Brand, the City Editor of *The Times*, and many others point to the unused balance of credit under this Act as convincing proof that there is nothing more to be done. I do not agree, because big new projects of a public character are not the kind of thing for which the Act is devised. Let us set against this the very recent report of the Chamber of Shipping Committee, which points out, the urgent need of expensive developments in many of our great ports, as one proof amongst many that the equipment of this country is not complete and up-to-date in all respects. Indeed, it is a bold and hazardous saying of my critics that our savings must drift abroad at 5 per cent because there is simply nothing worth doing in England at that price.

The Editor of *The Manchester Guardian Commercial* (May

29th) has written:—'Mr Keynes surely implies that there are opportunities for remunerative investment which the investing public have not the foresight to grasp, and which they will never grasp without the intervention of the Government. It is an argument which the Manchester Ship Canal, to take only one instance, effectively answers.' Certainly, this is what I imply, though perhaps I should substitute 'opportunity' for 'foresight'. Let me ask him to consider—for he is a very reasonable man—exactly whom he has in mind when he speaks of the 'foresight of the investing public'. Does he mean the average investor in trustee securities? Does he mean the great issue houses? (What pays them is to take a safe underwriting commission from a colonial government.) Is it worth the while, or within the power, of anyone to organise a new project costing £20,000,000 with the expectation of a return of 5 per cent? These persons 'exercising foresight' about new, costly, moderately remunerative projects do not exist. If there was no Manchester Ship Canal, does he suppose that a syndicate of private persons woud spring up today to construct it?

Mr Kiddy complains in *The Spectator* (May 31st) that 'the most extraordinary remedies' of my *Nation* article 'add to the complexities and dangers of the situation'. I am sorry. I respect Mr Kiddy's staunch principles. But vainly are his eyes cast backwards. Vainly does he treasure his copy-book maxims. (Condemn one, and he boils against you. Repeat one, and you are restored to his esteem.) The following extracts from his article afford a short but sufficient summary:—'The City views with profound concern...The City fails to comprehend...It is one thing to be entirely sympathetic with the deserving unemployed...Nor must there be lack of courage in expressing home truths to labour...It is felt in the City that there is all the more need for facing stern economic facts.' How remote one knows oneself to be from any kind of reality when one hears those dreary words,—milestones towards empty space!

A drastic reduction of wages in certain industries, and a

successful stand-up fight with the more powerful trade unions might reduce unemployment in the long run. If any party stands for this solution, let them say so. I believe that such a policy is not practical. Assuming, then, that the problem will not solve itself (which some maintain—I not amongst them), what more promising programme based on clear first principles, has anyone to suggest, than monetary reform coupled with an intensive encouragement of capital investment at home?

Keynes's reply to his critics naturally raised more comment, both in *The Nation* and elsewhere, and led to two more letters from Keynes, one to *The Nation* and one to *The Manchester Guardian*.

To the Editor of The Nation and Athenaeum, *21 June 1924*

Sir,

In reply to Mr Brand's letter in yesterday's *Nation*, I *do* agree with him 'that great difficulties face the application of Government aid to ordinary private *competitive* industry'. I have had in mind, in my contributions, to your columns, the development of what, in a broad sense, can be described as 'public utility' undertakings—though I should, for example, include in this description the mass-production of working-class houses. I join with Mr Brand in deprecating a policy of Government help to 'one shipbuilder against another or one steel manufacturer against another'. But this is just what the existing Trade Facilities Act does in certain cases. Perhaps you will allow me to take this opportunity of re-stating my reasons why the comparative failure of this Act is no argument at all against the policy which I have been advocating.

The Trade Facilities Act does not relieve those assisted of any portion of the risk of the enterprise—the Government guarantee stands behind, not in front of, the personal guarantee of the borrower. Thus the assistance given is limited to helping the borrower to borrow more cheaply than he would otherwise—say, at 5 per cent, instead of at 6 or 6½ per cent. This is all there is in it. It is a modest subsidy. It is not a risk-sharing or risk-shouldering scheme. It helps private enterprise to carry through projects of the kind which private enterprise undertakes unaided, but which are just at the margin of profit.

My point is that private organisation, for promoting public utility enterprises of large cost and moderate prospective profit and for carrying the risk of such enterprises, is simply non-existent. The Trade Facilities Act does not touch this complaint, which requires initiative on the part of the Government or other public bodies. The odd thing is that the present Labour Government is so bent on satisfying the highest conventional standards and on avoiding the least suggestion of socialistic tendencies, that they are proving themselves more tenacious of *laissez-faire* in this and some other matters than (say) Mr Baldwin or Mr Brand himself.

Yours, &c.,

J. M. KEYNES

To the Editor of The Manchester Guardian, *9 June 1924*

Sir,

Your City editor has given in today's *Manchester Guardian* what purports to be a lengthy paraphrase of my article in this week's *Nation*. But all my arguments have suffered a slight sea-change, with the result that it is not nearly so persuasive as my original version! I feel myself, in reading it, in the presence of the pantomime constable under warning that 'everything you say will be taken down, altered, and used in evidence against you'. So, as I can't expect you to reproduce my article *in extenso*, I must ask any of your readers who are seriously interested in the matter to refer to the original if they want to know what I said.

Yours, &c.,

J. M. KEYNES

As well, on 7 June Keynes contributed another anonymous 'Finance and Investment' column.

From The Nation and Athenaeum, *7 June 1924*

THE FALL OF THE FRANC—BANK RATE, STERLING, AND FOREIGN INVESTMENT

Considerable mystery surrounds the policy of the French authorities with regard to the support of the franc; and the mystery is deepened if anything by the official communiqué issued this week. We are told, and can well believe, that all the dollars sold to support the exchange during March had been bought in again by the end of the month, and that from then on to May 7th the Bank of France and the Treasury were able to lay in a store of foreign currency on top of the replenished credits. After May 7th, to counteract the renewed fall of the franc, the Bank of France began to utilise these credits once more, 'in particular on May 12th and 13th', and it has since followed the same policy, 'taking action, as far as possible, and as opportunity occurred, to correct the too sudden jumps of the exchanges'. Most Frenchmen, we imagine, will regard a fall from 67 to 89 to the £ within a month as belonging to the category of 'too sudden jumps'; and so heavy a fall could hardly have taken place if the Bank of France had made sustained and determined efforts to prevent it. The references to 'in particular on May 12th and 13th', and 'as far as possible', show that its efforts have been neither sustained nor determined. Doubtless it has doled out small quantities of dollars or sterling from time to time, but not such as to make any appreciable hole in the credits that were intact at the beginning of the month. Essentially it has held its hand. Why?

There are various possible explanations. Some hint at a malevolent desire to discredit the parties of the Left, by emphasising the exchange sequel to their victory at the polls.

Central banks, at their worst, are not likely to subordinate to such motives all considerations of public policy. Have the French authorities at last grasped the fact that it is impossible to maintain permanently a rate of exchange as high as 70 to the £, and that their best policy is to save their resources until a figure is reached at which enduring stability is feasible? We believe that we shall be nearer to the mark if we assume a calculation bearing some resemblance to this, yet shorn of all its wisdom. The French authorities will have seen clearly enough that they would merely dissipate their resources by supporting the exchange in the neighbourhood of 70. But we suspect that they are waiting not so much for the moment when stability is possible as for the moment when they may hope to repeat their silly triumph of last March. Let the exchange continue to fall until a heavy bear position is again disclosed. Then they can intervene with decisive effect; send the franc bounding up once more, plunge the bears into confusion and loss, replenish their foreign credits on the upward swing, and emerge from the operation with a handsome profit. That certainly is the way to make profits from an exchange speculation. It is not the way to promote the stability of the franc or the welfare of France.

'Lombard Street,' declared the Financial Editor of *The Observer* last Sunday, 'is gravely discussing the possibility of a rise in the Bank rate. It is admitted that internal trade and monetary conditions do not warrant such a move, but rather the exchange position...Such a measure would, of course, raise an outcry.' It would, indeed; and we sincerely hope that these views are not strongly represented in the Bank Parlour. It is really an outrageous suggestion that, at a time when the Government is striving desperately under pressure from every quarter to find something which will give a stimulus to trade, the Bank of England should take a step directly calculated to depress it. For let there be no doubt about it; the only channel through which an increase in Bank rate can exert any lasting influence on the exchange is that of a depression of trade and prices here. It is, therefore, idle for the Financial Editor of *The Observer* to argue that, 'in actual fact bank charges are but an infinitesimal portion of the burdens borne by business'. If the effect on trade were negligible, the effect on the exchange would be negligible also. In present conditions, the effect would certainly not be negligible. The raising of Bank rate is important, not so much in itself as in indicating that the volume of credit, which is what really matters, is about to be curtailed. It is thus a recognised warning signal, which reacts directly on business confidence, and business confidence is not so strong at the moment that we can lightly cast an additional strain upon it.

The chain of causation between Bank rate and the exchanges was set out with admirable lucidity in the Cunliffe Report[6] itself, in the section describing the pre-war system.

The raising of the Bank's discount rate and the steps taken to make it effective in the market necessarily led to a general rise of interest rates and a restriction of credit. New enterprises were therefore postponed, and the demand for constructional materials and other capital goods was lessened. The consequent slackening of employment also diminished the demand for consumable goods, while holders of stocks of commodities carried largely with borrowed money, being confronted with an increase of interest charges, if not with actual difficulty in renewing loans, and with the prospect of falling prices, tended to press their goods on a weak market. The result was a decline in general prices in the home markets, which, by checking imports and stimulating exports, corrected the adverse trade balance, which was the primary cause of the difficulty.

Hardly anyone, we imagine, would seriously maintain that we should today deliberately create the conditions thus portrayed

---

[6] The reference is to the *First Interim Report* of the Committee on Currency and Foreign Exchanges after the war (November 1918, Cd. 9182), known by its chairman Lord Cunliffe, formerly Governor of the Bank of England.

for the sake of giving 'a tonic to sterling'; but there are many advocates of the Cunliffe policy who hug the illusion that we can adopt the means, achieve the end, and somehow dodge the *modus operandi*.

As regards the exchange problem itself, the position is materially different from what it was a year ago. The pound was then round about $4.70, and we took the view that this rate was well above the true economic level and was a material factor in the depression of our export industries. We saw no reason, therefore, to deplore the fall which occurred last autumn; indeed, a considerable part of the subsequent recovery in our trade is, we believe, attributable to it. But the exchange is certainly down to its true economic level now; and, though a further fall might force out further exports, the stimulus of an over-depreciated exchange is at least as unhealthy as the deterrent of an over-appreciated one, though in a different way. The weakness of sterling during the past week is clearly associated with the collapse of the franc, and need not be regarded seriously. But the prolonged weakness over the past half-year is a more ominous sign, for the powerful seasonal influences have been in favour of sterling, and will shortly turn against it.

To what is this weakness due? To the speech of Sir Montague Barlow[7], answers *The Observer*. We prefer the answer of *The Times*, to the abnormal volume of external loans which have lately been floated in London. It is, indeed, difficult to see how we can hope both to pay our debt to America, and to lend abroad on the scale on which we have recently been lending, without unsatisfactory exchange reactions. It is common to regard the dollar–sterling exchange as the barometer of our national prosperity. It is really the barometer of our foreign investments,

[7] On 9 October 1923, Sir Montague Barlow, the Minister of Labour, in a speech on remedies for unemployment, suggested that the Government was considering currency and credit inflation as a possible policy.

more than of anything else, a fall of the barometer indicating that these investments are becoming excessive. To welcome and encourage every new foreign issue floated in the London market, and to seek to correct the inevitable exchange results by raising Bank rate is an almost imbecile policy. Surely the right course is to leave our trade unhampered, and to safeguard the exchange by diverting our flow of capital into home investment.

Chapter 4

THE RETURN TO GOLD AND FOREIGN LENDING

On 18 February 1924 the Prime Minister reassured the House of Commons that the Government was still guided as to future currency policy by the recommendations of the Cunliffe Committee, which included an eventual return to the gold standard at the pre-1914 parity. A fortnight later the Chancellor of the Exchequer, Philip Snowden, told the House that he appreciated the advantages of amalgamating the Treasury's wartime issue of currency notes with the Bank of England's note issue. As a result of these statements, after consultations within the Bank of England, Governor Norman suggested to the Chancellor that the Treasury set up a Committee to consider the amalgamation of the note issues and proceeded to suggest possible members. The Chancellor agreed and on 10 June the Treasury set up the Committee on the Currency and Bank of England Note Issues, 'to consider whether the time has now come to amalgamate the Treasury Note Issue with the Bank of England Note Issue, and, if so, on what terms and conditions the amalgamation should be carried out'. The Committee's members were Sir Austen Chamberlain, a former Chancellor; Sir John Bradbury, formerly Permanent Secretary to the Treasury; Sir Otto Niemeyer, then in charge of the finance side of the Treasury; Gaspard Farrer, a banker; and Professor A. C. Pigou. At the time the Bank of England, the Treasury and members of the Committee all accepted that these terms of reference would allow a review of the problem of restoring the gold standard—especially as the Cunliffe Committee had recommended in 1918 that amalgamation of the note issues should follow a return to gold.

On 4 July the Committee's secretary approached Keynes.

From N. E. YOUNG, *4 July 1924*

Dear Mr Keynes,
   The Chancellor of the Exchequer has appointed a Committee, of which Mr Austen Chamberlain is Chairman, to advise him privately whether the time has now come to amalgamate the Treasury Note Issue with the Bank of England Note Issue, and, if so, on what terms and conditions the amalgamation should be carried out.

Mr Chamberlain asks whether you would be willing to attend a meeting of this Committee at 10.30 a.m. on Friday next, 11 July, in the Conference Room at the Treasury. He suggests that, if so, it would be convenient if you would be prepared to make a general statement on the subject, on which you would then allow the Committee to ask questions.

I enclose a copy of the Interim Report of the Cunliffe Committee, which has been out of print until recently.

Yours very truly,

N. E. YOUNG

When Keynes appeared before the Committee on 11 July, all of its members were present except Professor Pigou. The Treasury transcript of the proceedings ran as follows.

From Committee on the Currency and Bank of England Note Issues, Minutes, 11 July 1924

COMMITTEE ON THE CURRENCY AND BANK OF ENGLAND NOTE ISSUES

Meeting held in the Treasury on
Friday 11 July 1924 at
10.30 a.m.
Present:
The Rt Hon. J. Austen Chamberlain, M.P. (*Chairman*)
Sir John Bradbury, G.C.B.
Mr Gaspard Farrer
Sir Otto Niemeyer, K.C.B.
Mr N. E. Young (*Secretary*)

Mr Keynes, called and examined

(CHAIRMAN) *I think our Secretary has communicated with you as to the terms of our reference, and asked you to be prepared to make a statement to us.* (MR KEYNES) Yes.

Would you begin by making a statement? The present plan of £1 Currency Notes and £5 Bank of England Notes side by side is anomalous in appearance, but it has no practical disadvantages of which I am aware. I do not attach much importance one way or the other to the proposal for amalgamation, as such, but it would be slightly troublesome to effect amalgamation, particularly at a time when the ultimate currency policy is unsettled. Therefore amalgamation would not be worth doing for its own sake unless it facilitated some other advantageous change.

The only important question to my mind is that of the rules controlling the aggregate volume of the two note issues. The present system is superficially like the pre-war system, that is to say there is a fixed maximum fiduciary issue of the two note issues together, just as there was a fixed fiduciary issue of the Bank of England note issue before the war. But in spite of the superficial resemblance, the present system is different from the pre-war system in two very important respects. The first one is the very familiar one that the maximum is liable to vary downwards from one year to another, and never liable to vary upwards. That is familiar. The other point I do not think is quite so familiar, although it is really obvious. It is that under the present system there is no means of increasing the non-fiduciary portion, so that, whereas under the pre-war system we had a fixed fiduciary issue and a fluctuating non-fiduciary issue varying with imports of gold, what we have in effect now is a fixed total issue. There can be no question either of the import or of the export of gold in the ordinary course in present circumstances. When the market was short of funds and the Bank reserve went down and so forth, in the pre-war system that automatically led to a replenishment of the basis of the currency. At present that cannot happen, and a system where the note issue is rigidly fixed in total is quite a different system from one where the fiduciary issue is fixed, but where it requires no great disturbance of the existing adjustments to enlarge the non-fiduciary portion.

(SIR JOHN BRADBURY) *To clear our minds on this point, you are really directing your observations to the position which exists so long as the exchange is below parity?* My remarks apply to the two issues taken in the aggregate, in a situation like the present in which the value of gold is in excess of the value of sterling. These provisions were of no great practical importance—in fact, were inoperative—until this year. Thus it is only quite lately that it has been worth while thinking about such points as what happens under the existing system when the actual note issue is quite close up to the permitted maximum.

I think that these are fatal defects—that although the actual note issue is very nearly equal to the permitted issue, that permitted issue should be liable to fall and not to rise, and that there should be no means of increasing it so long as sterling is depreciated. Therefore I do think it is important to modify the existing rules.

Nevertheless the question of modification seems to me to have little or nothing to do with the question of amalgamating the two issues which raises a different sort of problem. The existing rule is a relic of the time when it was the policy of the Government to carry out a progressive deflation, and this progressive reduction of the fiduciary limit was intended to enforce that progressive deflation. That policy, after falling gradually into desuetude, was expressly abandoned by the Government of the day just over a year ago when Mr Baldwin made his famous non-flationist speech. Unless, therefore, that policy is reversed, it would be foolish to maintain a rule the object of which is to enforce a policy contrary to what is the latest declaration of the policy of the Government in the matter. But even if that was reversed, even if we returned to a deflation policy on the lines of the Cunliffe Report, I still think that this rule would be a very inexpedient one, because we should surely carry out a deflation policy by curtailing credit, with the result that the demand for currency would contract automatically; and we should not think of tackling it by letting the currency limit become operative. The most that the currency limit could do would be to terrify us into doing what we intended to do anyhow, and, since there might have been some slight miscalculation in fixing the limit it might prove purely embarrassing. I cannot see how it could be useful.

(CHAIRMAN) *It would act as a signal, would it not?* It would act too late. If we waited until we were practically up to the currency limit it might be that nothing that we could do, short of inflicting general bankruptcy on the commercial public, would enable us to keep to the limit. We should have to act some appreciable time in advance, and in acting what we should look at would not really be this limit but the dollar exchange, the level of prices, the general state of credit, and all the reactions which we should have to bring about if we wanted to put a drastic deflation policy into operation. It seems to me that rigid limitation is unworkable. This view is not dependent on particular views on deflation or stability, and it is a mistake, for the reason I elaborated a few minutes ago, to think that this system of rigid limitation is the pre-war system. It is much more dangerous than the pre-war system, because the pre-war system was always capable of expansion without any very violent re-adjustment of the situation.

If the old rule is to be changed, the question arises what criterion can be put in its place. So long as the gold standard is inoperative, with the result that there is no question either of importing or of exporting gold, it seems to me clear that the criterion cannot for the time being relate to gold; it would be without serious significance to relate it to gold. If the criterion is not gold, I do not know of any alternative criterion which has been seriously put forward except the level of prices. But the difficulty of that is that we cannot easily—in fact, we cannot at all—apply that criterion, the criterion of prices, until we have decided whether our policy is to raise prices or to lower them or to keep them steady in the transitional period. I exclude the policy of any material rise in prices because I do not think anyone defends it.

(SIR JOHN BRADBURY) *You say 'transitional period'. Transitional to what?* Until there has been some final declaration as to what our ultimate currency policy is to be. I call it transitional because many people are in favour of a policy of stability of prices at present who are not in favour of stability of prices as a permanent policy. I did not want to raise that issue more than I need. Everyone who is not in favour of a very rapid deflation admits the existence of a transitional period. For many reasons, which I have printed in a book with which this Committee probably does not want to be troubled, I believe that deflation in the sense of lowering the price level—of course it is an ambiguous term—is contrary to the public interest, and I go further than that and I say that even if it were desirable, deflation at a rapid rate would probably prove socially and politically impossible in present conditions. If that view is accepted, we are left with a criterion which was explicitly adopted by Mr Baldwin, on behalf of the Government of the day, a year ago, of maintaining the price level steady. But whatever answer we give to the question I have just raised, whether our object is deflation or stability, the method of the Treasury and the Bank of England would be found in credit control rather than in currency control;—if only because currency control operates too late in the day to be effective. And therefore I think the function of any rule of currency limitation should be limited to the purpose of operating as a warning signal in the contingency, which one hopes will not arise, of credit control breaking down for any reason. So long as credit control is successfully conducted, the limitation on the volume of currency ought never to be operative; and if you have a limit at all it is only as a second line of defence and as a thing which might possibly strengthen the hands of the central authorities in the event of a serious collapse of their deliberate credit policy. If you use the currency limitation in that way, there should clearly be a reasonable margin between the permitted maximum volume of the note issue and the anticipated actual volume of the note issue, assuming for the moment that the criterion of price stability has been adopted. You do not want the warning signal to come into effective operation except for a fairly grave cause. The unforeseeable moderate fluctuations of the market you would not want to be complicated by this violent danger signal,—these you would deal with by the ordinary methods of the Bank rate and credit control.

I should like to say, at this point, that I do not myself attach importance to having any maximum at all, because if credit control does break down badly the damage is already done and it can only be undone by regaining control of credit. I do not think, for example, that the United States at the present moment suffers any danger or any inconvenience through having no operative limit to its note issue. There is, if course, a legal limit, but it is so very far from the actual issue that they are in just the same position as we were in a year or two years ago under the Cunliffe Committee, namely that the legal limitation is not a thing which enters into the calculations of the central authorities at all.

On the other hand, I do not see any very great objection to a maximum. It is a rule to which conventional opinion is accustomed, and I see that in certain circumstances it might act as a useful strengthener to the central authorities in endeavouring to do their duty. It is a thing intelligible to the public, to which the central authorities could refer when the reasons which actually govern them are more difficult to explain. I do not think it is of serious importance to the governing authorities themselves. I say that I see no objection to a maximum provided there is a margin sufficient to ensure that the limit will not be in fact operative unless credit control has really broken down, and also provided that the limit can be revised from time to time. I attach importance to this margin and to this power of revision, not only for the reasons I have given, but also because there is no constant mathematical relation between the level of prices and the demand for currency. The demand for currency depends on several things beside the level of prices; it depends, as has been long known, on the season of the year and on the briskness of trade, and it also depends, to an extent which has only been fully appreciated lately, on the point reached in the credit cycle and the general anticipations of the business world about the future course of prices. As an illustration of the extreme variability of the volume of the note issue in relation to the level of prices, in the two years between October 1920 and October 1922 prices fell by 30 per cent and the aggregate note issue fell by 14 per cent It might be, therefore, that in a certain condition of business psychology, a certain point in the credit cycle, the existing note issue would support a very much higher level of prices than we have now. For those reasons it is extremely difficult to achieve any result, whether with a gold standard or price stability, by fixing the level of your note issue;—if the maximum limit is to be operative you have to change it constantly at each season in the year and at each phase in the credit cycle, and if you knew enough to change the limit of the note issue accurately you would know more than enough to regulate the currency in other ways. It is the most difficult conceivable way to attain any result, to try to do it by regulating the note issue, because you are acting on almost the *last* event in the causal train. When a tendency is set up to cause rising or falling prices, the very last thing which happens is the movement of the note issue. It is like conducting a *post mortem*, like postponing all diagnosis until the *post mortem* and prescribing that steps should be taken to look after the patient as soon as it is ascertained for certain that he is dead. Of course, also, the appropriate volume of the note issue varies with the growth of wealth and population, and it also varies—a thing which may happen quickly or slowly—with changes in the banking habits of the community. If, for example, the Treasury were to take off the stamp duty on cheques, that might very appreciably alter the volume of note issue that was required to support a given level of prices.

(CHAIRMAN) *Do you really think that is so?* Of course, it is an estimate. But suppose cheques were more freely used for small payments—if you had not got to pay 2d. it might make a great difference.

In so far as notes are used in place of cheques, is it not because there are now small notes, and for that reason only, not on account of the extra penny duty? Before, you had to have either a cheque or a postal order for which you had to pay. Now you can put your hand into your pocket and pull out your ten shillings. Yes. I think that is why notes are used more now in that way, but my point is that if you take the stamp duty off cheques would be used.

I wonder. That does not matter. My point is that you may have changes of that kind in the facilities granted by banks or in the charges for them, which would make really a great variation in quite a short period in the extent to which people use currency notes for making payments. All this leads to the conclusion that if you insist on a fixed maximum for your note issue, this maximum should be appreciably higher—I should say by not less than 15 per cent; and I think even that is running it rather close—than you anticipated actual note issue. You ought not to aim at having the compulsory powers any nearer actuality than 15 per cent. There is a good deal to be said in favour of a margin of 20 per cent. A limitation of that kind would stand in the way of any serious inflation, such as has happened in many countries lately, or even such as happened in this country immediately after the War. It would stand in the way of any serious inflation without operating accidentally and without purpose in interfering with the considered credit policy of the authorities.

I have spoken so far as if the method of regulating our note issue would be in any case the method of a fixed fiduciary maximum. I agree with the Cunliffe Committee in thinking that a fixed maximum fiduciary issue is preferable to any of the other formulas in vogue in other countries. If the Committee is interested in any of the other formulas which have been suggested, I should be glad to discuss them, but the traditional English view seems to me to have everything to be said for it.

My practical conclusions, then, are that I see no particular object in combining the currency note and Bank note issues. On the other hand, unless there was some special purpose to be served, amalgamation would involve a troublesome bargain between the Treasury and the Bank of England, and there is also one incidental point I should like to mention—Sir Otto Niemeyer will be able to say whether it has any importance or not. I think it is an advantage of the present system that the Treasury has control over the securities of the Currency Note Redemption Account. In these days when the Treasury has big conversions and redemptions to be carried through, and is concerned in big market operations, the fact that a considerable volume of Government securities of one kind or another are held by what is technically known as 'Other Government Departments', of which the Currency Note Redemption Account is one of the largest, and that the type of security held in those funds can be varied quite privately, that facility is really of great importance to the Treasury in its operations. If you regard the Bank of England and the Treasury as virtually the same concern from this point of view, the change would not matter much, of course; but then I think you must make proposals of this kind on the assumption that these bodies are not necessarily the same thing. If they are the same thing, the whole discussion is of no importance whatever, but if this would mean that the Treasury would part with the control of the securities in the Currency Note Redemption Account to the Bank of England, I think it would be a retrograde movement. In the old days, when the amount of such securities was relatively small and when these operations were not being carried out except very infrequently, the matter was of no significance, but with their present magnitude and the operations the Treasury has in view in the next seven years, I attach a certain amount of importance to this point, because in practice that is the chief result which would flow from the amalgamation of the two note issues as such. I cannot see that amalgamation would make much difference, except that you would be handing over the control of this great body of securities out of the hands of the Treasury into the hands of the Bank of England. That is my first practical conclusion that amalgamation, as such, is not important, but there is more to be said against it than for it.

My second conclusion is that it is important to revise the present rule governing the volume of currency notes.

My third conclusion is that if you wish to keep the general principle of a fixed maximum, that maximum at the present moment ought to be about mid-way between the maxima that were established for the years 1922 and 1923, that is to say about 290 millions for the fiduciary issue of the Currency Note Account. I think that would be for the present a good practical compromise between various theoretical policies. As I have said, I should prefer no maximum; I should depend for price stability or deflation on the efficiency of credit control. There is another incidental point of Treasury interest I should like to bring up at this juncture. Suppose you had no maximum for the currency notes in ordinary circumstances, this would have no importance unless there is a complete breakdown of the central authorities over the control of credit; but it might be a very important point to the Treasury to be able to issue an unlimited volume of currency notes when dealing with its redemptions and conversions. It seems to me that suppose you have some big conversion scheme for the big 5% War Loan, and there was a certain percentage of holders who would not accept the general terms, it is important that the Treasury should be able to pay them off in currency notes and beat them down to accepting the Government terms, because there is nothing they could do with the currency notes. If the permitted maximum was intended to be a serious maximum there would be no margin for the Treasury to do that. It seems to me that the Treasury should be able to threaten to pay off a remnant of 25 or 50 millions in currency notes, as otherwise you might have a single big holder, or a very small group of big holders, or just a collection of people in the country, who could blackmail the Treasury in the most tiresome manner and possibly require special legislation. The loan is due on a particular date; these holders of 50 millions of the security would say, 'We do not accept your conversion terms; pay us off according to our bond', and there would be absolutely no way whatever by which the Treasury could legally pay them off. I think the inconvenience of that, particularly the inconvenience of the Treasury not having this weapon in reserve so that people could not even begin to talk in that way, is more important than the safeguard against the improbable contingency of the credit control breaking down,—particularly because my own belief is that if your first line of defence breaks down your second line of defence will break down simultaneously. It has nearly always happened in recent experience that the trouble has come through the first line of defence breaking down, through the authorities losing control of credit by reason of their excessive Government borrowings or in some other way, and I am not aware of a single example in which the first line of defence, that is to say credit control, has broken down in a modern community, where the situation has been saved in the slightest degree by having this second line of defence, a currency limitation. The rule of currency limitation is immediately waived. There are so many examples of that, and such recent ones, that it is hardly worth quoting particular cases.

In giving my practical conclusions, I should like to end up with one further point, namely, what my ideal system would be. My ideal system would be to hand over the country's reserves held to meet a foreign drain, whether those reserves consisted of gold or foreign balances or whatever they consisted of, to the authority controlling credit, i.e. to the Bank of England,

and I should place on the Bank of England the entire responsibility of controlling credit and maintaining their reserves at such a level as to maintain the parity of the standard, whether that parity was in terms of gold, dollars or commodities; and I would measure the failure of the Bank of England not by some arithmetical relation between the reserves and the note issue—which is a meaningless and quite illogical relation, since under modern conditions when the standard of value does not itself circulate, there is no reason why the one should bear any particular proportion to the other, but by any tendency of the standard to depart from its parity by more than the legal margin. That is the real fact of the situation for decades past. The relation of the amount of reserves to the amount of note issue is a fabrication. It relates to a system that existed a hundred years or more ago. It is kept up as a pure figment and no one ever works on these lines. The actual reserves you require are those necessary to meet unexpected fluctuations in your international position. There is no precise relation between the amount you require for that purpose and the amount of your note issue. The classical case in which this was argued out was the case of India, with which you are very familiar. It was not thought that the amount of the gold standard reserve ought to bear any particular relation to the note issue of India or the circulation of rupees. Sir Lionel Abrahams used to work out memoranda showing what on balance was the maximum net payment India might have to make abroad in a given period of time, and that was the only logical way of arriving at the reserve. That is the only way of arriving at the amount of reserve that the Bank of England ought to hold. I think it is a pure confusion to link that up with the amount of the note issue, and a confusion that may divert the authorities from their true purposes and may prove practically inconvenient. My system would be to link up the amount of reserve with the credit controlling authority and to put the responsibility on them to keep sufficient reserves to maintain the parity of the standard.

Having done that, I would issue without any arbitrary fixed limit such volume of notes as the state of credit required. Such issue would be automatic, and I would place it in the hands of the Treasury. I would place it in the hands of the Treasury because the profit belongs to the Treasury and you would therefore avoid awkward questions and difficult bargains, and secondly because it is helpful to the Treasury in their national debt operations to have under their control the great volume of securities held against the fiduciary issue.

There are three points I would like to repeat. One is what I mentioned at the beginning, that the fixed upper limit to the note issue is much more dangerous in present conditions than in pre-war conditions, since a fixed fiduciary issue is now in practice the same as a fixed total issue,—a thing which we never knew before the war; secondly, that in modern conditions currency control is a relatively unimportant second line of defence, the main line of defence being credit control—most of the conventional maxims about note issues have relation to the conditions of a hundred years ago and are empty words in relation to modern conditions. And thirdly, I would emphasise that most of what I have said this morning would be the same even if I were in favour of a hasty return to the gold standard. I do not think the subject matter of this Committee's discussions is very much connected with the question of stability of prices and the gold standard, because the only method of carrying out any policy is by credit control and not by currency control. It could only be a crazy person who would employ currency control for the purpose of achieving a gold standard, because a refusal to issue a volume of currency rendered necessary by the existing volume of credit would merely be general bankruptcy, and the first and biggest bankrupt would be the Treasury.

(CHAIRMAN) *Much of your argument has turned upon the present conditions under which gold cannot flow in as it used to do in old times. Would you agree that what prevents gold flowing in is the fact that if it flows in you cannot get it out again?* I should say that what prevents gold flowing in is that there is no purchaser in England who offers so high a price as purchasers in the United States.

At present there is an embargo on the export of gold? Yes. I do not think that embargo is the cause of the lower price offered for gold here than in America.

What would be the effect of lifting the embargo on the movement of gold? Would you mean by 'lifting the embargo', lifting the embargo as regards gold held in private hands, or permitting holders of Bank notes to take gold out of the Bank of England for export?

Taking gold out for export. I put aside gold for internal currency, which might or might not be included, but restoring the free market in gold for export. The first effect would be that a considerable amount of gold would flow, and the exchange would be immediately restored to parity. That would have many other consequences.

As the effect would be in a very short time to send the exchange to parity, do you think there really would be a great drain of gold? It does not follow that it would stay there. The immediate demand for gold would be limited to the extent to which the market was prepared to speculate on future requirements, and the extent to which the market would be prepared to speculate on future requirements would be smaller than what those future requirements would turn out to be. The market would never speculate to 100 per cent, partly because it would not be worth its while, and partly because it would never have confidence enough to do that. Therefore, as time went on various unforeseen requirements for dollars would be set up by this greater cheapness of them, and if no other steps were taken simultaneously, besides the removal of the embargo, to modify credit conditions and so forth, I should say that certainly after a time all the gold would have left the Bank of England and there would still be unsatisfied demands. If you were to offer more gold for sterling and make no other change, the demands for gold at this reduced price for export to America would be bound in the end to swamp you. Therefore that policy would have to be combined with a drastic credit restriction. You would therefore have to face the consequences of that. One of the first consequences of the restoration of sterling to par without any other change taking place simultaneously—I am assuming your instantaneous action—would be that all our exports would cost 12 per cent more in the world market than they cost now. That would mean in a great many cases that our export trade would be absolutely cut from under our feet for the time being.

On the other hand, there would be a correlative lowering of import prices of raw material and food? We should also tend to buy more, and the extent to which we should do that would depend on the confidence in this policy being permanently successful.

If your raw material and food prices fell, would not that tend to prevent the rise in prices of exports which you fear? Not at once, because you would not have wages falling automatically 12 per cent. Take the coal or iron and steel industries, where the imported goods they employ are insignificant. Even in the case of cotton goods the cost of the imported raw material in many cases is not more than about 30 per cent or something of that kind. So that a fall of 10 per cent in the raw material would only mean a fall of about 3 per cent in the finished product.

I put the question to you as if it were to be done with a stroke of the pen tomorrow; but now may I go to what is more practical? The embargo expires on the 31st December 1925. What would you do under those circumstances? This leads into rather big questions.

We are unable to keep them out. I hold very strongly that the Treasury or the Bank of England—whichever you like—must, I should say in perpetuity, keep a hold over both the import and export of gold. I should favour a permanent system of allowing both export and import of gold only by license of the Treasury or the Bank of England. That would mean that the rates at which gold was flowing in or out, and the level of prices and so forth, would be under their control. It might happen that for long periods together the licences would be granted to all comers without question, freely. You then have the advantages of the supposed free gold market. I have never heard what the advantages were, but they are often referred to. You would, at the same time, have no safeguard against being swamped with gold, which, I think, is the more likely contingency, or against suffering a sudden depletion of gold contrary to your policy. I see no reason whatever why the existing method of controlling gold imports and exports should not be made a permanent policy. I think there is a great deal to be said for it.

If you announced now, or between now and next December, that you proposed to introduce legislation to prolong, or to make permanent, the existing control over the export of gold, do you think that would have any effect on the position of our national credit? I think it would be unwise to say you would make it permanent unless you were at the same time announcing a permanent monetary policy in other respects. It would make people ask questions, and you would not know the answer to the questions. If you were merely to say that the existing arrangements are going to be continued for the present pending a final settlement of the currency policy, I think the effect would be nil. The number of people who are aware that this expires on a certain date is almost limited to the people in this room.

Do not you think that a great many people on becoming aware that it is necessary to prolong it would treat that as rather a serious declaration, rightly or wrongly? Would not they regard it as a confession on the part of the British Government of economic weakness? It would be a confession that it was not absolutely certain that we could return to the gold standard by the 1st January 1926. The opinion that we shall return to a gold standard on the 1st January 1925* is hardly held by anyone. That being so there is no reason to say anything particular just at present.

It would have to be said next year? This seems to me a question consequential upon other policies. I should pursue whatever was my exchange and currency policy, and should take this embargo off at the date when all my other policies had led to the result that the embargo was of no importance. Personally I should prefer to keep the embargo on even though it was not operative, as a safeguard.

It is an essential part of your views that we ought not to attempt to restore the old parity of the sovereign? No, that is not an essential part of my views. My own belief is that the policy I advocate—price stability—would almost certainly lead to a restoration of the parity of the sovereign, because I find it very hard to believe that American prices will not rise in time, unless they do improbable things. I am really at one with almost everybody on that point. I am against hurrying the day, but I regard it as probable that if we concentrate on a price stability policy we shall probably find ourselves at no very distant date at par. The peculiarity of my policy is limited to this, that

* This is what I said. There was a confusion about dates.

having got back to par I should like to accept the import of gold only by licence of the Treasury. That is to say, suppose there is a big wave of inflation in America which carries us back to par, I do not want to be carried on by that inflation. The advocates of the gold standard think it is very important that we should share in any inflation going on in the world generally. I want to stop at that point, and I think it is extraordinarily easy to stop at that point because the only way in which we have to alter our pre-war or present currency system is by saying—it is not a question of the import of gold—that the Bank of England should be the only party authorised to deliver gold at the Mints.

You would relieve the Mint of all obligation to coin at a fixed price? For all comers.

(SIR OTTO NIEMEYER) *And relieve the Bank of the obligation?* And I should also relieve the Bank of the obligation to buy gold at a fixed price. I should leave the Bank free to raise or lower its price. We should then be our own masters. If we did not want to share in the inflation that is hypothetically going on in the rest of world we should keep our prices stable.

(CHAIRMAN) *May I put a question in what I hope is a practical form? Do I understand that, from your point of view, we derived, as a nation, no advantage before the War from having an absolutely free gold market as contrasted with, say, the nominally free gold market of Germany which, in fact, was a controlled market?* The advantage we gained—you may call it consequential on that—was that our effective gold points were narrower than those of certain other countries such as France and Germany, and that made short-term loans and lendings on the London market by and to foreigners an operation more susceptible to small changes in the rate of discount than it could be if the gold points were rather wider; but it resulted not from the free gold market as such but from the narrowness of the gold points, and my policy would be that the Bank of England should announce limits corresponding to gold points for periods from time to time covering short loans. I think you can get the advantages of security in the minds of international borrowers and lenders if they have confidence in the rate at which they can get their money backwards and forwards by other methods than by the reception of gold in unlimited amounts. I think that the advantage of London was the certainty, over a period of three or six months, of the rate at which you could get your money in and out of England. That policy was contingent on the fact that almost the whole world was on a gold standard. If only a small part of the world was on a gold standard, that remains an advantage but a less extensive advantage. I think at present, under post-war conditions, which are different in very many respects from pre-war conditions, the danger of the pre-war system would be that New York, at certain times when money was very redundant as it may easily be under their present Federal Reserve System, would dump a lot of short money on London, relying on this way of getting it out again, so that any tendency towards inflation in America resulting from unduly cheap money would be at once reflected here in a way that we might not like at all. It would not always be an advantage to be a dumping ground for 2 per cent American money with an absolute guarantee that they could take it away at any moment. We should not know what to do with it. It would force our domestic rates down equally low. I think the absolute linking up of the London and New York money markets, while that has great advantages, is not such a safe thing as it used to be. In the old days the amount of floating funds in New York as compared with the size of the London market was not so menacing, as it would be now. One of the points of my policy is that, whilst I think there are other devices that the Bank of England can introduce for giving certainty to the market, the particular methods that secured certainty before the War are now dangerous.

(SIR JOHN BRADBURY) *Mr Keynes, do you, under present conditions, attach any importance at all to the fluctuation in the amount of the reserve in the Banking Department of the Bank of England?* You mean consequential on more Bank notes going into circulation?

The traditional pre-war policy of the Bank of England was to determine the credit policy of the Bank with regard to the movements in the reserve in the Banking Department. Under modern post-war conditions, do you attach any importance at all to those fluctuations as an indication for the purposes of determining the credit policy? At the moment when gold cannot flow in and out, none whatever. If gold flowed in or out, while I should attach some importance to the state of the reserve as one of the indications, I should not make it the sole criterion as under pre-war conditions.

One of the arguments for amalgamating the two issues is that the fluctuations in the volume of currency notes as well as the fluctuation in the Bank notes would be reflected in the movements of the reserve of the Bank of England? They are published every week now, and anyone who wants to know can make the calculation. That seems to imply that the Bank is so unacquainted with arithmetic that it is incapable of adding the two together.

I think you misunderstood the purpose of my question. No doubt the necessary calculations can be made; but the Bank of England, like other institutions, is susceptible to public opinion. If a variation of the Bank rate has to be justified to the public, to public opinion, the only justification before the War was that the increase had to be effected to protect the reserve of the Banking Department. My question rather is this: do you think in public opinion the old idea of the fluctuation of the reserve being an important barometer is a matter of any importance? Of very little importance. In so far as it is a barometer, I think it acts too late. If the Bank waits to put up its Bank rate, until it can have this justification for the public it will always put it up too late.

My point is this. So to speak we have now two barometers—the Treasury returns of the currency note issue and the ordinary Bank of England return. The skilled meteorologist has to compare the two and make the calculation from them. Would not there be some advantage, so to speak, in having only the one barometer by amalgamating the two, when the currency note return would be in the Bank of England return? I agree that to anyone at all skilled the business of adding the two together does not represent any difficulty. There are various financial weeklies which do the sum for the public every week. If the object is to make the public attach greater importance to it, I think it is obviously dangerous. I think it is dangerous for the public to say to the Bank of England, when the Bank wants to raise its rate, 'Why are you hampering trade when your reserve does not show any fluctuations'. I think it would be better that they should act in good time, and therefore to concentrate public opinion on the indication, which is a late-in-the-day indication, will weaken the Bank's position.

Is not it true that for the determination of credit the consideration of the Bank of England return, taken alone, is entirely useless? Taken alone, useless.

For the purpose of facilitating the consideration of these problems, could there not be something to be said for having, so to speak, an amalgamated return of the two? I think it would be just as useless.

(CHAIRMAN) *May I ask Mr Keynes this question? What are the indications upon which, in your opinion, the Bank ought to act? Set aside for the moment whether the relation of the reserve to the note issue is of any importance from the point of view of helping the public. What are the actual indications, arising long before that comes into operation as I understand, upon which you think the Bank ought to act?* May I illustrate that by what I should say about the Bank rate at this moment, which is very much under discussion. At this moment I should pay great attention to the ease with which the Treasury was able to get its dollars over the exchange. I should watch the level of prices in America. I should watch changes in the form of the assets of the 'Big Five' [clearing banks] as between advances, investments and discounts. I should watch the open market rate of discount. I should watch the new issues market, particularly the foreign new issues. Suppose that now or in the next three months I found that the Treasury was finding it difficult to get dollars, if I was told by bankers that cotton and wheat bills were coming on the exchange in heavy volume, if I saw American prices on the upward move rather than otherwise, I should be strongly inclined to put the Bank rate up. I should take into account the relative money rates here and in America, but I should take into account not less the money rates in Germany and France.

Supposing that the Dawes Report was to go through, so that confidence was increased, I should pay then more attention to high rates on the Continent, because I should think the political risks being reduced the English market would be more ready to take advantage of the high rates for money obtainable on the Continent. If all those indications, or a great many of them, were adverse, I should anticipate a combination of sterling exchange falling and American prices rising, and that combination would be almost certain to engineer a rise of prices here, which—possibly months later—would show itself in an additional issue of currency notes. But if I waited until the currency notes were pouring out as the final result of all this and let my exchange go against me in the meantime, and let the new issues market go on lending to New South Wales, and the private loan market go on lending to Austria and Germany, I should be in the soup. My only way out would be to try and bankrupt a lot of people.

(SIR JOHN BRADBURY) *I want to put this question to Mr Keynes on the credit policy. I take it you hold the view that the purchasing power, the unit of value, in this country ought to be determined entirely by whatever public authority controlled the issue of credit.* Yes.

Correct me if I misinterpret you. You do not under present conditions regard any kind of link with the commodity value of gold as a practical method for controlling prices, or any kind of link with exchanges? Well, I do not go as far as that. There are various compromises that are possible. One of the great objections to the gold standard is that I think that as time goes on, with methods of economising, gold will tend to be redundant, and one of the things I want to be protected against is inflation due to the depreciation of gold. If my opinion as to the relative abundance of gold is correct, a system of free convertibility into gold would be harmless. What we should require would be a system of licensing the import of gold for currency, so that when gold had depreciated in value we could lower the price of gold in terms of sterling, and we should then obtain for one pound sterling more gold than its equivalent on the pre-war basis of £3.17.10 per oz.

Would it be correct to say then that you think that the unit of value in this country should be maintained by credit control, plus the taking into account of various economic causes and tendencies, of which no doubt gold value should be one, but possibly not the most important? That is correct.

Of course that credit control becomes a very delicate operation? I do not think this difficulty is affected by what standard we adopt. I hold that the methods of credit control employed would be identical under my suggested scheme and under a gold system. When you have the credit system and no gold circulating I think the methods employed do not depend upon the aim, but are substantially the same whatever your aim.

May I put the point I want to get at in this way. The pre-war practice I take it regarding this very delicate operation of credit control, which you say must take place at a very much earlier time, before the currency limits come into operation, was left primarily to the Bank of England. On the other hand, the Bank of England was operating in the exercise of its credit control with that rigid currency system of the country, in the background if you like, as a menace in regard to which their policy must be developed. Now, the question I want to put to you is this. Supposing we got rid of that menace, the ultima ratio *of the currency control, or made it more remote, would you think that the duty of credit control could properly be left entirely to the Bank of England, in consultation, of course, with the Treasury and other people?* I should reform the constitution of the Bank of England in certain ways. I think I should develop the power of the Bank's Committee of Treasury. [One] might make the representation of the Treasury rather more formal than it is at present. There has been a great change since the war in the relations between the Bank of England and the Treasury. I should leave it ostensibly to the Bank of England and should develop the power of the Committee of Treasury.

You would leave the Bank formally a private institution, and allow it to exercise its control without any external control? I do not regard it as a private institution. I regard it as one of our Heaven-sent institutions by which through anomalistic methods we get the advantages both of a private and of a public institution.

I said 'formally' I think I would meet criticism by making a little clearer the relations between the Treasury and the Bank of England.

(CHAIRMAN) *Would you advise any Chancellor of the Exchequer to accept for himself and his successors the responsibility for the alteration of the Bank rate?* No. I think that the function of the Government and of the Treasury is to determine the policy, whether it is to be a gold standard or whatever it is to be, but the the technical means of achieving that ought to be left to a body in the position of the Bank of England.

(SIR JOHN BRADBURY) *There is one point on which I want to put a question to you. One of your arguments in favour of the policy for a fixed maximum for the fiduciary issue was that if the Treasury had power to issue Treasury notes in any volume it might facilitate operations in connection with the conversion of the public debt. Do you regard it as entirely consistent with the contract between the bondholder and public creditors of this country generally that that kind of pressure should be brought on the bondholder, i.e., that emergency currency should be made for the purpose of giving advantages to one party to the contract—the Government—as against the other party?* I should regard it as perfectly proper, provided that the Treasury were offering a fair bargain. I think it would be iniquitous to use this weapon to enforce on the bondholder a manifestly unfair bargain. I am considering a case where the great mass of the bondholders have agreed that the offer is a fair one. It is to protect the

Treasury from the blackmailing power of persons who demand that they shall be paid back.

(SIR OTTO NIEMEYER) *Is not that a part of their rights under the contract?* I think the propriety of using this weapon would depend upon the actual bargain you made.

(CHAIRMAN) *It would be a tremendous power to put in the hands of the Chancellor of the Exchequer or the Government for the time being.* It was a threat that Goschen used, and there were some people who were inclined to think he was driving a hard bargain.

(SIR JOHN BRADBURY) *What he threatened was to pay them in gold?* It is the same thing.

(CHAIRMAN) *Is it the same thing as paying them in currency notes?* So long as you maintain the value of your currency notes.

If they could issue 20 millions of currency notes for the purpose of paying off, would the value be retained? You offer them as good a bargain as they can get from anyone else. Supposing you were offering a conversion loan at 2 per cent and there were plenty of good securities at 5 per cent, of course, then they will defeat you. If you offered them a fair market price they would have to come to your terms. It would not suit them to buy goods. I do not think the threat would be used. I think the reserve power of using it might be of some importance.

(SIR OTTO NIEMEYER) *On this last point, if you assume a case where, say, a third of the bondholders had to be paid off by notes in the way you suggest, would not the effect be to penalise the other two-thirds who accepted your terms? I am assuming that you had to put this into force?* Yes, but I think that really assumes it is an unfair bargain. I think if you had one-third of the bondholders of a big issue demanding payment, I think that would be a proof that the bargain offered was an unfair one.

I am putting it as an extreme case, but pro tanto *if one had to issue further notes, the effect would be, to that extent whatever it may be, to depreciate the value of the securities which you are giving to the two-thirds who had accepted.* Let me put a case the other way. Supposing you had a single big insurance company or a big bank which held 25 millions of a loan which is falling due, and you offered them in exchange securities which were the equivalent of the market rates at the moment. If they said 'Unless you offer us $\frac{1}{2}$ per cent better we shall want payment in cash' you would have no means of paying them off. If this company were prepared to take payment in bank credits, cash at the Bank of England, there would be no difficulty, but suppose they were blackmailing and insisted upon payment in cash which they are entitled to, then you could not get that cash.

You suggest this power should be kept as a weapon for dealing with debt. You would limit it to that purpose. Would you be able to do so? I do not think there would ever be a question of it in any other circumstances, unless you lost control of credit. It would operate exactly in ordinary circumstances as a limit which was comfortably above your note issue. It is a very secondary point.

My point is rather different. In the case you are putting the state has a large debt to pay which she cannot raise money to pay, and this is the means of escape. Supposing the state wanted large sums of money for other purposes, would you get the same principle applying? I should call that a complete breakdown of credit control.

You think you could distinguish between the two cases. You think you could confine the use of the power to the case of debt repayment? I do not think there would be any difficulty in saying which was one case or the other.

(CHAIRMAN) *Do you think you can trust the Chancellor of the Exchequer not to fill his Budget deficit or for the purpose of his favourite scheme to use this if he has it?* I do not think there are any means of strapping down a really wicked Chancellor of the Exchequer.

Well, you would try to stop him as much as possible? No. I should try to throw him out of office. On your assumption that there might be a Chancellor of the Exchequer who was borrowing by inflationary means, he would not do it by actually paying out currency notes. He would borrow on terms that led to inflation of credit and did not represent real savings, and would be exactly similar to any other inflationary movement. My opinion is that if you had a Chancellor of the Exchequer with these wishes, the operation of the limitation of the currency note issue probably would not come into effect in his time anyhow. To depend on that for checking your Chancellor of the Exchequer would be depending on a remedy that comes much too late.

(SIR OTTO NIEMEYER) *Don't you think you perhaps put the point about the issue of currency notes a little high?* I did not mean to put this secondary point at all high; if I did, I withdraw it.

I wanted to be clear. Let me put my question in this way. As you know, the main assets of the Currency Notes Account are not convertible loans; the main assets are short-term securities such as Treasury bills. No doubt that could be altered, and of course there is a certain convenience in having this power for the purpose of conversion, though the Government controls very considerable other funds, as you know such as savings bank deposits. Still as you said, in so far as the Currency Note Account is concerned the power is useful. And yet, if they were held on Bank of England account they could be used by agreement with the Bank. I do not know how high you put this. Well, I do not think my opinion is worth very much, because I do not know how this thing works out in practice, but it seems to me, for example, that the Treasury should have large resources for paying off issues at maturity and in advance of their maturity.

There are the powers they have under the National Debt Acts and the deposits in the Post Office Savings Bank. I have no information as to the relative importance. If it is rather small, the importance is less, but the aggregate of the assets in the Currency Note Account are so large that I should have thought they would be of very great help in certain circumstances. The really difficult moment has not arrived yet.

The assets are roughly the same as the Savings Bank Account? I should think they are important. Hitherto you have been dealing with rather small conversions, but in the future, between now and 1931, you have some enormous transactions to carry through, and I should suppose that it would be technically helpful in spreading your operations over a long period to have all these reserves.

You would agree that the issue having been transferred to the Bank, you would get very much the same result in practice? I said that if the Bank could be considered as the same thing, the whole of this discussion is not of very much importance. It is merely a change of name.

You said you were in favour of strengthening the connection between the Treasury and the Bank. Would you go on to say there ought to be a Treasury representative on the Bank Court, as there is in many other foreign banks? I think that the Financial Controller of the Treasury ought to be in very close touch with the Committee of Treasury at the Bank without having any power of veto. Whether that is best achieved by making him an ex-officio member or more informally, I think those in closer touch could decide better than I.

You do not suggest that the Treasury or their representative should have the power of veto? No. I think the Treasury should only come in, in deciding what should be the parity of the standard. I do not think the Treasury ought to have a final voice in the method of obtaining parity.

I think you also said that one of the difficulties of amalgamation would be the precise bargain with the Bank of England. You remember that in the Cunliffe Report it is suggested that the Bank of England should surrender all their profits on the note issue. Assuming one was working on that basis, do you think there would be any great difficulty in negotiating with the Bank of England? It is not always easy to say what the profits of the Bank of England are.

The profits on the issue? Even that. The assets of this very large fiduciary issue would necessitate an amount of shifting of the particular assets between this fund and the total assets of the Bank of England. If you try and draw up a formal contract in these matters, which you are quite sure cannot operate disadvantageously to the public interest, you will find it very difficult. The Bank of England often for other reasons has to hold a certain amount of assets that are not very lucrative.

But it would not hold such assets as against the note issue. Why not?

Well, I am assuming that against the note issue they would have to hold Government securities. What kind of Government securities?

You would hesitate to leave to them the choice? Take the simple point that the Bank of England should have a mixed bag of securities—some short-dated, some long-dated, and some intermediate-dated. They do not all bear the same rate of interest. I should also think it is desirable that the Bank should have the power of moving securities backwards and forwards between its various accounts, so that the particular yield of the securities it holds against the notes is not necessarily an accurate measure of the advantages which the Bank of England gets from this. Again I do not attach great importance to this, unless there is something to be gained by it. I think these bargains are difficult to achieve. After all, the Treasury has had experience of bargains with the Bank of England and it is not easy to know exactly what the profit is.

You said there was no means of reducing the fiduciary issue? Of the aggregate.

The two put together? Yes.

Theoretically, you can increase the issue by buying gold? You could not in practice.

It would be too expensive you mean? Yes.

It could be done at a price, but the price would be unreasonable? Yes. It would be a silly thing to do.

I am not questioning that. It could be done.

(MR FARRER) *You made a great point about price stability, i.e., price stability measured in sterling?* Yes; measured in sterling.

If there is a great movement of prices outside this country, I suppose that you would say that is all regulated then by the course of exchange. Yes.

So that if you insisted upon maintaining price stability in this country, you might have a considerable variation in exchange and price movements outside? If there are considerable price movements outside. Supposing America was to indulge in a really big inflation and we did not, sterling would rise quite high above parity.

You would put price stability in this country as more important than exchange stability? Certainly. I think it would be better, both from the point of view of immediate internal conditions and our ultimate credit, that we should not follow America in any inflation that she indulges in.

Of course, it might be with other countries? There would only be a fluctuation in the exchange if the other countries had lost control of credit. I think it is disadvantageous to engage ourselves beforehand to share in any debauch that the rest of the world might be involved in.

That would involve possibly very big fluctuations in the exchange? Only if you were avoiding very big dangers of inflation.

Coming back to the rather practical point of this credit control, you gave Mr Chamberlain a great many reasons which ought to influence the Bank of England Directors in making these changes. Do you think from past experience, looking over the last forty years, that we have had a breed of people who are capable of taking all those considerations and acting upon them, or do you think we shall have to breed a superman to do it? My memory of events does not go back forty years, but I do not foresee any particular difficulty with it. I should not entrust this to the whole body of the Court.

You do not think you are anticipating Paradise in your suggestion. No. I am not changing the methods. If the Directors of the Bank of England are as stupid as some people think they are, our currency will break down in any case. I do not regard my system as intrinsically more difficult. What is more difficult is to manage a credit regime under which gold plays no part in circulation as compared with the medieval system when it was otherwise. That is where the difficulties come. This change, which I propose, I do not think complicates the task, and I should not have the smallest hesitation in thinking that there would be always half a dozen persons in the City well competent to look after it. Once they had started it, they would not find any particular trouble.

Of course, you have to educate your public as well as your City men. You have got to have the great mass of the people all through the country more or less understanding what their policy is. I think the policy is very easy to understand whether it is the gold standard or price stability. The difficulty is to understand the technical means of achieving it, and that has never been understood by the general public. There are two types of banking ability, the type of ability of understanding customers and not lending more than one ought to particular individuals, and on the other hand the central banking mind. You have the type of people who have risen in the world because of their capacity in the first direction, and then later in life they are put into this entirely different sphere of central banking. I should have said that at all dates there have been a considerable number of first-class men of the skilled central banking type of mind. It is on them I think that you would have to draw. If one reads the literature on the bimetallic and other past controversies, I think it is remarkable what an immense amount of ability of this type always has existed.

I suppose you would agree that both as regards credit and currency, the ultimate basis of everything is production. Unless we go on producing and selling at a profit we shall break down? That is the basis of wealth which is the ultimate thing. It is not the basis of [the] price level. You can have a high or low price level with any conditions of wealth.

(CHAIRMAN) *Following on the question Mr Farrer put as to the amount of ability required in the Bank of England for this, you would agree that the ordinary manufacturer, the merchant, even the ordinary exporter, is not a great student of these problems?* Yes.

Certainly the producer very often has very little knowledge at all, if any, of the method by which his accounts are really settled for sales or purchases effected? Very often not.

Do you not think he will be much more puzzled with a stable price and a fluctuating exchange than he would be with a stable exchange and a fluctuating price level? No, I do not think so.

May I say why? The price level will be for him the level of the goods in which he is dealing. It is true that his knowledge is centred on what he knows most about. The exchange, on the other hand, is a thing that he knows less of. He, therefore, wants to eliminate the possibility of what he intends to be a sale becoming a gamble in exchange. At present the price level of his particular commodity is made up of the movements of that commodity relative to other things, in regard to which he may be assumed to be an expert, and movements of the general price level of which he knows nothing. Many of the disasters of recent years have been due to the fact that the particular dealer in a commodity was at fault in the second, while being quite right in the first. With regard to exchange fluctuation, that only influences him in certain portions of his dealings, and by dealing in the forward exchange market he can hedge against it. You have the forward exchange market, through which he can insure against movements of the exchanges, but a forward market in commodities by means of which traders can insure against the risk of movements of prices is limited to two or three of the very biggest trades. Why I want price stability is that it will minimise disastrous losses to traders through no fault of their own, through events which were quite beyond their cognisance.

(CHAIRMAN) *Thank you very much.*

The witness withdrew.

After Keynes gave his evidence to the Committee and presumably in response to the trend of the questioning, as well as in response to recent speeches and articles by Sir Charles Addis, Sir Robert Kindersley and Walter Leaf, he took to the columns of *The Nation.*

From The Nation and Athenaeum, *19 July 1924*

THE POLICY OF THE BANK OF ENGLAND

I. *The new threat of deflation*

In recent weeks two influential directors of the Bank of England, Sir Charles Addis and Sir Robert Kindersley, and the chairman of the Westminster Bank, Dr Leaf, have advocated an immediate policy of deflation with the object of restoring sterling rapidly to its pre-war parity with gold,—thus reversing the policy of Mr Baldwin's 'non-flationist' speech of just a year ago, in which he declared that the right policy was to do all in our power to keep prices steady and on a level.

Of these three authorities only Dr Leaf explained details. His ideas of financial strategy are on the same general lines as M. Poincaré's and would prove about as successful. He believes that the problem of the exchanges can be solved by a temporary, violent agitation of the speculators. M. Poincaré's remedy for the franc was to cause the bears to rush for cover; Dr Leaf's remedy for sterling is to excite the bulls to rush into the open. He thinks that to attract floating funds to London and to cause a belief that sterling is going to appreciate will do the trick, without, apparently, other fundamental adjustments. It was alarming to discover the Poincarist mentality in high quarters here, but reassuring to find a little later that Dr Leaf's lightheadedness was not widely shared in the City.

For a few days Dr Leaf enjoyed a *quasi*-success in the daily newspapers. Mr Snowden, indeed, still sits on the fence, remarking that he must not 'rush in where angels fear to tread', telling a story that 'only two men understand the foreign exchanges, of whom one is dead and the other in a lunatic asylum', and declining to be drawn into a discussion; disappointing confessions from a Labour Chancellor of the Exchequer concerning an issue which almost all authorities from the Cunliffe Committee onwards are agreed in regarding as vitally relevant to employment. But in other quarters clear and decided voices were quickly raised in opposition. The Federation of British Industries petitioned the Bank of England to hear the views of industry before acting. The 'Big Five', led by the Midland Bank, are believed to have urged caution. The weekly press (for the division of opinion nowadays on really important issues is often not between parties, but between the daily press and the weekly press)—*The Nation, The Spectator, The New Leader,* and *The New Statesman*—weighed in with unanimous protests.

It is probable that for the time being the deflationist movement is scotched. To embark, indeed at this time of year and with the present tendencies of employment and sterling prices, on a campaign of rapid deflation to the extent of 10 or 12 per cent would be a crazy policy. In the early stages the excitement of the bulls might provoke a rapid upward movement. But before the final goal was reached, many other difficult and injurious things would have to come about. Let us consider—for the fortification of our position—four of the broad consequences of raising, deliberately and rapidly, the real value of our monetary standard by 10 per cent.

1. The real burden of the national debt would be raised 10 per cent,—equivalent to nearly £40,000,000 on to the Budget; for the payment of the fixed money interest on the debt would mean a greater real sacrifice by the taxpayer. This would come about by the revenue falling along with prices, whilst expenditure for interest charges would be unaltered.

2. Money wages throughout industry would have to be forced down by 10 per cent. This would not mean any reduction in real wages. Nevertheless the disturbance to industrial peace can be easily imagined.

3. If the improvement in the exchange value of sterling were to precede, and move faster than, the adjustment of internal prices, the cost to foreign purchasers of our staple exports, coal textiles, and goods of iron and steel, would have to be enforced by depression and increased unemployment in our export industries.

4. All producers of goods would receive warning that their commodities would (on the average) depreciate in price during the period of production, so that they would be better advised to cease or curtail output for the time being. All prospective purchasers of goods would be told that they would buy cheaper

by waiting and withholding their orders. All persons and companies contemplating new capital developments would put off their projects. For the fear of falling prices is bad enough;—the certainty *must* aggravate unemployment and retard productive activity.

A cheerful programme! Is it appropriate to the aspirations of a Labour Government? Would its execution enhance the prestige and the authority of the City? Would the public fall down and worship the gold standard with gratitude and awe?

These results would not follow from a rise of the sterling exchange in itself, if this were brought about slowly by the depreciation of gold, that is by rising prices in America. But they are the admitted results of a declared programme of forced deflation.

A new theory can never win its way in the field of practical affairs unless it is illuminated by vivid facts and supported by events. Those who subscribe to price stability as a deliberate policy are still in a minority; but recent weeks have shown what a weight of popular opinion, when it comes to practice, is thrown on their side.

II. *The Bank rate*

The policy of monetary control will be done an ill service if we allow the instrument of Bank rate to become associated in the public mind with the hated policy of deflation. Sooner or later—and perhaps fairly soon—a higher Bank rate may be required in order to preserve our position. When that time comes, the Governor of the Bank of England will need all the support he can get. There are always strong natural forces tending towards inflation. On this occasion monetary reformers have had to throw their influence against the fanatics of deflation, who would like to cut us with knives; next time it may be on the other side—against those who would intoxicate us with inflation. One has only to look back on Bank rate policy since the War to see that most harm has been done by not putting up the Bank rate soon enough.

It would be a serious blunder to raise the Bank rate now,—and a disastrous one if it was to be interpreted as a first move towards deflation. But I appreciate the underlying trend of events which is causing responsible authorities to be watching for the time when dearer money will be necessary. I think that they are right to be anxious, and that they should be helped to act promptly when the time comes.

The chief criterion for raising Bank rate in present circumstances can be explained quite briefly. Internal conditions at the moment—employment, the state of credit, the trend of prices—all favour cheap money. It is not likely in the near future that conditions will develop at home which call for measures of restriction. The danger signals on this occasion must be looked for abroad. If Bank rate has to be raised, it will be because our financial and economic relations with foreign countries are developing in such a way as to cause later, if they are not checked, a depreciation of the sterling standard.

The extreme cheapness of money in New York is a valuable assistance to us and may save the situation for a time by diverting funds from New York to London. This fact and the great importance of cheap money to the internal situation are powerful reasons for not acting prematurely.

But there are also strong influences working the other way. In spite of abundant funds, New York lends abroad very little, and London remains the chief centre from which the borrowers of the whole world endeavour to draw. Money may be abnormally cheap in New York, but it is abnormally dear in many parts of Europe; and European borrowers are more ready to borrow in sterling than American lenders are to lend in sterling. The Treasury has to purchase large amounts of dollars to meet the American debt, and it is doubtful whether we have yet adjusted our situation to this new burden. We are also reaching a season of the year when the financing of our imports, particularly cotton, is always heavy.

As a result of these influences the sterling–dollar exchange, left to itself, may—probably, not certainly—tend to depreciate. If this movement merely reflected falling dollar prices in America—as in the recent past—there would be no need to complain. But if an adverse movement of the exchanges were to be combined with a tendency of dollar prices to rise, some protective action on our part would be required. Such a contingency is not improbable. It is hard to believe that a few months of very cheap money in the United States will not initiate an upward movement of dollar prices.

The criterion for restrictive action, therefore, is to be looked for in simultaneous tendencies of the sterling exchange to fall and of dollar prices to rise. If this does not happen—and perhaps it won't—no action is needed. If it does happen, the particular method of correction to be employed should be worked out in such a way as to choke off credit to foreign borrowers as much as possible and to trade borrowers at home as little as possible. A situation, in which the external situation points to dear money and the internal situation to cheap money, is inevitably tiresome and difficult to handle. It is a problem of curing a maladjustment of the direction, rather than the amount, of credit, whilst doing as little indirect harm as possible during the process of regaining equilibrium.

From every point of view the only sensible policy, in the interests of the country, is to continue for the present Mr Baldwin's 'non-flationist' policy. This will not prejudge the gold standard question one way or the other. Indeed, a continuance of this policy will probably—by reason of the depreciation of the dollar—bring sterling back to its old parity in due course. It is only then that the controversy between the various monetary schools will really commence as a practical issue. In the meantime the mass of reasonable opinion would like to give trade and industry a chance to prosper, freed alike from the starvation policy of doctrinaire deflationists and from the intoxication policy of short-sighted inflationists.

Keynes sent early copies of his article to several people including Sir Austen Chamberlain, Reginald McKenna, Stanley Baldwin and Sir Charles Addis. Their comments are of interest.

From SIR AUSTEN CHAMBERLAIN, *18 July 1924*

Dear Keynes,

Many thanks for sending me your article. I am just off to the country, but I shall take it with me. I am afraid that on this occasion you have not made a convert of me.

Yours sincerely,
AUSTEN CHAMBERLAIN

From REGINALD MCKENNA, *19 July 1924*

Dear Maynard,

Many thanks for your article on the policy of the Bank of England. It is as good as only J.M.K. could make it. You are quite right in thinking that common-sense has been victorious for the time being. It is interesting for me to see that I took exactly the line you have taken in the last three paragraphs of your article.

Yours ever,
R. MCKENNA

From STANLEY BALDWIN, *22 July 1924*

Dear Keynes,

I always read the articles you are good enough to send me with interest.

I had meant to make a few observations on the 3rd reading of the Finance Bill, but in my position[1] I think I must wait till Chamberlain's Committee (the existence of which is unknown to the general public) has reported.

I want a holiday!

Yours sincerely,
STANLEY BALDWIN

[1] As Leader of the Opposition.

ACTIVITIES 1922–1929

From SIR CHARLES ADDIS, *21 July 1924*

Dear Keynes,

You are a most courteous opponent. I wonder sometimes if we are as far apart as we seem.

Had I a magician's wand I should cause a definite statement to be made, probably in reply to a question in the House of Commons, that H.M. Government has no present intention of interfering with the ordinary course of events by which on the expiry of the Prohibition Act the free export of gold would be resumed on the 1st January 1926.

Second, that as soon as possible thereafter the two issues would be amalgamated by the emission of Bank notes for £1 and 10/- in substitution for the existing currency issue; the limit of the fiduciary issue to be fixed later.

Third, that the Bank would convene at an early date the convention of central banks to concert measures for preventing undue fluctuations in the price of gold.

The effect of such an announcement, if people really believed it, would tend to raise the sterling exchange, probably sharply at first and later more gradually; but, of course, the effect of the announcement would not be permanent unless it were followed up by the appropriate action of the Bank. We must be prepared to use the Bank rate boldly if necessary. I do not think it will be necessary to raise it at present and it might not be necessary at all. It would depend on the relative mutation of prices here and in the U.S.

The way to resume specie payments is to resume. The fear of being denuded of gold in 1821 in England and in 1879 in America proved to be groundless. What happened was that nothing happened. It is not without the bounds of probability that before free exports were resumed, gold might be flowing *in* to this country.

Eighteen months is long enough as a warning to merchants to put their houses in order and adjust their forward contracts. Stocks are low which would mitigate the absolute amount of loss by depreciation. A fall in prices would raise real wages until nominal wages re-acted; they might not re-act at all if, in the interval, trade improved. The export trade might be expected to gain as much by a reduction in production costs as it would lose by a rise in exchange. The burden of debt would be increased, but this is not very serious so long as the payments are internal. The burden of the external debt would depend upon whether the increased gold value of sterling was due to rising dollar prices or falling sterling prices.

Why not wait! Well I would if I thought there was a better chance of getting back to gold later on. Last year it would have been easier to get back

268

to gold than it is now. Is there any reason to believe it will be easier in 1927 or 1928? I do not think so. It seems to me we are drifting in a state of uncertainty which is not good for trade. I think we shall have to depend more and more in this country upon our specialised manufactures, such as shipbuilding and the finer kinds of textiles, but also in our ability to supply the world with cheap freights, banking and insurance. In my own bank, the Hongkong Bank, we are financing through US credit about fifty million gold dollars a month of Eastern products to the States which were formerly almost entirely financed by sterling credits. I do not mean to say that the volume of trade is affected by this tendency but it does affect our commission industries where custom counts for so much. The tendency to fly from sterling, not only on the Continent but also in Egypt and Siam, has been more marked of late. We cannot expect to retain foreign balances here, note reserves &c. in fluctuating sterling. There are also the Dominions, who have a special interest in the matter, to be considered.

I regard, therefore, the case for a return to gold as urgent. I quite agree we should act prudently and with due regard to the circumstances. I do not agree with Leaf in his single proposal to raise the Bank rate to 5%, or with Schuster in his proposal to amalgamate the note issues before we have got back to gold. The policy must be judged as a whole and can only be successfully carried out by a series of interdependent acts. As a Director of the Bank of England, I am precluded from doing anything more than dealing in generalities. I cannot, at any rate at the present stage, advocate in public any particular plan of resumption. However much I might safeguard it by asserting that it was merely an expression of my personal opinion, there would be the usual insinuations that I was speaking for the Court; but I am under no restrictions in the freedom of private intercourse and I think you will admit that my plan offers the advantage of as little disturbance as possible. There is nothing to be done but to allow the Prohibition of Export of Gold Act quietly to expire when it comes to an end on the 31st December, 1925, and not to renew it. No legislation is required, except an Act to authorise the issue of £1 notes by the Bank of England; the Genoa Conference has already provided for the convention of central banks. The whole thing is largely psychological. If we say that we are going to resume the free export of gold and say it in such a way that people will believe it, you can take it as good as done. I think I ought to have your sympathy in the attempt to get back to gold since, as you justly observe, it is only after that that the real monetary controversy will begin!

Forgive this prolixity and believe me sincerely and always gratefully yours.

C. L. ADDIS

To SIR CHARLES ADDIS, *25 July 1924*

Dear Addis,

Very many thinks for your letter of July 21st. I am extremely glad to have a pretty full statement of your present point of view, and am relieved to find that you are not in sympathy with what I have described as 'Leaf's Light-headedness'

All the same, the proposals you outline do terrify me very considerably. I quite agree that if we think it worth while to make the necessary sacrifices there will be no insuperable difficulty in our returning to the former parity with the dollar within the next 18 months. I also think it not at all unlikely that this result will come about without any particular sacrifice on our part, merely by the depreciation of the dollar. Nevertheless, I do think it most unwise to anticipate events which cannot be foreseen with certainty. It seems to me that the relaxation of the embargo on the free export of gold ought to follow events and not precede them. To commit ourselves to such a thing in advance without knowing whether events would favour such a course or not, or whether we should be able in fact to carry such a thing through, strikes me as imprudent. But apart from the question of imprudence, the notion of what you describe as an 18 months' warning to merchants to put their houses in order strikes me as a ruinous proposal. Either the Government's announcement is believed and the future is discounted immediately in the rate of exchange, in which case we suffer all the torments of a violent and sudden deflation; or else the Government's announcement is disbelieved, or only half believed, in which case we have a slow movement with the expectation of a further movement in the same direction, the effect of which on trade and employment hardly bears thinking about. It is not simply a question of merchants and forward contracts and the like. As soon as the business world has good reason to believe that prices are likely to fall, no course is open to it except to contract its engagements, draw in its horns and go out of business as far as may be until the funest process is over.

To risk all these misfortunes merely for the sake of linking up the London and New York money markets, and so facilitating the work of international financiers—for this in my judgment is all it comes to—is going to lay the City and the Bank of England open to popular attacks the violence of which might be very great. It seems to me most unwise to act in such a way at the present juncture as to suggest that the interests of industry are being subordinated to those of international finance. I think this, although I agree with you that our profits from international finance are very great,—though I am not at all sure that we do not make more money out of the Americans and others in fluctuating conditions than in stable conditions, since they are generally wrong and we are generally right as to the prospective course of events. (This is not an argument I should use, but it is relevant when the question of the profitableness of international business is used as an argument.)

One further point. Are you quite sure that the rigid linking up of the London and New York money markets is all honey? The magnitude of the New York money market is quite different in relation to ours to what it was in pre-war days and in pre-Federal Reserve Bank days. The chances of redundancy of credit there on a great scale are also increased. Are you sure that you want London to be at any time the dumping ground of unlimited cheap American money liable to be withdrawn at a day's notice? It means that we should become without any power of helping ourselves, the victim of every inflationary boom that America may indulge in,—and that she will indulge in such from time to time is surely a probability.

However, all this is much too big a matter to discuss in a letter. The more I spend my thoughts on these matters, the more alarmed do I become at seeing you and the others in authority attacking the problems of the changed post-war world with—I know you will excuse my saying so—unmodified pre-war views and ideas. To close the mind to the idea of revolutionary improvements in our control of money and credit is to sow the seeds of the downfall of individualistic capitalism. Do not be the Louis XVI of the monetary revolution. For surely it is certain that enormous changes will come in the next twenty years, and they will be bad changes, unwisely and even disastrously carried out, if those of us who are at least agreed in our ultimate objects and are aiming at the stability of society cannot agree in putting forward safe and sound reforms.

I am now told by a good many friends that I have become a sort of disreputable figure in some quarters because I do not agree with the maxims of City pundits. But you know I ought not to be so considered really! I seek to improve the machinery of society not overturn it.

Ever yours sincerely,
[copy initialled] J.M.K.

In the next week's *Nation* a correspondent, who signed himself Monetary Reformer, took one statement from Keynes's article, that suggested that a policy of price stability would probably bring sterling to par with the dollar, at which time the controversy over monetary standards would really become a serious practical issue (above p. 266). He then went on to remark that if Keynes had said this in his *Tract* he would now have more influence in the City. Keynes replied immediately below the letter.

From The Nation and Athenaeum, *26 July 1924*

I fear that I must disappoint your amiable correspondent. My *Nation* article represented no change of view. If Mr Baldwin's 'non-flationist' policy, i.e., policy of price stability, is continued by general consent, those who favour this policy have no practical grievance. It is only if and when this course results in a return to parity with the dollar that, on the one hand, the removal of the embargo on the export of gold becomes feasible, and, on the other, the obligation of our Mint to receive unlimited quantities of gold becomes dangerous. That is what

I had in mind in writing the sentence which your correspondent italicises. I am aware how dreadfully easy it would be to recover what your correspondent calls 'influence in the City';—he must not tempt me to burn incense in that neighbourhood!

The same week, he contributed an unsigned leader on wheat.

From The Nation and Athenaeum, *26 July 1924*

WHEAT

Perhaps the most important events in recent weeks, transcending Dawes Reports, Housing Bills, Revolutions in Brazil, and Presidential Elections, has been the world-wide rise in the price of wheat.

In this country the price of flour has risen from 38s. a sack last March to 46s. 6d. today, or about 22 per cent. So far British wheat has not shared fully in the increase of price in the exporting countries. At a price of about 51s. per quarter, it is 3s. above the price of a month ago and 3s. 6d. above last year's price. It is also approaching its right figure in relation to other commodities, judged on the pre-war basis. Abroad, however, the rise has been much more sensational. Northern Manitoba wheat is now 10s. 6d. a quarter above its price of a year ago The rise in Argentine wheat has been about equivalent. The dollar price of wheat in Chicago is now 30 per cent above its price at this time last year, at nearly 128 cents a bushel as compared with 97 cents a year ago and 84 cents in 1913.

All through the past year the supplies of wheat available in the world have been ample, and the rise in price is entirely due to a prospective reduction of supplies rather than to any shortage at the moment. Indeed, the carry-over at the date of the beginning of the current harvest will be bigger than for many years past. The anticipations of the market are mainly due to two causes. In Canada the crop, whilst by no means bad compared with the average of previous years, will not reach the remarkable bumper figures of the past two years;—the latest estimate is for 319,000,000 bushels as compared with 474,000,000 last year. Elsewhere, and particularly in the United States, the fact that the price of wheat recently has been unremunerative to the farmers has led to a general curtailment of the production of this particular commodity, not anywhere on a sensational scale but appreciable in the aggregate.

It is too early as yet to say whether the final outcome of the harvest will be such as to justify the current predictions of the market or whether the high prices lately established will be sustained through the heavy selling period of the autumn months. But it is quite possible that we are on the eve of the fundamental adjustment which many authorities have been anticipating for the past two or three years.

It is clear that compared with the years before the War the price of wheat, and to a lesser extent of some other agricultural products, has tended to be too low as compared with the prices of manufactured articles, with the result that the agricultural sections of the international market have been considerably impoverished. Some part of the so-called lack of purchasing power overseas has been attributable to this fact. It has been difficult for the farmers to know how to readjust their relative economic situation, and the process has not been rapid. But the readjustment, if it has now arrived, will be an economic event of the first magnitude.

As regards Great Britain, the effects are likely to be of opposed kinds. On the one hand, the cost of our imported supplies will be immensely enhanced, as can be easily calculated from the figure of 29 million quarters as the approximate total of our necessary imports. On the other hand, the transfer of purchasing power into the hands of the farming communities of the world may have far-reaching effects in the stimulation of markets for certain types of goods. The change, moreover, opens out for British agriculture a prospect of relief from the depression which has long lain over it. Last September we ventured to predict, in the face of momentarily adverse tendencies, that our agriculture would obtain relief in this way before very long, pointing out that 'with the staple products of the world's harvests...it is often but a short step from a condition of apparently overwhelming abundance to one of dangerous scarcity'.

We draw the attention of our readers to a matter rather outside our usual field, because the readjustment between the interests of agriculture and industry throughout the world is the kind of event which often receives from the public much less attention than it deserves until the movement is almost over and is passing into history.

On 2 August 1924, at a session of the Liberal Summer School in Oxford, Keynes raised another issue which he had touched on earlier in the columns of *The Nation*, foreign lending. His remarks appeared in full a week later.

From The Nation and Athenaeum, *9 August 1924*

FOREIGN INVESTMENT AND NATIONAL ADVANTAGE

The established system, which we take as a matter of course, of being just about as willing to invest our savings abroad as at home, is not very ancient and is practised nowhere else. (France followed the same system for twenty years before the war; today Great Britain is in this habit unique in the whole world.) The belief that existing practice in this matter must coincide with the national advantage, which is a part of the orthodoxy of the day, certainly has historical roots. Whether it has also intellectual roots is the subject of my discourse today.

The hazarding of capital resources in foreign parts for trading, mining, and exploitation is an immemorial practice, which has generally proved of immense financial benefit to

275

nations with the courage, the temperament, and the wealth to follow it. For the English and the Scotch it has been, beyond doubt, the foundation of their national fortunes. The risks are recognised to be great, but the profits are proportionate. Nor are the total sums, which it is necessary to embark in such enterprises, a burdensome proportion of the public wealth. Nothing that I say here must be interpreted as casting a doubt upon the national advantage of investments of this kind.

The next development of foreign investment virtually began with the railway age,—that is to say, the use of British capital to build public-utility works abroad. The railways of the New World and even of parts of Europe could not have been built when they were, except with the aid of the mid-nineteenth-century savings of the British middle classes. These investments, too, probably, in their day, redounded to the national advantage. We did not, as a rule, lend the money to foreign corporations or governments. We built the railways ourselves with British engineering skill, with our own iron and steel, and rolling stock from our own workshops. We opened up lands and territories from which, indirectly by subsidiary enterprises, we drew additional wealth, and we made possible for ourselves the supply of cheap food from overseas. But already before the War such investments, which had extended beyond railways to harbours, tramways, waterworks, gasworks, and power stations, were becoming precarious. The practice was beginning of controlling the rates charged by such undertakings, and hence the profits earned, thus depriving the investor of the possibility of large profits to balance the never-absent risk of loss. But, further, a jealousy of the foreign investor was growing up, and a tendency to treat him with less than fairness. I believe that there are now very few countries in the world in which a public utility undertaking mainly owned by foreigners is secure of fair treatment. The cases of ruinously unfair treatment are so numerous that any typical pre-war investor in such things has suffered heavy losses.

The third leading type of foreign investment consists of loans to governments and local authorities abroad. These loans have a fairly ancient history, but on a great scale they also are quite modern. They reached their utmost limit of magnitude and of imprudence in France in the twenty years preceding the War. No investments have ever been made so foolish and so disastrous as the loans of France to Russia, and on a lesser scale, to the Balkans, Austria, Mexico, and Brazil, between 1900 and 1914. They represented a great proportion of the national savings of the country, and nearly all has been lost.

Indeed, it is probable that loans to foreign governments have turned out badly on balance—especially at the low rates of interest current before the War. The investor has no remedy—none whatever—against default. There is, on the part of most foreign countries, a strong tendency to default on the occasion of wars and revolutions and whenever the expectation of further loans no longer exceeds in amount the interest payable on the old ones. Defaults, in fact, are world-wide and frequent. The Southern States of U.S.A., Mexico, all Central America, most of South America, China, Turkey, Egypt, Greece, the whole of the Balkans, Russia, Austria, Hungary, Spain, and Portugal have all defaulted in whole or in part at one time or another.

Who can maintain that the indirect national advantages of such loans are great, many of which have been employed to wage wars and without which the wars could not have been carried on? There is much good sense in the attitude of American investors, who expect from 8 to 12 per cent interest on such loans, and do not like them even then.

Let me give one instance for which I happen to have the aggregate figures. British investors have advanced to the governments, local authorities, and public enterprises of Brazil about £250,000,000. This yields at present a precarious rate of interest of barely 4 per cent, and, allowing for the fall in the value of money since the investment was made, about $2\frac{1}{2}$ per cent.

Thus it is doubtful whether in the past loans to foreign

governments and public utility undertakings have been really advantageous. Yet in the future the motives tending towards repudiation, partial or complete, may become much stronger. At present many of our debtors, especially in the Dominions, borrow afresh each year more than the interest on previous loans. So long as this is the case, the motive to repudiation is clearly non-existent. But in the long run, partly from the mere operation of compound interest, partly perhaps from our not having so large a surplus to lend abroad, this will cease. Our difficulties on a grand scale will then begin. The representatives of the Soviet Government, lately in London, have expounded with their accustomed frankness the connection between the acknowledgment of old loans and the receipt of new ones. But it is only in their greater frankness (this, indeed, is the head and front of their offence) that they differ from many other governments.

In short, the nineteenth century, as in so many other respects, came to look on an arrangement as normal which was really most abnormal. To lend vast sums abroad for long periods of time without any possibility of legal redress if things go wrong, is a crazy construction; especially in return for a trifling extra interest.

What is the old-fashioned answer to this?—That the investor is capable of looking after himself; that present arrangements allow him to place his resources where they will bring him the greatest net return; that in this way the national income will become greatest.

Why do I question this answer?—Because I doubt (1) whether the investor is capable of looking after himself and whether the present organisation of investment is such as to protect the individual investor's self-interest; and (2) whether, even in so far as the individual gains, it follows that the national income as a whole is thereby maximised.

My remarks so far have been chiefly directed to the question of what advantages have actually been gained, in the light of experience, by foreign investment in its latest phases. No one who has examined typical lists of investments made by middle-class investors in pre-war days would lightly maintain that, in practice, the investor has proved capable of looking after himself. Large resources, painfully gained and saved, have been spilt on the ground. But there is also something to be said about the bias in favour of investment in particular directions caused by existing laws and practices.

I call attention in particular to the present operation of the Trustee Acts. These Acts in their present form provide an artificial stimulus on a great scale to foreign investment within the Empire. The phenomenon is a fairly recent one; imperial piety has silenced tongues and criticism; and its results do not receive enough attention.

Before 1889 Consols was the only security in which trustees could invest, failing special powers. The present state of affairs dates from the Colonial Stock Act of 1900, which, in effect, brought almost all the loans of colonial governments within the field of authorised trustee investments. Some further change, beyond the extensions allowed in 1889, was evidently required to compensate [for] the gradually diminishing volume of Consols and the steadily increasing volume of trustee funds. But since the War this ground holds good no longer, and it is only now, twenty-four years later, that we feel the consequences of the change.

Loans to colonial governments now amount to about £670,000,000 and to the Government of India £260,000,000— say £900,000,000 altogether. This amount is being added to at a great rate,—since the beginning of 1922 £60–70 millions a year, net addition. Thus we are not only reinvesting the whole of the interest due to us on existing loans (say, £35–40 millions), but adding to it nearly as much again.

It is not true that these great sums flow abroad as the result of a free and enlightened calculation of self-interest. They flow as the result of a particular social organisation which—for the most part unintentionally—gives a bias in this direction.

A considerable proportion of the growing wealth of the

community accrues in the hands of individuals or of corporations which by law or by strong custom and convention are compelled to invest the whole or the bulk of it in the trustee group of securities. They are limited in their choice to what securities are available within this group. It follows that, if, in any year, there is no net increase in the amount of home trustee stocks, the *whole* of the annual increased savings available for investment in this form is *compelled* to go abroad. If, by reason of the repayment of Government debt, there is actually a decrease in the available home securities, the compulsion to invest abroad is even more stringent.

Incidentally, it is worth noting that to pay off our own Government debt out of the proceeds of taxation, without at the same time providing a supply of home trustee investments to take its place, involves taking money by taxation out of the hands of persons who might invest in home enterprises of a non-trustee type and transferring it to another type of person who cannot help investing the proceeds in trustee investments abroad.

It follows from this that large sums may flow abroad without there having been a vestige of deliberate calculation on the part of anybody that this is the best way of employing the resources in the national interest.

There is a further reason why the Colonial Stock Act of 1900 favours unduly the exportation of capital. Some colonial governments undertake as a government service many public-utility enterprises, such as harbours, which are not so undertaken in Great Britain. It follows that money for such undertakings abroad can be raised more easily and cheaply in London than for similar and equally profitable undertakings at home. For example, loans for harbour works in New South Wales can be borrowed more cheaply in London than loans for the Port of London itself, merely because the former, being undertaken by the Government of New South Wales, represent a trustee investment, whereas the loans of the Port of London Authority, although a public body, do not fall within the trustee category.

In general, any service in the colonies which is socialised can be financed more cheaply by means of British savings than any service at home which is not socialised. Yet who would maintain that it is always in our national interest to finance the former rather than the latter?

Merely on the financial side, the Trustee Acts, by creating a monopoly with a bias against new home investments, are probably worth not less than £20,000,000 a year to the Dominions and India.

These are my most fundamental criticisms against such foreign investments as are made, not on their merits, but as a result of the Trustee Acts. But there is also another objection. The Trustee Acts lull trustees and others into a false sense of security. It is felt that all such investments are, in a sense beyond criticism. Yet it is really very doubtful whether, in the long run, they are as safe as is supposed.

In some cases these loans are becoming dangerously large in relation to the population and the wealth of the borrowing communities. So long as we renew maturing loans when they fall due, and lend in addition twice the amount required to meet the interest on previous loans, the capacity and integrity of the borrowers to meet their liabilities is obviously altogether untested. But this cannot go on for ever. Can we feel perfectly confident in every case that the obligations will be met in their entirety? I will not raise heat and controversy by instancing the name of any colony. But is it right to leave trustees to suppose that the long-dated securities of the Government of India are wholly free from risk,—that these are better investments, where safety is the first consideration, than (for example) the debentures, or even the first preference stocks, of English industrial enterprises whose names are household words?

Perhaps the limit of the absurdity, to which the Trustee Acts can lead, was reached early this year when £2,000,000 was borrowed by Southern Rhodesia on about the same terms as a large English borough would have to pay, more cheaply than the Port of London, and much more cheaply than most of our great industrial and commercial undertakings at home Southern Rhodesia is a place somewhere in the middle of Africa with a handful of white inhabitants and not even so many, I believe, as one million savage black ones. The security has no British Government guarantee behind it; yet unless such is implied the terms of the loan were farcical.

Thus the effect of the Trustee Acts is to starve home developments by diverting savings abroad and, consequently, to burden home borrowers with a higher rate of interest than they would need to pay otherwise.

A practical remedy is not far to seek. I would repeal the existing Trustee Acts and provide that no new issues, not carrying a British Government guarantee, should be added to the list except by special licence of the Treasury in each case. The Treasury should then use its power of licence to widen the list of admissible home investments and strictly to ration overseas borrowers. (Incidentally this would greatly assist the Treasury in protecting the gilt-edged market for its heavy impending conversions.) Further, the Treasury should be careful not to redeem debt, except when there is a need of new loans for home developments of a type suitable for inclusion in the list of trustee investments. This should be the criterion for the rate of reduction of the dead-weight debt. When there is no need of further liquid resources for investment in this particular sort of way, the money should be left in the hands of the taxpayer to find an outlet in other types of expenditure and investment.

I am afraid that I have not succeeded in separating so clearly as I had intended those of my arguments which relate to the private interest of the investor from those which relate to the public interest. But I will conclude with two of the latter type.

Consider two investments, the one at home and the other abroad, with equal risks of repudiation or confiscation or legislation restricting profit. It is a matter of indifference to the individual investor which he selects. But the nation as a whole retains in the one case the object of the investment and the fruits of it; whilst in the other case both are lost. If a loan to improve a South American capital is repudiated, we have nothing. If a Poplar housing loan is repudiated, we as a nation, still have the houses. If the Grand Trunk Railway of Canada fails its shareholders by reason of legal restriction of the rates chargeable or for any other cause, we have nothing. If the underground system of London fails its shareholders, Londoners still have their underground system.

With home investment, even if it be ill-advised or extravagantly carried out, at least the country has the improvement for what it is worth. The worst conceived and most extravagant housing scheme imaginable leaves us with some houses. A bad foreign investment is wholly engulfed.

My last argument relates to the reaction of foreign investment on our exports. It is often said to be the primary and sufficient justification of such investment that it stimulates our exports. This is quite true. But I see no special virtue in exports for their own sake, which are not required to pay for desired imports. The notion that the great thing is to get rid of goods out of the country is not sensible. Investment abroad stimulates employment by expanding exports. Certainly. But it does not stimulate employment a scrap more than would an equal investment at home.

Not only is there no special virtue in stimulating export for its own sake;—there is vice in it. For foreign investment does not automatically expand our exports by a corresponding amount. It so affects the foreign exchanges that we are *compelled* to export more in order to maintain our solvency. It may be the case—I fancy that it now is the case—that we can only do this by lowering the price of our products in terms of the products of other nations, that is by allowing the ratio of real interchange to move to our disadvantage. The more we have to force the volume of our exports, the lower the price which we have to accept for them.

A state of affairs, arising out of the arrangements of the

investment market and disconnected from the equilibria of trade and industry, which causes a bias in favour of, and may overstimulate, foreign investment, is capable of doing us a great deal of injury in the terms on which we conduct our international trade. It may be that we should do much better to be content with a volume of exports sufficient to pay for our imports, and to divert our surplus resources of capital and labour into the manifold improvements at home waiting to be carried out.

Our present system dates from a time when we had a surplus of savings which we could invest *much* more profitably abroad than at home and when the demand for our exports was highly elastic. The convention has continued, and its effects have been aggravated by the operation of the Trustee Acts, into a period when the benefit of such investment measured in rates of interest is greatly diminished, when the amount of our available surplus is diminished, and when the demand for our exports is weakened.

Last year we invested abroad about two-thirds of what passed through the investment markets, and probably between half and a third of our total savings. I believe that most of this could have been usefully employed at home, and indeed must be so employed in future, if our national equipment is to grow as fast as our population and our theoretical standards of life.

The issue of *The Nation* for 9 August also contained a letter from a Mr W. H. J. Woodward asking for an explanation for the rise in the Bank of England's gold stock since 1914, since when the commodity price of gold had been above the Bank's statutory buying price. Using a pseudonym he was to use in future, Keynes replied.

From The Nation and Athenaeum, *16 August 1924*

Sir,

Your correspondent Mr Woodward inquires where the Bank of England's new accessions of gold come from. I hazard two suggestions. Old ladies still fish golden sovereigns out of their stockings sometimes. Divers, each season, fish up quite a quantity of them out of the wreck of the 'Laurentic' off the coast of Ireland. Formerly the old ladies, latterly the 'Laurentic', have been the chief suppliers.

Yours &c.,

SIELA

At the suggestion of the editor of *The Manchester Guardian Commercial* and in response to some comments by 'A Stockbroker' in that newspaper, Keynes elaborated on his Oxford speech.

From The Manchester Guardian Commercial, *21 August 1924*

HOME VERSUS FOREIGN INVESTMENT

Further suggestions for revision of trustee list

In my address to the Liberal Summer School at Oxford I dealt briefly with several connected, but partly distinct, questions relating to our British policy of foreign investment. The interesting comments by A Stockbroker, in the *M.G. Commercial* for August 14, on what I had to say about the Trustee Acts encourage me to develop a little further this section of my paper.

My complaints against the present arrangements were, first, that they provide an artificial stimulus to overseas investment on a greater scale than is truly in the national interest, and, second, that they sometimes lull trustees into a false sense of security and are made an excuse for a lack of discrimination between one investment and another within the privileged list. I do not propose to repeat or develop here my reasons for these and other conclusions in my original paper, but, assuming that there is some substance in them, to consider what practical steps are desirable.

I suggested at Oxford that no new securities should be admitted to the trustee list unless either they carried a British

285

Government guarantee or they had obtained a special licence from the Treasury. I suggested, further, that the licence system should be used in practice to ration overseas borrowers and to widen the categories of admissible home securities. A Stockbroker, whilst sympathetic to some of my ideas, criticises very keenly any system of special Treasury licences as something which would never be tolerated in this country after our war experience of Treasury control of new issues. For this reason he would go farther than I did, and allow no additions to the list except where there is a British Government guarantee.

I admit that there is a great deal in what he says. A licence system would be troublesome to work in practice, and might be open to pressure on political grounds or to charges of partiality. I suggested it partly as a compromise, but partly because I attached importance to increasing the number of eligible home securities, yet feared that it might be difficult to define in advance precisely what categories should be included. On reconsideration, I think that my main object might be attained without introducing the objectionable system of licences.

I suggest, therefore, that the list of eligible trustee investments should be constituted in future on the following principles:—

(1) All existing trustee stocks would, of course, remain; but I would differ from A Stockbroker in also allowing replacement loans. I think that it would be anomalous to have a colonial government issuing two identical loans, one of which was non-trustee, yet the other a trustee investment for purely historical reasons quite unrelated to the security obtained by the investor. It would be better to let the old system gradually work itself out.

(2) All securities carrying a British Government guarantee would be in this list, but I should certainly include also British corporation and county stocks, subject to the same conditions as at present. (Perhaps A Stockbroker did not really mean to exclude the latter.)

(3) I attach great importance to giving the status of trustee

investment to the prior securities of the great public utility undertakings of the future. The danger of such enterprises being starved in favour of socialised public works in the colonies is one of my chief grounds of complaint against the present system. Just as in the past we have included the prior securities of British railways in the list, in spite of their being privately owned, so I should like to aid the flow of capital in the future into British ports, harbours, canals, motor roads, gasworks, waterworks, electric power stations, and the like, even though private initiative and methods of management continue to take some part in them. The prior securities of the Port of London, which I instanced, and of the Manchester Ship Canal, which A Stockbroker instances, are glaring cases. Centralised electric power stations, serving large areas within which they exercise exclusive rights, are likely to furnish in the near future important examples of what I have in mind. What will be the best way of dealing with these?

One way would be to include in the trustee list all bonds of public-utility undertakings of specified types which can be certified by the appropriate Government department as satisfying certain specified conditions. This might, in practice, get very near to the licence system which I suggested at first.

A second way might be found on the lines of the Trade Facilities Act, by which an actual British Government guarantee might be accorded in approved cases. A variant of the last, which is worth considering, might consist in charging the enterprise $\frac{1}{4}$ per cent per annum in return for a British Government guarantee, which would be paid into a reserve fund against which would be charged any outgoings in cases where the guarantee might become operative.

At any rate, the privilege of inclusion in the trustee list should be confined henceforward to home securities, since it is no longer in the least necessary to go outside these in order to obtain an adequate supply; nor should it be given in any case in which the security to the investor is not absolutely gilt-edged. If, on grounds of public advantage, it is thought desirable to give special encouragement to a capital investment, at home or abroad, which involves some risk, the trustee investor shall not be expected to assist without the security of a British Government guarantee.

The Governments of India and of the Dominions would, of course, be free to borrow, like anyone else, on the open market on such terms as their credit might be deemed to justify.

During the summer of 1924 the Commission of Gold and Silver Inquiry of the United States Senate asked Keynes for a memorandum on currency policy. After some discussion with John Parke Young of the Commission, Keynes finally replied.

To JOHN PARKE YOUNG, *15 September 1924*

Dear Mr Young

I have your letter of August 26th and enclose a brief memorandum for your Report. I have been in two minds whether to write anything, because it is so difficult to put one's views clearly in a short space. You will see that I have limited myself practically to one point. My feeling is that the United States will probably require a fairly severe dose of facts before they will have a ready ear for theories. If facts go in the opposite direction from what I anticipate, the situation will of course be changed. But if they go as I think they will, then will be the time for pointing out again the possibility of something a trifle more sensible than the existing state of affairs.

Yours very truly,
[copy initialled] J.M.K.

THE UNITED STATES AND GOLD[2]

The problem of the gold standard and of price stabilisation covers so wide a field, that one must either deal with it at considerable length, or select one or two points for special comment. Since I have written recently a book (*A Tract on Monetary Reform*) which gives my views on some parts of the subject, and since I hope in the course of the next year to write a further book which will develop these views more fully, I hope I may be excused if in this memorandum I limit myself to certain particular points, without arguing the general question.

The United States is admittedly accepting into her mints gold which she does not require. She is admittedly sterilising this gold from producing its full effect on the creation of credit and of prices. The results of this are: (1) to involve her in expense through the purchase of the gold and (2) to maintain the commodity value of gold at a higher level than it would otherwise have.

I think that this situation can be correctly described by saying that the United States is undertaking a valorisation scheme for gold, analogous to similar schemes which have been undertaken in the past for other commodities; that is to say, she maintains the commodity value of gold by taking off the market at a certain price such quantities of it as cannot find another buyer at that price. The scheme is unique in one respect, in that the bulk of the gold in the world is mined outside the United States, so that the valorisation scheme is mainly in the interests of foreign producers.

This policy on the part of the United States has not, however, been undertaken deliberately or explicitly, and it may be abandoned or it may break down at any time through the weight of gold influencing, after all, the creation of credit and the level of prices.

---

[2] Eventually published by the Commission in 1925 in a collection entitled *European Currency and Finance*. See below p. 370.

The reasons for this policy may be presumed to be: (1) that the United States, as a large holder of stocks of gold, is interested in protecting the value of these stocks; (2) that there is no alternative to the present policy, except to allow a serious inflation of credit to take place, or to make a new departure which might provoke criticism from conservative opinion; (3) because it is thought to be in the interests of the world that the gold standard should be restored, and that America's action is in the interests of herself and of other countries in that it prevents an obvious breakdown of the gold system during the transitional period; (4) because American opinion believes that the necessity of the valorisation scheme is likely to be temporary, and will come to an end shortly.

May I direct one or two comments to the two last of these reasons? As regards the third, if the United States is prepared to undertake the expense of providing the world with a stable gold currency, she would be performing a considerable service. I doubt, however, whether she would be prepared to do so if it would probably involve her in a permanent expense, one year with another, of perhaps as much as 200 million dollars per annum. Moreover, if the purchase of redundant gold has to be continued year in, year out, it will become more and more obviously absurd that the United States should pay this large sum in order to remunerate gold miners, mainly in South Africa, for laboriously extracting from the earth metal that is not wanted at the price.

It is doubtful therefore whether the third motive would operate unless the fourth motive operated also. At present this is the case, since, so far as one can judge, almost everyone in America believes that the present situation is temporary and will cease to exist as soon as an event known as 'the restoration of the gold standard' has taken place. This popular belief assumes that, if the currencies of other countries in the world were to be maintained at a gold parity, this would greatly increase the demand of those countries on the stock of the world's gold. I believe this to be a misapprehension. It is not lack of gold, but the absence of other internal adjustments, which prevents the leading European countries from returning to a pre-war gold standard. Most of them have plenty of gold for the purpose as soon as the other conditions favourable to the restoration of a gold standard have returned.

The following figures illustrate this point. The Cunliffe Committee fixed on the figure of £150,000,000 in the Bank of England and currency note reserves together as representing a sufficient figure for the maintenance of the gold standard in Great Britain. The actual gold reserve at present is £155,000,000. France has about the same amount of gold as before the War. Italy and Belgium have rather more than they had before the War. The Scandinavian countries and Holland have three times as much gold as in 1914; Switzerland two and a half times as much; and Spain five times as much. The Bank of Japan (in foreign balances and bullion together) has nearly five times as much. I do not think it can be argued that a single one of these countries requires a larger gold reserve than they now have in order to maintain a gold standard, even after allowing for the fact that gold has depreciated in value by 33 per cent. In the case of Russia, Germany, Austria and Hungary the gold reserves have been greatly depleted, but it is not likely that these countries would be able to afford, or even that they would think it worth while to afford, large purchases of gold in the near future; though they may absorb a certain amount gradually— particularly Russia. Moreover, the spread of the practice of keeping reserves in the form of interest-bearing balances in foreign centres, in place of barren gold, further diminishes the need of actual holdings of bullion on the part of progressive countries.

If none of the above countries absorbs large quantities of gold, where is the relief to the United States going to come from? In particular, Great Britain will always be in a position to avoid being forced to accept large quantities of unwanted gold, even in the event of the restoration of the gold standard, by anticipating debt repayments to the United States.

In short, I see no way of absorbing large quantities of gold unless either gold is again used in active circulation, which is not probable anywhere outside the U.S., or prices rise materially.

No doubt the actual amount of importations of gold into the United States will fluctuate from year to year and will be greater in some years than in others. But it seems to me that under the existing system, and unless she allows the redundant gold to take effect on her price level, the United States must look foward more or less permanently to receiving additional gold at the rate of between, say, 150 million and 300 million dollars per annum on the average.

If this view, or anything like it, is correct, I suggest that the United States will become discontented with the position sooner or later. When such discontent comes to a head there is an obvious remedy, namely to close her mints to the unlimited admission of gold and to constitute the American Treasury the only body which has the right to mint gold. This would not interfere with maintaining the full and free convertibility of existing and future United States currency into gold; nor would it prevent additions being made to the stock of gold if circumstances made this seem desirable. It would also be possible to make a concession in favour of American-mined gold if this was politically desirable, without incurring, in view of the relatively small amount of such gold, an undue expense.

In deciding not to keep her mints open to the unlimited reception of gold, regardless of whether or not the gold was required, the United States would, in my judgment, be protecting all her own interests; and I cannot but think it probable that this is the solution on which she will fall back sooner or later. The only reasonable alternative would be to continue the present valorisation scheme but to share the expense of it with other countries. If this could be arranged, which would be difficult, it might work for a time. But, even so, sooner or later it would be seen to be absurd to encourage in this way the mining of useless gold, and that too much was being spent for the mere purpose of keeping up appearances.

J.M.K.

15.9.24

On 27 September Siela made a second appearance in *The Nation*.

Sir,

'A. G. G.' has said in your last issue all that needs to be said on the personal side of the recent affair of the Prime Minister's motor-car. But does not this episode bring to a head the question of the emoluments of the Premiership as an issue of pressing practical importance?

In the eighteenth century the emoluments of office, direct and indirect, were so great that a political career might lead to great wealth. This undesirable state of affairs no longer existed in the nineteenth century, but the salaries were fixed at what, in terms of purchasing power, was a very comfortable figure. No compensation having been given in respect of income tax and super tax, or of the diminished value of money, what is still called £5,000 is worth less than half what it used to be worth; and this has come to pass just at a time when high office is being attained at least as often as not by men without private means; whilst after the War the Prime Minister was deprived even of his official right to a motor-car, merely because similar rights on the part of every jackanapes in the War Office had become a gross abuse.

Is it not essential in the public interest that the Prime Minister should be freed from pecuniary cares whilst in office and enabled to maintain a state of reasonable dignity and comfort? And is it not also essential that he should not be driven to cheap journalism, or the like, to maintain himself when out of office? It is not desirable that an ex-Prime Minister, who will almost certainly continue to perform public duties of high importance, should be compelled at the same time to earn his daily bread as best he can.

A suggestion in last week's *Spectator* that some private person should step forward to endow the Prime Minister is most unsuitable and contrary to the dignity of the state. If the office ought to be endowed, it is Parliament, and Parliament alone, that has the right and the duty to do it. I suggest:—

(1) that the Prime Minister's salary should be £5,000 free of income tax and super tax;

(2) that he should receive a house allowance sufficient to defray the expenses of running No. 10, Downing Street, including a motor-car;

(3) that every ex-Prime Minister who has held office for six months or more should receive, as of right and without question, a pension of £2,000 a year for life.

The abuses arising out of the absence of such provision are far greater than can possibly arise out of making it. Cannot the Liberal Party take steps in the coming sessions to push the matter forward?

Yours, &c.,

SIELA

In the autumn of 1924 Keynes faced another official committee. Late in July he was approached by the Assistant Secretary to the Committee on National Debt and Taxation. This Committee, under the chairmanship of Lord Colwyn, had been set up 'to consider and report on the National Debt and on the incidence of existing taxation, with special reference to their effect on trade, industry, employment and national credit'. After some correspondence with both the Assistant Secretary and the Secretary, during which the Committee received copies of 'Foreign Investment and National Advantage', Keynes appeared before it on 1 October.

THE RETURN TO GOLD AND FOREIGN LENDING

From the Committee on National Debt and Taxation, Minutes of Evidence,
1 October 1924

COMMITTEE ON NATIONAL DEBT AND TAXATION

ELEVENTH DAY

Wednesday 1 October 1924

Present: The Rt. Hon. Lord Colwyn (*Chairman*)

Sir Charles Addis, K.C.M.G.	Mr H. B. Lees-Smith
Sir Alan G. Anderson, K.B.E.	Sir William McLintock, K.B.E.,
Sir Arthur Balfour, K.B.E.	C.V.O.
Mr Henry Bell	Sir Josiah Stamp, G.B.E.
Mr J. W. Bowen	Mrs Barbara Wootton
Mr Fred Bramley	Mr R. G. Hamilton, *Secretary*
Professor Fred Hall	Mr G. Ismay, *Assistant Secretary*
Mr W. L. Hichens	

Mr J. M. Keynes, C.B., called and examined

Evidence-in-chief handed in by Mr Keynes

1. Income tax is especially deterrent to saving in so far as it falls on funds which naturally accumulate at compound interest and where no question of personal expenditure can enter in, e.g., the funds of insurance companies and the reserves retained by joint stock companies to provide further capital against an increase of their business. The latter in particular is increasingly the way by which industry secures additional funds. Since income tax is a tax on income as it accrues, whether in the hands of a corporation or of an individual, whereas super-tax is a personal tax falling upon individuals alone, a redistribution of the burden of taxation, by lowering the standard rate of income tax, bringing the super-tax limit lower, and increasing the super-tax rate, would be the most convenient way of exempting some forms of savings from taxation if it is thought to be in the interests of the community to do that. An expenditure tax, though perhaps theoretically sound is practically impossible. But our British distinction between income tax and super-tax might be so handled as to achieve to some extent the same object.

2. The criterion as to the amount of debt to be held in a short-dated form should, I think, be given by the appetite of the investment market for that type of security. The Government can borrow most cheaply by offering various types of bonds in such proportions as each is required by the

investment market and the money market. A large sum, probably a very large sum, can be borrowed more cheaply in the form of short-term debt periodically renewed, than in the form of long-term debt. It would be a sound policy to maintain the short-dated debt permanently at a high figure if that high figure could be kept afloat at a rate of interest lower (on the average) than the rate on long-term debt. In the case of short-term debt the capital value is guaranteed and the interest is fluctuating; in the case of long-term debt the income is fixed but the capital value is fluctuating. Abstractly there is nothing to be said in favour of the one rather than of the other. The idea that there is something unsafe in maintaining the short-term debt permanently at a high figure is based for the most part on false analogy. I may add that it would probably assist the steadiness of credit if the volume of the short-term debt were to be somewhat reduced in good times and somewhat increased in bad times.

3. Since it is sound policy always to have a certain margin in budgeting, it is right that a certain amount of debt should, if possible, be repaid every year. But it is not advisable to attempt blindly to repay large sums merely on the ground that the debt is something to be got rid of. The idea again is based on false analogy. Repayment of debt out of taxation is partly at the expense of other forms of saving. The higher the taxation becomes the larger is the proportion which is at the expense of saving. But even that part which is at the expense of expenditure is not necessarily in the public interest. If we confine our attention to that part which is at the expense of saving, the effect of the repayment of debt is to drive the savings into a particular channel instead of letting them find their own outlet. When holders of debt are repaid they will probably prefer to re-invest the money in bonds of the gilt-edged type. If, on the other hand, the savings are left in the pockets of the taxpayer there is no such presumption, and they may find their outlet either in industry or in any other way. In present conditions, therefore, a rapid repayment of debt affords an artificial stimulus to savings to flow into the channel of gilt-edged investments. At a time when there is a very heavy demand for this particular type of investment this may be sound policy. For example, if the Local Loans Authorities, or Borough and County Authorities, are involved in heavy expenditure for housing or public works, which they can only cover by borrowing in the gilt-edged market, then a simultaneous repayment of national debt by the Treasury may be just the right thing to do. But it is not necessarily right in all circumstances. If the supply of new gilt-edged securities is limited, thus indicating that the demand for capital by borrowers of that type is not extensive then repayment of national debt on a large scale may be very harmful. This sort of consideration should weigh more than the mere idea that blind repayment of debt must be good for its

own sake. To take money from industry and from individuals by taxation and give it back to the gilt-edged section of the Stock Exchange, regardless of whether there is a ready outlet for it there, is injudicious.

4. In an address which I delivered recently, and copies of which have, I understand, been circulated to members of the Committee, I gave reasons for thinking that the present Trustee Acts should be considerably modified. Some of the considerations which I urged may not be particularly germane to the inquiry of this Committee. But in so far as they are concerned with the renewal of the abnormally large amount of debt which falls due between now and 1929, the desirability of the Treasury exercising a more effective control over rival trustee issues, than it has at present, is worth emphasising. Both in the interests of the investors themselves and of the community as a whole and of the Treasury, I think it would be better to allow no securities in the future to enjoy the benefit of the Trustee Acts except home securities of certain specified types.

My anxieties under this heading are connected with those under paragraph 3. If our own national debt is repaid on a large scale, and if the bulk of the new issues of trustee securities consist of colonial obligations, the effect of these two things together, namely repayment of debt and the Trustee Acts, is to afford an artificial stimulation to foreign investment which may be exceedingly contrary to the public interest. Repayment of debt takes forcibly resources from the community at large and compels their utilisation in securities of the trustee type; and it may then happen that the bulk of the net additions to the list of trustee securities are overseas investments.

5. I have mentioned above that the Government will borrow most cheaply by supplying such types of bonds as the different sections of the investing public find suitable to their requirements. I suggest that there is one further type of bond not yet in issue which might prove popular with particular individuals and so enable the state to raise funds a little more cheaply. I suggest that there should be issued bonds of which the capital and the interest would be paid not in a fixed amount of sterling, but in such amount of sterling as has a fixed commodity value as indicated by an index number. I think that an official index number should be established for such purposes on the lines of the optional tabular standard recommended long ago by Dr Marshall, and that it should be open to anyone, including particularly the Treasury, to offer loans, the payment of the interest on which and the repayment of the capital of which would be governed by movements of the index number. I can say from knowledge that there are many investors, who wishing to take no risks would naturally confine themselves to trustee stocks, yet feel a natural anxiety in being compelled to invest their whole resources in terms of legal tender money, the relation of which to real value has been

shown by experience to be variable. Throughout almost the whole of Europe investors of the trustee type have been deprived in the past ten years of the greater part of the value of their property. Even here in England all such investors have suffered a very large real loss. We may hope that great instability in the value of the currency may not be one of the things which the future has in store for us. But it is natural that some people should be anxious about it. Unless, therefore, the Treasury hopes to make a profit through the depreciation of legal tender, it would lose nothing, and might gain something in terms of interest, by issuing such bonds as I have indicated.

3880 (CHAIRMAN) *Will you first of all amplify the points in your paper?* I should like, if I may, in dealing with the first heading of my evidence, to put the matter a little differently from the way in which I have put it in my written summary. In England historically the income tax has been, not a personal tax, but a tax on income as it accrued, in whatsoever hands it was. That is a point which is not always well understood, but it has been a very vital feature of our income tax system. We have gradually been compelled to depart from that system as the rates of income tax have increased, and it has become increasingly a personal tax. The personal side of it is represented most completely in the super-tax. I believe that this distinction between the tax on income as it accrues and the personal tax might be developed so as to take taxation to a certain extent off what we can presume to be savings, and throw a little more heavily on to that part of income which we cannot presume with equal likelihood to be savings. I would suggest that if it is desirable to move in that direction we might reorganise our system of income tax, and, instead of having two taxes called income tax and super-tax, have two taxes called 'standard tax' and 'personal tax'; that the standard tax should be like the old income tax and fall upon all income as it accrued, subject, as the old income tax was, to certain total exemptions at the bottom of the scale; and that the personal tax should absorb the fluctuating part of income tax and super-tax and should be avowedly a tax on individuals in proportion to their capacity to bear it. That would have the effect that corporations who are not spenders, except in so far as they pay dividends, would pay only at the standard rate on that part of their income which they put aside and did not distribute. The most obvious cases are insurance companies, where the money accumulates at compound interest, and industrial companies, which retain for further development of their business a certain part of their profits. In both those cases there is strong presumption that the income in question is saved and is not spent. If the standard rate of tax was to be lowered and the loss of receipts in that way was to be made good by regraduating the super-tax and bringing it down to incomes of much lower limit than £2,000 you would be exempting a certain part of income which goes to savings. I think it is difficult to know how much is now saved in that way and how much in other ways, but I am sure that important sums are now saved by corporations rather than by individuals, that is the tendency nowadays, and it is one which it may be worth while to encourage and of which our tax system ought to take account. In the old days, when income tax was at moderate rates and no steep graduation was necessary, there was much to be said for the old system. In the early days of super-tax, when the machinery of super-tax was in its infancy, it would probably have been very difficult to have worked a personal tax of the kind that I suggest. But in the present conditions it merely means an extension of our existing super-tax machinery under a different name, and with super-tax down as low as £2,000 and with further graduation below that point, a large part of our taxation is in effect personal tax, even that part which is collected ostensibly at the standard rate of income tax. We should get clearer and perhaps have greater simplicity in the end if we were to recognise that change, and it would have the advantage that money which accrued in the hands of corporations which could not be spenders, would be exempted.

3881 (MR BELL) *By corporations do you mean limited companies only?* No, I include, for example insurance companies, whether they are limited liability companies or not. But generally speaking, I should make exactly the same distinction as is now made by super-tax; that is to say, my personal tax would fall upon the classes of persons who, if they had large enough income, would now be liable to super-tax.

3882 *I was wondering whether the actual standard tax would fall equally upon a partnership? What is the present position as regards super-tax?*

3883 *Would the same facility for saving be granted to a private partnership as to a limited company for instance?* There are certain marginal cases at present which are dealt with under super-tax lines as carefully as the officials can. I am not very well acquainted with just where they draw the line.

3884 (SIR ALAN ANDERSON) *Private partnerships or the individual partners have to pay super-tax on the reserves held by the partnership.* (SIR JOSIAH STAMP) *And instead of extending the principle of limited companies to partnerships, you would extend the principle of partnerships to limited companies, and say that, in so far as you have limited companies which approximate in their true character to a partnership, they shall be deemed to be partnerships; but because there has been very grave abuse of the distinction between limited company and partnership in the past in regard to super-tax, therefore recent legislation has assimilated all limited companies with a few shareholders, to partnerships.* Perhaps I could answer Mr Bell's question by taking up the point just made by Sir Josiah Stamp. Hitherto the distinction between super-tax and standard tax has been the amount of a man's income, and therefore the arrangements to which he refers were quite distinctly of the nature of evasion. But suppose that the criterion which we have in our mind was whether the money was locked away in a form in which it could not be spent on current expenditure, then we should not object so much to individuals or partners who were in fact behaving in that way imitating the formal company, because they would have met our criterion.

3885 (MR BELL) *That is the only point I wanted to elicit—that they would have just as much advantage by putting to reserve as a limited company would.* I do not like to answer that quite definitely, because it is a technical Inland Revenue point. I should like to do that in so far as it is compatible with preventing evasion of taxation. In all those cases you must not go beyond a point, because it can be abused by those who seek to evade, and that is an Inland Revenue matter on which I am not an expert.

3886 *All I wanted to ask was whether they should be treated as a limited company in every way in which it can be done fairly and rightly?* I should aim at that, but I should have thought that any Inland Revenue authority would say that you would have to be stiffer with private partnerships just as you are now.

3887 *Would that be just?* As just as the present system.

3888 *I should have thought not. If you were going to put a premium upon saving and the holding of reserves it should be done equally with a private partnership as with a company?* It is not done at the present time. I did not raise that point, because I propose no change.

3889 *I mean standard tax, not super-tax?* I am making exactly the same point.

3890 (SIR WILLIAM MCLINTOCK) *There is a distinction between a limited company and a private company formed before 1914 and after?* Yes.

3891 *After 1914 certain private limited companies were treated as partnerships?* Yes.

3892 *This suggestion of yours would mean that all the pre-1914 companies would get off with a lower rate of tax and the amount placed to reserve would not be questioned, whereas in the case of the after-1914 companies, today the Inland Revenue go very exhaustively into all the circumstances of the case?* Yes, but I suggest that these questions are not really relevant to what I am trying to say.

3893 (SIR JOSIAH STAMP) *I think we are drifting rather too much into the technical difficulties of carrying out general principles. I would like to ask you whether something in the nature of a division between the normal tax and the super-tax as they have it in the United States would be possible?* I am inclined to have a somewhat higher standard tax than they have, at any rate at first.

I think it would be too great a change in the existing system to put the standard tax as low as in America. I should suggest 3s. in the £ as the figure.

3894 *That is to say, you would lower the present super-tax down to the class of those who in effect pay at the rate of 3s.* Yes.

3895 *It was started at £5,000, dropped to £3,000, and then dropped to £2,000; with every drop in the level a large number of people come in, and there is an inevitable loss, through evasion, every time?* I think that is the main objection to my proposal. Every tampering with the level of the standard tax leaves more room for evasion.

3896 *The Chairman will remember that the point where super-tax was brought down to a lower level was seriously considered by the Income Tax Commission?* But I think that now the situation is so different from what it was even a very few years ago, we have gone so far in this direction, that if there were other advantages to be gained I would risk this objection; but it is a great objection.

3897 (SIR CHARLES ADDIS) *With regard to the effect of income tax on companies' savings, is it your view that it acts by tempting companies to distribute a larger amount in dividends than they put to reserve?* No, I think it acts by diminishing the amount that they have available for reserve.

3898 *But not in the direction of encouraging increased distribution?* It may a little, but I do not think so.

3899 *Do you think in practice it has had the effect of reducing the amount of reserves?* Yes, I think so.

3900 *We have had evidence given here by Mr Layton that so far as he could judge, the reserves of the companies that he examined all kept pace with the increase in prices. Do you think that was correct?* I should have been surprised that you could get any sound statistical argument on that point, owing to the great changes by amalgamation and otherwise that have taken place in the character of companies in the past 10 years; but in any case it does not follow that the proportion put to reserve before the war was the really correct proportion.

3901 *Is there any real distinction in the position of a shareholder who receives a sum in dividends which might have been put to reserve, and himself invests it in some other industrial security?* I do not quite follow the question.

3902 *Supposing that a company, instead of putting to reserve, pays the amount in dividend and that the shareholder who receives that dividend invests it in some other industrial security?* It does not follow that he will. If he does, it does not make very much difference; but I am inclined to think that the new money for industry is being found more and more out of the reserves of existing companies. The tendency, in the case of a really progressive industry, is to pay the shareholders something to satisfy them and to retain as much as they possibly can in the business for the further expansion of that business. I think that is one of the most healthy ways in which additional capital for business is obtained, and I think that this suggestion of mine would leave more in the hands of the managers of the business, which they could retain in the business without disappointing their shareholders. They could in fact use it as an argument with the shareholders that it brings them within this lower rate of tax if they retain it in the business.

3903 *If you take two classes of shareholders: if you take class A, who receives the amount in dividend, and class B, where the amount is retained by a company and placed to reserve, the distinction is really between borrowed money and compulsory saving. In the case of A, he may save or he may not?* I think the argument is purely psychological. You might say that if you could earn 2s. and give your shareholder 1s., your 20s. shares will then be worth 21s., whereas if you gave him 2s., they would be worth 20s. Therefore your shareholder, by selling 5 per cent of his holding, could be exactly as he was previously; he would have obtained his 2s. But in practice people do not act in that way. If the money is retained in the business, it is much less liable to be spent by the shareholder releasing a portion of his holding than if it is paid to him as dividend; because he looks on the one as capital and he looks on the other as income. There is also a further point. The expenses of raising new capital are heavy, and one of the great advantages of increasing capital by retaining money in the business is that it is a very cheap way by which companies can increase their funds. If they have to issue new shares or borrow in the market, in modern conditions they have to give away a dangerously high sum in order to make a successful flotation. If they retain money in this way it costs them nothing; they have a perpetual regular flow instead of an occasional large but expensive issue.

3904 *The point I wanted to make was this, if I may make it clear. In the case of two shareholders, A and B, the one receives the dividend and the other has it invested for him. Would there be no inequity in taxing the one and exempting the other according to your proposal?* I do not think that any system of taxation is perfectly fair. I do not think that you would increase the existing unfairness. It exists in every case of the super-tax payer at present.

3905 *It seems to me that it would have the effect of encouraging a certain kind of saving, namely, compulsory saving, as against voluntary saving. I do not press that point, but there is a difficulty, I think?* It seems to me that you are imputing to a new system of taxation an inequity that exists at present.

3906 (SIR JOSIAH STAMP) *On that point raised by Sir Charles Addis, there is rather an assumption that super-tax is being lost at the present time on the amount retained by the company. But those sums are due not merely to people with incomes chargeable at a higher rate than the normal rate, but are also due to people chargeable at a lower rate and on the average probably there is not much loss, because there is no repayment to anybody on the money that is invested for them by the company. The shareholder may be hit by having the tax paid at 4s. 6d. in the £ on something for which he is only liable to 2s. 3d., and if you take the whole amount there is no statistical evidence to show that the real rate on the whole lot is higher than the normal rate. The thing is unfair in both directions. On this statistical point about reserves, supposing that the company makes £10,000 profit and looks at its balance sheet and sees that all its assets are intact, and says: 'We will pay £5,000 in dividend and put £5,000 to reserve', and that goes into the business, that is the kind of thing that ought to be encouraged?* That is my suggestion.

3907 *Now supposing the company looks at its assets and says: 'We have got some holdings in Dunlop that have depreciated in value; we must write that asset down', and they deplete their profit and loss account by £5,000, they show £5,000 profit and they pay that away in dividends, apparently they make no reserve, but do they not in effect do exactly the same as the first company?* Yes, I think so.

3908 *Then one way of doing it is to put it into reserve when it is obviously reserve, but we none of us know how large sums out of profits have been saved in the writing down of assets?* No.

3909 *Which makes it almost impossible to judge how much of current profits have been kept intact without distribution. It would seem to show that it is a favourable time, would it not, for an increase in capital when everything slumps in value. By the modern ideas of a balance sheet you compel everybody to put money on one side?* There is a striking instance of that in the case of banks.

3910 (PROFESSOR HALL) *That would apply, of course, to depreciation of plant as well.* (SIR JOSIAH STAMP) *That is a more regular thing, but this seems to show that industry is being particularly hit in the saving of capital at a time when capital values are being depreciated?* (MR KEYNES) Of course it does not always happen that companies do write down assets as much as they should.

3911 (SIR WILLIAM MCLINTOCK) *There are two methods. One company writes down a specific asset and reduces its value, probably they have only written it down to market value and then they hide it up in a big total; another company actually shows the reserve on the other side, and the result is exactly the same for the two companies?* Yes.

3912 *Would you consider there is an essential difference between the one which shows it as a true reserve and the one which writes it down to its market value as a legitimate business expense?* I think the existence of those two methods renders all estimates of amount nearly valueless on this matter.

3913 *I agree. They will have to reform their methods of stating balance sheets for statistical purposes.* (SIR JOSIAH STAMP) *What I want to know is whether you would allow the writing down of capital assets to be charged as a business expense?* (MR KEYNES) I think there is a great difficulty about it, because there is also the question of writing up. If you are to allow companies to write down depreciation of assets as a business expense then you must compel them to write up, and that would involve valuations on the part of Inland Revenue, which would probably be impracticable. I have always regarded the unwillingness of the Inland Revenue to allow writing down as a balancing item against the impracticability of compelling companies to write items up.

3914 (SIR ALAN ANDERSON) *You can practically choose now for a great many things, can you not, whether you will bring in the rise and fall, or whether you will not?* Also it seems to me that if you have writings up and down in accordance with fluctuations in the value of money and include these in income account, you would reach an impossible situation.

3915 (SIR JOSIAH STAMP) *I was going to ask you how you would avoid the appalling mess that Washington [i.e. the United States] has got into the last three or four years?* I do not quite understand the relevance to what I was proposing, because I was not suggesting any change in this particular respect.

3916 *We were on the question of the method of handling reserves in the different kinds of companies. I was wondering if you were going to have differential treatment at all?* Your point relates to the definition of profit. My suggestion does not really touch that.

3917 *You would allow profit to be defined as now?* Yes.

3918 *And you would get over all difficulties about exempting reserves or giving preferential treatment, by charging companies at a low rate of tax?* Yes.

3919 (MR BELL) *What would be the additional tax to the widow who lives in Ryde or the physician who lives in Harley Street? How is it to be made up?* It does not affect his position, because he is at present liable to super-tax.

3920 *I take it that the net result of this proposal would be that companies would be relieved of a good deal of taxation as long as they kept certain reserves intact. How will the revenue make that up?* It would be made up in various ways, partly by a general regraduation which will bring the super-tax limit down and partly by some increase in the personal tax all along the line. But the Harley Street practitioner would not be injured by that any more than any other individual of equal income.

3921 *But individuals would have to find the amounts of which industrial concerns are given the benefit?* Yes, wherever you relieve a particular sort of income from taxation you must make it up on some other sort of income, certainly.

3922 *Do you not fear that that might be a preferential treatment of one sort of people?* It depends how much public opinion was influenced by the desirability of exempting what are certainly savings. I think it may be that the encouragement to savings is rather a fetish sometimes; I do not think it ought to be pushed to its extreme point. But I am assuming that in existing conditions we want to do a little to help savings.

3923 *All sorts of savings equally?* All those that we can encourage without opening doors to evasion, and I think that confines rather narrowly the types that you can assist.

3924 *Would that really be possible in regard to individuals, do you think?* No, I do not think it would.

3925 *Then it would in effect be letting savings of a certain class of taxation off and not letting off another class of savings?* I am inclined, perhaps wrongly, to brush on one side all these minor questions of equity between individuals, because I think that line of argument leads always to abusing a new tax as against an old tax. Every tax that has ever been devised is packed full of these small inequities.

3926 *The inequity seems to me to be a pretty big one?* If these are emphasised it suggests that the new taxes, because they have them, have them more than the old taxes. If we were to go through the old taxes we should find just as many anomalous cases.

3927 (SIR ALAN ANDERSON) *I suppose there is an inherent objection to every new tax. You do not want to change the method of taxation?* There is always an objection to a new system of taxation. One never wants to alter our system of taxation for no reason at all.

3928 (SIR JOSIAH STAMP) *There is no enormous difference in the question of equity between one individual and another and the social value of savings. In your judgement, the social value of savings might be allowed to prevail?* Yes, but I sympathise with Mr Bell's point of view. I think there is a danger of going too far in the other direction.

3929 (MR BRAMLEY) *What would be the effect on the banks? Would your proposal tend to reduce the total amount of savings in the hands of banks, and increase the total amount of savings in the hands of companies?* I do not think so. Do you mean that it would increase the amount of the deposit accounts in banks? The alternative to the money being retained by the companies is that the investor would either spend it or invest it in some other way. Of the other ways in which they can invest it, putting it on deposit at their banks is only one of many.

3930 *The temptation would be to leave more money in the hands of the companies, would it not?* Not so much the temptation as the compulsion.

3931 *That would, of course, reduce the amount of bank deposits, would it not?* It would reduce the amount of money available for investment in other ways, and it is only in so far as interest-bearing deposits at the bank are a form of investment that they would be affected. It would not affect the amount on current account, and I should not think it would much affect the amount held on deposit; but it might.

3932 (MRS WOOTTON) *I understand you do not intend to alter seriously the present graduation of income tax?* No. I think that, if you were to merge super-tax and the fluctuating part of income tax, as I suggest, there are certain adjustments that one would inevitably think it wise to make; there are certain small adjustments which at present arise inevitably out of there being two taxes, which you would take the opportunity of correcting.

3933 *Your proposal is to relieve savings much more than to make any change in general taxation?* Yes.

3934 (MR BOWEN) *Would your proposal mean less revenue?* It would mean less revenue from a particular source, which would have to be made up from other sources.

3935 *Have you in mind what those sources would be?* My idea was that the total receipts from income tax and super-tax would not be diminished unless there were other reasons for diminishing them; that it would be a redistribution between income tax and super-tax payers rather than a relief of those classes; but if there was money which was available to relieve some class or other, personally I think the income tax payers are those who ought to receive it. I think that of the present taxes the income tax and super-tax are the most excessive.

3936 (SIR WILLIAM MCLINTOCK) *Assume that a lower rate of tax is applied to limited companies; they have a bigger sum available then for either distribution or reserve?* Yes.

3937 *If you assume that they pay a larger dividend by reason of the lower income tax, that higher dividend will in turn be subject to the higher rate of super-tax that you suggest?* Yes.

3938 *One may very well off-set the other?* I assume that the companies would to a certain extent increase their nominal rate of dividend.

3939 (SIR JOSIAH STAMP) *You do not think that they would retain in their business the whole of the difference?* No, I do not.

3940 *A great many of them already retain all they want and they would have no use for this money, and they would pay it out as a larger gross dividend?* Yes, and in so far as they paid it out as a larger gross dividend, no revenue would be lost.

3941 (SIR WILLIAM MCLINTOCK) *And the revenue would gain on the higher super-tax?* Yes.

3942 *That would be the tendency, would it not?* I think the tendency would be that a certain amount extra would be retained in the business.

3943 *A portion of it?* A portion of it. All this discussion has been based upon joint stock companies. But the case of insurance companies is very important, because the amount of the additional savings of the country that accrues in the hands of insurance companies per annum is something prodigious, and that part automatically accumulates at compound interest and it is an increasingly large source of savings. If they accumulated at a higher net rate of interest than they do now it would make a very material difference to the amount of savings. I attach more importance to that so far as the magnitude of the additional savings is concerned than I do to the other point.

3944 *Would it increase the bonuses paid by insurance companies?* It would increase them, certainly, if you mean the ordinary type of bonus which is a deferred bonus; it means that the insured person at the maturity of the policy receives a larger sum. If money is accumulating in the hands of the insurance company at a higher rate of interest there is a larger fund to be returned to the policy holder at the end of the period, and that is simply another way of saying that the bonuses are higher.

3945 *In that case no tax would ever be paid on those bonuses?* I do not say no tax; they would pay standard tax.

3946 *Except the standard tax. A limited company must distribute surplus profits at some future date?* Yes.

3947 (SIR ALAN ANDERSON) *Does not an insurance company pay income tax?* It pays income tax, certainly; that is the point of my answer; it would continue to pay standard tax.

3948 *When one takes out a policy one escapes the income tax on the premium?* Up to a certain point. The company pays income tax all the time.

3949 *When you answered about the doctor or the lawyer, the man who is making a personal income, I think you said that he was a hard case, did you not?* I said that he is a hard case now.

3950 *He is no worse off than a private firm now. You say they would be hard cases too?* They are a hard case, too. It is simply that anybody who is liable to super-tax, and who saves out of his income, is in a worse position than a company which saves correspondingly. My proposal slightly aggravates that inequity. But any scheme for helping savings that does not help all savings equally is inequitable in that way. That is an instance of my objection to Mr Bell's suggestions in some of his questions which are along these lines. No way of helping savings would help all savings to an exactly equal extent; therefore an element of unfairness is involved; therefore you must never help savings. This result is the danger of that way of arguing.

3951 (MR BELL) *Still, of course, it is the wish of all of us to be equally fair to all classes if we can. It is not a bad thing in itself to be rather careful?* No, certainly not; I agree with that; but I think that the perfectly fair person has to retire from all forms of action.

3952 (CHAIRMAN) *Will you proceed with the next point in your evidence?* There is the question as to what part of our debt we should be prepared to keep permanently in a short-dated form. I think popular opinion on that is often incorrect, because it is founded on a false analogy with the case of a private individual or of a company. It is clearly advantageous for a company to have its debentures of a long date, so that there may not be any risk of their falling due at a time when the company is embarrassed, or less easily able to raise money. I think the extension of that to the state is a false analogy. I see nothing unsafe in the fact that the amount of short-dated debt falling due for renewal year by year is one figure rather than another figure. My criterion would be determined by the amount of debt which could be kept floating one year with another in a short-dated form at a lower average rate of interest than if it were in long-dated form. I believe that the amount that could be kept floating on that criterion is very large, simply for the reason that there are a large number of holders of funds, particularly banks, to whom it is so advantageous to have debt which is regularly maturing that they are prepared to accept a lower rate of interest on it than on debt which does not mature in that way. In a long-dated debt the lender knows what interest he will receive annually for a long time ahead; he does not know for certain what the market value of his loan will be; in the short-dated debt he knows what the market value will be year by year in the near future; he does not know for certain exactly what rate of interest he will receive. From the point of view of the state it seems to be indifferent in which form they borrow, but there is a certain class of lenders to whom one kind is very much preferable and there is another class to whom the other kind is very much preferable, and I think the division between the two forms of debt ought to be determined by the proportionate appetites of those two classes of investors.

3953 (MR BELL) *In the result, I take it, you agree that there has been an enormous saving to the state by the cheaper form of borrowing on short-term security?* Very great indeed.

3954 (SIR JOSIAH STAMP) *Would you agree that the appetite will vary according as the times are good or bad?* Yes.

3955 *Would you settle it by the period of minimum appetite?* There is a certain difficulty there. It is in the interests of the trading community that the short-dated debt of the Government should be somewhat reduced in good times and somewhat increased in bad times. But those dates may not coincide with the dates at which it is most profitable for the government to convert its debt from one form into the other. You may, I think, have a dilemma sometimes between which objective to follow. If you can fund your debt more satisfactorily in good times, that is the moment to fund rather than in bad times.

3956 *Therefore you would not object to the step taken in reducing the huge floating debt that was frequently coming on the market in 1920 to more manageable dimensions?* No.

3957 *It was a source of great danger at the time, and was in constant competition with the gluttonous demands for money in the industrial market?* I think it was healthy, because it tended to direct new savings into the commercial market rather than into the investment market. It is a characteristic of good times that the new savings of the community ought to be put at the service of trade rather than flow into investments. If the Government at that time is floating long-dated loans to the investor and using the proceeds to repay the market its short-dated loans it does just what is wanted; it brings the new savings of the community into the service of commerce. On the other hand, in bad times, when the demands of commerce are reduced, the opposite is true; but I believe that the fluctuations which would be practicable in the volume of the floating debt as between good times and bad, would not be a very large percentage of the whole.

3958 *Not more than 10 per cent probably.* No, not more than 10 per cent.

3959 (MR BELL) *I am quite clear that there is a fallacy in the argument that a short-term debt is bad, but it seems to have been laid down almost as a financial principle that you must get rid of a short-dated debt of this kind. You are entirely opposed to that?* Yes, entirely opposed to it; indeed, I think if it were carried very far it would put our banking system into an extremely difficult situation. It would be driving bankers into a form of security which is not the most suitable for them.

3960 (SIR CHARLES ADDIS) *Can you make any suggestions as to the amount of floating debt that might be considered permanent?—Is it possible to arrive at an estimate?* It is rather difficult to give a figure, because one does not quite know at what point to draw the line, whether 1929 War Bonds are short-dated debt, whether 1932 Treasury Bonds are.

3961 *Might I take Treasury bills as an instance of floating debt?* I should certainly merge with Treasury bills all the National War Bonds which are of quite short-date—up to 1927/1928. I do not see anything very wrong in the present amount.

3962 *You do not think there is any danger with the amount at the present level?* No.

3963 *That is to say, if a demand were made for money, the Government could always command the situation by raising the interest on short-dated loans?* That is so, but supposing trade was to revive very definitely, I think it would be a sound policy if the Government tried to fund some of it and then was prepared to allow some to be reconverted into short-period debt later on. I do not think they should aim at a much lower figure than the present figure as an average.

3964 (MR BELL) *Might not the existence of the floating debt hamper the Government in any conversion scheme by making it more difficult to raise the cash if the conversion terms offered were not always accepted?* I think that assumes that we are always wanting to have conversion schemes, that the ultimate object of the Treasury is to convert everything. I do not think it would make very much difference. Supposing you had a certain part of the public naturally attracted by long-dated debt and a certain part of the public naturally attracted by short-dated debt, you do not get any rapid change between those two classes of investors, and therefore the market for the long-dated debt would be much the same at one time as at another. In fact by having mopped up all the really short-dated lenders into your short-dated debt, you have a more steady supply of lenders for your long-period debt.

3965 (SIR CHARLES ADDIS) *If the rate of interest on the short-dated debt eventually became the same as on the long-dated debt, would there not be competition?* If that happened, I should say it was a sign that the short-dated debt was getting excessive.

3966 *You would consider whether it was a good opportunity to fund. You would take the two circumstances together?* I think it is inevitable that you should. When the Government has been erring a little in one direction, it would probably be difficult to correct it, because it is just that difficulty which has probably led to the situation which is making the trouble.

3967 *In your view the management of this amount of floating debt would have to be increased and diminished in accordance with the fluctuations in the competition of trade for funds, would involve a certain amount of control?* It would involve a certain amount of intelligence.

3968 *You are not apprehensive as to the degree of intelligence that would be available for controlling credit in that way, are you?* I think it is quite impossible to write down certain rules in a book and then have the Treasury run by clerks from that time onwards by reference to the book.

3969 (PROFESSOR HALL) *I think you mentioned that you convert from short-dated loans to funded loans in times of good trade?* That is a secondary point. I should do that if it was not too expensive.

3970 *Would not that be rather an unfavourable time for funding?* It would; that is the difficulty. The reason for that is that during trade booms, owing to the nature of our credit system, the price of long-dated securities is unduly affected.

3971 (SIR ALAN ANDERSON) *Does it not come to this, that you would go on with the short-dated securities you have got now, unless you found you would save money by converting?* Yes, that is what it comes to.

3972 (SIR CHARLES ADDIS) *In times of commercial expansion do you regard the existence of the floating debt as tending to raise the rate of interest for business purposes?* No, I do not think it does that, but the existence of a floating debt affords an opportunity for diverting savings into the direction of business in the way in which I have indicated. It gives to the Treasury an opportunity, by funding its debt, of getting savings from the public and putting those savings at the disposition of commerce, and if it is practicable to do that, it is a good thing to do; but if it cannot be done, then it cannot.

3973 (CHAIRMAN) *Will you go on to your next point now?* My next point is the one to which I really attach most importance. It relates to times of repayment. I think some debt should be repaid every year in the interests of sound budgeting and sound finance generally. It is a sound principle to have some margin, and the policy of having a sinking fund of a certain amount is a way of insuring that. But when you consider repayments of debt on a larger scale than is required by such considerations, I think again there is a danger of applying the false analogy of an individual who is in debt, who would naturally wish to clear off his obligations at the first possible moment. The effect of paying off debt is to take money from the body of taxpayers and to place it at the disposal primarily of a particular form of investment. If a holder of Government debt is paid off he will probably want to reinvest in something of the same kind. Thus I should say that the main effect of debt repayment at a rapid rate is to divert the surplus resources of the community into the gilt-edged stock market. Sometimes this may be a very right thing to do. If the demand for capital which is offered in that particular form is brisk, then that is a good opportunity to pay off debt. But the policy of paying off debt regardless of the outlet is, I think, a very doubtful one. I think that probably mistakes were made on those lines in the 'nineties, though I do not know the history of that period well enough to be sure. I am clear that if at the present time upwards of one hundred million pounds of debt is repaid annually, that may take a larger part of the surplus of the community and put it at the disposal of the gilt-edged market, than is desirable. But I should look to the criterion of the demand for the outlet for savings in investments of the trustee type rather than to any other criterion in deciding how fast I should repay debt, once I had got a sufficient balance on the right side to satisfy the requirements of ordinary good finance.

3974 (SIR JOSIAH STAMP) *As a corollary to that point we have had the amount of diversion that excessive debt repayment introduces put to us in this form. You draw your taxes from businesses which are progressive but relatively obscure, and you deplete what they would otherwise have had for their development. You direct money by debt repayment, as you say, to the gilt-edged market, which is not big enough or extensive enough to absorb the sums so directed, and they seek the next best thing, which are debentures, and good industrial shares in very large undertakings. Therefore an excessive debt repayment has the effect of encouraging the financing of the largest and best known concerns and discouraging private enterprise?* I think that is true, but I should put even more strongly the point that it has the effect of encouraging colonial investments as against all types of English industrials.

3975 *And even against English debentures?* Even against English debentures; because colonial securities are considered by the public as nearer to the true gilt-edged type than even English industrials are.

3976 (MR BRAMLEY) *The continuation of the interest liability is a question of distribution, not of total wealth of the community?* Provided that interest is being met by taxation on the right class of the community, I do not think that ought to be a determining consideration. It is out of one pocket into another; whereas the other considerations that I have been mentioning have regard to the growth of the aggregate wealth of the community.

3977 (MRS WOOTTON) *What prevents this diversion from correcting itself? What prevents the tendency to invest in gilt-edged securities to straighten it out again?* The fact that there is very imperfect fluidity in the investment market. It is not true that capital seeks the channels of most lucrative investment by itself. It does nothing of the kind. The business of investment is most unsuccessfully carried on, because it is largely conducted by persons, namely, the individual investors, who know nothing whatever about it. It is lack of knowledge.

3978 (SIR JOSIAH STAMP) *It is conservatism too?* It is conservatism, obedience to convention, and lack of knowledge. That is inevitable, and those characteristics exist in the greatest degree in the gilt-edged type of investor. He goes into that class of security precisely because he, rightly, does not like to trust his own judgement. Therefore, you are putting the resources of the community, if you repay debt too fast, into the hands of the class of persons who have least courage and least skill in the utilisation of resources.

3979 (MRS WOOTTON) *There is not a sufficient margin also in the gilt-edged market?* The gilt-edged market is so enormously large as compared with the industrial market that there is not a sufficient margin. I am convinced that there is not a sufficient margin. I am convinced that the disparity in the size of the gilt-edged market and the other markets is much greater than is commonly appreciated.

3980 *Is that lack of fluidity constant, or does it increase and decrease?* I think it varies. At times when the general investing public have suffered misfortunes so that they have no courage, the lack of fluidity is much greater than when they have been having a rather fortunate time and are speculatively inclined.

3981 (MR HICHENS) *It has been put to us in evidence that if, by means, for instance, of a capital levy, we could pay off the whole of the debt and thus relieve the state of some £300,000,000 a year in the way of interest, that*

£300,000,000 would be available for other public purposes, such as education and so forth. Would you regard that as a fallacy or as a fact? The only valid distinction between a capital levy and taxes of the class of the income tax, is that one falls more upon those who hold wealth and the other more on those who earn incomes. That is to say, one is on the existing holders of wealth, the other is on the potential future holders of wealth.

3982 *That is to say, it might re-distribute the burden, it would not affect the magnitude of it?* It would re-distribute the burden in the interests of persons who are now earning their wealth, as against persons who have earned their wealth in past times.

3983 (MRS WOOTTON) *It might be better, might it not, for the state to extend it in certain directions, rather than in others, from a purely psychological consideration?* I think that would be very small, compared with the point that I have mentioned. The evil seems to arise when, in order to make the Budget balance, the rate of income tax upon current effort gets so high as to discourage that effort. I think the evil of discouraging that effort may be greater than the evil of disappointing the expectations of persons who earned their wealth in the past.

3984 (SIR ALAN ANDERSON) *In fact it is better to go on collecting money from income tax, so long as you are not pushing it too far?* Yes.

3985 (MRS WOOTTON) *There is a sort of convention that you ought not to spend out of the National Exchequer more than a certain sum, partly for psychological reasons. If you are relieved of the obligation of spending the amount of the debt interest, it might be possible to divert it to the other objects?* I doubt if that convention would last long if it was divorced from the real burden of taxation. I should not attach much importance to that argument in founding a permanent system of taxation for the country, because those conventions have a very short life. The position now is totally different from what it was a very few years ago.

3986 (MR HICHENS) *Another point of view that was put to us was that the question of debt repayment is not really a very serious matter, that the general public are used to a debt of £6,000,000,000 odd, and that, as it falls due, it will be a matter of no difficulty to replace it; therefore there is no urgency in redeeming the debt?* My view is that there is no urgency to redeem the debt unless the state has other important objects for which it wants the money; that is to say, if it is a question of replacing unproductive debt by productive debt, that may be a very strong reason for reducing the unproductive debt, but if there is no argument of that kind, reducing debt for its own sake I think is an undesirable policy, because it is not really increasing the wealth of the community, it is forcing the surplus of the community into a particular channel, which may not be the channel into which it ought to flow.

313

3987 (SIR ALAN ANDERSON) *You mean the argument in favour of the reduction of debt is primarily to retain the credit of the state so that it can borrow more if it wants to?* That is an argument which is used.

3988 *That is what you think, is it not: you would not do it, except for the credit of the state?* I would not call it the credit of the state. I would say that if the state has a demand for the money, if the state is itself in the gilt-edged market as a borrower, directly or indirectly, for productive purposes, then in order to make that productive borrowing easier there is a good deal to be said for paying off the debt. But if there is no natural outlet for the sums released by repayment of debt, then it is a mistake to repay debt.

3989 (SIR CHARLES ADDIS) *Supposing the demand for gilt-edged securities, both at home and abroad, was relatively small, the effect would be to drive money into industry, would it not?* The investor would be tempted probably into the second-rate bond, than which there is no worse investment.

3990 *Might there not be also a favourable result in the reaction on rates of interest from the reduction of debt?* It is a roundabout way of producing your result, to take money from industry in the hope that some of it may, by another channel find its way back there.

3991 (MR BRAMLEY) *May I just ask for information on this sentence in paragraph 3 of your paper: 'For example, if the Local Loans Authorities or Borough or County Authorities, are involved in heavy expenditure for housing or public works, which they can only cover by borrowing in the gilt-edged market, then a simultaneous repayment of national debt by the Treasury may be just the right thing to do.' Does that mean that if you could encourage local expenditure proportionately to the repayment of the debt, that would be an advantage?* Perhaps I can illustrate it in this way. I think about two years ago (I am not sure of my exact dates) various local authorities, county and municipal boroughs, and those authorities who borrow through the Local Loans Fund, had big schemes on hand which required large issues by them. At the same date we were in fact repaying Government debt at a very rapid rate. One of those things offset the other. I think it was quite a healthy thing. Money which had been repaid by the Government found an outlet in these loans of local authorities. At the present time, when local authorities have operations on foot on a much smaller scale, the amounts they are borrowing are relatively trifling. An equal repayment of debt therefore at the present time would be less advisable than it was in the circumstances of two years ago.

3992 (SIR CHARLES ADDIS) *You say: 'If the supply of new gilt-edged securities is limited, thus indicating that the demand for capital by borrowers of that type is not extensive, then repayment of national debt on a large scale may be very harmful.' Would you expand that?* Because it forces the surplus

THE RETURN TO GOLD AND FOREIGN LENDING

resources of the community into a channel where they are not particularly wanted.

3993 (MR HICHENS) *We have been told that there is a psychological effect, that if there is a large Government debt and the Government bondholders are people who are rather apt to look askance at it, money is being wasted by paying interest on the debt, whereas on the other hand if this debt were paid off and the capital were disseminated to industry, the same objection would not quite hold?* I think it is a relic of mid-nineteenth-century sound financial maxims which have extremely little application to the present day. But owing to the fact that the present application is so slight, conventional feelings of that sort gradually disappear. It is unsound to base the policy of the future on the decaying conventions of the past.

3994 (MR BRAMLEY) *I would like to be perfectly clear as to whether the evils arising from repayment of debt arise purely from the process of repayment or whether they are attached to some method of obtaining the means of repayment. Supposing the United States of America were to be inspired with a desire (this is merely supposition of course) to improve the credit of this country and they came along and said: 'We will make you a present of £2,000,000,000 sterling to help you out of debt', and we accepted it and repaid our debt to that extent, would that be a disadvantage to this country?* I think that the advantage of receiving a present of £2,000,000,000 would far outweigh the inconveniences of the financial problem of tidying things up with the proceeds.

3995 *But still, the evils arising from the process of repayment would remain the same, would they not?* I do not think that the evils of repaying £100,000,000 are £100,000,000.

3996 (SIR ALAN ANDERSON) *The evil is that the investors may waste some money?* Yes, the evil is not that you would lose all that £100,000,000, but that the £100,000,000 might not be used quite as well as it might be under other arrangements.

3997 *If the Americans gave us £2,000,000,000, we should have to do something with it?* It depends on what was offering, but here is a great benefit of £2,000,000,000, and however inadvisedly it was used, you would hardly waste all of it.

3998 (MR HICHENS) *At any rate, if the American chose to take some money out of his pocket and put it into yours, you would not mind if a little dropped on the way, whereas you might not think it worth while to change your own money from one pocket to another and lose some of it?* Precisely.

3999 (MR BELL) *There is considerable unanimity I think, in regard to the amount of £50,000,000 for the new sinking fund. All sorts of people say they think that £50,000,000 a year is a reasonable amount to pay off. Is that so, in your judgment?* I should say something round about that figure.

4000 (CHAIRMAN) *Will you pass to your next point?* My next point is closely connected with what we have been discussing. It arises out of the character of the present Trustee Acts. Until 1889 only Consols were available for trustees. During the 'nineties, great trouble began to arise because the amount of funds available for trustee investment was always increasing, whereas the volume of Consols was falling. To meet this certain alterations were made by the Colonial Stock Act of 1900 which greatly extended the range of trustee investments. At that time, the amount of colonial loans was not very great, and it is only comparatively recently that these have become very great. Now the colonies are prepared to borrow practically as much as we are prepared to lend them. The consequence is that if money is available in the gilt-edged market, and there is no new home investment to take off those surplus funds, they almost automatically find their way to the colonies. Thus the diversion of money into the gilt-edged market now creates an unduly strong presumption in favour of its leaving the country. The colonies have socialised a number of services which we have not socialised. Thus the money required for such services in the colonies is easier to borrow than money required for similar services in this country; and in many ways, which I have elaborated in a paper which I think some members of the Committee have seen, the extension of the Trustee Acts so as to cover nearly all colonial government securities, when at the same time the volume of home trustee securities is being reduced, creates a dangerous bias in favour of excessive foreign investment. The conditions which led to the extension of the Trustee Act no longer exist. It would not be wise or practicable to make any change as regards existing trustee securities, but I think that so far as future additions to the list are concerned, the rules ought to be tightened up very much. In a paper that I read lately I suggested that the Treasury should have a certain power of licence. That proposal has been much criticised, and I think there is force in the criticism. I should like to avoid that. I would therefore either abolish the Trustee Acts altogether, for which there is a great deal to be said, or if they are retained, I would allow as new trustee securities only home securities such as prior charges on railways and country and municipal loans, and I should extend the list so as to include a number of public utility services of the type of the Port of London, and so on. I attach considerable importance to this point, though of course if the volume of debt reduction is reduced, it is not so important as it would be otherwise. In any case there is not much prospect of the volume of home Government debt increasing, whereas the volume of investment which seeks an outlet in the gilt-edged market is always increasing. I think it is dangerous, therefore, that the surplus should tend to be drawn off into foreign investment, without more inquiry as to the relative advantage of the different channels of investment than is made at present.

4001 (SIR CHARLES ADDIS) *Do you advocate any control of the market in order to effect that object, apart from the repeal or the amendment of the Trustee Acts?* I am personally not so much afraid of allowing discretion to a central authority as some people are. That is why I originally suggested that the Treasury should have a certain power of licence. I think it is very difficult to define beforehand just what types of securities you will wish to include in the trustee list, and I believe that the Treasury could be trusted to use its discretion wisely. There are many people who believe that all officials and all bankers are devoid of intelligence and that no discretion should ever be allowed to them.

4002 *Would the amendment of the Trustee Act itself, in your judgement, produce any considerable effect? Would it not merely amount to this, that the colonies, who are eager borrowers, would borrow very much the same amount at a slightly higher rate?* I think that the rate would rapidly become somewhat deterrent to them. It would very much encourage them to float as much as they could at home. There are several colonies now where they are rather near the line. Canada is a little across the line. It is now cheaper for Canada to borrow at home than to borrow here; but there is always the danger in a new country where the rates are relatively high, that if you give them the benefit of our trustee rates, which are lower than theirs, you encourage them to borrow outside the country instead of at home. Besides, there is the United States market, which is likely to be attractive to them; and there again an extra half per cent in the London rate for colonial loans would increase the chance of the Americans being able to meet the requirements of the colonies at a competitive figure.

4003 (MR BOWEN) *Have you considered the effect of your proposals upon colonial markets and the effect it would have upon inter-colonial trade or trade between ourselves and the colonies?* I do not think it would have any great influence.

4004 *If the colonies require money—and we are told that they do—do you think this would act as a deterrent to their obtaining money and directly or indirectly affect their prospects of trade with the home country?* That raises the whole question of the use of our own resources. We have a certain surplus available for foreign investment which is best invested in that way. My criticism is not against all foreign investment as such, but a legislative contrivance which gives an undue advantage to it.

4005 *But we are up against public policy in some respects. If we are to encourage the colonies, do you not think it would have a ery injurious effect upon colonial trade, if you were to say to our investors: ' You must not invest in colonial investments'?* We should not say that.

4006 *But it would amount to that. It would very substantially restrict their operations, anyhow, and people who had money and who could invest only in* *gilt-edged securities, would be debarred from the colonial market altogether by your proposals. The colonial market would be open, therefore, only to the other people who had money to invest?* There are some people who think it primarily important to develop the colonies; there are others who think it primarily important to develop good conditions at home. It is a question of the balance between those two ideas. I believe that we ought to pay more attention than we have paid lately to the conditions at home, the return on which, in terms of public welfare, would be quite as great as the return we get from loans to the colonies.

4007 *I should be inclined to agree with you on that, but at the same time in making this distinction you make such a sweeping suggestion here that it would help my view if you would suggest any margin or line of demarcation. How far would it prevent trustees from investing in colonial stock?* The present law is that there are certain stocks to which trustees are limited if they are not specially empowered, but there are a great many investors in the gilt-edged market who are not limited in that way. Many trustees themselves are not limited in that way. It happens that there are now a number of colonial loans which, for technical reasons, because they stand above par and are redeemable within a certain number of years, are not available as trustee investments, and they consequently carry a higher rate of interest. It would not follow from my proposal that no investment would be made in the colonies. It merely means that a special artificial stimulus to investment there would be removed.

4008 *You think that if debt were repaid in any substantial sum above, say, £50,000,000 a year, all that would be directed onto the gilt-edged market again. Could you tell us why you have come to that conclusion?* Not all of it, but if a man holds gilt-edged securities there is a presumption that that is the type of security which suits him. Therefore, if you repay him, there is a presumption that he will reinvest the proceeds in a similar type of security.

4009 *But we have been told so often that there are people who invested in War Loan because of the national security at the time, not because it was a gilt-edged security. Could it be assumed that, if debt were repaid in larger measure than £50,000,000 a year, at least a great portion of the sum so repaid would find its way back into industry?* I should have thought that the proportion of holders of gilt-edged securities who held them for those reasons was now small. That was a strong reason for taking up the loans when issued, but it is rather a muddle-headed reason for going on holding them now. It does no injury to the state if a man sells War Loan. It did give assistance to the state when he subscribed to it.

4010 (SIR ALAN ANDERSON) *With regard to the Treasury having a voice in saying what should be trustee securities and what should not, it does not reflect at all upon one's confidence in the brains of the Treasury, but at first it would put them in an impossible position with regard to the colonies, would it not?* I think that the method would be that the Treasury would decide that over a given period of time a certain amount of loan was to be allocated to colonial borrowers, and they would then call a conference of the various colonial borrowers and arrange the division amongst them. In the case of the Australian Commonwealth, which is much the most important, it would probably take the form of the Commonwealth itself deciding how the amount was to be distributed between the Commonwealth and the various states. I think it would be much simpler to work if all except home investments were cut out, but I think it is going too far to say that the other arrangement is unworkable.

4011 (CHAIRMAN) *Suppose the Australian Government gets £4,000,000 loan from us, how is that £4,000,000 paid? Do they get it in the form of money or goods?* They get it in the form of goods in the end.

4012 *That bears on the point of whether there is an advantage in lending money for the sake of the home trade?* I do not think there is ever any advantage in getting rid of goods just for the sake of getting rid of them. An equal home investment would cause just as great a demand for labour.

4013 *Would there be the demand?* I am assuming that that is so. If there was no eligible home borrower on a sufficient scale then my objection to colonial loans would drop; but my argument is that there are outlets at home which, owing to the character of our organisation, at present do not get their fair chance as compared with colonial loans.

4014 (SIR ALAN ANDERSON) *You say that because of this inequity of the Trustee Act we are unfairly handicapped in favour of the colonies?* Yes, we are handicapping ourselves.

4015 (CHAIRMAN) *What is your next point?* My next point is one which may not interest the Committee at all. I am continuing the same line of argument that I was on before—that the cheapest way of carrying the national debt is to create the type of bond that the investor wants. I gave that as the criterion between short-dated, long-dated and intermediate-dated debt, because there are some people who want their interest fixed and some people who want their capital value fixed. But there is also another class of person, namely, persons who want to be free from risks arising out of variations in the value of money. I do not know how large that market is, but I know that such people do exist, and I think that the state could float a certain volume of bonds economically by catering for that particular class. My proposal would be that the Board of Trade or some suitable body should prepare an index number in accordance with the variations of which the interest and the capital of the loan would be paid. No one would be compelled to subscribe to such a loan except persons who fancied that arrangement. But particularly those, who are connected with corporations which have a very long life, have a natural anxiety on matters of this kind. I might perhaps speak for myself as Bursar of a Cambridge college. The colleges in the past have held the greater part of their property in the form of land. They have also held property, partly manorial dues, which have been fixed in terms of money. In the course of time all their property which was fixed in terms of money has ceased to be of significant value. They have been entirely dependent for their continued prosperity on the fact that their fortunes were not wholly committed to legal tender. Recently for obvious reasons there has been a strong tendency to sell their land and to invest in gilt-edged securities. They are therefore getting into the position, which is dangerous, of having their fortunes in legal tender instead of in real property. I think it is correct to say that in past history every long-lived institution which has had its property in legal tender instead of in real values has been ultimately ruined, because in the long run the value of any legal tender always falls towards zero, if you are considering considerable periods of time. There are other investing bodies, particularly those who are engaged in building up pension funds, who are interested in their fund having a given purchasing power at the end of a considerable period of years. Any pension fund in any part of the Continent of Europe which was invested in gilt-edged securities before the War, has now lost by far the greater part of its value. It has been the case in this country that all funds invested in this way prior to the War have lost a large part of their value. We may hope that that kind of misfortune will not occur in this country in future, but if you are considering a long period nobody can feel sure that it will not. Therefore there are certain investors who would be prepared to take a slightly lower rate of interest in order to insure themselves against that type of misfortune. In think it would be proper for the state to cater for that class, and I think it would also be advantageous to have an official index number of this sort, which could be taken advantage of by other borrowers than the state if they thought fit. The proposal I am making is nearly the same as one which was made by the late Professor Marshall when he gave evidence before the Commission on Depression of Trade in 1886, and again before the Gold and Silver Commision of 1888. I believe the advantages which were claimed for it then are even greater now.

4016 (SIR CHARLES ADDIS) *Would there not be a difficulty in regard to dealings in those bonds?* That would depend on their popularity.

4017 *You would have to make your estimate of what the changes would be in the years ahead?* You could assume that they would have a certain value on the hypothesis that prices would remain the same. As regards the future, you would have to make no more calculations than you have to make at present. Anyone who invests in gilt-edged securities as against ordinary shares, has to make the calculation of whether he thinks over a period of time prices are going to rise or fall.

4018 *You do not think there is much difficulty in regard to dealing with these?* It would be a little less easy to bury your head in the sand.

4019 (SIR ALAN ANDERSON) *And the interest would be settled each year?* Yes.

4020 (MRS WOOTTON) *Do you think there is any prospect of converting any of the existing debt to a bond of that kind?* I think there would be. I think many people would dislike them intensely. The element of variability of money income would not appeal to certain classes; there would be a complication about it; it would be more difficult to understand. On the other hand, I think there are types of investors who would like them very much, and it would depend on the number of such persons when you came to test the market.

4021 (MR BOWEN) *What would be the basis of your index figures?* I do not think it would make very much difference which of the standard types of index number was selected, but I should aim at something rather like the cost-of-living index number, than the wholesale index number; I should prefer a special index number for the purpose.

4022 (SIR CHARLES ADDIS) *You contemplate the issue of bonds for a considerable period of years?* Yes.

4023 (MRS WOOTTON) *May I put a question on another point? In an article which was written by you some time ago, you made a suggestion that instead of devoting sinking fund moneys to repay debt, the Treasury should lay out a sum, possibly £100,000,000 a year, on obtaining productive assets. Would you explain that, and could you at the same time give us your views on the proposal that was put up, that a similar sum should be earmarked for debt reduction or the acceleration of public works?* It is a big question: if you can spare me a few minutes I could develop it. My view is that in modern conditions there has been an insufficient supply of capital at moderate rates for public utility enterprises, which would absorb large sums of money. Owing to the control of profits and rates, and so forth, which is now popular, an investment in a public utility enterprise is very unlikely to yield the investor any unusual gains; he will never be allowed to obtain more than a certain rate of interest. On the other hand, he is not secured against loss. The result is that the inducement to the investment of money in large public utility enterprises is very much less than it was, for example, during the period of the railway boom, when our railways were built. In those days it was realised that it was a speculation, in a sense, but it was hoped that if railways proved a good thing, the investor would make a great deal of money. Supposing that steam locomotion was discovered today, the investor would know that, owing to the control of rates and so forth, he would never be allowed to make anything substantial; and, on the other hand, he might lose his money. I am, therefore, very doubtful whether, in present conditions, the railway system of England could be built by unaided private enterprise. I believe that considerations of this sort stand in the way at this moment of the development of our ports, of our transport system, and of our power system, and that the policy of leaving these to unaided private enterprise is a thing which is no longer practicable. As to the forms in which the state can help, I think there ought to be great variety. In the quotation to which Mrs Wootton referred, I do not mean to suggest that the Treasury should put this amount of money in directly, but that it should facilitate the investment of some such sum in various ways.

4024 *Guarantees?* Guarantees; and I think that a number of experiments might be made as to the best channel for doing this.

4025 (CHAIRMAN) *The Treasury give guarantees now?* We are drifting in that direction; it is already being done. I should like to do it more consciously and on a larger scale. I believe that the public utility enterprise is a thing which as an object of private investment we have killed already by our control of profits, and so forth, and we are liable to suffer because we are now in an interregnum period in which in half of our ideas we have a sort of semi-socialism and in another half of our ideas we still depend upon unaided private enterprise. Public utility enterprise is the sort of thing which particularly suffers in a situation of that kind. This is closely connected with this drift of money abroad to the colonies. In the colonies they have gone faster; they are not in that *interregnum*; the state assists all sorts of things which are not assisted here. I think that is dangerous, and I think that the situation wants looking into. I cannot think that there is so small a need for investment in public enterprise as is actually going on.

(CHAIRMAN) *Thank you very much.*

The witness withdrew.

Keynes appeared before the Committee again on 6 May 1925 to give evidence on a capital levy. His evidence appears as the Appendix to Part II this volume.

322

Keynes returned to the problems of investing abroad in a brief unsigned note in a Russian debts supplement to *The Nation* of 18 October 1924.

From The Nation and Athenaeum, *18 October 1924*

DEFAULTS BY FOREIGN GOVERNMENTS

The record of defaults by foreign Governments on their external debt are so numerous, and indeed so nearly universal, that it is easier to deal with them by naming those which have not defaulted than those which have.

All foreign Governments which have borrowed any considerable sum on the London market* have been in default in whole or in part on the service of their external debt within the past twenty-five years, with the exception of Chile and Japan. It should, however, be added that the defaults by Peru have been insignificant, and those by Uruguay not very important unless we go back to 1891.

The defaulting Governments include those of all the states of Central and South America, with the above-named two or three exceptions. Other important defaulters within the past twenty-five years include Mexico, China, Egypt, Turkey, Greece, Spain, Portugal, Russia, Austria, Hungary, Bulgaria, and Roumania.

Indeed, it is not an exaggeration to say that it has been very exceptional in the history of foreign investment for a foreign government to keep its engagements.

In addition to those countries which have technically defaulted, there are several other countries which have borrowed externally in terms of their own currency and have then allowed the currency to depreciate to less than half of the nominal value at which the loans were contracted, and in some cases to an infinitesimal fraction of it. The more important countries in this group are Belgium, France, Italy, and Germany.

* The Governments of Scandinavia and Holland, neither of which have borrowed more than relatively small sums, are amongst the exceptions.

When Parliament met at the end of September 1924 the Labour Government faced a vote of censure over its handling of the prosecution of a communist who allegedly had incited mutiny amongst the forces. The Government rejected possible compromises that would have avoided defeat in the House, lost the vote and appealed to the country in a general election called for 29 October. Keynes took no part in the campaign beyond a speech on 25 October at the Corn Exchange in Cambridge in support of the local Liberal candidate F. R. Salter and a widely publicised letter on his behalf.

To F. R. SALTER, *18 October 1924*

My Dear Salter,

I hope you will obtain much support as Liberal Candidate for the Borough of Cambridge. Liberalism has a part to play just as important as in the days of its full strength.

The man who looks ahead ought to vote Liberal. For if Liberalism was to decay, we should be left with one party representing Wealth and Conservatism up against another party representing Labour and Discontent. No Government lives for ever, and I can conceive nothing worse for all of us than a see-saw struggle on class lines between the Haves and the Have-Nots. We shall never get, that way, the evolution of a better society.

But the man who thinks of the tasks immediately ahead of us ought to vote Liberal too. Our most pressing problem is to mitigate unemployment and to raise our standards of output, of housing and of wages. To do this we must increase the mobility of labour between one job and another, organise more skilfully the employment of credit, and direct more wisely the use of our annual savings. (Personally, I attach great importance to improving the equipment of England herself rather than foreign countries.) By reason of their old fashioned dogmas and the class-interests they are compelled to serve, neither Socialists nor Tories are likely to do anything sensible and effective in the near future.

I imagine that the official Labour candidate has no chance of getting in, and that your real opponent is Sir Douglas

Newton. All voters with progressive sympathies, who care about peace and liberty and new ideas and commonsense, should join their forces to put you in against him. Mr Baldwin in his Election Address, has left so many loop-holes for protectionist measures that it will be imprudent for any free trader to vote for Sir Douglas.

There are some people in Cambridge who like stick-in-the-mud for its own sake. Let them vote for Sir Douglas Newton. But let everyone else vote for you.

Yours sincerely,

J. M. KEYNES

After the election returned a Conservative Government with a substantial majority, Keynes looked at the results more generally.

From The Nation and Athenaeum, *8 November 1924*

THE BALANCE OF POLITICAL POWER AT THE ELECTIONS

The statistics of the Election in round numbers, compared with a year ago, can be put in a nutshell, thus:—

(*a*) The number of those entitled to vote was 800,000 more than last year.

(*b*) The number of those who did vote was 2,000,000 more than last year.

(*c*) The Conservatives polled 2,000,000 more, Labour 1,000,000 more, and Liberals 1,000,000 less (after allowing for the constituencies where, this time, no Liberal was standing).

(*d*) Thus of the 3,000,000 new voters and Liberal deserters the Conservatives captured two-thirds and Labour one-third.

As usual, on our present electoral system, the turnover in power has been altogether out of proportion to the turnover in votes; 2,000,000 voters out of 20,000,000 decide the Government of the country. As a broad generalisation, 70 per cent of the electors are steady partymen who can be expected to give the same straight party vote every time. The distribution of this 70 per cent between the parties changes very slowly; at the present time perhaps 28 per cent is Conservative, 14 per cent Liberal, and 28 per cent Labour. Of the remaining 30 per cent, nearly 20 per cent abstain from voting, leaving us with the 10 per cent of wobblers who settle matters. Even the best political tacticians sometimes forget this. They pay too much attention to the party bondsmen and too little to the free men,—the unprejudiced, independent wobblers, who hold the head high and govern us by slightly inclining it to the left or to the right.

Now, owing to the geographical concentration of the strength of Labour in certain parts of the country, particularly in comparison with the Liberals, who are distributed more evenly, Labour's minimum representation is unlikely to fall at any time much below its present figure of about one-quarter of the House of Commons. But, on the other hand, it is, for the same reason, very much more difficult for Labour to obtain an absolute majority of the whole House. For example, if every single voter throughout the country who voted Liberal last week had voted Labour, the Conservative Party would still have had a comfortable working majority of more than fifty seats.

Thus, in order to get an independent majority, the Labour Party would need to capture not only the whole of the Liberal Party, but all the wobblers too. Actually, if the Liberal Party broke up, a considerable portion would join the Conservatives, and thus render the latter almost impregnable in many parts of the country.

What practical conclusions can we draw from this analysis? First, that whilst the Liberal Party cannot expect in future to obtain an independent majority in the House of Commons, it still commands a balancing power which will probably be decisive in one election out of every two.

Second, that it would need exceptional circumstances to give the Labour Party an independent majority,—such circumstances as the combination of several years of Tory misgovernment with a falling standard of life for the mass of the workers. Some sections of the Labour Party would like to stay in the wilderness waiting for the exceptional circumstances. Some day or other distressful economic conditions might yield them a brief opportunity to try extremist experiments. But, on the other hand, large elements in the Labour Party are capable of seeing that social improvements can only come as the result of clear thinking and cool action, and that the tumultuous exploitation of acute distress would give reforms a poor chance to succeed. New social experiments will not get a fair opportunity to prove their worth, unless they can be introduced in times of normal prosperity.

My third conclusion, therefore, is this. We are not likely to see, for many years to come, a progressive Government of the Left capable of efficient legislation, unless Radicals and Labour men stop cutting one another's throats and come to an agreement for joint action from time to time to carry through practical measures about which they agree. Probably not less than 10 per cent of the British electorate are natural Radicals. Their mentality and their feelings and sometimes their class sympathies are distinct from those of the typical Labour enthusiast. Their proper place is outside the Labour Party. They form a nucleus around which from time to time a substantial body of voters will collect. No important reforms will ever be carried in this country without their intellectual, moral, and numerical support.

On 6 November Keynes delivered the Sidney Ball lecture at Oxford under the title 'The End of *Laissez-Faire*'. He gave a revised version of the same lecture in Berlin in 1926 before publishing it through the Hogarth Press.[3]

On 11 December, Keynes travelled to Edinburgh to speak to the local Chamber of Commerce and Manufacturers. His topic was 'The Policy of

[3] It appears in *JMK*, vol. IX, pp. 272–94.

this Country towards Foreign Investments'. Keynes used most of the new material in the lecture in his second contribution to *The Nation* for 1925.[4]

From The Nation and Athenaeum, *17 January 1925*

SOME TESTS FOR LOANS TO FOREIGN
AND COLONIAL GOVERNMENTS

Recent columns of *The Nation* have contained several criticisms of the prevailing conventions in regard to loans to foreign and colonial governments. From the investment standpoint each proposition must, of course, be considered separately on its merits. But it may be useful to set out a few of the quite simple general principles which seem to me to govern the matter.

It has been common for writers in the financial press to take the line that, other things being equal, there is a positive advantage in foreign investments as against home investments, because of the stimulus which they afford to our export industries. This is surely mere fallacy. An investment at home provides just as great a stimulus to trade and to employment as an investment abroad. It is not a peculiarity of foreign investment that it should involve, directly or indirectly, the production and sale of goods. On the other hand, so far from there being a presumption in favour of foreign investment as such, there may be, in the present situation of this country, a fairly strong presumption against it. As a rule, an additional foreign investment does not cause, directly and in itself, a corresponding addition to our exports. This is only the case where the borrower expends the proceeds of his loan in purchasing British goods which he would not purchase otherwise. If this is not the case—and frequently it is not the case—the grant of a loan to an external borrower may produce a situation in which, *unless we export more*, our account does not balance. That is to say, market conditions are produced through the state

[4] His first on 'Inter-Allied Debts', which appeared on 10 January, is reprinted in *JMK*, vol. XVIII, pp. 264–8.

of the exchanges and the rate of interest which lead us as a country to press our goods more insistently than before on the markets of the outside world. In order to provide for our foreign investment we have to force on these markets a greater volume of exports. And in all probability, in order to do the larger business which is thus required of us, we must be content to sell our exports at a lower real price. Now, there is a certain volume of exportation which we can conduct at prices satisfactory to ourselves. But the more we have to export in order to cover our imports and our foreign loans, the less satisfactory this price will be. There is a great difference between foreign investments which are caused by a previous surplus of exports, which has put the international balance unduly in our favour, and foreign investments which are the result of convention and our investment arrangements and exercise a forcing influence on our exports in order to balance the account.

For these reasons, therefore, there is much to be said in favour of home investments, since they are much less likely to turn the ratio of real interchange with foreign countries against us. When we do lend abroad, the foreign or colonial loan must make out a strong case. In order to justify itself it must be exceptionally lucrative or likely to facilitate British enterprise abroad and the production of commodities of which we stand in need. There are many classes of foreign investment which have manifestly satisfied these criteria in the past. Foreign investments in mines and plantations, for example, must have justified themselves many times over. But it is not foreign investment of this type which is absorbing large sums today. We lend to the Governments of India and the colonies every year something like double the capital which we have put into *all* the coffee, tea, and rubber shares quoted on the London Stock Exchange. The latter investments are individually small; and even the sums which they absorb in the aggregate are trifling compared with the sums which a colonial government will think nothing of borrowing in a day. It is, therefore, mainly loans to foreign and colonial governments which must be examined with a critical eye and be called upon to justify themselves on every ground.

I suggest that there are certain broad conditions which such loans should satisfy, before they can be reckoned as satisfactory investments either for individual investors or in the national interest.

(1) It must be clear that the service of the aggregate foreign debt of the borrowing government is well within its financial capacity even in the event of the supply of new loans drying up and of the service of the existing debt having to be met out of current income. Any case in which a government appears to be borrowing substantially more than the equivalent of the service of its existing debt, and is therefore piling up indebtedness at compound interest, and has been pursuing this course for some considerable time, deserves extra-careful consideration, especially as to whether the whole of the sums borrowed are being invested productively so as to yield a progressively increasing income out of which the ever-increasing service of the debt can be safely met.

(2) It ought to be made a condition of any loan to a foreign or colonial government that there is a specific sinking fund attached to it which operates by drawings or by purchase in the market, so that the capital of the loan will be reduced year by year and be automatically extinguished by the due date. Many recent loans to foreign governments satisfy this criterion. If it had not been for this, the British investor would certainly have fared much worse than he has with his loans to the governments of South America. For, in the absence of a specific sinking fund, the probability of the loan's being repaid at the due date is extremely remote;—it will be refunded and the real repayment further postponed. When we turn, however, to loans to colonial governments we find that they rarely carry a specific sinking fund attached to them. In most cases there is a general sinking fund by which a certain sum is applied out of the budget towards the reduction or avoidance of debt. But this is no substitute.

Such general sinking funds may be applied either to internal debt or to new expenditure. They are a feeble guarantee for the repayment of the foreign lender. At the present time some colonial government loan falls due for repayment every few months, and is almost always refunded instead of repaid. If colonial government loans are to retain their present position in the list of trustee investments, the Treasury should at any rate lay down a regulation prescribing that in every case there shall be a specific sinking fund operating year by year in the market, so as to extinguish the loan to which it is attached by the date of the latter's maturity.

(3) It is relevant to inquire whether the country is borrowing abroad at a considerably lower rate of interest than it is paying at home. Thus British investors, for example, who are prepared to lend to the Commonwealth of Australia at a lower rate of interest than will content the people of Australia for similar loans, are surely in an unsatisfactory situation. There is a strong temptation to the Commonwealth Government, so long as the disparity of rates persists, to borrow abroad rather than at home. As soon as exchange rates have settled down there is an inducement to large British investors to transfer into the internal loans in exchange for the external loans. Moreover, there is no inducement for the gradual repatriation of the external loans into the hands of Australian investors themselves, which in the case of a country gradually growing in wealth is one of the most satisfactory means of discharging the external debt. In such circumstances, therefore, the foreign lender necessarily exposes himself to the possibility of some loss in the capital value of his investment through the tendency of the external and internal rates of interest to come together as time goes on.

(4) Fourth and most important of all, investors must never forget that in the case of external government loans there is no legal redress whatever in the event of default. This is a fact which in the past investors have often enough discovered to their disadvantage when it is too late. All kinds of circumstances can

arise when it is no longer to the interest of the external government to treat foreign lenders fairly. The temptation exists as soon as the service of the existing debt is a heavier burden than the benefit which can be derived from any probable future borrowings. This fact must render a loan to an external government a less desirable investment, other things being equal, than a mortgage or a high-class home debenture. Such loans, therefore, can never be regarded as satisfactory to the investor, unless they yield a materially higher rate of interest than can be obtained on the finest home debentures. There is also a further reason for an adequate margin in the rate of interest obtained, which applies, indeed, to all fixed interest investments. In the case of all investments in bonds and debentures there can never be any unexpected profit to compensate for the losses of capital which are bound to occur from time to time, even from the most carefully selected investments. The only fund, therefore, from which a margin can be obtained to average out such losses is in the surplus yield of interest obtainable on the bonds.

Let each investor test for himself his holdings of foreign and colonial government securities in the light of these facts. In the case of foreign government loans the investor has suffered so severely in the recent past that the market price may have fallen in some cases low enough to be tempting;—though it is difficult to be satisfied that the ever-present risk of default has been fully allowed for. I much doubt, however, whether the ordinary run of colonial government securities yield anything like the margin they should, on the above tests, in comparison with our own British Government securities.

If one looks back to pre-war days it is obvious that the conventional attitude towards Austrian and Russian Government loans, for example, was highly imprudent. In the case of Russia, in particular, everyone knew well that she had been borrowing excessively and satisfied none of the above tests. I am not sure that twenty years hence some of our present conventional canons of investment may not seem, in the light of subsequent experience, as ill-advised in their way (though not, I hope and expect, so excessively disastrous) as some of those of the pre-war period are now seen to have been.

With the election of a Conservative Government in October 1924, sterling rose strongly against the dollar on the foreign exchanges, largely for speculative reasons. This rise took it from $4.49 on 31 October to above $4.72 at year's end. In the new year it moved even higher. The rise in the exchange, plus the assurance of a stable Government for a full Parliament, gave the question of Britain's future exchange rate policy a new urgency in official circles and elsewhere. Keynes turned to the issue first on 21 February in his annual review of the speeches of the Clearing Bank chairmen under the title 'The Return Towards Gold'.[5] This article was extensively discussed in the Treasury.

Two weeks later he returned to the issue of currency policy after Bank rate rose to 5 per cent on 5 March.

From The Nation and Athenaeum, *7 March 1925*

THE BANK RATE

In May, 1924, the rediscount rate of the Federal Reserve Bank of New York stood at $4\frac{1}{2}$ per cent. Between then and August, 1924, this rate was reduced by successive stages to 3 per cent. The price level followed suit. In May, 1924, prices had been showing for a year past a declining tendency; but by July, 1924, the index number had turned round, and has been rising ever since. Between July, 1924, and the end of January, 1925, dollar prices rose by about 10 per cent,—a rise which, if it had occurred in pre-war days within an equal period of time, would have been regarded as almost unprecedented and in a high degree dangerous. The cheapening of money, coupled with an 'open market policy' on the part of the Federal Reserve Banks, which made money abundant as well as cheap, was, in vulgar language,

[5] *JMK*, vol. IX, pp. 192–200.

'asking for it'. During the same six months the aggregate credit created by the New York banks increased by the enormous figure of 30 per cent. As well as the above big rise of prices, an investment boom, the largest, measured in volume, ever experienced, duly followed.

In recent weeks a change in 'open market policy', following on some losses of gold and a tendency of the member banks to use more freely their borrowing powers from the central institutions, indicated that the Federal Reserve authorities might be beginning to take notice. On Thursday of last week, February 26th, the New York rediscount rate was raised to $3\frac{1}{2}$ per cent,—a small measure in itself (the rate has never fallen below $3\frac{1}{2}$ per cent in most of the Reserve districts), but indicating which way the wind was blowing.

Throughout the whole of this period the Bank of England rate had stood at 4 per cent. This figure is not strictly comparable with the American rediscount rates, since these usually stand below the market rate, whereas Bank rate here usually stands above the market rate. Nevertheless, the effective English rate has been about $\frac{1}{2}$ per cent above the effective American rate (corresponding to the difference of 1 per cent in the respective official rates). At the same time, the quantity, as well as the price, of credit has been kept almost stationary,—the deposits of the London Clearing Banks stood at the same figure in January, 1925, as in July, 1924, as compared with the increase, mentioned above, of no less than 30 per cent in New York. This did not prevent some rise in our prices sympathetically with the rise in America. But as against their rise of 10 per cent, our rise was only 4 per cent; whilst the dollar–sterling exchange has moved in favour of sterling by 8 per cent.

It is obvious that conditions have been almost ideal for an improvement in the exchange without the necessity for any drastic action on the part of the Bank of England. But if the tendencies in America were to turn round the least bit, even if the position there was to become stationary, it would make a great difference. It is not surprising, therefore, that the Governor of the Bank viewed seriously the movement in New York. A special meeting of the Court was summoned immediately, and the Bank of England's loan rates were raised forthwith by 1 per cent as a prelude to the raising of Bank rate.

This is not likely to be a popular consequence of the policy of a return to the gold standard. But those who think that gold is not the best criterion for the regulation of a credit system are not yet entitled to complain. Though our price level has not risen so much as America's, yet it has definitely risen. The interest on long-dated securities in London is so low, in relation to what borrowers are prepared to pay, that the London market has been unduly attractive to new issues of external loans, with the result that their total volume has tended to exceed the volume of the national savings available for this purpose. The use by the Bank of England of its power of putting on private pressure, behind the scenes, to prevent new issues is dangerous and unsatisfactory, and cannot be permanently effective. Four per cent is probably below the true rate of interest, and there is a presumption, therefore, against the continuance of such a low rate *so long as prices are rising*. There are, therefore, some good and substantial reasons for the Bank of England's action.

The one solid argument on the other side is to be found in the state of employment. The figures for unemployment are actually worse than they were a year ago,—mainly on account of the state of the coal, steel, and shipbuilding industries. This is a reason for being extremely critical of the present governance of our affairs. But although it may be necessary, once a slump has been allowed to occur, to allow to industry the stimulus of a substantial price rise from the bottom of the slump, it is not wise at the phase of the credit cycle which we have now reached, even if it is tempting, to try to cure unemployment by allowing actual inflation. I doubt if a 5 per cent Bank rate, which is not oppressive in itself, will do any measurable harm to employment, provided that the price level shows no tendency to fall. It will

335

do harm in one contingency only—and in that contingency it will do great harm—namely, if the rise in the Bank rate is interpreted by the business world as a prelude to falling prices.

This brings me to the point of real danger. We do not know for certain how to interpret the Bank of England's policy. If the policy is merely to keep our prices relatively stable, to wait for higher prices in America to carry sterling to par, and to proceed after that with the utmost caution and deliberation before committing ourselves to any definite action, then I see but little in a 5 per cent Bank rate to disturb the business world. If the business world could be promised that the Bank of England will do all in its power to protect them from a falling price level, even by lowering the Bank rate if necessary, then they can go ahead in quiet confidence. I agree, therefore, with Sir Josiah Stamp's contention, in the admirable letter which he contributed to Tuesday's *Times*, that industrialists should be given an assurance that no reversion is intended to the discarded policy of deflation, and that it is not the policy of the Bank of England to regard conditions in America and the foreign exchanges as more important than the needs of industry at home.

But if the policy is to restore the gold standard *coûte qu'il coûte* by the end of 1925, then the outlook is not so comfortable. It may well be that $3\frac{1}{2}$ per cent in New York will not do very much to check the incipient boom, and that the recent movement is not to be regarded as a first step by the Federal Reserve authorities to taking the position firmly in hand. But the opposite may also be the case. In this event the early removal of the embargo on the export of gold may involve a heavy sacrifice in the form of increased or continuing unemployment. The maintenance or raising of the Bank rate under conditions of falling prices would be highly injudicious in the present condition of British industry and trade.

Some people think that it is inconsistent to oppose a higher Bank rate at a time when prices have been falling and to support it, at a much later phase of the trade cycle, when prices have been rising. To be sometimes in favour of dearer money and sometimes in favour of cheaper money seems to them like being sometimes a Protestant and sometimes a Roman Catholic. But to think in this way is to overlook the very elements of the argument. What influences enterprise and employment is not the money rate of interest, but the anticipated real rate of profit over the period of the productive process; and this latter is compounded of the Bank rate and the anticipated movement of prices.

The essence of our industrial health, it seems to me, lies in confidence,—that is, in the business world being able to lay its plans free from anxiety lest their anticipated profit will be obliterated by a falling price level. Many writers in the press are arguing that the important risk to avoid is the risk of fluctuations in the American exchange. I think that they see things out of proportion. Only a part of our total production is materially affected by the dollar exchange; and for this part there is no difficulty whatever in insuring the risk very cheaply by dealing on the forward exchanges. On the other hand, almost all producers are affected by the sterling price level, and there is no means whatever of insuring against its movements.

Keynes's suspicions of 7 March that a change in policy was afoot were certainly strengthened by a meeting he attended at the Chancellor of the Exchequer's on the evening of 17 March. At that meeting, Keynes, Bradbury, McKenna and Niemeyer argued about the merits of alternative policies. The next evening, Keynes discussed the issues with the Commercial Committee of the House of Commons. His remarks appeared in *The Nation* for 21 March. The previous day, the Chancellor, Foreign Secretary, the Governor of the Bank and the Prime Minister met and agreed to announce a return to the gold standard at pre-war par in the Budget speech on 28 April.

From The Nation and Athenaeum, *21 March 1925*

THE PROBLEM OF THE GOLD STANDARD

The problem of the gold standard is often discussed as though it was a question of an automatic or self-regulated standard *versus* a managed standard. But this is not the real distinction between the orthodox party and the reforming party. The real distinction is one, not of method, but of object. The essence of a gold standard, in modern conditions, has very little to do with gold itself regarded as a commodity of intrinsic value. Its main object is to establish a uniform standard of currency, which shall be the same over a great part of the world, and which shall be independent of national politics. Unfortunately, these advantages cannot be obtained without the penalty of having to regulate our credit system, with all the far-reaching effects which this exercises over our industry and trade, with reference, not solely or even mainly to our own internal requirements, but to the conditions of credit in the world at large and more particularly in the United States. The main object of monetary reformers, on the other hand, is to evolve a standard of currency regulated primarily by reference to the requirements of the credit system at home and to the stability of internal prices, even when this is only possible at the expense of fluctuations in terms of the standards of other countries, for example, the mark or the dollar. Monetary reformers do not deny the great advantages of an international currency unit. But they think it better to evolve a good standard first (with the hope of universalising it later if possible), thus enabling our own credit system to run smoothly— which they deem almost a necessity for industrial stability; rather than to accept an unsatisfactory international standard, in the hope of improving it later on by organised international co-operation.

But whilst the *objects* of the two schools are thus contrasted, the *methods* of currency management, which each would have to employ to attain its object, are almost exactly the same. A fully automatic and self-regulating metallic standard has not existed in this country since the eighteenth century, and perhaps it was not fully automatic even then. The best, and indeed almost the only, example of such a thing in the twentieth century was the Egyptian currency immediately before the war. Where most of the business of a country is carried on by means of a credit system of the modern type, central management of the currency becomes a necessity. The best example of an attempt under modern conditions to reduce the element of central management to a minimum was to be found in the United States under their pre-war organisation prior to the establishment of the Federal Reserve System. This state of affairs proved so disastrous, particularly in the crisis of 1907, that it became the preoccupation of all thinking American bankers to evolve a managed system.

The course of events in England during the nineteenth century is instructive. The wars of Napoleon brought an inconvertible managed currency for a period of more than twenty years, just as the Great War has brought us the same thing for a period of more than ten years. Then, as now, the management, under the appalling difficulties of war and post-war conditions, was open to criticism. The relation of government finance to inflation and deflation was not fully understood. Then, as now, vicious war finance was allowed to breed inflation and virtuous post-war finance to breed deflation. Then, as now, the orthodox party proclaimed that the one thing necessary was to restore gold convertibility; and a little more than a hundred years ago the deed was proudly done. The results were shocking. We suffered twenty years of successive credit maladjustments and crises, the most disturbed and troubled we have ever known, barely escaping revolution. The growing discontents of the business world culminated in the famous reform embodied in the Bank Act of 1844. The peculiar Act is largely responsible for the myth about our having an automatic gold standard, which persists in the newspapers to this day. The reformers of that time, led by Lord Overstone, perceived that our troubles came from our pretending to have an automatic gold standard whilst really having an unmanaged credit system. Their solution consisted in laying down the principle that, whilst credit-money should still be allowed within limits, it should be made to behave exactly as it would behave if it were actually made of gold. This reform, if it had worked as its authors intended, would indeed have resulted in the virtual abolition of the credit system and the restoration of something very like an automatic gold standard. But in dealing with credit-money, the authors of the reform thought only of banknotes and forgot bank deposits. Thus the effect was not to crush the credit system, but only to drive it from note-issue banking into deposit banking; and the main ostensible object of the Act was quite defeated. The real reform thought only of bank notes and forgot bank deposits. of the Bank of England, and the adoption of the reformers' ideas about the Bank's discount policy, which were not embodied in the Act at all, gradually led to our at last obtaining a managed credit system. On this system, for fifty years, we flourished moderately.

I am afraid that this historical digression has been a little long. I return to my point that the credit system of this country will be a managed system *anyhow*. No one supposes that we can fix our normal gold reserve at (say) 40 per cent of our aggregate note issue and then leave it to the commissionaires of the Bank of England to announce that the Bank rate has gone up or down according as the reserve has fallen below or has risen above the percentage adopted as normal. To avoid sudden and injurious fluctuations, it will be necessary for the Bank of England to exercise the utmost foresight and to take steps long in advance of the actual inflow and outflow of gold, and, on the other hand, to ignore movements of gold when, in their judgement, such movements are due to exceptional and temporary causes. When the Bank Court thinks that it must act, its weapons will be Bank rate and, at times, the purchase or sale of Government securities. A managed currency, which aims at stability of internal prices and of internal credit, will operate in just the same way. The same amount of foresight will be necessary, and the instruments of action will be the same. Nothing will differ except the object. Under the gold standard the object will be to keep the percentage of gold in reserve within a certain number of points above or below a normal figure. Under the stable purchasing power standard the object will be to keep (say) the Board of Trade index number within a certain number of points above or below a normal figure. Apart from the initial difficulty of whatever is unfamiliar, I do not think that any more skill is required to work the one system than to work the other,—because in either case the technical problems, both of prognostication and of control, are essentially the same.

At any rate, on this occasion it is the monetary reformers who are the cautious folk. My concrete proposal is, after all, not very alarming—namely, that we should continue, broadly speaking, under the same legislation and employing the same methods and machinery of management as during the past two years, but with this difference, that we should have as our object the stability of internal prices and the adequacy of internal credit to the requirements of our own trade and industry, instead of the gradual deflation of our prices relatively to those in the United States. The new problem before the Bank of England would not be any more difficult than their present problem.

On the other hand, to declare at an early date that we bind our currency unit irrevocably to gold, is certainly rash. We should not be returning to the pre-war system. We should be taking the risks of a new and unknown predicament. For we should be trying to run a managed credit system disguised as an automatic gold standard, in the totally new conditions created by our indebtedness to America, the concentration of gold in America, and the establishment of the Federal Reserve System in America. Certainly we should no longer call the tune. A movement of gold to or from America, which would drain or swamp us, would be almost unnoticed by them. Certainly conditions in America would play a bigger part in determining our Bank rate and our credit conditions than the needs of our own trade. Certainly we should run the risk of having to curtail or raise the price of credit to our own industries, merely because an investment boom in Wall Street had gone too far, or because of a sudden change of fashion amongst Americans towards foreign bond issues, or because the banks in the Middle West had got tied up with their farmers, or because the American President was dead, or because the horrid fact that every American had ten motor-cars and a wireless set in every room of every house had become known to the manufacturers of these articles. Alternatively, we might be swamped with cheap American money upon which we could not rely.

With our industries in their present struggling condition and employment at its present level, I reckon it of the first importance that we should keep the control of our internal credit system in our own hands. We are not in a condition to stand shocks or storms. I think that we shall make a big mistake if we expose ourselves to them, merely for the convenience—for really it is little more—of a fixed rate of exchange with the dollar. Any important change in the cost of living and the general level of prices, whether up or down, will endanger industrial peace. Every contraction of credit, brought about by the external situation and not required to check an incipient boom at home, will take away from the employer the possibility of expanding, or even of maintaining, the amount of work on hand.

Mr McKenna, after defending the gold standard by pointing out its disadvantages, ended up with the naughty expectation that it will probably depreciate in the long run and so give us a little inflation without loss of apparent respectability. I think that his forecast is very probable. But I am concerned only secondarily with the long run of gold, whether up or down. My pressing concern is the the short-period fluctuations round the mean value, and with losing the control over our credit system, which we might have used, if only we paused to think, for the mitigation of the curses of unemployment and trade instability.

The worst of this controversy is that nine-tenths of it is carried on by people who do not know the arguments on either side. But perhaps that is true of all controversies. Nevertheless, one who is in the minority must make the best he can of what practical politics permit. The leaders of all three political parties have strapped on their blinkers and have decided to see nothing ahead except gold convertibility as our ultimate objective. Let me therefore offer three concrete proposals, not incompatible with their declarations, the adoption of which would reduce the risks I have been describing:—

(1) Whatever happens, the idea of restoring gold convertibility by allowing the existing embargo on the export of gold to lapse on January 1st next is needlessly rash. It would only serve to commit us in advance to do something in circumstances we cannot foresee, which we should not do voluntarily with our eyes open. Those who were in favour of the discarded policy of deflation naturally want to commit us in advance to the possibility of its reimposition. All those, however, who were opposed to the deflation policy of two or three years ago, should carefully avoid this trap. An announcement in advance of the impending removal of the embargo could have only two objects—to commit us to what we should not do with our eyes open, and to assist the immediate return of sterling towards parity by stimulating speculation on the exchanges. The second object is as foolish as the first; for speculation in favour of sterling will be followed by an equal and opposite reaction which will increase our difficulties later. It is desirable, therefore, to pass a Bill continuing the embargo *subject to the discretion of the Treasury* to remove it, when they judge it wise to do so. Is it not clear that the removal of the embargo should be the last stage of the transition—not to be accomplished until after sterling has been maintained at par *de facto* for some considerable time?

(2) The return to convertibility probably involves the amalgamation of the currency note issue with the Bank of England note issue. The terms of the amalgamation present some interesting problems. It would be well to get this question out of the way, before touching the embargo. If this is done, the future convertibility of the new note should be fixed, not in terms of sovereigns, but in terms of bullion. That is to say, the Bank

of England should be liable, not to cash individual notes in sovereigns, but to provide gold bullion against notes in amounts of not less than £1,000 at a time. This would avoid risk of the return of sovereigns into circulation.

(3) The right to send gold to the Mint should be restricted to the Bank of England, and the Bank's price for gold bullion offered by importers should be left to the Bank's discretion. This would enable the normal buying price for gold to be fixed somewhat higher than was the case before the War, above the fixed par of convertibility. It would also leave the Bank discretion not to buy additional gold if, in its judgement, we were in danger of being flooded. I attach great importance to this provision.

There would be room for an interesting Currency Bill on these lines. Being an impenitent economist, I should still be dissatisfied at the slowness of our statesmen to adopt the real cures, which lie to their hand, for some of our present evils. But if I was an industrialist, I should, if these suggestions were adopted, look forward to the near future with less anxiety.

Keynes's remarks before the Commercial Committee were the object of substantial editorial comment. *The Times* on 19 March devoted several paragraphs to the address and drew a correction from Keynes.

To the Editor of The Times, *19 March 1925*

Sir,

The three paragraphs in which your City Editor comments on my recent address to the Commercial Committee of the House of Commons mistake the drift of my argument.

My main concern was with the importance, in present industrial conditions, of retaining full control of our credit system, so as to regulate the supply and the price of credit by reference to our own conditions (including, of course, in these our export trade), rather than in sympathy with the course of events in the United States. Passing all this by, he develops the criticism that a managed stable-price currency would be liable to interfere with our competitive power in the international market. I do not follow the argument by which he reaches this conclusion. In fact, just the opposite is true. A stable-price standard is a much more sensitive instrument than is a fixed exchange standard (e.g., the gold standard) for adjusting a disequilibrium in our terms of international trade. For a movement of the exchange immediately shifts in the required direction the prices of all our exports in terms of foreign money; whereas under a fixed-exchange standard the same result can only be brought about by the long and painful process of altering the whole range of internal prices, loans, and wages, some of which are fixed in terms of money for considerable periods by custom or by contract. As an example of the same principle, Sir Basil Blackett pointed out the other day what great advantages of internal stability India has recently secured by allowing her exchanges to move. In our own case, if the exchange is allowed to fall at the same time that Bank rate is raised, our external competitive power is strengthened during the period of readjustment. But if, when the Bank rate is raised, the exchange is pegged, then our external competitive power is weakened, until the causal train set moving by higher Bank rate, including the lowering of money wages, has been at last completed. Indeed, the real criticism against the stable-price standard is that it is too sensitive in this respect, and I have made suggestions elsewhere (*Monetary Reform*, p. 190 [*JMK*, vol. IV, p. 150]) to remedy this.

Since you head your report of my address 'A Reply to Mr McKenna', perhaps I may repeat what I said to the members of the Commercial Committee—namely, that I agreed with nine-tenths of what Mr McKenna said, and that my purpose was to supplement his exposition and not to correct it. I do not think that he and I differ in any important respect about the risks and inconveniences of a return to a gold standard. But I take less comfort than he does from the thought that in the long run gold will probably depreciate and so give to business men the tonic of a little inflation under highly respectable auspices.

Yours &c.,

J. M. KEYNES

Keynes's letter, when published, produced a comment from the City Editor of *The Times* suggesting that a currency managed to stabilise British prices would undermine Britain's export competitiveness, as current events were proving, and that a return to gold at pre-war parity would be a better course even if it required painful adjustments.

To the Editor of The Times, *20 March 1925*

Sir,

I agree with your City Editor that we have had a managed currency lately. The management, however, has not been directed to establishing a satisfactory state of our own trade and credit 'regardless of the effect on the exchange'; but the opposite. We have been trying to raise the sterling–dollar exchange without sufficient regard to the effect on our own conditions. We have, in fact, succeeded, by attracting American money, in raising the value of sterling, as your City Editor justly points out, above the value to which our export trade is fully adjusted. I agree with him that the disappointing state of trade at this moment is partly due to this policy.

But whilst I quote the success with which recent management of the currency has attained its purpose, as an example of the efficacy of management, it is ironical to have quoted against me the results of a policy, the objects of which are just the opposite of those I advocate.

J. M. KEYNES

Keynes's second letter to *The Times* brought a comment from Wynnard Hooper which suggested that Keynes advocated management of the currency by the Treasury. Mr Hooper opposed such a course and also stated that he believed that price stabilisation was an impossible policy given human nature. Keynes naturally replied the day the letter appeared.

To the Editor of The Times, *25 March 1925*

Sir,

I hesitate to trespass upon your space yet again. This most fundamental problem of modern economic society requires a wider flight of thought and speech than I can expect you to accommodate. Confined within the birdcage of a column, one can but hop helplessly from one small perch to another.

But when Mr Wynnard Hooper gives, with your aid, much prominence to the statement that it is my policy to hand over to the Treasury the future management of our currency, I am compelled to send you a disclaimer. The passage in my *Tract on Monetary Reform*, which Mr Hooper detaches from its context, concludes an argument in which I maintain that he who manages the volume of credit is master, that the note issue merely follows suit, and that, therefore, when credit is managed the note issue needs no management at all and may just as well be left in the hands of the Treasury, who are anyhow entitled to the profit. Mr Hooper is so steeped in the old idea, that the management of the note issue is the essential thing, that he does not notice how I have deposed it by substituting the management of credit.

So far from wishing to diminish the authority of the Bank of England, I regard this great institution as a heaven-sent gift, ideally suited to be the instrument of the reforms I advocate. We have here a semi-independent corporation within the state, with immense prestige and historical traditions, not (in fact) working for private profit, with no interests whatever except the public good, yet detached from the wayward influences of politics. In the last resort, the Cabinet and the Chancellor of the Exchequer must have their way—in the future, as now and

347

always. But it must be the Bank of England which manages our credit system day by day and takes its orders from no one except in the most public way and under public protest. The Bank of England is a type of that socialism of the future which is in accord with British instincts of government, and which—perhaps one may hope—our Commonwealth is evolving within its womb. The universities are another example of the semi-independent institutions divested of private interest which I have in mind. The state is generally sterile and creates little. New forms and modes spring from fruitful minds of individuals. But when a corporation, devised by private resource, has reached a certain age and a certain size it socialises itself, or it becomes an abuse, or it falls into decay. As time goes on not a few of the institutions which a hundred years ago were individualistic experiments are socialising themselves. But none, perhaps, except the Bank of England—and (should I add?) *The Times* newspaper—has yet completed the process. I differ from the immediate policy of the Bank of England; but it is on the greatness and the prestige of this institution, which no one has done more to increase than the Governor who now holds office, that I rest my hopes for the future.

We still pretend to manage our currency as though we did all our business with lumps of sacred metal. But the pretence wears thinner and thinner. Those who advocate the deliberate management of our credit system from the point of view that our credit money represents not gold but the actual working capital of our industries must not be in a hurry; for they are proposing a big change in a sphere where those who must settle the matter are necessarily unfamiliar with the intricate reasons for the change. The reformers are impugning an orthodoxy and must expect, therefore, at this state to be met with 'moral' objections, with 'psychological' prejudices, and with appeals to the immutability of human nature as exhibited in the fashions of today. At present, to debate monetary reform with a City editor (or an ex-City editor) is like debating Darwinism with a bishop 60 years ago. But even bishops—so why not City editors?—move in the end.

J. M. KEYNES

Keynes also attempted to influence opinion in April with a pair of articles entitled 'Is Sterling Over-valued?'.

From The Nation and Athenaeum, *4 and 18 April 1925*

IS STERLING OVER-VALUED?

The chief reasons for anxiety in the near future, on the part of those who advocate an immediate return to the gold standard, depend upon: (1) whether at the present moment sterling is overvalued relatively to the dollar, and (2) whether business confidence and the present high level of prices in the United States are going to continue in a degree which will obliterate the overvaluation of sterling, or, at any rate, prevent the situation from getting worse.

The publication of the latest figures compiled by the Federal Reserve Board of the United States, as to the relative price levels here and in America, goes a little way towards answering the first question. The figures from February, 1924, to February, 1925, are as follows:—

	Great Britain		United States
	In sterling	Converted to a gold basis	
1924 Feb.	180	160	163
Sept.	172	158	156
Oct.	175	161	159
Nov.	176	167	160
Dec.	177	171	165
1925 Jan.	178	175	168
Feb.	178	174	167

Thus, in February, 1924, sterling prices, converted to a gold basis, were three points below American prices; but in February, 1925, they are seven points higher. This means that, between the two dates, the exchange has improved 6 per cent more than the relative price levels justified. The purchasing power parity theory of the exchanges as between two given dates is, for several reasons, not accurate; but these figures do definitely suggest that some overvaluation of sterling is ruling now. The indexes of prices for March, when we have them, will probably show an aggravation of the situation rather than otherwise.

There is, also, other corroborative evidence. The observed result is just what one would have expected as a consequence of the flow of funds from America to London on capital account, which we know to have taken place; whilst the exceptional difficulty which our export trades are finding in competing successfully in the international markets points to the same conclusion. If our exchanges were 5 per cent lower than they are, with our internal price level unchanged, our industries could afford to abate their prices 5 per cent in the international markets. The rise of the exchange, whatever may have been its cause, is at least a part of the explanation of the difficulties of our exporters. I believe that it would be much better for us, as well as much easier, to let our exchange adjust itself to the present level of our prices and our wages, which have now been fairly steady for some time, rather than to run the risk of having to force down the general level of wages by 5 per cent, at whatever cost to industrial peace. The theory, which some journalists put forward, that a return to the gold standard will, in itself, enable our exporters to offer more competitive prices in the international markets, has no reasonable foundation.

The other question, namely, whether the boom in the United States is going to continue, is still most difficult to answer. If prices rise there, then the return to gold may not involve us in any special difficulties in the very near future. But the reaction in Wall Street and the collapse of speculation in the grain markets have caused a definite setback. The prospects are much more uncertain than they were even a month ago. The Chancellor of the Exchequer has therefore done wisely to put off any decision until after Easter. The reasons for moving slowly and cautiously have grown decidedly stronger since the beginning of the year. If we go back to gold and if prices in the United States do *not* rise, we shall be compelled, at all costs, to force down money wages in this country;—which is not an attractive prospect. I do not see why we should gamble on the future course of American prices, instead of waiting to see what happens.

II

The Return-to-Gold Controversy raises two distinct questions. The one relates to permanent arrangements—the ideal currency of the future. The other relates to an immediate practical problem,—namely, whether it is prudent to tie up our price level in a particular way at this particular moment. In *The Nation* of April 4th I gave some reasons for thinking that our present price-level was too high to justify gold parity. I propose now to compare our level of money wages with those elsewhere in Europe. The following are some representative facts.

(i) The January *Bulletin* of the New York Federal Reserve Bank quotes the following daily wages, converted into gold at the current rates of exchange, paid in November 1924, by a large American company which has factories in the various countries compared:—

England	$2.28
Germany	$1.55
France	$1.35 (Paris)
France	$1.24 (outside Paris)
Belgium	$1.14
Italy	$0.96

(ii) *The Economist* for April 11th states that the skilled iron and steel worker receives weekly £1 18s. in Belgium, £1 13s. 7d.

351

in France, and £2 2s.6d. in Germany; whilst in England the average weekly wage for shorter hours and for the average of skilled *and unskilled* workers is £3 3s.

(iii) In so far as these figures are a measure of higher real wages in England, there is no reason to complain. In the United States, dollar wages are twice what they are in England. But the above unfavourable comparisons—unfavourable from the competitive standpoint—are partly a monetary phenomenon, due to the fact that the current rates of exchange overstate the relative internal value of sterling in terms of its purchasing power over articles of working-class consumption. In other words, if we sell a unit of export for $1, turn it into sterling, pay out the sterling in wages, and consider how much those wages will buy of articles of working-class consumption, as compared with pre-war days, we find that it will buy much less in England than in Germany, France, or Italy. The figures are as follows (the figures for England assuming that sterling is fixed at par):—

	Gold-cost of living (per cent of pre-war)
England	179
Germany	125
France	103
Italy	121

Gold wages are (in round numbers) 50 per cent higher in England than in Germany, and 100 per cent higher than in France, Italy, and Belgium. Real wages are also substantially higher in England, just as they were before the War,—but not nearly so much higher as gold wages are. Thus our difficulty in competing is largely due, not to higher real wages, but to the fact that relatively, the gold cost of living has risen much more in England than in Europe,—which is another way of saying that sterling, measured in its purchasing power over articles of working-class expenditure, is not worth its gold par.

I do not say that the maladjustment is all on one side. Prices in Germany and in Italy, and, above all, in France, are probably destined to rise,—though reparation payments will exercise a restraining influence in the case of Germany. But some of the maladjustment is on our side, so that gold cost of living and gold wages in England will have to fall somewhat, say by 10 per cent, relatively to those elsewhere, to restore equilibrium. I believe, further, that a considerable part of this overvaluation of sterling has taken place quite lately, that is to say, during the past year, as a result of the rapid improvement of the sterling exchange brought about by our monetary policy. It is the success of our monetary policy in using sentiment, more than deflation, to raise the exchange which is at the root of the difficulties of our export industries. Sentiment is a fading flower, and sooner or later we shall be compelled, if we peg our exchanges, to suffer the necessary relative deflation. When this has been accomplished, our export industries will feel better. But during the process we shall all feel very bad indeed. The return to gold may involve reducing money wages by (say) two shillings in the £ throughout industry. Does any one look forward with equanimity to the risk, even a small one, of this result?

There are three ways, and only three, in which we can get back to equilibrium:—

(1) By letting our exchanges fall until they are adjusted with our prices and wages—which would be wisdom;

(2) By gold depreciating abroad and prices not rising at home—which would be luck;

(3) By forcing our prices and wages down until they are adjusted with our exchanges—which would be misery.

The ascetic aspects of the third course have attractions for some. But the average industrialist, banker, or politician is not really anxious to submit us to a further course of deflation and of strikes and unemployment. Some of them are very uneasy. Others, whilst regretting that we have got ourselves into our present dilemma, by cultivating a misguided public opinion at home and abroad about the importance of dollar parity, feel, nevertheless, that it is too late to turn back and that we must now commit ourselves, with the best face we can, to gambling on (2). I admit that it is a gamble which may have a more than even chance of partial success. Nevertheless, most people now appreciate the dangers and the complexities of the case much better than they did a year ago, and sincerely wish that they had not talked so much about the blessings of hurrying back to par. It is in this chastened mood that the British public will submit their necks once more to the golden yoke,—as a prelude, perhaps, to throwing it off for ever at not a distant date.

Keynes's final contribution to the discussion of the issues surrounding a possible return to gold before the Chancellor's announcement came at a meeting of the Royal Statistical Society on 21 April. The paper under discussion was Alfred Hoare's 'The Bearing of Labour Unrest on the Path to be Taken to Sound Currency'[6]. Keynes's comments ran as follows:

From The Journal of the Royal Statistical Society, *May 1925*

Mr J. M. KEYNES said there was so much in Mr Hoare's shrewd and interesting paper with which he agreed that he would like to get out of the way a point with which he did not agree. He doubted the existence of any direct and necessary connection between sound money, or money of any kind, and a budget surplus. It was true that the restriction of credit could be used as an alternative to high Bank rate, and it was true that budget surpluses could facilitate the restriction of credit, but there was no other close connection between the two. The amount of the budget surpluses required for this purpose would be very small, and credit could equally well be restricted by other methods, e.g., by selling to the public securities which now formed part of the assets of the Bank of England or of the currency reserve. If, however, deflation was embarked upon, it would raise the value of money, and he agreed that in this case social justice might justify some taxation of the rentier to compensate the benefit which he would have received through the increased value of money. In order to do that, however, he would have to be isolated from the other income-tax payers, and that would be difficult

---

[6] For Keynes's obituary notice for Hoare, see *JMK*, vol. X, pp. 310–14.

without appearing to discriminate against the holders of Government securities.

The whole question of currency at this stage raised two distinct questions. There was the question of the ideal currency of the future. There was, also, the question as to whether this was the moment for tying up the price level in a particular way. He did not wish to say anything about the first big question, but to follow Mr Hoare in considering, rather, the immediate future of currency in its relation to industrial unrest.

A year or two ago most people agreed that it would have been unwise to have removed the embargo on gold. Mr Mason and Mr Hirst would, perhaps, have been in favour of removing it at any time, but they would have been in a small minority in holding that view. How far had the reasons that used to make the bankers averse to removing the embargo disappeared? The exchange was in fact very near parity, whereas before it was far from parity. At the earlier dates they feared lest the removal of the embargo might necessitate a policy of deflation at home. Was that fear removed by what had happened in the last year or two, or did it still exist? Personally, he believed there was a serious risk still, and he thought that, because the improvement of the exchange, so far as he could judge, had taken place only in part by an alteration of the price level in England. It had taken place to an important extent by influences of a temporary character affecting the normal flow of capital. If the exchange had improved by influences affecting the flow of capital and not by influences affecting the internal price level, this rendered our exports more expensive to the foreigner.

Mr Keynes thought that at the present moment the trouble of the export trade was partly due to the fact that manufacturers were suffering from an improved exchange without the compensation of lower prices at home. What were the special influences affecting capital that had brought about the result? *Firstly*, the changed attitude of Americans towards European investments, and particularly the fact that what Great Britain had said about her future policy gave the American investor a reasonable expectation that he would make a profit on exchange apart from the interest that he would get upon his sterling security. *Secondly*, the embargo exercised by the Bank of England on foreign loans.

On several occasions in the past he had spoken against the scale on which we had become accustomed to lend abroad; but only with the object that its place might be taken by loans at home. An artificial embargo brought about by authority of the central institution, and uncompensated by increased investment at home, played the devil with the export industries, without offering an alternative employment. If it were true that the present level of the sterling exchange had been partly brought about by these

355

influences affecting capital, then it followed that the end of the period of adjustments had not been reached—because these influences affecting capital must be temporary. In that case, the deflation of internal prices required to justify the existing level of sterling exchange was still ahead. If it were to happen that American prices were to rise and the value of the dollar to fall, the adjustment might be brought about without the need for deflation in this country; but in view of the control exercised by the Federal [Reserve] Board, this course of events could not be counted upon.

If there was a risk of deflation in order to control the situation, the arguments for an embargo that held good a year or two ago still existed. There was a serious risk that, if the embargo were removed, prices here would have to be forced down, and that was a prospect which no one had any right to open up. The country was not in a position where we could afford any such thing. In the present condition of the export industries and of employment a policy that might involve the forcing down of money wages by two shillings in the pound all round showed terrifying prospects, and Mr Keynes could see no wisdom in bringing about adjustment by that difficult means rather than by the easy means of adjustment of exchanges to internal prices.

The economic and social difficulties of forcing down prices in this country were so great that there were no advantages to be obtained from an immediate return to the gold standard to justify such a risk. He believed that to be the essence of the whole problem. The whole point was whether or not the country was running the risk of having to force down sterling prices; and if so the date of the removal of that embargo should be undoubtedly postponed.

Chapter 5

THE ECONOMIC CONSEQUENCES OF MR CHURCHILL

With the announcement by the Chancellor of the Exchequer in the House of Commons on 28 April of Britain's return to gold, Keynes's campaign against the gold standard naturally took a new tack. His first comment, which appeared in *The Nation* of 2 May, contained a mistake which he corrected in the next issue.[1]

From The Nation and Athenaeum, *2 May 1925*

THE GOLD STANDARD

Mr Churchill has done what was expected, and the experience of a hundred years ago has repeated itself. With one improvement;—Ricardo's Ingot Plan, rejected then, has been adopted now, and the public are not to have back their sovereigns.

But there is also another improvement,—one of no immediate significance, but perhaps of great importance to the ultimate evolution of our currency. The free mintage of gold has been suspended, and the right to tender gold bullion for conversion by the Mint into legal tender will belong, in future, to the Bank of England only. The Bank of England will be compelled by law to give gold bullion (in bulk) for its notes at the fixed price of £3 17s. 10½d. per oz. standard; it will not be compelled to give notes for gold bullion at a fixed price. Thus our legal tender can never be worth less than its gold parity; but it may, conceivably, be worth more. This wise provision protects us against two contingencies. If, by some unforeseen development in chemistry

---

[1] Keynes's mistake was pointed out to him by several people, including an audience member at an undergraduate lecture in Cambridge, and Hubert Henderson.

or in the mining of gold, or in any other way, gold suffers at some future time a catastrophic fall in value, we shall be unruffled; for our legal-tender money need not follow gold in a precipitate downward course. It also protects us from being flooded with gold from the United States or elsewhere, as the result of prolonged cheap money or of a changed reserve policy or in case of a war in which we are not engaged. I regard this protection as a matter of supreme importance in the new conditions, affecting the world distribution of gold, which now exist. If it were not for this provision, we should be compelled to follow any conditions of unduly cheap money which might occur in the United States, on the penalty of being swamped otherwise with a temporary flood of gold which we could not use and which would be liable to be withdrawn at any time. As it is, we need not accept in unlimited volume short-money overflowing from New York to the demoralisation of our own money market and of credit conditions here.

But, above all, the new law does not prejudice—in the event of gold tending to fall in value (which, in the long run, is much more likely than the opposite contingency)—the further evolution of our currency. It leaves open the possibility of a future regime—if thought and argument and experience tend that way hereafter—in which, as a compromise between old-fashioned principle and new-fashioned theory, we can have a currency of which the gold value cannot fall below its stipulated parity, but which, subject to this proviso, can be managed in the interests of the stability of home prices and the conditions of our own credit. Progress, in this case, can be continued, along such lines as the consensus of opinion may come to approve, without breach of continuity or of contract.

Thus, if we are to return to gold—and, in the face of general opinion, that was inevitable—the Chancellor and the Treasury and the Bank have contrived to do so along the most prudent and far-sighted lines which were open to them.

There is another matter which deserves emphasis. There can

be no doubt whatever of our ability to maintain the gold standard, once our decision is made. The critics of the return to gold have opposed this policy, because it is unwise, not because it is impracticable. We, in Great Britain, have our currency system fully under control; and the recognised instruments of credit management are fully efficacious to maintain sterling in terms of gold at any value within reason which we may select.

Nevertheless, we shall do well to remember that there is no means, in the long run, of maintaining this parity except by so managing our credit as to establish a gold price level here not higher than the gold price levels of other countries. For a time, it is true, there is another method, namely, by influencing the movement of capital; as, for example, by placing an embargo on the issue of new foreign loans in London (which we are doing now), or by paying preferential rates of interest on foreign balances (which we did during the War and for some time afterwards), or by borrowing in the United States (for which facilities are already arranged). These are all means by which the parity of gold exchange might be maintained, in spite of our internal price level being relatively too high. They are attractive, because they obviate, for the time being, high Bank rate and deflation of credit. They are justifiable to meet a temporary emergency—due to a political scare, for instance—or to frighten speculators. But they are dangerous and generally inadvisable, because they only put off the evil day, and, above all, because of their adverse influence on the export trades. For they are simply devices by which the internal price level, multiplied by the rate of foreign exchange, may be maintained at a higher level than will allow the export trades to quote competitive prices on the international market; and they achieve this through enabling us to pay our way by borrowing instead of by exporting. Our export trades are already in trouble because our exchange has been improved rather by the movement of capital than by the adjustment of internal prices. If we must have a gold standard, we had better play the gold standard game according to the recognised rules.

There remains, however, the objection, to which I have never ceased to attach importance, against the return to gold in actual present conditions, in view of the possible consequences on the state of trade and employment. I believe that our price level is too high, if it is converted into gold at the par of exchange, in relation to gold prices elsewhere; and if we consider the prices of those articles only which are not the subject of international trade, and of services, i.e., wages, we shall find that these are materially too high—not less than 5 per cent and probably 10 per cent. Thus, unless the situation is saved by a rise of prices elsewhere, the Chancellor is committing us to a policy of forcing down money wages by perhaps 2s. in the $£$. I do not believe that this can be achieved without the gravest danger to industrial profits and industrial peace. I would much rather leave the gold value of our currency where it was some months ago than embark on a struggle with every trade union in the country to reduce money wages. It seems to me wiser and simpler and saner to leave the currency to find its own level for some time longer than to force a situation where employers are faced with the alternative of closing down or of lowering wages, cost what the struggle may.

For this reason I remain of the opinion that the Chancellor of the Exchequer has done an ill-judged thing—ill-judged because we are running a risk for no adequate reward if all goes well. But now the decision is made, let us hope for the best. An upward movement of prices in the United States is not improbable. There never was a moment at which 'sentiment', as distinguished from technical conditions, was more important. The public and the business world of the United States are keeping in the form of bank deposits much more purchasing power than they have ever kept in this form previously, and enormously more than their convenience requires. Nothing is necessary to raise prices except that they should spend these funds or invest them in some other way; and there is nothing but the 'sentiment' of these depositors to hinder this. Once the mysterious spring is released which now holds them back, sterling might soon be worth par without any change in the level of sterling prices. It may even happen that our return to the gold standard may be, itself, the impulse which will release this spring of action.

The gold standard party have had behind them much that is not only respectable but is also worthy of respect. The state of mind which likes to stick to the straight, old-fashioned course, rather regardless of the pleasure or pain and of the ease or difficulty of the passing situation, and quite regardless of particular interests and of anything except the public good as they understand it, is not to be despised. How much preferable is this mentality to that of the financiers of France! But it is a state of mind, all the same, whose unsensationalism may deteriorate into an easy, ill-founded optimism and whose conservatism fails to notice how facts and theories are changing. Like other orthodoxies, it stands for what is jejune and intellectually sterile; and since it has prejudice on its side, it can use claptrap with impunity. This is the party of those who, in the words of Dr Johnson, 'without the instigation of personal malice, treat every new attempt as wild and chimerical; and look upon every endeavour to depart from the beaten track as the rash effort of a warm imagination, or the glittering speculation of an exalted mind, that may please and dazzle for the time, but can produce no real or lasting advantage'. Yet good new ideas are the most important thing in the world; and there is no economic field in which they can do more practical good than in that of currency and credit.

From The Nation and Athenaeum, *9 May 1925*

THE GOLD STANDARD—A CORRECTION

In the article which I contributed to last week's *Nation*, I expressed too rashly a commendation of the Chancellor of the Exchequer's 'Bill to facilitate the return to a gold standard'. The repeal of the provision of the Coinage Act, 1870, entitling private persons to demand the coinage of gold bullion, led me to think that the Treasury was wisely providing against our being flooded, at some future time, with redundant gold, which we did not require, to the demoralisation of our currency and credit. But I forgot Section IV of the Bank Charter Act, 1844, which obliged the Bank of England to pay for gold bullion in terms of Bank notes at the fixed price of £3 17s. 9d. per standard ounce. This provision is not repealed. Thus the position remains substantially as it was before. We are to be compelled to accept gold in unlimited quantities at all times, with whatever effects on the value of our legal tender, and even in circumstances where the Bank of England believes it to be contrary to our interests to accept any more.

This unfortunate decision strips away most of the reasons for consolation which I found last week. Unmitigated conservatism reigns at the Treasury. No word has been expressed even in favour of the famous Genoa Resolution and of aspirations towards an internationally managed standard; no word of notice for the theory, which is now as well established as anything can be, that the cure for cyclical unemployment is to be found in the control of credit; nothing indeed that could not have been said fifty years ago. This sterile, hard-boiled mentality may prove short-sighted politically, as well as scientifically. I agree with the orthodox party that the currency requires, more than most institutions, perpetual protection from cranks and from enthusiastic ignorance. Just because almost no one understands it, it must needs rely on prestige and dogma. But ideas in this field are now stirring everywhere; and no economic institution will be secure from ill-judged innovations unless it is progressive and intellectually defensible. The Report of the Committee on the Currency and Bank of England Note Issues will prove, in this respect, but a feeble bulwark, because it ignores or begs most of the important questions. This might have been an historic document. In fact it is somewhat trivial. The object seems to have been to say as little as possible, and the result is perfunctory.

On one matter, namely, the degree of the over-valuation of sterling, I should like to add something to what I have written in *The Nation* previously. The Committee state in their Report that last February, when [the] exchange was $1\frac{1}{2}$ per cent below par, sterling was probably over-valued by a 'significant' amount (let us say x), which they do not attempt to evaluate; and that, therefore, a return to par will not require a deflation exceeding $1\frac{1}{2}+x$ per cent. To bring this about, they cheerfully add, will not involve any 'further danger or inconvenience than that which is inevitable in any period of credit restriction and falling prices'.

Professor Cassel, in an interesting article just published,[2] has been bolder (and more useful) and has attempted to do the arithmetic. He finds that in February the value of x, that is to say, the over-valuation of sterling, was about 4 per cent. This was on the basis of the Federal Reserve Board's index numbers. The same figures for March yield a somewhat better result. But none of these figures are an adequate indication of the disequilibrium;—for the following reason.

The prices of some commodities, namely, the raw materials of international trade, for example, cotton or copper, *always* stand at or near their international price parity; nothing which happens to the exchanges or to credit can make their gold prices materially different in one centre from what they are in another. A further class of commodities, namely, manufactured goods

---

[2] In *The Times* Banking Number for May 1925.

which are imported and exported, cannot move, in any circumstances, very much above their international price parity; for, otherwise, the trade in them is killed. There remains a third class, of which houses, personal services, and railway charges are examples, which, for a time at least, can depart materially from their normal parity with the other two.

Now the purchasing-power-parity theory of the foreign exchanges maintains that, in the long run, even this third class must come into line; because, otherwise, the repercussion of the wage level and of the cost of goods and services, produced in the 'sheltered' trades but consumed in the 'unsheltered' trades, will so impair our power of competing internationally, that either the exchanges must fall or gold will flow out until the internal price level has been forced down all round.

When we are considering how severe a deflation may be required to balance the situation (failing a price rise abroad), the relevant question is how far the prices of the third class of goods are in excess of their normal parity with the first and second class. But the ordinary index numbers are largely made up from the prices of the first and second class, with the result that the disparity of price in the third class is watered down on the average of the three classes taken together. If, for example, the weight given to the third class is only a quarter of the whole, the true disparity may be three or four times as great as the result shown by the wholesale index numbers.

For this reason the cost-of-living index numbers, in which goods of the third class play a much larger part, may sometimes give a better clue to the real situation than the wholesale index numbers, which are made up so largely of the first class. I gave some figures bearing on this in *The Nation* of April 18th.[3] I give below a more complete table of the changes in the gold-cost of living in various countries, as compared with 1913, based on figures published by the Federal Reserve Board.

This table shows that these countries fall into three groups:

[3] Above, p. 352.

January 1925	Gold-cost of living (1913 = 100)
Holland	181
Sweden	179
Great Britain	176
Switzerland	170
United States	158
Canada	149
Australia	148
New Zealand	147
Spain	138
Belgium	137
Germany	124
Italy	123
France	103

the first comprising Great Britain and the other European countries whose exchanges have been restored to their gold parity; the second the United States and the Dominions; and the third the other European countries. It is obvious that the exports of the countries of the first group must be at a serious disadvantage, as compared with 1913, in competing with countries in either of the other groups. It is this table which gives the true picture of our difficulties and our prospects. The Committee on the Currency and the Chancellor of the Exchequer exhibit no sign of having considered it.

When the Chancellor of the Exchequer, Winston Churchill, mentioned Keynes's article of 2 May and its approval of the Government's policy in the course of the second reading debate on the Gold Standard Bill, Keynes also sent a correction to *The Times*.

To the Editor of The Times, *5 May 1925*

Sir,

The Chancellor of the Exchequer quoted me yesterday in the House of Commons as having written that the return to gold had been contrived along 'prudent and far-sighted lines'. I wrote this, unfortunately, under the misapprehension that the repeal of the right to the free mintage of gold would protect our currency from being flooded out in certain contingencies. But I forgot Section IV of the Bank Charter Act, 1844, which obliges the Bank of England to buy gold bullion in unlimited amounts at £3 17s. 9d. per standard ounce. We are therefore, unprotected in a spot where—I had prematurely hoped—a protection had been provided.

I can see no far-sightedness, but, on the other hand, much imprudence in the present circumstances of the world distribution of gold, in maintaining a provision to compel the Bank of England to buy gold bullion without limit at a time when, in the considered judgment of the Bank itself, it may be contrary to our national interests to do so. For this is not a case in which political pressure will influence the Bank contrary to its better judgement.

The Chancellor defended his proposal by arguing that if we were flooded with gold we could use it to pay off our American debt. Mr Churchill has been wrongly advised in this matter. The danger to be avoided is a flood of *temporary* American loans arriving in the form of gold. The Chancellor's proposal to use these funds to pay off our debt to the American Government would amount to replacing a funded debt to the American Government by a debt, repayable at call, to the American money market—an act of obvious folly.

The objection to a gold standard is that it sometimes exposes us to the disadvantages of deflation and sometimes to those of inflation. The first are those which we are risking in the near future; and there is nothing now to be done about it—we must just hope for the best. The second are, in my opinion, the likelier in the long run. Against these we could have guarded ourselves by repealing Section IV of the 1844 Bank Act, and thus giving to the Bank of England a discretionary power to protect our currency from serious depreciation. It is a very great misfortune that the new Bill does not do this.

I am, &c.,

J. M. KEYNES

On 7 May at the annual meeting of the Royal Economic Society there was a discussion of the national debt. Lord Holden was in the chair for the discussion, while the discussants were Keynes, Hugh Dalton, Owen Fleming, R. G. Hawtrey, Alfred Hoare, P. D. Leake and D. H. Macgregor. Keynes's comments ran as follows:

From The Economic Journal, *September 1925*

I see only two reasons for expediting the repayment of debt. The first is to facilitate the raising of funds on behalf of public bodies which require new capital for productive purposes. The second is to increase the amount of the national savings. The first reason does not hold good always, and I do not think that it is valid at the present moment. In 1920, on the other hand, when the housing programme was beginning and public bodies were requiring large sums for investment, I saw no harm but much good in the repayment of the debt. More recently the demand from public bodies has been much diminished. I have argued that the maintenance of a heavy sinking fund at such a time, in conjunction with the provisions of our Trustees' Act, unduly stimulates the flow of capital into the hands of public bodies abroad. I quite foresee a time arising when there will again be an outlet on a large scale for capital at home, and I think it would be good policy to hasten it by governmental activities on a much greater scale than at present. There would then be a reason for converting the dead weight debt into a productive debt. That would be my criterion rather than the repayment of debt as such.

The other ground, namely, the stimulation of saving, was mentioned by Dr Dalton. I quite agree with him that by no means all the money which is taken from the taxpayer in taxes for use in the sinking fund would be saved if those taxes were removed; whereas, on the other hand, almost all the holders of the debt will re-invest their money when they are paid off. If, therefore, there is reason for thinking that saving is on an inadequate scale, that is an argument for the sinking fund. At the present moment, I believe that the heavy rates of taxation militate against activity and the running of risks, and I do not think that the need for additional savings is so urgent as to justify heavier taxation in order to bring about this indirect stimulation of it. There, again, circumstances might change. But these are the two criteria which I should apply in determining the amount of the sinking fund from year to year.

The arguments on the other side seem to me to be partly æsthetic and partly an appeal to the potency of compound interest. For example, the tidying up of the published figures of the national balance sheet seems to make a considerable appeal to some people. Above all, anyone who toys with the national debt can produce a vivid picture of the accumulations of compound interest after a certain number of years. But although compound interest produces the most visible and impressive picture in the case of the national debt, it also works elsewhere in the community, and I would look, rather, to cumulative economic progress by the operation of compound interest in the community at large where it is less directly visible. You do not make compound interest more potent because you take money away from individuals and use it in this particular way. The burden of the Napoleonic wars was taken off our shoulders not by a sinking fund, but by the general progress of the community in the next hundred years. Now I should be very chary of allowing the apparent burden of the national debt to induce me to put on taxation so heavy that it might hold back the general progress of the community.

Another reason which often weighs, I think, is the false analogy between the debt of the individual and the debt of the state. There is no real analogy between the two. An individual's motives for clearing himself of debt may apply to the external obligations of the state; but they can have no application to its internal obligations. I think it would be better, therefore, if we were to confine our attention to the two criteria with which I began.

THE ECONOMIC CONSEQUENCES OF MR CHURCHILL

Keynes's *Nation* article of 9 May (above p. 363) came under attack in the next issue, when a correspondent who signed himself 'Economist' suggested that he had presented a distorted version of one of the arguments used by the Currency Committee by taking sentences out of order and adding his own gloss to the text. Keynes replied.

From The Nation and Athenaeum, *16 May 1925*

I have read the Report again in the light of the above letter, and can discover no misrepresentation. 'Economist's' point seems to be that the Committee's Report consists of a series of entirely disconnected sentences, and that one must not read any one of them in the light of any other. The Committee stated (*a*) that the credit conditions necessary to maintain parity would come about 'automatically and rapidly', and that this would mean no 'further change or inconvenience than that which is inevitable in any period of credit restriction and falling prices',—this being their *only* remark about the method of maintaining parity and its results; (*b*) that in February sterling was overvalued by a 'significant' amount; and (*c*) that, since at that time exchange was $1\frac{1}{2}$ per cent below par, the *extra* adjustment of maintaining parity, in addition to the adjustment under (*b*), would be $1\frac{1}{2}$ per cent. I brought these three statements into logical connection. If this is illegitimate, the Committee's Report is even more incoherent that I thought it was, and also more completely lacking in any discussion of the most important relevant issues. The real questions are: (1) How much is sterling over-valued, [and] (2) by what train of events will adjustment be brought about? Is it 'Economist's' contention that the Committee expressed no opinion whatever on these matters? My own view remains that they did quite clearly express the rather superficial view which I attributed to them. As for 'Economist's' last paragraph, there is not a word in the Report to suggest that the Committee do view credit restriction with serious apprehension, and it was that fact which I wanted to suggest by my word 'cheerfully'.

Later in the month *The Economist* of 23 May, in the course of a review of the materials submitted to the United States Senate's Gold and Silver Inquiry, compared Keynes's contribution (above pp. 289–93) with his letter to *The Times* of 5 May on Mr Churchill's contribution to the second reading debate on the Gold Standard Bill (above, p. 366). It then asked for an explanation of the apparent inconsistency between the documents. Keynes replied.

To the Editor of The Economist, *23 May 1925*

Sir,

In your review of an article, which I contributed last year to *European Currency and Finance*, you ask for an explanation of the discrepancy between my accepting therein the argument that we can get rid of redundant gold by anticipating repayments of American debt and my more recent rebuttal of this argument. There is no explanation—except the following, if this can be considered an explanation.

In the article under review I was considering the absorption of the annual supply of new gold; in my letter to *The Times* I was considering a flow of gold from America as the result of a flood of short loans from New York to take advantage of higher money rates in London. A proposal to check the latter flow by what amounts to using the American short loans to increase the net total of our permanent foreign investment, is obviously both futile and imprudent—as I pointed out. I assume that you agree with this. The objection to the same method in the former case is a little more subtle, and I overlooked it. In this case the method amounts to attempting artificially to increase the flow of our net foreign investment so as to permit the price level here to remain, more or less permanently, below its equilibrium level; in fact, to produce here much the same condition that the Dawes Scheme will attempt to produce in Germany. This might be practically feasible, and would not be open to the same immediate dangers as in the other case considered. Nevertheless, you will, I expect, agree—as I now admit—that this also is objectionable and unsound in the long run.

Yours, &c.,

J. M. KEYNES

In *The Economic Journal* for June 1925, Keynes returned to both the Report of the Committee on the Currency and the Gold Standard Act in two brief notes.

From The Economic Journal, *June 1925*

THE COMMITTEE ON THE CURRENCY

Report of the Committee on the Currency and Bank of England Note Issues. (Cmd. 2393.)   1925.

This Committee was appointed by Mr Snowden on June 10, 1924. At the outset the Committee's reference was limited to the question, 'Whether the time has now come to amalgamate the Treasury Note Issue with the Bank of England Note Issue, and, if so, on what terms and conditions the amalgamation should be carried out.' They heard witnesses about this from June to September, 1924. But at some later date—probably in January 1925—the Committee decided to interpret their task so as to include the general question of an immediate return to the gold standard. They did not, apparently, at this second stage of their proceedings, hear any witness except the Governor of the Bank of England.* In the end this broader issue became the main topic of their Report, and the ostensible subject of their terms of reference is relegated to a few sentences in the last two pages.

The Committee was a strong one, consisting of Lord Bradbury, Mr Gaspard Farrer, Sir Otto Niemeyer and Professor Pigou.† But one cannot say the same of the Report. Their attitude seems to have been that, since a return to gold was in any case

---

* The Committee state that 'proposals for substituting the price level of commodities in general for gold as the regulating principle of the currency have been fully and carefully explained in evidence before us'. Amongst the small number of witnesses examined I am the only one named who is known to be an advocate of this principle. When I appeared before the Committee, however, the only question on which I was invited to give evidence was that of the amalgamation of the two note issues. My evidence-in-chief was wholly directed to this matter, as also was most of my cross-examination, though wider issues came in a few times incidentally. There is no indication what the evidence was, which is referred to in the above sentence, or from what quarter it came.

† Mr Austen Chamberlain, who was the Chairman at the outset, resigned on accepting office as Foreign Secretary.

inevitable, it was useless to examine the objections and indiscreet to contemplate the difficulties. Consequently the less said the better (the Report could be printed *in extenso* in eight pages of *The Economic Journal*), and it was wiser to utter a few conservative banalities than to tackle large questions. But the reader must also feel, as he reads, that the Committee lacked intellectual interest in their subject, and were convinced from the start that there was little to be said on the subject which had not been said a hundred times already.

The result is that the Report amounts to next to nothing, and is more remarkable for its omissions than for what it contains. Two matters which they thought it worth while to discuss were the objection that the restoration of parity is technically impossible, which no serious authority has ever maintained, and the idea of fixing the exchange at 4·79 (the rate existing last February) rather than at 4·86, which no one has ever proposed. Amongst the points, on the other hand, which they thought not worth mentioning, I pick out the following in particular.

1. They dismiss without argument both the proposals for a devalued sovereign and those for a managed currency. This rules out most of the major problems, especially the importance of price stability, the future prospects of gold prices and the possible subordination of our credit system to that of the United States. Nevertheless, since a serious consideration of these questions would have led them far afield, the Committee's decision, to limit itself to the practical problems arising out of the proposal for an early restoration of gold, is intelligible.

2. But neither do they mention the proposals for international co-operation in the regulation of credit, so as to avoid cyclical price movements, which the Geneva [*sic*] Conference blessed in a famous resolution and of which Mr Hawtrey is the foremost advocate. One might have expected that they would have coupled their advocacy of a return to gold with a warning against its possible vagaries and a plea for an organised scheme to mitigate them. But not a word; not a hint even that gold is, or

could be, or ought to be, itself a managed currency. *A fortiori*, the Committee do not mention the possible connection between the working of the gold standard and the credit cycle, and between the latter and unemployment. They show no awareness of the fact that the connection between the management of the currency and the trade instability, of which unemployment is a leading symptom, is the main argument in favour of a managed currency, whether or not on a gold basis, advanced by its advocates.

3. No one was in favour of restoring gold convertibility a year ago—for the reason that to tie the sterling price level to the gold price level would have involved too violent a disturbance of the former. If we contemplate making the restoration shortly, the question for those who direct practical policy is to know how much disturbance it would involve now. It is not an easy question to answer, but it is impossible to act prudently without trying to answer it. The Committee produce no arguments and no figures and content themselves with the conclusion that 'we must still be prepared to face a fall in the final price level here of a significant, though not very large, amount, unless it should happen that a corresponding rise takes place in America'.

They do not tell the Chancellor of the Exchequer that this question of the parity between the internal price level and the external price level is really a question of the parity between one set of internal prices, namely, those of which the sterling price × the sterling exchange is *always* at or near the world price, and those of which the sterling price × the sterling exchange is not sensitive to the prices of similar goods and services elsewhere; and that it is partly the same problem as that of the disparity between the prices in what have come to be known as the 'unsheltered' industries and those in the 'sheltered' industries. An improvement in the sterling exchange necessarily lowers all the 'unsheltered' prices, and if this is unaccompanied by forces tending to depress the 'sheltered' prices to an equal extent, those who produce in the 'unsheltered' industries are in obvious difficulties, because they are selling at the unsheltered price level and, in part at least, buying and consuming at the sheltered price level.

It is not easy to measure the amount of the discrepancy between the two sets of prices. But it is certainly not measured by comparing the index number of wholesale prices here with a corresponding index number in America or in Germany. For such an index number is largely made up of unsheltered prices, which are necessarily, whatever happens, nearly the same in both index numbers; and the effect is to water down and to obscure any disparity between the movements in the sheltered prices here and elsewhere.

My own guess is that, compared with 1913, sheltered prices here are, at the present rates of sterling exchange, perhaps as much as ten per cent too high in comparison with the unsheltered prices, and that the injury thus caused to the competitive position of our exports in the international market is aggravated by the fact that in Germany, France, Belgium and Italy the sheltered prices are fully ten per cent too low. I base this guess mainly on the cost-of-living index numbers and the price-of-exports index numbers.

At any rate, whatever the answer, this is the essence of the practical problem; and a Report which ignores it is not to the point.

4. Assuming that there is some disparity between the two sets of prices, the next question must be directed to the causal process by which equilibrium can, or will, be restored. There are three alternatives:—

(1) the unsheltered prices may be raised relatively to the sheltered prices by a rise in world prices;

(2) the unsheltered prices may be raised relatively to the sheltered prices by a fall in sterling exchange;

(3) the sheltered prices may be lowered relatively to the unsheltered prices.

The first of these alterations is outside our own control—it may, quite likely, come to our rescue, but to depend upon it is a gamble. The second is that which I should have preferred as being calculated to restore equilibrium with the least possible disturbance to the course of production and to industrial peace. If we reject this and decide, on the other hand, to aggravate the disparity by *raising* sterling exchange, we are bound to consider by what causal process the third alternative can be brought about.

The Committee have made no attempt to analyse the facts; but, in so far as they discuss the matter at all, they contemplate that the necessary readjustments can be achieved by raising Bank rate. *How* this will come about—that is to say, by what intermediate steps—they give no indication. Do they mean that, by raising Bank rate and by curtailing credit sufficiently, unemployment can be intensified without limit until, even in the unsheltered industries, wages move downwards? If so, one is bound to admit the theoretical possibility. If not, what precisely is the causal process which they envisage?

I suspect that their conclusions may be based on theories, developed fifty years ago, which assumed a mobility of labour and a competitive wage level which no longer exist; and that they have not thought the problem through over again in the light of the deplorably inelastic conditions of our industrial organism today.

But I suspect also a further confusion of ideas. High Bank rate has two distinct sets of consequences—one, its effect on the international flow of capital provided it is high *relatively* to the rate elsewhere, and the other its effect on the internal credit situation. Now the efficacy of high Bank rate—from the purely financial point of view—for preserving the parity of the gold standard largely depends upon the first set of consequences. If Bank rate is made *relatively* high, the inflow of capital is stimulated and the outflow is retarded. If this tendency is set up strongly enough, the gold parity and the financial equilibrium are completely protected—at least for the time being—and there

375

may be little restriction, if any, of internal credit. But, in this case, the industrial disequilibrium may remain—because the greater the success of the Bank rate in producing the first set of consequences, the less is its success in producing the second.

For how would the process work out in practice? The high Bank rate is just as oppressive to the unsheltered as it is to the sheltered industries; and since the former are already working on a narrower margin of profit, it is they which are likely to go under first. Thus the high Bank rate *may* produce equilibrium (I do not say that it *must*)—not permanently, indeed, but for a longish time—by the progressive destruction of our weaker export industries and, at the same time, making good the deficit thus caused in our trade balance by diminishing, to the necessary extent, the net outflow of capital. Foreign investment provides a sluice, the due regulation of which by means of Bank rate can maintain the internal price level, for years together, either above or below the level outside—limited, nevertheless, in one direction by the volume of available savings, and by the other to the extent that we can live on our capital, or on what we should otherwise save. Since our available balance for new foreign investment has been, even since the War, of the order of £200,000,000 a year, we have this wide margin with which to provide for the closing down of of our export industries and the support of those who were previously employed in them.*

Now the Committee are half aware of this possibility and of the objections to it. They strongly deprecate the use of foreign credits for the support of the exchange. But they do not seem to notice that a high Bank rate, in so far as it attracts foreign short-loan money to London, does exactly the same thing.

The objections to the drastic restriction of credit at home are so pressing and so obvious in the present state of trade and employment, that there will always be a strong temptation to

* To avoid misunderstanding, let me add here what I have argued elsewhere, that, in any case, I should like to see some transference of resources from the export trades to capital developments at home, and the use of the above-mentioned margin to finance the latter. But to bring this about satisfactorily would require quite a different policy from the above.

the Bank of England to redress any adverse movement of gold to the maximum extent by attracting foreign money and to the minimum extent by restricting home credit. The recent declarations of the Chancellor of the Exchequer and the action of the Bank of England (at the time of writing) in squeezing up the bill rate, which is what counts in attracting foreign money, whilst leaving other rates unchanged, which are what matter to home credit, already point in this direction. And this is only natural, because the return to gold presents us with an unpleasant dilemma—the attraction of foreign money, which is admittedly unsound, or the restriction of home credit, which is deservedly hateful.

These few remarks go only a little way towards elucidating the problem. But we have a right to expect that the authors of a Report which recommends a high Bank rate as the panacea should present some sort of an account of how they expect their remedy to do the trick.

5. Ricardo recommended an appreciable margin between the buying and selling prices for gold, namely £3 17s. 6d. for the former and £3 17s. 10½d. for the latter. Sweden during the war took precautions to protect herself from a flood of redundant gold. The Genoa scheme for international credit control would be much facilitated if each country was responsible for its own stock of gold and was not free to unload its surplus at any time and in any quantity upon its neighbours. There are indeed many reasons—too many to discuss here—for reserving to ourselves, at this stage, some discretion to protect our currency against undue expansion. I attach very great importance to the Bank of England being relieved of the obligation to buy gold at a fixed price. Certainly the choice is of grave significance. But the oracle is dumb—the Committee do not mention it.

In presenting this Report at the same time as his Budget speech, the Chancellor of the Exchequer declared that 'it contains a reasoned marshalling of the arguments which have convinced His Majesty's Government'. From such a description one would expect an historic document which, whether one agreed with it or not, would take its place in the line of famous memoranda which have moulded our currency policy in the past—at any rate an armoury of up-to-date arguments in favour of old-fashioned expedients. But we find instead a few pages, indolent and jejune.

THE GOLD STANDARD ACT, 1925

The following comments may be made:—

1. After an interval of more than 100 years, Ricardo's Ingot Plan (first outlined in 1811) is, in effect, adopted by Section 1 (2) of the new Act. Ricardo's ingot was to contain twenty ounces troy of fine gold.* In these larger days the size is raised to 400 ounces—worth nearly £1700. Dr Bonar's most interesting article on Ricardo's proposals (*Economic Journal* (1923), Vol. XXXIII, p. 281–304) is worth re-reading in the light of the new Act.

2. The repeal of the right of members of the public to present gold for mintage (Section 1 (1)(*c*)) is not so important as it appears at first sight, because Section 4 of the Bank Charter Act, 1844, remains in force. This section runs as follows:—

'All Persons shall be entitled to demand from the Issue Department of the Bank of England, Bank of England notes in exchange for gold bullion, at the rate of £3 17s. 9d. per ounce of standard gold...'

Thus we are not to follow (at present) the precedent set by Sweden of reserving to ourselves a discretion not to accept unwanted gold in unlimited amounts. Nor are we to have the limited protection recommended by Ricardo of widening the limits between the buying and selling prices (he suggested £3 17s. 6d. for the former).

3. The new obligation placed on the Bank under Section 1 (2)

* Under the temporary clauses of the Resumption Act, 1819, the Bank was liable to redeem its notes in ingots of 60 ounces. Particulars of actual transactions under these clauses and also an illustration of Ricardo's ingot are given in *The Economic Journal* (1923), vol. XXXIII, p. 291.

to provide gold bullion by weight instead of sovereigns by rate avoids the slight uncertainty which used to exist as to the exact gold points owing to the possibility of the sovereigns obtained being below full weight. The points now depend solely upon interest, freight and insurance. The freight rate outwards has been recently raised to 5s. per cent. On this basis and at current interest rates Messrs Samuel Montagu and Co. put the gold export point at $4.843 to the £. The gold import point is stated to be in the neighbourhood of $4.90.

4. Convertibility from, and into, gold is limited to Bank of England notes. Currency notes remain legal tender, but are made absolutely inconvertible. Thus there is no way of obtaining gold for export except by acquiring Bank of England notes.

5. The Chancellor of the Exchequer announced that he had arranged borrowing powers under Section 2 of the Act with the Federal Reserve Board up to $200,000,000, and with Messrs J. P. Morgan up to $100,000,000. No charge will be made for the former if it is not used. For the latter a commission of $1\frac{1}{4}$ per cent is to be paid for the first year and half that amount for the second if the credit is not used. Thus £375,000 will be paid if the credit is not used at all.

Keynes returned to currency matters in *The Nation* on 13 June with a brief article on sterling.

From The Nation and Athenaeum, *13 June 1925*

THE ARITHMETIC OF THE STERLING EXCHANGE

The arithmetical effect on the foreign exchanges of the maintenance of a higher rate of discount in London than in New York is often overlooked. The following note is an attempt to indicate it.

In New York 90-day bank bills are discounted at $3\frac{1}{4}$ to $3\frac{3}{8}$ per cent. In London the discount rates on similar bills expressed in sterling are $4\frac{3}{8}$–$4\frac{7}{16}$ per cent; and it is reported that American banks can obtain somewhat higher rates, say $4\frac{1}{2}$–$4\frac{5}{8}$ per cent, on sterling bank deposits. So long as funds are available in New York in the hands of lenders who are indifferent where they hold them and look only to the yield obtainable after allowance for any exchange risk, this difference in interest rates must be approximately reflected in the premium on forward dollars, as compared with spot dollars, i.e., dollars for delivery against sterling at a future date must be worth about 1 per cent per annum more than dollars for delivery against sterling now. This is in, fact, the case, dollars for delivery in three months being 1 cent per £ (i.e., $\frac{5}{6}$ per cent per annum) dearer than spot dollars.

This difference between spot and forward rates of exchange corresponding to differences in interest rates, is now familiar. But it has not been noticed by writers in the financial press that, so long as confidence is felt in gold convertibility, the *forward* rate cannot fall below the gold-export point, and, there, that the spot rate must *exceed* the gold-export point by the amount of the premium on forward dollars.

In the above illustration, dollars three months forward have been taken,—chiefly because this is a date for which comparisons are easy and dealings active. This indicates that the spot exchange must be *at least* 1 cent per £1 above the gold-export point. But the same argument can be applied to a six months' transaction. Six months' sterling bank bills in London are discounted at $4\frac{5}{8}$–$4\frac{11}{16}$ per cent, and six months' dollar bank bills in New York are discounted at $3\frac{1}{2}$–$3\frac{5}{8}$ per cent. Thus dollars six months forward must be worth about 2 cents per £1 more than spot dollars; yet, as before, sterling six months forward must be worth at least gold-export point. Hence in so far as six months' transactions are practicable, the spot exchange for sterling in terms of dollars must stand at least 2 cents per £1 above the gold-export point.

In so far as the same disparity of interest rates applies to securities of longer date, and provided that suitable securities are available, the same argument continued would prove that the spot exchange for sterling must stand at least, as high as the gold-*import* point. The longer the date, however, the greater is the obstacle offered by such items as income tax and commissions. Moreover, the actual disparity between the rates of interest in the two centres is less in the case of somewhat longer-dated securities. Indeed, certain types of bonds, e.g., foreign government bonds, are cheaper in New York than in London. Even so, however, an effective difference of 1 per cent per annum in the rates of interest for periods up to six months is so great that one would expect, in anything like normal circumstances, that the exchange would certainly exceed the gold-export point by more than $1\frac{1}{2}$ cents per £1, which is its approximate level at present, and would probably approach the gold-import point. I have not examined pre-war records in detail, but I do not recall any occasion analogous to present conditions in which sterling interest rates could stand so high above dollar rates without drawing gold.

What requires explanation is, therefore, not that exchange should be so good as 4.86, but that it should be so bad. Owing to the operations of the forward exchanges, the rate of exchange, which can be considered favourable, is not absolute, but is relative to the effective difference in discount rates. If discount rates in London and New York stood at approximately the same level, then an exchange of 4.86 would probably indicate a satisfactory situation. But that it should, in present circumstances, be no higher than this shows either that New York distrusts sterling bills or that New York is, in fact, investing so heavily in this form already that, without distrusting sterling, the New York banks do not care to put any more eggs than they are, in fact, putting into this particular basket.

This last alternative is the probable explanation of the facts. The current level of the exchange, taken in conjunction with the difference of interest rates, suggests that the balance of ordinary payments is running so heavily against sterling that the proceeds of the full amount of bills, which America is prepared to take in response to the rate of interest, are absorbed in settling the account. The comparative stability round 4.86, which has been maintained lately, may be explained by the fact that at any rate below 4.86 the attraction to American banks to remit balances to London is very strong, whilst each movement of $\frac{1}{2}$ cent above 4.86 materially lessens the inducement.

If Great Britain's balance of international payments was level apart from borrowing in America, a difference of 1 per cent in the discount rates might be expected to attract gold from New York. Dear money in London, relatively to New York, *must* keep the sterling exchange above the gold-export point, until our credit is gone or our borrowing power exhausted. But the tremendous efficacy of this policy in supporting the exchange operates primarily by causing us to borrow in New York—just as much as though we were drawing on a loan from Messrs Morgan.

Soon after this article appeared Keynes began to think of approaching the subject on a more substantial scale. His first forum was the Committee on Industry and Trade which was set up during the summer of 1924 under the chairmanship of Sir Arthur Balfour. Sidney Webb had asked Keynes to be a member of the Committee on 24 July 1924, but he had declined.[4] Early in November 1924 the Committee asked Keynes to give evidence to it, but he asked to be excused until the Committee's investigations had become better defined. With the return to gold, however, he offered to give evidence

[4] His letter of 24 July 1924 declining Webb's invitation ran as follows.
Dear Mr Webb, One's natural inclination, on receiving such an invitation as is conveyed to me in your letter of to-day's date is to accept. But on reflection I feel great doubt whether I should do well to serve on the proposed Comm^ee. I am alarmed by the vagueness and wide scope of the proposed field of enquiry and sceptical as to the capacity of the usual type of Committee to deal with it usefully. The general upshot is, I suppose—Are the prospects of British Trade good or bad? There are some detailed aspects of this which certainly call for enquiry. But they are, in the main, difficult questions of fact which could only be tackled by a very small Committee of specially qualified persons with a good number of full-time investigators working under them. If—as I assume to be the case—this is to be a fairly large Comm^ee of the usual type, mainly composed of representatives of various points of view who will take evidence, I doubt if they will obtain within a reasonable period of time results proportionate to the labour involved. So very reluctantly and with many apologies, I must beg to be excused. Yours sincerely, J. M. Keynes.

on 15 May. He finally appeared before the Committee on 9 July, prepared to expand on the memorandum which he had submitted in May.

From the Committee on Industry and Trade, Minutes of Evidence

COMMITTEE ON INDUSTRY AND TRADE

THIRTY-FIFTH DAY
Thursday 9 July 1925

Present:

Sir Arthur Balfour (*Chairman*)

Mr John Baker, M.P.	*Secretary:*
Mr F. A. Hargreaves	Mr W. Carter
Sir Norman Hill, Bart.	*Assistant Secretaries:*
Sir John S. Hindley	Mr W. L. Buxton
Mr David Landale	Mr A. R. Fraser
Sir Peter Rylands	
Sir Hubert Llewellyn Smith	

Mr J. M. Keynes, called and examined

16,434 (CHAIRMAN) *Mr Keynes, you have given us a memorandum?* Yes.

Memorandum submitted by Mr J. M. Keynes

16,435 1. The purchasing-power-parity theory as stated by modern economists is very much the same thing as the parity between prices etc., in what are called the sheltered trades and those in the unsheltered trades. That is to say, a maladjustment of the internal price level in relation to the external price level mainly shows itself in the relations between those in the sheltered and unsheltered industries.

2. The prices of some commodities, namely, the raw materials of international trade, for example, cotton or copper, *always* stand at or near their international price parity; nothing which happens to the exchanges or to credit can make their gold prices materially different in one centre from what they are in another. A further class of commodities, namely, manufactured goods which are imported and exported, cannot move, in any circumstances, very much above or below their international price parity; for, otherwise the trade in them is killed. There remains a third class, of which houses, personal services, and railway charges are examples, which, for a time at least, can depart materially from their normal parity with the other two.

3. Now the purchasing-power-parity theory of the foreign exchanges maintains that, in the long run, even this third class must come into line; because, otherwise, the repercussion of the wage level and of the cost of goods and services, produced in the 'sheltered' trades but consumed in the 'unsheltered' trades, will so impair our power of competing internationally, that either the exchanges must fall or gold will flow out until the internal price level has been forced down all round.

4. When we are considering how severe a deflation may be required to balance the situation (failing a price rise abroad), the relevant question is how far the prices of the third class of goods are in excess of their normal parity with the first and second class. But the ordinary index numbers are largely made up from the prices of the first and second class, with the result that the disparity of price in the third class is watered down on the average of the three classes taken together. If, for example, the weight given to the third class is only a quarter of the whole, the true disparity may be three or four times as great as the result shown by the trade index numbers.

5. For this reason the cost-of-living index numbers, in which goods of the third class play a much larger part, may sometimes give a better clue to the real situation than the wholesale index numbers, which are made up so largely of the first class. I give below a table of the changes in the gold cost-of-living in various countries, as compared with 1913, based on figures published by the Federal Reserve Board:—

January 1925	Gold cost of living (1913—100)
Holland	181
Sweden	179
Great Britain	176
Switzerland	170
United States	158
Canada	149
Australia	148
New Zealand	147
Spain	138
Belgium	137
Germany	124
Italy	123
France	103

6. This table shows that these countries fall into three groups: the first comprising Great Britain and the other European countries whose exchanges have been restored to their gold parity; the second the United States and the Dominions; and the third the other European countries. It is obvious

384

that the exports of the countries of the first class must be at a serious disadvantage, as compared with 1913, in competing with countries in either of the other two classes.

7. There are two alternative ways of bringing about restoration of equilibrium. What may be termed the sheltered prices may be left as they are, whilst the foreign exchange may be allowed to fall somewhat, with the result that the unsheltered prices can rise and yet remain in the same relation to world prices as before. Or, alternatively, we may fix the exchange, thus tieing the unsheltered prices to world prices, and committing ourselves to a policy of somehow or other forcing down the sheltered prices (that is to say, unless the remedy comes about through a general rise of world prices). During the period when [the] exchange has been fixed and before sheltered prices have been forced down, the export trades feel the full blast. For they have to pay sheltered prices for much that they consume, yet cannot secure more than the unsheltered world prices for their products.

8. Failing a general rise of world gold prices which will raise the unsheltered prices, the great question now before the country is by what process of adjustment the sheltered prices can be brought down to the level of the unsheltered prices. On this point I have no satisfactory solution to offer to the Committee. It is not obvious by what peaceful method a general reduction of wages in the sheltered industries is to be brought about. Apparently the official policy is to bring to bear Bank rate and credit restriction in the event of disequilibrium reacting, as it must do in the long run, on our balance of trade. But the worst of this instrument for this particular purpose is that it falls with equal weight on the unsheltered as on the sheltered industries; and since the profits in the former show a narrower margin than those in the latter it is more likely to bring about a restriction of activity in those innocent industries rather than in those which it is necessary to attack. It is not obvious that the high Bank rate and credit restriction will bring about the necessary readjustment except by a process so long and so painful that the country as a whole would certainly not readily accept it.

16,436 *I understand, however, that you wrote it two months ago and would like to make a new statement to the Committee. Do you want to read your new statement?* No. I have notes, but I have not anything written out.

16,437 (MR BAKER) *May I ask how far it will differ from the memorandum we already have, if at all?* It will be in amplification of it. I propose to direct myself to the question of unemployment in its present phase and its relation to monetary policy. It seems to me that the diagnosis of the present state of unemployment is absolutely plain. The remedy is another matter. Unemployment is in its serious aspect confined to our export industries. There is not much abnormal unemployment in those of our industries which make entirely for home purposes. Rather paradoxically this great depression in the export industries is not combined with a general world slump. The conditions outside this country are not on the whole bad. You can find particular quarters of the world, such as China, where there are obvious difficulties in trade, but on the whole I should have said that the general trade situation in the world was fair to good. In the United States it is quite abnormally good. They are doing excellent trade on a level keel without any signs of inflation, and I see no recent evidence that trade is particularly bad anywhere in the British Empire. What we have to explain therefore is the combination of great depression in our main export industries with reasonably good trade in the world at large and reasonably good trade in our own home industries. I believe the explanation of this to be as plain as a pike-staff. We have raised the value of our money internationally during the past year by about 10 per cent, without materially altering either the wage level or the cost of living in this country. That means that our export industries receive in terms of sterling 10 per cent less than they would have received in similar circumstances a year ago, whereas what they are having to pay in wages, and what they can justifiably be called on to pay in wages having regard to the cost of living, is exactly the same as it was a year ago or at any rate not much changed. The result is that this margin of profit is converted into a loss.

I have prepared a table which seems to me to put the matter in a straightforward way. I have taken the cost of living in the United States, the cost of living in the United Kingdom, and the level of wages in the United Kingdom, and I have converted these into gold value; I have made the correction for the sterling exchange during the time it was below par and have modified the amount of that correction in accordance with the improvement in the exchange recently. If members of the Committee would not mind taking down a small number of figures I think I can make it clear. In March 1924 we were in very close equilibrium with the outside world. The cost of living in the United States in 1924 was 156. (I might say that all these figures are as compared with the pre-war figure of 100.) The cost of living in the United Kingdom was 157. The level of wages in the United Kingdom was 155. This is in terms of gold, of course.

16,438 (CHAIRMAN) *What was the level of wages in the United States?* There is no good index number of that. The date I have given you is March, 1924, when as I say there was almost perfect equilibrium. By June, 1924, the position was still much the same; the cost of living in America had fallen to 154, in this country it had fallen to 150, and wages had improved slightly to 157. So that an improvement of real wages had taken place, but we were still not out of equilibrium to any appreciable extent with the United States.

16,439 *Our trade was desperately bad both in March, 1924, and June, 1924?* It was very much better than now, and people were in an optimistic state of mind about the prospects.

16,440 *Was it better in actual figures?* The unemployment figures were much better, and the trade returns were much better.

16,441 *A shade better?* I am discussing the reasons for the abnormal unemployment and the worsening which has taken place in the past year. I think most people a year ago looked to an improvement. My own view a year ago was that things were decidedly taking a turn for the better, and there was no sign that our export trade had abnormal difficulties in competing—any more than they had for some little time past. By October the exchange had begun to improve as a result of the talk about the restoration of the gold standard, and we were beginning to get out of equilibrium, but not seriously. In October the cost of living in the United States was 157, while in this country it had risen to 162, and wages here were 164. By December most of the mischief had been done; the anticipation of the restoration of the gold standard had caused a big improvement in the exchange and by that date the United States cost of living was 158, our cost of living was 174, and our wages 172. By March of the present year the American cost of living was 158, ours 176, and wages 177. In April the American cost of living was still 158, our cost of living 172, and wages 178. For May and June I have not yet got the American figures, but I believe that they are practically unchanged. Our cost of living has remained unchanged, and with the correction for the exchange the figures for May and June are the same as for April, that is to say 172. Wages, for a full working week and making no allowance for short time, have risen a little to 180 in May, and 181 in June. The total result of this is that if you take the rate of wages and do not allow for short time there has been an improvement in real wages. Wages were a little below the cost of living in March of last year, and now they are nine points above. To that extent you may say that wages have been moving in the wrong direction apart from the external situation, but the main thing is that whereas our cost of living and wages were in equilibrium with the United States last March, they are now 10 or 11 per cent higher.

Of course the result is inevitable when that happens. We have improved our exchange 10 per cent, but we have not altered our cost of living, we have not altered our level of wages. If there had been a boom in [the] price level in America that might have lifted us out of our difficulty, but things on the whole there have run pretty level, and the result is therefore what we see. The position is aggravated by the fact that while we are on the wrong side in excess of the United States, taking the United States as the norm, European countries are very much below the United States. In the case of

Germany she is not so much below as she was, but she is still very much below; the stabilisation of the mark has been gradually resulting in an increased cost of living. The cost-of-living figures for Germany are as follows:—In March, 1924, 107; in June, 1924, 112; in September, which is roughly comparable with October, 116; in December, 123; in March, 1925, 136; in April, 137. April is the last figure available. That means it is not easy for Germany to pay quite such low money wages as she could before. Her cost of living has been raised 30 per cent, and her wages not so much, so that her material conditions have been worsening. That means that German wages will have to rise sooner or later. But Germany is still able to give a money wage which is 30 per cent below our money wage, and yet leave German workmen as well off in relation to pre-war as ours are. Their cost of living is 30 per cent below ours, and therefore their money wage may be 30 per cent below ours without the German workmen being badly off.

When you come to France it is more striking still. I do not altogether trust the French figures. I have not made a complete table, but it will be quite easy to follow without a complete table. Taking for example March, 1925, which is the latest date I have, the gold cost of living in France was 94, that is to say, actually less than pre-war.

16,442 (SIR PETER RYLANDS) *I took some figures out of Montagu's weekly report which gives about 110 for France. They fluctuated between 111 and 112, I think?* My figures are taken from the Federal Reserve Bulletin, which is always convenient for this purpose, and corrected for the exchange. My figures are for Paris. Possibly his are for other parts of the country.

16,443 *It may be that in the industrial parts of France it was a little different?* I say I do not trust these figures. I think they are too low to be true. I think your figure of 110 is much more plausible than my own figure of 94, and I would willingly substitute yours for this purpose.

16,444 *The figures I have got, translating them at the average rate of exchange, are 112 in May and 111 in April, 114 in March, and 116 in January?* I readily accept that. I think that is more plausible than mine. At any rate the cost of living in France, whatever the figure you take, is not very much above pre-war. The consequence is that there also they can take a money wage far below ours without their standard of living being actually depressed. I think, therefore, that our difficulties are fully explained by the fact that the gold equivalent of our money wages has been forced by the return to gold out of equilibrium with the rest of the world, and as our cost of living has also been forced out of equilibrium, though not quite to the same extent, it is very hard to force a reduction in the money wage until you have first forced a reduction in the cost of living—the two dovetail into one another.

When the return to the gold standard was being discussed two questions arose: the question of the merits of gold as an eventual standard, and the wisdom of doing it at the moment. I argued very hotly that a decision to return to gold at that moment involved as its corollary reducing money wages throughout the country 10 per cent, and I did not perceive by what *modus operandi* we were going to achieve that result. Therefore I thought this act to be an extremely foolish one until we had thought out by what means we were going to alter the internal price level, because nothing can be more certain than that a country cannot alter the external value of its money without altering the internal value. I thought it particularly dangerous because it aggravated the pre-existing situation. In the case of Germany when they stabilised the mark they were very much below the world level, so that it was not a specially dangerous thing for them to do. They could stand a relative rise of their money values; in fact it would help them towards equilibrium rather than otherwise. The evidence was that even a year ago having regard to everything that has happened since the war, the difference in our investing power and so forth, our internal money values were too high. In order to be in true equilibrium with the rest of the world we already had to reduce the money cost of living and the money standard of wages.

16,445 (CHAIRMAN) *Before the gold question arose at all?* Before the gold question arose at all. So that it was not, as in the German case, something which would tend to compensate a deviation in the other direction from equilibrium; it was something which was calculated to aggravate the existing disequilibrium. It is for this reason that the results have been so rapid and so very marked. There was no initial friction to overcome; it merely accelerated a movement that was already tending to take place.

16,446 *Should there be no compensating advantage in purchasing our foodstuffs abroad?* A certain amount.

16,447 *That will come?* That does come. Our cost of living has fallen 4 points converted into gold, and I should predict that that will go further, for I do not think that we yet have the full benefit of that.

16,448 *Then you come to the point of sheltered industries?* Even in the case of imported food, by the time it reaches the consumer very many home services have entered in in the way of transport, and retail delivery, and one thing and another, and if they are at a high level the benefit of purchasing the prime material at the ports at lower sterling prices has been watered down to a great extent so that you do not get anything like the full benefit in reduced cost of living.

16,449 *Apparently from what you say, in March 1924, before the question of the gold standard arose, we were living in a fool's paradise that could not be maintained in any case?* But that was a result of anticipation of a gold standard.

16,450 *You think so?* I think almost entirely. There had been an enormous movement of funds from America to this country to take advantage of the return of the gold standard which we had been announcing was going to take place. Anybody over there, who believed our announcements, had a profit in his pocket.

16,451 *That was a year ago last March?* Not a year ago: last March.

16,452 *At that time we were living under conditions where we could not do the world's trade on account of our cost?* I believe at that time we were out of equilibrium, but not seriously.

16,453 *We could not do the world's trade on account of our cost, and therefore it is not possible that the return of the gold standard has aggravated this point; it had to be faced in any case?* I think 10 per cent over the whole country is a very big amount; 2s. in the £ in any man's wages is a very big thing. I think that in March, 1924, we had overcome a very large part of the pre-existing disequilibrium which had existed earlier. I believe that if we had kept the exchange adjusted to our position at that date and had not raised expectations of a return to the gold standard, and had had easy money, we could have gone a long way towards abolishing unemployment by now. Things were favourable at that moment. I quite agree with you that we are not in equilibrium, that we are still on the wrong side, and it is very hard to measure how much that was. In my opinion 10 per cent is very big; 2s. in the £ reduction in a man's wages is a thing you can only achieve after a great row. It is not a thing you can slip into without anybody noticing it very much. The decision of the Government to return to gold was *ipso facto* a decision to reduce everybody's wages 2s. in the £. Therefore it was a decision to have a row with every industry in turn.

I regard that as the first stage of the diagnosis. How has the improvement of the exchange actually operated? It operates first of all by our export industries being in difficulties, and by unemployment in our export industries. That reduces our favourable balance of trade. The Bank of England then feels it necessary to counteract that unfavourable balance of trade. Their methods of counteracting it have been two: first of all by an embargo on foreign investment, which has recently been extended to colonial investment as well, and partly by offering rates of interest in London which attract loans from New York. The Bank of England has been creating a monetary situation in which the rate of interest for three or six months' money is 1 per cent per annum more than it is in New York—an absolutely unprecedented situation. So long therefore as an American banker believes that the gold standard is going to be maintained, and that he will be able to take his money away again without loss, he can get 1 per cent per annum more by lending his money in London than in New York. In fact, the gold standard has made our credit so good that we no longer have any need for exports! Credit is only useful to the borrower, not the lender; it is not usual to inquire very strictly into the credit of the lender; it is only on the assumption that we are a borrowing country that we need think about our credit being good. But our credit is so much improved that we have no difficulty in borrowing in New York whatever sum we require to make good the deficiency in our exports caused by unemployment in our industries.

16,454 *That is only a temporary method?* That is only temporary, and is obviously unsound in the long run. The Bank of England has no difficulty in preserving equilibrium for the time being partly by the embargo on foreign investment which reduces the amount we send out of the country, partly by attracting American money which increases the amount which comes into the country. That is one way or another a method of living on our capital, and is therefore unsound in the long run. The Bank of England therefore has to consider other measures to bring down the internal price level so that in the long run we shall be able to live, not by borrowing, but by exporting again.

What methods are open to the Bank of England to bring down the internal price level? There is really no method which does that to any large extent except the restriction of credit, and while that has not gone very far as yet, there are symptoms that there has been some restriction of credit. If the position goes on as at present and we are to continue with bad export trade, that restriction of credit will probably be intensified, if one correctly follows the policy of the Bank of England. How does the restriction of credit bring down internal prices? It brings down the prices of certain raw materials possibly by making it difficult for holders to carry them, and therefore compelling them to throw them on the market. But that is not the main feature, because it is not the price of raw materials that is the trouble. They are at the world price already. The trouble is the cost of wages and the cost of retail distribution, the cost of freight charges and so forth.

16,455 *And railway transport?* I include railway transport in freight charges. Restriction of credit does not directly affect this. The way it works is by limiting the opportunities of offering employment. That is to say, the method of the Bank of England is to intensify unemployment until the workers are prepared to accept lower wages. So that our policy has been first of all to produce a situation in which we were condemned to reduce wages 10 per cent and then finding that that does not happen of itself, as, of course, it could not, the only method open to us (the old-fashioned method of producing equilibrium) is deliberately to intensify unemployment until wages do in fact fall. That is the old theory of the Bank rate for bringing about equilibrium. Unemployment, one should remember, is produced in two ways, partly by exports being non-remunerative, and partly by credit being in short supply. I should say that up to this present stage it is the first of those factors which is the more important. The second factor, however, has been quite important; the embargo on foreign loans in particular, by restricting the capacity of borrowers to place orders has undoubtedly operated, and also the fact that new borrowers find it not easy to raise money, and that new issues are difficult to arrange, and so forth. All that tends to restrict opportunities for employment, and to intensify unemployment. So that as far as I understand the official policy of the Treasury and the Bank of England—though it is only a half-conscious policy—it is to intensify unemployment until wages do come down; and I think the Government in the recent debates, instead of apologising for what happened, ought to have pointed with pride to the comparative success of their methods up to date in that they had produced additional unemployment to the extent of 25,000, that that had already produced a greater willingness to accept lower wages, and that one would hope it would be sufficient to do the trick, or if it was not we should have to continue intensifying unemployment until willingness to accept lower wages was still more apparent than now.

16,456 *But the necessity for an alteration in our cost of production existed long before the return to the gold standard?* I do not think that it existed to any important extent.

16,457 *Trade was intensely bad at the end of 1923 and in 1924?* Yes, but my belief is that we had, given a continuance of easy money, turned the corner in 1924.

16,458 *But we had unemployment in 1922 and 1923 which was worse than even today?* It is only saying that the exchange was already too high at that date.

16,459 *No doubt you will deal directly with the alternative policy and tell us what you think might have been done?* The alternative policy would have been to have kept your internal price level steady because of the immense difficulties of altering it, and allowed your exchange to adjust itself to that.

16,460 *And adjust itself by trade?* Adjust itself by trade. My own opinion is that it was not so far from adjustment. The exchange would always have brought about true equilibrium and would have brought our internal prices to a competitive level with the outside world.

16,461 *We will say that from 1921 even we have not been in a competitive position?* If you go back as far as that we were in a world wide slump. I think that there was a certain period of time during which we, in common with the United States, were suffering from a cyclical depression which was a reaction from the previous boom.

16,462 *It was exaggerated by cost of production?* It was very violent, but it was a more or less normal experience. It was not that we were out of relation to the rest of the world, but that there had been a general disequilibrium between the different factors of production all over the world. America by their monetary policy emerged from that in the course of a year or two.

16,463 *Theirs was a much simpler problem?* Yes it was simpler.

16,464 *They did not owe money?* That is so; it was a bit easier for them. But we by our own policy aggravated the difficulties of our own situation, and that culminated in the policy of the last year. When one comes to the objection to what I interpret the official policy to be, I think that the great difficulty of producing a fall of prices by the intensification of unemployment is that when things reach a certain point the Government is inevitably pressed to do politically things which defeat its own object. On the one hand it will be having a tight credit policy at the Bank of England, and as soon as that tight credit policy begins to produce its effects those effects are so unpleasant politically that the Government begins to take other steps which counteract its own policy; so that you get the process of adjustment spun out much longer.

The next difficulty seems to me to be that you cannot reduce all wages simultaneously by the method of internal pressure as you can by the exchange. If all wages could be reduced simultaneously the cost of living would fall too, and real wages would very likely be very little lower than they had been before, and the working classes would not have suffered; so that if there was any machinery by which you could reduce all wages simultaneously the objections to the policy that I have been outlining would not be very serious. But that is not practicable. The difficulty I see is that those workers who are first asked to accept a reduction have a legitimate grievance because if you ask workers in a particular trade to accept a reduction they have no guarantee that the cost of living will fall and you are in the first instance, until it has fallen, throwing on them a reduction of their real wage against which they can legitimately protest.

16,465 *The reduction should be national really if it were possible?* I do not think you could do that. It is a wide question of course. The other difficulty is that the pressure that you exert falls on the weakest industries first, where unemployment is already greatest. Those industries are generally speaking the industries in which wages are already relatively low, industries where you cannot legitimately ask them in relation to other people's wages to accept less. The paradox is that you want to reduce wages first in those industries where there is least unemployment.

16,466 (SIR PETER RYLANDS) *Are those industries which would least affect the cost of living?* I think if you could put down railway charges, if you could put down retail trade charges, if you could reduce the wage of bakers—

16,467 *But those are not the wages you are talking about. Are you not talking about the wages of the iron and steel workers, and people like that?*

16,468 (CHAIRMAN) *Those are the wages you are talking of as being the least able to bear it?* Those are the wages least able to bear it. The leading instance is the coal industry.

16,469 (SIR PETER RYLANDS) *They would have the least bearing on the cost of living?* They would have the least bearing on the cost of living. They have very little effect on the cost of living and it is rather unjust to expect them to accept a reduction.

16,470 (SIR JOHN HINDLEY) *Do you say coal is one of the things that has least bearing on the cost of food?* It has very little. I do not remember its exact order in the Board of Trade's index number, but its position is not high.

16,471 *Surely from the point of view of transport it has some bearing?* It has some bearing certainly; all these things have some bearing; but it has very little bearing compared with the wages of bakers and other producers for retail, for example.

16,472 (CHAIRMAN) *The point will develop, I think, as we go on. Your point is the cost of food transport compared with the cost of manufactured goods transport, and coal for industry. It will have a big effect on the latter, of course?* The wages index that I am quoting, if it is of interest to the Committee to know what industries it is based on, consists of the wages of bricklayers and labourers, engineering fitters and labourers, dock labourers, railwaymen, woollen workers, cotton workers, miners and agricultural labourers. It is a very wide index.

16,473 *Have we not a totally new situation, which you refer to in your memorandum, in the existence of the higher wages in what are commonly called the sheltered industries?* That is my point precisely. It is the wages in the sheltered industries which are the problem, whereas the wages on which you are bringing pressure to bear are in unsheltered industries which are very likely quite reasonable already until the wages of the other industries may be brought down. If you could reduce the wages in sheltered trades that would reduce the cost of living and then you could then legitimately ask the colliers to take a lower wage.

16,474 *The trouble about the sheltered wage is that it is very largely tied up with special considerations, local considerations, and so on?* They are very difficult to get at, because if an industry has not any more than a normal unemployment it is very hard to see what pressure you can bring upon them to make them reduce their wages. Your instrument of unemployment tends to attack industries at the wrong end of the scale which are comparatively innocent ones. Why did the Bank of England and the Treasury make what I consider this mistake—because I think that throws light on the matter.

I think they made it for two reasons. In the first place they miscalculated the degree of disparity by attending to the inappropriate index number. They attended, I believe—I gather this from the not very clear remarks in the Report of the Committee on Currency [and Bank of England Note Issues]—to the wholesale index numbers. That is a point I deal with in my memorandum. If you want to know the disparity of English home prices it is perfectly useless to take prices of raw cotton in Liverpool, because the price of raw cotton in Liverpool is always the same, when corrected for the exchange, as the price of raw cotton in New York. It must be. The wholesale index numbers are largely made up of the international raw materials which are always at equilibrium, so that if you take that type of index number the disequilibrium you are searching for is very much watered down, and it will appear to be of the order of 2 or 3 per cent when it is perhaps really of the order of 10 per cent. What you ought to look at is the wages index number, the cost of living index number, and the Board of Trade index number of prices of our manufactured exports. Those three things give you the best clue. They would all have led to a conclusion of the order of 10 per cent as being the disequilibrium on the basis of gold parity. But I think the Treasury and the Bank of England have been influenced entirely by the Board of Trade wholesale commodities index number, and that showed a trifling disparity of the order of 2 or 3 per cent. I think that was the first part of their mistake.

I think the second part was that they believed there was some automatic or magical way in which high Bank rate would reduce wages, averting their attention from the fact that the only way in which it could do that would be by intensifying unemployment. I think they did this because they had not re-analysed the facts in the light of modern conditions. They were depending upon the orthodox theory of economic text-books, and that orthodox theory assumed mobility of labour and competitive wages. The way the argument ran was this. If the export trades get into trouble and there is unemployment, there will be a movement of labour from the export trades into the other trades which will bring down wages in the other trades by the competition of these other men offering themselves. The orthodox theory of the text-books assumed that when there is unemployment in the coal industry some of the colliers offer themselves as bakers, and this brings down wages in the baking industry, and so the conditions are very quickly averaged out between all industries, and you cannot have for any length of time this disparity between unsheltered industries and sheltered industries. That is to say they assumed that labour is free to move from industry to industry and from place to place, and that an unemployed man can get himself occupation by offering to work for a lower wage than the standard wage in one of the relatively prosperous industries.

16,475 (MR HARGREAVES) *By displacing another workman?* By under-cutting, and therefore with the result of bringing down the wages in the other more prosperous industries.

16,476 (MR BAKER) *It does not alter unemployment, but the wage rate?* It alters the wage rate. That theory has no relation to the facts at all, however. It is impossible of course for a collier to offer himself as a baker below the standard wages of bakers, that cannot in fact happen, partly because of the power of the trade unions in preventing the cutting of rates by the competition of unemployed labour from other industries, partly because the dole has reduced the extreme pressure to find employment elsewhere, and partly because labour for two reasons is very much less mobile both between places and industries. The reason it is less mobile between places is due partly to the condition of housing. A man has a house in the place where he has been employed, and it is a rash and dangerous thing for him to give up that house to go and seek employment in another part of the country where very likely he will not be able to get a house. The fact that he has a house in one place and no security of getting a house in another place pins him down and so limits his capacity to rove about and find employment elsewhere. The other thing—and I think it is an unavoidable and permanent factor—is that during a considerable part of the nineteenth century we were increasing at a rapid rate; everything was on a general crescendo, just as in the United States now; everything was increasing at the rate of 3 per cent per annum or something of that kind. That meant that when a given industry was too large and another industry too small you did not force a man out of the industry that had too much labour into the other, but you just stopped taking new men in for a certain period of time, and with the rapid general progress going on, the slack would be taken up not so much by driving men out of the industry as by simply stopping the intake for a bit. Then it was very much easier to bring your industry into equilibrium by just not taking on new hands—which you can do when the whole economic machine is stepping forward at a great pace—than by actually discharging men. One sees that illustrated in the case of railways. During the period when the railways were being rapidly extended, supposing the railway companies found themselves with redundant staffs they could right the situation by not taking on new men and using their redundant staff on new sections of line. If they are not opening new sections of line, if they find themselves with redundant staffs, there is no way of dealing with the situation except by sacking men. That is much more difficult both practically and humanly than stopping new men from coming into the industry. So that the old assumption about the mobility of labour and about the way in which a fall of wages in one trade would be reflected in others, in my opinion no longer holds good except in the very long run. I think it may be true that in the very long run it does operate. In the course of years low wages in unsheltered industries will react on the wages of sheltered industries, but it will not react quickly. Therefore the hypothesis on which the old theory was based as to the way in which you could bring about equilibrium between the internal value of your money and the external value of your money no longer holds good. I do not think that the authorities realised that we are now in a situation in which a forcible change in the internal value of money is extraordinarily difficult. We are in something much more like medieval conditions in which it was so difficult to change the internal value of money that when you were in disequilibrium with the external value you had what was called a debasement of currency, leaving internal prices the same and allowing the external value of your money to fall. The orthodox nineteenth-century theory of keeping the external value of your money to a certain gold parity, and making the internal value of your money follow suit, did not work badly in the conditions of that age; but of course they never tried in that age a forcible disturbance of 10 per cent. The change in the value of our money relatively to the value of other people's in any given period of time never approached that. So that they never set themselves so difficult a problem. Apart from that the conditions in which such a solution would work were much more nearly fulfilled than they are now. I therefore regard our present situation as the dilemma necessarily brought about by the monetary policy of the past year. We have committed ourselves to a policy of reducing wages 2s. in the £, unless something turns up in the external conditions of the world, without having any idea whatever as to the *modus operandi* by which that reduction of wages can take place.

16,477 *Had we not already locked ourselves up long before?* Not as long as our exchange could fluctuate, because we could always make the external value of our money what we liked. I do not know that there is any easy solution out of the difficulty. There seem to me to be three alternatives when I come to possible policies. One would be to allow the exchange to fall, which is the only wise course, but one which I suppose it is certain will not be taken. One must rule that out because it is impossible for the existing authorities to reverse the policy which they have adopted so recently. That is the first policy. The second policy is to intensify unemployment without limit until wages fall—which is the theory, as I understand, of the Currency Committee's Report—and the Bank of England has taken tentative steps in that direction. The objection to that seems to me to the probability, indeed almost the certainty, that political influences will interfere to prevent the completion of this long before it has reached its logical conclusion. The third policy is to pursue what, strictly speaking, is the unsound policy of gambling as it were on the chance of something turning up of an unexpected kind—which might quite well happen—which would pull us out of our difficulties as, for example, an inflation in America which was not accompanied by an inflation here—something which would diminish the value of American money and therefore revive our export industries and so bring back the necessary equilibrium. The third course is essentially unsound. It is the course which we are half pursuing now, viz., that of not following the sound policy to its logical extreme, but borrowing a good deal from abroad and hoping something will turn up. This gambling policy might take various forms. We might do our utmost to try to engineer something like an internal boom, flinging sound finance to the winds by programmes of capital expenditure and so forth, which would allow costive industries to discharge some of their labour into the booming internal industries. We could abandon all restriction on credit, we could remove the embargo on foreign loans, and when these various unsound policies produced their inevitable effect on our exchanges, when they began to cause a drain on the Bank of England, we could meet that by using our American credits and borrowing in America. That is to say, we could use our American credits to engineer a boom at home, and easy credit, and all the rest of it.

16,478 (SIR NORMAN HILL) *And lend abroad?* And lend abroad. Do something utterly unsound in the hope, as so often happens, that something would turn up; that the impulse we were setting going at home towards prosperity would in fact, in some way which we could not predict, take up the slack.

16,479 *But not in a permanent way?* Not in a permanent way, simply in the hope that we could carry on this policy for sufficient time to give us some chance of assistance from one of the innumerable things happening that one cannot foresee.

16,480 (CHAIRMAN) *Which of the sound principles do you suggest?* I think that the only sound policy is the first one, but I cannot conceive that the Government would so quickly reverse the policy it has undertaken. It is not practical politics.

16,481 *Will the Government be able to resist the first policy at all, if in effect we cannot do our export trade?* It is very hard to say. What I think is very likely to happen is that the Government will try a mixture of the second and third. The Bank of England will try to have a 'sound' policy and will greatly intensify unemployment, and the Government will neutralise all the things the Bank of England is doing by other things in the opposite direction, so that we shall not get the benefit of either thing. And we shall probably keep that state of things going for some considerable time, when either the unemployment will become so unpleasant that it will lead to a political upheaval which might result in a complete change of policies, or the present situation will drift on sufficiently long and in the end an adjustment will be brought about and then our troubles would be relatively over. Because these troubles are not eternal; they are troubles that exist during the period of maladjustment. If you could get the cost of living down, then people are not worse off than previously. It is simply the difficulty of seeing how that is to be achieved in any reasonable space of time.

16,482 *But our difficulty in exports is not competition with America, it is competition with the depreciated currencies like France?* Not entirely; it is aggravated by them. Until the improvement in exchange we could compete with United States coal in Canada and South America. The effect of the improvement in exchange has just made the difference that American coal has been brought to a level with ours. We are charging 10 per cent more for our coal than previously; the sterling price is 10 per cent heavier to a Canadian purchaser than it was before the improvement of the exchange. That just has the effect of letting in the American coal. It is very difficult to follow out all its consequences. It operates sometimes less than 10 per cent and sometimes more. Unquestionably the thing has been aggravated by the fact that apart from Germany the other continental exchanges have been working in an opposite direction, so that even if we had stopped where we were we would have been suffering some difficulties.

16,483 *We are bound to suffer, so much depending on our exports?* I think it is useless to pretend you can raise your exchange 10 per cent leaving your wages and cost of living where they were and not experience the effects on export industries which we are experiencing. The thing is a logical predictable consequence. While it is perfectly true we have many other troubles—and because we have other troubles this was a particularly dangerous thing to do in that it aggravated the existing bad situation—yet it is useless to avert one's eyes from the effect of the new policy of last year which has so much aggravated the whole situation. That is what I wanted to say.

16,484 (MR BAKER) *On the question of trade you say the United States of America trade is good?* Yes.

16,485 *It might be probably on the whole, but you would not call the iron and steel trade good when they are only working to 70 per cent of capacity?* In America?

16,486 *Yes?* Their 100 per cent is a very fictitious figure. They had some easiness in their iron and steel industry in the spring, but I should have said relatively speaking iron and steel in America was in very good order if you take as a rough test the prices of iron and steel shares on the New York stock exchange.

16,487 *Have they not gone down recently?* On the whole they stand high.

16,488 *I thought they had fallen?* They had a slight setback, but only slight, and part of that has now been recovered.

16,489 *With regard to your typewritten proof you seem to have modified that very considerably by what you have said in your oral evidence. I thought you were one of the people who were wanting a reduction in wages in the sheltered trades; I am not in favour of a reduction in wages. Also on another page you say you have no remedy to offer I think. You have given up your suggestion of dealing with the currency?* No, that is my first remedy, but I regard that as not practical politics at the moment. I still offer that for what it is worth, but I feel at the moment there is not much chance of its being acted on.

16,490 *I thought I had quite a number of questions to ask, but it seems to me from what you have said this morning your views are so much in consonance with my own feeling about the situation that I have not any questions to put to you.*

16,491 (SIR PETER RYLANDS) *I should just like to emphasise the point made with regard to the manner in which our internal value of the £ is below the external value. From what I understand you to say that arises from the lag in the effect of the fall in the price of imports on which the cost of living depends so far as affected by internal costs of manipulation?* It is partly that lag, but I think it is much more that those imported foodstuffs and so forth form only a certain proportion of the items that make up the cost of living.

16,492 *But supposing the wages all fell immediately, the internal value would remain the same as the external value?* Yes.

16,493 *But there is a lag; they do not fall until the cost of living falls?* And the difficulty is that the cost of living cannot fall until they fall.

16,494 *That is what I mean by the word 'lag'. There is a lag in the effect on the cost of living, and so upon wages, and wages not going down until the cost of living falls you get that disparity which you pointed out to the Committee was about 10 per cent. I take it that a somewhat similar phenomenon was going on in this country during the year or two preceding when the value of our £ was even then rising. I think I am right in saying that the exchange on New York was about 3.40 in about 1920?* You have to take in conjunction the movement of the exchange and the movement of American prices. You have to compound the two, and I have not in my mind the result of that composition.

16,495 *Very likely there was some tendency of the same sort going on even before March, 1920?* My memory of the figures is that we have gone through a series of waves in which we were in adjustment and out of adjustment, and the moments when we were out of adjustment were when America was exporting capital very freely. The effect of the large exports of capital by America was to put the exchange more in our favour than our position really justified. During the phases when America was exporting heavily we were suffering in a less degree the same difficulties as now. There were intermediate periods in which we were not suffering in that way.

16,496 *If anything there might have been the same tendency, broadly speaking, as now?* At certain dates, but I would not commit myself to the dates without looking up the matter.

16,497 *Turning to the Continent where there has been a steady depression of the currency at the rate of about 10 per cent per annum, the lag operating in the other direction has brought about the persistence of a higher value of the franc internally than externally.* Yes.

16,498 *With the result that today the internal value of the franc is, if anything, little more below the world's parity than the £ is above it?* Yes, but I should say a good deal more below in the case of France, and about the same in the case of Germany.

16,499 (SIR HUBERT LLEWELLYN SMITH) *Do you mean now in Germany?* Yes. Germany was, of course, very much below. I mean now in Germany.

16,500 (SIR PETER RYLANDS) *The Chairman says he thinks, and I must say I think, we are suffering most from Belgian and French competition in the iron and steel trade today. I take it that the cost of living in Belgium is not remotely different to the cost of living in France?* It is rather higher.

16,501 *You have given the figure of 137, which looks rather higher than anything I have seen.*

(SIR HUBERT LLEWELLYN SMITH) *That only shows that the Belgian cost of living has gone up compared with itself in 1913. The French cost of living must also be compared with itself. It has not any kind of comparison with the cost of living in Belgium.*

(SIR PETER RYLANDS) *You mean the index number may be based on something different.*

16,502 (SIR HUBERT LLEWELLYN SMITH) *It simply shows the percentage changes on the basic value of the French cost of living in 1913 and the Belgian cost of living in 1913?* Relatively to itself the gold cost of living in Belgium in May of this year was 131. That is very near to the figure you mention. That is to say, it is very near the German. It is not so serious as the French. It is more on the German level than the French level.

16,503 (SIR PETER RYLANDS) *There is no doubt that the wages in Germany and France are reflected more than the cost of living in this figure?* Yes.

16,504 *And measured in gold they are indubitably very much lower than those in this country?* Yes, without the real wages being particularly low.

16,505 *I take it you will agree that that is very largely responsible for [our] inability to carry on our export trade in the iron and steel industry at all events in competition with Belgium?* I do not know sufficiently about those trades to know how far Belgium in particular was responsible. I should have been inclined to think that France, Belgium, and Germany all played their part in that. If you say Europe, I agree. I dare say you are right about Belgium, But I cannot answer that on my own knowledge.

16,506 *It comes home to us every day of the week, of course. You have no policy to suggest at all that this Committee, for instance, could recommend, except a gamble?* Well, it is for the Committee to say what they could recommend.

16,507 *But you are here to help us, I take it, to come to some decision. You are not really in a position to suggest anything practicable?* Well, I say these are the three alternatives: to let the exchange go, to follow the policy of dear money and the intensification of unemployment, and, thirdly to hope that something will turn up and live rather a free life in the meantime. What I think will happen will be a compromise between the last two.

16,508 *I suppose it is an economic fact that this disbursement of about £1,000,000 a week in unemployment benefit and pensions and high Government expenditure, does create considerable activity in the home trade and help the sheltered industries?* Certainly.

16,509 *That in itself tends to strengthen the position of the sheltered industries and helps them to maintain their present rates and profits and remunerations?* Undoubtedly. That is one of the reasons why the old-fashioned repercussion of wages in one industry on wages in another does not have its full effect. Supposing the unemployed were not receiving the dole, retail trade would become so bad that there would be a tendency for wages to fall in the industries connected with retail trade.

16,510 *Can you hold out the slightest hope that the Continental position will improve from our point of view within anything like a reasonable time?* I think it will slowly tend in a direction favourable to us. I believe particularly in Germany there is a considerable chance of a rise in prices and wages.

16,511 *Belgian prices have fallen very materially during the last month, and manufacturers are not interested, and the country is not much interested in what is going to happen in five years' time, but we want to know whether there is any hope, do you think, that the internal value of the franc will rise during the next eighteen months?* If I was to predict at all I would predict that the movement would be in the right direction from our point of view.

16,512 *But you are not prepared to predict anything very violent or rapid?* I believe our own cost of living and wage level will tend to fall in the next six months. I think the pressure already put on will have some consequences, and I think that money wages in Continental countries will tend to rise, so that I should anticipate that there will be a smaller gap six or nine months hence than now. But I do not feel optimistic about the very big difference that exists being covered.

16,513 *I notice according to the Board of Trade returns the adverse balance of trade rose from £76,000,000 in 1923 for the first five months to £166,000,000 in 1925?* That is the visible balance of trade.

16,514 *That is the visible adverse balance. Do you think that is really covered by [in]visible exports, or do you think it is provided by balances left in this country, or other methods which might be described as living on our capital?* It is difficult to say. I wish I felt more confident about the Board of Trade invisible items. I do not know how they are compiled, but I think they are, to a considerable extent, corrections made on the best information available of previous estimates; so that if you start from a wrong basis the whole thing may be wrong. I think that the original estimates of invisible items on which the Board of Trade started may have been rather too low. On the other hand, whether they make enough allowance for the extraordinary fall in shipping income, for example, I do not know again. I think it would be very useful if the Board of Trade could compile an estimate which is as detailed as the American estimate. I think the American estimate is immensely better because it has a much firmer statistical basis than the Board of Trade estimate. The Board of Trade estimate is a good enough guess, I think—as good a guess as anybody could make who is having mainly to guess. Thus I do not put enormous faith in those figures, though I cannot provide any better ones myself. The other thing I would say is, that looking at it from quite another point of view, namely, on the basis of what amount of American money has come into this country, I should guess, without being able to stand cross-examination on the subject, that American money may have been coming in at the rate of, say, £50,000,000 a year.

16,515 *In deposit or sterling?* In the purchase of sterling bills, of one shape or another. If that is true, since this is the main item which makes up any deficit, it follows arithmetically that our invisible plus items fall short of our visible minus items by £50,000,000 a year. But I would not ask the Committee to attach any importance to that guess.

16,516 *But the figure of £166,000,000 in five months strikes the ordinary person as rather alarming. Do you not think it is at all alarming?* I think it is alarming, but I am very cautious about these figures. There are so many things to take account of. For example, take the rise in the price of rubber. A great part of it is directly or indirectly owned by Englishmen. That is a huge item. I only give that as an example of the things which one has to look out for. One must be very careful before one can be certain. But I agree with your suggestion that the position is alarming.

16,517 *So far as we are not in a position to make up a favourable balance of trade there is a reaction, I understand from what you say, upon the amount of business likely to be placed in this country by the borrower?* Yes.

16,518 *So that that is another adverse factor?* Yes.

16,519 (CHAIRMAN) *I would like to have a little further discussion with you on the question of what I call the locked-up position which you depicted to us. You say we have totally different conditions today. We have trade unionism very strong, the lines of demarcation between industries very clearly defined, the difficulty of transferring labour from one industry to another, accentuated by the housing question, and also by the 'dole', the unemployment benefit, and so on. How long are we going to be able to carry on in such a locked-up position?* It is very hard to say. There is one extraordinary instance I should like to mention to the Committee.

16,520 *I include the sheltered trades in what I call the locked-up position?* Yes. I think one most extraordinary fact—no doubt it is familiar to you—is that the number of men employed in the coal industry is as great as two years ago and the increased unemployment is due to new men having entered the industry in the last two years. That is partly due to the fact that there is a tendency for the localisation of the coal industry to move. South Yorkshire is employing more men than ever before; South Wales and Northumberland are declining. It does not happen that the South Wales and Northumberland miners move to the South Yorkshire coalfield; they remain in their former localities on the dole; and new labour from the agricultural population of South Yorkshire is drawn into the South Yorkshire mines. So that you have a case there which is very extraordinary, because it is not a difficulty of moving from one industry to another, but it is a difficulty even of moving from one coalfield to another.

16,521 *Of course, what might ease up our locked-up position would be if other countries were locked-up in the same way?* I do not know. Would that help it?

16,522 *That is a dreadful solution, but it is one that is contemplated?* I think it might aggravate our situation.

16,523 *But it is one that is contemplated a great deal by certain sections of the community?* Supposing the European steel industry were in a great state of depression and supposing their men were unable to obtain work in their country, it would intensify the situation rather than help it.

16,524 *I think it would myself, but it is advocated by many people that if other countries were in exactly the same position that would be of benefit to us?* No, I think it would intensify our situation.

16,525 *If we adopted your policy and let the exchange fall, how would that remedy the disparity between sheltered and unsheltered wages?* Because the export price level would rise to the internal price level. It would take the form of an increased demand for our exports; the export trades would have no difficulty in paying a level of wages as good as the internal wages.

16,526 *Would not there be a danger of the sheltered trades rising with them?* There might be a tendency in that direction.

16,527 *That would not help to reduce our cost of production?* If our exchange falls 10 per cent our gold level of wages falls 10 per cent on that same day.

16,528 *With regard to the Trade Facilities Act, do you think that has been a good method of trying to increase employment?* It all depends what one's policy is. If one's policy is to increase unemployment by dear money and then to prevent that by using the Trade Facilities Act to counteract its consequences, the thing is an absurd contradiction. I do not think there is any place for the Trade Facilities Act simultaneously with restriction of credit by the Bank of England.

16,529 *And the same with the Export Credits scheme?* The Export Credits scheme in the same way. Personally I rather like those schemes.

16,530 *You like them as temporary schemes?* I like them as temporary schemes. I would like to stimulate in all sorts of unsound ways a general state of prosperity in the hope that I could get a cumulative wave of prosperity going which would lap up the slack. I do not believe you can ever get straight by depressing things. I think there is always a lot of unused capacity in the country, and that prosperity is cumulative, and I would like to create unsound artificial prosperity in the hope that it would prove cumulative. But I do not like suggesting that because I admit fully it is only a temporary expedient and is essentially unsound.

16,531 *With regard to the Dawes Report, we have had a good many representations made to us by various industries some saying that it is beneficial and some that it is very detrimental. What is your view of its effect generally on the industries of this country?* I do not think it has had much effect yet, because Germany has not had an export surplus and she has met all her obligations under the Dawes Report out of money borrowed from the rest of the world. The Dawes Report begins to come into effect from next year onwards, and I think the way in which it will operate, if it is successful which I much doubt, will be by keeping the money level of wages in Germany down either at their present level or below it. We have been assuming so far that in Germany, as in Belgium, there is and there will be a tendency for wages to rise towards the international level. The Dawes Report will try to prevent that from happening and in so far as it is successful it means that the low level of money wages in Germany will be perpetuated.

16,532 *Of course it must bring great pressure on Germany to export and produce?* That is its whole object.

16,533 *In that connection what about the hours question, which must have a big effect on the question of production?* What matters is the money wage per effective hour.

16,534 *That means the production per hour really?* Yes.

16,535 *That will press the Germans into working longer hours, will it not?* I think very likely so, but of course how far you can press a country by external influence I do not know. Before long you make political difficulties, and every political party puts the blame on the foreigner, and the breaking point comes before long.

16,536 *The evidence we have had is that at the present time people in Germany, Belgium and France are showing great willingness to work longer hours individually, quite apart from any control from the top. That is bound to have a very big effect on our situation if it is continued, is it not?* Yes, I think it is. I have always thought that the stimulation of German exports was bound to be adverse to us owing to the fact that their staple exports overlap so very considerably with ours.

16,537 *On the other hand, there is the point that Germany in prosperity was practically always importing up to £80,000,000 more than her exports pre-war?* Yes, but under the Dawes Scheme the notion is to stimulate the exports without stimulating the imports. If you stimulate the imports you again defeat yourself. If Germany was an agricultural country it would all be different. Supposing the pressure on Germany was to cause her to export foodstuffs at low prices the effect on us would be quite different from what it is.

16,538 *On the question of subsidies to industry, do you think the provision of subsidies is any remedy for the present situation?* I must ask what is the concurrent policy. I think to restrict credit on one side and give subsidies on the other side is to get the worst of both worlds.

16,539 *What about the fiscal system? Is your reply to that the same?* It seems to me that protective measures must worsen the situation because the export industries must be injured by them. The effect of protection is to make the disparity between internal and external prices move further in the direction which is already on the wrong side. I can imagine protection being a remedy for some things, but as a remedy for this it seems unthinkable.

16,540 (SIR HUBERT LLEWELLYN SMITH) *I was unfortunately detained at another Committee, so that I have not heard everything you have said. In your memorandum, and I think in your argument, you rely a good deal, do you not, on these figures of the cost of living, for those reasons given?* I do, yes.

16,541 *Those figures are given in the Federal Reserve Bulletin, and in the April, 1925, number of the Federal Reserve Bulletin there is a very complete account of the sources from which they are drawn. You are probably familiar with it?* Not very. I am not an expert on the value of these statistics.

16,542 *I wanted to ask whether you had any occasion to test their comparability?* I said earlier, I think before you came in, that the French figures in particular I distrusted. They seem to me to be lower than they really should be.

16,543 *There are in fact, as we have had in evidence, omissions, and very*

406

notable omissions, of important articles, and there is the insertion of others which do not materially affect the cost of living? Then in the case of Germany the basis of compilation has been changed I think twice, which is always dangerous. If you are comparing for a period over 18 months, which was what I was doing, I think they are much more reliable than if you are comparing with pre-war. Also the differences are so large that there is room for considerable error without affecting the argument.

16,544 *I am not dealing with your argument, but I may say I have recently been trying to use these same figures and they fill me with a great deal of distrust. I wondered whether you were acquainted with an inquiry which the Ministry of Labour made periodically, based rather on a different system?* Before the War?

16,545 *No, since the war. It has now been handed over to the International Labour Office. They bring the local prices to bear upon the standard consumption of articles which are included in our own cost-of-living index. It has the disadvantage that you are estimating the cost of living in a European country on the false assumption that the workman consumes the same articles in the same proportion as the British workman; but having once got over that obviously incorrect assumption it has the advantage that you are absolutely standardised?* I do not like that method. I should distrust that method. You will remember there were some inquiries made by the Board of Trade before the war which did more than any other inquiries I have seen to confirm the theoretical point as to the objection to doing that. I remember the results, which came out about 1907, of those inquiries were that if you took the English diet, the cost of living was cheaper in England than in Germany; and if you took the German diet the cost of living was cheaper in Germany than in England.

15,546 *In the use I made of the results I found I had to allow quite a number of points for that error. We can in some cases measure it, because now the International Labour Office is continuing that inquiry and has taken a number of different standards. They have taken the British standard, and they have taken the Central European standard; France and Belgium is another group, and Southern Europe is another—though how well they have done it I do not know. They have worked out for those standards the figures that our Ministry of Labour used to work out here, so that you can make a comparison. I only wanted to ask whether you thought that those figures were comparable?* One of my difficulties is that I am not interested in the cost of living except as an indication of the sheltered prices level. Even if I knew the index of the cost of living quite accurately, still that would only be an approximate index to what I am after.

16,547 *I did for a kindred purpose try to estimate what was the difference between the real wages estimated by internal prices of articles of ordinary consumption and the gold value of wages. It was very much the same as your problem. I do not know whether I was right, but I got hold of France, Germany and Belgium, and I got an indication of about 15 points difference, London being 100?* That is 15 per cent then.

16,548 *It is 15 per cent on the London scale, but supposing Paris was only 60, it would be a good deal greater percentage. So I called it 15 points. I think these figures will give a good deal more discrepancy—more like 20 or 25. It is only a matter of statistical interest, But I made it a little less. I suppose you would compare it with the United States figure, would you, of 158 for gold?* It does not look to me so very different.

16,549 *It is interesting because they are based on a different set of figures?* Germany seems to me to be about 12 per cent (I am doing it very roughly), which is not very far from your figure.

16,550 *Without committing yourself to anything, you would not be surprised to find a figure of about 15 points?* Not at all. My French figures give more than that, but as I say I distrust the French figures.

16,551 *I distrust the figures too. They include paraffin, which no French workman uses nowadays, and they have left out coffee, which is an article of universal consumption.*

16,552 (SIR NORMAN HILL) *As I understand the general picture that has been put to this committee is that the War has affected radically our export markets, more especially in regard to the development of domestic production in the other countries. I understand that this is the picture that is put to us?* That is not the picture that I particularly have been putting today.

16,553 *I may not have fully appreciated the evidence, but the picture that I have got in my my mind from what we have heard is that many of our old customers are now busily producing what they used to get from us, and there is every likelihood of their going on producing; and that therefore our manufacturing industries are having to study new methods with the object of producing different articles, perhaps specialised articles, and finding new markets. That is the kind of picture?* I think there is something in that, but I should be more inclined to believe that the test is price. I believe that at the right price we could still find very big markets for our goods.

16,554 *Yes. It has been emphasised by a great many industries that there is still a demand but they are beaten in price. If that is the kind of problem that we have before us am I right in understanding from what you have told us that of your three plans Nos. 1 and 3 are temporary expedients?* No, I do not think No. 1 is particularly temporary. No. 1 is really maintaining our price level steady, and letting the exchange adapt itself to other people's price levels. That I should be prepared to continue permanently.

16,555 *But you are maintaining it steady in equilibrium with the States?* No. I would keep the price level in England at whatever it is, and maintain it at that level.

16,556 *No matter what happened in any country?* Yes.

16,557 *That would be a permanent policy?* Yes.

16,558 *Abandoning the gold standard altogether?* Yes.

16,559 *You would have nothing more to do with it?* Well, substantially it is abandoning it. I would have various provisions for preventing rapid movements of the exchange that had no real significance. I would not allow us to be blown about by every breath of wind. To that extent I would still be interested.

16,560 *If we had to abandon the gold standard policy do you think we should be all more comfortable in this country?* I ought to explain I have not been directing myself today to the ultimate merits of the gold standard. Everything I have said today would be consistent with the gold standard being the best standard. What I have been arguing against is linking ourselves to gold at a moment when it means a 10 per cent change in our price level.

16,561 *That is why I thought you were rather putting it forward as a temporary expedient?* Suppose the value of gold was to alter 10 per cent, the particular objections I have been raising today would cease to operate.

16,562 *You mean if it altered today.* I also take the view that from a permanent point of view there are objections to gold, but those are quite distinct from the particular point I have been urging today, all of which might have been urged by somebody who believed the gold standard was the ideal one.

16,563 *The third policy you mentioned was entirely an expedient?* Yes. I should like to say that quite apart from this money question my own view is that owing to changes in the external world such as you have been indicating, probably our export trades will be permanently on a lower scale in relation to population than they were in pre-war days. And I think we should do well to have a transference of labour to some extent from the export trades to non-export trades, and balance our reduction of exports by investing less capital abroad and more capital at home. As we happen to be a country which exported capital we have room to reduce our exports very materially and yet have plenty to pay for our necessary imports, merely by reducing our exports of capital and using more at home. So that my long-period policy would be the gradual transference of labour from export industries and a large programme of capital expenditure at home, which would absorb the savings which had previously found an outlet abroad.

16,564 *If you went in for that policy, or if you stuck to our policy of pushing our exports anywhere and everywhere as far as we could in the altered conditions, there will have to be a very big transference of labour?* Our exports are at present 20 per cent below pre-war, so I think a good part of it has been effected, but still I agree it is a fairly large transference.

16,565 *We are 20 per cent down in our exports, and you have explained that our unemployment is not fluid and is not adjusting itself. There are a great many gaps in a great many directions?* Provided we could have capital programmes at home and easy money conditions at home, I believe that it would be easy to make a beginning at absorbing that labour in home industries.

16,566 *Absorbing it in some home industries, but not the industries in which they had been working under the other policy of exports?* To a certain extent you would be stimulating the same industries, but making them slightly alter the class of article they produce. If we had any of the great schemes that have been proposed for capital development at home that would certainly stimulate the employment of labour in the coal industry and in the iron and steel industry because they would require the products of those industries.

16,567 *And possibly in directions quite different from the centres from which you were working the export trade in coal or iron?* To a certain extent, but it would not be like turning colliers into bakers.

16,568 *But you would have to solve what you say is now impossible, namely to get the superfluous miners of South Wales shifted to Yorkshire?* Yes, but if there is an intake for labour the business of transfer is not an insuperable difficulty. What I think is so extraordinarily difficult is to absorb labour out of industries when the other industries are not wanting any labour. You must first of all create a condition of demand for labour in the other industries.

16,569 *Because of the unemployment benefit and such things as that, you put forward the point that now labour is not fluid even in its own industry?* Yes.

16,570 *And because of the housing problem ?* Yes, but I think that would be greatly mitigated if there was a big demand for labour. To give an example of the kind of way in which it would work; if there was a big demand for labour the growing up population would be attracted only to industries that were in a sound condition, so that the coalfields in South Yorkshire would have to take active steps to transfer labour from other districts in order to get the labour they want. As it is, they pursue the line of least resistance and take in young men out of the growing up population.

16,571 *If we were working under your third policy it would be with the hope of bringing about the results you have indicated in your second policy?* Partly that, and partly, as I say, that various things might turn up which I cannot specify.

16,572 *And make it not so necessary?* Something might happen to the price level in America, or all sorts of things, that would make the situation less acute all round.

16,573 *If the unexpected does not turn up we shall have sooner or later to work under your second policy, shall we not?* Or under my first.

16,574 *We have had some very interesting evidence of what is happening in France, and we are told that there everybody is very eager to work and trying to make money, not much caring how long they work; there is no unemployment and everybody is very very busy indeed. Now if we take your first policy and we do what France has been doing since the War, is that a permanent policy? Shall we go on existing like that?* I am not quite sure how you interpret my first policy. As I say, the first policy I outlined in my original remarks was a policy of letting the exchange adjust itself to the existing price level. Suppose that something happened to the value of gold so that it was also adjusted to gold, then comes the further question whether we are to adhere to gold as a permanent standard or not. I am against gold, but for different reasons from those. So that my first policy has two branches, one of which would be permanent and the other not permanent.

16,575 *Does it differ from the French policy?* Certainly. The French policy has not been to keep their internal prices steady. Their index number has risen 100 points in a year and a half.

16,576 *They have not kept it steady because of what?* Because they have been inflating.

16,577 *You say keep it in equilibrium but do not inflate?* Do not inflate seriously.

16,578 *Keep it in equilibrium with the rest of the world?* No; keep it in equilibrium with itself. Keep it at the same level that you find it. I mean if our cost of living is 172, to have a state of affairs where it can remain permanent[ly] at 172 or thereabouts.

16,579 (CHAIRMAN) *When you say do not inflate seriously, what do you mean?* I say that because the world 'inflation' is used so very ambiguously. It is used sometimes for something which produces a rise in prices, and it is used sometimes for easy monetary conditions which may or may not produce an effect on prices. I feel it desirable to ease out credit conditions at this juncture perhaps a little rashly, and as soon as it began to have an important effect on prices I should draw in again. I should not allow it to go to any distance, but in view of the special conditions at the moment I should be prepared to be a little rash in the way in which I opened out credit facilities in the first instance.

16,580 (SIR NORMAN HILL) *I am afraid I do not quite follow all that you are putting to us. Is it right that sooner or later you are going to do what you say is so hard for political reasons—which you dealt with under your second policy? That is where we shall have to come to, is it not?* I think that we must. It is not the same problem. The one problem is not to divert labour out of the export industries, but to reduce wages in the other industries, so that the cost of living will fall, so that you can reduce wages in the export industries to a level at which you can support the existing condition of those industries. That is quite a different policy from the policy of the transfer of labour from export industries into other industries. That second policy of the transference of labour from export industries into sheltered industries you would have to bring about by some stimulation in internal conditions that might be rather unsound at the outset. That would be the way of doing it. The method of facilitating transference would be to make home industries boom. But if your object was to depress the internal trade in order that exports could survive, then the policy would be to depress internal industries. So that these two things really lead to the opposite conclusions.

16,581 *I was speaking as to the second policy and not as to the third policy. Let things alone and then pressure from the unemployed will bring down wages?* I think I have become confused as to which you mean by my second and which by my third.

16,582 *Was not your possible policy to leave things alone until wages come down?* But that is quite a different policy to the policy which I have been mentioning more recently, in my cross-examination by you. That is aiming at transference. If I had my way completely I should not regard the stability of the exchange as important, but, all the same, I should be aiming at a transfer from the export industries to the home industries by stimulating the latter.

16,583 *What was worrying me in my own mind was, can we avoid bringing down wages? Taking the world as it is, must we not either work longer or take less for the same hours? Is that the position?* It depends whether you are taking about gold wages or sterling wages. We have to bring down gold wages, but whether we have to bring down sterling wages depends on the exchange.

16,584 *It is what we get for the wages?* What we have actually done is to raise gold wages 10 per cent in the last year. I say that is the source of all our troubles. But there is often a confusion as to whether one is talking about gold wages or sterling wages. I suggest a policy by which gold wages can fall compatibly with sterling wages remaining the same.

16,585 (SIR HERBERT LLEWELLYN SMITH) *That is No. 1 policy?* Yes.

16,586 *That is the one which you say was hopeless?* Yes. That is the best policy.

16,587 (SIR NORMAN HILL) *Do you think that we can carry on [in] the world without reducing the standard of living here?* Yes.

16,588 *And without working harder?* I think the discussion is getting confused. Part of our difficulty may be that we have to consider the standard of living. I have not been addressing myself to that particular problem because I do not think the aggravation of the situation in the last year is due to that. That is part of our pre-existing difficulty. What I have been directing myself to this morning is not to our real wages being unduly high, but to the disparity between the value of money in this country and its value outside. Suppose the cost of living came down to the external cost of living, then wages could come down without any fall in the standard of life. In my original table it is not the discrepancy between 172 and 181 which I am dwelling on; it is the discrepancy between the 172 and the 158. The other is a separate argument.

16,589 (CHAIRMAN) *The 158 is the American figure?* Yes. In so far as it is purely a monetary phenomenon it may be cured without any bad effects whatever on real wages.

16,590 (SIR NORMAN HILL) *What you suggest by your first plan which you favour would enable the people in this country to go on living as we have been living since the war without working harder?* I think it is very hard to say. I cannot see any reason why we should not live just as well as we have been doing, if we went about it the right way.

16,591 *Without working any harder?* Without working any harder, provided we *all* worked. You see, I think that the whole situation changes enormously if you get things going, if you get full time worked everywhere and full employment everywhere. I think that would probably improve our conditions sufficiently to enable us to maintain our existing standard of life. I think that our existing standard of life is too high with unemployment and the rest of it as it is, but I am not clear, if our policy was wise in other directions, that there is any need for reducing real wages in this country.

16,592 (MR LANGDALE) *According to the cost-of-living and wages figures which you have given us, in March, 1924, the cost wages were 155, and in June, 1925, they were 181. That is a difference of 26 points?* Yes.

16,593 *The difference in the cost of living is only 15 points?* Yes.

16,594 *So that there is about 11 points margin. Wages might be reduced by 11 points without the figures being in any worse position than they were before?* Yes.

16,595 *That is about 6 per cent. That is a good load off the 10 per cent, is it not?* I was not thinking of that. There is more than 10 per cent between 158 and 181. I agree if these figures are reliable it would appear that at a time when money wages ought to have been coming down they positively have been going up.

16,596 *That has had nothing to do with the return to the gold standard has it?* No, I should not think it has.

16,597 *With regard to another point you refer to, you said that business in the outside world was fairly satisfactory. Those who are engaged in the export in this country to India and China find that the cost of production in Lancashire is too high?* As I said, I thought it was a question of price, but I should also regard China as being subject to particular conditions.

16,598 *China at the moment is in an unsatisfactory condition?* I have not heard any evidence to make me think that India is otherwise than normally prosperous at this moment.

16,599 *There is no doubt that the price of Lancashire goods is too high for eastern people. If Lancashire wishes to increase her export, or merely to do as much an export trade as before the War, her prices will have to come down?* My argument was that it was a question of price—the price we have to ask for exports in order to equal the internal cost—rather than any deep-seated serious lack of prosperity in other countries.

16,600 *Do you think we would be able to maintain this trade, or increase it, with the present 181 per cent of cost wages in this country?* As long as the level of gold prices outside this country remains what it is I think it is impossible. That is my argument.

16,601 *The wages will have to come down?* The question is by what *modus operandi*, by what course or process, will they come down? I say it is dangerous to put ourselves into a situation when they have to come down, because the only way of bringing them down is by intensifying unemployment until they do come down. If the business world takes the view that we are committed to this, and they must come down, then it ought to welcome unemployment, because that is the only way of doing it. It ought to do all it can to increase unemployment until wages do come down.

16,602 *Unemployment will be increased if your manufactures are too dear for you to sell?* Yes, but I think it is no good regarding that as an Act of God; it is the consequence of your own policy. I say, if that happens, you will have done it on purpose, because you must be assumed to will the consequences of your acts.

16,603 *That is due to your paying too high wages?* But you would not be paying too high wages if you had not improved the exchange by 10 per cent. When you willed that you would improve the exchange by 10 per cent, you ought to have willed at the same to reduce wages 10 per cent. There is no method of doing as you propose except by intensifying unemployment.

16,604 *You increased money wages 10 per cent?* You increased gold wages 10 per cent. You have not altered money wages very much. The effect of the improvement of the exchange is to increase gold wages 10 per cent.

16,605 *And to make your food cost low?* Yes.

16,606 *Generally speaking, you think you can maintain this 181 per cent above pre-war?* No, I do not, not if external gold prices are at their present level and the exchange remains at its present level. I do not think we can maintain gold wages at 181 if the external value of gold is somewhere in the 150's.

16,607 (SIR JOHN HINDLEY) *Do you suggest that we are really in a position to set the standard of living?* Who do you mean by 'we'?

16,608 *The country?* But we do not.

16,609 *As an industrial country depending very largely on exports, must we not follow rather than try to set the standard?* But the standard of living is not the same in the United States and in China. It is not the same everywhere. Our standard of living, I quite agree, must depend upon our own productivity, and we cannot set our standard of living independently of our productivity. But I do not think there is any law by which our standard of living must necessarily follow the standard of living in other countries.

16,610 *Do you think it is reasonable to compare the United States with Great Britain?* No, I do not think we can expect to have as high a standard of living as they can.

16,611 *As far as the United States is concerned her exports are more or less a luxury?* I would rather say that her essential exports are not nearly such a large portion of her total trade.

16,612 *Her prosperity is really dependent on her internal trade?* To a much greater extent.

16,613 *To a very much greater extent?* But our prosperity depends on our internal trade much more than people think.

16,614 (SIR PETER RYLANDS) *In discussions about the gold standard, I have heard people say that the argument in favour of returning to the gold standard was that it would lighten the burden of our debt to America, and cheapen the cost of things that come in. What would you say about that?* That is pure rubbish.

16,615 *Perhaps you would explain, because I think I am right in saying it is a very popular idea that by improving the exchange with America it lightens the burden of our debt and reduces the cost of things?* It lightens the burden of our debt in terms of sterling but not in terms of goods and services. The debt is fixed in gold and the burden of it depends upon what quantity of goods [and] services is equivalent to that amount of gold.

16,616 *The fact being that international trade is the exchange of units of effort and not of currency?* Yes, otherwise we could go on raising our exchange for ever until our external debt was nothing at all.

16,617 (CHAIRMAN) *The question of the importation of food is important in relation to the cost of living?* If everything comes down in proportion you are exactly as you were.

16,618 *Where are you to begin?* The restoration of the gold standard by lowering the sterling price of food does not do us a pennyworth of good if the value of sterling has been altered correspondingly.

16,619 (MR BAKER) *When we have this reduction in wages how much better off will the country be relatively—never mind the workers for the moment—than we were before we started reducing?* Not a penny the better off.

16,620 *All the fuss is to leave us where we were? Yes,* that is the best that can happen.

16,621 *If you looked at the matter so far as cotton is concerned, could you tell us the margin of difference between the reduced price of raw cotton and the increased price of cotton goods abroad if we raised the price abroad 10 per cent?* I have not worked it out. I think that the figures are worked out in certain publications of the cotton trade.

The witness withdrew.

Before he appeared before the Committee on Industry and Trade, Keynes offered *The Times* a series of articles on the consequences of the return to gold. On 8 July the editor of *The Times* accepted the series subject to his seeing the final version. On seeing them he wrote to Keynes.

From GEOFFREY DAWSON, *16 July 1925*

My dear Keynes,

I am rather embarrassed by these articles. They are extraordinarily clever and very amusing; but I really feel that, published in *The Times* at this particular moment, they would do harm and not good. Whether you like it or not, the gold standard has now been restored beyond all hope of recall. This being so, it seems to me that the only thing to be done is to make the best of it. I do not in the least mind publishing criticism of the Government in this or any other respect; but three solid articles seem to me to be rather over-doing it. Mill, to whom I showed the articles last night, suggested that you should be asked to cut them down into one. Personally I am against this, as I am sure would you be, for perhaps I appreciate their merits as a literary performance better than he does. But I really am reluctantly driven to the conclusion that I cannot take them as they stand, and that you had better let them loose elsewhere.

Yours sincerely,
GEOFFREY DAWSON

Keynes then offered the articles to Lord Beaverbrook, the proprietor of, amongst other newspapers, *The Evening Standard*.

To LORD BEAVERBOOK, *17 July 1925*

Dear Beaverbrook,

I have written three articles, under the general title of 'Unemployment and Monetary Policy' and the sub-titles of I.

THE ECONOMIC CONSEQUENCES OF MR CHURCHILL

The Diagnosis. II. The Policy of the Bank of England, and III. The Alternative Courses for the Government. The first two of these articles are, I think a little under 1,500 words, the third could, if absolutely necessary, be reduced to the same length. But it would be difficult, and it stands at present at about 1,800 words.

I offer you these for publication in *The Evening Standard*. It would, I think, be essential in view of the continuity of the argument that they should be published fairly quickly one after another—all three, that is to say, within about a week.

If you are interested in the proposal in principle I can send you copies of the articles to-morrow morning. In my opinion they are good journalism and are matters of popular interest. I think they would provide you with good texts worth developing in *The Express* and *The Standard* for some little time to come. The thesis of the first article is that Winston's policy has committed us to reducing everyone's wages 2/- in the £. The thesis of the second article is that the Bank of England's policy of credit restriction is a policy of bringing about the above result by deliberately intensifying unemployment. The third article makes two suggestions for treating the situation in a different way, compatibly with remaining on the gold standard.

Could you let me know about it as soon as possible. I shall be available on the telephone—Museum 3875. I suggest a fee of £50 for each article.

Yours sincerely,
[copy initialled] J.M.K.

Beaverbrook accepted the offer and *The Evening Standard* published them on 22, 23 and 24 July. Keynes expanded the articles into a pamphlet which the Hogarth Press published less than a week later under the title *The Economic Consequences of Mr Churchill* (*JMK*, vol. IX, pp. 207–30). Chapters I, III and V of the pamphlet correspond to the original newspaper articles.

Once publication of the articles began, Keynes continued his correspondence with Dawson.

To GEOFFREY DAWSON, *23 July 1925*

Dear Dawson,

As you may have seen, I have been printing a slightly abbreviated version of the articles which I sent you in *The Evening Standard*. I am also publishing an enlarged version as a pamphlet next week, under the title of *The Economic Consequences of Mr Churchill*. I will of course send you a copy of this for review in the ordinary way.

I don't quite agree with the implication of your second letter, namely that the only purpose of my articles is to write against the gold standard. My final conclusions were directed towards a remedy which was compatible with the gold standard. And I am sure we shall never find a remedy in the present state of affairs until, to some slight extent, we face the facts and admit what the real causes are. My object in the first two articles was to bring this out clearly.

I appreciate of course that what I was saying was not really compatible with the line which *The Times* is taking, yet I cannot but think that it may prove difficult as time goes on to keep up the bluff that the return to gold standard has nothing to do with our troubles with any sort of plausibility. However, I daresay that the best way is that I should write you a letter on the matter from time to time if, as heretofore, you will be able to find room for it.

Yours sincerely,
[copy initialled] J.M.K.

From GEOFFREY DAWSON, *26 July 1925*

My dear Keynes,

Many thanks for your letter. Yes, I saw the articles in *The Evening Standard* and shall look forward to the pamphlet.

Perhaps I did not make my meaning quite clear in rather a hurriedly dictated letter. Glad as I always am to see your extremely brilliant and amusing contributions in *The Times*, I felt that the publication of three long articles, even if accompanied by a leader in a different sense, would identify us rather too much with an attitude that we have always hitherto resisted. On the whole I think that an occasional letter is a better alternative.

Yours sincerely,
GEOFFREY DAWSON

Keynes's articles led to comments in the press and several flurries of correspondence. The earliest came when the City Editor of *The Morning Post* published a lengthy discussion of his articles on 27 July. Keynes picked him up on one matter.

To the Editor of The Morning Post, *29 July 1925*

Sir,

My attention has been called to a lengthy criticism of some articles of mine in your City Page on Monday. On the main issue I must refer your readers to my pamphlet, *The Economic Consequences of Mr Churchill*, which has just been published. But your City Editor makes one small slip which, perhaps, I ought to point out. He wrote: 'Because we are not out for debate with Mr Keynes, but only for the clarification of the situation, we shall not assert that price levels may not, at times, be affected by monetary policy, in which connection, however, it would have been better if Mr Keynes had made fuller acknowledgment of our cost of living having latterly tended to fall below the American level.'

But in the very article criticised I pointed out that a year ago the gold cost of living was 157 here and 154 in America; whereas the latest available figures are 180 here and 158 in America. Since I am not out for debate, I will not do more than assert that 'at times' 180 is greater than 158—indeed, just about as often as price levels are affected by monetary policy.

I must also state what your City Editor must surely know well, that to assert that the management of the currency in this country prior to the readoption of gold had my approval, is a gross travesty of my opinions. I criticised it repeatedly and vehemently.

419

It is typical of the silliness and utter lack of intellectual standards with which this controversy is carried on by City Editors, that, because I am in favour of managing the currency with a view to stability of prices, I am, therefore, supposed to be in favour of managing it with a view to instability of prices—sometimes I am said to have favoured deflation, as in your City columns, and sometimes inflation, as in the City columns of some of your contemporaries.

Yours, &c.,

J. M. KEYNES

The publication of *The Economic Consequences of Mr Churchill* coincided with two other events. One was the announcement of his engagement to Lydia Lopokova. Another was the publication of the Report of the Commission of Inquiry into an industrial dispute in the coal industry which had become more pronounced with the return to gold. The Report contained an addendum by Sir Josiah Stamp which argued that the recent difficulties in the industry were related to the exchange appreciation involved in the return to gold. The links between the pamphlet, the Report and Keynes's engagement are clear in the following letters.

From SIR JOSIAH STAMP, *28 July 1925*

My dear Keynes,

My *very heartiest congratulations*. Matrimony was all you needed to make you as near perfect as it's possible to be without being a nuisance.

I shall be delighted to lunch on Saturday.

Many thanks for the pamphlet, which is excellent in every way.

I was *most loth* to write my Coal addendum—it went against my grain to be embarrassing in any way to the Powers, but I didn't see how I could *honestly* escape it.

Yours

J. C. STAMP

From LORD BEAVERBROOK, *31 July 1925*

My dear Keynes,

Many thanks for sending me your pamphlet—which naturally possesses great interest for me—and for the additional figures in your letter. You have had a very good press—even from the newspapers which do not agree with us—and deservedly so. But the ranks of the unorthodox are being recruited rapidly—Sir Josiah Stamp being the latest to stampede. I think your 'unemployment' argument against the Bank of England policy, to which you gave prominence in your *Evening Standard* articles, has gone home.

I was delighted to see the news of your engagement in the press. Matrimony will bring you with a bound from youth into early middle age, and since, being older than you are, I already consider myself middle-aged, I am selfish enough to be glad at anything which reduces the disparity between us and brings you into my own class! I wish you every happiness.

Yours sincerely,
BEAVERBROOK

The link between unemployment and the gold standard certainly went 'home' as Beaverbrook put it, for the next month brought three powerful attacks on Keynes's position, as well as controversy elsewhere in the press and in the House of Commons. One came in the form of a long letter to *The Times* from Sir Henry Strakosch, the South African banker, which took issue with Keynes's views, while the other two came slightly later in the form of a long article in *The Financial News* by Lord Bradbury, Chairman of the Committee on the Currency and Bank of England Note Issues and an article in the *Westminster Bank Review* by Walter Leaf, chairman of the Westminster Bank. Keynes replied first to Strakosch.

To the Editor of The Times, *31 July 1925*

Sir,

Sir H. Strakosch's comments on my pamphlet *The Economic Consequences of Mr Churchill*, to which you give prominence today, are a nice example of the capacity to find 'good in everything'.

Sir H. Strakosch points out that on a previous occasion sterling rose to within sight of parity at a time when our internal price level did not justify it. This movement culminated at the date at which he begins his table—namely, December, 1922, to March, 1923. Our situation then, as he justly remarks, was very similar to what it was this spring. We were suffering accordingly and our unemployment figures were much as at present. If, at that date, we had restored the gold standard, the results would probably have been just what they are now. Since, fortunately, we did not make that mistake, we were able to recover equilibrium by a fall in the exchange without any marked disturbance, as Sir H. Strakosch also points out, to our own prices and wages. As a result of this our costs became adjusted to the international level, our unemployment figures fell by nearly half, and by the middle of 1924 it really seemed to most of us that we had turned the corner and were on the way to good times again. Then began the last and most fatal campaign to restore sterling parity. By the end of 1924, as Sir H. Strakosch's table shows, the exchange had again reached a level too high in relation to the internal value of money, and between December, 1924, and March, 1925, we worked ourselves into the same dangerous disequilibrium as a year [sic] before. This time, however, we have cut ourselves off from the exchange remedy and have left ourselves with no alternative but to beat down the level of wages. Hence our present tears. But why Sir H. Strakosch imagines that this little piece of history demonstrates 'the outstanding virtues of the gold standard' I have no idea.

His letter raises another hare more worth hunting. He points out that for two and a half years sterling wages and cost of living here and the dollar cost of living in America have been moderately steady, while the exchange has fluctuated sharply. If only we had had the gold standard all this time, he goes on to argue, the exchange would have been stable too and we should have enjoyed the best of every conceivable world! This is surely an extreme example of the fallacy that you can alter the exchange without altering prices. Professor Cassel has given reasons for the view that the fluctuations of the exchange during this period corresponded to the fluctuations in the volume of foreign investment by the United States. If the exchange had been fixed we should have been compelled in self-protection, even after the initial adjustment had been made, to have had alternately very cheap money and very dear money in London. Does Sir H. Strakosch think that this would have had no consequences?

The argument serves to bring out clearly the essence of our difference of opinion. I hold that in modern conditions wages in this country are, for various reasons, so rigid over short periods, that it is impracticable to adjust them to the ebb and flow of international gold-credit, and I would deliberately utilise fluctuations in the exchange as the shock-absorber. Sir H. Strakosch, believing that any other course is 'more appropriately called repudiation', would make exchange stability at 4.86½ the central object of policy and would leave prices and wages to be the shock-absorbers. In this case he must put up from time to time with unemployment and trade disputes and worse; but, looking as usual at the bright side of things, he will doubtless contrive to see even in these the final demonstration of 'the outstanding virtues of the gold standard'.

Yours &c.,

J. M. KEYNES

Strakosch replied to Keynes's letter, suggesting that the experience of the previous five years did not support Keynes's position and that unstable exchange rates were likely to be a greater source of internal instability than the gold standard. The City Editor of *The Times* went further when in commending Sir Henry's letter to his readers he suggested that the logical conclusion of Keynes's policy was either hyper-inflation on the German scale or inflation as in France and Italy. Naturally Keynes replied.

To the Editor of The Times, *5 August 1925*

Sir,

I am an advocate of managing the currency in the interests of the stability of prices and wages. Those who are opposed to this policy think it good tactics to represent me as being in favour of managing it at random. Some of them say that I am in favour of managing it as in this country before the restoration of gold parity, that is, in the interests of deflation; in your City page today I am represented as an inflationist, and the management of the German mark after the war as the 'logical conclusion'

423

of my proposals; and Sir Henry Strakosch seems to think that every inconvertible currency which has ever existed is an example of what I recommend. It is obvious that rational controversy is impossible with those who, whether from intellectual deficiency or emotional excess, are unable to distinguish between the policy of keeping the value of money steady and the policy of depreciating it to nothing.

To bring the issue back to the practical problems of the moment, and with the object, not of settling the gold controversy, but of elucidating it, let me ask the supporters of the official policy how they answer the following questions:—

1. Are we supporting the exchange by artificial interference with the export of capital and by borrowing in New York?

2. If so, how does this differ from the policy which we used to contemn the French?

3. Is it necessary (failing the depreciation of gold abroad) for the restoration of our financial equilibrium in these circumstances that money wages generally should be reduced?

4. If so, what steps are proposed with the object of reducing money wages?

5. If the limitation of credit facilities and the maintenance of dear money are the methods proposed, how do they achieve the object by deliberately intensifying unemployment?

6. In general, how are the working classes to be induced to accept lower money wages except by the pressure of lock-outs and unemployment?

7. If it is politically impossible (as in the case of the coal industry) to force money wages down by these methods, where are we going to end?

8. Would it be equally necessary to reduce money wages if the dollar exchange stood at 4.40 (as it did a year ago) instead of at 4.86 (as it does now)?

If the official party will face these questions fairly, and answer them frankly, we may begin to escape from the Monkeyville atmosphere in which our gold fundamentalists have enveloped us.

Yours faithfully,

J. M. KEYNES

Early August 1925 also saw Keynes giving a lecture 'Am I a Liberal?' (*JMK*, vol. IX, pp. 295–306) to the Liberal Summer School in Cambridge (on 1 August) and marrying Lydia Lopokova in London on 4 August.

Keynes's reply to Lord Bradbury's criticism of *The Economic Consequences of Mr Churchill* came on 18 August.

From The Financial News, *18 August 1925*

OUR MONETARY POLICY

It is a comfort to the author of *The Economic Consequences of Mr Churchill*, after reading a good many criticisms of his pamphlet, to see Lord Bradbury's contribution to *The Financial News*, which lifts the subject once again on to the level where rational controversy is possible. But the worst of Lord Bradbury's article is that it stops just when it is becoming most interesting.

If it is true that sterling prices are too high, then, he says, 'there are only three conceivable remedies—the reduction of sterling prices, the increase of our competitors' gold prices, or making the £ worth less than $4.86...If he (Mr Keynes) will not have the first and cannot have the second, he is inevitably thrown back on the third.' Quite true. Lord Bradbury argues, further, that the second alternative may not come off, owing to the United States successfully managing its currency in the interests of price stability and thus preventing a price rise. I agree. I think it an unreliable expedient, and I, therefore, coupled it with a second proposal, which Lord Bradbury ignores, for reducing wages, &c., 5 per cent all round.

But what is Lord Bradbury's solution? He, apparently,

accepts the first alternative, namely, 'a credit policy which will reduce sterling prices'. This, indeed, is the correct course for all members of the orthodox party. In this case I ask for a reply to the central issue raised by my pamphlet—How is he going to do it? I argued in my pamphlet that there was no way except through credit restriction; that this method was socially disastrous in [the] process and socially unjust in the result; and that it was probably politically impossible. The coal subsidy and the reduction of the Bank rate to $4\frac{1}{2}$ per cent have gone some considerable way, since I wrote my pamphlet, to confirm the truth of the last of these contentions.

I admit that the old prescription for curing an internal price level, which is too high, by dear money and credit restriction would certainly do the trick, if it could be carried to its logical conclusion. But I maintain that in modern conditions the medicine is so nasty that the patient cannot be induced to swallow it. Therefore, to embark on a policy which assumes that medicine on the old prescription *can* be administered is not sound statesmanship.

To embargo foreign loans and to reduce the Bank rate to $4\frac{1}{2}$ per cent is *not*, whatever else it may be—as, I think, Lord Bradbury will admit—the old prescription.

Our high money costs of production have turned the balance of international payments against us. Failing the application of the old prescription, we can only maintain the exchange by borrowing and by interfering with the normal export of capital. The Bank of England effects this by embargoing foreign issues even to the extent of requiring old loans maturing here to be paid off out of funds raised elsewhere, and by making special arrangements with the central banks of Holland and of the Union of South Africa to assist her with gold and with the New York Federal Reserve Bank to buy sterling bills.

Since we still have reserve resources and our credit is good, the Bank is able, in these and other ways, to raise very large sums for the support of the exchange, at a rate, I should guess, of not less than £100,000,000 per annum, which is enough to make good the wastage of nearly 500,000 men in unemployment. The Bank of England and the Treasury are not allowed, for political reasons, to execute the correct gold standard policy. Therefore, to keep up gold appearances they have to submit to expedients which in old days would have shocked Lord Bradbury out of his skin.

Does Lord Bradbury applaud this state of affairs? If not, should he not denounce the subterfuges of the Bank of England? And where does he think it will all end?

At the end of the month he wrote a long letter to *The Times* concerning Walter Leaf's article in the *Westminster Bank Review*.

To the Editor of The Times, *28 August 1925*

Sir,

Dr Leaf's recent article on Price Levels in Relation to Monetary Policy indicates that it is desirable to restate the problem from the beginning.

Goods and services fall into groups according to the sensitiveness of their gold prices to those of similar things elsewhere.

First come the staple raw materials of international commerce, of which wheat, cotton, copper, and export grades of coal are good examples. These must necessarily adjust themselves rapidly to changes in the international price level. Where there is a highly organised market, as in the case of cotton, the adjustment takes place within a few minutes. Let us call this Class A.

Next come (Class B) the articles on which the working classes spend their incomes, the price of which is measured by the index numbers of the 'cost of living'. Food makes up 60 per cent of these, and wholesale food is largely composed of Class A articles. Thus an improvement in the exchange soon tends to lower the sterling cost of living somewhat below what it would have been

427

otherwise; but not, at first, to the full extent—perhaps, at a guess, to half the extent—of the improvement in the exchange.

Next come money wages (Class C). Where there is a cost-of-living sliding scale, these will respond to a fall in the cost of living. But there is no automatic force to make them fall on the average as much as the cost of living. As a rule, there is no means of bringing down money wages except by the pressure of unemployment and trade disputes.

Next come various other types of home expenses which do not respond at all, in any direct way, to the improvement in the exchange and to the fall in the price of Class A articles. Railway freights, postage, insurance, local and Imperial taxes, debenture interest are examples of these, which we will call Class D.

Lastly come manufactured articles (Class E), the cost of which is mainly made up of the costs of the A, C, and D expenses which the manufacturer incurs. If Class A expenses are a large proportion of the whole, the manufacturer can cut his prices materially. But in so far as Class C and D expenses enter in he can only cut his prices, in advance of a price fall in these classes, by reducing his margin of profit. Those manufacturers whose goods are neither imported nor exported on a large scale (which we will call E1) are under no compulsion to reduce their prices in advance of a fall in their costs of production. Those, on the other hand, who are subject to international competition fall into two classes—those whose products are of a kind of which a largely increased supply of sufficiently identical quality *cannot* be quickly obtained from elsewhere (which we will call E2) and those whose products *can* be quickly obtained from elsewhere (which we will call E3). Thus the E1 manufacturers are best placed, whilst those E2 manufacturers whose A costs are in a large proportion of the whole are next best placed, and the E3 manufacturers whose C and D costs are a large proportion of the whole are the worst-placed. Our textile manufacturers are an example of those in a middle position. Our coal, iron and steel, and shipping industries are examples of the worst-placed class.

Now our problem today consists in the failure of the prices in Classes C and D to respond to the increased exchange value of sterling, and in the fact that until the prices in Classes C and D have fallen to the price level of Class A, the prices in Classes B and E are also maintained, in varying degrees, too high. It is these facts which constitute the 'overvaluation of sterling'. It is self-evident that a rise in the exchange value of sterling reduces the sterling cost of what we *buy* abroad below what it would have been otherwise. The question is whether it has affected adversely the gold price at which we can produce what we *sell* abroad. The 'overvaluation of sterling' consists in a rise in the money cost of what we produce for export above its equilibrium value. How then, does Dr Leaf seek to disprove the 'overvaluation of sterling'? He takes the index numbers of wholesale prices in England, which are largely made up of Class A articles, compares with them similar index numbers in the United States, and finds that the two are fully adjusted—as they nearly always must be. At the same time he ignores the prices in Classes B, C, D, and E—which are the sole cause of trouble. I have contended that our difficulties have arisen because the price of coal, for example, has fallen with the improvement in the exchange, whereas wages and other home costs have not fallen. Dr Leaf thinks that he can disprove this by producing figures which confirm my contention that the prices of coal and other articles in Class A have indeed fallen with the improvement in the exchange, and by ignoring the level of wages and other home costs. It would seem that Dr Leaf does not know what the controversy is about. This suspicion is confirmed by another passage in which he states that the importation of gold into London, as the result of dearer money here than in New York, proves that sterling is undervalued.

We do not possess index numbers specially compiled with the

object of indicating the price changes in each of my groups. But we have index numbers which are fairly satisfactory for the purpose. For Class A the usual wholesale commodity index numbers, whilst not ideal, since they include some articles which are not Class A, are reasonably reliable—the Board of Trade index here and the Bureau of Labour index in the United States being the most carefully compiled. (Dr Leaf's comparisons of various wholesale indexes vary according as they contain more or less Class A Articles.) For Class B we have the Ministry of Labour cost-of-living index, and for Class C Professor Bowley's wages index. For Class D we have nothing. As regards Class E, we have nothing for E1, but for E2 the Board of Trade's index of prices of manufactured exports is tolerable, and for E3 there is the Board of Trade's index of raw material exports (chiefly coal) and the Chamber of Shipping's index for shipping freights. What do these several indexes show?

In June, 1924, when the sterling exchange was 12 per cent below par, the indexes, converted into gold, were as follows (1913 = 100):—

(Converted from sterling into the equivalent gold value)

United States	Great Britain					
Whole-sale index	Whole-sale index	Cost of living	Wages	Manu-factured exports	Materials for exports	Shipping freights
145	143	150	157	164	154	110
A	A	B	C	E 2	E 3	E 3

These figures indicate that Class A was, as usual, nearly adjusted to the outside world; that world shipping freights were already seriously depressed; and that prices in Classes B, C, and E2 were already on the high side. Thus, as I said in my pamphlet, we had a serious problem, even when sterling exchange was 12 per cent depreciated, in the relatively high level of prices in Classes B and C, and E2—which already showed itself in unemployment and depressed exports. (The allegation that I attribute all our troubles to the gold standard is a myth in my case, as Sir J. Stamp has shown it to be his. I expressly limited this influence to the worsening of our position during the past year. Indeed, a prominent part of my argument was directed to showing that the return to gold was particularly rash just because we already had other troubles which we could not afford to aggravate.)

What had the position become in June, 1925, with the exchange at par?

United States	Great Britain					
Whole-sale index	Whole-sale index	Cost of living	Wages	Manu-factured exports	Materials for export	Shipping freights
157	158	173	180	191	156	101
A	A	B	C	E 2	E 3	E 3

Thus the wholesale index was still adjusted; Class E3 had been compelled to abate its prices by almost the full extent of the improvement in the exchange, and in the case of freights by considerably more, the shipping industry having to support not only the exchange burden, but also an aggravation of the depression in the international freight level. On the other hand, the divergence of the prices in Classes B, C, and E2 from those in Class A was seriously aggravated.

In June, 1924, the ratios of the price levels in the British A, B, C, and E2 classes respectively to the American wholesale index were 99, 103, 109 and 113 per cent. If we consider the abnormally low costs in certain European countries, and the impairment of our position through the war, this was sufficiently serious. It was, therefore, rash to adopt an exchange policy, the first effect of which would certainly be to increase the discrepancy and to widen the gap to be bridged by painful social adjustments. The result of such a policy is that in June, 1925, the same ratios had become 101, 110, 115 and 122 per cent. I believe that the last two of these ratios are about 10 per cent higher than they need have been if, during the past year, we had concentrated on stability of internal prices and had left the exchange to look after itself. However that may be, it is these high figures which are at the root of our troubles. In the United States there is evidence that the corresponding ratios have fallen, rather than risen, during the past year. As regards Europe, the B and C ratios have fallen in France, Italy, and Belgium, and have risen in Germany; but in all these countries they are still much below 100.

When I wrote my pamphlet on *The Economic Consequences of Mr Churchill*, I did not foresee that such plain and evident matters—namely, that our relative money costs are too high and that the return to gold parity has aggravated this—would be denied. The exact percentages are open to dispute; but I believed, and still believe, that the main facts are incontrovertible. Perhaps I should have learnt from my experiences after the Treaty of Versailles what passionate moral indignation a state-ment of economic truth can provoke. Nevertheless Dr Leaf's assertion, that sterling is actually undervalued, still takes my breath away.

Lord Bradbury has truly pointed out in an article in *The Financial News* that there are three remedies open to us:—(1) a reduction in sterling costs; (2) a rise in our competitors' gold costs; (3) a fall in the sterling exchange; though one might add (4) a permanent reduction in the volume of our foreign investment such as would render a complete return to our former favourable international balance of trade permanently unnecessary. If (1) proves politically impracticable, if (2) does not occur, and if (4) is by itself inadequate, I have no doubt that sooner or later (3) will become inevitable. But since it is very unlikely that this third alternative will be accepted except as the result of bitter experiences, it seemed worth while to make suggestions for a remedy on the lines of (1) and (2). The orthodox remedy is, of course, to bring about (1) by means of credit restriction. I argued in my pamphlet that this method would be socially disastrous whilst it was going on and socially unjust in its results, and also that it was probably impracticable politically. I suggested, therefore, that we should aim at an all-round 5 per cent reduction of money wages by agreement pending a fall in the cost of living, and that we should, at the same time, release gold in the hope of raising prices elsewhere. The first of these suggestions has been ignored by my critics. I daresay that it is not practical politics. Nevertheless since it is very probable that we shall remain on the gold standard for the present, I suggest that it is our business to seek a remedy along the lines either of (1), (2), or (4).

What in fact are we doing? The coal subsidy and the reduction of Bank rate indicate that the authorities have abandoned, for the present, the attempt to reduce sterling prices. Mr Churchill, in the House of Commons, even has the audacity to represent himself as a defender of the present level of money wages against my nefarious plans to reduce them. Meanwhile the Governor of the Bank of England, converted at last to the methods of his *confrère* at the Bank of France, exercises his ingenuity to cover our adverse trade balance by preventing the export of capital and by borrowing abroad. The last named policy may be a first half-unconscious step in the direction of (4), that is to say, a permanent curtailment in the scale of our foreign investment. But the right way to achieve this result cannot be, in the long run, by means of an embargo, but by the deliberate organisation of investment at home, resulting in an increase in the rate of interest, at which foreign borrowers can sell their bonds here, above the corresponding rate in New York, and, above all, by the organised transfer of labour out of the export industries.

What we need, expressed in one sentence, is to reduce our C and D gold costs relatively to similar costs elsewhere. The mistake which we have made in raising the exchange, also

433

expressed in one sentence, is that we have increased the amount of the necessary reduction by at least 10 per cent, without any plan as to how to effect the reduction.

If I was in authority but was committed to the gold standard, I should try to get some help from each of the remedies (1), (2), and (4). I should do what I could, short of restricting credit (which might be very little) to reduce prices in Classes B, C, D, and E. I should export as much gold as possible with a view to raising prices elsewhere. I should take steps, other than the embargo, such as an alteration of the Trustee Act and the encouragement of expensive new capital projects at home, to reduce the existing pressure towards overseas investment. I should try with might and main to shift labour out of the export industries (especially coal). And, in the face of a hard task, rendered much harder by muddleheadedness, I should trust, for the rest, to luck, and hope for the best.

But it will be difficult for the authorities to apply any remedies at all if, like Dr Leaf and Mr Churchill, they deny the existence or the nature of the disease.

I am yours, &c.,

J. M. KEYNES

On 3 September, two days before his letter on Leaf appeared in *The Times*, Keynes went off to Russia to meet Lydia's family and to act as the official representative of the University of Cambridge at the Bicentennial Celebrations of the Academy of Sciences held in Leningrad and Moscow between 5 and 14 September. While in Moscow Keynes gave two lectures, 'The Economic Position in England' and 'The Economic Transition in England'. These appear below.[4]

THE ECONOMIC POSITION IN ENGLAND

1. Money wages in England are 80 per cent higher than before the War. The cost of living of the working classes is 73 per cent higher. Thus real wages have improved about 4 per

[4] The second has strong parallels to 'Am I a Liberal?' (*JMK*, vol. IX, esp. pp. 303–6).

cent. Since working hours have been somewhat reduced, and since the intensity of work is also—according to most observers—less rather than more, the position of the working class is improved.

2. At least this is the case for those who are in work. The black spot is the large proportion of unemployment. From 10 to 12 per cent of the workers are without employment, including near 1 million adult male workers. Even the position of these, however, is much better than it would have been in similar circumstances before the War; for a married unemployed worker receives from the state about 40 roubles a month.

3. The unemployment is not equally distributed throughout industry, but is concentrated in those trades which compete for their markets with foreign goods—in particular shipping, shipbuilding, coal, iron and steel, engineering and textiles. In those industries which depend on the home market and supply goods to satisfy the very considerable purchasing power of the working classes, the position is entirely satisfactory. For example, in the building industry the whole of the productive capacity is employed; and the tobacco industry, the beer industry, the artificial silk industry (which makes the stockings which every English factory-girl and shop-girl now wears) are making greater profits than ever before.

4. The explanation of this situation is the obvious one—with sterling at gold parity, British prices and wages are too high relatively to world prices. I reckon that British wages would have to fall nearly 20 per cent to be in equilibrium with those in France, Germany, Italy and Belgium, and nearly 10 per cent to be in equilibrium with the world situation as a whole. The problem how to bring about this reduction is as much a political as an economic problem. Not much progress has been made as yet towards its solution.

5. The result is that the industries of the country fall into two groups—what are called the 'sheltered' industries which are exceedingly prosperous and comfortable and the 'unsheltered'

industries which are in great distress. The high prices of the goods produced by the prosperous 'sheltered' industries make wages and other costs in the 'unsheltered' industries so high that the latter are handicapped in competition with their foreign rivals.

6. This disequilibrium between the two groups is the fundamental problem for Great Britain; and this problem has been gravely aggravated by the restoration of the gold standard. A year ago sterling was 12 per cent depreciated compared with gold, and this depreciation provided a sort of bounty to the export industries. Now, when sterling is at par, the 'sheltered' industries maintain the same prices and wages, whilst the 'unsheltered' industries, which sell for export, realise 12 per cent less in sterling for what they sell than they realised when sterling was depreciated. The result has been to reduce some of them almost to bankruptcy.

7. The correct remedy would be a fall of wages in the 'sheltered' industries. But since employment is good in these industries and the trade unions strong and determined to accept no reductions, it is very difficult to put pressure on them. On the other hand, in the 'unsheltered' industries, where the pressure of unemployment and bad trade exists in a high degree, the wages are already relatively low, so that these industries have a good case before public opinion and in justice for not suffering a further reduction.

8. The first example of an attempt to reduce wages—namely in the coal industry—has had a surprising result. This industry is the most exposed of all the 'unsheltered' industries. Accordingly the mine-owners were able to prove that if they continued to pay the present wages they would become bankrupt. On the other hand, the mine-workers were able to prove that, if the wages were lowered, their standard of life would be unjustly reduced below the standard in other industries. The other trade unions supported the mine-workers and declared that they would order an almost general strike if the Government insisted

on the reduction. The Government, at a loss to know what to do, made the surprising decision to appoint a Commission to examine the case, and meanwhile for the Government themselves to pay the difference between what the mine-owners offer and what the mine-workers demand! This costs the Government at present about 20 million roubles a month.

9. The disequilibrium naturally results in brisk imports and reduced exports, thus impairing the balance of payments. This is being temporarily remedied by the Bank of England in two ways—partly by bank credits from America, and partly by prohibiting the financiers of the City from making new foreign loans. This prohibition now extends even to loans to other parts of the British Empire. This state of affairs also has its reaction on Russia and makes impossible what would in any case be difficult, namely new loans to Russia.

10. There is one other aspect of the case which has its application to Russia, namely the growth of population. The high level of unemployment and the difficulty in transferring labour out of the unprosperous industries into the prosperous industries is not a little due to the excessive growth of population and to the fact that the number of younger workers entering industry every year is much greater than the number of old workers going out. I believe that the poverty of Russia before the War was due to the great increase in population more than to any other cause. The War and the Revolution reduced the population. But I am told that now again there is a large excess of births over deaths. There is no greater danger than this to the economic future of Russia. There is no more important object of deliberate state policy than to secure a balanced budget of population.

11. In conclusion I emphasise that the economic problem of England is essentially a problem of solid and economic disequilibrium and not primarily a problem of poverty or of a lack of technical capacity to produce wealth.

14 September 1925

THE ECONOMIC TRANSITION IN ENGLAND

Great Britain, not less than Russia, is suffering an economic transition in the early stages of which we are now living. An American economist, Professor Commons, one of the first to recognise the nature of this transition, distinguishes three epochs, three economic orders, upon the third of which we are entering.

The first is the epoch of scarcity, whether due to inefficiency or to violence, war, custom or superstition. In such a period there is the minimum of individual liberty and the maximum of communistic, feudalistic or governmental control through physical coercion. This was, with brief intervals in exceptional cases, the normal economic state of the world up to (say) the sixteenth or seventeenth century.

Next comes the era of abundance. In a period of extreme abundance there is the maximum of individual liberty and the minimum of coercive control through government; and individual bargaining takes the place of rationing. During the eighteenth and early nineteenth centuries Europe won its way out of the bondage of scarcity into the free air of abundance, and in the latter nineteenth century this epoch culminated gloriously in England in the victories of *laissez-faire* and historic liberalism. It is not surprising or discreditable that the veterans of the Liberal Party cast backward glances on that easier age.

But England is now entering on a third era, which Professor Commons has called the period of stabilisation and has truly characterised as the actual alternative to Marx's communism. In this period, he says, there is a diminution of individual liberty, enforced in part by governmental sanctions, but mainly by economic sanctions through concerted action, whether secret, semi-open, open or arbitrational, of associations, corporations, unions and other collective movements of manufacturers, merchants, labourers, farmers and bankers.

The extremes of this epoch in the realm of government are

438

Fascism on the one side and Leninism on the other. For my part, I accept neither. Yet state socialism offers no middle course, because it also is sprung from the presuppositions of the era of abundance, just as much as *laissez-faire* individualism and the free play of economic forces. Therefore I direct all my mind and attention to the development of new methods and new ideas for effecting the transition from the economic anarchy of the individualistic capitalism which rules today in Western Europe towards a régime which will deliberately aim at controlling and directing economic forces in the interests of social justice and social stability. I still have enough optimism to believe that to effect this transition may be the true destiny of a New Liberalism.

It happens that England has today in the position of her coal industry an object lesson of the results of the confusion of ideas which now prevails. On the one side the Conservative Government is pursuing an orthodox nineteenth-century policy based on the assumption that economic adjustments can and ought to be brought about by the free play of the forces of supply and demand. They still assume that the things, which would follow on the assumption of free competition and the mobility of capital and labour, actually occur in the economic life of today.

On the other side not only the facts, but public opinion also, have moved a long distance away towards the epoch of stabilisation. The trade unions are strong enough to interfere with the free play of the forces of supply and demand; whilst public opinion, albeit with a grumble and with more than a suspicion that the trade unions are growing dangerous, supports the trade unions in their main contention that coalminers ought not to be the victims of cruel economic forces which they never set in motion.

The idea of the Conservatives, that you can, for example, alter the value of money and then leave the consequential adjustments to be brought about by the forces of supply and demand, belongs to the days of fifty or a hundred years ago when trade unions were powerless, and when the economic juggernaut was allowed to crash along the highway of progress without obstruction and even with applause.

The orthodox economics, which we have inherited from the nineteenth century, assumes a high degree of fluidity of the economic organism. It depends on what I would term the *principle of diffusion*—the principle that, when any disturbance is introduced at any point in the economic organism, it diffuses itself fairly rapidly through the whole organism until a new position of equilibrium has been reached. It has always been admitted that the economic organism is partly rigid and that friction may delay the process of diffusion. But it has been supposed that the organism has sufficient fluidity and mobility to allow the principle of diffusion to be a good working hypothesis.

That a great measure of diffusion still takes place, I do not deny. But the ease and rapidity of diffusion is—in England at least—much less than it used to be. I put this down to three main influences:

1. A rapidly progressive community possesses much more mobility than a stationary or slowly progressive community. In the case of the former equilibrium can be restored by (for example) a particular industry growing more or less fast. It is much easier to retard the rate of growth than actually to drive capital and labour, which are already in an industry, out of it. I attach immense importance to this. I do not think that Englishmen sufficiently realise to what an extent their nineteenth-century methods depended on the fact that the country was living in a continuing economic crescendo. The orthodox economic assumptions work much better in the United States than in England precisely because in the United States the crescendo of progress still continues.

2. The growth in the power and authority of the trade unions both to maintain wages and to exclude the entry of new labourers into a trade.

3. The growth of a sort of humanitarianism, exemplified in the 'dole' to the unemployed, which interferes with the natural pressure of economic forces on individuals.

These influences have, between them, introduced a considerable degree of rigidity into the British economic system. Yet the authorities still frame their policies on the assumption that a high degree of mobility and diffusion still exists. Hence our tears and troubles.

It is not an accident that our first difficulties, which will last long and take many different forms, should centre about monetary policy. For no feature of our pre-war system depended more fundamentally on the principle of diffusion than did our pre-war gold standard regulated by means of Bank rate. The first and most important step, in my judgement, is to establish a new monetary system based on a stable level of internal prices, which will not ask from the principle of diffusion more than it can perform.

But this is not the only item in my new economic programme. I believe that there are many other matters, left hitherto to individuals or to chance, which must become in future the subject of deliberate state policy and centralised state control. Let me mention two—(1) the size and quality of the population and (2) the magnitude and direction of employment of the new national savings year by year.

Some of you in Russia will not agree with me in seeking help in these matters from a reformed and remodelled Liberalism, which above all, shall *not*, if my ideal is realised, be a *class* party. Leninism—so it seems to me—is at the same [time] a persecuting religion and an experimental technique. Capitalism too is at the same time a religion, which is much more tolerant, however, than Leninism is, and a technique which, from having been experimental, is now perhaps in danger of becoming obsolescent. On the religous side it is not for me, who am a free-thinking heretic, to speak. But the experimental technique is necessarily a matter of most high interest. We in the West will watch what you do with sympathy and lively attention, in the hope that we may find something which we can learn from you. For we too have new problems to solve.

15 September 1925

On his return from the Soviet Union Keynes wrote three essays under the title 'Soviet Russia'. These appeared in *The Nation* for 10, 27 and 24 October before the Hogarth Press published them in December under the title *A Short View of Russia* (*JMK*, vol. IX, pp. 253–71).

Keynes's return also brought a renewal of his agitation over official financial policy. On 12 October he journeyed to Manchester to speak to the Manchester Branch of the Federation of British Industries the next day. Two days later his speech appeared in *The Manchester Guardian Commercial*.

From The Manchester Guardian Commercial, *15 October 1925*

Mr Keynes said that if the Treasury and the Bank of England had listened to the advice which the Federation of British Industries had pressed on them at frequent intervals during the past three years employment today would have been exceedingly good. The F.B.I. had been all through not only moderate and reasonable in its officially expressed policy, but right.

We may also differ about the cure [continued Mr Keynes], but we cannot differ about the character of our difficulties. It is no longer true that there is a world depression. The United States has never in its history experienced such unmitigated prosperity as at the present day. It is not true that our principal customers are abnormally impoverished, unless it be in China. Home trade is good on the whole. Wheat, sugar, cotton, copper, steel, oil, and coal—to take some of the commodities which to us are the most important in the world—are in abundant supply. It is not true that we are technically inefficient. We are not backward in the new industries—artificial silk, motor-cars, oil-driven ships, electrical engineering. In all those things we hold our own with the whole world. The foundations for prosperity exist.

The reason why unemployment does not diminish and

certain industries are half-bankrupt lies in the fact that our manufacturing costs of production, measured in gold, are higher than those of our chief industrial competitors. That is the result of our having used financial devices to fix the gold value of sterling at a value above that which, in fact, it has measured by its command over home services.

These excess costs of production may be divided into two parts. One part is due to the fact that the real wages of our workers are higher than those in the rest of Europe. The other part is because our cost of living, when converted into gold at the current rate of exchange, is higher than the corresponding cost abroad, so that we have to pay our workers higher money wages before they are dead level with wages elsewhere. Thus the second factor has nothing to do with the efficiency or inefficiency of capital or of labour, but is just a symptom of monetary maladjustment.

So far we all agree. But when we come to the cure, one can distinguish three schools of opinion. The first school I will call the pious school. The pious school thinks that the monetary factor is not very important one way or the other. It stresses the high level of taxation and the high real wages of our workers, their relatively short hours, and their tendency to ca'canny. In its hysterical moments it is occupied with something said to be prevalent in this country which it calls Communism. According to this school, there is very little that the Government can do except to economise drastically in its own expenditure. Apart from Government economy there is nothing to be done except to exhort everybody in terms of copybook maxims. We must forget party differences, we must all pull together, we must work much harder, employers and employed must be at peace, those whose wages are relatively high must be willing to reduce them for the benefit of others, and the old country will pull through yet.

The ablest representative of this school in the daily press is, perhaps, the City Editor of *The Morning Post*. Gentlemen who write to the newspapers belong to this school more often than not. So does Mr Baldwin, except in the matter of governmental economics—about which as a sensible man he has no illusions. The first leader in today's *Times* is a perfect example of this philosophy. All the same, this school, I am afraid, though vocal and more than respectable doesn't cut much ice. In practice its precepts boil down to demands for reduced Government expenditure and reduced real wages. Now, though it is not good manners to cast doubt on such admirable sentiments, I do doubt whether these measures are practicable and even—in general— desirable. I do not believe that important economies in Government expenditure are possible except in the fighting services—while the latter, though desirable, are not compatible with our present foreign policy of guaranteeing distant frontiers against the Turk, and of undertaking to defend Germany disarmed against France in the plentitude of her military power—two steps in the highest degree imprudent.

As for our real wages, while they are higher, I am glad to say, than in the rest of Europe, they are not so high as in the United States. I am not convinced that they are higher on the average than we can afford. Ca'canning is a degrading and antisocial practice. Wages are too high in particular grades and particular industries relatively to others. But I sympathise with the working classes in resisting a general reduction of real wages. I am sure that no material reduction is possible in the near future without engaging on a social struggle of which no one could foretell the outcome.

The second school is the strait-laced school. This school recognises the existence of monetary disequilibrium and would like to cure it by carrying out, pretty ruthlessly the orthodox rules of the pre-war gold standard. If British prices are relatively too high, this means that credit is relatively too abundant. If the markets for capital and goods are left perfectly free and unrestricted, as they ought to be—so runs the teaching of this school—gold will flow out and credit will be restricted until equilibrium has been restored. This may involve temporary sacrifices, but they are necessary and worth while.

The ablest exponent of this philosophy in the daily press has been the distinguished and well-informed City Editor of *The Manchester Guardian*. Now the fault of this school is that it depends too much on applying to new conditions rules which were drawn up with a view to old conditions, without considering in sufficient detail how they will work out in these new conditions. The only method by which the high Bank rate and credit restriction can lower prices is, so to speak, by deliberately organising a depression. These measures aim at depriving the business men of sufficient cash for carrying on at the existing level of prices; and rely on this to effect the necessary reduction of prices.

Now in conditions of boom or incipient boom it is necessary and desirable to use this method to damp down business enthusiasm. But at a time of depression deliberately to organise more depression simply breaks the heart of the employer of labour. Moreover, when it is wages which which the policy aims at reducing, it may, in modern conditions of organised labour and impaired mobility of labour, merely produce the depression without bringing about an adequate reduction of prices. The reason why we are still full of unemployment when the rest of the world is recovering from the depression of 1921 is because for three years past whenever business was raising its head the Bank of England has seized the opportunity to restrict credit and so organise a depression with a view to lowering prices in the interests of the dollar exchange. When the adjustment has at last been affected, this school will have done its worst and its best for the time being. But, meanwhile, the consequences of this policy are disastrous. Indeed another five years of this policy might bring us to the edge of revolution, if revolution is ever possible in this country.

The third school I will venture to call the sensible school. It has included the Federation of British Industries, Mr

McKenna, Sir Alfred Mond; and the leading weekly newspapers, *The Nation*, *The New Statesman*, and *The Spectator*. I even notice a slightly greater wisdom in the weekly *Manchester Guardian* than in the daily. This school believes that prosperity is more important than the dollar exchange, that prosperity is cumulative, that prosperity by allowing production up to capacity and full-time employment may enable us at the same time to pay present real wages and, nevertheless, reduce our costs. This school, therefore, would set itself in every possible way to organise prosperity instead of depression, would stimulate new capital developments of every kind, would encourage the business world to launch out, and would give it the confidence and the credit to do so.

Up to the date of the reintroduction of gold convertibility this spring, it was easy to combine these aims with an absolutely sound financial policy. It is not so easy now. The prosperity policy will probably lead in its early stages to a loss of gold, perhaps on a large scale, and we must be prepared to take no notice of this, which would, in normal times, be incompatible in the long run with a sound gold-standard policy. It involves a risk. Nevertheless, the risk should, I think be taken. Having made the mistake of returning to the gold standard before we were ready for it—the only remedy is to be found in not taking the gold standard too seriously for the time being.

In classifying the schools of opinion I have not yet placed the authorities of the Bank of England—for that reason that I simply do not know where they stand. At one time I thought that they belonged to the strait-laced school. But their latest actions no longer bear this out. Lenin and Mussolini have at least explained what they were at. But our despots are dumb. The veiled prophetess of Threadneedle Street speaks in the riddles of Bank rate, the City reverently accepts her word, but no one, it seems, has any idea what the old lady really means.

The recent policy of the Bank of England is capable of two opposite interpretations. The Bank of England may wish quite deliberately to lose a certain amount of gold in order to have a good excuse for curtailing credit once again, and for raising the Bank rate to 5 per cent after an interval. The object of the recent recoil of Bank rate may be *pour mieux sauter*.

On the other hand, it may mean that at last the Bank has come over to the sensible school, that the object of the present cheap money is to revive trade, that we can rely on a continuance of cheap money until trade does revive, that gold will be allowed to flow out on a large scale if necessary without any restriction of credit ensuing, and that the Bank's resources in America will be used if they are needed. If this is the policy, our prospect may be fairly bright.

Take Manchester for example. If Lancashire was producing up to capacity, would it not be possible to reduce costs materially, without any reduction of wages? Is this not a better programme than to curtail credit in the hope that the resulting unemployment will lead to a fall in real wages? Cheap money is a dangerous thing. Cheap money in the right conditions can work wonders. I would run the risk of cheap money at the present juncture. With abundant cotton plus abundant credit is not a remarkable revival in the textile industries perfectly possible?

It may be that the Bank of England has no steady or thought-out policy at all, but lives empirically day by day—by cunning rather than science. It is absurd that we do not know. For the immediate future of this country depends on the answer. The premature return to gold renders what I call the prosperity policy more difficult and more risky than it would have been otherwise. I urge, all the same, that the Federation of British Industries should use its influence to make sure that it is the prosperity policy and not the suicide policy which wins the day.

The Guardian Commercial's report of Keynes's speech led to two further letters from Keynes.

To the Editor of The Manchester Guardian Commercial, *17 October 1925*

Sir,

In your otherwise excellent report of my speech at the F.B.I. luncheon, Manchester, the other day, you attributed to me the dreadful expression 'ca'canning'. I did not know how to pronounce the word, and I did not know its derivation, but I did, I think, know how to spell it. The mistake had, however, the result of bringing me from a correspondent the whole story. I send it to you in case there may be some others amongst your readers besides myself who learn something from it.

My correspondent writes:—

This is made up of two words 'calling' spelt in Scotch cain and the und [*sic*] canny, a word which as a good Englishman you no doubt apply to all Scotchmen, good and otherwise. Ca'in is the participle of the verb to call and 'canny' is an adjective. The phrase you should have used was therefore 'ca'in canny'. Further 'a' in *Ca'in* is pronounced as in *calling*.

I would only add that the last sentence is to me ambiguous. Am I to pronounce *ca* as *car* or as *caw*?

I am, etc.,

J. M. KEYNES

To the Editor of The Manchester Guardian Commercial, *26 October 1925*

Sir,

I am afraid that I am still in error about 'ca'canny'. My letter which you published last week has brought me another correction from a further correspondent, who writes this time as follows:

The verb in *to ca'canny* has nothing to do with the word to call (vocare—spelt also *ca* in Scots). In this phrase it means to work, drive or knock—e.g. my mither ca's the mangle. In the well known Scotch song beginning, 'Ca' the yowes to the knowes', the word is used in the sense of *drive*—not *call*, i.e. 'Drive the ewes to the knolls'—(and I your lover will go with you). A Scots expression puns on the two meanings:—Ye can ca' me (call) what ye like if ye dinna ca' (knock) me ower (over)'.

I am, etc.,

J. M. KEYNES

The *Manchester Guardian*'s and *The Commercial*'s City Editor's comments on Keynes's speech drew two more letters.

To the Editor of The Manchester Guardian, *19 October 1925*

Sir,

Your City Editor argues today that my recommendation to maintain Bank rate at 4 per cent, in spite of the loss of gold, is somethat risky. No doubt this is so. But the policy of last spring has produced a situation in which *no* course is open to us against which there are not considerable objections.

He, I understand, advocates dearer money and the restriction of credit if the outward flow of gold continues. May I ask him whether he advocates this in order to tempt back the American balances which have been flowing away, or in order to curtail credit at home in the hope of reducing prices? If his object is the former, could we not attain the same end, namely, short-period borrowing from New York, by using the Bank of England's credits with the New York Federal Reserve Bank, leaving our own Bank rate where it is in the interests of trade recovery? If, however, his object is the latter, may I ask him to particularise a little the causal train by which he thinks dear money and credit restriction will lower prices?

We agree, I think, that the trouble is the high level of British costs of production when expressed in terms of gold. Will dear money cure this, except by the process—as I expressed it the other day—of organising depression; that is to say, of increasing losses and bankruptcies amongst employers and unemployment amongst workers, in the hope that both parties will eventually abate their demands under the overwhelming pressure of their misfortunes? In what way will dear money and credit restriction tend towards a lower cost of production, unless it be thus?

If this is the way in which dear money does its job, isn't it sensible not to be strait-laced?

Yours, &c.,

J. M. KEYNES

To the Editor of The Manchester Guardian Commercial, *2 November 1925*

Sir,

Your City Editor's account of my opinions published last week is one to which I cannot, for several reasons, conveniently reply in an adequate manner within the limits proper to correspondence. In a few respects he misrepresents me. In other passages he raises solid and important arguments.

Yet most of this is really irrelevant to the essential difference between us, which is something broader. He stands firm on the past; I am trying to grapple with the future. He thinks that we have nothing to do but to follow the good old rules. I think that things have changed, and that the presumptions as to fact, upon which his rules depend, no longer hold. I am doubtless wrong and rash in many matters, and will be corrected by experience. But I am trying with all my wits, now in this direction and now in that, to face up to the new problems, theoretically and practically, too. Your City Editor is blind as a bat—so it seems to me—to the shifting scene, though so much abler than the other bats. For this reason, what he writes is—except from the debating standpoint, which one can always enjoy—to me absolutely uninteresting and unsignificant. I know it all before-hand; for I was brought up on it and taught it for years. If only I could convert him, not to my opinions and recipes, but to my state of mind! Then, whether we agreed or not, we should be able to discuss with exhilaration and with profit the difficulties

450

ahead. So I appeal to him to step out of his coffin, discard his strait-laced shroud, and join the ranks of the living.

Yours, &c.,

J. M. KEYNES

The remainder of the year brought one more letter from Keynes's pen—not on the gold standard. In June 1924 Keynes had taken part in a deputation to the Prime Minister to lobby against the authorities' proposals to commute tithes (see *JMK*, vol. XII). The deputation was not successful.

To the Editor of The Times, *21 November 1925*

Sir,

As the Bursar of a college which is one of the largest owners of impropriate tithe, I have followed closely the proceedings on the Tithe Bill. In my opinion the feature of the Bill which deserves the closest attention is the method of valuation which the Government have seen fit to adopt.

Tithe is at present a form of real property of which the annual value in terms of money fluctuates in a way which cannot be foreseen with certainty. It is proposed to compel the owners by legislation to accept in lieu of it a fixed money annuity. With one class of owners, the clergy, an agreed bargain has been reached, in which rating concessions play an important part. With another class, the lay rectors, amongst whom are the Colleges of Oxford and Cambridge, no agreed bargain has been reached.

The question has arisen, therefore, how to fix the amount of the money annuity, failing agreement. The Colleges have proposed that the question of valuation should be submitted to an independent arbitrator, who would hear evidence. The course taken by the Government has been to ask the opinion of a single authority, of much eminence, but not an expert in this particular matter, and to whose appointment for this

451

purpose the disadvantage (or advantage) attached that the Government knew beforehand what his opinion would be, since they had obtained it on substantially the same matter a year previously. This gentleman has not heard evidence from the parties concerned; nor has he based his decision on the present net annual value of the property in question. He has looked into the future and has decided that the value attached to tithe must be calculated by reference to what its value would be on the assumption, which he deems reasonable, but which the owners dispute, that the prices of corn will fall rapidly during the next 15 years to their pre-war level.

The method of arriving at a fair figure is a question of some general importance, because several other analogous transactions are on the programmes of the various political parties—e.g. coal royalties, the coal mines themselves, railways, rural and urban land under Mr Lloyd George's schemes. Suppose, for example, that the same method were to be applied in fixing a money annuity receivable by landlords in lieu of future rent. Let us suppose that the decision is left to the judgement of a single individual, the bias of whose opinion is known beforehand. Let us suppose further that this individual expects agricultural prices to fall steadily to two-thirds of their present level, and calculates the annuity on the basis of what rents would be if this assumption is realised. Would not landlords feel aggrieved at being expropriated from a considerable part of the present value of their property on the ground of a disputed and unverified expectation that something might be going to happen some years hence which would cause rents to fall? Might they not reasonably demand that such a settlement should be preceded by an open and impartial examination of their case?

Compulsory expropriations of property in return for a fixed money annuity are very much in the air just now. Whether the valuation embodied in the Tithe Bill is right or wrong in itself, have the Government seriously considered the nature of the precedent which they are setting? As a Bursar I am disgusted at a measure which, as I believe, robs the Colleges of Oxford and Cambridge of expectations worth £100,000 or so. As an economist I realise that the establishment, by a Conservative Government, of a precedent of this kind, which may be much quoted and often acted on in future, is a matter of more importance. The passage of this Bill and the light way in which our complaints as to its justice have been handled by Ministers mark, I think, an important transition in the attitude of public opinion towards property rights. It means that, in future, property will be liable to expropriation not at an arbitrated figure, but at such price as may seem to the Government of the day to be convenient on broad political grounds. For my own part, I believe that expropriations of particular forms of property may become increasingly necessary in the public interest; but I believe also that the mode of fixing the compensation payable in such cases should partake of the attributes and formalities of the public administration of justice—which have been conspicuously lacking in this case.

Yours, &c.,

J. M. KEYNES

Chapter 6

1926: FURTHER ECONOMIC CONSEQUENCES, THE FRANC AND THE RUPEE

With the new year Keynes turned his attention to the French financial situation. The first result was an article 'An Open Letter to the French Minister of Finance (whoever he is or may be)'[1] which appeared on 9 January. A week later he replied to press comment on the article.

From The Nation and Athenaeum, *16 January 1926*

THE FRENCH FRANC: A REPLY TO COMMENTS ON 'AN OPEN LETTER'

In last week's *Nation* I wrote an open letter to the French Minister of Finance. My argument ran:—

(1) Is not a rise of franc prices inevitable in any case, and will not this rise, when it occurs, materially ease the problem of the Budget?

(2) Would not a material increase in the rates of taxation over-burden the French taxpayer beyond endurance? Is it not better to depend on improved collection of the existing taxes?

(3) Meanwhile the important and practical measure is to prevent the franc exchange from running away and to use the Bank of France's gold for this purpose if necessary.

Thus I made one prophecy: prices will rise; and three counsels: collect the taxes, peg the exchange, and trust to time. The reaction of the financial editors of London and Paris to these observations, throws light on the psychological difficulties of the French situation. Let me take six samples in order.

[1] *JMK*, vol. IX, pp. 76–82.

The Times

The Times argues that, because M. Poincaré's policy of improving the exchange *down* to a parity with prices failed, the policy of bringing prices *up* to a parity with the exchange would also fail. If I point out in reply that the two policies, being the exact opposite of one another, might perhaps produce opposite results, I shall, I fear, only lay myself open to the charge of 'cleverness' For *The Times* continues: 'The financial problem is much more likely to be solved by straightforward methods than by clever tricks. A reduction of expenditure, or higher taxes, or a mixture of both, is the proper method of restoring permanent order to the finances of our Ally.'

Does *The Times* realise that the story about Frenchmen paying no taxes is a myth? France is already one of the most heavily taxed countries in the world. Mr Moulton, in his admirable and impartial volume on *The French Debt Problem*, calculates that in 1924, with taxes lower and collection less efficient than now, the revenue actually collected equalled 20 per cent of the national income as compared with 18·5 per cent in Great Britain. I think that he has underestimated the French national income, and that the true percentage was not so high as he calculates. Nevertheless, when we remember that the income per capita in France is not much more than half what it is in Great Britain, I suggest that it is not reasonable for *The Times* to expect a solution from 'the pressure of a resolute public opinion' in France demanding a programme of higher taxes.

The Morning Post

The Financial Editor of *The Morning Post* is 'entirely in accord' with my two main proposals to peg the exchange and to collect the existing taxes. But he does not like the idea of rising prices. 'We must confess that for our own part we would prefer to see the stabilisation of the French exchange unaccompanied by any welcoming of a rise in internal prices.' I reply that the rise of prices *will* happen by mere lapse of time, unless the franc exchange is greatly improved, and that a material improvement of the franc is not only doomed to failure, but would, if it were successful, render the Budget problem incapable of solution. The export trades cannot permanently retain their present advantage unless the franc exchange goes on falling ever further. For it only requires time for internal prices to catch up. French prices are rising every month. May I not legitimately point out that in this respect time is on the Treasury's side?

The Manchester Guardian

The City Editor agrees with me: 'Mr Keynes's prescription is a simple one and one which will commend itself to most external students of French finance.' But he wonders whether Frenchmen will ever be persuaded to use their gold reserve 'for the only purpose for which it can ever have been designed'. The leader-writer in the same issue doubts whether any effective scheme for attaining financial equilibrium will ever pass the French Chamber, so that all words are wasted. He is very possibly right.

Le Figaro

M. Romier sees 'the logic of my system'. But his objection is short and to the point. If an attempt were made to stabilise the exchange before the Budget is balanced and before external and internal prices are in equilibrium, he believes that all the gold in the Bank of France would disappear abroad. Here is a clear issue. I do not agree with him at all. The disequilibrium between external and internal prices is an aid, and not a hindrance, to stabilisation at present levels. In my opinion, the Bank of France might have to sell some gold to prove that it was in earnest. But as soon as confidence was established in the Bank's intentions, the danger would be, not that the flow of gold would continue indefinitely, but that the franc exchange would improve too much and too fast. It would be desirable that the Bank of France should not only sell gold at (say) 28 francs to the dollar, but should also buy dollars at (say) 26 francs; and I should not be surprised if in the first three months the Bank were to buy more dollars than it sold gold.

Le Temps

I am not very clear about the comments of *Le Temps*. They contend that a rise of prices would aggravate, and not lighten, the budgetary burden, because the expenses would rise more than the receipts. It is evident that some of the budgetary expenses would rise. But since from a third to a half of these expenses are fixed in terms of francs, the contention of *Le Temps* needs more proofs than they supply. They conclude that I am too pessimistic about the eventual equilibrium level of prices and the exchange. If so, is not this an argument for stabilising the franc at *not worse* than 30 francs to the dollar? *Le Temps* does not say a word about my proposal to use the Bank's gold for this purpose.

L'Information

M. Robert Wolff's important article offers the most interesting comment. He argues that I have exaggerated the proportion of the debt service to the total expenditure. If he is correct in putting the debt service for 1926 at less than 13 milliards, his criticism is well-founded. I was under the impression that, including sinking funds and pension debt, the figure approached 22 milliards, and that, leaving out pensions (which probably ought to be left out for this purpose), it approached $18\frac{1}{2}$ milliards. He argues from this that, whilst I am right that internal prices will and must rise somewhat, they need not rise nearly so high as I indicate. He adds—which is also news to me—that, even as things are, the Budget very nearly balances. From this, he proceeds to the logical conclusion that France can reasonably hope to stabilise the franc at a better figure than the 25 to 30 francs to the dollar which I indicated. He does not commit himself to a precise level, but seems to hint at 20 francs.

Now one might have supposed that M. Wolff, seeing that he is not averse to my general line of thought and only criticises me for being too pessimistic, would concur in my proposal that the Bank of France should at least see to it that the franc does not fall *below* 30 francs to the dollar. But no! He sees no objection to using the Bank's gold for this purpose, provided such measures are postponed until *after* all the psychological causes which are leading to the export of capital have disappeared!

O unchanging France! O wide and vasty Channel! To a Frenchman the gold reserves are always for ornament, not for use—the family jewels. To an Englishman they are always for use, and not for ornament—the family cash. It was so before the War; it was so during the War; and it is so now. On this point my English critics all support me; on this point my French critics all reject me. *The Manchester Guardian* is right. The French gold is purely ornamental and might just as well plug the teeth of the public for any use it is.

But I suspect other motives also in this universal reluctance in Paris to fix the franc exchange. Too many people think that they have an interest in depreciation. A situation is being created, as erstwhile in Berlin, where the whole Parisian population are in some way or another bears of the franc. Every exporter, every holder of a foreign security, every waiter who owns a dollar bill, is better pleased when he reads in his evening paper that the franc has weakened than when he reads that it is stronger. The waiter calculates that his dollar bill is worth another franc; he forgets to calculate that his tips are worth less in dollars. So too the investor. Perhaps these secret, never expressed, predilections are a more important factor than is recognised. If Frenchmen *want* to prevent the franc from falling, they will use their gold. If not, not.

In the same issue he remarked after a letter over possible political difficulties in the French case.

From The Nation and Athenaeum, *16 January 1926*

The difference, as I see it, between the French and English situations, is this. Here equilibrium requires lower prices, in France higher prices. Now it is very easy for politicians here to say that prices ought to be lower, but very hard for them to *do* it. On the other hand, it is very difficult for politicians in France to say that prices ought to be higher, but very easy to *do* it. Thus in practice it will be easier to secure equilibrium in France.

Two weeks later he returned to the same issue with further information.

From The Nation and Athenaeum, *30 January 1926*

SOME FACTS AND LAST REFLECTIONS ABOUT THE FRANC

One of the peculiar features of the present financial position in France is the difficulty of getting reliable data on matters of fact, such as the existing amounts of the debt service and Budget deficit, which one would have expected to be matters of common knowledge outside controversy. My recent articles on the position of the franc have brought to me several most interesting letters from French correspondents, which have helped to clear up some of my own doubts. (Why are the private letters which reach me from France ten times more sensible and informing than the big newspapers? Is it that in France the influence of wise counsellors and of those who know is even more completely obliterated by the politicians than elsewhere?)

First, as regards the service of the debt. M. Caillaux assessed this in the article which he contributed to *The Banker* early this month at 22 milliards. Mr Moulton (*French Debt Problem*, p. 110) put the actual pension charge in 1924 at 3·6 milliards, and the actual interest charge on the debt at 16·5 milliards, which is in fair agreement with M. Caillaux's figure, which avowedly included not only the pension debt but also the sinking fund, though not the debts to Allied Governments. On the other hand, this figure has been criticised by other authorities, who estimate the current interest on the internal debt at less than 13 milliards. The available facts seem to be as follows. The interest on the internal debt at April 30th, 1925, was made up of:—

	(million francs)
Long-term debt	7,451
Short-term debt	2,693
Floating debt	2,763
Total	12,907

Since that date a part of the floating debt has been converted into a 4 per cent loan with interest guaranteed in terms of gold, and about $7\frac{1}{2}$ milliards of short-term debt, carrying 6 per cent interest, has matured and been replaced by *Bons de la Défense* or *Dépôts au Trésor* which carry less than 5 per cent interest. A further part of the floating debt has been replaced by advances from the Bank of France, which carry a still lower rate of interest. Thus the present service of the internal debt, exclusive of sinking funds, is below, rather than in excess of, the above figure. At the present rate of exchange this is equivalent to about £100,000,000, which is certainly not excessive; and if we allow for the disparity between internal prices and exchange, it is the equivalent of (say) £170,000,000.

The actual sum charged on the Budget of the current year for the debt service as a whole is 19,817 million francs. The difference between this total and the figure given above is made up (approximately) as follows:—

	(million francs)
Interest on external 'commercial' debt (calculated at 94·77 francs to the £)	1,078
The pension charge	5,144
Sinking fund charge (in round figures)	700

Since the interest charge on the British national debt in the year's Budget amounts to £305,000,000, I agree that the service of the French debt does not absorb so excessive a proportion of the national income, comparatively, as I was inclined to suppose. It seems that the service of the internal debt (apart from sinking funds) is not much more than 7 per cent of the national income (taking the French national income in 1926 at 180 milliards).

Let us now turn to the question of the deficit on the Budget. Under the peculiar system prevalent in France, the outgoings of the Exchequer are not accurately known until months or even years after the event. In the calendar year 1924 the receipts were 29·5 milliards. The latest estimate of the outgoings is 33 milliards, leaving a realised deficit of 3·5 milliards; that is to say, just about the same deficit as some prophets are anticipating on Mr Churchill's Budget. The French position during the current year is in some respects worse and in some respects better than this. On the one hand, some of the supplementary estimates which really belong to 1925 will not have been voted by the Chamber until 1926; some increase of official salaries, long overdue, is probably inevitable; and the above figures include but a trifle for sinking funds, and nothing at all for the inter-allied debts. On the other hand, the additional taxation already voted in 1925 has still to produce the greater part of its results; and the substantial rise in internal prices during the past twelve months has scarcely had time to affect the yield of the taxes. Lastly, the effect of the Dawes receipts on the Budget, regard being had to the complicated principles of their division between numerous special accounts, is quite incalculable. The upshot is that probably not even the French Minister of Finance (whoever he may be) knows either his income or his expenditure for the current year within (say) 10 per cent. In these circumstances, a Budget statement, in the English sense of the term, is out of the question. He is a rash man who expresses any definite opinion as to the amount of the French deficit. M. Doumer himself puts the figure at 3 milliards without sinking funds and $4\frac{1}{2}$ milliards with them. The Finance Committee of the Chamber is slightly more optimistic. It looks as though the truth may lie anywhere between 3 and 6 milliards. If the latter figure proves nearer the facts than the former, I am confirmed in my previous conclusion that budgetary equilibrium will not be achieved except with assistance from a further rise of prices.

In my first article I expressed the opinion that the note issue of the Bank of France was already adequate to support a higher level of internal prices than rules at present. Several critics have questioned this; and further inquiry has persuaded me that they have some truth on their side. I underestimated the amount of gold and silver circulating in France before the War. It is calculated that the total circulation of France before the War in bank notes and coin together was about 10 milliards. The note issue of the Bank of France now stands at about 51 milliards. Taking the present price level at 5 times pre-war, the circulation, uncorrected for other factors, is, therefore, roughly in equilibrium. These other factors are, on the one hand, that the territory in which the franc circulates is increased, and, on the other hand, that the hoarding of notes may be less than the hoarding of notes *and coins* used to be, also that the *Bons* which constitute the floating debt may serve some of the purposes of bank notes. But I confess that it appears doubtful, in view of the above, whether the present circulation of notes would support a price level much above five times pre-war. If the equilibriums of the Budget and of the exchange require—as, in my opinion, they well may—a higher price level than this, then it would be useless to repine at a corresponding further inflation of the note issue. It would be essential, however, to take effective steps to stabilise the exchange, before permitting the slightest inflation.

The idea, that an expansion of the note issue must necessarily undo any measures which may be taken to stabilise the exchange, is mistaken. On the contrary, some further expansion is probably inevitable and even desirable in the long run, unless the exchange value of the franc is raised substantially above its present figure. There are such powerful economic factors at work tending towards a further expansion of the note issue that an expansion will probably occur in any case. The psychological effect of this on the exchange may be serious, unless steps have first been taken to stabilise the latter. France's danger is lest every increase in the note issue may precipitate a fall in the exchange, and every fall in the exchange involve after an interval a further increase in the note issue. French opinion believes that the way to stop this endless progression is to cry *No more inflation*. I am of the opinion that this policy starts at the wrong end, and is probably for that reason unrealisable. And if it were to be successful, it would produce the symptoms of deflation. The level of external prices will inevitably drag up internal prices somewhat. If this is not compensated by an increased volume of notes, it will be compensated by diminished production and by unemployment. Thus, forces have been already set in motion which render some further rise of prices, and consequently, if the above calculations are correct, some further increase in the note circulation scarcely avoidable, even in the public interest. I maintain, therefore, that the first step is to prevent further exchange depreciation. I do not see that anything has occurred as yet to render this objective difficult to attain.

Thus, although I make concessions to my critics on some important points, each of these concessions does not weaken, but confirms, my original conclusion that the practical first step is to fix the exchange with the Bank of France's gold behind it. If the figures put forward by my critics are correct, time will come to the rescue sooner than I thought, and with less strain to the social system, whilst the policy of exchange stabilisation will be all the easier and the safer to accomplish. If, however, my critics are too optimistic, an undertaking to prevent the franc exchange from falling below its present level is provided, nevertheless, with a wide margin for safety.

On 18 January *The Banker* asked Keynes to write a brief appreciation of *Lombard Street* to mark the centenary of the birth of Walter Bagehot. Keynes agreed, submitting the article on 6 February.

From The Banker, *March 1926*

BAGEHOT'S *LOMBARD STREET*

One hundred years have passed since the birth of Walter Bagehot, and more than fifty since *Lombard Street* was written. No book on banking and the money market has ever attained such a position—an undying classic, outliving the facts it describes and the controversies to which it contributes by reason of its author's sweet persuasive ways, its perfect examples of a certain kind of English writing, and its truth to human nature. It lives by goodness, art and truth, the three immortals, born, by accident as it were, out of a plain description of ephemeral fact.

Its destiny might surprise the anticipations of the author. Bagehot wrote *Lombard Street* as a piece of pamphleteering levelled at the magnates of the City, to knock into their heads two or three important facts. He feared, as he wrote it, how unpopular it would make him in bank parlours. 'I fear,' he writes in the preface, 'that I must not expect a very favourable

465

reception for this work. It speaks mainly of four sets of persons—the Bank of England, joint stock banks other than that Bank, private bankers, and bill brokers; I am much afraid that neither will altogether like what is said of them.' I expect he was right. Not much of value has been written on these matters in the last century which was acceptable at the time to the financial powers.

Bagehot's immediate purpose was practical, and much of it has been attained. But in the last thirty years the book has achieved a secondary destiny. It has become the one book in the library of economic literature which every economic student, however humble, will have read, though he may have read nothing else. In some ways it is but ill-suited for such a use. Part of it deals with obsolete facts, and part with obsolete controversies, and much of the remainder is extremely difficult. Yet everyone can read it with pleasure, if only on account of certain striking passages and its impact of intense reality. Bagehot has painted an unfading picture of the shrewd men who in the 'sixties and 'seventies consolidated the power of London as the financial centre of the world. No one has contributed more than he to the prestige and glamour of Lombard Street in the world at large. Men and forms, manners and methods have changed. But it is his picture of that hidden kingdom which still holds and satisfies the general imagination.

Bagehot wrote in the first flush of the modern international money market; he was the first to describe its intricate and elegant features, the first to appreciate its novelty, its possibilities and its dangers. 'Most men of business,' he wrote, 'think—"Anyhow this system will probably last my time. It has gone on a long time, and is likely to go on still." But the exact point is, that it has *not* gone on a long time.' In particular he was concerned with the position, the responsibilities, and the control of the Bank of England. In point of law and history the Bank is a private institution worked for the profit of its shareholders like any other joint stock company. People still talked like this in 1870. 'It might be expected,' Bagehot says, 'that as this great public duty (of keeping the reserve) was cast upon the banking department of the Bank, the principal statesmen (if not Parliament itself) would have enjoined on them to perform it. But no distinct resolution of Parliament has ever enjoined it; scarcely any stray word of any influential statesman. And, on the contrary, there is a whole *catena* of authorities, beginning with Sir Robert Peel and ending with Mr Lowe, which say that the banking department of the Bank of England is only a bank like any other bank—a company like other companies; that in this capacity it has no peculiar position, and no public duties at all.' It was Bagehot who first insisted that by force of circumstances, whether we like it or nor, the Bank of England had become a national institution with national responsibilities, and could no longer function with primary regard to the profits of its shareholders.

The fundamental duties of the Bank of England, according to Bagehot, were three—to operate with a degree of caution and impartiality beyond what could be required of an ordinary enterprising business, to maintain and build up the reserve in ordinary times, and to use the reserve without stint or limitation in times of panic. Bagehot's right policy in times of panic was, perhaps, his most characteristic and significant contribution to the practice of the day—though already in 1825 the Bank had rescued the situation along these lines. In times of panic no one but the Bank of England has the power to come to the rescue. In such a time, 'the holders of the cash reserve must be ready not only to keep it for their own liabilities, but to advance it most freely for the liabilities of others... The ultimate banking reserve of a country (by whoever kept) is not kept out of show, but for certain essential purposes, and one of those purposes is the meeting a demand for cash caused by an alarm within the country. It is not unreasonable that our ultimate treasure in particular cases should be lent; on the contrary, we keep that treasure for the very reason that in particular cases it should be lent.' It was Bagehot who hammered this hard truth into the hard heads of the City of London, who made it part of British tradition and prejudice. No other principle or practice has contributed more than this one—for no other financial centre has ever learnt it—to the prestige and leadership of London.

Bagehot's view has long prevailed, but even now we sometimes speak in the old way. Labour politicians demand the nationalisation of the Bank of England; Dr Leaf predicts that appalling disasters would ensue from such an act. They both waste their words. Bagehot nationalised the Bank of England fifty years ago. We may differ about what our monetary policy ought to be, but whatever it is, the Bank of England stands as an instrument of incomparable power to carry it out.

But if the Bank of England is a national institution bearing the ultimate responsibility for the mercantile solvency of our economic system, is its traditional method of government suitable and appropriate in all respects? Bagehot thought not, and proposed important changes. Within the last ten years there has been a certain movement in the direction of carrying out some of Bagehot's ideas—the constitution of the Committee of Treasury has been somewhat changed, the rotation of the office of Governor has been almost abandoned, a joint-stock banker has been admitted to the Board, and a permanent office of high rank has been created in the Comptrollership. Nevertheless, the problem remains substantially what it was, and it is still worth while to recall what Bagehot wrote. He described the management of the Bank thus:

1. The directors, self-elected from amongst the younger members of a limited range of old-established firms, none of them professional bankers—'Many years since I remember seeing a very fresh and nice-looking young gentleman, and being struck with astonishment at being told that he was a Director of the Bank of England.' They are still to be seen.

2. 'The older members of the Board, that is those who have passed the chair, form a standing committee of indefinite

powers, which is called the Committee of Treasury... A strong Governor does much mainly from his own responsibility, and a weak Governor does little. Still, the influence of the Committee of Treasury is always considerable, though not always the same. They form a cabinet of mature, declining, and old men, just close to the executive; and for good or evil such a cabinet must have much power.' This is not far from the truth today.

3. The Governor and Deputy Governor, though shifting, are so constantly present during their term that there is no room under them for a permanent official of influence. 'Under this shifting chief executive there are, indeed, very valuable heads of departments. The head of the Discount Department is especially required to be a man of ability and experience. But these officers are essentially subordinate; not one of them is like the general manager of an ordinary bank—the head of all action.'

So Bagehot sums up thus:

'In theory, nothing can be worse than this government for a bank—a shifting executive; a board of directors chosen too young for it to be known whether they are able; a committee of management, in which seniority is the necessary qualification, and old age the common result; and no trained bankers anywhere.'

There are compensations, of course—'Steady merchants collected in council are an admirable judge of bills and securities. They always know the questionable standing of dangerous persons; they are quick to note the smallest signs of corrupt transactions; and no sophistry will persuade the best of them out of their good instincts.' 'Nevertheless,' Bagehot concludes, 'the policy of the Bank has frequently been deplorable, and at such times the defects of its government have aggravated if not caused its calamities.'

Yet Bagehot was perplexed to find a remedy. Should the Governor be permanent, and perhaps nominated by the Crown, as in some continental countries? There is a great deal to be said for 'monarchical' management in business. Yet he doubts the

469

expediency of such a course. Bagehot's analysis of the objections to it is one of the finest of his passages on business psychology.

First, he would be too powerful. 'A permanent Governor of the Bank of England would be one of the greatest men in England. He would be a little monarch in the City; he would be far greater than the Lord Mayor. He would be the personal embodiment of the Bank of England; he would be constantly clothed with an almost indefinite *prestige*. Everybody in business would bow down before him and try to stand well with him, for he might in a panic be able to save almost anyone he liked, and to ruin almost anyone he liked. A day might come when his favour might mean prosperity, and his distrust might mean ruin.'

And, secondly, Bagehot does not believe that 'we should always get the best man for the post; often I fear that we should not even get a tolerable man'. And if the Governor were to be a man of inferior judgement, in that case, Bagehot points out with great subtlety and truth, it is in the nature of his office that a considerable time might elapse before he was found out. 'A Prime Minister, or a Chancellor of the Exchequer, or a Secretary of State, must explain his policy and defend his actions in Parliament, and the discriminating tact of a critical assembly— abounding in experience and guided by tradition—will soon discover what he is But the Governor of the Bank would only perform quiet functions, which look like routine, though they are not, in which there is no immediate risk of success or failure.' 'A large bank is exactly the place where a vain and shallow person in authority, if he be a man of gravity and method, as such men often are, may do infinite evil in no long time, and before he is detected.' In short, the Governor's traditional silence may allow a misunderstanding or shallow mind to escape discovery.

After all this, Bagehot's final proposal may seem a little lame. He proposes that the *Deputy* Governor shall be permanent, that the London bankers should not be altogether excluded from the Court of Directors, and that the Committee of Treasury should consist of the most competent instead of the most senior.

I have quoted enough to show how Bagehot's main strength lay in his characterisation of the psychology of the City, of the springs of motive and the practical behaviour of bankers and business men. There are many other passages which invite quotation. Let anyone who has not read the famous portrait of the private banker of fifty years ago turn to the unforgettable description of that enviable station. 'There has probably very rarely ever been so happy a position as that of a London private banker; and never, perhaps, a happier.' Yet I must add two more passages to what is becoming, as every article about Bagehot must become, an anthology.

The conservatism of big business. 'A man of large wealth, however intelligent, always thinks, more or less—"I have a great income, and I want to keep it. If things go on as they are I shall certainly keep it; but if they change I may not keep it." Consequently he considers every change of circumstance a "bore", and thinks of such changes as little as he can.'

'We must not confide too surely in long-established credit, or in firmly-rooted traditions of business. We must examine the system on which these great masses of money are manipulated, and assure ourselves that it is safe and right. But it is not easy to rouse men of business to the task. They let the tide of business float before them; they make money, or strive to do so, while it passes and they are unwilling to think where it is going.'

Bankers under criticism. 'The Bank Directors now fear public opinion exceedingly; probably no kind of persons are so sensitive to newspaper criticism. And this is very natural. Our statesmen, it is true, are much more blamed, but they have generally served a long apprenticeship to sharp criticism...But a Bank Director undergoes no similar training and hardening ...He is not subjected to keen and public criticism, and is not taught to bear it. . .He is apt to be irritated even by objections to the principles on which he acts, and cannot bear with equanimity censure which is pointed and personal. At present I am not sure if this sensitiveness is beneficial.'

On 9 February, at the invitation of C. P. Scott, the editor of *The Manchester Guardian*, Keynes spoke to the Presidential Dinner of the Manchester Reform Club. His speech, entitled 'Liberalism and Labour' appeared in *The Nation* of 20 February (*JMK*, vol. IX, pp. 307–11).

Keynes sent an advance copy of his speech to H. N. Brailsford, the editor of *The New Leader*. The subsequent exchange of letters is of some interest.[2]

From H. N. BRAILSFORD, *26 February 1926*

Dear Keynes,

I ought to have written earlier to thank you for sending me an advance copy of your speech at Manchester.

I think I should have commented on it much more fully, had not Ben Spoor and to a less extent Snowden, spoilt the chance of a reasoned discussion by approaching it in exactly the wrong way.

I can quite understand your feeling that it is the trade unions in the Labour Party which make co-operation difficult with people who think as you do.

My difficulty is twofold. Firstly, though I have none of the real hatred against Lloyd George which Massingham felt, I think him, both by his record and his character, an utterly impossible ally. I suppose everybody who has had dealings with him has sooner or later caught him in what one can only call in plain English a lie; often the stupidest kind of lie. That was my own experience and I know it was Massingham's. He amuses me so much that I cannot be angry with him, but still one has to say at some point 'Never Again'.

My second difficulty is the doubt how far people with your intellectual outlook are typical of any fair proportion of the Liberal Party. I cannot believe, for example, that the so-called Radical group is nearer agreeing with you than the stupidest of our trade unionists. I used to know Runciman fairly well, and like him as a human being, but surely his vision of life is nowhere near yours. And the same thing is true of other abler people like Wedgwood Benn and Pringle.

[2] For further material on Keynes's views on Brailsford, see Keynes's correspondence with Kingsley Martin in *JMK*, vol. XXVIII.

If people who think to any extent as you do formed a group with which we could negotiate, I should support the idea strongly.

Our trade union people are so barren of ideas outside their own limited area of action, that they always sooner or later follow the intellectuals in the Party.

Sincerely yours,

H. N. BRAILSFORD

To H. N. BRAILSFORD, *28 February 1926*

Dear Brailsford,

I appreciate your points. Indeed, I feel them myself. But time, in my opinion, still has some work to do before it would be useful to form any separate group. At present everything is politics, and nothing policies. We must do the best we can with the former during the interregnum whilst we are trying to make progress with the latter. It is the latter which really matters, but it needs time.

Yours sincerely,

[copy initialled] J.M.K.

BROADCAST THE BUDGET!

From The Radio Times, *26 February 1926*

On 15 February, in response to a request three days earlier, Keynes finished a piece on broadcasting the Budget speech. It is clearly important that broadcasting should not lend itself to propaganda, and, above all, that this great national monopoly should never become a propagandist instrument of the Government of the day.

This fact has been so well appreciated by those responsible, that the evolution of broadcasting in this country has proceeded on ultra-cautious lines wherever any question is concerned which could be regarded as controversial or political.

I grant the wisdom of this. Yet, all the same, if every political matter is to be excluded for ever, we may be losing one of the best opportunities now available of doing something for the political education of the big public.

There was a day when political meetings, even where front-rank statesmen were not performing, excited a degree of interest, which is quite out of fashion now; when political oratory up and down the country, indoors and out of doors, played a predominant part in forming public opinion. Then, with the growth of the press and the press telegram, newspaper reports of proceedings in Parliament and of political meetings elsewhere were remarkably full—quite different from the snippets which are all anyone gets now. The leading statesmen of the day could reckon on full reports of their big speeches in the leading organs of the press.

Now, for reasons that it is not quite easy to analyse, this state of affairs has passed away Political speeches are no longer good copy. Even ex-Prime Ministers find that their biggest platform appearances may receive but scanty notice, even in *The Times*. A sensational statement or rash words will be extracted from their context. But no statesman today, except, perhaps, the Prime Minister of the hour, is in a position to expound his ideas before the big public in coherent or continuous argument.

It may be that the interest of the general public in practical politics is so far dead that broadcast speeches will make unpopular programmes, just as reported speeches are supposed to make bad journalistic copy. If, after experience, this proves to be so, that may be a valid reason why the British Broadcasting Company may have to put political orators on short rations.

But this would be quite a different, and, perhaps, a more solid, reason for keeping politics out of broadcasting from that which is the ground of the existing policy, namely, the desire to avoid controversial matter. I suggest, therefore, that it will be an immense loss to the cause of political education in this country if, in these days of declining public interest in political meetings, and of declining publicity for reports of political speeches, broadcasting is to take no part whatever in spreading political information and political argument.

I think that what is wanted is gradually to evolve some system fair to all parties, by which broadcasting can become the organ of all of them, and not merely of the Government of the day. But if such a system is to be evolved we must not be too afraid. We must be ready to make experiments—whilst not less ready, at the same time, to meet criticism of these experiments on the ground of alleged unfairness to any particular class of opinion.

There will be an opportunity in a few weeks time to make a very interesting experiment on these lines. I hear that there is an idea on foot to broadcast the Chancellor of the Exchequer's Budget speech in the House of Commons.

I cannot imagine a better occasion on which to inaugurate a broader policy than has been permitted hitherto. The Budget speech is largely informatory, and only secondarily controversial. It is a statement to the public as a whole of how the national finances stand. There is no other political event in the year which offers so large a proportion of pure political information, which everyone, of whatever party, is equally glad to have.

But there is another advantage. The Budget speech is exciting, because it may contain surprises which will have been kept secret up to the last moment. The public will be willing to listen to a good deal of matter, which it is good for them to hear, but which, in other circumstances, they would find dull, because their interest is maintained by expectation and curiosity about what is to come. Mr Churchill, for sure, can be relied on not to miss the dramatic opportunities which every Budget speech presents.

Personally, I did not like Mr Churchill's last Budget, and it

475

is more than likely that I shall not like this one. But I do not feel that the Government will be laying itself open to any charge of unfair discrimination on a matter of political controversy if they allow this experiment to be made.

Only two safeguards seem to me to be necessary. The consent of the two other party leaders in the House of Commons ought first to be obtained; and one or two competent critics of the Government policy should be allowed to have their say at an early succeeding date.

To broadcast the comments which the Opposition spokesman may make immediately after the conclusion of the Budget speech would not be enough. The public would be bored by that time, and the Opposition would not have had time to collect their thoughts or to marshal their arguments. But I am sure that everyone would feel that due impartiality had been observed if, for example, one or two ex-Chancellors of the Exchequer from the Opposition parties were to be offered the opportunity to broadcast their criticisms and comments.

It has long been the custom to allow public buildings to be used for political meetings, subject to strict impartiality of treatment. This is a precedent on a small scale for the far more important problem of politics and broadcasting.

Late in March, in the light of his previous contributions to discussions,[3] Keynes appeared before the Royal Commission on Indian Currency and Finance which was then examining witnesses in London. Before he appeared before the Commission, he submitted a written memorandum on the Commission's proposal for a gold standard for India.

[3]   See *JMK*, vol. 1 and vol. xv, chs. 2–5.

*From the Royal Commission on Indian Currency and Finance,
Minutes of Evidence.*

ROYAL COMMISSION ON INDIAN CURRENCY AND FINANCE

HEADS OF MR J. M. KEYNES'S EVIDENCE

1. I see no advantages in a gold currency over a gold exchange standard except to placate Indian opinion.

2. If there are no great disadvantages and the matter is one of comparative indifference, it is better to placate Indian opinion than to thwart it, even though Indian opinion is misguided.

3. The measure of the possible disadvantage depends on
(a) the effect on the international value of gold;
(b) the effect on the London money market;
(c) the effect on the international position of silver;
(d) the financial cost to India.

4. I do not lay great stress on (a). £103,000,000 could be spared from the world's gold reserves, and need have no effect on prices or on the supply of credit. Any effect which the withdrawal might have would be the result of avoidable policy not of necessity.

5. (b) If the gold is to be provided mainly by selling sterling securities from the Indian gold standard or paper currency reserves or by raising a loan in London, the strain on London may be severe—though no more severe than from any foreign loan of comparable amount no part of the proceeds of which are directly spent in Great Britain. It appears to me, however, that it would be wrong to oppose the change on this ground. It is a consequence, and part of the risk, of London's undertaking international banking on a gold basis. One's banker has no right to complain when one draws a cheque on one's balance, even though it inconveniences him and he knows that you are going to spend it stupidly.

6. (c) The possible effect of the change on silver is much more important and dangerous than its effect on gold. Assuming that the scheme is successful in getting gold into circulation and that the gold replaces silver rupees in circulation and in the paper currency reserves, the effect on the value of silver may be disastrous.

I suspect that the current supply of silver from the mines is somewhat inelastic—partly because an important proportion is now produced as a by-product of lead and copper. The demand for silver on a large scale is mainly from India and China. If India steps out from under, China will have to choose between doing the like or suffering a collapse of her exchanges. I should think it not unlikely that China, faced with the prospect of being alone in the world in the use of silver on a large scale, would be forced to move towards gold. What would happen to silver then? If for several years India meets her own normal demand for silver by melting rupees, I should not be surprised to see silver fall to half its present value in terms of gold. All the silver interests in the world would be up in arms. And, not least important, India would by her own act have depreciated by perhaps 50 per cent the predominant store of value of her own people. This forecast may be over pessimistic but the figure of 24d. suggested in the commission's questionnaire strikes me as very optimistic. In any case the proposal now under consideration is obviously calculated to make the price of silver fall seriously. As soon as this is felt, will the Indian public thank the politicians who have been clamouring for it? In my opinion, India still has a considerable interest in the stability of silver. For the gold market £103,000,000 is no great matter: but for the silver market the silver in the equivalent value of rupees is overwhelming.

7. (d) If I am right in supposing that the release of the silver in £103,000,000 worth of rupees might halve the price of silver, the gold required would cost about three times the value of the silver released: that is to say, the changeover would cost India

about £67,000,000 in terms of real resources. Now suppose India has £67,000,000 to play with, can one easily conceive a more senseless way of using it? Are there not a hundred better ways of using such a sum?

8. The proposition impresses me, therefore, as being a plan to spend some £67,000,000 in destroying the purchasing power of the favourite store of value, namely silver, of the great mass of the population. This is very foolish indeed and perhaps dangerous—sufficiently foolish and dangerous, in my judgement, to justify the Government of India in turning it down. I think that it would show a want of courage to accept a proposal contrary to Indian interests, for fear of being supposed to refuse it out of a regard for British interests. It is of course not improbable that the attempt to put gold into circulation in India would prove a fiasco—so that a gold currency could be offered as a gesture having no important practical consequences. But it would be wrong in principle to gamble on this from the mere desire to make a gesture.

9. I should like to say in conclusion that stability of internal prices in India is, in my opinion, much more important than stability of foreign exchanges. I attach very little importance to a legislative enactment fixing the rupee at 1s. 6d. On this criterion, however, whilst there is not much to choose between a gold standard with gold circulating and a gold exchange standard, some advantage lies with the gold exchange standard. Moreover, the gold exchange standard, whilst open to most of the objections against a pure gold standard, does at any rate secure most of the advantages, such as they are, as economically as possible and without a waste of resources.

10. I believe that the Royal Commission would do well to do nothing.

19 March 1926

Keynes appeared before the Commission on 22 March.

From the Royal Commission on Indian Currency and Finance, Minutes of Evidence

ROYAL COMMISSION ON INDIAN CURRENCY AND FINANCE

THIRTY-EIGHTH DAY
Monday 22 March 1926

Present:

The Right Hon. Edward Hilton Young, P.C., D.S.O., D.S.C., M.P. (*Chairman*)

Sir Rajendranath Mookerjee, K.C.I.E., K.C.V.O.

Sir Norcot Hastings Yeeles Warren, K.C.I.E.

Sir Reginald Mant, K.C.I.E., C.S.I.

Sir Henry Strakosch, K.B.E.

Sir Alexander Robertson Murray, C.B.E.

Sir Purshotamdas Thakurdas, C.I.E., M.B.E., M.L.A.

Professor Jahangir Coverjee Coyajee

Mr William Edward Preston

Secretaries

Mr G. H. Baxter

Mr A. Ayangar

Mr John Maynard Keynes, C.B., called and examined.

12,921 (CHAIRMAN) *You have been good enough to come and help us on the subject of our enquiry this morning. You are a Fellow and Bursar of King's College, Cambridge, Editor of the* Economic Journal, *and Secretary of the Royal Economic Society, and you were a member of the Chamberlain Commission in 1913–1914?* Yes.

12,922 *You have been good enough to let us have a short memorandum⁴ of the principal headings of your evidence. What is your opinion as regards the relative advantages of a gold currency standard and a gold exchange standard?* I am aware of none except the political advantage of placating Indian opinion. I have seen arguments as to the likelihood of a gold currency bringing gold out of hoards. It is the only solid argument I have seen in favour of a gold currency. It is difficult to express an opinion on that, but I see no reason to accept it. A gold currency might quite possibly have the opposite effect in that gold would be a little easier to obtain than otherwise.

⁴ Above, p. 477–9.

12,923 *By providing more gold you might encourage the tendency to hoard?* You would increase the facility for obtaining gold in small quantities.

12,924 *As a matter of fact, at present there are no difficulties in obtaining metallic gold for ornaments, etc?* I am not well informed as to the size of the units in which gold can be conveniently purchased. I was under this impression that a gold currency might slightly facilitate the obtaining of gold in very small quantities.

12,925 *By increasing the facilities for obtaining the smallest possible unit in the shape of gold coin?* Yes.

12,926 *The smaller the gold coin the greater that opportunity?* Yes.

12,927 *What are the possible disadvantages of a gold currency system such as is proposed in the memorandum which has been submitted to you for your consideration?* I hold strongly that if there are no great disadvantages and if the matter is one relatively of indifference, then it is better to placate Indian opinion by conceding what is desired even though one may think oneself that Indian opinion is misguided. It is not so much a question of deciding what is ideally best, in my opinion, as in judging whether there are grave disadvantages in the proposed scheme. The measure of these possible disadvantages seems to me to depend, first of all, upon the effect on the international value of gold; secondly, the effect on the London market; thirdly, the effect on the international position of silver; and fourthly, the financial cost to India.

12,928 *Take these in order—first of all, the effect on the international value of gold.* I do not lay great stress on that. The figure of £103,000,000 has been suggested. I think that could be spared from the world's gold reserves, and need have no material effect on prices or on the supply of credits. I emphasise the word that it *need* not, because I quite agree that it might. It would depend upon the policy pursued. I mean that I see no reason why a policy should not be adopted which would prevent a gradual withdrawal of that amount of gold from having any sensible effect. Gold is now not used in circulation to any extent worth mentioning anywhere. The amounts of the gold reserves of the world are arbitrary within wide limits. There is not much reason why they should be the present figure rather than another figure. We could support a much higher price level with the existing reserves, and equally, we could also have a much lower price level without materially affecting them. The price level depends not on the quantity of gold in the world, but on the policy of the central banks as regards their reserve proportions.

12,929 *The policy by which the disturbing effects might be avoided would be the policy of the central banks of the world?* Yes.

12,930 *And it is they who might, in your opinion, avoid the disturbing effects by reducing their reserves.* It seems to me that it might easily be done because this sum is not very large spread over some time in relation to the normal movements of gold.

12,931 *You said that in your opinion £103,000,000 could be spared from the gold reserves. Where would it come from, in the first place?* It would probably come first of all out of the current production of gold. There is a production of gold at present in excess of the non-currency demands, so that in the absence of a scheme of this sort I should expect the bank reserves of the world to be on the increase, so that part of these requirements could be provided merely by avoiding an increase in the gold reserves in the banks. It is suggested in the memorandum this would be spread over ten years. If it is spread fairly evenly over the ten years I should not be surprised if the whole amount could be provided in that way. If the earlier years took more than their quota from the £103,000,000 it might be necessary to have some reduction in the reserves, but it would be nothing worth mentioning in relation to the aggregate of those reserves.

12,932 *Is the general question of the future of the world's gold supply a matter on which you feel able to assist us?* Do you mean the future production of the mines?

12,933 *The relation between the world supply and demand for gold in the foreseeable future.* I take a heterodox view of this. I think it is a matter devoid of importance, because I think the world's demand for gold is just whatever the world chooses. The world's demand for gold is not a fixed demand. Supposing the United States Federal Reserve Bank decided to work to a normal percentage of 80 per cent, you have one demand; and supposing it works to a normal percentage of 60 per cent, you have another demand; and similarly in the case of the Bank of England or the Reichsbank, or the Bank of France. I cannot conceive but that these banks will in fact, over periods of time, adjust their proportions to whatever the supply is. So that I do not regard demand as anything which exists independently of the supply, but as something which is so artificial that it will adjust itself, or can adjust itself if skill is exercised, whatever the supply turns out to be.

12,934 *Have you any opinion about the other side of the book,—the question of supply?* I do not think, my opinion is worth much on that.

12,935 *That is not a matter which you have gone into?* I know no more than is common knowledge.

12,936 *Turning back for one moment to the demand and the question of the United States, in your opinion is it a practicable policy which can be foreseen in the foreseeable future that the central banks of Europe should be able to make substantial reductions in their proportion of reserves, particularly taking into account the effects of that upon the general confidence in the present state of the world?* I think it is entirely a matter of taste. In our own case the present fixed amount of the fiduciary issue of the currency notes and the Bank of England together has the effect of locking up and rendering completely useless by far the greater part of our gold. It is just a matter of taste how much of our gold we choose to make useless. If we choose to make useless £25,000,000 or £50,000,000 less in the course of the next few years, we could find nearly all the gold required by India in excess of the current production of the mines without the loss having any consequences whatever. There is no rhyme or reason behind the present arrangement.

12,937 *Shall we say it is a matter of convention; but confidence is sometimes based upon convention and not upon reason?* Yes; but this would not require any such constant convention. The public take what they are told. If the fiduciary issue is fixed at one figure or another public opinion a week later will be just as content with the one as with the other.

12,938 *Then the second possible disadvantage to which you referred was the effect on the London market. Will you enlarge on that?* I think there the question depends on the particular means by which India raises, not so much gold, as the resources to pay for the gold. I imagine it is possible that that might be done to a considerable extent by selling sterling securities out of the Indian gold standard or paper currency reserve, or by raising additional loans in London. In that case, if the sales were fairly rapid the strain on London might, in my opinion, be quite severe; but no more severe than from any other foreign loan of an appreciable amount, no part of the proceeds of which are spent in Great Britain. I think, however, that it would be wrong to oppose the change on this ground, or to let it weigh appreciably. It is a consequence and part of the risk of London's undertaking international banking on a gold basis. If India is not free to realise the sterling securities in the gold standard and paper currency reserves absolutely whenever she likes, it is obviously a wrong policy to have such securities as part of the reserve at all. One's banker has no right to complain when one draws a cheque on one's balance even though it inconveniences him, and he knows you are going to spend it stupidly.

12,939 *As regards the sale of securities, there might be an analogy between that and a draft upon one's balance, but as regards the raising of supplementary credits, if that were necessary, in London, I suppose the analogy for that would be more in the nature of starting an overdraft?* Certainly I think that new credits are a different question. About that I hold, not only in the case of Indian loans but about all foreign loans, that the principle of the controlling of foreign loans is a right one, and one towards which we shall move. We are at the moment living in a state of reaction against the controls of the War period, and at a time when financial rectitude is believed to be whatever happened in 1914; but that will not last very long.

12,940 *As regards the sale of securities, that may be said to be as the right for India?* Yes.

12,941 *The raising of credits could never be a matter of right?* No. That matter must be a matter of agreement. I think the Treasury or the Bank of England would be absolutely justified in making difficulties about such a loan, if it appeared likely to embarrass the London money market.

12,942 *The parties to the agreement would negotiate from the point of view of their own interests?* Yes.

12,943 *Would it be possible to raise credits of the magnitude required directly in London without necessity for the concurrence of New York?* So far as I can see, it would be possible for India to raise the whole amount required in the earlier part of the period at any rate by the sale of sterling securities out of the existing reserves.

12,944 *That is £50,000,000 in the first year, is it not?* Is it as much as that? I am speaking subject to correction, because I have not got in my head the total of the reserve.

12,945 *£15,000,000 at the outset and £35,000,000 in the first year or two?* Perhaps you could tell me for my guidance what the aggregate of the sterling securities of the two reserves is? It is £40,000,000 in the gold standard reserve, is it not?

12,946 *It is 80 crores.*[5] Then it would go a very long way.

12,945 *£15,000,000 at the outset and £35,000,000 in the first year or two.* Then I think perhaps that is not quite correct. Perhaps you could tell me for my guidance what the aggregate of the sterling securities of the two reserves is? It is £40,000,000 in the gold standard reserve, is it not? *not that suggest that it would be necessary to supplement the sale of securities with credits?* You have got securities for 80 crores and certain sales of silver. It looks to me rather a close thing; I agree that it would be imprudent in all probability to take this step unless you did see your way to borrow something.

12,949 *To back it up?* The amount of the loan need not be very great.

12,950 *To generalise that question somewhat, do you think it would be possible to carry this policy through without the substantial concurrence of the New York money market?* I think it would be much better to have the concurrence of the New York money market; but it appears to me almost unthinkable that you would secure it because of the reasons which I come to later, of the effect on silver.

12,951 *Perhaps that will come out more definitely in connection with your third heading?* Yes; but I concur in the drift of what you are suggesting, namely, that some loan would probably be required, and that London would

---

[5] One crore of rupees equals ten million rupees.

be justified in making difficulties if simultaneously there were large sales of sterling securities held by India. Therefore, the position of the United States is significant.

12,952 *Just before we pass away from gold, I should like to ask you a further question. How in your opinion would any unfavourable consequences react actually upon the interests of the Indian community? Supposing that your anticipations that this drain of gold would be carried out without disturbance were unfortunately not to be realised, and supposing there were to be a disturbance, what then?* In London?

12,953 *Yes, a rise in Bank rate?* I can hardly imagine that the disturbance would be serious enough to have much reflex on India. I think that it would not be to the advantage of India that we should have dear money here, but it should not require any very desperate measures on our part. I should have thought it would merely mean that a certain percentage of our normal foreign investment should take this form for a period. It would not mean that we should need to do anything more drastic than to make foreign investments in this form instead of some other form.

12,954 *I will put the question rather more clearly. Would the disturbance to the world's gold markets, and particularly in London, be a disturbance which India could afford to neglect, as having no effect upon Indian interests?* If the disturbance was great, it would have an effect on Indian interests; but I should not anticipate a disturbance sufficiently great for it to be necessary for India to consider that from her own point of view very seriously.

12,955 *Then with regard to silver, which you mentioned just now, what in effect would be the disadvantages on the international position of silver?* In my opinion the possible effect of the change on silver is much more important and dangerous than its effect on gold. Assuming that the scheme is successful in getting gold into circulation, and that gold replaced silver rupees in circulation in the paper currency reserves, the effect on the value of silver might be disastrous. I suspect that the supply of silver from mines is somewhat inelastic—but you will probably be receiving expert evidence on that from other sources—partly because a large proportion—I have heard the proportion of 50 per cent mentioned—of silver is now produced as a by-product of lead and copper. The demand for silver on a large scale is mainly from India and China. If India steps out from under, China will have to choose between doing the like, or suffering a collapse of its silver exchange. I should think it is not impossible that China, faced with the prospect of being alone in the world in the use of silver on a large scale for currency purposes, would be forced to move towards gold. In that case what would happen to the silver? If for several years India was meeting her own normal demand for silver by melting rupees, I should not be surprised to see silver fall to half its present rate in terms of gold. All the silver interests in the world would be up in arms; and, not the least important, India would by her own act have depreciated by perhaps 50 per cent the predominant store of value of her own people. This forecast may be over-pessimistic; but the figure of 24d. suggested in the Commission's questionnaire strikes me as very optimistic. In any case the proposal now under consideration is obviously calculated to make the price of silver fall seriously. As soon as that is felt, will the Indian public thank the politicians who have been clamouring for it? In short will the present public opinion, such as it is, in favour of the change, be an enduring one? In my opinion India still has a great interest in the stability of the value of silver. For the gold market, as I have already explained, £103,000,000 is no great matter; but for the silver market, the silver in the equivalent value of rupees is overwhelming.

12,956 *You say that India still has a considerable interest in the stability of silver. You are referring to the interest in the large amount of silver held as a store of value?* Yes.

12,957 *Is there any other substantial interest which is present in your mind?* No.

12,958 *You referred to the connection between the price of silver and the lead and copper markets. I wonder if you would amplify that at all, to make it clearer to us how the two will react on one another?* I understand that a considerable amount of silver is now obtained in the course of refining lead and copper Though this is not the case in all the mines from which silver comes, it is the case in a great number that lead and copper are their main products, though they make their profits sometimes out of the relatively small amount of silver which they obtain incidentally. If silver was to fall in price heavily, it would be a matter of embarrassment to those mines, and would diminish their profits, and might put some of them out of action. But as the value of the silver they produce is not very great as compared with the value of the lead or copper they produce, it would probably have to be a very severe fall in the price of silver before any great proportion of those mines would be put out of action. It might be that the fall in the price of silver would be compensated for by the rise in the price of lead and copper. I am not an expert on this matter; but my impression is that a fall of 20 per cent in the price of silver might diminish the new supply of silver surprisingly little; so that in order to bring about equilibrium between demand and supply when the Indian demand was removed, a very heavy fall indeed in the price of silver would have to take place.

12,959 *It would be against the market both ways?* It would be against the market both ways; and there would be a further aggravating circumstance, you must remember. If a policy of this kind were to be announced, the world's confidence in the future price of silver would be undermined, so that it would become a less eligible article for a store of value than previously. You might, therefore, have a great tendency to sell on the part of people who would otherwise be hoarding silver; with the result that you would not only have the Indian currency demand removed, but you might have a considerable part of the demand for silver as store of value throughout the world removed. It might well happen, when it was seen that the price of silver was doomed to fall, that there would be a strong tendency to change over from silver to gold in all parts of the world where silver is still held in large quantities as a store of value; so that a certain fall in the price of silver might precipitate a much greater fall. If the best opinion held that silver would fall from 30d. to 24d., I should expect that to precipitate such a flood of silver on to the world's markets, and to offer such a strong incentive to bear speculation that at any rate in the first instance, silver would fall to a great deal less than 24d. This seems to me much the biggest point from India's point of view. To introduce this great instability into the silver market, might have consequences of a really disastrous kind, when you consider what part silver plays in the life of India. It is a step which ought not to be taken lightly, but only for very grave cause.

12,960 *You referred to the reaction on Chinese trade. Could you explain to us how the full consequence would be realised in Indo-Chinese trade of a fall in the value of silver?* Of course it would make it extremely difficult for China to import until the new equilibrium had been reached. The amount of her own money which she would have to offer for goods in the international market would be very greatly increased; and if China were simply to remain on her present basis, during the whole period of the change, there would be severe obstacles in the way of any manufacturer or trader who was accustomed to ship goods to China for sale there. On the other hand, there would be for the time being an artificial stimulus to export from China, and any markets which were in competition with the Chinese exports would be also interfered with. I have not clearly in mind exactly how far Indian interests are in either of those positions. I know they are to a certain extent, but I am not conversant with the precise figures, which no doubt you have from other sources.

12,961 *You suggest that they might be forced to move towards gold? It has been put to us in evidence that China is really incapable of moving in any direction under present conditions.* That sounds to me very likely, but here one is looking forward over a period of ten years. In former days before the War when China was in a more settled condition, there was a great deal of talk of moving towards gold, and they had Commissions of Enquiry similar to this one. Though I should imagine it is true at the moment that China would be incapable of any change, you have to remember that silver does not circulate in China by edict, but by custom. The ordinary private life of China goes on amazingly unaffected by political events. It is impossible for me to predict in what way a move of this sort, once it had got going, might influence the opinion of the ordinary merchant in China. It would certainly influence it to this extent, that he would be less willing to keep stocks of silver on hand. Like everybody else, he would dislike holding a depreciating store of value, so that you might have a tendency for rich men in China to move over towards keeping their reserve in some other form than silver even if the Government was quite incapable legislatively of taking such a move.

12,962 *That would result in what I might call a demand for commercial gold in China?* It might be gold. They might be more anxious to keep their money in the banks on a gold deposit basis. I do not know what form it would take.

12,963 *If it took the form of gold, undoubtedly the circumstances would have to be taken into consideration as to how far it would affect the situation as regards the world gold market?* I should think it would. I think one can be sure that the Chinese business men, who are very shrewd and by no means removed from general knowledge on these matters, would not be anxious to hold a depreciating store of value. So that the ultimate reaction of the relative values of gold and silver of a move of this sort on the part of India, if the world took it seriously, could hardly be exaggerated. As I say, I lay much more stress on this side of the matter than on the purely gold side.

12,964 *In contemplating that for several years India would be meeting her own normal demand for silver in the way of the rupee, were you considering the suggested possibility of an import duty on silver?* I was not clear what form it would take, but was assuming that in some way or the other the Indian Government, being a seller of silver, would reserve the local markets for its own demand. It might be by selling silver a little cheaper than it could be imported, or it might put an import duty on silver—I think that the latter course would have a great deal in its favour. But I do not base my argument necessarily upon such a course.

12,965 *Would the import duty serve to protect the value of the Indian holdings of silver against the otherwise possibly inevitable decline to which you referred?* Quite possibly, if it was a very heavy duty it would no doubt protect them to a considerable extent. But there has always been a considerable export of silver from India over the land frontiers, and if people who were accustomed to do that trade were finding that the value of silver in the outside world was very much below that of the Indian silver it would probably affect confidence in the value of silver in India itself. In the case of an article like silver which is largely useless, and is kept as a store of value and not for use, the influence of opinion on its value is of an order of importance quite different from what it is in the case of something which is consumed year by year.

12,966 *It has been suggested to us in the evidence that the desire for silver is so strong, and the habit of using silver as a store and for ornament is so inveterate, that the cheaper silver is the more it will be bought; and it does not matter how far it falls in that case. Does that seem to you to be a circumstance which should be taken into consideration?* I think that is one of the hoary old maxims about currency affairs which are all false. It is always said that people are very conservative in matters of money, and will never adapt themselves to a new situation. All experience, in my opinion, shows to the contrary. It is most astonishing to see the way in which the public will rapidly adapt themselves to a new situation in currency matters. One example which always struck me, because it was always quoted in advance to the contrary, was that of Egypt. Egypt was always represented as the one country which would never handle anything but hard metal; in fact there was no country in which paper currency was introduced more easily during the War period.

12,967 *Although the public may be uninstructed in India, you have a large professional class of extremely intelligent dealers and brokers?* No one is uninstructed in that sort of matter.

12,968 *Not even the Indian ryot?* I should doubt it.

12,969 *You say all the silver interests of the world would be up in arms, but I gather one must add to that, in view of your previous analysis, in common interest to the people as well?* I include those as silver interests.

12,970 *Would that have special relation to the reception of any proposals in the United States?* Yes.

12,971 *You have already mentioned in the course of a previous reply that that is a matter to be taken into serious consideration?* Yes.

12,972 *Would you explain that and tell us what you think about that matter, as to what the view of the United States would be on the subject?* I think great play would be made in the United States with the history of the Pittman silver. It would be pointed out that when India was in difficulties in this matter, the producers in America were prevented from obtaining profits they might have obtained, and the American Government behaved with extreme handsomeness towards India. In view of that, a move tending towards the depreciation of silver would be regarded by American opinion as something which India was certainly entitled to do, but not something for which it was entitled to invite American assistance. In the present state of opinion in America I am sure there would be a difficulty in raising a loan—which would not anyhow, be particularly attractive to America from the Americans' selfish standpoint—for the express purpose of making difficulties for two of America's leading products.

12,973 *To put it baldly, though the gold interests in the United States might see no objection, the silver copper, and lead interests would have a very strong objection?* Yes; moreover for the gold interests the project would be a matter of indifference, because unless it is going to increase materially the value of gold, it does not do them any good and, as I have explained, I see no reason why it should materially increase the value of gold.

12,974 *The fourth disadvantage to which you referrred is the expense or financial cost to India.* What it would cost India depends upon the price she realises for her silver, and the price at which she sells out her sterling securities or is able to borrow. Taking the simple question of silver, if I am right in supposing that the release of the silver in 103,000,000 pounds' worth of rupees might halve the price of silver, I calculate very roughly that the gold required would cost three times the value of the silver released; that is to say, the changeover would cost India somewhere about £67,000,000 in terms of real resources. If we suppose that India has £67,000,000 of real resources to play with, can one easily conceive a more useless way of using it? Are there not, in the opinion of everybody, a hundred better ways of employing such a sum? The proposition, therefore, impresses me as being a plan to expend some £67,000,000 in destroying the purchasing power of the favourite store of value of the mass of the population. Such a step, with all its risks and unforseeable consequences, strikes me as very foolish indeed, and perhaps dangerous—sufficiently foolish and dangerous to justify the Government of India in turning it down. I think it would show want of courage on the part of the British advisers to accept a proposal contrary to Indian interests for fear of being supposed to refuse out of regard for British interests. We have the curious position that probably hardly any Englishman conscientiously believes that this scheme is in India's interests, but a good many, from praise-worthy motives, are prepared to support it out of deference to what they believe to be misguided Indian opinion. The danger is not that British opinion will be unreasonably allowed to ignore Indian opinion. The danger is that misguided Indian opinion will be allowed to have too great a weight. Of course, it is possible, and it is not improbable that the attempt to put gold into circulation in India would prove a fiasco, so that the gold currency would be introduced normally as a gesture without having important practical consequences; but it would not be right to gamble on that probability just in order to make a gesture.

12,975 *As regards that last point, would it be possible to announce such a policy without at any rate some of these reactions on the silver market to which you have already referred?* No, I think that is true. I think that even the announcement would produce some of the consequences. But if in fact the new scheme did not come into operation to any great extent, those consequences would work themselves out before long.

12,976 *No important expense would be incurred, as you suggest, if this scheme were to prove a fiasco?* No.

12,977 *The only expense incurred, I imagine, would be if credits had been established beforehand, which would cost something?* Yes. But it seems to me it would be rather a strange policy to introduce a scheme of this kind in the hope that it would prove a fiasco.

12,978 *Casting back for a moment to your figure of £67,000,000, perhaps it is rather a question of mechanism and detail, but could you explain to us in what form that expense would come home to roost on the Indian taxpayer?* It would come home to roost in that he would not receive the interest on the sterling securities now held if he sold them; and he would have in some shape or form to pay interest on any loan which was raised.

12,979 *What in your view is the general ideal to set before oneself in an attempted solution of any problems of Indian currency?* Well, I should like to say in conclusion that stability of internal prices in India is, in my opinion, much more important than stability of foreign exchange, though I agree that great instability of the exchange is in itself a disadvantage. I attach very little importance to a legislative enactment fixing the rupee at 1s. 6d. In so far as the stability of foreign exchange is important, while there is not much to choose between a gold standard with gold circulating and a gold exchange standard, some advantage lies with the gold exchange standard. Some sales from time to time of sterling securities by the Government of India in order to adjust the exchange position can be effected with less disturbance to the internal situation than the withdrawal or the pumping in of the equivalent quantity of gold. Above all, the gold exchange standard, whilst it is open to most of the objections against a pure gold standard, does at any rate secure most of the advantages, such as they are, as economically as possible, and without a waste of resources.

12,980 *May I ask you a question on that, before passing on? Would you describe what are the principal advantages which can be gained by the exchange standard as well as by a gold standard with gold currency?* The linking up of India with the prevailing standards of the outside world, and the prestige attaching to a currency which is interchangeable in terms of gold.

12,981 *I am afraid I interrupted you just now?* I was going to say that, if my advice were asked, I should advise the Royal Commission to do nothing whatever. I think that the present situation in India is the best possible obtainable at the moment. That is to say, there is for practical purposes reasonable stability of the exchanges, and India maintains her freedom in the event of future happenings rendering any alternative course more desirable. I think that the present moment is a bad moment for making a change, and that almost any positive course recommended now is likely to be bad. We are at the moment in a state of reaction on currency matters, not at all to be unexpected after the debauches of the War and post-war period. The world has seen the disadvantages and the abuses of unregulated currencies, and it is trying to seek salvation in conservatism, in going back, not in my opinion to the reality, but to the appearance of what existed in pre-war days. It is not impossible that out of this something wise may be evolved, but it is going to be very difficult. We are not at the end of currency discussions, but at the beginning of them. The future currency of the world is going to be determined not by what has happened in the last two or three years, but by what is going to happen in the next 10 years. It is impossible to say what the experience of the countries which are going over to the gold standard is going to be. I think that India will be well advised to hold her hand until some experience has been gained. At present, in the event of serious fluctuation in the value of gold, either upwards or downwards, India is free to avoid the disadvantages of that fluctuation just as she avoided a part of it during the boom and the slump of 1920 and the subsequent years.

12,982 *She avoided them by allowing a change in exchange to a greater extent?* Yes. In my opinion India should pursue her present course—that is as long as nothing special happens in the outside world—of maintaining practical stability in the neighbourhood of 1s. 6d.; of in any event not allowing any sudden change from 1s. 6d.; but in the event of gold becoming unstable in the outside world—and no one can say it will not—of maintaining legislative freedom to adjust her exchange to the event in the outside world, and so preserving the stability of her internal prices.

12,983 *The present state of affairs has been strongly criticised before us on the ground that it allows all matters of currency policy to be entirely in the arbitrary discretion of the currency authorities—at present the Government of India and the Secretary of State in Council?* If you include in the term 'authorities', whatever central bank authority is in control of India, I should say that would always be the case. The notion that gold standards work by themselves without interference by the authorities is a myth.

12,984 *It is said that by adopting some regularised form, either of gold standard or gold exchange standard, the system can be made to work automatically, and less at the discretion of authority than at present?* The exercise of authority would be more concealed; but I think the course of affairs will still be governed by the policy of the Secretary of State in buying and selling bills, and by the policy of the banking authority in the matter of its rate of discount, and its willingness to increase or diminish the basis of credit.

12,985 *Supposing that a currency system is adopted under which the currency authority accepted the obligation to buy and sell some means of international payment at a fixed price, would the Secretary of State's operations still continue to affect the matter?* I cannot see that the essential situation would be any different from what it was in the years immediately preceding the War, when the Secretary of State, or rather the Government of India, was under a legal liability one way to maintain fixity, and had a fairly binding practice in the other direction also.

12,986 *It is said that there was a practice, but it was by no means binding; and that if the legal liability is made to pull both ways, it will largely reduce the opportunity for the exercise of discretion by the currency authority. That would be so, I imagine, would it not, although it would still leave the element of management which is contained in the operations of the banking authority?* Yes, I think it somewhat reduces it. Supposing it is held that the most important thing about currency is that no element of human purpose or contrivance should enter into it, I think this does somewhat diminish the element of human purpose and contrivance; but in my opinion it would be just as foolish to try and get rid of purpose or contrivance as it would be in such a matter as how much land should be ploughed for wheat in a year. It is just as silly to say you will have your currency governed by blind force as to say you will have the amount of your harvest governed by blind force.

12,987 *In considering that general proposition, do you think that any special consideration should be given to the circumstances of the history of Indian currency, and—what is no doubt the fact—that some of the circumstances of the history of Indian currency, have produced a sort of special lack of confidence in currency regulation?* I should have said precisely the other way. India has had a considerable experience of regulation; and while criticism has been levied against the responsible organ of the Indian Government, just as against every other organ of the Indian Government, in fact India has done extremely well. The currency history of India for the last 15 years or so is more favourable than that of any other country in the world. India has actually had experience of these things being done without anything very dreadful occurring, but quite the contrary.

12,988 *Would the opinion you have just expressed affect the question of the possibility of entrusting larger powers in the control of Indian currency to a central bank?* I have always been very much in favour of that. I wrote a memorandum on a central bank for India for the Chamberlain Commission, and the views I expressed there I still maintain.[6]

12,989 *Then I imagine that one, as it were, has co-ordinated those two opinions by saying that you would continue the present system, but introduce a central bank to manage the present system in place of the Government of India?* Of course, since I wrote that memorandum a great deal has been done in that direction. India has not gone the whole way; she has embarked on a

[6] *JMK*, vol. xv, pp. 151–211.

path that is rapidly leading the whole way; but I imagine that the biggest thing not done is the handing over of the paper currency reserve to the bank.

12,990 *Such a measure as handing over the paper currency reserve to the bank would, I imagine, be quite consistent with the general views you have expressed as to the continuation of the present position as regards control of Indian currency?* Yes. When I said that I wanted the present state of affairs to continue, I was not meaning in all these details of internal organisation.

12,991 *Now as to the gold standard reserve, would the unification of the gold standard reserve and the paper currency reserve under the control of a central bank be consistent with your general opinion?* If you have a coin of any sort circulating in the country, you have to maintain a reserve for meeting expansions in the demand for the currency inside the country itself. The rupee portion of the paper currency reserve is at present held for that purpose. If gold were to circulate in India, you would have to hold a gold reserve also with that object in view. If, however, your actual circulation is composed of notes or tokens, you need your reserves entirely for external purposes, for meeting the fluctuations in your balance of trade which could not be redressed otherwise except by rather drastic measures. The policy governing your reserve ought to be different according as you are holding your reserve to meet the internal drain or the external drain. In my opinion the virtue of the Indian system as it was developed by Sir Lionel Abrahams was that those two purposes were kept more distinct than in any other country. They were not kept entirely distinct, because the sterling resources in the paper currency reserve were also part of India's precaution against an external drain. I think that more recently the distinction between the purposes of the two reserves has been further blurred; and if everyone's mind was perfectly clear there might be advantages in consolidating the two reserves into one. But so long as people are inclined to confuse the reserve which you keep for the internal with that which you keep for the external drain, I think there are advantages in the Indian system of having different names for the two; or, at any rate, for parts of the two. A great deal of rubbish is talked about reserves in England, because historically our reserve was held to an important extent for the internal drain, whereas now it is kept almost entirely for the external drain. We have not, as India has, different names for the two. The result is that a great deal of argument which would be quite sound if we were holding the reserve for the internal drain is still alleged as sound when we no longer keep our reserve for that purpose. In England we suffer because historically our reserve has been held to an important extent as a precaution against the internal drain. India's double reserve helps her in that way.

12,992 *If the maintenance of a double reserve has these consequences, that it makes either or both less efficient for fulfilling the purposes for which it is intended, then I suppose it would be rather a heavy sacrifice to clarity of ideas to maintain the separation?* Yes; if that was so.

12,993 *In your opinion might that be so or not?* I do not think it has been so.

12,994 *The organising of the reserve in a single or a double form?* I do not think it has had any bad consequences so far.

12,995 *Does not it necessitate keeping a larger reserve in both, for instance?* I do not see why it should.

12,996 *Anyhow, the minimum which is necessary?* I have the impression, as I have said, that the management of these two reserves has been more blurred in post-war days than it was in the pre-war days. At the date when I was more closely connected with Indian currency affairs than I am now I think the distinctive purposes of the reserves were quite clearly kept in mind, and the reserves were held at appropriate figures having regard to those considerations.

12,997 *You see no objection to the unification as long as the currency authority is sufficiently instructed, as it were, in the elements of the science which he has to work as to realise the purposes that this reserve is to serve?* Granted that assumption, I see no great disadvantage; but on the other hand, I do not see any very great advantage. There is a very strong tradition for allowing a freer hand for that part of your reserve which is not called the currency reserve. The essence of all reserves is that you should have a free hand with them. I fear that if you were to transfer the resources of the gold standard reserve into the paper currency reserve you probably would not have such a free hand to use them in an emergency as you have now. The gold standard reserve is absolutely free. If you put it into the paper currency reserve you quite likely tie it up in the same way as the latter.

12,998 *That would rather depend, would not it, upon the legal formula as regards the relation between reserve and circulation? The disadvantage would be that you had not machinery of sufficient elasticity to permit you to use the reserve?* But I am afraid no one but myself has ever proposed a formula which would be sufficiently elastic. In my opinion, there should be no legal proportion whatever, so that the whole of the currency in your reserves may be available. You can get rid of the legal proportion as soon as the internal drain is not a danger; for the only remaining purpose of the legal proportion is to render some part of your reserve useless.

12,999 *What is your opinion in this connection of the method, which is typically that of the Reichsbank, I think, of permitting reduction of reserves subject to tax?* I think it is better than nothing, but I always regard that as a rather humbugging contrivance, because the surplus profits of state banks

495

nearly always go to the government, and it does not matter two straws to the authorities of the Reichsbank whether they do pay this fine or not. It generally comes out of the government, which is entitled to a share of the surplus profits. It is a contrivance for moving a little in my direction while keeping up the appearance of the old formulæ. The proportionate reserve, or fiduciary reserve, and all these devices were invented when you were keeping your reserve to an important extent against the internal drain; so that when your gold was moving out your need for currency in other forms would be automatically contracted to a certain extent, and the legal proportion enabled to prevent the bank from counteracting that by re-issue. When you are not holding your reserve for the internal drain but for the external drain, the situation is entirely different, and this new situation has not been very profoundly examined from that point of view. I fear, therefore, in the present state of opinion that if you imprison in the paper currency reserve the resources that India is holding for external purposes they will be likely to come up against some of these rubrics.

13,000 *Is not that difficulty adequately, if not somewhat cumbrously, met by provisions for suspending the legal basis of the reserve in times of special emergency?* Provided it is understood that you always break your rules whenever you want to, I agree that there is less objection to them.

13,001 *That is the substance of the matter?* On the other hand, there is no great advantage.

13002 (SIR PURSHOTAMDAS THAKURDAS) *Can you tell me what you think is the ideal system of currency for India in the circumstances in which you know India is at present?* I think a system like the present in which stability of the exchange is aimed at in normal circumstances, but in which India is free to depart from the present level of exchange if it is in the interests of the internal stability of prices for her to do so. I would not have her allow the question of the rate of exchange to overbear every other object, but I think it is important that she should maintain the liberty to have a different exchange from the present one if the maintenance of the present exchange would cause internal prices either to rise or fall to a marked extent.

13,003 *Then I understand that with regard to the return that the cultivator should get for his crop in rupees which you would insure for a period of years—say five years—you would regulate sterling exchange in such a manner that the cultivator would continue to get the same return in rupees and nothing substantially more nor less?* Yes; I should do that, except that I should take the standard value of money on a rather broader basis than crops. Crops would be a great part, but I would have it rather broader. Also I would not do anything to counteract minor changes, and it would be impossible for me to do anything to counteract the changes due to the harvest. That you have implied in suggesting a five years' period.

13,004 *I put a five years' period because you named a five years' period before the Babington-Smith Committee [JMK, vol. xv, p. 293]. That is why I named it.* I had forgotten I had named that period.

13,005 *For that purpose, in order to think it out and to avoid any injustice to any of the major interests concerned, it would be necessary to have a complete set of figures representing the minimum cost of living, and the economic cost of growing certain major crops which would leave a fair margin to the cultivator— would not it be necessary to do that?* If it was done in a very precise way, such as has been proposed for certain other countries, I agree you would have to have a broader basis of statistics; but there are all kinds of degrees possible in this. I think India is extremely well placed and better placed than any other country for aiming at the same sort of objects in a much less precise way and with a much broader brush; that is to say, not aiming at counteracting small movements or following small movements at all. To keep the stability of the exchange as a normal objective, India is able to do without any disturbance of her existing situation, whilst permitting a fluctuation of the exchange in the event of the value of gold suffering a major change.

13,006 *You would have to reckon with fluctuations in world prices which would be of course outside the control of the Indian currency system. Take only one article in which India is substantially interested, namely, cotton. Cotton has this year gone down in America. I understand (you may take it from me) that cotton has dropped in India to the extent of 50 rupees a bale?* Yes.

13,007 *Would it not be necessary to ascertain what should be the minimum price to be paid to the cultivator in order that you may not injure his legitimate interests in a substantial manner?* I should not be influenced by the prices of one crop, even if it was as important as cotton. If the same thing was happening all round, then I should be prepared to take action; but I think it is very important that you should not take action in the interests of a particular group of cultivators.

13,008 *Take cotton, or jute, or seeds, or rice. Those are four of the important crops. Take any one of them or altogether. In order that the growers of these should not suffer, and they form the major part of those concerned whose interests should be watched, do not you think that we ought to have some basis before we try to regulate exchange by internal price levels?* I think that if that policy were to be adopted it would want going into in a good deal of detail. I quite agree to that. You would have to think out quite clearly what were the main indicators of price fluctuation which for India were important. I was only meaning to say at this stage that I do not think that by the adoption of this policy you need settle anything very precisely. I should not in the case of India at the present stage of things, aim at avoiding anything except major price changes which were quite obvious to everybody—there would be no doubt that the value of money had gone up or down, as the case might be.

13,009 *What was in your mind when you said 'major price changes' which would be obvious to everybody?* I think if the index prices that are now compiled—no doubt they are rather rough index prices—had moved 10 per cent, the Government of India ought to consider whether the exchange might not be allowed to fluctuate a halfpenny or a penny; but, even so, I would do it gradually.

13,010 *Would you take the present index number as a fair basis?* No; if I was doing anything precise I would modify my index number, but I think that the latest Indian index numbers are not bad.

13,011 *You would be prepared to recommend that they should be relied upon for a start. Is that what I understand?* I think they are a fairly satisfactory guide to major movements.

13,012 *In America they have got separate index number for major crops which are exported?* Yes; in America they have index numbers which are very much more elaborate than in any other country, and which I think are much superior. There are two reasons for that. In the first place, the Bureau of Labour index number is elaborately weighted according to the importance of the different articles. America has a census of production and consumption which is sufficiently precise to enable pretty accurate weights to be given. In most countries it is difficult to give accurate weights because one does not know enough. The second reason is that the manufacturers in America are much more willing to make returns to the Government, so that America has pretty satisfactory numbers for certain manufactured and semi-manufactured goods; whereas, in most countries the index numbers are faulty because it is practically impossible to take enough account of the prices of manufactured and semi-manufactured goods.

13,013 *Would you agree that India is far, far behind America in this matter? Index numbers in India compared to those of the nature which you have just mentioned as existing in America, are of a comparatively crude nature?* Yes; but on the other hand, India being a simpler country in its organisation you can go much further, whilst having nothing but the prices of the main commodities, than you can in America.

13,014 *Did I understand you to say India being a simpler country in its organisation?* Yet; the number of articles which really matter are much fewer in number.

13,015 *The major crops being fewer is what you have in mind?* The consumption of manufactured articles in great variety of shapes and forms being a less important part of the consumption. A mere food index in India would go a long way, whereas a mere food index in the United States is very inadequate. I am simply illustrating what I am saying, that you do not need such complication as they need.

13,016 *You really think, therefore, that the present index numbers and other figures available in India are fair guides and you would utilise them for the purpose of the ideal that you have named?* I think they can, and ought to be, improved; but I am prepared to trust them in a general way as indicators of major movements.

13,017 *Would you take the present basis as being a basis showing a fair return to everybody concerned, either in agriculture or in manufacture? Would you take the present basis of index numbers as the basis which should be maintained, or would you put it up or lower it?* If one is going into it in as much detail as that, you ought to have specified to me which index number you are referring to.

13,018 *Take the index number of cereals, which is round about 130 as compared with 100 pre-war?* I would not take the index number which was only an index number of cereals.

13,019 *What would you take as the basis?* I would take broader index numbers which are compiled. My chief practical difficulty would be, I think, in knowing what to do when the index numbers for different parts of India moved differently. My information is—I do not know that I can substantiate it today—that whilst for any precise scientific regulation where movements of a small number of per cent mattered, the Indian statistics are inadequate; yet if you merely need a general indication to the authorities as to whether prices on the whole are moving seriously up or seriously down, for such purposes they are adequate.

13,020 *Up to what point would you allow fluctuations before [the] Government interferes by regulation of exchange to control further fluctuations?* My difficulty in answering that question is this. I am not quite sure whether I am being examined on what I proposed in my evidence-in-chief, namely, an intermediate system for India in which this sort of general aim was blended with some of the general aims which have prevailed in the past.

13,021 *You yourself said a scientific system for India is neither feasible, nor is the material for it available. Therefore I should have thought that we were discussing the other one which you thought was both feasible and immediately available to put in practice?* If that is clear, then I can answer.

13,022 *I took it from your earlier answer that you strike out the scientific basis as not being feasible; but there is a rough and ready one which you think is good enough to allow the Government to go ahead on?* Yes. I was not suggesting in my evidence-in-chief that you should have what sometimes has been called the tabular system for India—that is to say, in which it should be the duty of the Government to keep a composite index number within a certain range of fluctuation. I was not suggesting that. I was suggesting something much more like what it seems to me has happened in recent years;

499

that is to say, so long as there are no important movements in the outside world, exchange stability is regarded; but when there is an important movement in the outside world, the stability of internal prices is allowed to have some influence. For that purpose I think the Indian index numbers as currently compiled are an adequate guide.

13,023 *I also asked if you would tell me at what point Government should adjust the exchange?* Well, I hesitated in answering that, first, because I wanted to be clear on this point. I have a further ground for hesitation, that if you are dealing with a system where the Government is not bound legislatively to keep to a certain figure, I think it would depend very much upon the causes of the fluctuations—the general circumstances; and in particular, whether the change was one which had originated in India, or whether it was one which had originated outside India. If it was one which had originated in India I should be more chary in interfering with it. I should think it more likely that it had sound foundations. But if it was a change which had originated in the outside world, if something that had happened in New York and London was reacting on Indian prices in a way which was quite unnecessary from the internal Indian point of view, then I should be much more ready to meet that by allowing the exchange to fluctuate a penny or so than if it was a case arising in the first set of circumstances. I would not like to say 5 per cent or 10 per cent, because I think that the controlling authority should have regard to the attendant circumstances.

13,024 *It may lead to this, may it not? Supposing that there was a shortage of wheat in the world, and you found that the prices of wheat in the world market were soaring, the Government of India would regulate wheat prices locally by manipulating the exchange?* I should be against that.

13,025 *You would be against that?* Yes.

13,026 *You would allow the wheat crop in India to share the boom prices in the world market?* If I thought it more desirable that it should not I should deal with an individual thing like that by an export duty.

13,027 *You would put on an export duty so that local prices should be regulated by that?* If the movement was of such magnitude that I thought it would be disastrous for certain districts of India, I would put on an export duty such as many countries have done. I would not introduce currency regulation for this purpose. What I should introduce currency regulation for would be something of a general kind in the outside world not due to a particular harvest of a particular crop, but due to a general tendency of prices to go up or down to an important extent. For example, 1920 is a typical sort of case. If prices in the outside world were booming, as they were in 1919 and 1920, or slumping as they were in 1921 and 1922, I should have thought that an indication that the Indian exchange ought not to be kept steady. If, in such circumstances of the outside world, the stability of exchange was to be put first, that would bring about fluctuations of internal prices which would be contrary to Indian interests.

13,028 *Any such regulation would necessitate expert knowledge about various world crops and world markets? It could not be done by the officials that you referred to in your memorandum regarding the state bank before the Chamberlain Commission?* I think the kind of thing that I am contemplating would not require more knowledge than you would expect them to have. One has to remember that all this sort of matter is much more discussed and written about than it used to be. In fact, the danger will be that the officials of the state bank will spend too much time reading the enormous mass of weekly and monthly literature on these matters than that they will read too little.

13,029 *Whom would you entrust with this work of watching and regulating, so as to know when to act?* Well, I think that the ideal arrangement is a central bank, which is in close touch with the Finance Department of the Government.

13,030 *You think the commercial community would be able to anticipate the regulation with intelligence, or would it come as a surprise to them?* You can answer that question better than I can.

13,031 *How do you mean?* I think you have more experience of the people in question.

13,032 *Would that be a system capable of being followed by the ordinary public, or would it not be known to them only when notified publicly as the decisions of persons in charge?* I think it would appear in this sort of way—that there was a severe boom or slump in the outside world, and that as a consequence of this the authorities in charge of the exchange were allowing the level of the rupee to act as a brake against the reaction of those outside forces on India. I think that those major movements such as I am now considering are things which are extremely well appreciated by a wide opinion now-a-days. I think the situation is different from what it would have been even ten years ago.

13,033 *So far as the currency in India is concerned, you recommend no changes; you would keep on silver rupees and paper currency notes as at present?* Yes.

13,034 *You think that would be the ideal system for India, or would you recommend any change; are you aiming at any other ideal?* No; I do not think so. I think that the further popularisation of the note is desirable, but that seems to be going on very well. I should have nothing in particular to suggest about that. The progress since the days when we first used to study these matters has been almost beyond knowledge.

13,035 *The progress seems to be satisfactory as far as it goes?* Yes.

13,036 *You said you did not believe that gold currency would lead to a greater popularity of paper currency?* I said I did not see why it should.

13,037 *That would perhaps depend upon the psychology of the people?* Yes.

13,038 *And also, to a certain extent, upon how the people would take to notes after gold currency is available as far as inspiring greater confidence is concerned, would not it?* You are suggesting that if the note was convertible in terms of gold that would increase confidence in the note?

13,039 *That is it. If people feel that they have only to go round to the Treasury or bank whenever they want any gold coin it has been repeatedly said to us that it would considerably increase the confidence of the people in the paper currency.* That is conceivable. I am not as much up-to-date in these matters as I used to be. In former times when circles existed it used to be held that doubt about the convertibility of the note into rupees, as it was then, did stand in the way of its popularity. My impression was that by now any doubts about convertibility had really been dissipated, and that was no longer a matter greatly affecting the circulation of the notes in India; but it is not a matter on which I can speak with any authority.

13,040 *Would you be disposed to challenge Indian opinion if it was fairly unanimous on this point?* I should, on the ground that I know they are in favour of the change for other reasons. I should therefore consider them biased on the matter.

13,041 *Will you tell me what those other reasons are which you have in your mind?* I should like to try to elucidate them, but it is difficult. I think Indian opinion has a feeling that a gold currency is, so to speak, the smartest sort of currency; it is the most *chic* thing, and that India is, by some malicious contrivance, being deprived of this outfit.

13,042 *I wonder if you have seen that emanating anywhere from responsible quarters in India, or is it your impression from a general reading of the newspapers?* I have read a great many pamphlets and memoranda and books on this matter, and that is the impression which that reading makes on me.

13,043 *With reference to silver, India will not need for some years to come silver for the coinage of rupees, and that would have a depressing effect on the silver markets of the world. Is not that so?* Yes.

13,044 *I do not suppose that anybody will contend that India should continue to buy silver in order to help the American market?* I do not contend that.

13,045 *Suppose the people in India continue to take paper currency freely within the next five or seven years. The Government at present have a large number of rupees in the Treasury. There are 90 crores there. Supposing another 60 crores come in during the next five years. What would you recommend the Government to do? Would it be necessary for them to part with some of this silver which would be lying idle in the Treasury?* Yes. I quite agree with the suggestion contained in the question. I think, quite apart from any proposals which this Commission may make, the position of silver is precarious. Any important change of habit on the part of India would upset silver. It is just because it has so few natural supports at the moment, that I gave the evidence I did earlier this morning.

13,046 *I only wanted to ask you what you would then recommend the Government of India to do? Would you then say that they must keep the silver and not dispose of it, as perhaps they would do in the ordinary course when they were convinced that so much silver was not necessary?* It is difficult to express a definite opinion on these hypothetical circumstances. I have expressed the opinion that India has a great interest in the stability of silver. I adhere to that, but I can quite conceive circumstances arising in which silver would really be past saving, and if that were so I should deprecate the Government of India wasting resources in trying to achieve a probably unattainable stability for the metal—silver.

13,047 *What would happen at that time to the silver that they had? Would not they have to sell it?* I should have thought that it is not likely there would be any great occasion for selling silver unless there was a change of habit as regards the hoarding of it in India. Leaving that out of account, I do not see why anything should happen which should cause the Government of India to melt a great deal. You are suggesting that the progress of the use of notes might be so great that less rupees would be required in circulation. Unless that happened very rapidly, the natural increase and the natural wastage and so forth would, I should have thought, absorb the rupees that were being released by the increased use of notes. What you are suggesting is that conceivably, but not probably, the Government of India would be in the position of wanting to sell silver on an important scale.

13,048 *You say it is conceivable. Supposing it did, in fact, happen within the next seven years. Do you not think the Government would be quite justified in selling silver then?* Certainly.

13,049 *Would you, then, give any weight to the interests of America or of any other country?* I should give no weight to the interests of America in such circumstances—not the slightest; but I should still think, if I had any influence with the Government of India, that they ought to pay some regard to the stability of the metal from their own point of view. I do not suggest that, in any circumstances, India should pay the slightest attention to American opinion, unless they are wanting to borrow in America. There is no other reason.

13,050 *There has been a suggestion made before this Commission that the question of transferring the note issue to the Imperial Bank or to a central bank should be considered. Do you still hold the views which you put forward before the Chamberlain Commission regarding the formation of a state bank?* Yes, I still hold those views.

13,051 *I see you said there, on page 60 of the Report of the Chamberlain Commission: 'First, as regards the relation of the Bank to the Government. The creation of such a bank as is here proposed certainly increases in a sense the responsibilities of Government.'*[7] *Do you think such a central bank would also increase the responsibilities of Government?* In this passage here I am distinguishing between two senses of responsibility, and I am saying that in a sense it increases the responsibility of Government, but that in another sense it does not. I think I still agree with it so far as I still remember what is here.

13,052 *That is brought out further on page 61, where, in the last paragraph but one you say: 'The choice lies between a good deal of responsibility* without *thoroughly satisfactory machinery for the discharge of it; and a little more responsibility* with *such a machinery'?*[8] I think that fairly represents my view.

13,053 *And you confirm that today?* Yes.

13,054 *You would be opposed then, to any suggestion that the central bank should work absolutely without any sort of direction from the Finance Department?* I think it is very difficult. It is not desirable. The Indian Finance Department is such a very big factor in the situation in their operations that it would be an inefficient way of conducting the bank not to be in very close touch with them, and if you are in very close touch with them it is impossible that they should not be taking a certain responsibility. That had better be faced at the outset.

13,055 *It has been pointed out that central banks in important European countries have very little, if any, government control. Do you think there are sound reasons for having a different system in India?* To which of the countries are you referring?

13,056 *In many important countries, we were told, the central bank is more or less independent of the government?* It all depends whether you mean formally or informally.

13,057 *Formally?* You could not have a more extreme case than the Bank of England, which formally is a private company, but that does not in any way represent the facts.

13,058 *And there is a sort of persuasion, and perhaps a spirit of trying to see each other's point of view. The Bank of England, at a certain juncture during the War, did absolutely refuse to issue paper without gold backing, and the Government had to issue their own paper—the Bradbury note?* I do not think that is quite a full history of the matter. I should have said, if we are to take the War period as bearing on it, that it is the Chancellor of the Exchequer who has the last word in the end.

13,059 *The Government may have the last word by issuing their own paper?* Within very wide regions the Government of the day has the last word in the end.

13,060 *What happens if the Bank Directors are opposed to doing it?* The Bank Directors have the power of resigning and making a great public scandal about it in the last resort, but in practice, short of a great public scandal, I should say that it is the Government of the day which has the last word.

13,061 *Do you suggest that what you recommend for an Indian central bank has its counterpart in any country in Europe?* I think we are in a very transitional state in England in which the formal situation is more remote than it used to be from the actual situation. That is also the case in several other countries. There is a struggle going on as to where the equilibrium of power should lie. In the United States the precise relation of the Federal Reserve Board to the United States Treasury is in process of evolution. It is impossible to make an up-to-date exact statement of what it is at any moment.

13,062 *You suggest a Board of three—the Governor, the Deputy Governor, and a representative of the Government, and then you recommend three assessors as representing the Presidency Banks, as they were then?* That is all out of date now.

13,063 *Would you make the Imperial Bank, as it is constituted at present, the central bank, or would you start another bank as the state bank?* I have not clearly before my mind the exact charter of the Imperial Bank, so that I cannot answer that question now. I should require to prepare myself on the point.

13,064 *I only wondered whether you would convert a bank, which is admitted to be a commercial bank into a central bank? Would you entrust a bank which borrows money, and lends money, and opens branches all over the country, and in fact which has the largest number of branches in the whole of India, with the power of note issue?* I think I should be unwise to answer, without preparing myself, questions as to the way in which the Imperial Bank could be developed.

13,065 *Regarding the ratio to be fixed, I think you say in paragraph 9 of your memorandum that you 'attach very little importance to a legislative enactment fixing the rupee at 1s. 6d.'. I daresay you may be aware that at the moment the ratio in the Indian Statute is 2s.?* Yes, I am aware of that.

13,066 *Which is absolutely inoperative, and prevents gold from being tendered to the Government?* Yes. I think that inoperative provision ought to be removed.

13,067 *To that extent, at least it is necessary for the Government to make a change, even though your recommendation of doing nothing may be fully complied with?* Yes, I agree.

13,068 *What is the ratio you would have substituted?* I should substitute no ratio.

13,069 *No ratio at all?* No.

13,070 *At what rate would gold be tendered to Government?* It would be possible for the Government to fix, as I think it used to at one time, a buying rate from time to time, which would be in suitable accordance with the actual exchange of the moment. I would leave the Government to fix its buying price by enactment and not have it tied to a price.

13,071 *By enactment?* By executive order, I mean.

13,072 *The basis for the action to be the regulation of internal prices?* The question of the prices at which they buy and sell gold is exactly the same as the question of the prices at which they fix the exchange. Therefore, if I am in favour of a certain latitude as to the rate of exchange, I am clearly in favour of the same latitude as regards the price of gold.

13,073 (SIR REGINALD MANT) *You said in reply to the Chairman that you thought that in future the demand for gold for monetary purposes would practically be regulated by the supply?* Yes.

13,074 *Do you share the view that in the past prices have been regulated, broadly, by the supply of gold available?* In pre-war days, yes, but with modifications. I think the gold reserves in 1914 would have been much less in relation to prices if the South African gold had not been pouring out since 1900. I think the South African gold did not produce its proportional effect on prices, because the central bank took advantage of the greater ease with which they could get gold to increase their reserves more in proportion than they would have done if it had been more difficult to do so. But I agree that before the War the supply of gold did exercise a dominating influence on the price level. Before the War, however, gold was in circulation in many countries, so that the requirements of gold in circulation had a strong causal nexus, with the level of prices. Now that is no longer so.

13,075 *You do not anticipate any large return of gold to circulation?* No I do not. The one country which is in a position to put gold into circulation without any cost, namely, the United States, does not in practice find that gold is used except in quite limited parts of the country. The greater part of the United States, which is quite free to use gold if they want to do so, do not.

13,076 *If prices can be kept steady by the control of central banks irrespective of the supply of gold, it is equally open to them to raise or lower prices if the supply of gold remains steady?* Within limits. I should not have given the same answer if the amount of gold in question had been ten times as great. All these things are within limits, but those limits are sufficiently wide to allow of the absorption of less than 100 millions of gold. If you are dealing with much larger sums, it is another question.

13,077 *What I am considering is the prospect of the world's prices being practically in the hands of the banks or other authorities which control the volume of currency. According to your view, in the future world prices will practically be managed prices?* I think so.

13,078 *You think they would be managed by some sort of international agreement or international committee?* I should hope so, but I think we are a very long way off that. You can have a state of affairs where the level of prices is dependent upon the action of banks, even although the action of banks is not taken advisedly or in collaboration. I think the dominating influence at present is the Federal Reserve Board in the United States, and the great difficulty in the way of an extension of international co-operation is that it must mean the Federal Reserve Board voluntarily resigning some portion of its present power. The present political conditions in America are such that it would be difficult for it to do that. It is already open to the charge of acting contrary to American interests under international influences. Although I think that charge is completely unfounded, it is the sort of thing to which you have to pay some attention. I believe we could have a great measure of control by an international body of banks at this moment if the Federal Reserve Board was prepared to surrender some part of its present power. I do not see it doing that easily.

13,079 *But looking forward, as other nations come back to a gold standard, presumably the world's reserves of gold will be distributed more widely than they are at present?* I do not know that they need be.

13,080 *You do not think they will be?* Not necessarily. If you had a perfect gold standard you would not need any gold at all. If you had perfect international co-operation it would be unnecessary for anyone to have any gold reserves, and as you tend further and further in that direction the smaller is the part which gold reserves play in the matter. I think it is possible that we shall eventually move to something which we call a gold standard, in which actual gold plays scarcely any part. I personally have been against that particular evolution because I think that the task of paying lip service to gold greatly aggravates the difficulty of the technical problem; but in so far as international co-operation is developed, the attention to gold will be more and more in the nature of lip service, and it will be more and more a matter of indifference as to what gold reserve any given country holds. I think there will be anxiety on the part of countries to save money and to have as little gold as possible rather than to have as much as possible.

13,081 *The regulation of prices will be under some form of international control?* Yes, but I think it will probably be in rather a loose way, such as I have been suggesting in the case of India. Certainly it would be in that form first of all. The tabular standard would come later. In the first instance it would be a control which was aimed at avoiding major movements. It would not be tied to any prices formula.

13,082 *That would be the international position. What I understand you to recommend for India is that she should stand outside it?* I think she should wait and see. None of these things which we have been discussing are really in sight at present. The actual future of the gold standard, I think, is quite uncertain at the moment. If I was in India I should wish to wait, being under no compulsion to make a change, until I saw what happened. We are in very early days at present. It is not a year since this country came on to a gold standard, and I think it is needlessly rash for a country which has its liberty to take a movement at all at this moment.

13,083 *You do not want India to tie herself to world prices at present?* I do not see why she should, no.

13,084 *Later on it would be open to her to come into the international pool, or not?* Yes, and if an international pool was under serious discussion I think India ought to be represented at the meetings and ought to be one of the parties to it, but I think she should go to that meeting with a free hand.

13,085 *With regard to your recommendation that we should practically maintain past practice, I think you modified that to some extent in your reply to Sir Purshotamdas Thakurdas, when you said you would have no legal rate of exchange fixed by statute?* Yes. The old practice was to have a legal rate one way but not the other; that is to say, a legal rate at which gold was accepted, but at no legal rate at which it was paid out.

13,086 *You would not recommend a legal rate both ways?* No. I should prefer to have liberty both ways.

13,087 *Do you contemplate unlimited sales or receipts of gold or gold exchange under the system you recommend? I will just explain that in the past the amount of gold or foreign exchange to be sold in the shape of reverse councils was an arbitrary amount fixed by the Government. It has been suggested to us that in a new system unlimited amounts of foreign exchange should be provided?* I think that they should be provided at the rate that was fixed for the moment. Suppose that the rate was 1s. 6d.: I would supply exchange freely at the appropriate parity with that, but I would maintain the liberty to alter it. I think the system which prevailed after the War of rationing exchange was thoroughly vicious. I am an admirer of the Lionel Abrahams system of pre-war days, in which you tried to work out rather carefully what reserves you required in order to meet the maximum probable fluctuation of India's foreign trade position within a short period, and then used those reserves freely; but I should not make great sacrifices in order to preserve an exact parity of exchange if, for other reasons, I did not think it was worth while.

13,088 *I understand you would have no limit in selling foreign exchange until it became a question of altering the rate?* Yes, and I should be strongly in favour of making any alteration, not catastrophically but by small degrees. If there were indications that there was going to be a severe drain, I should lower my exchange by $\frac{1}{8}$d.

13,089 *You would never inform the public how far you were going to alter it?* No, because I should not know myself. I agree that the objection to that is that you may have bear speculation arising, but I think you must have sufficiently large reserves to be able to look after that. That is so with any arrangement of this sort.

13,090 *Would not it introduce an undesirable element of uncertainty in trade and commerce?* It is undesirable, but I think it is not so undesirable as the uncertainty of prices. I think it is an evil.

13,091 *Dealing with the two reserves, the paper currency reserve and the gold standard reserve, you have said that the former is intended primarily for internal conversion and the other for external purposes?* I said the silver in the paper currency reserve was intended for internal purposes.

13,092 *For internal purposes it is only the silver in the reserve that would be required?* In older days the amount of sterling securities in the paper currency reserve was very trifling. It is the increase in the sterling securities in the paper currency reserve which has slightly blurred the distinction which used to be clearer. Formerly the greater part of the sterling resources were in the gold standard reserve. There was some gold, it is true, in the paper currency reserve which you might hold as serving the other purpose, but the bulk of the paper currency reserve was rupees. Now there is a greater proportion of the paper currency reserves which it might be argued is held for external purposes, so the distinction is not so clear as it used to be.

13,093 *Is it not a fact that the paper currency reserve serves a dual function, in holding silver resources for internal purposes and holding also a considerable amount of gold or sterling resources for external purposes?* Yes. I think now that is so—that part of the paper currency reserve must be reckoned as being a reserve against external drain.

13,094 *The only distinction between the two reserves is that one is maintained for two purposes and the other is maintained for one purpose?* Except that you have this considerable sum of 40 millions sterling in the gold standard reserve which is freely available without any reaction upon anything and which you can use untrammelled by ratios or rules of any sort. I think that is a great advantage. In the use of the second line of your reserve for external purposes, which is in the paper currency reserve, you are more hedged about. Moreover one would hope that it would only be in very exceptional circumstances that the second line would be in question.

13,095 *Which are you calling the first line?* I am calling the gold standard [reserve] the first line, but I may be talking old-fashioned language, because I have noticed a tendency to keep the amount of that absolutely fixed in recent times, and a greater willingness to fluctuate the sterling resources of the paper currency reserve. I think the old-fashioned method is better.

13,096 *In practice the paper currency reserve is used as the first line, and gold standard reserve is kept as an ultimate reserve?* That is so lately. But I doubt whether that would be done if it were a matter of an important movement.

13,097 *You would rather see the gold standard reserve used as the first line?* Yes, and I think it would be used first if the large sums were involved over a short period. I do not think you can argue from recent custom what would happen in more severe circumstances.

13,098 *In the memorandum which you wrote for the Chamberlain Commission you recommended that the paper currency reserve shoud be made over to a bank but that the gold standard reserve should be retained by Government?*[9] Yes. I had forgotten that I recommended that. It depends upon the nature of the responsibility. I think in this Report I was contemplating that the Government would be under legal obligation to maintain exchange at a fixed figure, and I think I recommended this as a consequence of that.

13,099 *It would not quite fit in with your theory that the gold standard reserve should be used as the first line of defence?* Yes, I am of opinion that it would, because I was contemplating in that Report that the legal liability in relation to the currency would remain with the Government.

13,100 *The bank would be merely responsible for maintaining the internal convertibility of the note?* No, I do not think that was my recommendation. I am sorry I have not read this through quite recently. If the Commission wish to know just how much I hold to this, I should have to read it through.

13,101 *I merely wanted to know whether you still hold that, if a central bank were constituted and entrusted with the note issue, the responsibility for maintaining exchange should remain with the Government and not be imposed on the bank?* There are two points I should like to make about that. When I was writing this I was contemplating that there would be a legal value of the rupee in terms of sterling, and that the responsibility would lie on the

[9] *JMK*, vol. xv, pp. 191–2.

Government for preserving that. I was also making in a sense a compromise suggestion, because at that time India was much further from the central bank idea than she is now. There was the complication of the Presidency Banks and so forth. I was in a position of difficulty as to how far it was possible to recommend that the Government should hand over to a body which was still non-existent the responsibility for keeping the law, so to speak. Now there are two changes. I am not recommending that there should be the same legal liability to maintain an exact rate of exchange, and India has progressed much further in the central bank direction, so it is less experimental. Therefore I answer this point with less confidence. What my final answer would be would depend upon the question just how much the Government was concerned in the bank. If an attempt was made to pretend that the central bank was something independent of the Government, I should still be nervous of giving them the whole of the final responsibility for the exchange, but if the central bank was, whilst administratively an independent entity, nevertheless in a sense a full organ of Government, then I should be inclined to centralise the whole thing and to put the whole matter in the hands of the bank. But I could not give a final confident answer unless I had before me the precise proposal as to the relations of the new bank with the Government.

13,102 *If the bank were not entrusted with the responsibility for maintaining exchange there might be some conflict between their discount policy and the exchange policy of the Government, might there not?* I think it would be most important that they should be pursuing an agreed policy, wherever the final responsibility lay. It would be hopeless to have the bank responsible for the discount policy and pursuing a line which was not in accordance with the line of the Treasury in their responsibility for exchange. I agree with that completely.

13,103 *Then there will have to be either complete responsibility or complete control? Either the bank must take over both, or the Government must control the discount policy of the bank?* I think in a sense that is true, but at any rate in English conditions, and I should have thought in Indian conditions, things are not quite so cut and dried in practice, and you can have two bodies which maintain their respective spheres of responsibility and of power and yet necessarily always work together. It is the fundamental question of the relation between any central bank and any Treasury. In a sense in any country it is quite unworkable that the two should be in antagonism. Therefore you might say, as a logical consequence of that, that one must be in subordination to the other, but I hope that is not true in practice, but that you can have two bodies neither of which is subordinate to the other but which must always act in co-operation with one another. It is a dilemma which you get in other spheres of government. My view in this country of the future of regulation would be that the Treasury and the Bank of England would be neither subordinate to the other but would always be pursuing the same policy. That may sound impossible, but I do not think it is.

13,104 *What I am trying to feel my way to is how your argument as to the varying rate of exchange would fit in with the proposals which have been put before us for making over the responsibility of maintaining exchange to a central bank. It would be simple enough to make over that responsbility if we had a legal rate of exchange which the bank would be bound to maintain, but I do not see quite how the future arrangement would work out if the rate of exchange was variable.* You may pretend it is the liability of the bank, but if there is any doubt as to the power of the bank to implement it the Government comes in at once. I think it was always contemplated under the pre-war arrangement that India might be subjected to such a severe strain that she would have to borrow. The moment there is a question of borrowing the credit of the Government comes in. I think the notion that the Government can get rid of responsibility on to the bank, and that avoidance of responsibility can continue not only in good times but in difficult times, is a misapprehension. As soon as any real problem arose the Government would have to be in such relations to the bank again as to make itself responsible, because the bank has no ultimate authority of itself.

13,105 *In any case I suppose Government would retain the responsibility for varying the rate of exchange under your scheme?* Yes. I conceive a central bank not as something which is independent of the Government in the sense in which a Bombay cotton mill is independent of the Government, but as an organ of the Government which has a certain independence of the executive; that is to say, that it is not a subordinate department of the Treasury, but is an organ of the Government on a level of authority with the Treasury. I think there is apt to be a confusion between the Government as a sovereign body getting rid of responsibility, and some particular department of Government like the Finance Department, which at present has responsibility, having less responsibility. I think the change would mean that the Department of Finance woud have less responsibility than it has now, but the Government of India, in a broad sense, would have just the same amount of responsibility as it has now. It is impossible to conceive a sound system in which your central bank was really a private thing and was not subordinate to the sovereign instructions of the Government.

13,106 *I just want to clear up that last point I put to you. In any case the responsibility for varying or altering the rate of exchange must rest with the Government?* It might rest to outward appearance with the bank as an organ

512

of Government, but I should not be able to conceive a situation in which the bank could fluctuate the exchange contrary to the wishes of the supreme authority of the Government.

13,107 *That is much the same thing. The Government must retain responsibility?* It seems to me unthinkable that it should not. I cannot imagine India having a central bank which could say that the exchange should move a penny, when the Viceroy-in-Council was of the opinion that it should not.

13,108 (SIR HENRY STRAKOSCH) *I would refer you to paragraph 4 of your memorandum where you say you do not lay great stress upon the withdrawal of 103 millions sterling from the currency reserves of the world. Would your opinion be unchanged if you also consider that there is needed, especially in more primitive countries, an addition to the currency annually? In that connection I may just say that before the War there was an annual addition to the currency in India of something in the neighbourhood of 20 to 25 crores?* If this figure of 103 millions is in fact too small a figure—if the actual figure is much larger—that would affect me; but I think it can be somewhat larger without affecting me. If you mean that this is a miscalculation, that what India would really require would be a very much larger amount, I would have to reconsider my opinion. I was taking this figure as a good estimate.

13,109 *I do not suggest it is a miscalculation, but I suggest that in addition to the 103 million sterling which will be needed to stock India with a gold currency there will be needed annually an accretion to that currency?* Within the next 10 years?

13,110 *In the past there has been an annual accretion to the currency of India of something in the neighbourhood of 20 crores?* I am not clear whether you are suggesting that India will need for currency purposes more than 103 millions in the first ten years.

13,111 *That is so; I do suggest that.* I should have to reconsider what I have been saying. I have been speaking on the basis of the 103 millions being roughly right.

13,112 *If, as you suggest in a later part of your memorandum, owing to the severe fall in the price of silver a country like China might switch over to the gold standard, that would obviously require a further withdrawal from the gold currency reserves of the world. Would you in that case also be of the view that it would not affect the purchasing power of gold?* I agree that a point comes when you reach a figure so large that it would be difficult to supply it without a change of policy, but I think there is a fairly wide margin. I agree that if you were talking about 500 millions it would be another matter.

13,113 *To go further, you said in your evidence that a withdrawal of that gold need not affect the supply of credit and gold prices. I suppose you would agree—in fact I think you said it—that the reserve needed to assure the external value of a currency is the amount of foreign payments which have to be made on balance at any given time?* After making some allowance for what one can borrow at short notice.

13,114 *That is to say, the gold reserves in a gold standard country have to be big enough to enable a temporary adverse balance of trade to be righted before the orthodox means of contracting the currency have their play?* Except that I should expect countries to hold foreign balances as part of their reserve—at any rate a good many of them—as they do already. The measure of the gold reserve you must keep is what you require to meet short-period fluctuations, after taking account of any foreign balances that you hold, and a conservative estimate of what you can borrow at short notice.

13,115 *You would also agree that the greater the volume of trade of a country the greater the possible temporary adverse balance of payment?* Except there are many other factors. The variability of Indian exports as compared with British exports is greater than in proportion to their absolute amount.

13,116 *What would be the psychological effect of reducing the gold balances held? If the view is held that the gold reserve should be big enough to right a temporary adverse balance of payments, then it would be an easy matter to induce the currency authorities in the gold standard countries to reduce their gold security reserves as you suggest?* I think that the danger of the central banks pursuing what I should regard as a misguided policy, and thereby allowing a withdrawal of gold for India to have more effect than it need, is a very real one.

13,117 *But human nature being what it is, would they not feel extremely uneasy if they saw their reserves dwindle to a point where they felt that their adverse balance of payments could not be met? Is not that a factor which would have to be taken into account?* I confess that the personalities of the central banks of the world do alarm me.

13,118 *It is not only the central banks but the general public. Have not the general public a great deal to do with it? If the general public became alarmed when they saw that the gold reserves were dwindling would they not immediately react to that position?* I feel that unless there is some change of opinion in these matters we are done anyhow. This does not seem to me a larger amount, spread over the period that it is, than amounts which will often be coming along. Something that one cannot predict will constantly put a strain comparable to this on the gold standard, and if the governors of the central banks are so fixed in their minds as to what proportions they want, and are so unwilling to use their gold reserves that they cannot accommodate themselves to a demand of this magnitude, I do not see much future for the gold standard.

13,119 *I think you have said that if ideal conditions in international trade were to obtain then you could afford to reduce your gold reserves?* Yes. I am assuming that in that case the practice of holding foreign balances would be increased.

13,120 *I take it that would mean a long process of education?* Yes, I think it would, and if you concentrate those balances too much in one place it adds to your dangers from that place; and as regards the place—for example, London—where foreign balances are held on a large scale, the requirements of that place for gold would be greater, I agree.

13,121 *You would not think it unreasonable if people did attach importance to the holding, in these circumstances, of substantial gold balances to secure the external value of their money?* I should think it foolish if they held these with the idea of never using them.

13,122 *Then, in the next paragraph, you draw a picture of a banker having to pay out balances due to his customers. If I may, I should like to complete the picture. If you had a big creditor of a bank withdrawing his balance for the purpose of buying, let us say, a collection of old masters, and if the bank for that reason had to curtail credit to its other customers upon whom the trade of the big depositor depends, would not that hit the big depositor?* I think the big customer might be well advised not to do it, but I think there are limits to the extent to which his banker can press that point on him. I think he would be entitled to resent it if his banker pressed the point.

13,123 *That is to say, greatness, even in the matter of bank balances, imposes responsibilities?* I have expressed the opinion already that India would be ill-advised to press for this. I think it would be wrong of them to do it, but it seems to me to strike at the root of international banking if we make any difficulties.

13,124 *Now to turn to another point. Supposing India was content to link her price level to gold? What would be the criterion in your view, when you come to consider at what point you are to stabilise permanently your exchange?* I should take something as near as possible to the existing situation.

13,125 *That is to say, you would examine whether internal prices had sufficiently adjusted themselves to the external value of the money?* Yes.

13,126 *Do you see anything in the point which has been put to us by a number of witnesses, that to fix the external value of the rupee at 1s. 6d. would damage certain interests, especially those of the cultivator and exporter?* As compared with?

13,127 *With a lower ratio.* I think whenever you arbitrarily alter the exchange you benefit some interests and injure others.

13,128 *But at this stage?* I have not examined the level of prices in India in detail recently, but so far as my knowledge goes I see no injustice in talking about 1s. 6d.

13,129 *You are aware that the exchange has ruled at 1s. 6d. gold ever since this country went back to the gold standard?* I am not aware of the exact period.

13,130 *But can one not suppose that, during that period, internal prices would have adjusted themselves to the 1s. 6d.?* I think it is reasonable to expect that adjustment to this figure is fairly complete.

13,131 *What would be the effect if one were to fix the external value at 1s. 4d. having regard to these circumstances?* If it is true that things are adjusted to 1s. 6d., one would be introducing an arbitrary disturbance which I should very much deprecate.

13,132 *There is the question of the hoarding of money in India. I take it you will agree that the hoarding of money is detrimental to India's interests from every point of view?* Yes.

13,133 *Both from the point of view of managing the currency and also economically?* Yes.

13,134 *Could you suggest a way of educating the people of India to hoard in things other than precious metals?* That is a very old problem. It is evident that India is absorbing a very much greater volume of securities than used to be thought possible. Everything that can be done to encourage that ought to be done. It looks as though in recent years great progress has been made. I have not the Indian experience that would enable me to make suggestions.

13,135 *You would say that to offer India a gold currency would not have any effect in that direction?* I cannot see how it could. I should have thought it would tend the other way, if anything.

13,136 *You would say, I suppose, that to give them a gold currency in India would not teach them anything?* I think it is a retrograde measure.

13,137 (SIR RAJENDRANATH MOOKERJEE) *I understand that your chief objections to a gold currency scheme are, firstly the disastrous effect on its value, and secondly the opposition of silver interests?* No. My two chief objections are the effect on the silver market, and the cost to India.

13,138 *Did you not also lay stress on the interests of other countries being affected in any way?* I lay very little stress on that. The two points I lay stress on are (c) and (d) in my memorandum.

13,139 *The hoards of silver in India are principally composed of coin, are they not?* I do not know. I always understood that there was a bigger store of silver not in the shape of coin. I am not aware of the relative magnitudes.

13,140 *Anyhow, we have been told by the Government that in addition to 90 crores of silver in their reserve they may be estimated a maximum of Rs. 100 crores with the public?* Yes, but I am not aware of what the estimate is of the amount of silver hoarded not in the form of coin.

13,141 *The proposal in the Memoranda of the Finance Department is, that even with the introduction of gold coin and a gold standard, the silver rupee would remain legal tender?* Yes.

13,142 *The silver coin and silver rupees are generally in the hands of the cultivators, who number 224 millions out of the total population of India of 320 millions. These cultivators, as you know, will not be able to exchange their silver for gold coins for two reasons. First of all, dividing up the total silver coinage between these 224 millions of cultivators we find that each man's share comes to about 5 rupees. Taking an average of four persons to a family, a sum of 20 rupees is not big enough for them to wish to go and change it into gold. Also it is not convenient for them to do so as they want to use their silver hoards in times of necessity. They can take out one or two or three silver pieces when they want to buy food. If they possessed just one gold coin it would be very difficult for them to get it changed in smaller coins in a remote village 40 or 50 miles from a city. Therefore, they would rather keep the silver in their store than change it into gold, besides a rupee will remain a rupee and buy a rupee's worth as it does now.* You are arguing that there is no real demand for gold coin in India, and that it is not suitable for India. I think that is quite possible.

13,143 *Therefore the contention that this silver would come out for conversion into gold, and thus accumulate into the Treasury, is not quite correct?* I agree that if there is no real demand in India for a gold coin, and if the scheme is a fiasco, it will not have very serious consequences.

13,144 *Therefore there will not be any such disastrous effect on the silver market as you apprehend?* I am assuming that if it is successful it will be disastrous, but if it is unsuccessful it will be less disastrous.

13,145 *But it cannot have a disastrous effect on the silver market if silver is not changed into gold?* If most people in India do not want gold coins, and wil not have anything to do with them, then I agree that the offer to them of gold coins will not have very serious consequences. On the other hand, the risk would have been run for no very useful purposes.

13,146 *As regards the second point, the opposition of silver interests, do you remember that, with the formation of the Latin Union in 1865 and the adoption of the gold standard by Germany in 1871, silver prices fell from 65d. per ounce in 1869 to 31d. in 1893? Did the members of the Latin Union and Germany give any thought to what effect their policy of the demonetisation of silver would have on India's stores of silver?* As you are probably aware, it was a very great controversy at the time, and there was tremendous opposition in all countries to a step which would depreciate silver, but I agree with your main suggestion that the prospective depreciation of silver did not carry decisive weight—at least not with France and Germany. It was a very great historical controversy, and the views of India were freely expressed and weight was given to them; but I agree with your suggestion that the final course adopted by the Continental countries was not much influenced by what India said.

13,147 *They did not think of India when they did it?* I think they did consider the disadvantages of depreciating silver, because there was a very powerful and vocal party which expressed that opinion; but the final decision went contrary to those arguments.

13,148 *Again, with the triumph of the gold standard in 1896 I believe, in America, and the adoption of the gold standard by Japan and Russia in 1897 silver depreciated further to about 22d. in 1908. That means that in the course of about 40 years India's stores of value in silver, depreciated to ⅓rd of their value in 1869, through the deliberate action of other countries. Why should India now show any scruples about the effect a particular policy proposed to be adopted by her may have on foreign authorities or foreign interests?* I do not think they need if it is for an important advantage. My argument was on rather different lines. I was suggesting that India was herself one of the greatest holders of silver in the world, and that it was the Indian silver interests which ought to be regarded and not the foreign silver interests.

13,149 *Do you refer to the producers of silver in Burma?* India is one of the greatest owners of silver in the world, and therefore India, as I say, has an interest in considering the value of silver.

13,150 *The domination of silver in her currency has cost India huge losses in the past. If she chooses now to break away from silver, in order to safeguard her future and come into line with gold standard countries and is willing to undergo a temporary sacrifice what objections would you still have to the proposed gold scheme?* I think she must weigh the consequences. I do not at all say that India ought to support silver at all costs. I agree that the past experience of India in relation to silver has been unfortunate in many ways. I think it is a pity that India is such a large holder of silver; but, that being so, she must not forget it. Silver must not be treated as a foreign interest. Silver is very greatly an Indian interest, and from that point of view I think India would be well advised to go very cautiously. If there were great advantages in a gold standard I should weight them against the disadvantages of depreciating silver, and I might quite likely come down in favour of a gold currency. My whole argument is conditioned by my assumption that there are no great advantages in a gold currency, and that being so it would be short-sighted to do something which would react heavily upon Indian holders of silver merely in order to satisfy what may be an ephemeral phase of public opinion in India.

13,151 *Do you think India has advanced sufficiently in banking habits to be able to work successfully in a paper control system, which has been rejected by England on the grounds that the time was not yet ready?* I am in favour of an exchange standard and the use of paper currency and rupees according to the experience and practice of the country. I am not clear how the question of the development of a banking habit is relevant to that.

13,152 *A banking system must be introduced to a large extent among the people, so as to get them accustomed to the drawing of cheques, the working of the discount rate and so on?* I do not think that much affects the matter.

13,153 *You are against the gold standard?* Yes.

13,154 *You say it is 'a barbarous relic'?* Yes; that is a correct quotation.

13,155 (SIR RAJENDRANATH MOOKERJEE) *But perhaps for a barbarous country like India the barbarous relic may prove a blessing.*

13,156 (SIR ALEXANDER MURRAY) *So far as regulation of prices in India is concerned, does it make any difference whether we have a gold standard with a gold coin, or the old gold exchange standard and a regulated rate of exchange?* Very little, I think.

13,157 *It is immaterial?* Practically.

13,158 *We could have a gold standard without a gold currency?* Yes.

13,159 *Personally you do not favour a gold currency?* No. If I am arguing on the basis of it being certain that India wants to have a gold standard of some kind, I should then prefer the gold exchange standard to the gold currency standard.

13,160 *You think gold is better in the central reserve, so to speak, rather than in circulation?* Yes.

13,161 *You consider it wasteful in circulation?* Yes.

13,162 *Earlier in your evidence you differentiated between the reserve which England has today—the type of reserve which is really against [an] external drain and the type which India should still have, which should be against an internal drain as well as an external drain?* If India had a gold currency she would need gold against an internal drain just as she needs rupees against an internal drain now.

13,163 *We have had it put to us that in the past England adopted the process of keeping a reserve against internal as well as external drain; that is to say, when it had gold coins in circulation. Germany had to do the same thing when it went on to a gold standard in the '70s. Did Germany not prohibit the use of small notes in order to get gold coins into circulation? It has been suggested to us that just as Germany and England had to go through that stage before they came to the present stage, surely India is entitled to go similarly through the gold coinage and circulation stage?* I think if India wants to go through every stage she had better start with cowries.

13,164 *I only want your opinion on that point, because it is an argument that has been put to us in India.* You mean the idea is that India is to begin by making all the mistakes that it is possible to make and to adopt in turn all the obsolete currencies?

13,165 *India has been on a gold exchange standard. England has now reached the gold exchange standard practically. It has been suggested that India, not having gone through the gold currency stage, ought now to go through the gold currency stage in order to familiarise her people with the gold coinage?* Nobody would make the same proposals as regards cotton machinery or motor cars, would they?

13,166 *I am glad to have your opinion on that point. In connection with the ratio of exchange, I think in olden days you favoured the sovereign as being the suitable coin on the 1s. 4d. basis? Supposing the ratio is altered to 1s. 6d., what is your opinion in that connection now?* At 1s. 6d. the sovereign is an inconvenient unit. I think you would need a gold coin which represented a more convenient number of rupees.

13,167 *Does that suggest to your mind an Indian gold coin—either a 10 or 20 rupee coin?* I think of this as a mere matter of convenience. I have no particular feeling one way or the other.

13,168 *Have you a feeling in favour of a high valued gold coin?* It depends on how serious you are in your wish to get gold into circulation. If you want to get gold into circulation I should have a relatively small unit, say 10 rupees or less. If you hope the people will take as little gold as possible then I would have a larger unit.

13,169 *Your view in that connection would be that India should therefore have a large valued coin?* I would have as large a unit as possible, because the less gold flows into circulation the better.

13,170 *In the old days it was really the sovereign that circulated more than the half-sovereign?* I believe so. I believe there were hardly any half-sovereigns in India.

13,171 *I gather from your examination that you are prepared to give India a gold currency practically in order to placate Indian opinion, and even although Indian opinion may be misguided. How do you arrive at Indian opinion? You said you arrived at it, I think, by reading various publications, but do you recognise the difference between opinion in India and Indian opinion at home with which you are more familiar?* Yes. I do not pretend to assert as a fact that Indian opinion is in favour of it. I mentioned it because it is often said that it is, and that seemed to me, if true, the most solid argument I have heard in favour of gold currency. Therefore I devoted myself to answering what seemed to me the most solid argument. But it may be that Indian opinion is not in favour. I am only going by the type of communication which this Commission has probably had in large quantities, and which I also receive through the post.

13,172 *If you were to take a country like England, with a high standard of education where probably 80 per cent of the people are urban as against 20 per cent in the country...?* Frankly my opinion is that Indian opinion is in favour of it, in the same sense in which British opinion was in favour of the gold standard a year ago. In this matter there is always only a small minority of the public who take any intelligent interest in it. If you take good class academic opinion in India, which I think ought to have some deference paid to it in a matter of this sort as representing true Indian opinion, I should have said that the weight of good academic opinion in India was in favour of a gold currency. Many professors who I consider deserve respect in other matters have expressed that view, and although I disagree with them on that I do not think their opinion ought to be swept on one side.

13,173 *I appreciate that. You think that the academic opinion in India, although of very small volume, is of such value that it ought to be carefully weighed as against the unexpressed opinions of 80 or 90 per cent of the population?* Yes, I think it ought, because it is not only Indian academic opinion but there is also a considerable volume of Indian business opinion to the same effect. I think all the methods one has of gauging Indian opinion would lead to the conclusion that Indian opinion, so far as it is intelligent and articulate supports this.

13,174 *At home they have not accepted the best academic opinion?* They have accepted the weight of academic opinion.

13,175 (MR PRESTON) *It is quite evident that you are aware of another side of Indian opinion regarding the propositions which the Commission have placed before you in the memoranda other than was evident to us. Therefore may I say that it will not come as a surprise to you if I were to state that the phase of Indian opinion which has been placed before you in that memoranda is not the only one which is existing in India?* I am glad to hear it.

13,176 *Or in other words that there is a very heavy weight of opinion also in India which is not represented by that memoranda?* I am very glad to hear it, but I can only say that not much of it has come my way.

13,177 *The gold exchange standard which we had functioning in India from 1893 to 1914 was simple, public, automatic, and brought great advantages to the land of India, did it not?* I think it was the best currency system then existing in the world.

13,178 *And had it not been for the War it is reasonable to suppose that that system would still have been in force?* I think so.

13,179 *And there would have been no need for the Babington-Smith Committee or probably for this Commission?* I think that the conclusions of the Chamberlain Commission would have held.

13,180 *This other weight of opinion recognised that that gold exchange standard had been beneficial to the land of India had it been properly managed. They have come to the conclusion that during the War it was mismanaged. For our purposes now it is immaterial whether it was or was not, but, really speaking, it was about two-thirds on the way towards a simple gold standard, was it not, in its application?* Yes, quite two-thirds of the way to a gold standard, but to a gold currency not so far.

13,181 *Let me call it a simple gold standard?* More than two-thirds of the way.

13,182 *The consensus of that other opinion today, in so far as I can read it, is that they have no desire whatever to be guilty of, or to demand, any action from the authorities on this side which, in her claim for gold, would be detrimental either to this country's or to India's interests. They have also in view that, in her demand, they would not be guilty of any action which would in any way jeopardise the existing securities in the paper currency reserve or the gold standard reserve. What they desire is simply this—that it should be authoritatively constituted, that there should be a free and unrestricted import of gold and output of gold. In pre-war times the sovereign was the universal tender in India. The parity was 15 to 1, or the 1s. 4d. such as we knew it. Therefore the upper gold point was put down as 1s. 4$\frac{5}{32}$d. The export point was put at 1s. 3$\frac{27}{32}$d., and, whilst we allowed gold to come in, Government never accepted the responsibility of giving gold on the other side for rupees. Therefore what they now desire is that inequality, if I may call it so, should be rectified. So that, taking the changes which have happened since then, and taking the great changes and the difficulties which are in evidence here on this side, and of which you yourself have spoken this morning, would it not be a reasonable and a fair proposition in answer to their demands to grant the concession which they now desire, namely, that our existing system should be so altered as to lead to a free import of gold and a free outflow of gold?* Yes, I think so. If it is settled that India is to have a gold standard of some kind, and if the feeling in India in favour of greater facilities for getting gold is to be met, I agree with you that the wisest way of doing it would be to have a statutory selling price for gold on behalf of the Government, as well as a statutory buying price. That is assuming that the gold standard is to be established.

13,183 *Then they go further than that. They state that in their demands Government should only sell her council bills to the exact amount of their requirements. Consequently Government, having sold her council requirements, which for the last year were about 40 millions sterling, the off-take for gold would not be more from this market or from the world's markets. We have it in evidence that it is from five millions to ten millions. Would that meet with your approval?* I should not have thought that the net takings of gold, if the Government had a statutory selling price, would be much different from what they would be if it had not a statutory selling price. That is your point.

13,184 *The point is this. In the memoranda* which you have got there they*

* Appendix 95 (B). [Not printed.]

present to you a bogey of 103 millions of gold? That is on the assumption of a gold currency, but I think there is one point where I should differ from what you are suggesting. If the Government is to have a statutory selling price for gold it will have to hold a permanent gold reserve in India in order to meet that liability, and the amount of the normal aggregate of that gold reserve would be in addition to India's other gold requirements. Therefore, whilst it would be less than 103 millions, I think the statutory selling price for gold would mean some addition to India's net gold requirements in the first instance. After that reserve had been once built up, I do not see why it should mean any further increase.

13,185 *What I am trying to arrive at is this—that the annual off-take from this market would never, on the average, exceed five millions to ten millions of gold?* I cannot say as to that, but I see no reason why the annual off-take should be increased. I do see, however, a reason why the initial requirement would be greater. The Government would have to hold gold in order to make sure of being able to meet its statutory liability to sell gold at fixed prices.

13,186 *Then the idea underlying their request in that particular respect is this—that in the event of a falling away in exchange, and exchange falling to a lower point, her gold standard reserve is still intact?* Yes.

13,187 *So that this extra off-take would not be required in any way whatever to maintain the exchange parity?* You would require an additional reserve, because you would have an additional requirement. The gold which India kept in India to meet its statutory liability to sell gold at a fixed price would be additional to the reserve which she would have to keep to meet external drains.

13,188 *It would in its operation become additional?* But once that initial reserve had been built up I do not see that any more gold would be required than is required at present.

13,189 *I would like to obtain your opinion on this silver bogey. From the best information which has been placed before us we gather that the total amount of rupees outstanding today is about 250 crores—possibly 300 crores as an outside figure, of which there are nearly 90 crores in the Government Treasury chest. Prior to the War it was always the policy of the Government of India to maintain about 20 crores as a working balance. Taking India's trade today at about 100 per cent increased volume, and with the increase in population, and the possibility of increased trade, would it be unreasonable to suppose, as is the evidence which has been tendered to us, that the working balance would be a minimum one at about 40 crores, in comparison with the 20 crores in pre-war times?* My opinion would not be worth anything unless I could look into it more carefully.

13,190 *Assuming that the 40 crores was a fair estimate, that would leave in our paper currency reserve about 50 crores. We have ascertained in evidence that the annual absorption of rupees is in the region now of nine crores per annum. On that assumption the excess stock would barely give us room for five years' requirements?* The arithmetic seems to be correct.

13,191 *If that were the case would you say that the bogey of the selling of India's rupees was warranted or not?* I see no reason to expect that India would be selling rupees if a gold currency is not introduced, or, if a gold currency, being introduced, is inoperative.

13,192 *The memoranda which have been placed before you suggests the sale, in view of that balance figure, of what they look upon today as redundant rupees. Assuming that our annual absorption is in the region of nine crores, with an increasing figure, is the reason for the suggestion of that sale apparent to you or not?* If I follow you rightly, you are going on a different assumption. The memoranda assume that gold will be introduced into India as the currency, and will circulate to an important extent. You are assuming it will not circulate, and therefore that the demand for rupees will go on as heretofore. So naturally the two assumptions lead to different conclusions. If no change is made in the way of introducing a gold currency, I quite agree that the present apparent redundancy of rupees in the reserve would be absorbed in due course.

13,193 *Therefore this idea of a wholesale selling of rupees would not be warranted?* But that idea of a wholesale selling of rupees is made on a different hypothesis.

13,194 (SIR HENRY STRAKOSCH) *We have been told by some witnesses that the time is not yet ripe for India to establish a real central bank because its present banking organisation is too limited. Do you see anything in that point?* No.

13,195 *Would you not rather say that a central bank would be very helpful in expanding the commercial banking organisation?* Yes, I should.

13,196 (SIR REGINALD MANT) *When you advocated a variable rate of exchange I assumed that there would be no place in your system for a legal tender gold coin?* No.

13,197 *I understood from your subsequent replies that you did contemplate that?* No. I was doing that on a different hypothesis. I said assuming a gold standard is to be established in India then I thought that the statutory selling price might be introduced. If, as I consider the better policy, a legal gold standard is not introduced, then there is no place for the statutory selling price.

13,198 (CHAIRMAN) *We are very much obliged to you for your very valuable assistance.*

The witness withdrew.

A Government wage and profit subsidy had held the coal mining dispute of the summer of 1925 in abeyance while a Royal Commission under Sir Herbert Samuel examined the problems of the industry. While the Commission sat, both the Government and both sides of industry prepared for industrial action when the subsidy expired in April 1926. The Samuel Commission reported on 11 March 1926, recommending certain longer-term changes such as nationalisation of royalties and amalgamations of uneconomically small pits as well as a reduction in money wages. The owners, demanding wage cuts and longer hours, rejected any government reorganisation of the industry. The miners rejected both wage reductions and longer hours. In these conditions of deadlock, Keynes made a suggestion.

From The Nation and Athenaeum, *24 April 1926*

COAL: A SUGGESTION

The acceptance of most of the Coal Commission's recommendations by all the parties concerned has cleared much matter out of the way. The issue is being narrowed down, until it is becoming possible to see more clearly the general lines which almost any settlement must follow.

The dimensions of the problem. In the last quarter of 1925 the amount of the subsidy varied from 4s. 7d. per ton in South Wales to 1s. 7d. per ton in the Eastern Division, and averaged 3s. per ton for the whole country. This enabled the mines to make a trading profit averaging 1s. 7d. per ton for the whole country, and not less than 8d. per ton in any district. The Report of the Commission shows that an improvement of 3s. per ton in the net proceeds would enable all but the worst mines in every district to continue without actual loss, and the better mines to earn a normal trading profit averaging about 1s. 6d. per ton. Thus in round figures we may say that the economic problem of the mines is to raise the net proceeds by 3s. per ton. Anything much less than this would knock out whole areas, whilst anything much more would tend to perpetuate over-production and to hinder the gradual transference of activity to the newer and better mines and districts.

The sources of the improvement. It is agreed that in the long run the only sources from which this necessary improvement in the net proceeds can come are three—(1) lower wages, (2) economies resulting from the Commission's miscellaneous recommendations, and (3) higher prices to the consumer. The Commissioners have proposed that the contribution from lower wages should be about 10 per cent, which would work out at an average of about 1s. 3d. per ton. They have not specified how much they expect from the other two sources, an omission which gives a certain vagueness and lack of precision to their intentions. I suggest that rough justice would be done if we were to start off in framing a concrete scheme of settlement with the idea that we might get 1s. per ton from each of the three sources. It is evident, however, that whilst an agreement could make sure of the contribution from wages, the amount of the contributions from eventual miscellaneous economies and from higher prices is bound to be problematical beforehand, and will only emerge with certainty in course of time. An important part of the immediate practical problem is, therefore, to tide over the dubious period immediately ahead of us.

The form of Government assistance. Obviously the economies to be obtained from putting into force the Commission's miscellaneous proposals cannot be effective until after an interval of time. This fact is the only, but sufficient, justification for a continuance of Government assistance. The subsidy should be framed with the sole object of providing for this interval. It follows that its initial amount should be governed by a conservative estimate of what these economies will yield, that it should gradually diminish over the period which they will take to mature, and that it should be the same for good districts and for bad. The last condition is important. So long as the subsidy could be regarded as primarily a subsidy to wages, it was, perhaps, natural to give a bigger subsidy to the worse districts. But nothing can be more injurious in the long run than a device which endeavours to put the worst pits on a level with the best;

and a subsidy on these lines has in fact seriously aggravated the present plight of the industry. Unless, therefore, there is good reason to anticipate that the worse districts have a prospect of securing materially greater economies than the better districts, the only sound principle for further Government assistance is a flat contribution per ton of coal raised. The actual figures would be better filled in, here as in the rest of this article, by those who know more about the details of the industry than I do. But I suggest as a basis of negotiation that the Government should pay a uniform subsidy of 1s. per ton, falling by 1d. a month. This would not cost the Treasury above £6,000,000.

The amount and the method of wage reductions. The national settlement should be on broad lines and might consist of an agreement that the aggregate reduction in the wages bill should not in any district exceed the equivalent of 1s. per ton, that the position of the worse-paid workers should be protected by subsistence minima as at present, and that district settlements should be subject to ratification nationally. Subject to these conditions, the details should be referred to the districts for individual negotiation, and the masters and men should be free, if they can, to bargain a lesser reduction of wages than the above against the men meeting the masters' ideas on various matters other than wages. Further, recruitment of new hands into the industry should be prohibited for the present, and some reference to the cost of living standard might be introduced into the minima. The miners know that, unless the subsidy is to continue indefinitely, the choice lies between accepting a modest reduction of wages and facing (whether with or without a strike) widespread unemployment, and I believe they prefer the former.

The future of prices. There remains the future of prices. It is difficult to render this element precise because there does not appear to be justification for a uniform increase of price over all classes of coal. Household coal is already high enough; commercial coal used at home ought not to be raised much;

export coal, on the other hand, is well below its economic price. The crux of the export districts' problem is, indeed, whether they can raise their prices without losing the trade. This is probably a more essential and difficult element in the case, even than the wages question. Yet it is one about which, except from the lips of Sir Alfred Mond, we hear far too little. So long, however, as private enterprise continues, this must remain a problem for the mine-owners to solve themselves. If they cannot solve it, the industry must disappear or it must accept nationalisation. The apparent incapacity of the owners to tackle this problem firmly is one of several indications that we are dealing with a decadent, third-generation industry. The inclination of the owners at the outset to throw the whole brunt of their difficulties on to wages is the reason for the widespread popularity of the men's cause—so long as they fight it in a spirit of reason and social sense. On the other hand, the Government must not forget that the price problem of the coal exporters has been created largely by Mr Churchill's gold-standard policy. The extent to which it is now essential for them to obtain higher prices by better selling methods is almost exactly equal to the lowering of sterling prices attributable to the rise in the exchange. It is true that many of our export trades have failed so far to solve the problem which Mr Churchill set them a year ago. It may be that a Chancellor of the Exchequer, who is blind to economic cause and effect, has set old-fashioned private industry, which is not organised in combines or cartels, a problem which it is incapable of solving. So-called conservative finance, which consists in turning two blind eyes to the wrong end of the telescope, is more likely than anything else to lead old-fashioned industrial organisation into trouble. But the problem having been set, our export industries must stand or fall by their success in solving it. In the case of coal it looks to an outsider as though, failing international agreement, the exporters might derive some relief, temporarily at least, by arranging for themselves a pool, somewhat on the lines of the

Tinplate Pool which is familiar enough in South Wales, by which a scheme of quotas, of standard prices, and of penalties is drawn up. This might, with necessary modifications, be better suited to the special conditions of the industry than the alternative of organised short-time on the lines of the Lancashire cotton mills. The employers in the export districts must at any rate take the responsibility of introducing some method or other of improving prices. After all, several of our staple export trades would be by now in the same plight as coal if other employers had shown themselves as helpless.

Here, then, are the elements of the problem. The precise amounts and forms of the contributions to be secured from each of the three sources are a legitimate subject for negotiation and for reasoned debate. After all, the real differences of opinion, which still remain, are surprisingly small. Everyone, including the miners, knows that some reduction of wages is inevitable and no one supposes that the reduction suggested by the Commissioners can be exceeded. Everyone expects that the essentials of the miners' demand for a national settlement must be conceded to them. Everyone, including the Treasury, is well aware that the continuance of some kind of subsidy is inevitable. Everyone, including the owners, expects the latter to practise a little more self-help and willingness to reorganise their house than they have shown hitherto. Even the amounts of each of the three factors can probably be guessed already by the leaders on either side within a few pence. If the will for a settlement exists, it cannot be impossible to draft one.

When the existing agreement in the coal industry expired with the subsidy, the owners locked the miners out on 1 May. The result was not only a mining dispute but also a General Strike which lasted from 3 to 12 May.

During the strike, Keynes wrote two notes. The first, which exists in Lydia's handwriting, was cabled for publication in the *Chicago Daily News*, where it appeared in a slightly modified form on 6 May.

To the Chicago Daily News, *6 May 1926*

The strike situation ought never to have arisen—for two reasons. The leaders on both sides honestly wanted to avoid it, although some of their less responsible followers may have been not disinclined for a try-out. When both parties want to avoid something only clumsiness and stupidity can bring it about. But there was another reason, and here the fault lies, I think, with the Government. Negotiations should never have been broken off, even though it cost a short prolongation of the subsidy, until the men had had put before them a concrete proposal on lines approved by impartial opinion in conformity with the Commission's Report, had had time to consider and discuss it and had deliberately refused it. This they have never had. If the miners had deliberately refused a fair and generous offer, it is most unlikely that the Trades Union Council would have supported them with a General Strike.

Now by fatal blundering we are out of the atmosphere of reasoned discussion. But let not American opinion misunderstand. On the whole working-class sympathies are solid with the men. But there is no excitement, no passion, not a flicker of revolutionary feeling. That is not the atmosphere of London today. The atmosphere is first one of depression and helplessness and dismay at the failure of reason and common sense.

I suppose that even now a patched-up settlement might come at any time. But if not I see no reason why the present situation might not continue for a few weeks. In the end the forces of law and order are certain to prevail. On some terms good or bad offered by the Government the men will go back. But such a termination will settle nothing. The problem of evolving a better way of conducting our business in an industrial society as complex as America's but no longer assisted out of its difficulties and mistakes, as England used to be and as America still is, by a crescendo of material progress, will remain for future solution.

I am inclined to predict that the future political effect of the present breakdown will be a considerable increase in the parliamentary strength of the British Labour Party. I should expect Labour to win impending by-elections in doubtful constituencies. Mr Baldwin comes well out of the negotiations, so far as temper and good will count. He made the best speech in Monday's debate in the House of Commons. He fell down through his lack of fertility and resource and his failure to offer any constructive suggestion. But above all he will have lost what was perhaps his chief asset, namely his reputation for being a safe man under whose quiet rule nothing serious would ever happen. The breakdown will bring it home to public opinion that inactive good will and unimaginative common sense are not enough and that the solution of Great Britain's social problem needs restless intelligence and constructive imagination.

The second note Keynes wrote exists in several drafts entitled 'Reflections on the Strike' and 'A Symposium, I, from J. M. Keynes'. The draft entitled 'Reflections on the Strike' appears to have been cabled to America for publication in *The New Republic*. However, it never appeared, as Keynes held it back when 'The Symposium' planned for *The Nation* failed to appear on 8 May because of the continuance of the General Strike.

REFLECTIONS ON THE STRIKE

Sir John Simon tells us that the Strike involves breach of contract. Lord Birkenhead declares that the quarrel must not be ended until it is recognised that there is 'one Government and one Government only in this country'. Everyone speaks of 'the attack on the Constitution'. All this is true or partly true. But those whose minds are filled with these ideas and phrases are not thinking or saying the things which it is important to think and say. The strikers are not red revolutionaries; they are not seeking to overturn Parliament; they are not executing the first movement of a calculated manoeuvre. They are caught in a coil, not entirely of their own weaving, in which behaviour, which is futile and may greatly injure themselves and their neighbours, is nevertheless the only way which seems to them to be open for expressing their feelings and sympathies and for maintaining comradeship and keeping faith. The strike is a protest, a demonstration, an expression;—though its aim and meaning be obscure, so that it is not easy for anyone, certainly not for the strikers themselves, to explain adequately what it is a protest against, an expression of. Unlike Sir John Simon, it is inarticulate, unlogical, ill calculated. Certainly I cannot put it into words. But my feelings, as distinct from my judgment, are with the workers. I cannot be stirred so as to feel the T.U.C. as deliberate enemies of the community, who must be crushed before they are spoken with.

Subsequent developments have revived the impression which the Report of the Coal Commission made on me when I first read it but which I afterwards tried to suppress out of deference to the opinion of others as to its diplomatic value—namely that the Report was in some ways very weak and woolly. It would have been better if the economic issues had been more sharply emphasised and if a more definite and concrete scheme of action had been propounded. There was too much diplomacy in the Report. Diplomacy is too difficult an art for human men. It is just because it was too diplomatic that diplomatically it has failed.

Of course it is important to reduce the cost of production of coal by every possible practicable improvement. But too much emphasis on this side tends to obscure the other side which for the moment matters much more,—namely that there are too many men in the industry, that even with the men now employed there is serious overproduction, and that, in the absence of any pool or other concerted action, this over-production has resulted in a cut-throat competition which has driven down prices, mainly in the export trade, to a level which cannot yield a living wage. Improvements from reorganisation, etc. are all very well. But the urgent problems of the trade are to transfer men out of the industry, to curtail production and to raise export prices. These matters are not ignored in the Coal Report. But they are not, as they should have been, dragged out of the detail into the limelight. If they had been, it would have been impossible for the owners to have gone on up to the last moment with the proposal of an eight hours' day.

The eight hours' day as a policy for the future, after the redundant labour in the industry has been placed elsewhere, might be defensible. But as a temporary policy for the present it is half-witted. To meet a condition of overproduction by increasing production 14 per cent! Or, alternatively, to meet excessive unemployment by throwing a further 14 per cent of the men on to the dole! It is as though the Lancashire cotton mills were to propose as a solution of their troubles that the spinners should work overtime. A temporary five-hour day might help the coal industry. But a temporary eight-hour day is a ludicrous plan. If all the miners were to work eight hours, we could not sell the coal produced even if we were to capture the entire export trades of Germany and the United States. We must not forget that up to almost the last moment the only concrete proposals made to the miners were along these lines.

If the T.U.C. is given a pretext for calling off the strike now, it might be possible for them to claim it as something of a success, considered as a demonstration, owing to the completeness with which the men have come out. This fact is the main obstacle to reasonable negotiations. For many supporters of the Government believe that the T.U.C. should be given no honourable opportunity of calling it off until by lapse of time it has become an evident failure. This section of opinion, which has much influence in the Cabinet, in effect casts its influence in favour of prolonging the strike until the men show signs of breaking—which may take some time. Is it more important to settle the strike or to discredit it? Is it better to raise the strike now on peaceful terms, the unions withdrawing in good order, or to break it a month hence by economic pressure by destroying the loyalty of the men to one another? That is the matter of controversy today. I think that those who believe that the future peace and prosperity of this country require the latter make a great mistake.

After the General Strike had ended, but while the miners remained out, Keynes made another suggestion.

From The Nation and Athenaeum, *15 May 1926*

BACK TO THE COAL PROBLEM

Sir Herbert Samuel's proposed *concordat* for the settlement of the coal dispute is very good, so far as it goes. It introduces some further elements of definiteness which were unfortunately lacking in the Report of the Royal Commission. That Report contained most things somewhere, but it did not throw the limelight into the right places.

The new *concordat* has narrowed the issues down a degree further. The question of hours is almost eliminated (the mine-owners are still entitled to raise the question of hours as being relevant to that of wages before the proposed National Wages Board), and attention is concentrated on the arbitration of wages. The lowest paid men are entirely protected from reductions. The important measure of forbidding new recruitment into the industry is made definite. The closing of pits is more explicitly envisaged, and the measures proposed for helping men whom this will throw out of work have become precise. The only objection from the point of view of the miners lies in the one remaining element of indefiniteness—the amount by which their wages may be reduced. But they gain so much in other directions that they will be exceedingly ill-advised to reject, or even to seek amendment of, the scheme. Sir Herbert Samuel deserves the thanks of the country for his labours.

Nevertheless in the enthusiasm with which we greet the

termination of an impossible situation we must not overlook the grave and difficult problems which still face the arbitrators, even when the point at issue is confined to the level of wages. They still have to decide what contributions to acquire from the three sources which I distinguished in *The Nation* of April 24 [above p. 526] namely, how much from wages, how much from other economies, how much from higher prices for the product.

The fault of the Report and one of the faults of the owners has been the undue stress which they have laid on 'other economies', the report relying too much on the economies of re-organisation, etc., and the owners relying too much on the alleged economies of the eight-hour day. The latter is now ruled out, and it would be rash to expect very much from the former, at least in the near future.

We are back, therefore, on the price of product which means, in the main, the price of export coal. Now there are only two ways of bettering the price—by reducing the output and by selling-price agreements whether national or international.

How much reduction of output will raise the price of export coal by (say) 2/- per ton? In other words, will an increase of price diminish the consumption of coal or drive the trade elsewhere comparatively much or comparatively little? It is probable that the diminution of world consumption would not be very great. But we should inevitably lose some trade to our competitors. How much it is impossible to say until we try. To some extent, perhaps, we set the world price. In so far as this is so, we may lose less trade than we expect.

If we could agree with German exporters to fix a minimum price for exported coal, the improvement of the price might be achieved with a minimum of disturbance in other directions. This will obviously be very difficult and perhaps impossible. But in any case the first step towards it must be the formation of some kind of cartel amongst our own coal-exporters, which is totally lacking at present; moreover a cartel once formed might do a good deal to maintain prices even if no arrangement was reached with Germany. I should, therefore, put the formation of a cartel of British coal-exporters in the forefront of the remedies. Whilst, however, reduction of output and an export cartel are indicated, it seems unlikely that the National Wages Board will be able to discover quantitative certainty in these directions. On what principles then ought their deliberations to be governed? I venture to suggest that the thoughts of the arbitrators should flow along the following channels.

(1) In the long run it is essential to reduce the cost of production of British coal by every practicable improvement. But too much emphasis on this side tends to obscure the other side which for the immediate future matters much more—namely, that there are too many men in the industry, that even with the men now employed there is serious overproduction, and that, in the absence of any pool or other concerted action, this overproduction has resulted in a cut-throat competition which has driven down prices, mainly in the export trade, to a level which cannot yield a living wage. The urgent problems of the trade are, therefore, to transfer men out of the industry, to curtail production and to raise export prices.

(2) It follows that, so far from fixing wages at a level which would enable most collieries to continue to produce at present prices, they should be fixed at a level which, even for collieries which are not below the average, assumes some rise of selling price to enable them to make both ends meet, and involves the closing down, temporarily or permanently, of a not inappreciable number of less efficient collieries. Wage reduction on a more dramatic scale will not even help the employers in the long run, but will merely perpetuate and aggravate the existing overproduction.

(3) In these circumstances the criterion of what wages the trade can bear can only be applied in a very indefinite way. The answer depends on the level of selling prices, which in its turn, depends on the volume of output, which again depends on the level of wages, so that we can only proceed to the equilibrium position by the method of trial and error.

(4) I conclude that the National Wages Board must be largely influenced by the alternative criterion, namely the amount of wage reduction which the men can reasonably be asked to accept having regard to the cost of living, the hardships and dangers of their life and the level of wages in other industries. There is no paramount national object to be served by forcing the export of coal to a point when the selling price does not afford a reasonable wage, any more than in the case of cotton or any other commodity.

(5) Finally the employers are wrong in their contention that the workers in bad districts should receive permanently much lower wages than those in good districts. Temporarily some confusion in this direction may be justified to avoid too sudden a dislocation. But the principle is altogether unsound and its operation should be discouraged. If it is acted on over a long period, it aids mines in bad districts at the expense of what may be in fact superior mines in good districts. The present system of district ascertainments already exercises a bad influence in this direction. The wage areas ought to be as large as possible, not as small as possible, and should perhaps apply to coal of different kinds and for different uses and markets rather than to geographical districts.

The trouble in the coal trade is not to be settled by good will alone. The Report of the Royal Commission left untouched the most ticklish part of the problem, namely, the quantitative problem of the discovery of the new equilibrium points of output, prices and wages. And Sir Herbert Samuel's admirable memorandum only passes it on to a still uncreated body.

The General Strike produced problems for the recently reunited Liberal Party. During the strike, all agreed that the strike went beyond the limits of constitutional action, but there was substantial disagreement as to whether negotiations with the Trades Union Congress should cease until the union unconditionally surrendered or whether they should continue in some form, thus implying bygones were bygones. After the strike a letter from Lord

Oxford to Lloyd George appeared, taking the latter to task for refusing to attend a Shadow Cabinet meeting on the grounds of his dissent from certain 'unconditional surrender'-style statements from other Liberal leaders since the previous meeting. Lloyd George in reply defended himself in a conciliatory manner. Inevitably, the discussion spilled over into the columns of *The Nation* where Keynes's letter appeared after three weeks of comment.

To the Editor of The Nation and Athenaeum, *12 June 1926*

Sir,

The many whose feelings have been painfully divided in this quarrel must be touched by Sir James Currie's letter in your issue of June 5th, and by other expressions in the same vein. May I—now that the acuteness of the controversy is diminished—endeavour to state frankly how I, for one, have been influenced?

Mr Lloyd George has been responsible in the past for wrong and disastrous policies. Lord Oxford has always been sensible and loyal, never forefeiting trust or esteem. Lord Oxford is doubtless right when he says that Mr Lloyd George is a bad colleague. Yet Mr Lloyd George has other obvious qualities. He is naturally and temperamentally a radical, happiest when his lot lies to the left, in spite of excursions in other directions. He is a great politician—an engine of power for the big public. When Mr Lloyd George is in a bad mood he can work more havoc than any other politician in the world. But when he is in a good mood, he can do great service.

Now Liberals knew all about Mr Lloyd George's past and about his character and his temperament two years or more ago when the two wings of the party were being 'reconciled'. Many radicals wondered then whether it would be possible to work with him, whether he would not develop some fatal tendency. It was decided that it was worth while to try. Lord Oxford, Mr Runciman, Sir John Simon, and the rest welcomed him back, and did not disdain to use the almost fulsome expressions of esteem which Mr Lloyd George quoted at Manchester the other day. It may have been that these words were entirely insincere, and that, when a year ago Mr Runciman said that no man living was more entitled to be honoured than Mr Lloyd George, and when Sir John Simon thanked God for him, they meant the opposite of what they said. But that was the moment, it seems to me, for Sir James Currie to rub his eyes and to remember the Coupon Election, the Treaty of Versailles, and the Black-and-Tans in Ireland. For these events happened before the 'reconciliation', and not after. That also was the moment for an ultimatum about his separate party funds if the surrender of his funds was considered to be a *sine qua non* of co-operation.

If, therefore, Mr Lloyd George is to be expelled now from the counsels of the Liberal Party, it must be for something which he has done lately, some confirmation from his recent conduct of doubts provoked by his past actions. Lord Oxford, though not some of the others who have lately sat in judgment, purported to act on these lines. But Lord Oxford in his first letter and in his subsequent communications has only half tried to make out a convincing or even a coherent case. Indeed, those who have supported him hardly pretend that what he has told us constitutes by itself any adequate justification for his action, and ask us, rather, to rely upon a general presumption that he must have had his reasons—a presumption which we would probably accept, if it were not destroyed by the flood of unsubstantial and unsubstantiated gossip with which they accompany it, gossip which they seem to think very damaging but which, where it does not lack foundation, is in fact not damaging at all.

All the same, if I disliked the recent trend of Mr Lloyd George's policy, his attitude during the strike, his strivings to work out a radical policy, his desire to orientate the Liberal Party with a view to an eventual co-operation with Labour, I should, whilst thinking privately what I chose about the wisdom of Lord Oxford's recent action, nevertheless stick by Lord Oxford on general political and personal grounds and try to make the best of a bad job.

But if, as is the case, the contrary is true, if I support the line which Mr Lloyd George has taken lately and find myself thoroughly agreeing with him on policy for the first time for years, would not Sir James Currie think me guilty of bad behaviour, if, to pay off old scores, I were to join with those who mistakenly supposed that his attitude during the strike had furnished a good opportunity for doing him in? Would it not be politically dishonest for one, who agreed with Mr Lloyd George during the strike, to side against him in the recent crisis on no more evidence than is furnished by Lord Oxford's letters? It seems to me that there was absolutely no choice in the matter with whatever pain in regard to old associations and whatever doubts about new ones.

The line of fissure in the Liberal Party has shown once more what always must happen so long as politics are taken seriously— that personalities come second in the end. Lord Oxford is a whig. Mr Lloyd George is a radical. The Liberal Party is strongest when these two elements in it, which have always existed side by side, can work together. The great merit of Lord Oxford is that he is a whig who is free from prejudice against radical projects, and, though he initiates nothing, will always give open-minded intellectual hospitality to ideas from other minds. But this passive rôle is useless by itself. If the recent manoeuvre to oust Mr Lloyd George had been successful and the full authority of the party had become vested in the tenth-rate fellows at Liberal headquarters, the Liberal Party must necessarily have died of inanition.

One day last week Lord Oxford wrote to Sir Godfrey Collins that it was 'absurd to suggest that his attitude was inspired by an unwillingness to advance along radical lines'; and on the same day Sir Godfrey Collins issued a statement that Mr Lloyd George had retained his chairmanship of the Parliamentary Party by the support of Liberals 'who hold their seats by Tory votes and at the sufference of the Tory Associations in their divisions'. Both these statements may be true. But if they are intended to suggest that Lord Oxford is really the radical and Mr Lloyd George still a Tory coalitionist, the suggestion is not true. I believe that today Mr Lloyd George is a good radical, that he can give valuable assistance, within the Liberal Party, to the working out of a new radical programme, from which some day Labour will be glad to borrow; and that his willingness to cultivate personal relations with the leaders of the right wing of the Labour Party, which might develop in favourable circumstances into active collaboration, is not only right and reasonable in itself, but is a necessary accompaniment of an outlook for the future of the Liberal Party which is the only justification for its continued existence. These are political, not personal, matters. If Lord Oxford is not willing to contemplate co-operation with the Labour Party in any probable circumstances and desires that the Liberal Party should continue in a state of intellectual quiescence, let us divide, amicably but as soon as possible, into two separate parts. But if he is willing to contemplate such co-operation and, as he has said, 'to advance along radical lines', then, without pretending to a personal cordiality or to a daily intimate intercourse which he cannot sincerely assume or maintain, let him encourage Mr Lloyd George to stir the radical pond and to exchange ideas with Mr Philip Snowden, ready in due course to subject to benevolent criticism whatever may be fished out of the waters, troubled or otherwise.

Yours, &c.,

J. M. KEYNES

Keynes's letter of 12 June, along with previous correspondence with Margot Asquith over the same issue, led to a temporary estrangement from the Asquiths: Keynes and Lord Oxford did not meet again during the latter's lifetime.

Keynes's letter of 12 June also led to two further letters.

To the Editor of The Nation and Athenaeum, *3 July 1926*

MR RUNCIMAN'S LETTER

Sir,

In Mr Runciman's disclaimer (in your issue of June 26th) regarding a commendation of Mr Lloyd George which I have attributed to him, he advised me to verify my reference. I have done so, and find in the *South Wales News* of May 30th, 1925, substantially the words which I had quoted at second hand, and some more in the same vein. I assume, therefore, that his letter is not intended to disclaim the words. If Mr Runciman means that his subsequent actions have proved these words to have been a conventional insincerity, though doubtless uttered with the best of motives, that I certainly accept. Indeed, I suggested this explanation in my original letter.

In spite of so many words about persons, it is, in truth, policies and not persons which are drawing the lines of division. It would be very agreeable if politics were a tea party. If they were, I am not sure that I would not sip with Mr Baldwin as lief as anywhere. But alas! it is not so.

Yours, &c.,

J. M. KEYNES

The second was in answer to a question from W. M. Crook of London, N.W. 1, who asked Keynes to define whig and radical.

To the Editor of The Nation and Athenaeum, *28 June 1926*

Sir,

Thank you for showing me Mr Crook's letter. A whig is a perfectly sensible Conservative. A radical is a perfectly sensible Labourite. A Liberal is anyone who is perfectly sensible.

Yours, &c.,

J. M. KEYNES

542

While Keynes was in Berlin to deliver the final version of *The End of Laissez-Faire* (*JMK*, vol. IX, pp. 272–94) as a lecture, he also made further comments on the General Strike. On the last day of his visit, 24 June, he spoke to the English Seminar of the University of Berlin on the strike. His notes ran as follows.

THE GENERAL STRIKE

A General Strike must be either a revolution or a demonstration. The paradox of the English Strike is that it was neither. In consequence essentially senseless.

The leaders knew this. They wanted to prevent it. As soon as it was started they were anxious to get out of it with as little loss of credit as possible. In fact the leaders of the Labour movement were in an impossible situation. Thomas recently on record as saying if a General Strike succeeds God help England. Ramsay MacDonald always openly against it but on general and on practical grounds.

Thus the Strike only came about by a chapter of accidents.

First. The Labour Movement had long played with the idea. It was a natural development of the strike idea itself. Sympathetic strikes had been getting increasingly common. They had been fairly successful. The General Strike was thought to be just a further step on. Thus the T.U.C. was theoretically committed to support miners in advance.

There was a greater latent danger in this than was realised because of Triple Alliance having previously let down the miners on Black Friday.

Loyalty the essence of trade unionism. Shame for Black Friday might lead loyalty to outrun expediency on the next occasion. All the same the leaders had no intention to use the strike except as a threat.

Meanwhile Baldwin's mishandling had brought matters without a solution in sight up to Saturday April 29 with the subsidy at an end on following Monday. Even on Saturday morning no one expected a General Strike actually to occur.

543

The history of the next two days is obscure and disputed. The following is the best account I can give.

On Saturday morning the executive of T.U.C. proposed a noncommittal resolution to the Executive.

Amendment from body of men.

Issue of threat.

Without consulting the Cabinet P.M. continues negotiations. Miners' attitude is stiffened.

Negotiations all through Sunday.

T.U.C. leaders practically agree to call off strike unless miners agree in principle to reduction of wages.

Cabinet meets; objections raised to negotiations under strike threat.

P.M. leaves Cabinet sitting to speak with Thomas.

Formula agreed. Thomas tries to collect miners' leaders.

P.M. returns to find Cabinet in insurrection.

Attempt of *Daily Mail* operation.

Negotiations broken off.

No means of saving faces.

Strike begins.

Strike anecdotes

Extreme loyalty of Unionists

(Silver band at Cambridge)

Almost no disorder

Papers (had none) greatest difference to daily life

Broadcasting

Train service very slow

Everything essential can now be done by motor transport

Much sympathy with miners

Football match

Experiences of undergraduates (tips at Dover)

No skilled occupations

Surfeit of fish through rapid unloading

Driving lorries

But after a few days war atmosphere intensified.

Intense depression—lack of news.

544

Everyone wondering where his duty lay.

Military mind gaining control which means in England—I
expect everywhere—complete collapse not only of intellect but
of ordinary intelligence and of daily common sense. All the
people who are too stupid to be of any value or importance in
peacetime began to feel themselves essential and even to find
themselves in charge.

Great issue of negotiations or no negotiations which meant
saving faces or no saving of faces.

Collapse of strike.

Meanwhile whilst carrying a brave face in public Labour leaders
becoming increasingly defensive. Their position impossible.

Samuel memorandum provided a pretext

Simon speech (though bad law) a third

Various rumours as to Gov^t. intensifying campaign.

Strike suddenly called off.

Baldwin's services at this stage.

Railwaymen

Dockers etc.

Trade unions received a severe blow.

Direct action discredited.

But non-revolutionary character of British labour movement
established.

Perhaps Parliamentary Labour movement strengthened rather
than otherwise.

The whole thing an episode perhaps not of first importance
in evolution of Britain's industrial problem.

 Cessation of crescendo

 Excessive labour supply

 Decay of old-fashioned private enterprise

 Wrong distribution of capital and labour between industries
 aggravated by return to Gold Standard

I am not very cheerful about the future

 Business men narrow and ignorant, unable to adapt themselves

 Old-fashioned orthodoxies respected everywhere

Technical problems too difficult for working-class leaders
    But we still have a big margin for mistakes
So that whilst I am not very cheerful, I am not very depressed
either

During June Keynes made two contributions to *The Nation* on subjects
less directly related to the General Strike. The first was a reaction to an earlier
declaration by Herbert Hoover against attempts, such as the Stevenson
scheme for rubber, to control the output or the price of particular raw
materials.

From The Nation and Athenaeum, *12 June 1926*

THE CONTROL OF RAW MATERIALS
BY GOVERNMENTS

A few months ago Mr Hoover, Secretary for Commerce in the
Administration of the United States, declared economic war
against those foreign governments which might control the
supplies or the prices of raw materials. His declaration had
special reference to the scheme of rubber control enforced by
the British Colonial Office and the governments of certain
Crown Colonies, but he also specified cotton, camphor, coffee,
iodine, nitrates, potash, mercury, and sisal. Since few people
inside or outside of the United States credited him with sincerity
of principle or impartiality in the matter, in the sense of
supposing that he would have been equally indignant at similar
action taken on behalf of American interests, but assumed that
his main object was to employ the preponderating power of the
United States to beat down the prices of foreign goods imported
by them, the response which he evoked abroad was one of out-
raged indignation at one more example—so it was supposed—
of the willingness of Americans to cover up purely commercial
and selfish objects under high-sounding principles. We sometimes forget that the United States is still enjoying, more

uncritically than we are, a phase of civilisation in which, so far from there being any opposition between commercial greediness and high principle, they are practically the same thing. But whether or not European opinion did him an injustice, the indignation aroused prevented at the time any cool discussion of the important questions at issue—and it may be useful to return to them now.

There are various ways in which a country may seek to improve the terms on which it exchanges its own products for those of foreign countries. It may impose import duties on foreign products or export duties on its own products. Its merchants may form combines or pools for marketing on monopolistic lines. Its producers may make formal or informal arrangements for limiting their output with a view to securing a better price. Finally, its government may enforce a restriction of output or of export, or may produce the same result, so far as the consumer is concerned for the time being, by buying up stocks to hold them off the market.

These measures will be more or less successful in achieving their intention according to the urgency of the outside world's demand for the products concerned and the measure of independence of the country adopting them from the necessity for foreign goods. But, further, they will, in general, be more successful for a short period after their first adoption than they will be in the long run. For there are very few cases in which the outside world cannot make other arrangements given time. Thus, more often than not, measures to restrict or control international trade will, if they are intended to be permanent or to secure abnormal profits, defeat themselves in the long run and be open to the double disadvantage that they injure the customer at the beginning and the producer at the end. The important exceptions to this general principle, where the producing country can expect to make a monopoly profit year in and year out by taxes or restriction of output, can almost be counted on the fingers of one hand. There is the South African diamond cartel which keeps the price of diamonds at a fancy figure; but in this strange trade one might argue that the restriction was as much in the interests of the consumer as of the producer, since no one would want diamonds if they were cheap. There is the long-established control of the price of nitrates by the Government of Chile through an export tax, to which definite limits are set by the competition of synthetic nitrate. There is the case of Indian jute where similar opportunities may exist. There is the Franco-German potash combine. And there are certain minor commodities, where something which approaches a world monopoly exists or has existed, such as platinum, bismuth, cobalt, and quicksilver. Whilst the control of the last-named of these by the Rothschilds, at a time when it was the only known remedy for a mortal disease, may be reckoned as an anti-social act; nevertheless, the list as a whole exhibits how relatively unimportant to the world such cases are.

There remains, however, quite another category, to which, as it happens, most of the recent acts of governments belong— where the object is neither permanent nor aimed at securing an exceptional profit but is temporary, and is aimed, on the other hand, at avoiding an exceptional loss. The nervous systems and financial strength of the markets in many staple commodities are such that a miscalculation on the part of the body of producers as a whole, leading to an overproduction which amounts to a comparatively small percentage—say, 10 per cent—of the total production, can cause an altogether disproportionate fall of price. Now in some cases this fall of price leads rapidly, without any organised or concerted action on the part of the producers, to a curtailment of output which will soon restore prices to the normal. But in other cases, where the fixed plant is a large proportion of the total cost or where the complete process of production is spread over a long period, possibly years, as in the case of rubber planting, so that any curtailment will not take effect for a correspondingly long time, this is not so. The product continues to come forward in quantities which the market is unable to absorb, and, if nothing is done about it, the price falls to a level which means a ruinous loss and perhaps bankruptcy not only to the inferior producers but to the main body of producers. If this process is allowed to work itself out, forces will be set in operation which will mean in course of time a curtailment of output much greater than is required, with a corresponding rebound of prices at a later date to a level which is as excessive as the former price was insufficient. In the long run this violent oscillation in price and in supply will be as injurious to the consumer as to the producer. Obviously the world will be better off on the whole if it can be prevented.

The reader will notice that a combination of conditions is required to bring this situation about—an inability of the market to carry surplus stocks and an inability of the producers, acting separately, to restrict production quickly. Now it is not sufficiently realised that the commodity markets of the world are almost never able to carry any material surplus of stocks at a price anywhere near the estimated normal. They are organised to carry the risk and the expense of looking after stocks in course of production, in transit and between harvests—stocks, that is to say, which are expected to pass into consumption within the year. But a short calculation will show that it is in the nature of things that they cannot hold truly redundant stocks unless they are tempted by a reduction of price ruinous to the producers. Market statistics indicate that a pure speculator will seldom run the risk of carrying stocks, particularly on a falling market, unless he has an expectation of profit of at least 10 per cent per annum, and, if professional dealers in the commodity have been weakened and discouraged by losses on their normal holdings as a result of the initial price fall, the possibility of much more profit than this is required to tempt anyone in. In addition to this, the actual outgoings for warehousing, insurance, interest and deterioration will often amount to nearly another 10 per cent per annum. Thus if it seems that the stocks may not be absorbed for more than (say) two years, there is a reason

549

for prices to fall as much as 40 per cent below the estimated normal price.

On the other hand, the producers, acting independently, may, if they have laid their plans for a given scale of production, and have already incurred a large part of the costs, find it better [sic] worth while to continue at a loss rather than to close down. Curtailment will not be worth while unless it results in a better price; yet one individual's curtailing will, in itself, scarcely affect the price which he will get for the balance of his output.

Where the industry is in a few strong hands, the necessary curtailment may be arranged by agreement. But if there are many, small, and perhaps ignorant, producers, and if, besides, the industry is the main occupation of the place, so that its bankruptcy involves the general ruin of the country and no one has any alternative occupation to which he can turn, then it seems to me both inevitable and right that the government should intervene. It is *laissez-faire* gone crazy to maintain the contrary.

Now the government, when it acts, has to decide in which quarter it will attack. It can supplement the deficient carrying power of the market by buying up stocks—the Bawra organisation for dealing with Australian wool during the war, the Bandeong tin pool of 1921 by the Government of the Straits Settlements and the Dutch East Indies, and the various coffee valorisation schemes of the Sao Paulo and Brazilian Governments have been of this character. Alternatively, it can restrict output or at any rate export, as in the case of the Rubber Restriction Scheme and the imminent Cuban Sugar Restriction. The Egyptian Government has applied both methods at different times to the case of Egyptian cotton. The former class of action is, for obvious reasons, much more popular with producers, and sometimes it may prove the right course. But it is much more dangerous for the government, since, unless great skill is exercised, a lasting condition of overproduction may be encouraged, until the stocks have reached a level where the government can carry no more.

I argue, therefore, that there is all the difference in the world between a case where a government is endeavouring to exploit a monopoly or a position of economic advantage, and where it is endeavouring to protect one of its staple industries from bankruptcy and the consumer from violent oscillations of price below and above the normal selling price. In the former class the cases where it will be successful in the long run and will not in the end defeat its own objects are somewhat rare. Anyhow, these attempts at national profiteering tend to impoverish the world as a whole, and are examples, if anything is, of bad international practice. In the latter class the consumer is benefited in the long run, and if they are carried out judiciously, the world as a whole is richer. For it would not have benefited consumers of rubber in the end, if all new rubber planting had been stopped and existing plantations abandoned to the weeds of the tropics.

Let us examine Mr Hoover's position in the light of this argument. As a member of the Republican Administration which is committed to one of the highest protective tariffs in the world, he cannot be opposed to this kind of governmental interference to raise prices or to injure foreign producers. As an administrator of the Webb Act, which provides that American exporters shall be freed from the restrictions of the Sherman anti-trust law against combines at home, he cannot be an opponent of the exploitation of the foreigner by private monopoly. As a colleague of Mr Mellon, on the one hand, Secretary of the Treasury, and on the other hand, the power behind the Aluminum Company of America, which controls the price of aluminium throughout the world, he must be able to control his indignation against such practices. As a subordinate of President Coolidge, who supported but a few weeks ago a measure which would advance financial aid to farmers who desire to hold crops in expectation of a rising market, he must at least have learnt to suffer these notions in silence. Finally, as an advocate of the Cuban Sugar Restriction, he has seemed to fall in with my argument as to the essentially reasonable character of measures of this kind.

If the Eastern rubber producers aim at maintaining permanently a price level above the eventual cost of production elsewhere, Mr Hoover is justified in encouraging production in new districts. He is also entitled to denounce tariffs and all public and private instruments of international monopoly as examples of bad international practice, provided he is ready to apply his principles impartially all round. But I think that he would do well to make an exception in favour of all schemes the primary object of which is not to make abnormal profits but to avoid abnormal losses. If he is interested in general principles, he might think the matter over again with this criterion in view.

The second looked back on the first fourteen months of Britain's gold standard experience.

From The Nation and Athenaeum, *26 June 1926*

THE FIRST-FRUITS OF THE GOLD STANDARD

The currency discussions which preceded Mr Churchill's first Budget a year ago ranged over two distinct questions—whether gold is the best available objective standard for our money, and whether it was wise to link our existing money to gold at a parity which was about 10 per cent higher than the level to which wages, the cost of living, and the wholesale prices of raw materials were then adjusted. The first was a long-period problem not likely to be settled for many a year yet. The second was an immediate practical issue. Consequently, what we were busy in arguing early last year was mainly the second question. That, after a year's experience, is also the subject of this article.

Let me remind the reader how last year's argument ran. If all transactions expressed in money were to be changed by 10 per cent simultaneously, then no harm would be done. But in practice, so the argument ran, this does not happen. Some prices, of which the wholesale prices of raw materials entering into international trade are typical, adjust themselves rapidly. Others of which the cost of living is typical, are stickier and move more slowly. Others, of which wages are typical, are stickier still. Others, of which interest on the national debt and a number of other budgetary commitments are typical, being contractual and only alterable by something in the nature of repudiation, do not move at all. The evils arise from these differing rates of adjustment and from the fact that it is extremely difficult to accelerate the slower moving ones except by methods of deflation or of repudiation, which are objectionable in other ways. Pending the adjustment, our export trades, which are producing at one level of costs and selling at another, will be seriously depressed and unemployment aggravated; whilst when the adjustment is complete the problem of the Budget will remain permanently heavier because, measured in money, the revenue will fall off whilst much of the expenditure is fixed. Last year I particularly emphasised the difficulty of reducing money wages and the permanent aggravation of the weight of the national debt.

How do these arguments look after a year's interval? Wholesale prices have fallen 13 per cent, the cost of living has fallen 4 per cent, and money wages have fallen by less than 1 per cent. Meanwhile wholesale prices in the United States have fallen 6 per cent. Thus relative wholesale prices have fallen, as they were certain to fall, by the greater part of the amount of the rise in the exchange; the cost of living has been stickier; and money wages have been even more recalcitrant than one would have expected, inasmuch as they have scarcely moved at all. Allowing for the fall of gold prices in the outside world, the maladjustment of international gold prices with our cost of living is scarcely diminished, whilst the maladjustment with our rates of wages is actually worse than it was. Thus our exporters have had to sell at lower prices measured in sterling, whilst many of their costs, especially wages, have fallen very little. At the same time, although the full burden on the Budget still lies in the future, the revenue is already failing to show the resiliency which, given a stable price level, the normal course of progress and population might be expected to produce.

The indirect results have also been what they were bound to be. In a year in which the productive activity of the United States has exceeded previous records, we have had a million unemployed and all the penury of a slump. The export industry, namely coal, the greatest proportion of the costs of which are wages, and which for reasons not connected with currency was already our weakest point, and therefore least able to endure a further handicap, has been reduced to the verge of ruin. Our largest group of export industries, namely textiles, though more self-reliant than coal, are, in spite of the comparative cheapness of wool and cotton, almost in despair at their losses. The outputs of iron and steel have been maintained with the assistance of subsidised coal; but no profits have been earned. The results have been what a year ago I feared they would be, but worse than I dared or cared to prophesy.

The wonder is, not that our exporters are in difficulties, but that their position is not worse than it is. When we compare the level of gold wages here with what it is in Germany, France, or Belgium, it seems a miracle that our exporters who compete with these countries do any trade at all. Currency comparisons surely demonstrate that we must still retain a large body of specialised production where no one can touch us, and that, currency difficulties apart, the efficiency of our manufacturers must compare favourably with that of foreigners. They even suggest the possibility that our trade unionists do more work in an hour than is commonly supposed.

Meanwhile, the Government, without sufficient resolution to

face the full effects of its policy, has been content to retard rather than to hasten the processes of adjustment. The coal subsidy had no other object than to put off the evil day. The Bank of England's policy of deflation has been severe enough to aggravate unemployment and effective enough to balance the international account by attracting foreign balances to London, but not severe enough to end the period of transition or to effect the more difficult adjustments. Mr Runciman, it is true, in a speech which provoked general admiration for its brazen courage, felt able on the morrow of the strike, to thank God for the gold standard. Yet, all the same, the lively hopes of last year's optimists have faded away.

Mr Churchill could scarcely avoid the question altogether in this year's Budget speech, which he would probably have preferred to do. But I venture to think that the calibre of the defence he offered was not worthy of his office. He did not mention the one solid advantage which, in my opinion, the gold standard has gained, namely, the improvement of London's position as a centre for holding international balances,—there can be no doubt that foreign financial centres are more willing to deposit their surplus resources in London than they were before the return to gold. Mr Churchill's defence began with the calculation that since the dollars which we owe the United States for our purchases and our debts work out at a smaller figure in sterling than they would if the dollar exchange value of sterling was lower—which is indeed an arithmetical certainty—therefore we have 'saved' the difference! He forgot that we have 'lost' an equal percentage on all our exports.

He followed this up by claiming that the adjustments in international price levels have been completed—by which he meant, presumably, that the sterling prices of export coal and other articles of international trade had fallen to the new sterling parity with the international price level. Poor innocent, to think that this was the adjustment which we feared it might be difficult to effect! The predicted trouble was attributable, of course, to the fact that the sterling price of export coal would fall rapidly, whilst the sterling wages of miners would fall much more reluctantly, if at all. This was the problem of adjustment. Mr Churchill points triumphantly to the fall in the price of export coal (and similarly of other materials) as a proof that the problem of adjustment of the coal trade (and similarly of other trades) is now complete! How can it be possible for one who knows so little what he is talking about to govern our course wisely?

Both the above fallacies were pointed out by Mr Pethick Lawrence in the course of the Budget debate. Mr Churchill had an opportunity to reply. He did not take it.

The economy campaign against social services, the Budget problem, the continued depression of employment, the losses of the export industries, the last aggravation of the coal problem which has rendered it seemingly insoluble, are the first-fruits of the gold standard.

On 1 July *The Times* published a letter from Sir Josiah Stamp on the effects of the Eight Hours Bill for the coal industry on employment. In his letter Stamp compared the effects on employment of three alternatives: existing wage rates and hours, a reduction in money wages to the 1921 level and existing hours, and the longer hours proposed in the Bill. In his discussion of the third alternative he suggested it would lead to greater output, some fall in coal prices and some diminution of coal production offset by an expansion elsewhere induced by cheaper coal. He, therefore, supported the Bill. On reading Stamp's letter, Keynes wrote to him.

To SIR JOSIAH STAMP, *1 July 1926*

Dear Stamp,

I cannot follow the arithmetic of Section 3 of your letter to today's *Times*. You estimate under (1) that on the present basis there is a gap of three or four shillings to be made up. If, as I take it, your argument under (3), though ambiguous, is on the assumption that the longer hours are to be worked for the same aggregate wages as at present, your economy of between $\frac{1}{9}$ and $\frac{2}{3}$ is more than taken up in liquidating the existing deficit, and none of it is available for a fall in price which will absorb the increased output. It would thus appear that the output under an eight-hour day on these assumptions would have to fall below the present output. Thus you would surely have a very large addition to the unemployed. On your figures none of the additional output could be absorbed, and the whole of the increase due to the longer working day, and more too, would be reflected in fewer men employed.

Perhaps I have not understood you. But it seems to me self-evident that if the economy of the eight-hour day is not much more than half of the gap which has to be bridged as it is, the output of coal under that regime must be less and not more than at present, so that the whole of the longer hours would be reflected in increased unemployment.

Yours sincerely,
[copy initialled] J.M.K.

From SIR JOSIAH STAMP, *3 July 1926*

My dear Keynes,

I am sorry I was North when your letter came. I had not thought it necessary to 'reconcile' the 3/- to 4/- under (1) with (3). The profits per ton are 'ascertainment' profits & cover or include a lot that is relatively inert (i.e. bank & debenture interest, amortisation, pitsucking charges, &—valid for some considerations—preference charges). Therefore a net absolute necessary for satisfactory ordinary capital charge can be got with much lower gross margins per ton with the higher output, & as the differences are say as 18 to 28, there is scope for an argument on my lines. But I don't know the net figures well enough to be at all certain of this, though I *am* quite sure that one cannot reason from the apparent (ascertainment) profits per ton as a constant over all volumes.

And, of course, I am just as uncertain as you probably are about questions of elasticity of demand & price. I hope I have understood your criticism.

Yours,
J. C. STAMP

P.S. I suspect I have to thank *you* for the initiative in my Cambridge Sc.D. If so, I can't tell you how much I appreciate it & what keen pleasure it has given me.

J.C.S.

To SIR JOSIAH STAMP, *6 July 1926*

Dear Stamp,

Your answer does not satisfy me. What it amounts to is that your estimate of 2/- a ton economy from the eight-hour day is not complete, and that there would also be some further economy from using the overhead more intensively. The Commission's Report is not quite explicit about this, but the figure of 2/- which they quote as the owners' own estimate of the economies on the eight-hour day seems to be intended as a total figure. Certainly it seems to be more than could be accounted for by wages alone. However, be this as it may, any additional economies on overhead could not possibly be more than 6d. For it would only be this amount if an increased output of 10 per cent could be obtained without involving any additional cost whatever except for wages. Let us, therefore, estimate the economy of eight hours at 2/6 instead of at 2/-. How does the argument then stand?

Some part of this will have to be sacrificed in order to get off the additional output. From the experience during the subsidy, and the other evidence as to the inelasticity of the demand for coal, it certainly seems probable, as I think you will admit, that a considerable part of the economy would have to be sacrificed in the price if the eight-hour day is to result in any appreciable increase in aggregate output. This means that the economy from the eight-hour day largely washes itself out in providing for the additional output, and leaves little over to bridge the existing gap.

This brings me to the point where your comparison between Remedy 2 and Remedy 3 seems to me to be logically deficient. A reduction of wages to the 1921 level would involve a reduction of cost, all of which would be available towards bridging the existing gap. The eight-hours day, on the other hand, has to squander much of the original gain in looking after the additional output. Thus, a sacrifice by the men in the form of working longer is likely to be less efficient towards bridging the existing gap than a comparable sacrifice by the men in accepting a lower aggregate wage.

Your letter does not persuade me that my previous opinion that the eight-hour day was a balmy remedy for what is already a state of over production was a mistake. Do you think that you are entitled, on the evidence and on the argument of your letter, to have your authority quoted in the House of Commons by the Prime Minister and others as an advocate of the eight-hour day, as against the arguments of the Commission, and as one more piece of evidence that economists always differ.

Yours ever,
[copy not signed or initialled]

Keynes must have included a postscript to his letter of 6 July referring to a forthcoming piece in *The Nation*, or another letter which has not survived intervened, for Stamp's next comments ran as follows.

From a letter from SIR JOSIAH STAMP, *10 July 1926*

Miners' wages. I will study *The Nation* to write, whether I agree or not! But as I am knocking about in Scotland from tomorrow for some days it may not be this week.

I've got your point clearly, & it is not quite on the same line as my own. I can see. I agree that I am not entitled—to use your word!—to be quoted by the P.M. in the sense indicated after the line he has taken over the Yorkshire terms.[10] But more later.

The article in *The Nation* referred to by Stamp appeared on 10 July. It was unsigned. However, its presence in the scrapbook of signed and unsigned *Nation* articles kept by Keynes's mother and the relationship of its content to the correspondence with Stamp suggest Keynes was the author.

From The Nation and Athenaeum, *10 July 1926*

MR BALDWIN'S QUALMS

It is said that Mr Baldwin is feeling keenly the recent attacks upon his behaviour from some of the Labour men. No man in

---

[10] The owners in the rich west Yorkshire coalfield had resorted to a low scale of wages more appropriate to a poorer area.

politics minds abuse, however scurrilous, if it is totally unfounded. Of course, Mr Baldwin does not deserve a word of
the vulgar attacks which have been made against his personal
honour and his personal sincerity. But he has a bad conscience.
And it is right that he should have a bad conscience. Mr
Baldwin's bad conscience is the explanation of the flounderings,
the inconsistencies, and the vacillations of the Government's
policy for the last two or three weeks. Mr Baldwin has been,
in effect, defeated in his own Cabinet. He has been too weak
to defend from some of his colleagues the working-men who had
genuinely placed their trust in him. If he had been asked at the
conclusion of the General Strike whether the owners' policy,
now officially adopted by the Government, was the sort of thing
which he had in mind when he promised the miners 'a square
deal', he would probably have repudiated the suggestion with
indignation. He is sufficiently aware of this to be uneasy—to
plunge in the traces in a way which strains the nerves of his
colleagues on the box seat who thought that they had the reins
firmly in their hands. He still desperately hopes to find a way
out which is consistent with his promises and his professions.
Two debates have been proceeding simultaneously—the debate
between the Government and the Opposition, and the debate
between Mr Baldwin and his conscience. Members of Parliament
naturally find it a little confusing when speeches which belong
to the latter debate are suddenly interjected into the former.

Meanwhile, have the debates in Parliament disclosed any new
argument for the eight hours day to rebut the conclusions of the
Royal Commission? We have discovered none, except the
argument which the Commissioners did not overlook—that some
degree of elasticity in the hours worked by certain grades of
labour or in exceptional conditions would be technically
desirable.

There are three possible grounds on which to advocate a
general increase to eight hours for all grades of labour—that it
is a good diplomatic threat, not intended to be carried out in

practice, for bringing the men's leaders to heel, or that it offers the possibility of a solution which, rightly or wrongly, the men themselves would really prefer to lower wages, or that it is on its merits, despite the Royal Commission, the right solution of the problem. The validities of the two first reasons only the event can test. But we hold that it is a grave error—certainly not 'a square deal'—to propose any solution which cannot be defended on its merits, and can, therefore, only put off the evil day.

Once more, then, we must return to the merits of the eight hours solution. No one denies that some substantial number of pits ought to be closed down. The crux of the economic problem of the mines, as distinct from the diplomatic problem of getting the men back, lies in the difficulty of bringing this about in an orderly way and in the still greater difficulty of absorbing in other industries the men who will thus be thrown out of work in addition to those who are unemployed already. It is as plain as day that the eight hours proposal must gravely aggravate these difficulties, and that this is the final and unanswerable argument against introducing it at this juncture. The coal industry is suffering from an overproduction—an overproduction which may not exceed 5 or 10 per cent of the whole, yet which, in the absence of joint selling arrangements, is sufficient to knock the bottom out of the market. To prescribe in such a case a measure, the first of which will be to increase production by 10 or 15 per cent, *must* be wrong, unless there is reason to think that the economies of more intensive production will in themselves allow a reduction of price sufficient to absorb a substantial part of the additional output.

Sir Josiah Stamp, in a letter to *The Times*, which has been quoted in the House of Commons in support of the Bill by the Prime Minister, the Chancellor of the Exchequer, and the Minister for Mines, seems to argue that this is so. Sir Josiah Stamp is a high authority whom we respect. But his argument in this case appears to be marred by a blunder.

The so-called eight hours proposals which are being made to

the men are not, as their description might suggest, a proposal
that the men should work longer hours at the same hourly wage
as before. They are a polite cover for a proposal to reduce hourly
wages coupled with an option to the men to make this up, if
they choose, by working longer hours. Since most miners can
already work more hours a week if they are so disposed, the
proposal is not much different, from their point of view, from
a mere reduction of wages; it merely gives an opportunity for
arranging their hours of work in a way at present forbidden. This
part of the so-called economy or the eight hours solution is
entirely a lower-wages, and not a longer-hours, economy, and
could be brought about, without a similar risk of overproduction,
by a straightforward cut in wages such as the Royal Commission
recommended. The owners claim, however—probably with
justice—that there are some additional economies from a greater
technical efficiency and a more intensive employment of overhead
which an eight hours' day will make possible. These are truly
longer-hours economies. The question is—will these economies
in themselves permit a lowering of prices sufficient to sell the
whole or the greater part of the additional 30,000,000 tons which
a universal eight hour day by the men now employed might be
expected to raise? This is the essential question which the Royal
Commission examined and answered in the negative. Mr
Baldwin's Cabinet seems to be intellectually unequal to asking
the question, far less to answering it. The Mining Association
have estimated the lower-hourly-wages economies *plus* the true
eight-hour-day economies (as defined above) at an average figure
of about 2s. per ton. The Royal Commission thought it might
be a bit more—say, 2s. 3d. Of this, the reduction of hourly wages
is responsible for not less than 1s. 6d. Thus the true eight-
hour-day economies amount on the average to 6d. or 9d. per
ton at the most. Is a reduction in price of this amount going
to enable the industry, in the present state of world markets,
to sell an additional 30,000,000 tons or anything approaching
that figure? The Royal Commission thought not, and we have

not seen a ha'p'orth of argument to the contrary. Where has Sir Josiah Stamp gone astray? Unless we have quite misunderstood him, he has, in comparing the eight-hour solution with the straightforward reduction of wages recommended by the Commission, taken credit for the whole 2s. to 2s. 3d. as being available for price reductions to carry off the additional output; whereas the true figure in a comparison between these two courses is 6d. to 9d.

Thus the arguments of the Commissioners have escaped entirely unscathed from the recent intensive discussion of this feature of their Report. If, on the other hand, the owners intend, as seems probable in several districts, to demand after a few months' interval, *both* an eight-hours day *and* a reduction of 10 per cent in aggregate wages, this goes far beyond what the Royal Commission recommended, or what the Government and owners' propaganda is disclosing to the public, or what the men can reasonably be asked to suffer.

Mr Baldwin's manifest qualms as to whether the men are getting 'a square deal' are not unfounded.

The next week Keynes returned to the French financial situation. Since January the franc had fallen to new lows on the foreign exchanges, as successive governments grappled with the situation and subsequently failed to keep the confidence of the Assembly. In May, the Government of the day had appointed an expert committee to advise on means to improve the situation. It reported on 14 July, and at the time Keynes wrote the franc had fallen even lower amidst uncertainty as to whether or by whom the report would be adopted.

From The Nation and Athenaeum, *17 July 1926*

THE FRANC ONCE MORE

There have been three truths which it has been found unpatriotic hitherto to admit within France—leaving to foreign critics an artificial monopoly of wisdom. Two of these are now officially accepted, and possibly even the third is knocking at the door of the Chamber.

The first truth is that the franc will never recover its old parity and must be devalued. The second truth is that the new value of the franc must be fixed, not at the end, but at an early stage, of the scheme of financial reform. The third truth—the one which is still officially disreputable—is that the Bank of France's gold is the appropriate resource for supporting the franc at its new value.

The Experts' Report has been spun out of cotton wool and is not meant to be clear. Nevertheless, it has succeeded in bring to the front the essential problem of the French Treasury. Granted that the franc is to be pegged somewhere between its present internal and external values, wherein does the difficulty lie? It does not lie in the volume of the notes. Even on the criterion of internal value, the volume of notes in issue is not particularly excessive. It does not lie in the inadequacy of the gold reserve. The Bank of France holds £139,000,000 in gold, which at the present rate of exchange represents more than 50 per cent of the note issue. The difficulty lies in the menace of the floating debt. The fear is that, if the franc is pegged, the holders of the floating debt will demand repayment and will then, directly or indirectly, spend or invest the proceeds abroad, taking advantage of the facilities to exchange francs into foreign money at a fixed rate of exchange. The political controversy in France seems chiefly to range round the problem how to ward off this danger.

In my opinion the danger is greatly over-estimated. If the franc is pegged the holders of the floating debt will be less, and not more, anxious than at present, to remit their funds abroad. When the profits of an ever-depreciating exchange cease to exist, the pressure on the part of holders of franc money claims to change these into foreign money claims will be diminished not increased. Nevertheless, the contingency must be faced, because otherwise the public will not feel the necessary confidence that the new value of the franc will be maintained. No modern country, which uses, as we all do, paper money and bankers' money, can maintain the value of this money against a general belief in the minds of the public that its value is going to fall.

What devices for warding off the menace of the floating debt are the various parties in the French Chamber putting forward? I hear of three—the forced consolidation of this debt, which is M. Tardieu's plan; the capital levy, which is M. Blum's plan; the foreign loan with the Bank of France's gold in the second line of defence, which is the plan of the Experts and of M. Caillaux.

The forced consolidation of the debt would undoubtedly be effective in removing this particular menace. But the arguments against it impress me. These are that a measure of semi-repudiation is hardly the way to restore confidence, and that it throws the whole of the sacrifice still required on a particular category of wealth which has already been hard hit by deprecia-tion, whilst those citizens who have created the present trouble by their action in remitting their investments out of the country will escape entirely. There is also the strong objection of principle against an overt and deliberate breach by the state of a specific contract.

M. Blum's capital levy would be less technically effective, because months and even years would pass by before its proceeds could be collected. In principle I am not opposed to a capital levy. But it is not the appropriate remedy for the present crisis.

The arguments against M. Caillaux's foreign loan are that it presumes a settlement of the inter-allied debts in a hurry, possibly on more onerous terms than might be obtainable later on, and that it is distasteful and burdensome for France to incur obligations to foreign lenders. I sympathise with these objec-tions. I believe, indeed, that a foreign loan is unnecessary—but on one condition, namely, that the Bank of France is ready to use its gold. In the most favourable circumstances the foreign loan will not exceed the Experts' estimate of £40,000,000. This sum could be taken from the Bank's gold as a special *masse de manœuvre* and still leave £100,000,000 intact against the notes. This is the right solution for those Frenchmen who find a foreign loan distasteful. But if it be true that public opinion is implacably hostile to this, and would consider it a sign of weakness, then in my judgement M. Caillaux's programme is the next best alternative. Therefore, whilst I should sympathise both with M. Tardieu's aversion to a foreign loan and with M. Blum's affection for a capital levy, I should vote with M. Caillaux, hoping with some confidence that the mere display of the loan would be enough, and that France would be in a position to discharge it at an early date.

Mr Churchill's debt settlement with M. Caillaux this week shows that at least one of France's war-time creditors is not in a mood to take advantage of her present difficulties, but rather to stretch concessions to help her. Those of us who believe that the total cancellation of the inter-allied debts should have been a cardinal point of the proceedings of the Paris Conference in 1919, and that M. Clemenceau and M. Klotz and M. Tardieu made a disastrous mistake in grasping at phantom milliards from Germany instead of getting rid of real burdens from the shoulders of France, are bound to welcome the developments of these latter days. But France, like the rest of us, must expect to pay some price for rearing up a race of politicians who have neither aptitude nor inclination to understand the economic facts of the modern world.

There remains the question of the Budget. Here also I think that M. Caillaux is right. In their demands for new revenue or new economies the Experts appear unduly austere. In some articles which I wrote six months ago I argued that a higher internal price level was inevitable, and that the effect of this in diminishing the real burden of the national debt would come to the rescue of the Treasury in the long run. To critics of my supposed advocacy of *la vie chère*, I replied that I was offering not advice but prophecy, and that there was nothing wrong in taking advantage of the inevitable. The internal price level has been rising rapidly since I wrote, and the process of adjustment is not yet complete. I would now re-emphasise a corollary to my former prophecy. If the franc is stabilised somewhere between 160 and 170 to the £ sterling, internal prices are bound to rise much beyond their present level. In due course this rise of prices may require an increased note issue. It is important to face this possibility beforehand, lest otherwise a belated alarm is provoked by the inevitable consequences of the inevitable.

When *The End of Laissez-Faire* appeared, a commentator in *The Westminster Gazette* suggested the appointment of an Economic General Staff along the lines suggested by Sir William Beveridge in *The Nation* in December 1923 and January 1924[11]

To the Editor of The Westminster Gazette, *17 July 1926*

Sir,

In your leading article of 12 July, in which you comment on my recently published volume, *The End of Laissez-Faire* (Hogarth Press, 2s.), your contributor 'J. A. S.' argues that one of the most pressing tasks of the modern state is to remedy economic ignorance—inevitable ignorance due to the vastness and complexity of the modern world, and avoidable ignorance arising out of the aptitudes and inclinations of politicians. He therefore supports the appointment of a body on the lines of the Economic General Staff proposed some little time ago by Sir William Beveridge.

I am sure that this is right. A whole series of events here and elsewhere have proved that the modern statesman needs to be supplemented by something additional to and a little different from the Civil Service. We shall never enjoy prosperity again

[11] W. H. Beveridge, 'An Economic General Staff', *The Nation and Athenaeum*, 29 December 1923 and 5 January 1924.

if we continue indefinitely without some deliberate machinery for mitigating the consequences of selecting our governors on account of their gifts of oratory and their power of detecting in good time which way the wind of uninstructed opinion is blowing. It is this need which I had in mind, amongst some other things, in the latter part of this sentence from my book:

'Perhaps the chief task of Economists of this hour is to distinguish afresh the Agenda of Government from the non-Agenda; and the companion task of Politics is to devise forms of Government within a Democracy which should be capable of accomplishing the Agenda.'

Yours, etc.,

J. M. KEYNES

On 9 August Keynes addressed the Independent Labour Party's Summer School at Easton Lodge, Dunmow on 'The Future Balance of British Industry'. No extensive record of his remarks has survived, nor have any of his speech notes.

With the autumn Keynes returned to the subject of sterling in the columns of *The Nation*.

From The Nation and Athenaeum, *23 October 1926*

THE AUTUMN PROSPECTS FOR STERLING: SHOULD THE EMBARGO ON FOREIGN LOANS BE REIMPOSED?

The period of autumn pressure, when Europe is a seasonal debtor to America, has come round for the second time since the gold standard was restored. It finds us with depleted resources after half a year's coal strike, yet gaily lending almost as usual to smarten up the emporiums of our trade rivals—Tokyo, Hamburg, or wherever it may be. At the same time—since every day brings even the coal strike a day nearer its end—we all nourish a hope that afterwards a trade revival may come our way at last. It is a time, therefore, to look round and measure the prospects.

If we are to employ our population, though not at full stretch, yet reasonably well, we must hope for an increase of the national productive activity by, say, 10 per cent. For this we shall require an additional working capital of perhaps £100,000,000, some part of which will be spent abroad in purchasing raw materials, and most of which will have to be found through the intermediary of the banking system. This sum is not beyond the capacity of our current savings over six months, if the surplus beyond what is required to finance normal capital improvements at home is available. But if the banks are to find the real resources which industry will need without resorting to inflationary methods, the new savings of the public must be drawn into their hands in exchange for other assets—such as Stock Exchange investments now owned by the banks, undigested new issues financed by the banks, overdrafts by corporations, and the like, which can be repaid out of the proceeds of the issue of public loans. Thus the resources to finance a revival of trade must be mainly found through the diversion of the current savings of the public into these channels, instead of into new foreign issues of the type now popular. The ability of the banks to finance this revival will also be conditioned by the policy of the Bank of England. It is essential that the latter should not be restricting the basis of credit, and, if prudently possible, should be slightly expanding it.

We may jeopardise our revival, therefore, if we allow our not very abundant flow of new savings to be drained away into foreign loans, and, generally speaking, if we allow the balance of current international indebtedness to tend against us rather than for us, with the result of pushing the Bank of England, not only towards dear money, but to a restriction of the volume of credit. If this happens, there will be no revival of trade. It is one of the fatal traps latent in the gold standard that one of the easiest methods of protecting it at any given moment consists in checking trade. Traders and manufacturers spend their working capital some months on the average before they recoup themselves out of the proceeds of sales. To prevent them from spending is, therefore, an efficient temporary expedient for diminishing our international indebtedness and thereby retaining our gold.

Experience shows that a policy of *laissez-faire* in these matters means taking no action until the mischief has been done and then allowing the so-called 'natural forces' thereby generated to administer a sharp rebuff to all enterprising persons. Let us, therefore, examine the autumn prospects for our international cash account and for the sterling exchange, with a view to seeing whether it is safe to let matters take their course.

The balance of trade

For the first nine months of 1926 the excess of imports over total exports has been £43,000,000 greater than for the same period of 1925—almost the whole (£42,000,000) of this deterioration having occurred in the last two months of the period, August and September. Since the published trade returns reflect business activity some little time in arrear, the deterioration is certain to continue during the last quarter of 1926, whether the coal strike is settled or not, and will probably reach or exceed £75,000,000 by the end of the year. Furthermore, new foreign issues during the first nine months of the year have been £31,000,000 more than in 1925, during the greater part of which year the embargo on such issues was still in force. Thus we are already £74,000,000 down on the two visible items of trade and new investment taken together. A comparison with 1924 yields much the same result.

What is the effect of these changes on our ability to invest abroad? The Board of Trade has compiled an estimate of the invisible items in our favour in 1924 and 1925. It is possible, in my opinion, that this is an underestimate. To avoid undue pessimism, therefore, let us increase the official estimate of our miscellaneous financial and trading profits by £60,000,000 per annum—which is probably an excessive allowance. On this assumption, and taking the invisible items at the same rate per annum in 1926 as in 1925, the international balance sheet for the last three years works out as follows:—

	(£ million)			
			1926	
	1924	1925	Jan.–Sep.	Oct.–Dec.*
Net favourable balance of 'invisible' items	447	474	355	119
Excess of 'visible' imports over exports	324	386	317	140
Balance available for foreign investment	123	88	38	−21
Actual foreign issues on the London market	134	88	72	

* Forecast.

This table indicates that at present we have no surplus for foreign investment, and that we must be providing for about half of our recent loans by reborrowing in the form of temporary balances and bills held by foreign banks in London.

Are there any favourable influences to modity this conclusion? Some there certainly are. Our shipping earnings have increased in recent months. Government receipts from reparations and interest on allied debt are a little larger. The restoration of the gold standard has probably increased our profits on international banking business. On the other hand, for the fact that some of our leading imports are relatively cheap—especially cotton, but also sugar, wheat, and maize, I have tried to allow in my forecast of the excess of imports during the last quarter of the year. Moreover, we are no longer receiving abnormal profits on the sale of rubber—a very large item not long ago. Taking all into account, and remembering that we have added £60,000,000 per annum to the official estimate of our invisible earnings in order to correct a possible underestimate of this item, no one, surely, can maintain that our surplus for foreign investment in 1926 as a whole will exceed £50,000,000 at the best, a figure which the actual issues on the London market have already exceeded, or can deny a risk of its sinking to zero.

The awkwardness of this for our future prospects is aggravated by the circumstance that the effect of foreign issues is generally delayed, some part of the proceeds being at first deposited with London banks or invested in sterling bills or used to pay off indebtedness previously incurred. The growth of London's international banking business also adds to our risks, since it may cause a greater proportion of the autumn pressure of European indebtedness to America to fall on London than has been the case lately. Against this, however, we can probably reckon on the United States Federal Reserve Board doing what it can to ease our seasonal difficulties, and on its refraining from embarrassing us by raising the Federal Reserve discount rates, unless the American internal situation urgently requires this, of which there seems no sign, but quite the contrary, at present.

Should we restore the embargo?

Taking all the features of this complex situation into account, is it sensible to allow foreign investment to proceed unhindered? The austere philosophers of *laissez-faire* reply that, if we lend too much, this will bring its own remedy in due course. Certainly. But the remedy will take the form of a reduction in the basis of credit, which will check indiscriminately foreign lending and home business. If this remedy has to be taken, the trade revival we hope for will not happen.

The orthodox doctrine of leaving foreign investment to take care of itself on the assumption that if it is in the least degree more profitable or less troublesome to the individual to lend his money to Tokyo than to finance the employment of labour in the North of England, then the former is preferable, whilst if practised to excess it will 'bring its own remedy'. These notions purport to be very wise and intellectual. They accord with the repopularised motto of leaving everything to the resultant of individual business men acting each on his own and for himself 'without interference from government'. They are obsolete and dangerous, all the same. I did not criticise the embargo on foreign investment which preceded and accompanied the restoration of the gold standard. I did not believe that this restoration would obviate the use of the embargo in future. I think that a central control of the volume of foreign investment is a permanent necessity for Great Britain, just as much as a rational Bank rate policy. Meanwhile, I should like to see the embargo reimposed at once.

The embargo is not a perfect instrument and might be much improved. It is not entirely fair, and it is not entirely effective. But it is broadly efficient on the whole in attaining the desired end of checking new foreign investment by the great body of ordinary investors. We ought to devise a permanent centralised control for the regulation of foreign investment. The interesting pamphlet on Australian loans, lately published by Mr Russell Cooke and Mr Davenport, shows how badly the Trustee Acts are working in regard to Dominion issues.[12] We need a regular official plan for the control and rationing of this and other foreign investment business. Meanwhile, the embargo, though crude, is the best instrument we have.

My argument, put shortly, is this. A trade revival at home will require real resources on the one hand and an undiminished basis of money credit from the banking system on the other. But, unless we can strengthen our international balance sheet, we are in danger of temporarily running short of the former and of putting the Bank of England in a position where the desire to protect its gold will cause it to restrict the latter. By checking foreign investment immediately we can lessen both dangers.

---

[12] S. R. Cooke and E. H. Davenport, *Australian Finance*, dedicated to the Imperial Conference 1926, (London, 1926).

Moreover, if we do this, the Bank of England can feel sufficiently confident about the underlying solvency of our position to allow its gold to flow out for the time being and even to use its American credits, if necessary, without these movements being allowed to impair the reserves of the joint stock banks.

Is it wrong to exercise foresight? Does the individual sub-scriber to a Tokyo loan in response to large-scale newspaper advertisement consider the possible reactions of his investment on employment in the North of England three months hence with such care and understanding that those at the centre, the Treasury and the Bank of England, are absolved from the duty of taking thought? I suggest that this is not a case where the irresponsible actions of individuals are best left alone to produce what consequences they will.

On 13 November Keynes returned to the same theme in an unsigned note.[13]

From The Nation and Athenaeum, *13 November 1926*

The view, which we have expressed strongly in *The Nation* to the effect that there had better be no more foreign government loans for the present, has, we understand, been accepted in responsible City circles. An exception will be made in favour of the Bulgarian loan, which is to appear shortly under the auspices of the League of Nations. But other applicants will be quite definitely discouraged. Thus in effect, probably by agreement rather than by open compulsion, the old semi-official embargo has been largely restored.

During November and December Keynes's energies were largely devoted to the reorganisation of the Lancashire cotton industry.[14] However, he made one more interjection on financial matters. On 20 December the City Editor

---

[13] Attributed to Keynes in the 'marked copy' of the issue in the Keynes Papers.
[14] See chapter 7, below.

574

of *The Times*, commenting on a report of an agreement concerning acceptance commissions by New York banks, suggested that recent reductions in similar rates in London were not good for either the market or the banks. Keynes wrote immediately.

To the Editor of The Times, *20 December 1926*

Sir,

Your reference today to the reduced rates for acceptance business now charged by the London banks raises a question of some importance. For many borrowers 90-day acceptances and bank advances are alternatives, the choice between which is mainly determined by the cost. The cost of the former is measured by the market rate of discount for bank bills *plus* acceptance commission *plus* stamp. The cost of the latter generally bears a more or less fixed relationship to Bank rate— e.g. $\frac{1}{2}$ per cent or, at most, 1 per cent above Bank rate. Thus the comparative expense of the two methods of borrowing depends on the margin between the market rate of discount and the Bank rate. Now, I think it is correct to say that recently this difference has been narrower than it used to be, the strict management of the money market and the tight control now maintained by the Bank of England being the chief cause of this. The result is that, if the acceptance rate is maintained at the former figure of $\frac{1}{4}$ per cent for 90 days, this method of borrowing compares unfavourably with bank advances. For example, commercial bills are quoted today at $4\frac{9}{16}$ per cent discount, which, with acceptance charges as above and stamp duty, adds up to $5\frac{3}{4}$ per cent discount, equal to slightly more than 6 per cent interest to the borrower, which is not a competitive price as compared with the cost of bank advances. The shortage of commercial bills, doubtless a consequence of this state of affairs, has led to the anomalous position of their commanding a discount rate lower than that on Treasury bills.

Unless there is some flaw in this calculation, is it right to criticise the banks for bringing down their rates for acceptance business to $\frac{1}{8}$ per cent? Is it not a very sound move in the interest of keeping the London commercial bill market alive?

I suggest that the action of the banks in cheapening the cost of borrowing by means of bank acceptances is specially to be welcomed just now for the following reason. The volume of bank advances is abnormally high. Yet if there is to be a revival of trade they must probably go higher. Their present high level may be due in part to the decay of acceptances consequent on the latter's relatively high cost. If acceptances can be brought down to a competitive level, this may bring a very necessary relief to the pressure on bank advances.

For business where their special experience is essential, the $\frac{1}{4}$ per cent charged by the acceptance houses is doubtless reasonable. But this does not apply to the case of customers of the banks who, if they do not use acceptances, will take out an advance. There is no reason why the banks should charge more for the former method of accommodation than for the latter at a time when it is the former which it is in the interest of themselves and their customers to encourage.

Yours, &c.,

J. M. KEYNES

Keynes's letter drew comment from the City Editor and another correspondent signing himself 'Acceptor', both taking issue with Keynes's facts. On 24 December, Keynes drafted a reply. It was never published and it is unclear whether it was ever sent.

To the Editor of The Times, *24 December 1926*

ACCEPTANCES *VERSUS* BANK ADVANCES

Sir,

It is evident that the facts are pretty obscure to outsiders like you and me. I did not infer, as I see I should, from your original statement (Dec. 20) about the reduction of the bankers' acceptance commissions to $\frac{1}{8}$ per cent that this suggested discrimination against home borrowers. On Dec. 22 you added that the reduction applied only to leading German banks. Your correspondent 'Acceptor' today (Dec. 24) states in correction that it applies to foreign banks generally. Whether it *never* applies to home borrowers, is still unclear. Further, on Dec. 20, you quoted the New York *Evening Post* to the effect that certain London banks have been accepting American *financial companies*' bills for nothing. Today you tell us that the London money market is stricter than it used to be in insisting that bills must also be used to finance goods in transit or in storage, and also—which I take leave to doubt—that bank advances are seldom used for these purposes. It would be useful to know precisely for what borrowers and for what purposes the banks are lowering their commissions.

The criticisms of 'Acceptor' against a gratuitous discrimination in favour of foreign borrowers as against domestic borrowers seem to be entirely sound. If this is all the banks have done or intend to do, my praise was premature. But this does not affect the point of my letter, the only point on which I am entitled to have an opinion, namely that a state of affairs in which a bank acceptance is more expensive than a bank overdraft tends to kill the domestic bank bill; that this is an anomaly and a misfortune, since there are many purposes for which such bills are appropriate and convenient for all concerned; and that it is a double misfortune at the present time when the banks are somewhat overloaded with advances. I am not concerned in any controversy about the wisdom of competition between banks and accepting houses. But I suggest that, if the banks would extend to English borrowers of unexceptionable credit the concessions which they are making to Americans and Germans, they could ease their own position and that of their customers in the event of a trade revival.

[draft not signed or initialled]

577

Chapter 7

INDUSTRIAL REORGANISATION: COTTON

As in the case of coal, the cotton industry in Britain in the 1920s was finding it extremely difficult to adjust to changing market prospects which resulted from the rise of overseas competitors and the problems associated with the return to gold. On 24 October Keynes began to write an article on the industry. It appeared in *The Nation* just under three weeks later.

From The Nation and Athenaeum, *13 November 1926*

THE POSITION OF THE LANCASHIRE COTTON TRADE

The heavy fall in the price of raw cotton since the beginning of September may prove to have been, for the world as a whole, the most important economic event of the year, not excepting the British coal strike. More than one third of the cotton spindles in the world are in Lancashire. Lancashire alone, if she worked full-time, could consume 1,500,000 more bales of American cotton this year than last. It is, therefore, an occasion to examine the causes of Lancashire's present plight.

The coal industry and the cotton industry have pursued in face of their common difficulties diametrically opposite policies. The coal industry has ruined itself by uncontrolled over-production, thus bringing down prices to an unremunerative level, and is now engaged in an attempt to chase the price further downwards and to aggravate the overproduction by establishing an eight-hour day uncompensated by the closing of pits. The cotton industry, on the other hand, has ruined itself by organised short-time extending over five years, which, by increasing overhead expenses, has raised its cost of production above the competitive level. Nevertheless, both these policies, opposite though they be, are based on a common fallacy. For both are founded on a belief that, if only the industries hang on, 'normal' times will return when they may again hope to employ all their existing plant and labour on profitable terms. Neither industry has attempted what the Germans are calling 'rationalisation', that is to say, the concentration of demand on the most efficient plants, which are worked at full stretch and the rest closed down.

Has there been a world-wide slump in the cotton trade?

As compared with the volume of its pre-war export trade, Lancashire has lost about one third of its business. In the *best* post-war year the exports of piece goods have never reached two-thirds of the 1913 figure, and, with the exception of the slump year 1921, have been very steady between 59 per cent and 63 per cent of 1913:—

Piece goods (exported) (millions of square yards)

		1913	7,075
1920	4,425	1923	4,140
1921	2,902	1924	4,444
1922	4,182	1925	4,434

These figures are noteworthy and depressing. In 1921 there was evidently an abnormal slump of short duration which could be appropriately met by organised short-time, such as had proved effective in former days. But short-time has been continued ever since that year down to the present date. Is it right to assume that the pre-war scale is 'normal' and that the steady figures prevailing since 1922 are 'abnormal' and transitory?

Lancashire has comforted itself by blaming the continued depression through these years on a variety of external circumstances—such as the high price of cotton, the alleged reduced purchasing power of the international market, the disturbances in China, and so forth. Doubtless at all times unfavourable factors can be discovered. If, however, we put the question to the test of the world consumption of cotton, what do we find? Is it true that Lancashire has been suffering from world-wide causes which have affected all producers alike?

World consumption of all kinds of cotton for the years ended July 31st (thousands of bales) (International Cotton Federation figures)

	1913	23,000	
1921	17,595	1924	20,430
1922	21,167	1925	22,294
1923	22,143	1926	24,681

This table shows that for the world as a whole there was something of a slump in 1923–24 as well as in 1920–21, but that this was recovered in 1924–25 and 1925–26, with a total consumption comfortably in excess of the pre-war figure.

The totals for 1912–13 and 1925–26 can be analysed as follows:—

	(Thousands of bales)	
	1912–13	1925–26
Great Britain	4,274	3,022
Germany	1,728	1,148
France	1,010	1,179
Russia	2,509	1,752
Italy	789	1,037
India	2,177	2,064
Japan	1,588	2,816
U.S.A.	5,786	6,395
Others	3,139	5,268
Total	23,000	24,681

These figures convey some very important information, which should be broadcasted throughout Lancashire and thrown on every cinema screen and advertised on every hoarding. We find, as we should expect, a falling-off in Russia and Germany ($1\frac{1}{4}$ million spindles in Alsace have been transferred from Germany to France), and a fair (but not sensational) increase in the United States. Indian mill consumption, which experienced a bad year in 1925–26, is but little changed, and, on the average of post-war years 1919–26, was a little better than before the War. What of the rest? Those amongst whom Lancashire numbers many of her customers—France, Italy, and the others—are making a good deal more for themselves, whether under the protection of tariffs or for other reasons (such as two shifts in the twenty-four hours), than they used to do—having consumed 7,484,000 bales, i.e., 30 per cent of the world's consumption, in 1925–26, as compared with 4,928,000 bales, i.e., 21 per cent of the world's consumption, in 1912–13. At the same time Japan has increased her business by nearly 80 per cent during the same period in which Lancashire's has fallen off by 30 per cent. Indeed Japan's gain, measured in bales, which is, however, not an accurate guide to output, almost exactly balances our loss.

These figures surely show that during the last two years at least there has been no slump in the world's consumption of cotton, but sound progress, and that Lancashire has suffered a definite loss of trade since the War, partly because her customers now make more for themselves, and partly because Japan has been capturing her business. Is not Lancashire deceiving herself when she advances other explanations?

In order, however, to appreciate the full force of these figures, we must analyse them further. For, uncorrected, they confuse together two branches of the trade which are pursuing opposite courses. If we take the consumption of Egyptian cotton as an index of the state of the fine cotton trade, we find that Lancashire's proportion since the War has been as high as it was before, and that in 1923–24 and 1924–25 it was better. This section of the trade, moreover, has been working full-time. The conclusions of this article do not apply, therefore, to the finer branches, where technical skill and the absence of organised short-time have enabled our spinners fully to hold their own.

If we separate off the 22,000,000 spindles in Lancashire which have been working full-time on the finer counts, we are left with about 36,000,000 spindles which have been, for five years past, working half-time or not much more on American and coarser cottons. In this great industry, the greatest of British exports, we appear to have lost, not just in an isolated year, but as a phenomenon extending over the whole of the post-war period, something approaching *half* of our former trade (say, 45 per cent).

The consequences of short-time

Ever since 1920, the Lancashire spinners of American and miscellaneous cottons have been meeting their inability to market their goods on the old scale, not by closing down the weaker firms and the more inefficient plants, but by *everyone* working short-time—thus adding the embarrassment of high overhead costs to the embarrassment of high labour costs (which, with no reduction of wages since the restoration of the gold standard, have been 10 per cent more burdensome in 1925–26 than before). The less Lancashire sells, the shorter the time she works, the higher therefore her costs—a cumulative progress towards perdition only limited by the rate at which other countries can erect new spindles.

The crushing effect of short-time work on the competitive position is strikingly illustrated by the following. In the half-year ending July, 1926, Japan actually consumed, for the first time in history, a greater weight of raw cotton than was consumed in Great Britain. Yet the number of spindles in Great Britain was more than ten times the number in Japan. This figure has to be modified to allow for the smaller weight of cotton required to spin a given length of yard in the finer counts. After allowing for this, it seems, on the test of cotton consumption that Japan's spindleage has had an output between $4\frac{1}{2}$ and 5 times the output of comparable spindles in Great Britain using comparable cotton.

This conclusion is closely corroborated by the statistics of hours worked. Until May, 1923, the normal working week in Japan was 132 hours, when it was reduced to 120 hours, i.e., two daily shifts of 10 hours each. The actual average weekly hours worked recently have not been less than 118. In Great Britain the corresponding figure for the last half year has been 28 hours per week. Thus a Japanese spindle has been worked between $4\frac{1}{2}$ and 5 times as intensively as a comparable Lancashire spindle.

The consequences of this on overhead costs are obvious. When we add to this the difference in wages (Japanese male hands earn on the average about 3s. 3d. per shift, or, say, £1 per week, and female hands 2s. $6\frac{1}{2}$d. per shift, or, say, 15s. a week), it is evident that in this branch of the trade Lancashire is not on a competitive basis and only gets the business in excess of what her competitors can handle.

The comparison with Japan is, of course, the extreme one. But comparisons elsewhere are the same in tendency. In Germany there has been a good deal of short-time amounting at present to about 20 per cent; also some short-time in Poland and Czechoslovakia. But in France, Italy, Belgium, Switzerland, Holland, and Sweden practically full-time has been and is being worked. In the United States the spindles employed on American cotton have been worked twice as intensively as those in Lancashire.

Lancashire, finding herself at a disadvantage through tariffs and relatively high labour costs, has proceeded to put herself at a greater disadvantage still by increasing her overhead costs; and to meet the additional burden of the restored gold standard she has taken no steps whatever. The result is that the rate at which she is losing her trade (always excepting the finer branches) is only limited by the rate at which other producers can erect new spindles. Lancashire starts with so large a percentage of the total spindleage of the world that she cannot lose her trade other than gradually. In the four years between 1921 and 1925 Japan increased the number of her spindles by 50 per cent. But since in 1921 Japan's total spindles numbered only 10 per cent of Lancashire's (exclusive of those spinning fine counts), this represents a fairly slow process, even allowing for the difference in the hours worked.

The prospects ahead

Lancashire's first need is to face these figures. If they are substantially correct, the termination of the short-time policy is urgently called for, and the substitution for it of a 'rational-ising' process designed to cut down overhead costs by the amalgamation, grouping or elimination of mills. The failure so far to eliminate weak mills is largely attributable to the banks, who have been too ready to protect old loans by new ones. There are said to be two hundred Lancashire mills on an unsound financial basis. It may be that only the bankers of Lancashire are in a position to take the first step to break down the unorganised individualism which was well enough for an ever-expanding industry, but spells universal loss when some curtailment is necessary.

As it happens, Lancashire has just had a great stroke of luck, which may make a revision of policy much easier than it would otherwise have been. Owing to a cotton crop in the United States which has broken all records, raw cotton has suffered a catastrophic fall of price. It costs today about two thirds of what it cost a year ago, although the price then was already moderate on post-war standards. It will be paradoxical if this fall of price does not stimulate consumption considerably. The cotton trade of the world is justified in expecting an increased turn-over during the next year or two. Now since the unoccupied spindles outside Lancashire do not amount to any formidable figure,

Lancashire can rely on obtaining a fair proportion of this coming year's business, in spite of her costs being above those of her competitors. Thus a fortunate accident has given her a breathing-space in which to reorganise her affairs.

But it will only be a breathing-space, which it would be imprudent to treat otherwise. The danger is lest Lancashire may consider the revival of trade, when it comes, to be a justification of her past policy, and a return of the 'normal' times for which she has been waiting so long. But in truth the times will not be normal. There will be a temporary recovery based on raw cotton well below the cost of production, and on the time lag, before cheaper producers can increase their spindleage. Present prices for raw cotton will not last for long; nor will the present limitations on spindleage elsewhere.

The mishandling of currency and credit by the Bank of England since the war, the stiff-neckedness of the coal owners, the apparently suicidal behaviour of the leaders of Lancashire raises a question of the suitability and adaptability of our business men to the modern age of mingled progress and retrogression. What has happened to them—the class in which a generation or two generations ago we could take a just and worthy pride? Are they too old or too obstinate? Or what? Is it that too many of them have risen not on their own legs, but on the shoulders of their fathers and grandfathers? Of the coal owners all these suggestions may be true. But what of our Lancashire lads, England's pride for shrewdness? What have they to say for themselves?

Keynes's article had an immediate impact: the Manchester evening newspapers of the day before *The Nation* appeared were full of criticisms from leading cotton men. On 16 November the Short-Time Committee of the Federation of Master Cotton Spinners invited him to come to Manchester to discuss points raised in his article. On 19 November, Keynes accepted their invitation and met the General Committee of the Federation three days later. The discussion was private but at the end of the meeting a communiqué appeared which made it clear that Keynes was advocating a cartel, enforced by the Federation and the banks, with transferable quotas to allow the concentration of production in the most efficient firms.

The previous Saturday's issue of *The Nation* had contained several letters on the problems of the trade and Keynes's analysis. In the case of two letters, Keynes appended brief comments, but he did promise a more substantial discussion of matters the next week. His two comments were in response to letters from Frederick W. Tattersall and Fred A. Tomlinson.

From The Nation and Athenaeum, *20 November 1926*

I am grateful to Mr Tattersall, from whom in the past I have learnt much of my cotton statistics, for his criticisms and additions, particularly when he agrees with me on my main conclusion. I plead guilty, however, on only one point—my slip in saying that Japan had consumed a greater *weight* of cotton than Lancashire. For I added that 'Japan's gain measured in bales is not an accurate guide to output', and in comparing the intensity of Japan's employment of her machinery I hope that I made a sufficient correction. Further, Mr Tattersall's arithmetic is surely wrong when he reduces Japan's increment of production from 80 per cent, as stated by me, to 44 per cent. Japan used Indian bales before the war, as well as after; indeed, her proportion of American bales has considerably increased since the war: so that the effect of Mr Tattersall's correction is to make her percentage increase *greater* than 80, not less.

As regards potential consumption, does Mr Tattersall deny that, if all the Lancashire mills capable of using American and similar cottons were to be worked forty-eight hours a week for a year, Lancashire's consumption of these cottons would be quite 1,500,000 bales greater than in the year ended July last?

Mr Tomlinson's details about hours are very interesting. But so far from overlooking the system of two shifts abroad as a factor in the situation, I expressly mentioned it as one of the causes of Lancashire's difficulties. If Mr Tomlinson complains that I did not sufficiently emphasise it, I reply that it seemed to me premature to talk about two shifts in Lancashire so long as short time is being worked! The implication of Mr Tomlinson's argument is to corroborate my contention that a twenty-eight-hour week gravely increases the cost of production. To my demand for a forty-eight-hour week, it is scarcely a defence of the twenty-eight hour-week, to reply that what we really require is a fifty-five-hour week. Doubtless Mr Tomlinson does not intend it as such. But it is a red herring to talk about fifty-five-hour weeks and double shifts so long as organised short time continues. Surely the first step in the right direction is to get rid of the latter.

From The Nation and Athenaeum, *27 November 1926*

THE PROSPECTS OF THE LANCASHIRE COTTON TRADE

I appreciate the spirit in which Lancashire has taken my article in *The Nation* of November 13th, written by an outsider to the industry. My article has brought down on me a flood of critical and supplementary information in print, in letters, and by word of mouth. The Committee of the Federation of Master Cotton Spinners has done me the courtesy of asking me to meet them. The result is that I am better informed about the details and practical difficulties of the problem than I was a fortnight ago. My purpose in this article is not to answer criticisms in a controversial spirit, but to put again my contentions, enlarged, but not materially changed on essentials, as they are after having heard Lancashire's point of view.

I must begin by contradicting two widespread misapprehensions about my previous article. I did not maintain, what would have been absurd, that Lancashire's difficulties are wholly or mainly due to short-time. Short-time has been the *result* of Lancashire's finding her competitive position worsened and her markets narrowed from quite other causes, some of them altogether beyond her control. My point was that, her competitive position being already worsened by these other causes, the palliative of short-time was suicidal because it had the effect of aggravating her inferiority, so that Lancashire's progression to perdition is progressive.

Nor did I maintain that Lancashire, instead of organising short-time, ought to have worked the whole number of her spindles full-time during the last five years. So far from denying the necessity for restriction of output, my point was that a lasting curtailment, save in exceptionally favourable years, was probably inevitable, but that organised short-time, whilst well adapted for a temporary curtailment, was a disastrous expedient with which to meet a lasting one.

On the statistical side my figures have been supplemented and corrected in some particulars, but not so as to affect the argument materially. No one denies that in the American branch Lancashire has lost between a third and a half of her pre-war trade. No one denies that this is due, not to a world-wide depression in the consumption of cotton goods, but to our customers and our competitors alike gaining ground on ourselves. There is only one important qualification to this, which I did not bring out in my previous article, namely, that our loss of trade in India is not entirely due to the competition of Japanese and native Indian mills, but also in part to a diminished aggregate consumption of cotton goods in that country, as shown in Mr Tattersall's letter to last week's *Nation*.

At my meeting with the Committee of the Federation these conclusions were not seriously contested. Indeed, I think that some of the members were more pessimistic than I was. Furthermore, no one in Lancashire defends short-time on its merits. It is agreed that such a policy continued over a long period is economically unsound and must ruin everybody in time; though possibly a contributory influence in favour of the short-time policy, which is seldom mentioned, is to be found in the machinery of the dole. Short-time, as it is worked in Lancashire, is, from one point of view, an ingenious device for securing the maximum subsidy for the industry out of public funds. Thus the loss which it brings on the country as a whole is much greater than the loss which it brings on those in the industry itself.

In face, then, of this large measure of agreement, how is it possible for the local press to sum up the situation by saying that few people can be found in Lancashire to accept my conclusions?

I have no doubt about the explanation. There is a fearfully uneasy conscience abroad throughout the American branch. Everyone knows in his bones that the present policy is all wrong. *But no one can think of any practicable alternative.* Lancashire does not really disagree with me when I say that their present policy is leading them progressively to perdition. They know that, if they cannot work full-time with raw cotton at its present price, they will never work full-time again. It is when I seem to suggest that I know an alternative, that I have a way out, that they disagree with me—which is expressed by saying that short-time is undoubtedly wrong, but that anyone who opposed it does not know what he is talking about. Lancashire, in short, must go to hell her own way; for any other route to any other destination is, in the circumstances, 'theoretical'.

In speaking to the Committee of the Federation I said that the practicability of an alternative depended upon how seriously the leaders of the industry felt about the necessity of a change. After visiting Lancashire my impression is that many of them, if not all, are fully alive to the actual facts of the existing situation. Nor is there much for anyone to tell them, which they do not know already, about the complex causes of the situation. What, in my opinion, Lancashire is not yet fully alive to, is the exact reason why a remedy is so difficult or why it must take a certain form.

The problem of surplus capacity

The method of building up a growing industry by individuals adding spindle to spindle and mill to mill when they see profitable opportunities to do so, works perfectly well. But—a point which is familiar to students of other industries and other places, but is a new idea to Lancashire—this system includes no provision whatever for reversing the process, except the slow and dragging cure which time brings at last by decay and obsolescence.

Let us suppose that there are 36,000,000 efficient spindles in existence. Let us suppose that the demand at prices which pay interest and depreciation on the value of a spindle as measured by cost of replacement, will only occupy 30,000,000 spindles save in exceptionally favourable years. What will happen in an unorganised industry? Competition between the owners of the 36,000,000 spindles will drive down prices towards the point at which no contribution at all is left towards overhead expenses. Each individual will accept not the price which yields him a normal return, but the price which is preferable to abandoning his plant altogether and closing down his organisation. If this goes on for long, the mills which are financially the weaker, though not perhaps technically inefficient, will become bankrupt. But even this will not bring a solution. The spindles of the bankrupt mills will not cease to exist. They will be sold at a low price and thus transferred into stronger hands on terms which will enable the competition to persist in conditions too severe for other businesses to earn their interest charges. And so the losses will continue until the gradual growth of demand over a long period or the obsolescence of the older spindles restores equilibrium at last.

The policy of organised short-time delays this result but by increasing working costs and aggravating financial losses all round it leads to a still greater loss of trade. It suits no one except those who stand aside from loyalty to the Federation's orders.

Now this problem of excess productive capacity is not a new one in the world at large, and there are recognised ways of tackling it. All these are variations of the cartel, the holding company, and the amalgamation, such as I outlined at Manchester last Monday. By these means, and by these means only, can the surplus capacity be withdrawn from competition and held in reserve against future requirements, so that the rest of the industry can earn normal profits meanwhile.

This analysis of the situation is not yet a living thing in the mind of the average cotton-spinner. The nature of the remedy is repugnant to his intensely individual temperament and traditions. It is not clear that there is anyone in Lancashire with enough authority or initiative to set the ball rolling. There is no obvious way to bring in the recalcitrant minority. These are the 'practical' difficulties in trying to get off the 'bus, even though the passengers see well enough where the 'bus is going to.

The present prospects

Nevertheless, I do not believe that short-time will last much longer. The trade is sick of it. They feel increasingly that it is a mistake. Moreover, it is not loyally observed. At the first breath of the revival of demand, which the present low price of cotton will surely bring as soon as merchants are convinced that the bottom has been touched, it is likely to be abandoned. With the coal strike finished and cotton so cheap that it is much below its cost of production, there will be nothing more to wait for.

Whatever else may follow, the abandonment of organised short-time will be the first step towards putting the industry on a sounder basis. But this will not cure—it may even aggravate—the financial unsoundness of the industry, which, in my revised opinion, is a bigger factor than short-time in causing its present disorders. The financial clean-up of an industry, which was, in many cases, overcapitalised in the boom and has been losing money for five years, is just as necessary as is the concentration of production. Both these things must come, whether or not the industry feels ripe for 'rationalisation'. But neither of them in themselves will solve the problem of surplus capacity. That is why I ventured, in all diffidence, to suggest to the industry that the idea of cartels, holding companies or amalgamations deserved consideration. The formation of holding companies at the bottom of the slump is not likely to prove unprofitable to those who have the pluck and the initiative to take the lead. It will facilitate the financial clean-up as well as help to solve the problem of surplus capacity. If the formation of a cartel is attempted, it will not be absolutely necessary, however desirable, for everyone to come in, any more than with organised short-time. Experience elsewhere shows that a cartel can sometimes be successful even where it does not cover the whole of the industry. But for any important move forward the sympathy and the assistance of the banks will be essential.

On 26 November John Ryan, a member of the committee attempting to form a Cotton Yarn Association to reconstruct the spinning section of the trade, wrote to Keynes enclosing some literature on the Association and offering to send a small delegation to London to discuss its plans and aims. To this Keynes replied.

To JOHN RYAN, *30 November 1926*

Dear Sir,

I have your letter of November 26, for which I am very much obliged, sending me full particulars about the Cotton Yarn Association. I am very glad to have these particulars, since, whilst I already knew about the Association in a general way, I had not seen the full details.

I have now read carefully all that you have sent me, and I am ready to agree that this Association probably represents by far the most hopeful move in the direction which, in my opinion, is essential for the recovery of Lancashire's prosperity. With a few modifications, I believe this Association, if it is formed, could go a long way towards achieving the objects which I sought to obtain by my proposal for a cartel. I should much like to have an opportunity of discussing the matter with the members of your Committee, and of making such suggestions as have occurred to me. If any of your members are likely to be in London in the new future. I should be delighted if they would lunch or dine with me here for the purpose of a talk. Unfortunately, at the moment I am not a position to name a day. Up to December 9 I shall be engaged in Cambridge. The week after that I may have to go to Paris to represent the International Chamber of Commerce at a Conference, but the day has not yet been settled. Subject to that I shall be in London the whole of the week beginning December 12. If you could be so kind as to suggest one or two days convenient to your Committee, I could then let you know later on how they would fit in with this projected visit to Paris.

Yours faithfully,
[copy initialled] J.M.K.

Ryan replied on 3 December suggesting that if the Committee could release part of Keynes's letter of 30 November to the press it would strengthen its cause. Keynes authorised a statement paraphrasing the second sentence of the second paragraph of his letter. This appeared in the newspapers on 9 and 10 December. Keynes met a deputation from the Committee for three hours on 16 December.

After the meeting Keynes prepared another article for *The Nation*.

From The Nation and Athenaeum, *24 December 1926*

THE COTTON YARN ASSOCIATION

A week ago the Federation of Master Cotton Spinners finally abandoned the false expedient of short-time. They did this, if I interpret their mood rightly, not as a surrender to the forces of disorganisation and beggar-my-neighbour competition, but to clear the ground for some more effective plan of joint action. The possibility of such an alternative now depends, having regard to the practical politics of the industry, on whether there is enough public spirit amongst the Master Cotton Spinners of Lancashire to bring to birth the embryonic *Cotton Yarn Association*. The Articles of this Association are sufficiently comprehensive to serve as the framework for a real reorganisation on modern 'rationalised' lines, and also to bring about many obvious long-desired reforms, the need of which no one disputes, but which single individuals, acting separately, are powerless to effect. The Association has already half the industry behind it. The more active spirits are putting their hopes in it. If it fails, no one will have the heart to begin anything else;—in which case we can but look forward to a slow, cruel process of loss and bankruptcy which will leave no one un-hurt,——perhaps mitigated at first but probably aggravated in the long run by a temporary revival of demand based on abnormally cheap cotton.

The project for the *Cotton Yarn Association* has now been under discussion and in course of development for some six months by a Committee representing about two thirds of the American section of the spinning trade. It is estimated that the number of spindles spinning American yarn for sale (i.e., excluding those spinning other cottons or specialties of yarn for use by associated concerns) is about 28,000,000. So long ago as last August 233 companies, owning 70 per cent of this total number and representing 93 per cent of those who replied to a circular letter, had declared themselves in favour of the proposed Association in principle. This initial success was followed, however, by a disappointment. The promoters of the Association, which takes the form of a limited company with share capital, considered that the participation of 70 per cent of the industry was necessary to success. But when it came to inviting subscriptions not much more than one third responded in the first instance. The number of the supporters of the scheme has, however, increased gradually in recent weeks, until nearly 15,000,000 spindles, or about a half of the whole industry, have come in. It remains to overcome the opposition, or more probably the lethargy, of those controlling another 5,000,000 spindles before the Association can begin to function.

The powers of the Association are wide; its purposes at present not very precisely defined. It will accomplish much or little according to the spirit in which it is managed and supported. Before I catalogue the purposes which it *may* fulfil, I had better restate, in the light of recent discussions with the leaders of the industry, the elements of its problem.

(1) For various reasons, some perhaps avoidable, other certainly unavoidable, Lancashire has found, since the War, a worsened competitive position and diminished markets for her American cotton goods. The loss of markets is not disputed; nor its magnitude; nor, in any responsible person's expectation, apart from temporary spurts or booms, can anything in the near future short of a miracle restore the demand to its pre-war level. A controversialist driven into a corner can sometimes be found to deny this. But such is not the opinion of the industry itself. Spinners know that nothing which they can do themselves and no permanent, lasting change in outside circumstances, which is in the least degree probable, will enable them to sell at a profit 50 per cent more yarn in the next three years than in the past three years.

(2) The industry is faced, therefore, with the problem of surplus capacity, with which so many of our staple exports are faced at this moment. The prevalence of the complaint is due to many causes, but the culminating fact was, of course, the restoration of the gold standard. It was easy to predict beforehand that this measure must be followed by one or other of two things—either a struggle to reduce costs, partly wages in the industry itself, partly charges by other industries, or else an obliteration of profits followed eventually by an adjustment of the scale of outputs to the reduction of outlets. But it was not

easy to say which of the alternatives would prevail. The coal industry has chosen the first alternative so far, but will probably be driven to the second later on. The cotton industry, on the other hand, has chosen the second alternative, being at present in the stage of the obliteration of profits and of feeling its way towards the adjustment of output.

(3) The Lancashire spinners of American cotton have been peculiarly defenceless for dealing with surplus capacity. The large number of independent units (some 330 separate firms within one small geographical area), a long tradition of competition, secretiveness, and non-co-operation, heavy overhead expenses on capital account which are always running, whether the mills are busy or not—these and other factors have caused the spinners to suffer most from conditions which have impoverished all branches of the trade alike. Previous experience had provided them with only one expedient—that of short-time as recommended by a Committee of the Master Cotton Spinners' Federation, subject to a periodic ballot of its members. For five disastrous years this remedy has been tried in vain. Last week it was abandoned.

Since the idea of curtailing output was not fundamentally vicious (as some critics, but not I, seem to think), it will be useful to consider why the policy of short-time broke down so badly. The reasons were undoubtedly the following. In the first place, short time practised by mill A tempered the force of competition for mill B; yet, since there was no penalty if mill B took advantage of this to work longer than the hours recommended, the temptations to disloyalty have proved irresistible to many spinners. In the second place, the Short-Time Committee has worked without any proper statistical basis;—its own constituents have refused it the necessary information, in particular the state of their order books, so that the Committee, working in the dark as to the immediate prospects, has always been a few weeks out of date in its ideas and its prescribed hours of working have often been out of touch with the real situation, sometimes in one direction and sometimes in the other, a maladjustment which has made loyalty difficult even for those who would have liked to be loyal. The withholding of relevant and even essential information from the Short-Time Committee by its own constituents has been carried to a point which an American or a German business man would deem incredible. The secretiveness practised by our business world, from the Bank of England downwards, would be excessive in criminals seeking to evade justice, and is, in fact, a major factor in British inefficiency. In the third place, the American branch of the trade is itself highly complex and includes many sub-branches, not all of which have equal order-books or like prospects at a given date. But the short-time policy as practised hitherto has made no allowance for these differences, prescribing for all mills alike uniform working hours, which may have been excessive for some sections but were certainly inadequate for others. In the fourth place, short time, being essentially an expedient to meet a temporary situation, has done nothing whatever to adjust the scale or the direction or the costs of the industry to permanently changed circumstances. It leads to nothing—except a slow bleeding to death.

(4) In course of time the illness of surplus capacity has led to a complication, almost worse than itself, namely financial exhaustion. Excessive competition, resulting from surplus capacity, has, in many cases, brought the level of profits below that of interest charges and other unavoidable outgoings. The resulting losses have been provided out of bank loans and other resources which ought only to have been used as current working capital. The consequence is that the normal borrowing capacity of the industry has been exhausted in meeting losses, and is not available for new business. A large part of the industry has lost its working capital and is so heavily mortgaged that no means to replenish it is in sight. In short, the spinners, as a class, are frightfully hard-up, which leads to the pest of what is known as 'weak selling'. There are always spinners with no money at

the bank and accounts due at the end of the week, who have, therefore, much less than a normal bargaining resistance, so that they cannot carry stocks of yarn even for a matter of days, and must just take what they can get on the nail. Thus, on the top of a surplus capacity, which abolishes normal profits, since it makes it worth while to accept any price which is better than closing down, 'weak selling' carries the trouble a stage further and leads to prices which are worse than closing down. Nor do these low prices help towards the recovery of markets, since concessions made in such circumstances are liable to be absorbed by the other factors in the trade. Moreover, they encourage hand-to-mouth buying, since only so can the buyer take full advantage of the weakness and necessities of the seller. All the spinners whom I have seen are agreed that this involuntary selling by financially necessitous mills is causing the final loss of blood which no one can suffer and live. Not even the best-placed mills can make profit from this. Nor will they when bankruptcy overtakes the worse-placed, since the spindles do not disappear along with their owners, but are merely transferred into other hands at a lower capitalisation. It is a case where joint action is in the interests of every unit in the trade.

There are, therefore, three objectives before the industry which are in the following order of urgency in point of time though not perhaps of ultimate importance—the elimination of weak sellers and replenishment of working capital; the adjustment of surplus capacity to the actual and potential demand; the securing of organised economies and improvements which may lead later on to the maintenance, and perhaps to the recovery, of markets. I believe that this is the correct order of events and that the industry is right in being more preoccupied at the moment with the recovery of 'margins' than with the recovery of markets. Markets can never be recovered by selling at a loss but only by being able to sell profitably at a reasonable price. The first step towards this must be the avoidance of further losses and the financial rehabilitation of the industry.

We can now return to the proposed Cotton Yarn Association.

How can this Association help the spinners? No one can say that a very new experiment will be successful. But the Association will have sufficient powers, in my opinion, to do what is needful, if they are rightly used. Its leading features, stripped of all detail, are the following:—

(i) The members will be pledged to loyalty to the Association's orders under penalties both financial and personal.

(ii) The members will undertake to furnish prompt and complete statistics to the Association, including duplicate copies of every contract booked.

(iii) The Association will fix a minimum price, below which members will be forbidden to sell, adapted to every type of yarn by the method familiar to Lancashire of points 'on' and 'off' a standard basis. It is not yet clear whether this minimum is to be fixed so as to yield normal profits to the normal mill, in which case the basic price will probably prove to be the maximum as well as the minimum, and will work out as a cut-and-dried system of price fixing, or whether it is to be fixed at a protective minimum. It appears to me very important that it should take the latter form, thus leaving room for the normal play of competition; that is to say, the Association's minimum should be aimed not at the cheap, competitive producer, but solely at the weak seller. It should be a minimum which it would not be worth anyone's while to undercut on purpose.

(iv) The Association will, in the light of the full statistics in their hands, fix separate quotas of output for each distinct section of the trade. As in the case of prices, these quotas should be fixed, not below what some of the stronger spinners might reasonably wish them to be, but protectively, so as to avoid what, in the light of the combined statistics of the trade, is obviously a senseless overproduction beyond what the market can absorb at prices which will cover costs. It is desirable that these quotas should be made transferable with a view to the concentration of production, and also that production should be permitted in excess of the quota on payment of a modest fine.

(v) The Association, which will have an initial capital of not less than £200,000 (namely, £1 per 100 spindles) will be authorised to raise loans. This side of its possible activities is not developed in its original prospectus. I see here, however, an invaluable opportunity, which I must not stop to develop in detail in this place, of working out a scheme of co-operative credit by which the prime necessity of finding fresh working capital for the industry may be satisfied. Moreover, if the Association could undertake to lend with suitable safeguards against stocks of yarn valued at the Association's minimum price, this would be by far the most effective protection against involuntary 'weak selling' and against forced unfaithfulness to the minimum price.

(vi) The Association will be free to establish an Inquiry Bureau for the information of spinners as to the standing and engagements of manufacturers, yarn agents, and merchants, to work out standard forms of contract which will protect spinners' interests as those now used do not, to bargain with other and better organised sections of the trade, to study foreign markets and foreign requirements, and generally to promote a healthy and efficient industry which can regain in the new conditions some measure of the prosperity and pre-eminence of the past.

Is not such an Association a constructive effort in tune with the spirit of these times, which is at least worth a trial by men otherwise desperate? Has a spinner a sufficient motive for standing out? I do not see that he has. The Association will have powers and facilities to achieve whatever was reasonable in the discarded short-time policy, free from the disabilities of the old Short-Time Committee. It will have practically all the powers of the typical continental cartel. It may be that amalgamations and larger units will be required for full efficiency. But the Association will provide a framework within which these can be gradually organised. It is a movement started within the industry by some of its own leaders of their own initiative, which has already gone three-quarters of the way towards securing the necessary support. Every spinner who is still standing out ought to ask himself just why he is doing so.

I suggest that the Association deserves the open approval and practical assistance of other interests which are concerned with the prosperity of Lancashire—in particular the banks. What have the banks done so far to help solve the crisis? Nothing whatever, so far as I can hear. Their main preoccupation appears to have been to use their special knowledge and position to secure that, when bankruptcy is at hand and the crash comes, they shall be somewhat better secured than anyone else. They have been more concerned to get mortgages against their advances than to see that these should be used for their proper purpose of financing current business and not merely to meet losses. If the banks have an answer to this, I do not know what it is. For they seem to be a species of deaf mutes. If only they could hear what is said and make an intelligible reply! Perhaps they can. If so, here is their chance. If they lend their powerful influence to the Association's support, it will assuredly be launched and a new chapter begun.

In the New Year Keynes went further on the Association's behalf. On 4 January he returned to Manchester to address a meeting of spinners of American cotton. Prior to his speech, he met representatives of the weaving section. Keynes's notes for his speech ran as follows.

My first incursion into this subject destructive.
But no one has a right to destructive criticism unless he is prepared to give his assistance to any attempts at construction which he may find going on.
The Cotton Yarn Assoc[n].
Probably no need to explain its main outlines.
What are the objections?
The objectors are somewhat silent.
But I have made enquiry by word of mouth and read what the press has to say.
Let me put the opposition case as well as I can and weigh how much it is worth.
1. The Assoc[n]. comes too late. The argument of the optimists.

We have touched bottom.

We have only to wait a matter of weeks for a revival of trade probably accompanied by an upward turn in the price of cotton. The impairment of spinners' margins is a usual accompaniment of a falling price for the commodity. But it is a passing phenomenon and must not be attributed to other causes. Just lately spinners in Italy, Japan and India have been feeling the wind nearly as much as here.

There is not a word in this with which I disagree. I think—fortunately—that it is all true. It will be astonishing if abnormally cheap cotton slowly rising in price towards its proper value does not stimulate demand. It will be astonishing if Lancashire does not get its share of this. In which case we may normally expect some recovery of margins.

But I do not draw from this the conclusion that the Assoc^n. is not needed. On the contrary I look on this prospective revival as something which may produce a favourable atmosphere for the Assoc^n. in its difficult early stages,

For the stimulus from cheap cotton slowly rising is obviously temporary. It obviously will not cure the industry's deeper troubles. It gives a breathing space of which advantage must be taken—and not treated simply as a means to put off the evil day. Moreover the Assoc^n. can confer on the trade, I think, positive advantages. It is a great mistake to consider it merely a rainy weather device.

2. The influence of the Association will be towards higher prices; whereas Lancashire's only chance of repairing her position is by asking at all times the lowest possible prices. Whether or not this is a reasonable objection, depends on what the price policy of the Assoc^n. is to be. I think that the promoters of the Association would do well to make their price policy somewhat clearer than in their original prospectus. This prospectus seemed to suggest that the price-fixing policy would be aimed at securing margins which would give everyone normal profits even if short-time were being worked and mills were

capitalised at the fairly full figure of 50/- a spindle. This seems to me to be going the wrong way to work. The remarks about this in last Thursday's *M.G. Commercial* are quite sound, I think. The minimum price should be a very low protective minimum with plenty of room for competition above it. It should be a price not intended to deter genuine competitive practice but only to cut out involuntary weak selling.

But this argument serves, I suspect, to cover up something else not nearly so reasonable. Lancashire industry is a complex affair. There are plenty of people in Lancashire who would like to keep the spinners in a weak competitive position. In some of the criticisms of the Yarn Assoc[n]. which I have seen I think I can detect the voice of others than the spinners.

Now I don't agree at all with the idea that it is in Lancashire's interest to cut prices to an indefinite extent. Manufacture is meant to pay its way. No one can build up a healthy or progressive business on losses. The suggestion that it is really prudent to try to win back markets by selling at a loss is cant. If the Assoc[n] fixes prices which will stop the spinning industry from bleeding to death, it will do good to *all* branches of the trade and not only to the spinners.

Therefore I do not trust this objection very far. No one can make improvements or show enterprise who is on the edge of bankruptcy. I regard the recovery of a reasonable margin as the first step towards a healthy industry capable of making an effective attempt to hold and recover markets.

3. The industry is riddled with unsound finance; some of it the result of the overcapitalisation of the boom period, some of it is the accumulated losses of several bad years running, some of it—undoubtedly—is the result of inferior management. A thorough financial clean-up is overdue. The Association is an attempt to avoid this clean-up. In proportion as it succeeds, it will just put off this return to wholesome conditions. The weaker managements might be eliminated; lost capital might be written off; and the industry might pass into stronger hands on a basis

of a capitalisation so low that it can compete on favourable terms with the whole world. Leave matters alone for another two years and this is what will happen—so runs the argument: loss and injury to individuals no doubt, but salvation to the industry and those who live by it in the long run. The Association is really—looked at frankly and cynically—an attempt to save those who had much better not be saved.

This brings us in my opinion to the crux of the whole matter. The question of supporting or opposing the Association really hangs on this. Is it in the interests of the stronger firms and of the industry as a whole that bankruptcy should be allowed to do its work?—until reconstructions and the passing of spindles at a very low capitalisation into stronger hands has done its work.

A solution of this kind is the counterpart of the way in which Lancashire industry was built up. The arguments in favour of it are by no means negligible. We must try to apply very clear thinking to it. In the first place there are obviously going to be reconstructions, Association or no Association.

In the second place the process of bankruptcy is going to be very disastrous for everybody. Is it desirable that Lancashire should spend this coming year of cheap cotton in a process of neighbour-begging?

But in the third place—and this is the real point—suppose every spinning establishment in Lancashire was capitalised on the basis of 10/- a spindle, would all be well? In my opinion the real problem would remain exactly as it is.

If high capitalisation and bad management were the essential troubles, reconstructions and bankruptcies might be the right solution. But they are only secondary troubles. The real trouble—and this is the beginning, the middle and the end of my argument—is surplus capacity—not necessarily permanent but at least prolonged and with no end in sight.

Now when there is surplus capacity in an industry, there is no solution merely by writing down capital. Unless there is some concerted effort, *everyone* will lose money until there is a concerted effort. The more bankrupt concerns come into the market, not the better but the worse it will be for those who are still solvent.

The problem is not new. It has happened many times before in every industrial country. It is only to Lancashire that it is novel. There is overwhelming evidence for the view that in such circumstances there is no solution for anyone except in united action—either something like this Yarn Assoc^n. or more drastic amalgamation into trusts.

I venture to predict that the survival of an industry organised as Lancashire now is, which suffers from surplus capacity, is simply impossible.

If you refuse to do anything now, you will just lose your money for a year or two more and then be driven to just the same thing in the end.

May I say a word to the banks—those professional deaf-mutes as I have called them, some distinguished representatives of which I see here in person. I don't think there can be the slightest doubt on which side their bread is buttered—on the side of this Yarn Association without any manner of doubt.

There may be some parties in Lancashire who might plausibly regard the process of widespread bankruptcy as serving their own private interests. But not the banks. The banks are to a large extent the proprietors of the weaker concerns in question. If half the mills in Lancashire, the financially weaker half, were to be liquidated and sold off at something between 10/- and £1 a spindle, how much would the banks lose?

Is it not worth the while of the banks to consider whether they should not give this Association their enthusiastic support?

I have heard no argument to the contrary except that it is against their traditions ever to do anything whatever in any conceivable circumstances—that they are, in fact, to change my metaphor, professional paralytics.

I tell them to have courage, to rise from their beds and walk, to resume the functions of hearing and of speech.

After all in Germany in parallel circumstances the banks would be represented on the boards of most of the companies concerned. I do not advocate this. I think there are great advantages in the English system—but not if it is carried to extremes.

After all not much is asked of the banks. Only two things that I am aware of—that they should publicly declare their support of the Association, and that they should use their influence with their customers to persuade them to join;—though perhaps I might add a third thing to consider sympathetically with the management of the Association the possibility of devising some measure of co-operative credit, a point to which I attach much importance though I must not take time in enlarging on it today.

Since the Liverpool and Manchester brokers are represented today, perhaps I may say a word to them too. It is obvious that they are interested in the reformation of the credit of the spinners. I suggest that they too like the bankers would be acting in their own interests if they use their influence in support of the Association.

The interest of the weaker spinners and of all those who have lent money to them seems to me to lie with the Association beyond all possibility of doubt.

What I want to urge once more before sitting down is that it is also in the interest of the strongest non-turnover mills. In other industries it has generally been the strongest elements in the trade which have organised cartels. For there is only [one] thing in the world which can prevent the highly efficient, strongly financed mill from making money—namely the existence of surplus capacity. And to deal with the problem is the object of the Association.

After Keynes's speech, the meeting passed a motion supporting the Association. There was one opposing vote.

In the ensuing weeks Keynes continued to give the Association support and advice. He also encouraged individual manufacturers, who wrote to him, to join it.

On 8 January Professor G. W. Daniels of Manchester University gave Keynes another opportunity to support the Association. Speaking on 'Industrial Combinations' to the Association of managers of Textile Works in Manchester, Professor Daniels criticised the Cotton Yarn Association as not having the stability necessary to achieve its objects or the ability to assist materially in the larger object of restoring the competitive position of the industry. On reading a report of the speech. Keynes wrote to *The Guardian*.

To the Editor of The Manchester Guardian, *10 January 1927*

Sir,

Professor Daniels's very interesting lecture on industrial combinations in relation to the cotton industry underestimated, judging by your report, what to my mind is the essential point. Cartels abroad have fallen, as Professor Daniels recognised, into two distinct classes. The first class have aimed at some monopoly advantage, generally by exploiting the home market behind a tariff wall, more rarely by taking the full profit of a material monopoly such as potash. The second class have come into existence as a means of mitigating the evils of surplus capacity. Pre-war economic text-books dealt mainly with the first class because they used to be the predominating type, the problem of surplus capacity not being so prevalent formerly as it is now. Nevertheless, there were several examples of the second class in pre-war days, and the so-called 'rationalising' cartels and amalgamations of latter-day Germany, of course, belong to it.

Professor Daniels's objections amounted, however, to an argument that the conditions for a successful operation of the first type of cartel do not exist in Lancashire today. This is not relevant to anything I have proposed. Nor did he illustrate his argument by reference to the bleachers' and dyers' associations or to the artificial silk industry.

The Lancashire textile industry, so far from being peculiarly unfitted for combined action, is, in fact, one in which combination has been remarkably successful in each branch in which it has been tried—too successful, perhaps, so long as there are other, unorganised, sections to prey upon. Professor Daniels's lecture suggested that he is not one of those who fail to recognise the existence of the problem of surplus capacity. If so, does he not think that concerted action is essential? As a practical man, does he see any likelihood of such action in the near future, except via the only movement on foot—namely, the projected Cotton Yarn Association?

Certainly Lancashire's best hope as a world market lies in the discovery in one direction or another, of real economies—which selling at a loss is not. I initially approached the problem, as he does, from that point of view, and denounced short-time because, so far from being a real economy, it definitely increased the real cost. I have never abandoned that standpoint. But further inquiry convinced me that the first step towards increased real efficiency must be found in some organisation which could restore the solvency of the spinners, could establish a proper statistical basis for their policy, and could stand up to the better-organised sections of the trade. This is the beginning, not the end, of salvation but it is a beginning, and the Cotton Yarn Association comes much nearer to supplying it than anything else in the least likely to be started. If Professor Daniels knows anything better and more likely to happen let him tell us.

How difficult it is to do anything where something like unanimity is required between opposed temperaments! There were always two elements of opposition—the pure stick-in-the-muds and those whom I have called the bankruptcy party, who think that they see some advantage to themselves in the ruin of their neighbours. But the more subtle obstructionists are now in the field—those who are reasonable enough to admit the force of the arguments for doing something but oppose any actual plan on the ground that it is not the ideal solution and the pseudo-critics, of whom a leader-writer in last Thursday's *Manchester Guardian Commercial* offers a first-class example, who adopt an all-embracing agnosticism and declare that the subject is so vast and our ignorance of it so profound that any action whatever is out of the question. Your leader in last Wednesday's *Manchester Guardian* struck, if I may say so, the right note—namely, that there is nothing to be afraid of in the Cotton Yarn Association and that it is in the circumstances 'a risk worth taking'.

Yours, &c.,

J. M. KEYNES

During the following month the Association was successfully launched. Keynes welcomed it in an unsigned note in *The Nation*.

From The Nation and Athenaeum, *26 February 1927*

The Cotton Yarn Association, the objects of which have been explained and supported by Mr Keynes in these columns, was, after many doubts and difficulties, successfully launched in Manchester on 18 February. The Association had set itself to secure the adhesion of 19,000,000 spindles, which would represent 70 per cent of the American yarns spun for sale. They have in fact obtained 20,692,595 spindles, which is about 76 per cent of the industry. This result is a great success for Mr H. Dixon and Mr Ryan, the Chairman and Secretary of the organising committee. The Association has a stiff task in front of it, and it is doubtful how much loyalty in adversity it will be able to command. We hope that, so far as its minimum price policy is concerned, it will keep the official figure below what spinners can normally hope to obtain. It starts, however, in a decidedly favourable atmosphere. There is no doubt that the revival of business in Manchester since the beginning of the year has been in respect of volume on a really substantial scale, though profit-margins have remained unsatisfactory, and scarcely began to recover until the last week or two. Some authorities estimate that the volume of output in the American section, both spinning and weaving, has increased from 60–65 per cent of capacity at the end of last year to 75–80 per cent at the present time. This should have a favourable influence over export statistics in due course.

Life for the Association proved difficult, however, as a decline in demand set in during 1927. Keynes commented on the problem late in August.

From The Nation and Athenaeum, *27 August 1927*

THE PROGRESS OF THE COTTON YARN ASSOCIATION

Seven months ago the Lancashire spinners of American cotton came to the belated conclusion that joint action and even some surrender of the individual right to cut prices might be better than an indefinite continuance of financial loss. It was not an undisputed conclusion—there were a good many people, especially amongst other sections of the industry, who thought that a fair dose of bankruptcy would clear the air and be more in accordance with the traditions of Lancashire, and anyhow that an attempt on the part of the spinners to stop losing money would be incompatible with the prosperity of Lancashire as a whole. Nevertheless 75 per cent of the mills were persuaded to join the newly founded Cotton Yarn Association, binding themselves to conform to its rules and practices.

The Association has been managed with great energy and ability. The first step was to grade what is in fact a highly diversified industry into separate sections which could be treated in a uniform manner without serious inconsistency, and to organise proper statistics. The next step was to prescribe standard working hours per week for each section which should conform to the buying power of the market in the light of statistics, and to fix minimum prices for the several grades of yarn which would aim at protecting the spinner from actual loss. The short-time rules differed from the arrangements in force prior to the existence of the Yarn Association in that the statistical basis was securer, the hours to be worked were not uniform for the whole industry but were adapted to the state of demand in each section, and the members of the Association were bound, and not merely recommended, to observe them. The minimum price policy approached dangerous ground, and had been much criticised in advance. It was feared that the minimum would rise to the level of spinners' hopes and desires rather than fall to a merely protective level. In fact the prices have been fixed reasonably, and, whilst they leave room for small differences of opinion, no one has pretended that they represent more than the barest living wage for a typical firm. Finally the system of transferable quotas has been instituted whereby the concentration of production in the hands of the strongest producers is facilitated. At present this system is in its infancy. Nevertheless several transfers have been already negotiated, by which for a payment of ½d. per spindle the right to work additional hours has been transferred from firms short of orders to other firms better placed for securing them. Nor has the Association been afraid to exercise authority over its members—a firm has recently been fined £300 for selling below the prescribed minimum price—and it has been supported, on the whole, with much more loyalty than the critics of the scheme anticipated.

Nevertheless, in spite of so much energy, loyalty, and apparent success, the Association is now at a crisis of its fortunes. A point has been reached at which the opportunities of the spinners outside the Association to obtain all its benefits without paying any part of the price are becoming intolerable. In present conditions a membership of 75 per cent of the industry is doubtfully sufficient for effective operation.

The main reason for this is—I am sorry to say—that the pessimists, amongst whom I have been numbered, have so far proved right. That is to say, in spite of some months of very cheap cotton (not so cheap now), and a record world production of goods spun from American cotton, the Lancashire spinners have never been within sight of being able to employ all their machinery. During a short spurt in the spring of the year demand brought up average output to nearly 85 per cent of capacity. Since then the falling away has been so serious that a figure of 50 to 60 per cent is nearer the mark, and for some important descriptions of yarn the figure is between 40 and 50 per cent. Now so long as average production was round 80 per cent the existence of 25 per cent of the industry outside the Association was not very serious. Assuming that this numbers of non-members could, under cover of the Association, work 100 per cent by just under-bidding its minimum prices, the members of the Association could still work 73 per cent. But if average production falls to 60 per cent, then if the non-members use these methods to work something like full-time, the members are left with only 46 per cent of their capacity employed. Thus the greater the amount of necessary short-time, the larger the percentage of the industry which the Association needs to control.

These figures and the similar story told by the statistics of exports certainly indicate that all the different interests centred in Manchester ought to reconsider their methods and make a concerted effort to develop and recapture business. But to suppose that the right way to do this is to ruin the spinners by encouraging the forces of disorganisation to produce a situation where everyone sells at a loss, is surely most misguided. Whether or not the opinion is correct—in maintaining which I found myself in the minority when I was last in Manchester, but which is perhaps gaining ground—that a proportion of idle machinery will continue for some time to be the rule except only in abnormal and temporary conditions of demand, at any rate this is the situation which does now exist and has existed for some years. Lancashire will do better, therefore, to organise herself to deal with the problem of surplus capacity so long as it continues to exist, than to keep up a perennial illusion that all will be well to-morrow. With this object, the chief contribution to efficiency and economy of working which the spinners as a body are able to make can lie in no other direction than in facilitating a concentration of production. In other respects the recovery of markets and the resuscitation of Lancashire's trade must necessarily depend on the energy and ability and public spirit of the other factors in the industry.

Actual experience of the Association's methods and the progress of events since its formation have greatly strengthened opinion in its favour—so much so that the Midland Bank in their last *Monthly Review* have committed themselves to the view that 'the failure of the Yarn Association would be a disaster for the trade'. If the Association commanded a membership of practically the whole trade, it could by a combination of pre-scribed hours and transferable quotas move steadily towards the appropriate degree of concentration of production. Nothing seems more certain, therefore, than that it is in the interests of the spinners as a whole to strengthen the Association. But the trouble is that these considerations do not seem to weigh against the obvious advantages to the outside firm. For not only can they get for nothing the advantages for which a member seeking a transferable quota is ready to pay. But by just underbidding the Association's minimum price, they can obtain for nothing all, and more than all, the advantages of the Association's regulation of output. Here is something being done in the general interest. I should like to offer a small prize for the best name to describe those who, in spite of the perilous position of a great industry to which they themselves belong, steal the advantages without joining in the subscription. But the practical problem is how best to persuade, cajole, or compel them to come in.

First there is coercion by legislation. Where a trade association represents a large majority of an industry, the Board of Trade should, in my opinion, have power at its discretion, on the application of the Association, to extend certain of its rules to the whole of the industry, subject to an opportunity to consumers, to operatives, and to the minority of the industry to show reasons to the contrary. If such powers could be brought into existence, here would be a case for their application.

Second, there is coercion by public opinion. In a concentrated area such as Lancashire, something might be hoped from this. The Yarn Association is in fact endeavouring to mobilise opinion, especially amongst shareholders. Meetings have been held in the last fortnight at Oldham, Royton, Blackpool, Ashton-under-Lyne, and Rochdale, in each case with the Mayor of the town in the chair. Nevertheless, public opinion, though strongly sympathetic, is still passive on the whole. The press and the banks from being lukewarm have become friendly, but they have not yet become active. So far—perhaps better things are in store—the Federation of Master Cotton Spinners' Associations has not done what it might; and, so long as this is so, the apathy of outside bodies can scarcely be condemned. It is to be hoped that the round-table conference between representatives of the Federation and of the Yarn Association, which is to meet shortly, will find that they can agree on drastic action in the common interest.

Third, there is coercion by retaliatory measures, taken by the Association or by others interested, particularly the banks. It is evident that the banks could do a good deal if they chose. The powers of the Association in this direction are seriously limited by its lack of financial resources. All such methods are, however, obviously undesirable in themselves. It would be much better, if only it were possible, to set in motion through Lancashire a sufficiently overwhelming wave of feeling that the concerted action for which the Yarn Association stands is a necessary thing in the general interest, and that those who steal its fruits are wanting both in fairness and in public spirit.

In an attempt to increase the coverage of the Association by enlarging its membership, it held a meeting in Manchester Town Hall on 6 September. Keynes was the main speaker. His notes appear below.

Mr Lord Mayor,

I feel myself here today in a very delicate and unenviable position. I am not a cotton man. I am not a professional orator.

The problem before us for discussion is a very broad one, where there is no need of the subtleties of an economist. I have nothing novel or sensational to propound. I am just an individual bold enough or foolish enough to offer himself up for this sacrifice—and in that spirit I hope you will accept me!

My presence here is a sequel to a previous visit to Manchester some eight months ago. A good deal has happened since then. Important fresh experience has been gained—some of it encouraging, some of it most depressing. The encouraging—very encouraging—event has been the emergence, out of the cloud of words in which we were then moving, of a constructive organisation. *Action* has begun. And I take it that we are here today, Mr Lord Mayor, to promote future action—a more active and vigorous policy of construction. Our task, therefore, is a task of *persuasion*—to persuade and unite the public opinion and the press of Lancashire on a course of action.

The first step to agreement is to discover just where we disagree. Let me, therefore, put the broad argument step by step. No-one disputes that Lancashire has lost something approaching one third of her pre-war export trade in American cotton goods. This state of affairs has persisted for several years. During the past year—a period of abnormally cheap cotton during which the aggregate world production of American cotton goods has been on the largest scale ever experienced—Lancashire has spun not only much less American yarn than before the War, but actually less than in the preceding year which included the months of the General Strike. Lancashire's proportion of the world consumption of American cotton, which 20 years ago was around 30 per cent, fell from 16 per cent in 1925–26 to 13 per cent in 1926–27. It seems to me to be scarcely possible to exaggerate the seriousness of the situation, and—therefore—the need to support anyone who has a constructive policy to suggest.

Let me put in a few sentences the deplorable facts of the Lancashire trade in yarns and cloths made from American cotton:—

Thousands of looms are standing idle

2,000,000 spindles silent

20,000,000 spindles working three days a week

40,000 mill workers unemployed and most of the rest on half wages

4,000,000 spindles under moratorium schemes

Shareholders not only with no dividends but having to pay heavy calls on their shares

Banks refusing further advances even to technically efficient concerns

Sheds and mills not being kept in good repair owing to heavy capital losses.

Now it follows from the figures just given that Lancashire's mills are not fully employed. It would be an exaggeration to say that they have been three-quarters employed on the average of the last six months. But let us take this figure—75 per cent production—for the sake of illustration. Furthermore no-one now expects—particularly since the rise in raw cotton prices—that anything is going to happen suddenly to increase the demand to capacity. No-one supposes that Lancashire's production will exceed 75 per cent on the average of the rest of this year. Does anyone disagree with my argument up to this point?

In this case there seem to me to be two legitimate objectives before the spinners—in seeking which they deserve outside support—namely to prevent the surplus capacity from leading to a cut-throat competition which will cause further financial losses and widespread distress through Lancashire; and, secondly, to spread the necessary amount of short-time fairly—I emphasise *fairly*—through the industry. Does anyone advocate cut-throat competition, pricing below the cost of production? Whom can such methods benefit in the long run?

This meeting is agreed, therefore, that *organised* curtailment is necessary. If so, should it be spread fairly? Or unfairly? Should everyone agree to take his share? Or—relying on the fact that legal compulsion is at present impossible—should a minority of individuals try to make money for themselves by taking advantage of the loyalty of the majority? Now I can understand a few individuals holding this view,—though I confess I was surprised to find a leading article in last Thursday's *Manchester Guardian Commercial* encouraging the 'independents' to continue on their way so long as it pays them, and sneered at any appeal to the general interest. For if three-quarters of the trade curtail and if there is no legal compulsion on the minority to do so and no retaliatory methods are practicable, is it not obvious that it *must* pay the minority to stand out so long as they can. But if they are encouraged to do this, must not the Yarn Association break down sooner or later? If we do not want this, should we not do everything possible to bring the independents in? Undoubtedly it pays the minority to stand out. That is the essence of the difficulty. It seems to me that either the Yarn Association is a bad thing for the spinners as a whole, in which case the sooner it is closed down the better. Or, if it is a good thing, then it is the duty of the independents—and in the long run their interest—to come in.

As Mr Kendrick points out in a powerful letter to today's *M.[anchester]G.[uardian]*—one of the best contributions yet to this controversy—the power of the Yarn Association to help the trade would be immensely increased if it were a 100 per cent association. Spinners should be engaged in a competitive contest with the world not with one another. It is only common sense to have a policy. Only through the Association is this possible. It seems to me to be fearfully short-sighted to take advantage of the Association's existence and not join it. The Association, therefore, deserves and requires the support of shareholders, banks, the strong sanctions of the industry and of public opinion in urging the independents to recognise that sturdy individualism can have a bad side as well as a good one, and that unity is sometimes strength. I believe that the Association, if it comprises practically the whole industry, might initiate a new epoch of prosperity for spinners.

But I should leave more than half of my task of persuasion undone if I were to stop here. I have not the slightest doubt what is the true explanation of the latent opposition to the policy of the Yarn Association. It has been expressed very clearly in a statement recently issued by Mr Bootham speaking on behalf of the Amalgamation of Operative Cotton Spinners. It is a feeling that the policy of the Association is a *defeatist* policy— that, in Mr Bootham's words, 'they are not really working for a return to anything like the pre-war volume of trade'.

Well, personally I think it is unlikely that it is in Lancashire's power to recover in the near future her pre-war volume of exports. But I am certain that it is a complete mistake to believe that it is not the policy of the Yarn Association to retrieve the situation to the utmost degree possible. What the Association has been attempting with very great ability and energy in very difficult circumstances—is to do one thing at a time. It is quite useless to expect an industry, which has been trying desperately to save itself from bankruptcy and to get any business which can be done at a profit, to be laying well thought-out plans for future expansion. So far as the spinners are concerned, the first thing has been to get them on their legs and to build up an organisation capable in course of time of securing a concentration of production.

The real defeatist policy in my opinion is that of the opponents of the Association—of those who think that Lancashire can only hold her markets if the spinners produce at a loss. For if this were true, it is absolutely certain that sooner or later Lancashire *will* lose her markets. To build up trade on the losses of a large section of the industry is to build on a quicksand. It would be a suicidal policy for the other sections of the trade to survive on the losses of the spinners. I can imagine nothing more short-sighted. The prosperity and financial strength of the spinners is the only possible foundation for the prosperity and financial strength of Lancashire as a whole.

Nevertheless, public opinion, though it may express itself

618

wrongly, generally has its roots in common sense. It would, indeed, be fatal for Lancashire to acquiesce in defeatism. And whilst the Yarn Association, so far from being a defeatist move, is a first and essential step of a constructive character, it is certainly not enough by itself—if only because it embraces only one section of the trade—and in this opinion I know that prominent members of the Association agree with me. The Association has necessarily been chiefly engaged at the start in salvage. We need something more positive and more comprehensive. Has not the time come for the cotton textile industry as a whole to take stock of what is really a very bad situation?

I suggest, Mr Lord Mayor, that this meeting should not limit itself to the very necessary duty of rallying opinion to the support of the Yarn Association, but that it should invite the summons of what one might term an unofficial Royal Commission on the state of the industry. Such a conference as I have in mind should include responsible representatives from every section of the industry including the operatives who might play a very valuable and important part, for you here in Lancashire have the unique advantage that the operatives know almost as much about the industry as the masters and have opinions well worth listening to. But it must not be too large in numbers. It should have an adequate staff and funds and be prepared to work very hard.

The Lancashire textile industry is so highly specialised, broken up into so many sections, so strongly monopolised in some parts and so disorganised in others, that, if no concerted action is taken, things may drift from bad to worse, just because it is not in the interest or in the power of any one individual or any one firm to do what is in the interest of the whole. I venture to say that there is no-one even in Manchester who understands the cotton trade from top to bottom. Indeed there is so much secretiveness and suspicion that it is almost impossible for anyone to know all the facts. We need, therefore, a pooling of knowledge and, if possible, to secure a whole series of agreed economies at every stage of the handling of the goods, which may be insignificant separately but add up to a figure which may make just the difference between being on a competitive basis and being above it.

The Cotton Conference—if I may so style it—should have exceedingly wide terms of reference.

(1) Its first task should be to ascertain the facts. It should set out to discover just what the costs are at every stage of production and to compare these costs with corresponding costs abroad and with what they were here before the War. Then, at last, one might have some definite idea as to where and how costs can be cut, so as to put Lancashire on a competitive basis with the rest of the world.

(2) It should consider whether a separate overhead organisation for each mill can be afforded in these days of high salaries. May it not be that overhead expenses have become top-heavy and that Lancashire is not taking full advantage of the economies of management which her local concentration ought to facilitate? Have the higher staffs and their salaries been cut as they should have been from the inflated basis on which they were put in 1920? Is the industry carrying more directors, managers, salesmen and middlemen of all kinds than are really necessary? I speak as an outsider to the industry—I do not know. But I can see that there may well be a body of vested interests strong enough to keep up the overheads to an unnecessary figure.

When an industry has reached a certain age and has ceased to progress, there will always be many individuals occupying key positions, some of them redundant, some of them incompetent, some of them just overpaid, who are likely to be discomforted by any change and therefore resist it. It is acquiescence in such a situation which before now has caused great industries to dwindle and decay.

(3) The comparative importance of outside expenses such as freight and transport charges, tariffs on dyes and local rating should be carefully estimated with a view to collective agitation where it is justified.

(4) By no means least important, the financial organisation of the mills should be considered,—not merely the reconstruction of individual mills in difficulties, but the question of reforming the general methods by which mills obtain their capital.

(5) Lastly there is the question whether Lancashire's traditional organisation for marketing and merchanting at each stage should not be overhauled and brought up to date. May it not be that the Manchester Exchange—the seething turmoil of which has been a matter of so much pride—is, in some respects, today a very wasteful and uneconomical way of transacting business? Does the merchant system encourage the merchants to care about turnover as much as the interests of the rest of the industry require? May it not be something that the maximum profit *plus* safety to the merchant is found at a lower level of turnover than is required by the maximum profit of the industry as a whole? Is there room for some collective propaganda and display for Lancashire goods abroad? Again I do not know. And I am not sure that anyone knows.

Are not these matters worth some hours of collective discussion? Is there the least chance that they can be taken up successfully by any individual? It is at least possible that a Cotton Conference, which means business, which was courageous and intelligent, might initiate something useful. Possibly something permanent might grow out of it—a central office of information, conciliation, discussion and organisation, representing both masters and employees—a Cotton Parliament so to speak. Lancashire men are lions against the rest of the world, but—in my experience— they are terribly afraid of one another. But the times are evil—very evil indeed. Why should not the different interests—*all* the different interests—pluck up courage for once to speak to one another frankly, truthfully and constructively across a table?

The Manchester meeting did not succeed in its goal. Keynes reflected on the result in November.

From The Nation and Athenaeum, *19 November 1927*

THE RETREAT OF THE COTTON YARN ASSOCIATION

A fortnight ago the Cotton Yarn Association relieved its members of the obligation to observe a percentage of short-time and a scale of minimum selling prices. Thus after six months' attempt at regulation, the market in cotton yarn has been again abandoned to unfettered competition and unrestricted supply. In view of previous articles which have appeared in *The Nation*, readers may be glad to have a short summary of the events of the past year.

Exactly a year ago (November 13th, 1926) I wrote an article in *The Nation* attacking short-time in the cotton industry as practised by the Federation of Master Cotton Spinners, arguing that this method was futile in face of a more or less lasting surplus capacity. I gave figures to show that the prospect of Lancashire's recovering her pre-war trade was remote, and concluded: 'Lancashire's first need is to face these figures. If they are substantially correct, the termination of the short-time policy is urgently called for, and the substitution for it of a "rationalisation" process designed to cut down overhead costs by the amalgamation, grouping, or elimination of mills.' This article obtained an unexpected degree of attention in Lancashire, arousing indignation, in some quarters on the ground that it was wrong to act on any other assumption than that Lancashire would recover her pre-war position, and in others on the ground that short-time was the only practicable remedy. It ended in my being invited to meet the Short-Time Committee of the Federation.

At this meeting (November 22nd, 1926) I was challenged to suggest an alternative. I replied that, the existence of surplus capacity being granted, I knew of no methods of curtailing the scale of an industry except bankruptcy, cartels, or amalgamations, or variations of these three, and continued:—'Bankruptcy would not take place without a grave struggle; and losses on the part of those made bankrupt would react on those not made bankrupt...In a cartel the individual businesses maintain their separate identity. They are each allotted quotas by the cartel managers. These quotas are transferable...The remaining type which has been appropriate in certain industries, are amalgamations, either complete amalgamations or, more probably, holding companies which buy a great number of mills in order to close down some of them, strengthen their finances, and concentrate the business on those that remain.'

In the discussions which followed this meeting it emerged clearly that there were no individuals in Lancashire ready to take the initiative to form an amalgamation, but that there was in existence an active Committee with ideas analogous to that of the cartel. There was nothing else constructive in the field; and the plans and personnel of this Committee seemed to represent, as they still do, the best hopes of the future.

Out of this Committee emerged the Cotton Yarn Association. There was a danger that the Association's policy might be no more than the old short-time practices *plus* an attempt to fix prices unduly high, but there was reason to hope that the Association might develop along cartel lines leading eventually to a concentration of output.

The first task was to persuade spinners owning 19,000,000 spindles—which proportion of the industry (in the neighbourhood of 70 per cent) was fixed on as representing the minimum effective membership—to join up. After three months' hard work by the Committee this objective was just achieved, and on April 22nd, 1927, the members were alloted their quotas, which varied according to the class of yarn spun. This was followed on May 13th by a list of minimum prices to be observed by the members, and later in the summer by an arrangement which made the allotted quotas of output transferable between members. At the same time the statistical side of the Association's work was developed and perfected, so that for the first time full details of output, stock, and unfilled orders were available to guide the management in fixing the allotment of quotas. Thus a complete machinery was set up for the operation of a cartel.

If the demand for Lancashire's output of American cotton goods had been maintained at even 70 per cent of capacity, the Cotton Yarn Association would probably have been successful. Last winter most spinners were anticipating this level of output. But my own more gloomy forecasts were nearer the truth. Demand sank to 50 or 60 per cent. In such conditions a cartel covering not more than 70 per cent of the industry was not strong enough for effective operation. Outside firms could, by undercutting the Association's minimum prices by a fraction of a penny, secure far more than their due proportion of the business going. Thus the efforts of the Association to curtail output redounded, especially in certain sections, much more to the advantage of non-members than to that of members.

Clearly this was an impossible situation. Either the Association must increase its membership or it must release its members from their restrictions. At a crowded meeting held in Manchester on September 6th, with the Lord Mayor in the chair, a new campaign was launched to bring in the minority. At the same time it was proposed that all sections of the industry should support an 'unofficial Royal Commission' to discover how Lancashire could reduce her costs and regain her markets.

This meeting was followed by prolonged negotiations in a Committee, convened under the auspices of the Federation of Master Cotton Spinners, representing both the Yarn Association and spinners outside the Association. After endless hours of wrangling and substantial concessions by the Association from their own ideas of sound policy, a compromise was threshed out by which an agreed system of short-time and minimum prices should be observed both by members of the Association and by non-members. The Federation recommended this solution to the trade; the members of the Yarn Association honoured the bargain reached by their representatives; but the non-members repudiated the bargain reached by theirs. So the attempt at a concordat had proved entirely abortive.

In view of this no course was open to the Yarn Association except to release their members—for the time being at least—from all restrictions, and to return to unfettered competition until the air was clearer. I am sure that this course was right and in some ways preferable even to the success of the compromise, since the latter almost abandoned the cartel idea and was little better than a return to the futile short-time practices of 1926 and earlier years.

The future is obscure. Bankruptcy is beginning, but whether this will clear the way or only make things worse, is hard to say. Perhaps the Yarn Association may revive its cartel functions later on with more hope of success. Perhaps its leading spirits will feel that the best chance now lies in some closer form of amalgamation and that a smaller number of mills coming together more intimately, e.g., with common financial arrangements, might be stronger than a larger number more loosely associated.

One thing at least has been accomplished in this year of wordy warfare. Most people in Lancashire now recognise the existence of a problem of surplus capacity. What was assailed, when I suggested it a year ago, with a storm of mingled interest and indignation, is now commonplace. An important paper by Mr Barnard Ellinger on 'Lancashire's Declining Trade with China', read before the Manchester Statistical Society on November 9th, confirms the extreme seriousness of the position and the necessity of new methods, but it does not suggest that the bankruptcy of the spinners is the highway to success. On the other hand, no one has yet propounded any fourth alternative to the three original alternatives of bankruptcy, cartellisation, or combines.

I have paid several visits to Manchester in the past year in conditions where I have had exceptional opportunities of hearing opinions from all quarters; and I have always come away with a feeling of intense pessimism. I am not surprised at the breakdown of the loyal efforts which have been made with so much ability and good temper by Mr Lincoln Tattersall and his fellow directors of the Yarn Association and Mr John Ryan, their Secretary. There is something desperately discouraging—insensitive, stale, unadaptable—in the atmosphere of Lancashire today towards any constructive effort—an atmosphere much more ominous in my opinion than the statistical facts of the industry. It is hardly an exaggeration to say that the efforts of the Yarn Association have been watched even in more or less impartial quarters with a curious, half-malicious hostility which would scarcely be deserved even if the Association's ideas were intellectually misguided.

The atmosphere is compounded of several different elements which it is difficult to distinguish and describe. First of all, of course, there is the temper of the minority spinners, sturdy, independent, greedy, short-sighted, as full as Guelphs and Ghibellines of local jealousies and passions and ruthlessness to neighbours across the way, born of ancient feuds and ancestral struggles to survive. The Capulets of Royton will not lie down with its Montagus. On the other hand, the leaders of the operatives play a waiting game, and will not readily subscribe to any policy which aims at a regulated curtailment.

Next there are the innumerable other elements in the vast cotton industry, who have been accustomed too long to enjoy a mediocre prosperity at the expense of the spinners' losses, and whose immediate interest might be affected unfavourably by a strengthening of the spinners' position—who rather prefer, in fact, to see the spinners weak and tender to the touch. Manchester itself is, of course, a lily of the field so far as spinning is concerned. Oldham, Rochdale, and Royton are apart from Manchester, and Manchester's direct sympathies are not primarily with the spinners. The export houses and warehousemen, the strong and prosperous spinners and manufacturers of fine cottons, the leaders of the monopolistic finishing trades, the great engineering firms, all these have a certain contempt for the small men, the spinners of American cotton. Yet it is well to remember that these small men occupy a key position in what is still the greatest export industry of the country.

Then there are the moralists who remember the unholy goings on of the boom period, reflect that Nemesis follows, and perhaps half-welcome her. Finally, there is a respectable body of academic opinion which has been taught (and teaches) to distrust monopolies, combines, and the like, and wonders, perhaps with reason, whether the existing combines do not contain unwholesome elements which one would not wish to see one more section of the industry learning to imitate. Thus and with these ingredients, good and bad and indifferent, phlegm and spleen and frog's brains, and rosemary for remembrance, is the witch's cauldron filled. And it is all, to my mind, very depressing and very ominous too.

All through the year *The Manchester Guardian* has warmly supported those who have been trying to do something. For this reason the division of Manchester opinion and the lack of any general will to action is all the better illustrated by the perverse attitude of *The Manchester Guardian Commercial*. A year ago, when this controversy first began, they deprecated combines; they do not like short-time; they are opposed to cartels, and have sniped at the Yarn Association from the outset; yet, as a final completion of the closed circle of negatives, they objected, in an article last week (November 10th, 1927) which, in view of previous articles, can only be described as impudent, to the Yarn Association's retreat, and—after having done nothing to help the Association to win through—blame its reluctant abandonment of regulations which were penalising its own members against outsiders. At the same time the existence of a surplus capacity problem is now unreservedly recognised. The sterile unhelpfulness of the Manchester atmosphere could not be better shown.

In a comment on Keynes's article *The Manchester Guardian Commercial* suggested, under the title 'The Conversion of Mr Keynes', that he was showing signs of accepting that newspaper's point of view. Keynes replied.

To the Editor of The Manchester Guardian Commercial, *27 November 1927*

Sir,

I am afraid that I cannot respond to the politeness of your article last Thursday under the title 'The Conversion of Mr Keynes', for the article seems to me to be wanting in candour.

A year ago I advocated amalgamations in the American cotton spinning industry. In reply you wrote (November 18, 1926): 'At the risk of being included among those who in Mr Keynes's eyes are too old or too obstinate to live in the modern age, we venture to doubt whether his suggestion of amalgamation is immediately applicable to the cotton trade as it exists today—or, at any rate, to the American section of the trade.' You went on to give your reasons—namely, that amalgamation must be *preceded* by individual firms being brought to a state of maximum efficiency (obviously an impossible requirement when the object of amalgamation is to remedy inefficiency); whereas at present, you went on, this is not the case—'not, as is generally thought, because of excessive loan and interest charges but rather because of high labour costs. It is for the trade itself to decide whether these are due to lower efficiency among those employed in the trade or—as is more likely—to old and inefficient plant and machinery'. You reiterated the same standpoint in several successive articles—namely, that combination is no good as a remedy for inefficiency and overproduction, but is only appropriate for individual firms already organised at maximum efficiency, which, we all agree, is not true of the American cotton spinners today.

When a year later I recur tentatively to my original suggestion of amalgamations as an alternative to a cartel to meet the present troubles, you pretend to welcome 'the conversion of Mr Keynes' to the 'lines which we ourselves advocated a year ago'. I say that this is wanting in candour.

Further, you opposed the attempt of the Yarn Association to secure an agreed regulation of prices and output, and you now oppose the cessation of the attempt. This also oversteps the due bounds of controversial inconsistency.

We have a problem where all the possible alternatives are open to objection, and the task is to find the least objectionable. In such a case there is plenty of room for honest difference of opinion and keen debate. But there are certain standards of controversy which one expects a reputable journal to maintain.

Yours, &c.,

J. M. KEYNES

On 17 January 1928 the Royal Statistical Society discussed a paper by Professor G. W. Daniels and John Jewkes, entitled 'The Post-war Depression in the Lancashire Cotton Industry'. In the course of the discussion Keynes made some observations.

From The Journal of the Royal Statistical Society, *part II, 1928*

MR J. M. KEYNES said that Professor Daniel's paper raised so many points of interest that he would only select one or two of the more striking. His most remarkable conclusion, if it could be substantiated, was to the effect that the margins in the American section were greater than before the War, and greater than in the Egyptian section, after allowing for changes in prices. On the face of it, that ran counter to almost universal experience, and Mr Keynes thought that Professor Daniels's results ought to be modified a good deal, because he had corrected his price changes in margins by means of the *Statist* index number of wholesale prices. It was no good to correct by reference to the *Statist* wholesale index charges which excluded rates, commissions, etc., but were in the main wages and salaries of one kind or another. It was useless to correct changes in wages and salaries by means of the *Statist* wholesale index. The figures of any industry worked out on that basis would disclose very unexpected results. Even if the cost-of-living index number were used the facts could probably be understated, and the wholesale index number appeared to bear no proper relation to what was relevant. If, indeed, it were the case that the spinners were getting more than pre-war in the sense that they were getting larger contributions towards increased profit, they would not be in the condition in which they were in today.

That miscalculation, if it was one, was perhaps connected with the over-emphasis which Professor Daniels laid on the recapitalisation of the industry during the boom period. It was quite clear that some very imprudent things were done, and the industry had suffered from this boom in many indirect ways. Some of the shrewdest people in the industry had left it. Instead of the industry being owned and controlled largely by people who knew and understood it, a large body of outside shareholders and directors were substituted for them.

Mr Keynes believed Professor Daniels would have kept nearer to the truth if he had tried to break up the composite figure which a cotton spinner called his 'margin' Professor Daniels's conclusion would only follow if, when other items had been subtracted, the balance left for interest and depreciation had gone up more than in proportion to the replacement cost of a new spindle. It was known that that was not the case. To get a rough idea of the order of magnitude, with a normal mill spinning a medium count, if the fixed capital stood at 20s. a spindle, 1d. per lb. would have to be set aside for interest and depreciation would be 5d. If mills were succeeding in getting that 5d. which the boom period presumed, that would be a tremendous factor in the situation. In fact a mill would be lucky if it got 1d., and very few mills got 1d. at the present time. Also, that 1d. only represented interest and depreciation on the pre-war replacement prices of the spindle, whereas to cover today's cost a surplus of $2\frac{1}{2}$d. might be needed.

All that part of the paper about the boom period, while very interesting in itself, seemed to Mr Keynes to have next to no bearing on the main problem under discussion, and it would appear that there were some serious inconsistencies in Professor Daniels's view as to how far the overcapitalisation was leading to high prices.

Sir Sydney Chapman had pointed out that on page 177 it was said that high capitalisation required high prices. On page 180 Mr Daniels suggested that the trouble was that the mills were not in a position to cut prices as they should. On the other hand, the truth was very well put forth on page 171, where it was pointed out that the actual capitalisation of the mill did not in the least affect earnings and was irrelevant. On page 181 it was pointed out that it was the overcapitalised mills that were the worst as regards price cutting. The right story was given on page 171 and the wrong story on pages 180–81. Mr Keynes was a little sorry that Professor Daniels had so much emphasised the financial problem because although it was a very real one, it had been an obstacle in the way of the education of opinion in Lancashire. Anyone who had lived in Lancashire during the boom period had been so much shocked at what was going on that he was now disposed to attribute a great part of the present troubles of the industry to those past historical events. But if the average of the whole industry, even at the present time, were considered, it would be found that the spindles were not on an average valued at their replacement cost. If the whole of the ordinary capital were written off, the whole of the trouble would not be wiped out; it was necessary to probe further. Mr Keynes agreed with almost every word that Mr Ellinger had said. Mr Ellinger had published a very important paper showing that spinners were not charging a high price for spinning on world standards, and there was no reason for supposing that they were the real sinners. There were at least three hundred mills of which the aggregate capital was less than that of Messrs Coats. It was evident that under modern conditions an industry organised in an out-of-date manner would not produce the best results, but the sort of economies that could be got by reorganising the spinning side by itself could not possibly make enough difference for Lancashire to recapture markets. Something more drastic had to take place, and the difficulty was that it was nobody's business to take the steps, and no one was in a position to do so. Anything that could be any good would upset vested interest in many directions.

There was probably no hall in Manchester large enough to hold all the directors of cotton companies; they ran into thousands. One of the first things should be to dismiss the vast majority of these people, but the persons to whom this proposal would have to be made would be precisely those directors. It might be of benefit to the shareholders, who were otherwise in a hopeless position. If any section of the industry were taken it would be found that a large proportion of those concerned believed that their interests were bound up with the continuance of the present state of affairs, and therefore there was a real risk of nothing being done and the industry going downhill. That was why it was important to try and discover the really weak spots and do something, where it was possible to be practical at all. The cotton industry was not one in which it could be hoped that the ideal course would be taken at present.

So far as the spinners were concerned, Mr Keynes thought that they had to tackle the problem of over-capacity, and they would also have to form a combine within themselves to make the necessary economies. Outside that there was the problem of the cotton industry as a whole, and how to regain trade. Attention was concentrated on the spinners because they formed the weakest unit, and therefore the losses of the industry as a whole had fallen on them disproportionately. Mr Keynes would like that weak unit to be made stronger, and if it were made stronger there might be some chances of the other units, no longer able to live on the losses of the spinners, waking up themselves.

After 1928 Keynes continued to take a friendly interest in the cotton industry. When in January 1929 the Bank of England formed the Lancashire Cotton Corporation, with much of the management coming from the Cotton Yarn Association, Keynes welcomed the move.

From The Nation and Athenaeum, *2 February 1929*

THE LANCASHIRE COTTON CORPORATION

One is disposed to murmur with Galileo—It moves all the same. And quickly too, if we view the situation in perspective. The movement to reorganise the Lancashire industry of American cotton spinning which took shape two years ago in the formation of the Cotton Yarn Association, has borne fruit today in the registration, under the auspices of the Bank of England, of a vast combine which will absorb at the start approaching one third of the whole industry—and perhaps much more before long— and will have at its command the best brains in the business and adequate financial resources to rationalise, economise, and experiment. As one who has been in close enough touch with this movement to know something of the difficulties and obstacles which have been overcome, I think it should be recognised how much Lancashire and the country owe to Mr Lincoln Tattersall and Mr John Ryan, whose wisdom and skilled diplomacy and indomitable patience and good temper have steered their ambitious project to success. They now have—in conjunction with Sir Kenneth Stewart and their other colleagues—quite a different task to accomplish, namely, to achieve a business success as great as the diplomatic success already to their credit.

The financial structure of the new concern is very interesting. Most of the mills to be taken over are so heavily indebted to their banks as not to be in a position to resist any reasonable proposal supported by the latter. This has been the engine to secure the assent of boards to a scheme, which, however advantageous to creditors and shareholders, involves all the directors (several hundreds of them), in deprivation of office. At the same time the scheme is tender to shareholders and unsecured creditors, all of whom will get something and retain some tangible interest in the prosperity of the new combine, although most of them would on a forced liquidation get much less than nothing. The arrangements are also such as to allow time to shareholders for the discharge of their liabilities in respect of share capital not yet called up, and to give them a valuable asset in exchange for such calls when they are made.

The most ticklish question, however, related to the treatment, not of the weaker creditors, but of the stronger. Would the banks, in particular, who hold in many cases a first mortgage on the physical assets of the mills, saddle the new concern with an obligation to pay heavy debenture interest from the start, whether it was earned or not? Or would they allow it a breathing space and seek their security in its future business success rather than in its present physical assets? This has not been satisfactorily settled without a struggle. But in the end the banks and other prior creditors are to be satisfied with $5\frac{1}{2}$ per cent convertible income debenture stock, on which interest will be payable only if it is earned, so that the combine will be freed from all fixed interest charges in respect of the indebtedness of the companies absorbed. This was a matter of great importance, since it is exceedingly likely that the combine will not succeed in earning the interest on these income debentures until it has had time to reorganise its constituent members and to try out its new ideas. Thus there was a danger that it might be compelled in its early years to pay away liquid resources in debenture interest which it had not earned. But under the scheme adopted, the combine will have no fixed liabilities whatever, except in respect of the new money which it will raise. And here also it has a favoured position at the outset. Pending the issue of first debentures, the new money required (perhaps about £2,000,000) is being put up by the Bank of England on easy terms, the exact details of which have not yet been published, subject only to the directorate of the Corporation obtaining the Bank's approval. This incursion of the Bank of England—somewhat late in the day but wholeheartedly in the end—into the field of rationalisation is in itself a matter of much interest and, in my opinion, of congratulation. There are other matters on which the post-war policy of the Bank of England has been gravely at fault. But in two spheres the present Governor has deserved unqualified praise—for his powerful and unselfish support of the European reconstruction schemes sponsored by the Financial Committee of the League of Nations, and for the friendly relations which he has established with the Federal Reserve System in the United States. His present action had added a third, where, failing decisive intervention by the Bank of England, the separatist interests of the Big Five might have caused disastrous delays or spoilt the details of the plan.

Another ticklish question was whether the various interests concerned would allow a really drastic writing down of the spindleage to be taken over. Here, again, after a struggle, sound business principles have prevailed. The mills taken over are to be valued according to their age and condition, but by reference to a basis which will leave the combine with its plant standing in the aggregate well below present replacement cost and at a much lower figure than the plant of its competitors in any part of the world. Indeed, the total loan and share capital of the whole thing will be extraordinarily small compared with its national importance—probably of the order of some £10,000,000 or less than a tenth of the present market capitalisation of the single firm of Courtaulds.

Thus it is fair to say that the purely financial side of the problem of the American cotton spinners in Lancashire has now been solved. They can devote themselves with unembarrassed minds to their technical and marketing problems.

It has been clear from the outset that a combine on these

principles was the right line of evolution. My first rash incursion into the affairs of Lancashire in November, 1926, was to advocate this. Failing a combine, but as a possible first step towards it, it seemed that some kind of cartel might prevent the industry from bleeding to death by continued selling below cost price. The Cotton Yarn Association's unsuccessful attempt at a cartel paved the way for the present more drastic scheme—a scheme which always lay, I think, from the beginning at the back of the minds of those responsible for the Yarn Association. For the cartel could scarcely be more than a means of avoiding losses, and nothing less than a combine could effect economies in production.

To this technical problem the best part of the industry can now devote itself, freed from financial embarrassments. How much can it hope to achieve? No one can say beforehand. In technical experience, in size, and in financial strength the new combine will start at a considerable advantage over its competitors in every country. There is reason to hope that it may be able to effect economies, over what the separate mills could accomplish, ranging from a fraction of a penny a pound in the coarser counts up to several pence in the finer. The economies will come from several sources, and most of them are likely to be small taken separately. To dispense with five hundred directors and reduce the host of independent managers, salesmen, and secretaries will be something to begin with. The bulk buying on the one hand of cotton and other stores, together with financial resources to take advantage of the right moments to buy, and the bulk selling of yarn and disposal of waste on the other, with some elimination of agents and brokerages, may be worth a good deal. For example, a concern which buys 500,000 tons of coal a year is in a very different position to avoid intermediate charges from one which buys 5,000 tons. But it may turn out that the larger advantages will come from certain other directions which can only be explored gradually. The specialisation of individual mills on spinning a uniform product is one example. A further integration with other branches of the cotton industry—the combine proposes from the start to absorb a considerable number of looms—may be the beginning of a movement which will transform the whole structure of Lancashire's traditional organisation. But we must give it time and not expect results too quickly.

The Lancashire Cotton Corporation is a signal example of a piece of work where the hope of quick large profits for individuals has played a minimum part and the interest of carrying through a durable, constructive effort has been uppermost.

Keynes's article required one reply to a letter signed 'Critic' which appeared in *The Manchester Evening Chronicle* for 19 February.[1]

To the Editor of The Manchester Evening Chronicle, *19 February 1929*

Sir,

My attention has been called to a letter published in your issue of February 13 accusing me of having 'made a great howler' in my recent article in *The Nation* on the Lancashire Cotton Corporation, on the ground that I said that the new combine might be able to effect economies 'ranging from a penny or two a pound in the coarser counts'.

If your correspondent will kindly read the actual text of my article in *The Nation*, which appeared on February 2, he will find that the correct version as printed is as follows 'ranging from a fraction of a penny a pound in the coarser counts.'

J. M. KEYNES

Keynes's final contribution to the discussions was that of a professional economist.

[1] The mistake had been in *The Evening Chronicle*'s report of Keynes's article.

To the Editor of The Manchester Guardian, *25 April 1929*

Sir,

Since it seems probable that the Cotton Yarn Association will be wound up at an early date, it becomes a matter of considerable importance that some means should be found of continuing the Association's statistical work. Doubtless the formation of the Lancashire Cotton Corporation, with the result that a solution is being sought through the method of the combine rather than by looser methods of association, means that the major purposes for which the Cotton Yarn Association was originally formed are now superseded. But this is not the case so far as relates to their statistical work. This must have been of very real value to the industry. Cannot some means be found to carry on this necessary work, either by maintaining an *ad hoc* body solely for this purpose, or by transferring the present machinery to some existing body? Would it be practicable for the Statistical Bureau of the Chamber of Commerce to take on the work?

Yours, &c.,

J. M. KEYNES

Chapter 8

INDUSTRY, ECONOMY, CURRENCY AND TRADE

Keynes began 1927 with a series of speeches. On 4 January he spoke on the cotton industry in Manchester (above, pp. 601–6). The next day he addressed the London Liberal Candidates Association at the National Liberal Club. The full text of his remarks survives.[1]

LIBERALISM AND INDUSTRY

I am sure that the recent malaise in the Liberal Party has been due to something much more important than personalities, and rightly considered, much more encouraging. It is due to the fact that the subject matter of Liberalism is changing. The destruction of private monopoly, the fight against landlordism and protection, the development of personal and religious liberty, the evolution of democratic government at home and throughout the Empire—on all those issues the battle has been largely won.

Today and in the years to come the battle is going to be fought on new issues. The problems of today are different, and, in the main, these new problems are industrial or, if you like, economic. Now, this change, which will be a disturbing thing for all the historic parties, is partly a result of the victory of democracy, and of the new self-consciousness and the new organisation of the wage-earning classes. But it is not entirely psychological in its origins. It is due also, as I believe, to the arrival of a new industrial revolution, a new economic transition which we have to meet with new expedients and new solutions.

[1] It was published later in the year in a collection of papers entitled *Liberal Points of View*; edited by H. L. Nathan and H. Heathcote Williams.

The main political problem of today is the safe guidance of the country through this transition and towards the establishment of an economically efficient and economically just society in the changed conditions. There is a dual aim before the statesman—a society which is just and a society which is efficient; and more and more in terms of our old solutions we are feeling ourselves confronted with a dilemma, a seeming contradiction very often between the policy which appears to be just and the policy which seems to be in the interests of efficiency.

On these issues between the Tories and Labour there is a sharp cleavage on both points. They disagree as to what is just; they disagree as to what is efficient; and so they can engage with conviction and enthusiasm on the business of cutting one another's throats.

But Liberals are in a more difficult position. They are inclined to sympathise with Labour about what is just, but to suspect that in the ignorant blind striving after justice Labour may destroy what is at least as important and is a necessary condition of any social progress at all—namely, efficiency.

It is useless to suppose that we can pursue ideal justice regardless of ways and means in the economic world. No one can look at the evolution of society and not admit to himself that some measure of social injustice has often been the necessary condition of social progress. If society had always been strictly just, I am not at all sure that we might not still be monkeys in a forest.

The task of the statesman is to see to it that the best possible compromise is achieved between our ultimate aims and our practical means of reaching them. The great danger of today, as I see it, is lest the immense destructive force of organised Labour should, in its blindness and ignorance, destroy the opportunity for the contrivings of science and constructive industry before these have had time to guide the transition along sound lines. The Labour Party is organising an immense force to ends which may be right, but by dubious paths which may lead not to construction but to a destructive loss of the opportunities which would otherwise exist.

It is the task of Liberals, as I conceive it, to guide the aspirations of the masses for social justice along channels which will not be inconsistent with social efficiency; and a party which pursues that task with sincerity and devotion will exercise an influence over the future of this country altogether disproportionate to its numerical strength or to its Parliamentary position.

The very extreme Conservatives, led by Sir Ernest Benn and his friends—with whom, I am afraid, some so-called Liberal leaders may partly sympathise—Sir Ernest Benn and his friends would like to undo all the hardly-won little which we have in the way of conscious and deliberate control of economic forces for the public good, and replace it by a return to chaos. I cannot believe that that can be the policy of the Liberal Party if its aspirations are as I have described them.

The more moderate Conservatives, under Mr Baldwin, try to temper the same logic with mercy and expediency; but the result is that they have no plan, which leaves them at the mercy of the noisy anti-trade union, anti-communist, anti-everything man who has always been the muscle and brawn of their Party.

The Labour Party has got tied up with all sorts of encumbering and old-fashioned luggage. They respond to anti-communist rubbish with anti-capitalist rubbish. I do not believe that class war or nationalisation is attractive or stimulating in the least degree to modern minds. I was talking to a prominent Labour politician not long ago somewhat on these lines, and I ventured to say that perhaps the old gag about the Conservatives being the stupid party ought now to be applied to Labour. 'No,' he said, 'not the stupid party—the silly party.'

The consequence of all this is that, whether in or out of office, the business of orderly evolution seems likely to remain in Liberal hands. If we cannot carry out our policies ourselves, we can at least develop them and hope with some confidence that others will steal them.

What are the great changes of which I have been speaking, which have made this alteration of programme so essential? They are partly psychological and they are partly material. The industrial wage-earning classes are now, as a delayed result of the franchise reforms of the last two generations, on the road to political power, which means that they are able to force to the forefront of practical politics the industrial problems which especially concern them individually, just as each previous class which has attained political power in this country has made its own problems the dominant problems of the age.

It is not only that. It is also that the optimistic *Zeitgeist* of the nineteenth century has given way to a pessimistic *Zeitgeist*. The spirit of the age is not optimistic as it used to be. We are disappointed with the results of our existing methods of carrying on. We used to think that private ambition and compound interest would between them carry us to paradise. Our material conditions seemed to be steadily on the up-grade. Now we are fully content if we can prevent them from deteriorating; which means that the working classes no longer have sufficient hopes in the general trend of things to divert their attention from other grievances. We no longer have sufficient confidence in the future to be satisfied with the present.

But it is not only psychological changes which are responsible; there are also great changes in the world of things associated with these changes in the world of feelings and of desires. The old picture, the old schematism as to the actual nature of the economic world we live in is hopelessly out of date; the picture of numerous small capitalists, each staking his fortune on his judgement, and the most judicious surviving, bears increasingly little relation to the facts. I have been spending some time lately in conference with the spinning industry of Lancashire. They are living industrially in the old world; and they are suffering intolerable pains from their failure to adapt themselves to the conditions of the new economic world. Businesses are increasingly owned by the public, who know nothing about the details of the true financial position of the concern, and they are run in their daily management by salaried persons who, perhaps, are risking little or nothing of their own fortunes. There has been a series of three articles in *The Economist* in recent weeks, analysing the distribution of the share-holding of the great combines amongst shareholders. It is a remarkable result that it is innumerable small holdings, averaging £300 to £400 each, which make up the great combines of today—concerns which one thinks of as representing the wealth of financial magnates rather than of small investors. But these small investors who own these businesses have no power whatever of controlling them and no knowledge whatever of their real position. How remote that is from the old picture of owners staking their fortunes on their judgement, and the most judicious surviving.

Moreover, the day of the small unit is over, partly for technical reasons, even more for marketing reasons. To get the market is half the task of the modern businessman, and modern methods of capturing markets are hopelessly inapplicable on the small scale of the old competitive industry. In fact, under modern conditions the wastes and expenses of cut-throat competition and the beggar-my-neighbour business, which we used to applaud so whole-heartedly, are so devastating that every go-ahead and prosperous industry spends half its time trying to get rid of them; and those industries which still persist in small units and free competition—like coal and cotton, to take two prominent examples—are rapidly going bankrupt and will continue to go bankrupt until they alter their ways.

But there is another important feature in this transitional age. Methods which were well adapted to continually expanding business are ill adapted to stationary or declining industries. You can increase the scale of industries by small additions arranged by individuals. If there comes a need to shift from one industry to another, to curtail particular industries by small decrements, just as they have been expanded by small increments, no corresponding method is available to isolated, unorganised, individual effort. Combination in the business world, just as much as in the labour world, is the order of the day; it would be useless as well as foolish to try to combat it. Our task is to take advantage of it, to regulate it, to turn it into the right channels.

I was told today by a friend who lately visited an asylum that he had commented to the authorities on the small number of warders that seemed with safety able to take charge of such a large number of dangerous lunatics. 'How is it,' he said, 'that it is safe for you to run this concern with such a small staff?' 'Oh,' came the answer, 'lunatics never combine'. I wish I had heard that story soon enough to repeat it in Manchester yesterday.

What is the remedy for the serious evils which we are suffering consequent upon our failure so far to adapt ourselves to the economic transition in which we are living? Certainly not backward to chaos. Certainly onwards towards order, towards society taking intelligent control of its own affairs. But equally it is not to class war, it is not to spoliation, it is not to the highly centralised system of state socialism. We need the maximum degree of decentralisation which is compatible with large units and regulated competition.

I could give you a long list of the sort of directions in the economic and industrial sphere where we have got to be prepared to take a line which in the old days would have been thought unorthodox. First of all, and this is perhaps the least controversial, it must be the avowed and deliberate business of the Government to make itself responsible for the wholesale collection and dissemination of industrial knowledge. The first condition of successful control and of useful interference of whatever kind from above is that it must be done with knowledge—which it has never been hitherto. An immense amount of economic and industrial knowledge is to be had for the gathering by a body with the authority and with the resources of Government. Of all modern industrial countries we are now the most backward in that respect. The industries themselves do not know what they should know about their own affairs. Each individual spends his time concealing from his friends the facts about himself which it would be useful for them to know, just as it would be useful for him to know the corresponding facts about them. It is pure waste and inefficiency to try to do without the pooling of knowledge. There is no country in the world in which the secretiveness of businessmen and their unwillingness to pool their knowledge is a greater factor of inefficiency than it is in this country. The Government, in my opinion, should make it a deliberate act of policy to break down that secretiveness, that failure to secure the collection of knowledge which is important and relevant to industrial society as a whole.

But it must not only collect and distribute facts which will be useful to the business world itself. The Government of the future ought to regard it as one of the prime tasks of statesmanship to be prepared beforehand with facts and policies for industrial mishaps and maladjustments before they occur, to see them coming along and to be provided with some sort of manner of handling them before it is too late. Just as it has been formerly supposed to be the business of the Government to have foresight where diplomacy and war are concerned, and not to wait until the last moment before taking any steps, so in the industrial world it ought to be the business of the Government to be forewarned and forearmed against every industrial misfortune which might befall the country.

We have two signal examples lately, the treatment of currency policy and of the coal question, in which the Government was taken by surprise and had to begin too late to collect the knowledge which, if they had had it earlier, might have materially altered their initial policy.

I have said that this is the least controversial of the directions in which progress seems to me to be now required. My next point follows on what I was saying a few minutes ago about the new distribution of the ownership of big business. Governments must consider it their business to take some responsibility for seeing that the vast body of private investors are able to invest their savings with a reasonable degree of knowledge and security and in the directions most conducive to national prosperity. They might also find some way of restoring a greater association of financial interest with activity in the industry and responsibility for its daily management. This is peculiarly a case in which we are living between two worlds. In fact, big business is coming to be owned by the man in the street, but we run our affairs on the assumption that the owner is the man who is directing it, who is consciously and knowingly taking the risks, and so forth. If that is carried much further it is bound to end in all sorts of disasters and misfortunes, and, in my opinion, it is time that, in such matters as the reform of company law, publicity of accounts, and so forth, the Government shall feel a responsibility to adjust things to the new state of affairs which has arisen.

It must also be prepared to experiment with all kinds of new sorts of partnership between the state and private enterprise. The solution lies neither with nationalisation nor with un-regulated private competition; it lies in a great variety of experiments, of attempts to get the best of both worlds.

In England there have been made already without due recognition a good many experiments in that direction. We want to carry forward that natural evolution more deliberately, knowing what we are doing, and doing it on purpose. The Government must recognise the trend of soundly run business towards trusts and combines. It must be prepared to recognise their existence as beneficent institutions in right conditions; and it must adopt an attitude towards them at the same time of encouragement and regulation. In some quarters there is supposed to have been a traditional Liberal Party attitude towards trusts, to harry them out of existence if possible—their existence was to be made difficult. I believe that policy (if it ever was the policy of the Liberal Party) is a wrong policy in modern conditions. It should be not discouragement, but encouragement for them to live and exist in right conditions conducive to the general welfare. So far from their being any natural incompatibility between the two, I believe that these great concerns run by salaried persons with a sufficient degree of decentralisation may, if they are handled by politicians and statesmen in the right manner, become a pattern and model of the way in which the world of the future will get the best both of large units and of the advantages that might be expected from nationalisation, whilst maintaining the advantages of private enterprise and decentralised control.

I must not linger for any length of time on any one of the several points which I lay before you, because I am attempting an outline, not a complete exposition, of far too big a subject. It is not only in the direction of the regulation of capital that the state must be prepared for new functions. It must be prepared to regard the regulation of the wages of great industrial groups as being not merely of private concern, and it must quite deliberately in its wages and hours policy treat the gradual betterment of the economic welfare of the workers as the first charge on the national wealth, and not leave it to the accident of private organisations and of private bargaining. But in this age of transition it is not only wages and hours which are going to determine the health and prosperity of the labouring classes. The problem of the education and the mobility of labour is going to be at least as important. The haphazard methods of the past by which different groups of industry have been recruited is, perhaps, one of the major causes of the present scale of unemployment. It is not so much that there is no work to be done, but that men drop into occupations with no knowledge, by mere accident of circumstance and parentage and locality, often finding themselves in the wrong market, trained for something for which there is no demand, or not trained at all. There is no remedy for that by unregulated private action. It must be the concern of the state to know and have a policy as to where labour is required, what sort of training is wanted; and then when there are maladjustments, as there are in the coal industry, to work out plans for the transfer of labour from localities and trades where there is no demand to other localities and other trades which are expanding and not declining. That is one example of the general policy which Government has to be prepared for—namely, the deliberate regulation from the centre in all kinds of spheres of action where the individual is absolutely powerless left to himself. Leave individuals to go on doing what they are doing more or less satisfactorily, even though individual action is not perfect—where it exists and is functioning, leave it alone—but do from the centre those things which, if they are not done from the centre, will not be done at all. I have given several examples of that, and as the machinery gets built up and the policy is developed, not a year will pass without an important addition to the spheres where it may be usefully employed without any detriment to the advantages of our existing form of society.

The conditions for me and for many others of sustaining any live interest in party politics are, first of all, that my party should see the broad outlines of this new industrial problem, that it should be prepared to adopt an active policy towards it, and be ready to evolve new methods and a new attitude on the part of the state, and particularly that it should be ready to co-operate with Labour whenever Labour is inclined to help with our active policy—a by no means impossible contingency unless we are going to have a Tory Government for ever.

It is a vast programme that I have briefly outlined—one of great practical and technical difficulty, but it is what really matters in the political world today. It is *the* task lying to the hand of the new Liberalism. An attempt is now being made to work out some first outlines of such a policy by the Liberal Industrial Committee, initiated by the Liberal Summer School and encouraged and supported by Mr Lloyd George. It is far too soon to foreshadow an unwritten report; but perhaps I have indicated some of the lines, not exactly on which we are going to report, but along which some of us are tackling the problem, the type of action which is passing through our minds and is receiving an impartial consideration.

Perhaps I ought to stop there, but I should like in all sincerity to add another word. Many of those who, without disrespect, I may call the old Liberals, are blind to this new problem, are suspicious of and hostile to any policy directed towards solving it, and they are not ready to co-operate with Labour on any likely terms. If that is true (I may be doing individuals an injustice) it means that on the economic issue they are Conservatives. This is compatible with remaining good Liberals on the old issues— free traders, supporters of self-government in democracy, moderation in armaments, the liberty of the subject, and so on—all the great good old causes—it means that they remain good Liberals in respect of the things which mattered most twenty-five years ago, but that they are Conservatives in respect of the new problems which are now in the centre of the picture.

A party cannot live by its past, however distinguished. If this wing had captured the Party it would have died of inanition within five years, for it would not have differed on anything which was of first political importance at the moment from the more moderate Conservatives. Apart from free trade, Mr Baldwin is probably as good a Liberal as many of them. He is a Conservative because, like them, he has not a vestige of a plan or an idea for the new problems of today.

In my judgement, there is no sufficient purpose for a Liberal Party, no reason why it should continue to exist, except to contribute, firstly, to international peace in all its aspects, and, secondly, to the gradual evolution of a reformed economic society which shall be acceptable, just, and efficient in the changed conditions of the age. The test of a man's Liberalism today must not be his attitude towards the questions which were important a generation ago, but to those which are most important to the generation coming.

Keynes returned to industry on two more occasions in the ensuing weeks. On 18 January, he took the chair for a discussion on 'State Control of Industry' at a meeting of the British Institute of Philosophical Studies. On 16 February he took part in a broadcast discussion on 'University Men in Business', the script of which survives.

UNIVERSITY MEN IN BUSINESS

SIR ERNEST BENN: *We are going to have a conversation or discussion—I am not at all clear how it ought to be described—on the question of 'University Men in Business'. We are to have the advantage of hearing Mr Maynard Keynes and Mr Ernest Walls, and it is my function to stand, or sit, between these two experts and, as chairman, keep them in order.*

Mr Walls as the Managing Director of Lever Bros. Ltd. will speak with very exceptional authority on the subject from the point of view of the business man. No one can tell us better than he can what it is that business looks to secure from the universities. On the other hand, we are fortunate in being able to hear Mr J. M. Keynes on the other side of the question; and he will be able to tell us how the universities look at the matter, and what it is that the universities can give to the business life of the nation.

There are all sorts of great big questions involved in this discussion. First, the difference between education and instruction. Is a university education the basis upon which a business career can be subsequently built and to which business knowledge can be added, or is it suggested that the universities can actually teach a man how to do business? But there are bigger and more immediate questions. There is the vital matter of industrial peace, a matter which is exercising the minds of every serious citizen today. Surely no one will deny that industrial peace would be easier of achievement if both branches of the industrial army possessed a higher degree of education?

I notice in a recent discussion on this same question a reference to the class instinct of the undergraduate. Class instinct is surely a bad thing, and I hope that Mr Keynes will be able to show us that the universities are able to break down, and not in fact to build up, anything in the nature of class instinct. As a business man without a university education, I have always suspected a certain snobbery developed by the universities which drives most of their products into professions—the civil service, the arts and other sidelines in human endeavour. Surely the main line of human endeavour must always be the production of the material requirements of the human race, and that is business.

As I hope Mr Keynes may be able to tell us that the universities are looking more and more to business as a profession and as a career, so I hope Mr Walls will be able to assure us that business men are looking more and more to the universities to supply the recruits for the business of the future.

My job, however, is not to carry on this discussion—merely to introduce. My instructions from Mr Sieveking were to introduce for five minutes. Having to the best of my ability complied with that command, I am now going to ask you to listen to Mr Walls.

MR WALLS: *In your kind introduction, Sir Ernest, you said that my function would be to state as far as I can what appeared to be the requirements of business—what business calls for from the universities. I fear it is a little difficult, apart from the immensity of the subject, because I am myself prejudiced, as I am bound to say at the outset, in favour of the university man in business, as my own career has been that I entered business immediately I came down from the university and have remained in the same business ever since. As far as I am personally concerned, any success I have had in business I put down entirely to my university training.*

CHAIRMAN: *Entirely?*

WALLS: *Yes, I think so. I think I would say entirely. Where I think the universities can help us in business especially is in the direction making the career of business more of a profession than it is today. You said just now that the universities are turning out men for certain professions such as the church, the civil service, the law and so on. Apparently today it is expected that an undergraduate at the end of his career will leap straight from the university into business and settle down immediately into it. No one expects the same thing of a lawyer or any other professional man; and I think that this gap between the professional life of business and the previous training is the greatest difficulty that we have to face, and—to be perfectly frank—the universities do not, as it seems to me, make any real effort to fill that gap.*

My point about the professional character of business, I think, is well reinforced by the experience of the present time when more and more important positions in business are being occupied by professional men—lawyers, for instance, are becoming more and more business men—and this I take to be on account of their professional training. The present day business world is largely made up of limited liability companies in which the directors are in effect trustees for shareholders. Then again business is being done on a very much larger scale than has ever been the case and, in addition, we have in every direction amalgamations and combines which are not only national, but are tending to become international, so that the men who will be required to direct and organise these modern types of business must be professional in the sense that they have been definitely trained for the position they will occupy and have had the advantage of the highest education which we can give them. In a word, what modern business calls for is a professionally trained business man and the question is: Can the universities provide him in the same way that they have successfully supplied the older professions?

CHAIRMAN: *What do you say to that, Mr Keynes?*

MR MAYNARD KEYNES: The men whom the universities have supplied to the business world in the past, have belonged to two quite distinct types. There are, first of all the sons of wealthy business parents who are sent to a public school and a university with the idea from the outset that they will at the end of it all, find a safe berth in the family business or in some other concern where the family has influence. This will work out according to programme, unless the young man shows himself quite unusually incompetent. He has no great incentive to stretch his energies in any direction which is not naturally agreeable to him. The degree he takes will not be too much scrutinised. For him, the university is a pleasant and delightful interlude without much serious bearing on his future career.

The other type consists of undergraduates with no family or other influence in the business world, who are faced with the necessity of earning a living immediately after the conclusion of their university career, and have nothing but themselves to depend upon. These young men are naturally, as a rule, pretty serious workers. They measure themselves against their contemporaries; and those who know them through their three university years can probably form a shrewd judgement at the end of that time, both about their brains and about their temperamental suitability for one walk of life or another.

Now, in the past, the majority of university men in business have belonged as a rule to the first type. I hold no brief for these. I hope the university does them no harm: I think it may do some of them quite a lot of good. But it is not for what they have learned at their university that they have been selected for a business career, and I don't think that it's the universities who should be blamed, if parental affection had encouraged them to lead too easy a life when they were young and has put them in too safe a job when they were grown-up. Indeed, my own opinion is that hereditary influence in higher business appointments is one of the greatest dangers to efficiency in British business. So many of our industries are now reaching a difficult age. They are becoming second and third generation businesses. They are getting into the hands of men who didn't create them and who couldn't possibly have created them.

I fancy, however, that the other type, those who have been deliberately chosen on the ground of their university record, is going to become increasingly important. There has always been a certain number of this type entering business, but it is a comparatively new thing for them to do so in large numbers. In the case of the University of Cambridge (about which I know most), it dates from the development of the University Appointments Board, which is an organisation the whole purpose of which is to keep in touch with the requirements of the business world and to make sure that no one is recommended from Cambridge who isn't well suited to the job offered, not only by his intellectual attainments but by character and temperament. A man's university career ought to be a testing time. Universities can reasonably claim to be judged by the success of those who are selected because they have passed successfully through this testing time, and not by those who have passed straight on through family influence, quite irrespective of what they may have done at the university or what their university thinks of them.

CHAIRMAN: *Have you in mind any examples of men who have been selected on the sole ground of their university success?*

KEYNES: Well, Sir Ernest, there is one very big concern—the Shell Oil Group, which has now been taking men from Cambridge regularly through the Appointments Board for some twenty years, so that they have now had time to estimate the success of this method from pretty long experience. Sir Robert Waley Cohen, Director of the Shell Group (who, by the way, is a good specimen himself of the university man in business) in speaking to his shareholders recently after a visit to the East, told them that the thing which stood out and impressed itself on him more than anything else was the remarkable staff by which the Company was served. 'Many of them,' he said, 'joined us originally straight from the university, and they constitute today a highly trained and intelligent body of men who are serving our interests with devotion and ability. There is more active competition in the oil business today than at any time within my memory. But we are holding our own, and I think we owe this, as much as to any other single factor, to a unique staff.' The Secretary of one of the Argentine Railways, who has been taking Cambridge men lately, reports that the only difficulty the Company has is that other people are so anxious to snap their men up. I know another great company trading in India and the East which is now almost exclusively staffed by men of good academic attainments, mostly from a single Cambridge College, judging by results certainly one of the most prosperous concerns in the country.

CHAIRMAN: *Well, Mr Walls, what have you to say to that?*

WALLS: *Those are very useful examples, Mr Keynes. What I would be interested to know is what kind of vocational training, if any, followed the university course in these cases.*

It seems to me that there is probably required for business something in the nature of such vocational training (either immediately following the university career or overlapping with it), in the same way that the lawyer has a specialised legal education, for example; and this is a point on which I am sure Mr Keynes you can give us some very useful suggestions, for I feel strongly that it is here that the real gap exists. Of course, for highly specialised work—engineering, chemistry and so on—vocational training of university type exists, and I imagine it is realised by everybody that for such careers it is absolutely essential; but I am thinking more of the commercial side of business rather than any specialised part and, indeed, more of what we might call commerce than what would be classed as production.

Then, there is the international side of business and the utter lack of foreign languages amongst our business people. We have gone on for several generations in our insular pride without finding it necessary to learn any other language than our own. This is hardly likely to continue to be possible, all the more so if one of the features of the immediate future is the internationalisation of business, which will certainly bring great demands in the direction of language.

KEYNES: My own view, Mr Walls, is that it is a mistake for the universities to attempt vocational training. Their business is to develop a man's intelligence and character in such a way that he can pick up relatively quickly the special details of that business he turns to subsequently. I am sure that the special training you speak of is something that can only be taught by

654

business men to business men. I agree with you about languages; and there, I think, the universities are open to criticism and, perhaps, the schools even more. Every young man ought to have mastered either French or German (preferably both) by spending some of his vacations abroad, by the time he leaves the university.

CHAIRMAN: *In that case it will be vacational and not vocational training? Where, then, would you draw the line? Does chemistry come within the category of vocational training? What about engineering, electrical engineering? Where do you stop?*

KEYNES: I doubt if any of these things come into the scheme that Mr Walls mentioned. The engineering laboratory at Cambridge, which trains a great number of men for business, is a totally different thing from an actual engineering works. The chemistry we teach is a necessary foundation for the commercial chemist, but, fortunately for its educational value, it is in itself something totally different from the work of the average, commercial chemist.

WALLS: *I think the greatest complaint which I have come across myself amongst business men when they are talking about this question of university men and the alleged failure of university men to make good in business, I think the greatest objection I have come across is that the university man when he comes down and enters into business, is apt to take a theoretical view about the various questions and problems that come before him—*

KEYNES: What do you mean by 'theoretical'?

WALLS: *What do I mean by 'theoretical'? I think the business man calls theoretical any effort to deal with a problem in a general way rather than bringing it down to what he would call 'Brass tacks'.*

KEYNES: May not a training when they are young to look at the world rather more broadly, help them to take a more profound view of things when they have added business experience to their education?

WALLS: *The difficulty is this. A young man of 23, say, entering a business without any knowledge of that business, is immediately pitted against other young men of the same age who have had a good many years in the business and know all manner of practical details connected with the business—facts and figures and so on, of which he is obviously completely ignorant. It is one of the difficulties, I think. A university man will get the essential facts and figures in a very short time, but in the early stages he is likely to be subject to criticism. Possibly the answer is in an intermediate period of vocational training for business following the university—I agree with you, Mr Keynes, that it is not the university's function to give this training and that it must be linked up with actual business. But there is, I think, undoubtedly amongst business men a feeling that the university man is rather apt to look on the practical questions with too airy a view, his head rather in the skies. That may possibly be a self-protective device of the business man.*

One last point is this. I feel strongly myself that we want university men in business, properly trained and ready for business, because business itself is in such desperate need. When we have over a million unemployed as a regular feature of our national life it cannot be said that the business men of the country, whatever their difficulties, have really succeeded in paying a national dividend. And many of our existing business methods need considerable reinforcement at the present time if we are to compete successfully with America, for example. There seems a need of new points of view, and it is to the young men who have had the advantage of the finest education and training that we know how to give them that we ought to be looking for the reconstruction of British business.

KEYNES: What we do want in this country is some general scheme of training worked out by the big businesses themselves. I believe that large engineering concerns, like Daimlers and Metropolitan-Vickers, already have an elaborate and well thought-out scheme for training their university apprentices. I rather think that Sir Hugo Hurst of the General Electric Company was the first man in this country to set up a regular training scheme in the business for producing commercial

INDUSTRY, ECONOMY, CURRENCY AND TRADE

material from the universities. I believe that is the right line, rather than to try to drive university teachers to attempt something for which they have no real qualifications.

CHAIRMAN: *I remember one of the first Mayors of the London Boroughs who on election said that he hoped to discharge the duties of the h'office without partiality on the one 'and or h'impartiality on the h'other. That was twenty-five years ago, but it's a statement of the principles of good chairmanship which I have never failed to remember. As Chairman, I can agree with both of these distinguished debaters, or I can discharge my duties equally satisfactorily by differing from both of them. And in a way I do differ, at all events on some points from what has been said by Mr Keynes and Mr Walls.*

It seems to me that we ought to have started by defining business. We have talked about industry: we have talked technicalities. But we don't seem to have on the table, as it were, a very clearly defined notion as to what business is. The world at the moment is full of producers who know how to produce, who want to produce their own products, and who don't seem to me at least, to pay much attention to what the consumer wants. I would define business as bringing the producer and consumer together—to me the most difficult function in the whole of the work of providing us with the necessities of life.

But that by the way. I want for the moment to do a little quarrelling with each of my friends.

Don't you think, Mr Keynes, that you are a little bit hard on what may be described as the hereditary business, though it is, of course, true that there are cases where pampered sons are jobbed into father's business, and this goes on.

KEYNES: I am not referring to the extreme cases. They drop out soon enough.

CHAIRMAN: *But have you made enough allowance for the fact that some businesses at least are really more than one life's work? For instance, in my business of publishing and journalism, it is now commonly supposed that you must have enough printers' ink in the blood to succeed in it. I feel that there is a great deal in that. One life is often too short a time to know all there is to know about the intricacies and complexities of many of our trades. Only a few weeks ago, I heard a Scotchman make a twenty minutes' speech on the herring, from the boyhood of his grandfather to the evening of his own life devoted to the study of the herring, and at the end he calculated that he was just beginning to understand something about that useful and modest commodity. You can name concerns where the family tradition is the basis of the business.*

Now, turning to Mr Walls, I am going to quarrel even more definitely with him.

He said his success was entirely due to his university training—a most serious statement for one of our princes of commerce to make: I ventured to interrupt him and make him repeat the word 'entirely'. I know nothing of his business except as an observer and admirer. He is associated in my mind with two great big things—good soap and good advertising—and I should like to hear from him what the University of Oxford did in giving him a training in either.

KEYNES: I am surprised that you do not consider Oxford a good training for advertising.

WALLS: *Answering your point, Sir Ernest, we need in all industry efficient production of goods and efficient marketing of goods. That I think is what you mean by 'good soap and good advertising'. Now as regards production with which the technical side of business is mainly concerned I think it would be universally agreed that we require in our managements the highest scientific skill attainable— the highest standards of scientific education and training.*

CHAIRMAN: *But this is that point I made as to defining the nature of business. I should say that your technical man really belongs to a higher grade of labour. He is concerned with production; he may be concerned with the industry, but not with business.*

WALLS: *I agree, I agree. And I endeavoured in my remarks to differentiate between production and business or if you like the commercial side of business: the two things are distinct.*

Then, of course, you come to the advertising side, if you regard that as commerce—

CHAIRMAN: *I regard that as the essence of the commercial side of business.*

WALLS: *Well then if we are to take advertising and selling as the essence of business and in an age where production is always overtaking demand they are certainly of prime importance, is it not in this field especially that you want a clear mind, a man with his brains trained to think, to generalise and analyse situations, perhaps more than in any other branch of business? What business men are apt to think is that the marketing of goods is a spectacular corner of business; that if you are a born showman, if I may use that term, you will be able to sell anything. My own view about the selling problem of business is that, first of all, it is an analytical question and that the whole subject can be made, and in many directions is being made, a very scientific job indeed; but if it is, then you want men who have had a considerable training in the art of analysis and of clear thinking. Apart from that you want something else, which is the biggest need we have in business. You want the creative ability. Everybody is born with a creative instinct, and that instinct can be developed in many ways, but the finest way of developing it so as to bring the best results is by suitable education. This need of creative ability I would count our greatest need in business today; and while, of course, there will always be geniuses arising who possess that ability inborn to an extraordinary degree, it is perfectly certain that in some measure it is an inborn faculty and can be to a considerable extent trained and developed successfully, and to a much greater extent than at present. Creative ability and imagination—these are the great needs of the business of the future:—Can we look to the universities to supply them in the business men of the future?*

CHAIRMAN: *Well, Mr Keynes, it seems to me that I shall have to appeal to you from the Chair, even if you do come from Cambridge, to put in a word for advertising and salesmanship. Mr Walls' modesty seems to need correcting. Surely, if you look to America, where business and industry have succeeded in a way unknown in any other country and at any other time, advertising has developed to an extent which we don't begin to understand here.*

KEYNES: Well, Sir Ernest, advertising has become a highly intellectual business. That is a reason why the universities may be useful in regard to it. But I think Mr Walls put his finger on the practical difficulty when he dwelt on the problem confronting the university man immediately on his leaving the university and arriving at his business appointment. Obviously he will be extremely 'green' at first. He will naturally be an object of some amusement.

CHAIRMAN: *Yes I agree.*

KEYNES: Half the trouble would disappear if business men would pay him, in spite of that, a reasonable salary from the beginning (having regard to the expense of his education), and find some way of training him for the higher work of the business. For example, if the managing director can give such a man a post as his private secretary and let him see from the inside all his own problems and all the matters that arise in running a big business. Experience of a year or two of that kind will probably do more to make him fit to take his place than years in other departments.

WALLS: *I would rather see him starting with all his training, at the bottom of the ladder. Of course he is going to mount it much faster than the untrained man ever could do.*

KEYNES: In the case of small business, a university career is of more doubtful advantage. If a man is to run the whole thing himself, he must begin when he is young and when he is still content with very small earnings...[*A page of typescript is missing at this point*]...*think the discussion has only served to indicate the outlines of this great question and to show how much there is in it. There can be no doubt that in these days business men are more in need of learning than any other class, because their responsibilities are, perhaps, greater than those of most people. Equally, I think, the universities have something to learn about business, and to me it is really good to know that the great centres of learning are thinking more and more about their responsibilities*

660

to the business world and the development on better lines of this most important of all social services.

If as a result of to-night's talk nothing more happens than that a million listeners will henceforth connect the two ideas of education and business, the trouble, such as it is, involved will have been amply worth while. A million seeds full of promise of good will have been sown, and we may look for even better things from both education and business in coming generations.

May I, as Chairman, in conclusion, on behalf of everyone of the listeners, express our deep sense of obligation both to Mr J. M. Keynes and Mr Ernest Walls for all that they have told us from their respective and equally authoritative points of view.

Keynes did not neglect his traditional interests, however; he made his annual speech to the meeting of the National Mutual (*JMK*, vol. XII) and continued his regular survey of the speeches of the chairmen of the clearing banks with an article in *The Nation* on 12 February under the title 'Mr McKenna on Monetary Policy' (*JMK*, vol. IX, pp. 200–6).

In his article of 12 February, amongst other things, Keynes discussed the movement of sheltered and unsheltered prices since mid-1924. This section of the article drew a critical comment from D. T. Jack of the University of St Andrews, who argued that the same movement had occurred in the United States and suggested that this should affect Keynes's argument. Keynes replied in the next issue.

To the Editor of The Nation and Athenaeum, *19 February 1927*

SHELTERED AND UNSHELTERED PRICE LEVELS

Sir,

In your last issue, Mr D. T. Jack endeavours to work out some figures for the U.S. to compare sheltered and unsheltered price levels corresponding to those which I published for the U.K. in your issue of February 12th. He thinks that his figures show that the relative movements have been much the same in the two countries, and asks whether this conclusion would affect my argument.

There is first of all the question of statistical fact. I depended on a fairly wide range of known figures, some of which appeared explicitly in my table, and others of which corroborated these. Those which appeared explicitly included wages and cost of living. Those which corroborated the general conclusion suggested by these figures, namely, that the sheltered value of sterling had remained practically unchanged during the last thirty months, included 'rent, rates, cost of social insurance, railway charges, and the various items on either side of the national budget which are practically fixed in terms of money'. For the U.S. Mr Jack cites only the cost-of-living figures. For these he has no data later than June, 1926. Over the twenty-four months for which he has figures, it appears that, whilst, as one would expect, their movements both up and down have been smaller and slower than those of wholesale prices, their relative position has been practically unchanged, namely (to repeat his quarterly and half-yearly figures of the ratio of sheltered prices to unsheltered in U.S.), 117, 115, 110, 110, 114, 115. During the period in which the U.S. ratio of sheltered prices to unsheltered, as calculated by Mr Jack, moved from 117 to 115, the U.K. ratio, as also calculated by him, moved from 104 to 116. These figures do not support his contention that the relative price movements have been much the same in U.S. as in U.K. Such plausibility as his conclusion has is, therefore, mainly derived from the figure which—since the actual figure is not yet available—he has had to invent for December, 1926. *If* this figure proves to be correct, then it will be true that the cost of living in U.S. has agreed with that in the U.K. in not following wholesale prices downwards during the twelve months of 1926. At present even this result is hypothetical and unproved. By inventing a different figure for December, 1926, he could have produced an opposite result.

Suppose, however, that the figure of the U.S. cost of living when known supports Mr Jack's anticipations, and suppose that the other indicators of sheltered values in U.S. which he does not know would, if known, tend to the same conclusion, would these facts, if realised, affect my argument? Not materially, in my opinion.

In the first place they would not affect the conclusion that the disequilibrium caused by the return to gold remains uncorrected. In the second place, they would show, at the most, that those of our manufactured exports which compete with similar exports from the U.S. are not at a greater disadvantage than they were a year ago. The U.S., however, is not our chief competitor in our staple export trades; and a considerable part of the U.S. exports consist of the raw materials and agricultural products, the price of which is reflected rather by the fall in the wholesale index number than by the steadiness of the cost-of-living index number.

Mr Jack would have produced a stronger and better established case if he had pointed out that the gold cost of living in Germany, France, Italy, and Belgium rose during 1926, in spite of a fall of wholesale prices, largely as the result of financial measures, analogous to ours, affecting currency and the exchanges. These measures have undoubtedly improved our competitive position relatively to theirs, especially in the case of France. On the other hand, prior to this, our relative disadvantage was overwhelming.

To summarise the net result on our relative position of all the international price changes of the last eighteen months affecting the products of our customers on the one hand and of our competitors on the other, is impossible in any precise terms. I was not attempting this; I had not overlooked the European deflations when I concluded that, in our own case, the position as regards equilibrium between our sheltered and unsheltered price-levels 'is assuredly no better than it was eighteen months ago'. Of course, this is not the only factor in the situation. Indeed, one of my principal conclusions was the possibility of our return to prosperity, though not to our previous scale of exports, without ever restoring the old equilibrium.

Yours, &c.,

J. M. KEYNES

The same week that Keynes's letter appeared, *The Nation* published an article entitled 'Books and the Public' in the hope of opening a discussion of the problems of the book industry. Two weeks later, Keynes made his contribution to the discussion.

From The Nation and Athenaeum, *12 March 1927*

ARE BOOKS TOO DEAR?

The editor of *The Nation* has initiated a discussion in these columns as to the health of an industry, of which the national importance is altogether out of proportion to its size—the book trade. No one, I think, could maintain that too few books are published. So far as fertility is concerned, there is every appearance of health. Few authors of merit nowadays are prevented from seeing the light. But are enough books bought? Do books play the part in occupying our leisure hours which they ought to play? Are the rewards of authorship (and, incidentally, of publishing and bookselling) what they ought to be in a self-respecting community which honours as it should this profession (and those essential aids and adjuncts to it)?

The answer is certainly—No. As for booksellers, to all intents and purposes outside London, Cambridge, Oxford, Edinburgh, and a very few large provincial towns, there are none—none, that is to say, where you can reckon (within reason) on finding what you want on the premises. I hope that the editor will get some publisher's travellers to tell us where in England they can hope to get orders on the large scale. Even in the whole of the metropolitan area are there above a dozen bookshops worthy the name? If so, let us hear their addresses. I should think that to

664

allege one first-rate book shop in the county of Middlesex per half-million of inhabitants would be to overstate the facilities.

Publishers, on the other hand, like authors, are not lacking in numbers. But are they, as a class, prosperous? I hear not. Apart from educational works and text-books and bookstall trash and trade publications, do all the publishers in London added together make enough money to keep one big draper alive? Each book they issue mops up working capital and represents an appreciable risk. I doubt if the profits they can earn are at all proportionate to the difficulty and precariousness of the business.

What of the authors? They are a humble tribe, pleased enough (too often) to see themselves in print without paying for it. They hardly hope, outside the small but not select band of best-sellers, to support a wife and family on the proceeds. Heaven knows (and the editor, and they themselves) that the contributors to *The Nation* are badly paid enough; yet most of them probably draw appreciably more per word than they could hope to earn from a bound book. Heaven knows (and the manager) that the circulation of *The Nation* is small enough; yet there are very few books indeed which even approach it in circulation. How many authors are there in England who can reckon on earning from their books above £500 a year on the average? Very, very few. I fancy that the compositors may do better out of the business on the whole than any of the other factors of production.

Now all this is profoundly unsatisfactory. It means that the power of ideas in this country, expressed otherwise than through the popular press, is negligible. Where does the fault lie?

For a long time I was in the habit of maintaining that the fault lay with the publishers. I have become convinced that they are not the guilty ones. The fault lies, first and foremost, with the public—with their wrong psychology towards book buying, their small expenditure, their mean and tricky ways where a book, the noblest of man's works, is concerned.

The question is largely one of arithmetic. Let me do a sum,

by way of illustration, which will exhibit the economics of book production. I will take a volume, recently published, where I know the figures. The book is a substantial one, above four hundred demy octavo pages, containing more than 160,000 words, bound in a good cloth binding, a book which would normally be published not below 15s. net.

One important item in the cost of production remains practically unchanged whatever the size of the edition, namely the binding, which cost in this case about one shilling a copy, though a cheaper binding could have been had for ninepence. Once the book was set up in type and put on to the machines, the cost per copy for printing and paper was about tenpence a copy. Thus what economists call the 'marginal cost of production', that is to say, the cost of producing each additional copy over and above (say) the first five hundred copies of a book, which would normally be published at fifteen shillings, was not above two shillings a copy. There are indeed very few books of which the marginal cost of production after the initial expenses have been paid exceeds two shillings; for most books—I should say for the vast majority of books bound in cloth—this figure lies between one shilling and two shillings and sixpence. The actual published price will generally be from five to ten times the marginal cost thus calculated.

It was computations on these lines which used to make me think that books were much too dear and that the publishers were at fault in maintaining their conventional price level much too high. But before we fly to this conclusion, let us pursue our arithmetic further.

The initial costs of this book for composition, &c., were about £150, without allowing anything for the author, for the publisher's profit and overhead expenses, or for advertising. A figure somewhere between £50 and £200 would probably cover the initial costs of the vast majority of books. This expense is irrespective of the number of copies produced or sold. £150 is 3,000 shillings. Thus spread over an edition of 500 copies, the cost is 6s. per copy; for 1,000, 3s.; for 3,000, 1s.; for 6,000, 6d.;

for 9,000, 4d.; for 18,000, 2d.; and so on. Thus up to a sale of (say) 2,500 copies the average initial cost falls very rapidly. After (say) 5,000 copies the additional economy becomes almost negligible, amounting to a very few pence at the most.

Now let us add our marginal costs to our initial costs. We reach a total of 8s. per copy for an edition of 500; 5s. for 1,000; 3s. for 3,000; 2s. 4d. for 9,000; 2s. 2d. for 18,000.

On these data what is a reasonable price to charge? Is 15s. reasonable? Let us calculate, on the basis of this price to the public, how much the different parties are going to make out of it. First of all, we must deduct the expenses of distribution in the shape of the bookseller's and wholesaler's discounts. We shall not be over-estimating this, if we put it at one third. Nor is this excessive, in comparison with any other retailing business—especially for a non-standardised, non-staple, seasonal trade. One third of what we pay for most things which we buy in shops go to the expenses and profits of distribution and not of production. Only on condition of the public becoming much larger, more reliable purchasers than they are at present could this charge be reduced.

Thus we have 10s. left for the costs of production, the costs of advertisement, the expenses and profit of the publishers, and the royalties of the author. Deducting costs of production as above, this means a lump sum of £50 on an edition of 500; £250 on 1,000; £1,050 on 3,000; £3,450 on 9,000. Before we divide this lump sum between the different claimants, let us compare the results of publishing at prices of 7s. 6d., 10s. 6d., and 24s. with those at a price of 15s.:—

Size of edition	Lump sum available, as above, at a published price of			
	7/6	10/6	15/-	24/-
500	−£75	−£25	£50	£200
1,000	nil	£100	£250	£500
3,000	£300	£600	£1,050	£1,950
9,000	£1,250	£2,100	£3,450	£6,150

Now, first of all, would it *pay* the publisher and the author to reduce the price below 15s.? The expectation of sales, allowing a little for the increased risk, must be *three* times as great as at 15s., to justify a price of 7s. 6d., and *twice* as great, to justify a price of 10s. 6d. On the other hand, 24s. will pay with *half* as great a circulation. The question for publishers is the degree of response of the public to lower prices. The circulation of most books falls into two parts—sales to public libraries, circulating libraries, and the author's friends and regular supporters, which part is very little affected by variations in the price within fairly wide limits; and casual sales to the general public. Sales in the first category (best-sellers apart) for most books of good reputation probably lie between 250 and 1,000. Now if the potential sales to the general public capable of being stimulated by low prices and high advertising were of the order or 5,000 copies or more—as surely it ought to be—it would be worth while to make a bid for these. But in practice, I fancy, the potential public demand for a solid book of the type under consideration is more likely to be from 500 to 2,500, and will only exceed the latter figure in the case of an exceptional success. In general, therefore, you cannot increase the circulation of a book threefold by halving its price. The result is that it probably pays publishers in most cases to charge as high a price as custom permits and as will not frighten away the reliable first-category buyers. Indeed we have reason to be thankful for publishers' moderation in not spending a few pence per copy on illustrations (which are supposed by the public and by authors to cost much more than they actually do), and another penny or two on a smart binding and, with these slight ostentations as an excuse, raising the price of my hypothetical book to 24s.

Thus, from the purely business point of view, there is no case for reducing the price of the book, unless and until the potential book-buying public is very greatly increased. Let us next consider whether, things being as they are, the author or the publisher is being over-remunerated.

Let us suppose that the publisher has agreed to pay the author a royalty of 15 per cent of the published price on the first 1,000 copies sold (i.e. 2s. 3d. per copy on a 15s. book), 20 per cent thereafter up to 2,000 copies, and 25 per cent after 5,000 copies; then on sales of 500 the author receives £56; on 1,000, £112; on 3,000, £412; and on 9,000, £1,537. The book, you must remember, is a solid one, such as would occupy most authors two years at the least to write; and sales for such a book above 3,000 quite an exceptional event. Authors, anyhow, can be acquitted of avarice.

What is left for the publisher's expenses and profits? We cannot put the normal cost of advertising per copy sold at less than 1s., and up to 2s. may be worth while; some publishers might consider these figures too low for any book worth pushing. For the sake of illustration, I will put advertising costs at a lump sum of £50, *plus* 1s. per copy sold. This leaves the publisher with −£81 on sales of 500, +£38 on 1,000, +£438 on 3,000, +£1,413 on 9,000; not *net* profit, but *gross* profit, from which all his own overhead expenses have got to be deducted. Now if sales of 9,000 were a common event, instead of a rare event to be averaged out against the sales of 1,000 or less, this rate of profit could clearly be reduced. If on the other hand, sales of 2,000 to 3,000 represent in practice a very decided success, it is evident that, averaging these with sales of 1,500 and less, the profits of this type of publishing are moderate. Indeed, it is likely to be so, for competition is keen. But the wide range of possible profits brings out an important and unfortunate fact—publishing is a *gambling* business, kept alive by occasional windfalls.

I conclude, therefore, that so long as the normal circulation of the typical good book, outside the narrow best-seller class, is not above 3,000 copies at the best, it is uneconomic, and indeed impossible if author and publisher are to gain a living wage, to reduce the price of books. If, on the other hand, the potential sales under the stimulus of low prices were to rise to the order of 9,000 or more, then the price of books could be approximately halved.

Is it not a thing to be ashamed of, having regard to the wealth and population of the English-speaking world, that editions are on so miserable a scale? How many people spend even £10 a year on books? How many spend 1 per cent of their incomes? To buy a book ought to be felt not as an extravagance, but as a good deed, a social duty which blesses him who does it. I should like to mobilise a mighty army, outnumbering Froth-blowers and Gugnuncs and Mustard Clubmen, an army of Bookworms, pledged to spend £10 a year on books, and, in the higher ranks of the Brotherhood, to buy a book a week.

Ten days later Keynes, in a letter to the Editor supplemented his article on the book trade.

To the Editor of The Nation and Athenaeum, *22 March 1927*

Sir,

Since I wrote in *The Nation*, of 12 March, an article on the price of books an interesting article in singular conformity with the conclusions I there reached, published in the issue of *La Bibliographie de la France* of 1 October last, has come to my notice. According to this article the cost of book production in France in terms of paper francs has increased about seven times, which is equivalent to an increase of about 40 per cent in terms of gold. The prices of books, on the other hand, have increased about threefold, so that in terms of gold the prices have fallen about 40 per cent. Thus, allowing for the change in the value of money, the price of books in France is now about half what it was before the war, perhaps even somewhat less than half.

What is the explanation of this relative fall in price? asks *La Bibliographie de la France*. The explanation is to be found in the greatly increased circulation of books amongst all classes of

French readers and abroad since the war. This authoritative organ states that editions are on a notably increased scale compared with what they were formerly. Possibly, it adds, increased publicity has played some part in this. But whatever the cause, they estimate the normal circulation of a successful French book at four or five times its pre-war figure.

This is a remarkable and enviable state of affairs. How far the increased circulation is due to the fall in the price of books, which fall may have occurred in the first instance as the result of a price-lag at a time when the franc was depreciating; or how far the fall in price has been made possible by the increased circulation, it is impossible for an outsider to say. In either case, French experience corroborates very closely the conclusion which I reached in my article as to the connection between the volume of sales and the price which it is economical to charge. My conclusion was to the effect that prices could be halved if circulations could be trebled. If the facts of *La Bibliographie de la France* are correct, sales in France have been increased between three and fourfold, whilst at the same time relative prices have been reduced by somewhat more than half.

Yours, &c.,

J. M. KEYNES

On 30 April Keynes contributed a brief note on the Government's recently published Finance Accounts.

From The Nation and Athenaeum, *30 April 1927*

A NOTE ON ECONOMY

The Finance Accounts for 1925–26 show that in that year the Treasury paid to the Bank of England £1,095,199 for the management of the debt, i.e., for posting dividend warrants and registering transfers, &c. This seems a good deal to pay for clerks' work and printing.

I suggest that here is an item on which champions of economy might fix their attention. During the same year the *total* salaries and expenses of the threatened departments (not the *net* economy through transferring their functions, which will be at best a small fraction of the total) were as follows:—

	£
Department of Overseas Trade	377,407
Mines Department	186,749
Ministry of Transport	124,436
	£688,592

The following figures are also useful for purposes of comparison:—

Salaries and Expenses in 1925–26	£
Treasury and Subordinate Depts	325,422
Home Office	382,222
Foreign Office	188,885
Colonial Office	170,800
	£1,067,329

Thus economical and efficient business men, in the shape of the Bank of England, spent more money on posting the dividends and registering the transfers of the public debt, than was expended on the salaries and expenses of the extravagant and red-taped staffs of the Treasury, the Home Office, the Foreign Office, and the Colonial Office added together. I wonder what Somerset House could do the work for, if they were asked to tender?

He returned to the question three weeks later.

From The Nation and Athenaeum, *22 May 1927*

A NOTE ON ECONOMY: II

Since I called attention in *The Nation* of April 30th to the large sum paid to the Bank of England for the management of the national debt, the matter has been taken up in the House of Lords by Lord Arnold, and this week in the House of Commons also. Mr Churchill's reply was on reasonable lines. He told the House that some reduction in the charge had been effected since the last published figures, and that 'since attention has been called to this matter in the press and in the House of Commons he is having it made the subject of careful examination'. On the figures now given it would be surprising if no further economy is possible. It appears that some 2,250 clerks are employed to deal with 2,500,000 stock accounts, involving 9,000,000 coupons, 750,000 transfers, and the other business attendant on these. It follows that: (1) each coupon and transfer costs on the average about 2s. in round figures for clerks' work, printing, stationery, and postage; (2) each clerk manages to deal with about eighty coupons and seven transfers a week, which, on the basis of a 45-hour week, means that a clerk spends about half an hour (or—to allow a margin of 100 per cent for errors in the calculation—let us say a quarter of an hour) contemplating the beauties, which are undoubtedly considerable, of each printed dividend warrant. These calculations are crude and doubtless lacking in exactitude. But they offer a *prima facie* case for a further investigation.

The main purpose, however, of my original note was not an attack on the Bank of England, but a defence of the Civil Service, and an effort to expose the pettiness of the recent attacks on the efficiency and economy of the latter. For what would be said if the figures given above had been found true about a Government Department instead of about a vested institution? I sought by a striking example to deal a blow at the myth, which is coming to be so widely accepted, that Government Departments are extravagant and inefficient compared with large non-governmental institutions. Civil Servants, in my experience, work harder, are better educated, and are paid less than the officials of great companies. I should like, some time, to challenge Lord Inchcape to a detailed comparison between the numbers and cost of the higher staff of the P. and O., including the board of directors, and those of the Treasury and the Board of Inland Revenue.

The danger is that, under the stimulus of an economy campaign, which is largely spurious, the Civil Service may be rendered inefficient by being understaffed and underpaid. We all of us complain at times about the mistakes of the Inland Revenue. But in fact the staff of this Department—having regard to the difficulty, the delicacy, and the magnitude of its work—maintains an amazing standard of ability, courtesy, honesty, and efficiency on standards of pay which would be very low in a private business. As Sir Josiah Stamp said on Tuesday, 'in the case of direct taxation an increase of staff could at any time in the last fifty years have yielded results much greater than the expense involved'. Undoubtedly it would be a popular move with income tax-payers to decrease the number of those clever and inquisitive people who try to make them pay what they should. But it does not follow that this is an 'economy' which would be economical. So in other departments—particularly in the case of the Ministry of Transport. These spurious and petty economies can only have the effect of crippling the Civil Service. One suspects that this, rather than economy, is in fact the half-deliberate object of some of the attacks now being made. In raising my query about the Bank of England, I wanted to find out if some of the champions of so-called economy would be equally enthusiastic about a saving materially greater in terms of money than those which they were pressing forward, but which did not have the incidental effect of crippling the Civil Service. I find, as I suspected—I do not here include the Chancellor of the Exchequer—that they are not.

But just as I want to increase, rather than diminish, the efficiency of the Civil Service, so also I should think it regrettable if my illustration was to develop into an attack on the Bank of England—as certain supplementary questions in the House of Commons half suggested. We are each entitled to our differences with the Bank and to criticise its policy with all the language at our command. But we must distinguish between the fleeting policies of Governors and the Bank as an institution. The preservation of the integrity, strength, and prestige of the Bank of England is vitally important. Those who believe that a wise management of currency and credit is essential to the prosperity of the country must feel this even more strongly than others. For we have in the Bank of England the only possible instrument of such management.

When the Colwyn Committee, to which he had twice given evidence, appeared, Keynes devoted himself to a review article for the next issue of *The Economic Journal*. He also led a discussion of the Report at the Tuesday Club on 9 March.

From The Economic Journal, *June 1927*

THE COLWYN REPORT ON NATIONAL DEBT AND TAXATION

This Report is, in the main, a vindication of the British system of taxation as it now is. Each tax in turn is considered, popular fallacies about each are dissipated, and the Committee conclude that all is for the best. In only two cases do they hesitate—the sugar duties and the stamp duties. They pick out the former—rightly, in my opinion—as probably the first national tax which ought to go. As regards the latter, they do not do more than express a hesitation, a doubt whether these duties may not slightly interfere in a way which does harm rather than good with the free mobility of capital. It is satisfactory, however, to see that the Committee are justly severe on the argument that, if the reduction of the duty on cheques from 2d. to 1d. were to increase their use at the expense of the note circulation, this would justify a reduction in the level of our normal gold reserves. For this is a popular fallacy which overpasses the limits of excusable error.

675

With this vindication of our tax system most economists—especially in the light of the new statistical evidence with which the Committee support it—will, I think, concur. When we discuss or criticise the efficiency of government and the ability of officials, we seldom do full justice to Somerset House, one of the best run and most useful institutions in the country, a remarkable creation of the British genius for administration. It is impossible to read the contributions to the proceedings of the Committee by Sir Richard Hopkins and Mr W. H. Coates, of whom the latter is now unfortunately withdrawn into private business, and of the part obviously played in the preparation of the Report by the Committee's secretaries, Mr G. R. Hamilton and Mr G. Ismay, one of whom, however, is now, I think, with the Customs, without feeling that Somerset House understands its business.

The most important practical conclusion to be drawn from the vindication is that we are not, at the present time, beyond the limits of direct taxation as an efficient fiscal instrument, as many, not unnaturally, have supposed us to be. Our direct taxes are exceedingly unpleasant to the rich individuals on whom their full weight falls, and they probably have some unfavourable reactions on the national savings, since they transfer wealth from the class which is the most likely to save its surplus,—though even this objection will be mitigated if the Government, to whom the money is transferred in the first instance, itself saves it in some shape by directing it into productive channels. But apart from these consequences there is little or no evidence of the indirect harm which is often attributed to high income tax and death duties. As Professor Pigou puts it in evidence, 'from a distributional point of view, it would plainly be best to take nearly all your money from the rich people, but that might be so bad from a productive point of view that the poor people would in the end be damaged'. It *might* be, and the rich always hope that it is. But the Committee conclude that, at present at least, it is not.

In particular the Committee endorse, practically without reserve, the unanimous opinion of the economists who have evidence that income tax is not shifted and does not lead to higher prices to the consumer, as against the almost equally unanimous opinion of the business men to the contrary. The *data* at the disposal of Mr Coates have enabled for the first time the *a priori* conclusion of the economists to be subjected to a statistical test—and the test whatever it may be worth is very interesting indeed—from which it emerges undamaged. The Committee 'conclude that the broad economic argument' (that income tax is not shifted) 'is true over practically the whole field and for practically the whole of the time, any exceptions being local or temporary and insufficient to invalidate it'.

There are many other popular fallacies, put into circulation by those who suffer from high taxation, which, as I have said above, the Report seeks to disperse. There is no evidence that post-war income taxes have driven individuals or businesses abroad on a scale worth troubling about, or that death duties break up businesses through the strain of finding ready cash to meet them, though the troubles of landed proprietors are partly admitted. In short, the Committee have reached the unpopular conclusion that our taxation is not too high—from which it follows, though this they do not underline, that it would not be right to diminish admittedly useful expenditure, on such things as education and social insurance and health services, merely in order to reduce it.

The Committee's final summing-up is worth quoting:

The burden of direct taxation, while we do not wish to belittle it, is less crushing than is frequently represented. It does not, with trivial exceptions, enter directly into prices, and its indirect effects are not such as substantially to affect the general price level. It has a materially adverse effect on savings, but this does not hold good so far as the receipts are applied to payments on account of the internal debt. Again, it has widely diffused psychological effects, and has been responsible for a good deal of discouragement, while trade has been suffering from long-drawn-out depression due to wider

Relating Direct and Indirect Taxation to Specimen Incomes

N.B. The taxpayer is assumed to be married and to have three children under the age of sixteen

Income	Income tax and super-tax — Income wholly earned (£ s. d.)	Income tax and super-tax — Income half earned half investment (£ s. d.)	Death duties — Income half earned half investment (£ s. d.)	Inhabited house duty (£ s. d.)	Total direct taxes — Income wholly earned (£ s. d.)	Total direct taxes — Income half earned half investment (£ s. d.)	Tea (s. d.)	Sugar (s. d.)	Tobacco (£ s. d.)
1903–4									
£50	—	—	8 0	—	—	8 0	13 0	12 0	16 0
100	—	—	1 5 0	—	—	1 5 0	14 3	14 0	1 2 0
150	—	—	1 18 0	4 6	4 6	2 2 6	15 0	14 6	1 6 0
200	1 16 8	1 16 8	2 9 0	7 6	2 4 2	4 13 2	15 0	15 0	1 8 0
500	16 0 10	16 0 10	6 1 0	1 5 0	17 5 10	23 6 10	15 0	15 0	1 18 0
1,000	45 16 8	45 16 8	16 6 0	3 0 0	48 16 8	65 2 8	15 0	15 0	2 1 0
2,000	91 13 4	91 13 4	32 14 0	4 15 0	96 8 4	129 2 4	15 0	15 0	2 9 0
5,000	229 3 4	229 3 4	103 11 0	9 0 0	238 3 4	341 14 4	15 0	15 0	2 16 0
10,000	458 6 8	458 6 8	251 17 0	15 0 0	473 6 8	725 3 8	15 0	15 0	2 16 0
20,000	916 13 4	916 13 4	549 9 0	28 0 0	944 13 4	1,494 2 4	15 0	15 0	2 16 0
50,000	2,291 13 4	2,291 13 4	1,607 5 0	55 0 0	2,346 13 4	3,953 18 4	15 0	15 0	2 16 0
1913–14									
£50	—	—	8 0	—	—	8 0	12 3	6 2	1 1 0
100	—	—	1 5 0	—	—	1 5 0	13 4	7 2	1 10 0
150	—	—	1 18 0	4 6	4 6	2 2 6	14 2	7 6	1 15 0
200	7 6	11 8	2 8 0	7 6	15 0	3 7 2	14 2	7 8	1 17 0
500	12 0 0	17 4 2	8 3 0	1 5 0	13 5 0	26 12 2	14 2	7 8	2 10 0
1,000	37 10 0	47 18 4	20 10 0	3 0 0	40 10 0	71 8 4	14 2	7 8	2 15 0
2,000	75 0 0	95 16 8	49 19 0	4 15 0	79 15 0	150 10 8	14 2	7 8	3 5 0
5,000	291 13 4	291 13 4	144 10 0	9 0 0	300 13 4	445 3 4	14 2	7 8	3 15 0
10,000	758 6 8	758 6 8	371 17 0	15 0 0	773 6 8	1,145 3 8	14 2	7 8	3 15 0
20,000	1,591 13 4	1,591 13 4	935 5 0	28 0 0	1,619 13 4	2,554 18 4	14 2	7 8	3 15 0
50,000	4,091 13 4	4,091 13 4	2,588 4 0	55 0 0	4,146 13 4	6,734 17 4	14 2	7 8	3 15 0

1918–19

£	(1)	(2)	(3)	(4)	(5)	(6)	(7)	(8)
100	—	—	1 4 0	4 6	1 4 0	1 8 0	2 14 0	2 5 0
150	—	—	1 16 0	7 6	2 0 6	1 12 0	3 1 6	3 6 0
200	—	—	2 9 0	7 6	2 16 6	1 15 0	3 5 6	4 2 0
500	33 15 0	43 2 6	7 6 0	1 5 0	51 13 6	1 15 0	3 6 6	4 9 0
1,000	146 5 0	165 0 0	17 14 0	3 0 0	185 14 0	1 15 0	3 6 6	6 0 0
2,000	450 0 0	487 10 0	42 19 0	4 15 0	535 4 0	1 15 0	3 6 6	6 13 0
5,000	1,787 10 0	1,787 10 0	127 0 0	9 0 0	1,923 10 0	1 15 0	3 6 6	8 3 0
10,000	4,187 10 0	4,187 10 0	377 19 0	15 0 0	4,580 9 0	1 15 0	3 6 6	9 0 0
20,000	9,437 10 0	9,437 10 0	933 0 0	28 0 0	10,398 10 0	1 15 0	3 6 6	9 0 0
50,000	25,187 10 0	25,187 10 0	3,826 19 0	55 0 0	29,069 9 0	1 15 0	3 6 6	9 0 0

1923–4

£	(1)	(2)	(3)	(4)	(5)	(6)	(7)	(8)
100	—	—	1 3 0	—	1 3 0	1 1 0	3 10 0	2 15 0
150	—	—	1 15 0	—	1 15 0	1 2 8	4 3 0	4 0 0
200	—	—	2 5 0	5 0 0	2 10 0	1 4 0	4 8 0	4 15 0
500	15 3 9	18 0 0	6 17 0	12 6 0	25 9 6	1 4 0	4 12 0	5 0 0
1,000	106 6 3	117 11 3	17 6 0	2 10 0	137 7 3	1 4 0	4 12 0	6 15 0
2,000	308 16 3	331 6 3	49 15 0	4 15 0	385 16 3	1 4 0	4 12 0	7 10 0
5,000	1,346 6 3	1,346 6 3	205 14 0	9 0 0	1,561 0 3	1 4 0	4 12 0	9 13 0
10,000	3,571 6 3	3,571 6 3	592 0 0	15 0 0	4,178 15 3	1 4 0	4 12 0	10 4 0
20,000	8,321 6 3	8,321 6 3	1,808 9 0	28 0 0	10,157 15 3	1 4 0	4 12 0	10 4 0
50,000	23,821 6 3	23,821 6 3	6,394 12 0	55 0 0	30,270 18 3	1 4 0	4 12 0	10 4 0

1925–6

£	(1)	(2)	(3)	(4)	(5)	(6)	(7)	(8)
100	—	—	1 2 0		1 2 0	11 0 0	1 17 6	2 15 0
150	—	—	1 14 0		1 14 0	12 0 0	2 3 9	4 0 0
200	—	—	2 5 0	Inhabited	2 5 0	12 9 0	2 5 3	4 15 0
500	10 3 4	14 6 8	6 15 0	house	21 1 8	12 9 0	2 7 6	5 0 0
1,000	81 3 4	97 16 8	17 3 0	duty	114 19 8	12 9 0	2 7 6	6 15 0
2,000	264 10 0	281 3 4	64 18 0	abolished	346 1 4	12 9 0	2 7 6	7 10 0
5,000	1,095 15 0	1,095 15 0	316 3 0	by	1,411 18 0	12 9 0	2 7 6	9 13 0
10,000	2,995 15 0	2,995 15 0	890 17 0	Finance	3,886 12 0	12 9 0	2 7 6	10 4 0
20,000	7,370 15 0	7,370 15 0	2,253 18 0	Act, 1924	9,624 13 0	12 9 0	2 7 6	10 4 0
50,000	22,120 15 0	22,120 15 0	6,621 18 0		28,742 13 0	12 9 0	2 7 6	10 4 0

Total taxation: percentage of income

Alcoholic drinks £ s. d.	Entertainments £ s. d.	Cocoa, coffee and chicory, dried fruits, patent medicines and table waters £ s. d.	Total indirect taxes £ s. d.	Total taxation: Income wholly earned £ s. d.	Income half earned half investment £ s. d.	Income wholly earned Direct %	Indirect %	Total %	Income half earned half investment Direct %	Indirect %	Total %
2 5 0	—	1 0	4 7 0	4 7 0	4 15 0	—	8·7	8·7	0·8	8·7	9·5
3 0 0	—	2 0	5 12 3	5 12 3	6 17 3	—	5·6	5·6	1·2	5·6	6·8
3 10 0	—	3 0	6 8 6	6 13 0	8 11 0	0·2	4·3	4·5	1·4	4·3	5·7
4 5 0	—	4 0	7 7 0	9 11 2	12 0 2	1·1	3·7	4·8	2·3	3·7	6·0
5 5 0	—	4 0	8 17 0	26 2 10	32 3 10	3·5	1·8	5·3	4·7	1·8	6·5
8 0 0	—	4 0	11 15 0	60 11 8	76 17 8	4·9	1·2	6·1	6·6	1·2	7·8
14 10 0	—	4 0	18 13 0	115 1 4	147 15 4	4·8	0·9	5·7	6·5	0·9	7·4
29 0 0	—	4 0	33 10 0	271 13 4	375 4 4	4·8	0·7	5·5	6·8	0·7	7·5
29 0 0	—	4 0	33 10 0	506 16 8	758 13 8	4·7	0·3	5·0	7·3	0·3	7·6
29 0 0	—	4 0	33 10 0	978 3 4	1,527 12 4	4·7	0·2	4·9	7·5	0·2	7·7
29 0 0	—	4 0	33 10 0	2,380 3 4	3,987 8 4	4·7	0·1	4·8	7·9	0·1	8·0
2 0 0	—	1 0	4 0 5	4 0 5	4 8 5	—	8·0	8·0	0·8	8·0	8·8
2 15 0	—	2 0	5 7 6	5 7 6	6 12 6	—	5·4	5·4	1·2	5·4	6·6
3 5 0	—	3 0	6 4 8	6 9 2	8 7 2	0·2	4·2	4·4	1·4	4·2	5·6
4 0 0	—	4 0	7 2 10	7 17 10	10 10 0	0·4	3·6	4·0	1·7	3·6	5·3
5 0 0	—	4 0	8 15 10	22 0 10	35 8 0	2·6	1·8	4·4	5·3	1·8	7·1
7 10 0	—	4 0	11 10 10	52 0 10	82 19 2	4·0	1·2	5·2	7·1	1·2	8·3
13 10 0	—	4 0	18 0 10	97 15 10	168 11 6	4·0	0·9	4·9	7·5	0·9	8·4
27 10 0	—	4 0	32 10 10	333 4 2	477 14 2	6·0	0·7	6·7	8·9	0·7	9·6
27 10 0	—	4 0	32 10 10	805 17 6	1,177 14 6	7·7	0·3	8·0	11·5	0·3	11·8
27 10 0	—	4 0	32 10 10	1,652 4 2	2,587 9 2	8·1	0·2	8·3	12·8	0·2	13·0
27 10 0	—	4 0	32 10 10	4,179 4 2	6,767 8 2	8·3	0·1	8·4	13·5	0·1	13·6

C1 (£ s. d.)	C2 (£ s. d.)	C3 (£ s. d.)	(£ s. d.)	(£ s. d.)	(£ s. d.)	—					
2 15 0	5 6 0	10 0 0	9 17 6	9 17 6	11 1 6	—	9·9	9·9	1·2	9·9	11·1
4 5 0	7 0 0	11 6 0	13 2 6	13 7 0	15 3 0	0·2	8·8	9·0	1·4	8·8	10·2
5 5 0	7 6 0	14 0 0	15 9 0	15 16 6	18 5 6	0·2	7·7	7·9	1·4	7·7	9·1
5 0 0	11 6 0	15 0 0	15 17 0	50 17 0	67 10 6	7·0	3·2	10·2	10·3	3·2	13·5
7 10 0	17 0 0	15 0 0	20 3 6	169 8 6	205 17 6	14·9	2·0	16·9	18·6	2·0	20·6
11 15 0	1 10 0	15 0 0	25 14 6	480 9 6	560 18 6	22·7	1·3	24·0	26·8	1·3	28·1
20 0 0	2 0 0	15 0 0	35 19 6	1,832 9 6	1,959 9 6	35·9	0·7	36·6	38·5	0·7	39·2
36 0 0	2 10 0	15 0 0	53 6 6	4,255 16 6	4,633 15 6	42·0	0·5	42·5	45·8	0·5	46·3
36 0 0	2 10 0	15 0 0	53 6 6	9,518 16 6	10,451 16 6	47·3	0·3	47·6	52·0	0·3	52·3
36 0 0	2 10 0	15 0 0	53 6 6	25,295 16 6	29,122 15 6	50·5	0·1	50·6	58·1	0·1	58·2
6 0 0	7 6 0	8 3 0	14 1 6	14 1 6	15 4 6	—	14·1	14·1	1·2	14·1	15·3
10 0 0	9 0 0	9 0 0	20 3 6	20 3 6	21 18 6	—	13·5	13·5	1·2	13·5	14·7
12 0 0	10 0 0	9 9 0	23 6 6	23 11 6	25 16 6	0·1	11·7	11·8	1·2	11·7	12·9
12 0 0	14 0 0	10 6 0	24 0 6	39 16 6	49 10 6	3·2	4·8	8·0	5·1	4·8	9·9
18 0 0	1 0 0	10 6 0	32 1 6	140 17 6	169 8 6	10·9	3·2	14·1	13·7	3·2	16·9
28 0 0	1 12 0	10 6 0	43 8 6	356 19 6	429 4 6	15·7	2·2	17·9	19·3	2·2	21·5
50 0 0	2 5 0	10 6 0	68 4 6	1,423 10 6	1,629 4 6	27·1	1·4	28·5	31·2	1·4	32·6
100 0 0	2 15 0	10 6 0	119 5 6	3,705 11 6	4,297 11 6	35·9	1·2	37·1	41·8	1·2	43·0
100 0 0	2 15 0	10 6 0	119 5 6	8,468 11 6	10,277 16 6	41·7	0·6	42·3	50·8	0·6	51·4
100 0 0	2 15 0	10 6 0	119 5 6	23,995 11 6	30,390 3 6	47·8	0·2	48·0	60·5	0·2	60·7
6 5 0	3 0 0	6 0 0	11 17 6	11 17 6	12 19 6	—	11·9	11·9	1·1	11·9	13·0
10 3 0	4 0 0	6 6 0	17 9 6	17 9 6	19 3 6	—	11·6	11·6	1·1	11·6	12·7
12 3 0	5 0 0	6 9 0	20 7 6	20 7 6	22 12 6	—	10·2	10·2	1·1	10·2	11·3
12 0 0	12 0 0	6 9 0	20 19 6	31 2 6	42 0 6	2·0	4·2	6·2	4·2	4·2	8·4
18 0 0	1 0 0	6 9 0	29 2 6	110 5 6	144 1 6	8·1	2·9	11·0	11·5	2·9	14·4
28 0 0	1 12 0	6 9 0	40 9 6	304 19 6	386 3 6	13·2	2·0	15·2	17·3	2·0	19·3
50 0 0	2 5 0	6 9 0	65 5 6	1,161 0 6	1,477 3 6	21·9	1·3	23·2	28·2	1·3	29·5
105 0 0	2 15 0	6 9 0	121 6 6	3,117 0 6	4,007 18 6	30·0	1·2	31·2	38·9	1·2	40·1
105 0 0	2 15 0	6 9 0	121 6 6	7,492 1 6	9,745 19 6	36·9	0·6	37·5	48·1	0·6	48·7
105 0 0	2 15 0	6 9 0	121 6 6	22,242 1 6	28,863 19 6	44·2	0·2	44·4	57·5	0·2	57·7

causes; on the other hand, some of the psychological effects have been actually beneficial. In our opinion the present taxation—even in conjunction with the loss of material wealth due to war expenditure, which lies behind the national debt—is not one of the main causes of industrial difficulty ...So far as taxation is concerned, we think that, if general conditions improve and times become more prosperous, the burden will be carried with comparative ease. We base our conclusions, not on preconceptions, but on the long analysis contained in the foregoing part of our Report, in the light of which they must stand examination. We may perhaps remark that the view which we take is more optimistic than the view which attributes to taxation a very large responsibility for the present industrial position; for, while there is little prospect of any great lightening of the tax burden in the early future, there is legitimate hope that in many respects more general conditions, both at home and abroad, may improve.

There is one interesting anomaly in the distribution of the burden of taxation which emerges from the Committee's inquiry, but to which they do not invite particular attention. The Committee have endeavoured to calculate for various years the percentage of his income which a normal member of each income-range class pays in direct and indirect taxation taken together. The table is of such very great interest that I reproduce it in full on pp. 679–81. From this it appears that recent concessions to small income-tax payers have had the effect of bringing down the aggregate taxation paid by those with incomes in the neighbourhood of £500 to a much lower percentage of their income than is paid either by those who are somewhat poorer or by those who are somewhat richer than themselves. Whereas a man with an earned income of less than £200 or more than £1,000 pays in taxation at least 10 to 11 per cent of his income, the man with an earned income of £500 pays only 6·2 per cent. The anomaly has always existed to a certain extent, but recent tax changes have increased it.

As regards the taxation of the very rich, the Committee make clear how advanced this now is by estimating what annual insurance premium would have to be paid in order to defray the death duties. For example, a man with £1,000,000 invested at

5 per cent, who wishes to leave his million intact for his heirs, has to pay away altogether about £36,000 from his nominal income of £50,000, leaving him with £14,000 per annum for himself. The number of millionaires in Great Britain would seem, by the way, to be of the order of 250, and the number of those with more than £50,000 a year somewhat more than 500. This strikes one as rather small compared with the army of nearly 9,000 individuals who admit to having an income of more than £10,000 a year. Nearly 30 per cent of the income of the very rich comes from directors' fees and other so-called earned income. It is obviously now almost impossible to become a millionaire except by means of increments of wealth which in one way or another escape tax.

The Committee follow Mr Coates in estimating the national savings (in 1924) at £500,000,000 per annum, which, allowing for the change in the value of money, is they think, about £150,000,000 less than the corresponding figure before the War. This is very near to the estimate of Professor Bowley and Sir J. Stamp for the same year, namely, £475,000,000. Mr Coates, who claimed that his aggregate was correct within 10 per cent, explained that the details were made up as follows:

	£ million
Internal new issues for investment in the United Kingdom	89
Internal new issues for investment abroad	135
Addition to National Savings Certificates	3
Increase in Treasury holdings of bonds tendered in payment of eath duties	9
Investments sold by the banks	35
New houses	35
Profits not distributed by companies and private traders but invested in own businesses; and miscellaneous	194
Total	500

This is a net addition after allowing for the depreciation of obsolescent goods, and it does not include such things as house furnishings. The figure is a very considerable one. The national

683

wealth at the present time, so far as it can be measured in money, probably does not exceed £24,000,000,000; so that, on the above computation, it is increasing at about 2 per cent per annum, at which rate it will have increased by 50 per cent within twenty years from now. During the same period the increase of the population is not expected to exceed 5 to 8 per cent. Thus we have a prospect of abundant resources available for new housing and new public utilities, if only we can learn how to absorb and employ them.

The most interesting item in Mr Coates' table, and possibly the most accurate, since it is based on definite figures in the hands of Somerset House, is the amount retained in the business by companies and private traders, namely, £194,000,000. I should like to add that, whilst his total is very likely about right, the logic of the table is open to criticism. Having rightly

	£ million
British joint stock banks and foreign banks with offices in London (including an estimate of £100 millions of Treasury bills)	750
Bank of England	70
Post Office Bank (£285 millions less £120 millions in guaranteed or other securities nor forming part of the dead-weight debt) and Trustee Savings Bank (£80 millions, less £30 millions)	215
Government securities purchased for depositors through the Savings Banks (£210 millions) and Trustee Savings Banks (£30 millions)	240
Treasury note reserve	240
Ways and Means Advances (Public Departments, £160 millions less amount included under Treasury Note Reserve), say	70
Insurance companies, approximately	350
Railway companies	80
Add to preceding items to bring to par value	277
Balance of Treasury bills not included above, and held by various concerns, bill brokers, and others needing liquid resources, largely as part of the floating money system of the country	300
Held by private persons liable to estate duty	2,350
Held by foreigners, trusts, charities, trade unions, joint stock companies, etc.	1,650
Total	6,592

excluded the amount devoted to the sinking fund, since this releases resources for investment under his other headings, why does Mr Coates include the addition to National Savings Certificates and the bonds tendered for death duties? The correct addition in respect of the activities of the Exchequer seems to me to consist in the amount of productive capital expenditure by the state not covered by his heading of 'internal new issues'.

Mr Layton's estimate (August 1924) [above, p. 684] as to who holds the internal national debt emphasises the above conclusion as to the importance of the activities on capital account of institutions as distinguished from individuals.

Before we leave the statistical material of the Committee's Report, Mr Coates' very interesting estimate of rates of profit on turnover, given in his Memorandum on 'Incidence of the Income Tax', printed in the volume of appendices must be mentioned. Mr Coates points out that calculations of rates of profit on turnover are particularly valuable for comparative purposes between different dates and different industries because they are free from the difficulties of capital valuation and of changes in the value of money. His results can be summarised as follows:

	Average rate of profit per cent of turnover	
Industrial group	1912–13	1922–23
Cotton	7·00	2·47
Wool	8·19	9·78
Iron and steel	7·49	7·74
Miscellaneous metal industries	6·10	5·22
Food	5·07	7·11
Wholesale distribution	3·90	4·14
Retail distribution	8·48	5·14
Average of the seven groups	5·80	5·43

Whilst the reader will do well to consult the original for the details, the essence of the results is given above. Mr Coates analyses elaborately the dispersion round the median and the mean, showing that the median is, in general, somewhat below the mean, being for the seven groups 4·61 in 1912–13 and 4·11 in 1922–23. The main additional point which emerges from this analysis is the *magnitude* of the dispersion, which is so considerable as to do some damage to the conception of the Representative Firm. The figures for the seven groups taken together are as follows:

	Median	Lower quartile	Upper quartile	Mean deviation from median
1912–13	4·61	2·53	7·67	3·59
1922–23	4·11	1·24	8·46	6·01

Thus whilst profit on turnover is, on the average, much what it was, it is decidedly more irregular than before the war as between one business and another. The unprofitableness of the cotton industry since the war is brought out very strikingly.

These results have been made possible by the large number of detailed accounts now available in the hands of the Inland Revenue Department. 'The number of accounts furnished voluntarily', Mr Coates tells us, 'now approaches a quarter of a million'. Of what incomparable value to economic study and to the science and practice of administration the continuous analysis of this material and publication of the results would be. With but a little development the Statistical Department of Somerset House could furnish us with a continuous census of production and curve of profit for the whole of British industry. Hundreds of thousands of pounds spent on this embryo department would be well spent. As it is, we have an occasional tit-bit of information thrown us in an appendix to a Report on another subject by a gentleman who is no longer an official. I suspect that the scandals of economy are far greater and far more permanently injurious to the public good than the scandals of extravagance ever were.

Upon two main sections of the Committee's field of inquiry I have not yet touched,—the capital levy and the sinking fund.

The Committee have dealt with the former in a most judicious manner—obviously aiming at, though not reaching, a unanimous Report. They admit no objections to a capital levy on grounds of general principle. They accept a memorandum from Somerset House in which 'the Board of Inland Revenue, while they view the levy as a task of the first magnitude, do not regard the inherent difficulties as too great to be overcome'. They indicate that at the right time and in the right circumstances, which may have existed immediately after the War, they would support a levy. But they reject it on the ground of its disappointing yield in terms of its net results in return for what would undoubtedly involve a very considerable psychological and business upset. Finally, they attach great importance to the extent of the public support for such a project. The Board of Inland Revenue, at the same time that they admit the practicability of a levy, 'illustrate by reference to the success of the excess profits duty and the failure of the land values duties the primary importance of the attitude of the taxpayer to any large scheme of new taxation. They point out very forcibly the dangers that might befall the administration of a levy, either if there were systematic obstruction or if there were widespread anxiety'.

The number of individuals with a capital of more than £1,000 is estimated at 1,500,000; of those with more than £2,500 at 900,000; and of those with more than £5,000 at 500,000. The scale of levy suggested by the Labour Party, which exempts estates below £5,000 and takes proportions ranging from 5 per cent to 60 per cent on the rest, would probably yield about £2,500 millions. A levy which would yield £3,000 millions was the most drastic which received support in any quarter.

Now what would this be worth to the Treasury after allowing for loss of revenue from income tax, super-tax and death duties? These necessary reductions bring down the budgetary benefit from a gross figure of £150,000,000 (allowing interest at 5 per cent) to a net figure of £60,000,000. It is the magnitude of this reduction from the gross saving to the net which has taken most people by surprise. This net figure of £60,000,000 is equal to about 1s. on the income tax. Most people will agree with the Committee, I think, that—at least when income tax is not above 4s. in the £—it would be wiser for a Chancellor of the Exchequer to put 1s. on the income tax than to attempt to impose a capital levy on an exceedingly drastic scale.

The illusions under which many of us have rested in the past as to the possibilities of a capital levy are a special case of a general tendency to exaggerate the importance of the national capital as compared with the national income. The former, even if we include in it the whole of the land and natural resources of the country, is not above six years' purchase of the latter. Capitalists and socialists suffer equally from these illusions as to the importance of the existing stock of wealth. It is the flow of current income and current savings which truly matters.

Throughout their Report the Committee turn down every single one of the bright ideas submitted to them both by the present writer and by others. Quite likely they are right to do so. Bright ideas within the realm of taxation are seldom worth while. There is nothing to be done wisely except to raise all you can in straightforward direct taxation and the balance from luxuries and drugs in wide, general use. I do not dissent, therefore, from the negative attitude towards change of the greater part of the Report. It is only when the Committee come to their own bright ideas, their sole constructive proposals, which centre round the sinking fund, that I find them speaking with a real want of wisdom.

At present the standard rate of the sinking fund is £50,000,000 per annum, though for reasons pointed out by the Committee this is not generally equivalent to more than about £40,000,000 net reduction of debt. They propose that this amount should be raised immediately to £75,000,000 per annum, and as soon as possible to £100,000,000. The Minority Report goes further and recommends £150,000,000. Finally, Professor Hall, in a Report of his own, raises it to the equivalent of £300,000,000. To aim at a sinking fund of £40,000,000 per annum or thereabouts can, I think, be justified on grounds of prudent budgeting. This represents about 5 per cent of the total Budget, and a margin of this amount can be defended on the ground of being on the safe side one year with another, and having some surplus to meet contingencies. Any figure in excess of this, however, can only be justified on the ground of the importance of reducing the national debt as quickly as we can. In what follows, therefore, I shall, in order to make the argument concrete, be comparing a sinking fund of £100,000,000 per annum with one of £40,000,000. The difference betweeen the two, namely, £60,000,000, happens, as we have seen above, to represent 1s. on the income tax.

The Committee do not elaborate any adequate philosophy of the national debt. Doubtless they would not dispute that it is not a question of the amount of the national wealth but solely of its distribution. We should not be a penny the richer, either for waging war or for social reform, if, like Germany, we had practically no internal debt. If 'paying off the debt' really made us richer, the case for a capital levy would, of course, be overwhelming. In fact, however, it is simply a question of the distribution of the current national income between individuals, and of the tax instrument as a factor in modifying this distribution. Now the effect of heavy taxes in modern conditions is generally in the direction of bringing about a more equal distribution of income. The Committee in fact show that the effect of high post-war taxation has been somewhat in this direction. For this reason the 'capitalist'—to use a convenient abbreviation—is apt to be opposed to high taxation, and the 'socialist' to be in favour of it. Nevertheless it is not easy to argue *a priori* from this what their respective attitudes to a heavy sinking fund will be. For the immediate effect of a heavy sinking fund is to aggravate the burden of taxation, whilst the manner in which the eventual release of budgetary resources will be employed, say twenty years hence, is problematical. *A posteriori*, it seems, the capitalist is disposed to favour a heavy sinking fund, partly out of his ingrained habits of 'prudence' and of preferring the possibility of future benefits to the certainty of present ones, and partly out of a feeling that a stiff sinking fund at any rate locks away for the time being available budgetary resources from being spent on the doubtful boons of so-called social reforms; whilst the socialist also favours one, partly because, by mere confusion of thought, he thinks that the £1,000,000 daily interest on the national debt is in some sense 'paid away to the rich' in a way in which it would not be if the debt is gradually paid off. Both parties are reinforced by the good and the virtuous who, out of false analogy with private debts, 'feel that it must always be a sound thing to pay off debt'; so that the economist, who asks in an intellectual spirit what after all is the object, is left lonely.

The weakness of the Committee's treatment of the question is to be found in its being based neither on psychological and political grounds nor, on the other hand, on scientific grounds. An additional annual burden on the Budget of £60,000,000 is a very important one. It is far in excess of any possible economies, other than from drastic disarmament. It is three times the sugar duty; it is nearly half of the total yield of rates throughout the country. If we have £60,000,000 per annum available either from an increased yield of the existing taxes or from unobjectionable new taxes, there are many things of great public advantage which we could do with the money. If the local rates throughout the country were half what they are now, would anyone seriously propose to double them in order to increase the sinking fund from £40,000,000 to £100,000,000? It is odd to find all parties agreeing that a large sinking fund has the first claim, that it is to be preferred, in the words of the Committee, to any other 'new expenditure of whatever nature',—unless it be for very strong reasons. Yet the only arguments which the Committee adduce are of the flimsiest description.

They are two in number. The first is to pave the way for future conversion operations by reducing the rate of interest on Government loans. The second is to provide against 'the possibility of a future national emergency'. I say that these reasons are flimsy, because the possible benefit from the first is quantitatively very small, and because the second supposed advantage is mainly based on a fallacy.

As regards the first, the Committee have been at pains in a previous section of their Report to show that the supposed savings to be obtained from conversions over the next twenty years are much smaller than is commonly supposed. Apart from this, the extent to which the yield on British Government stocks can be divorced from the world gilt-edged rate of interest is comparatively small—at any rate until the aggregate of the British debt has been reduced to so low a figure, as, for example, it was at before the Boer War, or as that at which the United States now stands, that it has a scarcity value for investors who for various special reasons cannot look elsewhere, a result which could not be achieved even with a sinking fund of £100,000,000 per annum for a great number of years to come. Whilst we can possibly look forward to more important savings as the result of a fall in the world rate of interest, a reduction of ½ per cent in our rate below the world rate as the result of a heavy sinking fund, which is probably the utmost we could achieve in that way, would effect a saving of only £11,000,000 per annum in the course of more than twenty years. Even this would not affect the amount of the national wealth, but only the budget problem.

As regards the capacity to wage a future war, this will depend on the flow of national income at the time and on our ability to make the whole of the surplus available by taxation, by the commandeering of resources and in other ways. It is hardly to be supposed that our policy of largely depending on loans adopted in the late war will be repeated in the next one; and even if it is, the difference between a large and a very large internal debt should make a scarcely appreciable difference. It is not as if the sums paid off over the twenty years will lie by, so to speak, ready to be re-borrowed when they are needed. They will have been used like the past flow of other resources, and nothing will be available at the time except the current flow of resources.

What then would constitute good grounds for a large sinking fund? I see three important reasons which might carry weight in different circumstances. In the first place, the savings of individuals might be inadequate to the national needs, so that it would be necessary for some saving to be effected through the agency of the Treasury. A compulsory transfer of resources by means of taxation from individuals to the state and the employment of the proceeds on reduction of debt might be the best way of bringing this about. A variant of this state of affairs would exist if large capital expenditures were being made on great public utilities in excess of what could be borrowed from investors at a reasonable rate. A large sinking fund, of which the proceeds were devoted to productive expenditure, thus gradually converting the dead-weight debt into a productive debt, might be a sound policy in such circumstances. The Committee, however, do not argue that either of these conditions exist at the present moment. For my part, I should like to see increased capital expenditure on public utilities; and if this policy were adopted, I would support a larger sinking fund, but not meanwhile.

A third reason for hastening the repayment of the national debt might be based on the expectation that the future burden of $£x$ on the taxpayers is likely to be heavier than a present burden of $£x$. Is this in fact likely? I should have thought that the opposite is far more likely. As stated above, the expectations appear to be in favour of an increase in national wealth of 50 per cent and in population of 5 to 8 per cent in the next twenty years. With normal progress of scientific invention and business and economic technique, it is not very optimistic to expect the yield of our present taxes to increase by 1 per cent per annum on the average. If this is so—and would not most people agree that it is?—is there any case for burdening the present generation of taxpayers or in postponing useful expenditure in the supposed interest of those to come? The Committee do not anywhere meet the point that, if heavy taxation is the evil to be remedied, a sinking fund aggravates this evil for many years to come, and the eventual benefit will only accrue at a time when it will be worth less than it is worth now.

The prospect of falling prices as a reason for paying off the debt quickly is considered by the Committee and dismissed. But they have not thought it worth while to mention the increase in the burden of the national debt, which occurred whilst they were sitting, as a result of the return to gold—preferring to cast a decent oblivion over the consequences of that act.

If the burden of the internal national debt is a matter of great importance, the lightening of which is worth serious sacrifices and inconveniences, the history of this burden as affected by price changes deserves more attention than the Committee have given it. (The point is more stressed, however, in the Minority Report.) The following calculation, worked out by the present writer, is based on some figures given by the Committee in their Appendix XXVI. The Committee's figures are based on the *Statist* index number. This is not the most suitable for the purpose, but it will give a sufficiently accurate general idea of what has been happening. We raised between the beginning of the War and March 31, 1920, an internal debt of £5,900 millions at an average price level of 202. The nominal total has not been reduced by any significant amount since that time. By March 31, 1925, the price level had fallen to 165; and at the end of 1926 it stood at 146. Thus the burden of the war debt in terms of war-£s (i.e. at a price level of 202) has been as follows [see p. 694].

Thus a sinking fund of £100,000,000 per annum for twenty

	Index number	Debt in terms of war-£s (millions)
Average price at which war debt was raised	202	5,900
Its burden at March 31, 1920	308	3,900
Its burden at March 31, 1925	165	7,200
Its burden at Dec. 31, 1926	146	8,100

years will only succeed, assuming no further change in the price level, in bringing the real burden of the debt back to where it was in 1920. More than a third of the burden of what is now owed in respect of the war debt is due not to the expenses of the War, but to the fall of prices since this debt was incurred. The further fall of prices since the return to gold has added many hundreds of millions to the burden of the debt. Sinking funds of even £100,000,000 a year are neither here nor there whilst this sort of thing is going on. But, as I have said above, this is a subject on which the Committee have thought it better to preserve a discrete silence.

Whilst, however, I dissent from the Committee's pious ejaculations in favour of sinking funds, I feel, as perhaps they did, that there is not the same harm in these ejaculations as there would be if there were the slightest chance of their being followed up by action. There is no subject more academic (in the misused sense of that word) than sinking funds; nor any serious risk in practice of sinking funds being excessively indulged in. Perhaps the Committee felt that only by talking about a sinking fund of £100,000,000 shall we induce Chancellors of the Exchequer to keep any margin at all on the right side.

The Minority Report is not a very helpful document. It is not clear that the minority differed from the majority on the merits of any question to an extent which could not have been put right by footnotes. But the signatories were evidently anxious not to commit themselves too precisely in black and white. Their only definite proposal consists of an addition of 2s. in the £ to the tax on investment income, the proceeds to be applied to the reduction of debt.

In 1927 the Liberal Summer School was held in Cambridge between 28 July and 4 August. As the Liberal Industrial Inquiry was then proceeding, many of the lectures given reflected its concerns, with Keynes's on 'The Public and the Private Concern' being a good example. Keynes's speaking notes have not survived, but fortunately one newspaper report was fairly full.

From The Manchester Guardian, *1 August 1927*

'The Public and the Private Concern' was the title of a paper which Mr J. M. Keynes read to the Liberal Summer School this morning, under the presidency of Sir Herbert Samuel. The paper was a most comprehensive survey of the whole field of modern business, public and private, with some special reference to the increasing area in which the one is difficult to distinguish from the other. It did not attempt to formulate any theories concerning individualism or socialism. It simply sought to demonstrate what really is happening.

Mr Keynes disclaimed any orthodoxy in one direction or the other when considering the functions of government towards industry. He said: 'As soon as anyone comes to examine the facts it becomes evident that every sane and sensible person regards a great deal of public enterprise as unavoidable, necessary, and even desirable, and, on the other hand, there is an enormous field of private enterprise which no one but a lunatic would seek to nationalise. The line of demarcation between the two is constantly changing in accordance with the practical needs of the day. As to where precisely this line should be drawn no great question of principle is involved at all.'

Mr Keynes went on then to examine what actually exists. First of all he found that the great medley of socialised, semi-socialised, and other state-regulated enterprises from which the private-profit motive had been partly or altogether removed controlled no less an amount of capital than £3,500,000,000. Among the figures making up this sum were £100,000,000 in the case of docks and harbours, £100,000,000 controlled by water boards and other analogous bodies from which all the methods and criteria of private enterprise had already disappeared.

Then the Ecclesiastical Commissioners administered at least £50,000,000, the colleges, schools, and universities £100,000,000, and the Charity Commissioners something exceeding £100,000,000. Building societies had accumulated in driblets more than £200,000,000 and co-operative societies another £200,000,000. Moving steadily in the direction of normal private enterprise one found bodies, of whom the railway concerns were the chief, with capital raised privately under an Act of Parliament which laid down conditions as to rates which might be charged and profits which might be earned.

The capital of all these contributed to the stupendous total of three thousand five hundred millions, which was two-thirds of the total capital of large-scale undertakings in this country. That, then, was the first fact to bear in mind—that two-thirds of the typical large-scale enterprise of this country had already been removed, mainly by Conservative and Liberal Governments, out of the category of pure private enterprise. Here was all this diversity developed by experience to meet real problems and actual situations. What did the socialist think he would gain by assimilating it all to the model, say, of the Post Office? On the other hand, was the individualist prepared to scrap all that had been done and to hand over this vast capital to uncontrolled individualism?

'To my mind', said Mr Keynes, 'the real problems of the next ten years is neither a great reduction of the existing principle of public concerns nor a great extension of that principle, but a deliberate and persevering attempt to discover how to run the best enterprises which are already public concerns efficiently and to the public advantage. We have allowed all these concerns to grow up without ever considering them very deliberately. Many of them have a form of organisation which is by no means the most suitable. I suggest that we should give up pretending that there are no public concerns. We should take a good look at that great body of public concerns which we already have and learn to handle them wisely and efficiently. Then it will be time enough to consider whether we ought to add widely to the scope and field of their operations.'

Mr Keynes considered next how the existing public concerns might be overhauled and set in order. He thought that Cabinet Ministers should have as little as possible to do with these concerns, whose gigantic operations should be kept separate from the state budget. He was doubtful, too, whether a committee of a town council was particularly suitable for running productive enterprises whose proper geographical boundaries might not be identical with local government frontiers. Public enterprises, so far as their organisation and management were concerned, might take a leaf out of the book of the private concern.

He advocated the running of these public services, national and local, by boards whose members, chosen solely for their business capacity, were adequately remunerated. This board would be very much like a private board of directors, and in that way the advantages of public ownership and responsibility would be combined with the technical methods of management which private enterprise had evolved as the most efficient for large-scale affairs. The board should be as free from daily interference as the normal board of directors was.

He admitted that the public boards that already existed were not encouraging. The managers were not appointed because of business capacity, and the underpaid officials had no career before them. We needed to open up an attractive career in business administration to all the talents.

'I do not see', he said, 'why we should not build up in this country a great public service running the business side of public concerns recruited from the whole population with the same ability and the same great traditions as our administrative Civil Service. There would be one great general recruitment for all the great public concerns, with room for the rapid promotion of exceptionally efficient men and satisfactory prizes for those who reached the top.'

It seemed to him that the pressing concern was not barren controversy as to whether we should pretend that there were no public concerns or whether we should pretend that there should be no private ones, but rather the making of our existing public concerns living things with a great tradition of service.

Mr Keynes next traced the evolutionary process which has been going on in private concerns, bringing about the joint-stock company of diffused ownership and salaried management, which had moved half way from the typical private concern to the public concern. One of them might have 20,000 shareholders, but the active people were the financiers behind them. Big business began to consist, to an alarming extent, in the exchange of inside information between the insiders. The tendency of business towards this state of things was on the increase, and it all meant that many of the advantages which used to be claimed for unrestricted private enterprise no longer existed. And yet there were people who talked as though the only question was whether business should be run as the Post Office was run or whether it should be run like the barber's shop round the corner.

What then, Mr Keynes went on to ask, were the next steps to be taken in view of these facts? For one thing, he thought that the existence of diffused ownership or businesses by people who knew little or nothing of them, coupled with the tendency to monopoly, called for greatly increased publicity. One should be told what was going on, both in particular and in general. The traditional secretiveness of the British business man should be broken down. The shareholders were entitled to a drastic reform of published accounts, and of the information which auditors might sign as representative of the facts. The public, as buyer, was entitled to know what profit was being made. At present indignation was diffused because the public did not know what firms were making excessive profits and what firms were not. He could imagine no greater contribution to industrial peace than accurate knowledge concerning the profits of industry. Statistical research of an adequate kind would contribute enormously to economic science and to a right psychology.

Publicity would combat the dangers of monopoly. He would prohibit nothing and publish everything. Public opinion would do the rest in nine cases out of ten. He believed the task of Liberalism was to be realistic about the facts as they existed. 'Let us at least', he ended, 'avoid the hot air with which the controversialists of the two other parties try to asphyxiate one another.'

In answer to questions, Mr Keynes said that one of the forms of publicity he had in mind was something similar to the census of production, but fuller and more frequent. The Food Council, with the threat of legislation always in the background, indicated how the thing might work. He was asked how the capital to finance public services was to be raised, and told his questioner that the matter would be fully dealt with in the report of the Liberal Industrial Inquiry.

After the morning session the School rested from its labours till Monday morning. In the pleasant weather the members were entertained by Mr and Mrs Keynes in the Fellows' Garden of King's College.

During the Summer School Hubert Henderson had spoken on 'Industry and Taxation'. In the course of his paper he argued that an active policy of capital development, a reduction in local rates financed by the central government and improved standards of education and public health were more important needs than any that could be met by reduced direct taxation. After the Summer School, Henderson was criticised by the Liberal Council, a point noted by W. M. R. Pringle, a former Liberal M.P., in a letter to *The Guardian*. Keynes replied to Mr Pringle.

To the Editor of The Manchester Guardian, *14 October 1927*

Sir,

The paragraph published by the Liberal Council to which Mr Pringle refers in your issue of 13 October, as a piece of 'careful and scientific thinking' to 'correct the sloppiness' of Mr H. D. Henderson is the following:—

We almost hesitate to introduce to Mr Henderson those distinguished political economists who hold the theory that the purchasing power of money is diminished by its velocity of circulation. It hardly seems a confusion of thought to hold from that theory that £100 spent directly by a business man has a higher purchasing power than the same sum subjected to the triple process of payment into and out of the Treasury and expenditure by a War Loan holder.

This is, of course, a piece of the wildest nonsense, the appearance of which in print is barely credible; as any economist——or anyone else—whom Mr Pringle may choose to ask will readily tell him.

May I also take this opportunity of asking Mr Hirst a question with reference to his letter on 'Liberals and Economy' in today's *Manchester Guardian*? For it is important that there should not be an appearance of difference of opinion between Liberals unless there really is one. I take it we are all agreed, first that expenditure on armaments should be considerably reduced, and secondly that there should be the greatest possible pressure towards administrative economy and the avoidance of waste in every department of state. But I am not clear from Mr Hirst's letter whether he goes farther than this—that is to say, whether he advocates a step backwards in expenditure on the social services, such as national insurance, public health, and education, and on those kinds of productive capital expenditure which fall within the province of the state, such as roads. Could he elucidate this point? for the first move in a successful campaign of economy is precision as to what services are to be economised.

Yours, &c.,

J. M. KEYNES

Mr Hirst replied that he believed that road development was relatively unnecessary, that reductions in taxation were possible without impairing public health services and education, and that popular tax reductions would help the Liberal Party regain its former predominance. The next day Mr Pringle replied that Keynes's letter showed that he did not defend Henderson's position. Keynes replied.

To the Editor of The Manchester Guardian, *19 October 1927*

Sir,

Why does Mr Pringle think that I disagree with Mr Henderson? Mr Henderson argued that taxation merely transferred purchasing power and did not affect its volume, and that, therefore, the real objections to heavy taxation arise in other ways, which he proceeded to enumerate. When I heard Mr Henderson make the speech which Mr Pringle criticises I thought he was wasting the time of his audience with a truism. I find that I was wrong. The Liberal Council is guilty of the crude fallacy which Mr Henderson was exposing, and supported it by an argument which is admittedly nonsensical.

The really important question is, of course, whether the Liberal party is to call a halt or to demand a step backwards in the programme of education and social reform which it was carrying out in the great days before 1914. I think it would be rash to promise the electorate Mr Hirst's 'popular reductions of taxation' unless we see our way to effect them without interfering with our social programme.

Yours, &c.,

J. M. KEYNES

Ten days earlier, Keynes had written to *The Sunday Times* on a comment it had made on an article in *The Nation*. Owing to a slip, the letter did not appear until 23 October.

To the Editor of The Sunday Times, *9 October 1927*

Sir,

In your Political Notes of 9 October you speak of me as having 'blown sky-high' the arguments in favour of the Labour Party's 'surtax'. This probably refers to a leading article in *The Nation* for 24 September. I agree with that article. But I did not write it. The leader was an unsigned one, for which Mr H. D. Henderson, the editor, has, therefore, the responsibility. The attempt of the authors of the 'surtax' to answer him has not been successful. They would do better to admit their blunder.

J. M. KEYNES

By the time Keynes's letter on Labour's surtax proposals had finally appeared, however, Keynes had made an extended comment on the proposals.

From The Evening Standard, *22 November 1927*

WHY LABOUR'S SURTAX IS BAD FINANCE

When political parties or Chancellors of the Exchequer find themselves obliged to propose new taxation, they generally try to do so in a manner which is unprovocative and even apologetic. No one likes taxes. Taxes need defending. The milch-cow must be handled gently if she is to yield her milk.

Not so the Labour Party in its present mood. Their surtax is conceived not as a necessity but as a demonstration—something new and horrible, full of pain for the rich, full of trouble for Somerset House, an instrument of wrath. Its advent represents the defeat of that half of the Labour Party which would like, as the Americans put it, to operate on the constructive side, and the victory of those who think that the next step is to make things worse, not better.

It is meant to be as upsetting as possible. Anyone whose only object was to raise revenue to finance good causes would never dream of proposing the surtax. That is why Mr Philip Snowden, whose 'attitude' was so perfectly indicated by Low in *The Evening Standard*, and Mr Graham—two good radicals, two bad revolutionaries—have, so far, had nothing to do with it.

It is a piece of propaganda, not taxation. And bad propaganda, too—because it alienates the considerable number of people who are quite ready to stomach high, and even increasingly high, taxes if they are truly required to finance good purposes, but are not attracted by the idea that the next step is to make things worse.

There are several good reasons why the surtax is bad finance—whatever it may be as propaganda.

We have at present an income tax and a super-tax which only

work because in Somerset House we have gradually built up an instrument of amazing efficiency, such as exists in no other country, neither in Moscow nor in Berlin, nor in Paris, nor in Washington. These taxes now constitute between them an elaborate system of graduation, of special allowances, and of discrimination between earned and unearned income which it would be difficult to improve. An important simplification in the machinery of collection has been lately embodied in the Finance Act, and will come into force next year, by which the two taxes are more nearly merged in one. (As part of this change the super-tax is to be called henceforward the surtax—a possible source of some fine confusions to come, when taxpayers are served notice on behalf of Mr Churchill to fill up their returns to surtax!)

Both income tax and super-tax have been reduced in recent years from levels to which Conservative Chancellors of the Exchequer had raised them. Both could be raised again, if there was a sufficiently good reason, without any serious disturbance or new machinery. Assuming that we wish to raise more revenue by direct taxes on income, no one but a lunatic or a wrecker would seek to impose a third new tax cutting right across the other two. I can conceive of no motive for such a proposal, except that it looks, and is, more tiresome.

I do not agree with those who think that our high direct taxation is a major cause of our industrial troubles, and that it is more important to reduce it than to do anything else. The Colwyn Committee on National Debt and Taxation showed on high authority how much imposture there is in such arguments.

I have no sympathy with those who would like to call a halt in education and other social policies in the interests of the super-tax payer. For sufficiently great benefits to the country let us be ready to bend our necks beneath new burdens. But it is surely unprecedented for a political party to go about threatening us with a new tax without telling us how they are going to use it. The old demagogy, which used to cry out in a loud voice the benefits to be received and slipped in the taxes afterwards, was, at least, better suited to the weakness of human flesh than the new demagogy, which reverses the process.

Finally, there is the question of the yield of the new surtax. Mr Lees Smith, its principal author, estimated it at £85,000,000 because he had misunderstood the meaning of a figure which he had obtained from the Inland Revenue. When the editor of *The Nation* pointed out that a tax averaging 2s. in the £ on the unearned incomes of individuals in excess of £500 could not yield more than half this sum, Mr Lees Smith, instead of drawing back, from what had been an honest mistake, proceeded to support his old figure by new explanations, of which the most amusing is the claim that, although the yield might not be £85,000,000 now, it will have risen to that figure by the time the Labour Party comes to office! It is certain, in my opinion, that the estimate of yield is a blunder, and could not be fully substantiated even if the tax were to be extended to company reserves as well as to individual incomes.

Perhaps, however, this mistake about the yield will provide an emergency exit. Mr Ramsay MacDonald began by being very cautious about the surtax. His tortuous mind only took it up after (1) he knew that Mr Snowden (who had lately attacked his Protocol policy) did not like it, and (2) evidence had accumulated that the estimate of yield was indefensible. If it were to happen that the surtax is not a popular success, or if, for any reason, he were to become reconciled with Mr Snowden, then he will be able to discover that he was only led to accept it by being deceived about the estimated yield.

During October 1927 Keynes also gave two talks. On 12 October he spoke to the Tuesday Club on 'The Balance of Trade' using material from his article which was to appear in *The Economic Journal* in December. The article appears below, with a supplementary note Keynes added three months later.

From The Economic Journal, *December 1927*

THE BRITISH BALANCE OF TRADE, 1925–1927

Great Britain's visible import surplus (i.e. excess of total imports of goods and bullion over total exports) has been increasing steadily for five years. It was £150,000,000 greater in 1924 than in 1922, and it looks like being £85,000,000 greater in 1927 than in 1924. Meanwhile the volume of new foreign issues on the London market has not shown a corresponding decline. Whilst formerly our apparent surplus for net additional foreign investment generally exceeded (taking one year with another) the volume of new foreign issues, since 1924 the reverse has been the case. As the accounts must necessarily balance somehow, it would be a matter of much interest to know in which of the undisclosed items the balancing changes have occurred. In particular, has Great Britain been diminishing the (net) balance of short-period indebtedness due to her from foreign countries?

The relevant figures, based on those published by the Board of Trade except as indicated in the footnotes, are as follows:—

	£ (million)					
	1922	1923	1924	1925	1926	1927*
Net non-merchandise surplus	375†	375†	410	438	465	465
Net merchandise deficiency (i.e. excess of imports of goods and bullion over exports)	171	203	324	384	477	410
Net surplus on income account	204	172	86	54	−12	55
New foreign issues of capital in London	136	136	135	88	111	116
Assumed increase (+) or decrease (−) of other capital items required to balance the account	+68	+36	−49	−34	−123	−61
Bank of France repayments to Bank of England	5‡	5‡	5	6	7	37

* Excess of merchandise imports and new foreign issues estimated on basis of figures for first ten months; and non-merchandise surplus assumed to be the same as in 1926.

† Board of Trade estimates for 1922 and 1923 revised (1922 +50, 1923 +70) to match their revision of their old estimates for 1924, 1925 and 1926.

‡ Estimated.

It used to be believed—probably with good reason—that the Board of Trade's estimate of the net non-merchandise (or invisible) surplus was much too low. It still rests on a precarious basis of guesswork, and the Board of Trade does not yet attempt to collect definite facts on the lines followed by the United States Department of Commerce. Nevertheless there have been two substantial revisions upwards since the end of the war, and I know of no reason for thinking that it is now more likely to err in one direction than in the other. The most substantial source of error in any given year is to be found in the amount of the profits (or losses) made by British merchants, importers and speculators in dealing in raw materials, which, on account of the frequent occurrence of wide price fluctuations, they may have, in fact, bought at different price levels from those appearing in the trade returns, or which have not been shipped to this country at all. For example, fluctuations in the cost of raw rubber alone are quite capable of affecting the international financial position of Great Britain by as much as £25,000,000 or even more between one year and another.* How far the Board of Trade attempts to deal with these fluctuations I do not know. But it must be difficult for them to do more than make a rough allowance for the larger and more notorious items.

At any rate, since the Board of Trade have now raised their figures so greatly (their revised estimate for 1926 being £140,000,000 greater than their old estimate for 1922), and since the big fluctuating item of rubber has contributed a much lower figure in 1926 and 1927 than in 1925, it is unlikely that the true surplus for the last two years, 1926 and 1927, available for (net) foreign investment has been much greater than the apparent surplus of about £42,000,000. During these two years, however, public issues in London on foreign account have amounted to

* In 1924 the average price of rubber was 1s. 2d. per lb., in 1925 2s. 11d., in 1926 1s. 11¼d. and in 1927 about 1s. 6d. Assuming that British shareholders and merchants are interested in 240,000 tons of rubber per annum in excess of British consumption, then our rubber profits were (say) £45,000,000 greater in 1925 than in 1924, £25,000,000 less in 1926 than in 1925, and £12,500,000 less in 1927 than in 1926.

more than £220,000,000,† or (say) £180,000,000 after deducting the repayments made by the Bank of France. The question as to how this difference has been financed is the main subject of this inquiry.

In the first place, the proceeds of new foreign issues are a very imperfect guide to the net total volume of our investment in long-dated foreign securities. There are, first of all, the sinking funds for the repayment of previous foreign loans. It would not be difficult to make a fairly accurate estimate as to the annual amount of such repayments; but I am not aware that any reasoned estimate of these payments—so backward are all our financial statistics—has ever been made. My own guess, however, as to the sinking fund and other annual debt redemption payments (i.e. exclusive of loans paid off at maturity) would be small—less than £10,000,000 per annum. Apart from such repayments the London Stock Exchange is an international market where many securities are quoted which shift in large amounts from one country to another. Great Britain has long been accustomed—though not now on so large a scale as before the War—to invest substantially in the United States. There are certain securities which pass freely between London, Paris, Amsterdam, Berlin and Vienna. Various parts of the Empire buy back, as they grow richer, their own securities which have been financed by British capital in their early days. And—as a feature chiefly characteristic of the last two or three years—we have been buying domestic continental securities especially in Germany, and Americans have been beginning to buy a few domestic British securities (though the burdens of double income tax continue to impede greatly this class of transaction).

The gross volume of these transactions backwards and forwards must be very large. It is, therefore, possible that the net balance one way or the other might also be large. Indeed, it is probable that our normal pre-war foreign investment was

† These figures, which are based on the totals published by the Midland Bank, exclude, so far as possible, new loans to repay old ones.

a good deal larger than the new foreign issues in London. Whether or not the reverse is now true, it is hard to say; and it is so difficult to make a reasoned estimate as to the amount of the net balance that an attitude of complete agnosticism on the whole subject might seem attractive.

All the same, I think it is legitimate to draw tentative conclusions as to the order of magnitude of this net balance. The very absence of tangible evidence as to the amount of the various transactions involved suggests, I think, that their net result is not likely to be very large in relation to the big figures appropriate to the present discussion. Moreover, it is certain that there are substantial items on both sides of the account; so that if the net difference is to be large, the gross items must be very large indeed—so large as scarcely to escape general observation and some sort of rough computation.

Let me particularise a little further. On one side of the account there are the purchases of foreign investments by ourselves otherwise than through the new issue market. Two or three years ago our holdings of American securities stood at a low figure, since we had sold almost the whole of our pre-war holdings during and after the War, whilst the risk of loss arising out of a return of sterling to parity deterred repurchases prior to our return to the gold standard in 1925. There is much evidence, however, that more recently British investors, particularly insurance companies and investment trusts, have been returning to their old favourites. It is, therefore, probable—indeed almost certain—that we have bought more American securities than we have sold during the last two or three years. This conclusion is corroborated by the figures of the U.S. Department of Commerce, who calculate that in 1926 there was a net movement of American stocks and bonds outwards to foreign countries generally amounting to £25,000,000 ($636,000,000 sold and $509,000,000 repurchased); and add expressly that the evidence of their questionnaires shows that 'British investors are gradually reverting to their pre-war custom of investing in American securities'. In addition to this movement, American new issues of loans to foreign governments have generally stood at a slightly lower price than similar issues in London, with the result—as it is commonly supposed—that there has been a steady stream of such bonds from New York to London. Moreover, since two or three years ago we had very few of the domestic securities of continental Europe, it is probable that during the period of European reconstruction we have purchased more of such securities than we have sold, especially from Germany. Finally, Paris, which was a buyer of international securities during the flight from the franc, is more likely to have been a seller on balance during the period of recovery.

On the other side of the account there are the sales of securities from ourselves to investors abroad. There is probably a steady stream, nowadays, of sales to the Dominions. But it is quite certain that such sales are not large in any one year. There have been re-sales of their own high-yielding government securities to continental countries; but for the reason given above such purchases on continental account are more likely to have been made in New York than in London. Finally, there are the sales from London to New York of international securities and also of some domestic British securities. The last-named may be substantial; but owing to income tax and other considerations, such purchases are concentrated on a limited number of securities; and we should surely have heard more about it than we have, if it had been taking place on the scale of tens of millions per annum or anything approaching this.

On the face of it, therefore, it would seem that the two sides of the account of the sale and purchase of securities to and from foreign countries, other than new issues, are more likely to be nearly balanced than they are to be widely different. I see no reason to think that the one side has exceeded the other during the last three years by £100,000,000 or even £50,000,000. Even a difference of £20,000,000 would be hard to substantiate. It is indeed just as probable, indeed more probable, that our purchases of securities, other than new issues, from foreigners have exceeded our sales, as that our sales have exceeded our purchases.

I conclude that a *prima facie* case exists for the view that our net foreign investment during the last three years—apart from the balance of short-period borrowing and lending—may have exceeded our available income surplus by some figure not less than £150,000,000, and perhaps in the neighbourhood of £200,000,000; from which it would follow that we have adjusted the position by diminishing our liquid assets or increasing our short-period obligations by a similar sum. This is after allowing for the Bank of France's repayments to the Bank of England.

Is such a conclusion consistent with the direct evidence as to the international movement of short-period balances? If it is contradicted by such evidence, then the statistical foundations on which we have raised it are not strong enough to justify obstinacy. But if it is not contradicted, then our conclusion may represent about as good an approximation as the character of the data permits.

For a consideration of the movements of short-period balances, the two and a half years since the return to the gold standard may be divided into three intervals. Immediately prior to the return to gold, foreign, and in particular American, balances were believed at the time to be flowing to London in speculative anticipation of the improvement in the exchange. It may be presumed that, after the anticipation was fulfilled, profits were taken and that these balances flowed out again. But at the same time their place was taken by normal and quasi-permanent foreign banking balances which were re-established in London after the restoration of the pre-war gold parity. Having regard to the magnitude of the foreign balances of central and other foreign banks, as to which some figures will be given below, one might expect this movement by the middle of 1926 to have increased the total foreign balances in London by a large amount as compared with the end of 1924 (when the speculative movement in anticipation of the return to gold had hardly begun), and even by a substantial amount as compared with the middle of 1925. I know of no actual figures to substantiate this. But City opinion, basing itself on general observation of the facts, does not doubt that the return to gold (whatever its other consequences) restored the position of London as a depositary, along with New York, of foreign balances. Over and above this return of quasi-permanent balances, this period also covers the flight from the franc when abnormal private French balances in London were rapidly increasing—the major part of the collapse of the franc having occurred between October 1925 and July 1926.

The second period—say, roughly, from the middle of 1926 to the middle of 1927—was marked by the portentous piling up of foreign balances by the Bank of France and the French Government. These balances are believed to have approached a total of £200,000,000 by the end of this period and it is said that some £80,000,000 out of this was located in London. We must not attribute the whole of this flow to the period subsequent to the middle of 1926, since to an important extent official purchases of sterling on French account represented the taking over of sterling previously purchased by Frenchmen on private account. But we may fairly attribute the major part of it to the period subsequent to the middle of 1925, since there is no reason to presume the existence in London in the early part of 1925 of large floating balances on French account, whether public or private.

Thus whilst the return of normal foreign bank balances to London overlapped the reflux of balances on account of exchange speculation, and similarly the growth of official franc balances overlapped the reflux of private French balances, nevertheless, if we take the whole period from the beginning of 1925 to the middle of 1927, it is reasonable to assume an increase of at least £100,000,000, and probably more, in foreign balances in London, in addition to the repayment of £50,000,000 by the Bank of France to the Bank of England which has been already allowed for.

We come finally to the period since August 1927, when money rates in London have been established on a basis appreciably higher than corresponding rates in New York as a result of the reduction of the Federal Reserve rates to 3½ per cent and the maintenance of the Bank of England rate at 4½ per cent. In comparing British and American money rates it is always a matter of much difficulty to know which to choose as being most truly comparable. In this case, however, different methods of approach yield much the same answer, as is shown below.

The *Federal Reserve Bulletin* for September 1927 chose as its basis of comparison the New York time loan rate (90 days) with the London bill rate (90 days). But it will be better to give also the London time loan rate and the New York call loan (renewal) rate:—

	Deposit rate (90 days)		Three-months bill rate	Call loan rate
	London*	New York†	London‡	New York§
July 1926	4·75	4·37	4·31	4·27
August	4·75	4·75	4·36	4·52
September	4·75	4·94	4·53	5·02
October	4·75	5·00	4·69	4·75
November	4·75	4·75	4·74	4·56
December	4·75	4·68	4·47	5·16
January 1927	4·75	4·50	4·23	4·32
February	4·75	4·44	4·14	4·03
March	4·75	4·44	4·33	4·13
April	4·66	4·44	4·23	4·18
May	4·50	4·37	3·62	4·26
June	4·50	4·50	4·35	4·33
July	4·50	4·37	4·34	4·05
August	4·75	4·12	4·34	3·68
September	4·75	4·12	4·32	3·80

* Supplied by a bank.
† Time loan rates as given by *Federal Reserve Bulletin*.
‡ Mid-monthly three-months bill rate as given by *London and Cambridge Economic Service*.
§ Renewal rate.

This table is, I think, conclusive as to the movement of relative rates in the two centres. In the autumn of 1926 it was possible to use a free balance with slightly more profit in New York than in London. In the spring of 1927 London was, on the whole, offering a little more than New York—up to $\frac{1}{4}$ per cent higher. In June 1927 rates were as nearly as possible level in the two centres. Since August 1927 London has been $\frac{1}{2}$ per cent higher than New York. This is a very substantial difference as these things go—particularly in the autumn, when New York rates are almost always higher than London rates. It is evident, therefore, that international balances, in so far as they are influenced by interest rates, must have had a preference for New York in the last half of 1926, a slight preference for London in the first half of 1927, and a substantial preference for London since August 1927.

It is scarcely to be supposed that this shift of relative rates in the autumn of 1927 as compared with the autumn of 1926 can have been without influence on the movement of international balances. But there is a mitigating consideration of which we have not yet taken account. If the rate of exchange between London and New York was absolutely fixed—instead of fluctuating, as in fact it does, between the gold points—there is a large supply of floating resources for which even a small difference in the relative rates of interest would be a determining consideration. In view, however, of the fluctuations which actually occur, a possible difference between the rate of exchange at which funds are remitted and that at which they will be brought back again is a relevant factor. If we take 4·85 and 4·89 as the gold export and import points respectively for sterling (this is not exact, but near enough for the present purpose), this is a difference of about ·82 per cent. Thus when the sterling exchange stands at 4·89, an American bank which remits funds to London runs the risk of having to remit them back, again at 4·85 and thus losing ·82 per cent on the exchange as an offset against any gain in interest. For a long-period investment this hardly counts, but spread over three months it is very large. These figures, however, represent the extreme measure of the exchange deterrent as against the interest incentive. When sterling is at 4·85 there is no exchange deterrent; if the remitter anticipates satisfactory interest rates in London for some time to come and is, therefore, prepared to spread any exchange loss over a longish period, the deterrent is much diminished; and in any case the true measure of the deterrent is not its possible maximum but its mathematical expectation (i.e. the amounts of possible exchange losses multiplied by their probabilities). Moreover, it is generally possible to insure against exchange loss by means of a forward exchange transaction for less than the possible maximum of loss.*

The fact remains that as sterling creeps up above 4·85, high interest rates in London become less and less effective in drawing short-period investments from abroad. It is evident that with exchange at 4·85 a difference of $\frac{1}{2}$ per cent in interest rates in favour of London might be extremely powerful in drawing funds. If short money would not flow in these conditions, it would indicate either that our power of maintaining the gold standard was distrusted or that we had borrowed already a large proportion of the world's floating funds. Thus funds will flow in the first instance on a scale adequate to cancel out any adverse international balance on other scores, and, when this has been accomplished, their continued movement shifts the exchange upwards. As the exchange rises the remittance of funds becomes less and less attractive until a position of equilibrium is reached where the incentive of dear money is no longer strong enough to draw any additional funds in face of the deterrent of possible exchange loss. It is impossible to say *a priori* just where this point of equilibrium will be found, because the exchange deterrent is of varying significance and importance to different classes of lenders and borrowers; but during the last two months ex-

* I have gone into the details of this in *A Tract on Monetary Reform* [*JMK*, vol. IV], chap. III.

perience seems to indicate that it lies somewhere in the neighbourhood of 4·87. The present indications are that the existing difference of interest rates is exceedingly effective in maintaining the exchange above 4·85, but that it would need a greater disparity, or a greater confidence in the duration of the present disparity, to drag it up to 4·89. As funds flow under the attraction of dear money, the exchange rises; as the exchange rises the cost of insurance by means of a forward exchange transaction (i.e. what is called the 'swap rate') increases; and, according to recent experience, this continues until for a three-months transaction the 'swap rate' about balances the gain in interest. When this point has been reached a further improvement in the exchange is dependent on the inflow of 'unhedged' funds, i.e. short-period investments which for one reason or another are prepared to ignore the risk of exchange fluctuations.

We have stated the argument in terms of the dollar exchange; but corresponding calculations, each with its appropriate critical point, also apply to the movement of funds between London and the chief continental financial centres.

The argument so far makes it probable that funds have moved under the influence of dear money sufficiently to liquidate any debit balance; but we have no clue as to the magnitude of such movement. The movements must have occurred in three ways:—

(i) by causing trade bills to be carried in New York instead of in London;

(ii) by causing London banks to borrow in New York or American banks to lend in London;

(iii) by attracting (non-American) international floating balances in London.

As to each of these we have a certain amount of indirect evidence.

That trade bills have been held back this year is the prevailing impression in the City. *The Times* wrote on October 24, 1927:—

American banks, instead of sending sterling cotton and grain bills to London for discount immediately they are ready, have lately shown a tendency to keep them as investments, and to remit them for collection at maturity. It is calculated that the British banks hold at the present moment not much more than one half the amount of American grain and cotton bills which they had in their portfolios two years ago. The American banks have been induced to do this by the higher rate of discount which prevails in London.

The slack movement of raw cotton to Liverpool is partly responsible. But the effect of relative interest rates is confirmed from America by an interesting passage in the *Boston Evening Transcript* (quoted by *The Manchester Guardian*, Oct. 1927):—

The comparatively low interest rates prevailing here [United States] have led British banks to make extensive short-term loans at American banks, by means of which the London banks have prepared themselves to take care of cotton and other acceptances made by their customers, the British manufacturers, as these come along. That is to say, such purchases are, for the moment, being financed wholly in dollars, and the reckoning in pounds has been set over for 60 or 90 days.

What bankers know is that the names of British banks have been behind important borrowings at short term here. Why on earth would the British banks have opened these dollar credits if it was not for the financing of autumn purchases? The conclusion seems inescapable. Moreover, it was given direct official sanction on Tuesday by a prediction in the Federal Reserve Bulletin that 'the decline in rates charged on bankers' acceptances in New York' would have precisely this 'tendency to attract a larger volume of the financing of exports to the banks of this country'.

As to lending by American banks in London, it is difficult, or impossible, to obtain quantitative estimates. That it does occur and sometimes on a substantial scale, is certain. But it is doubtful whether such transactions are very large, because it is precisely this type of transaction which would be most deterred by the level of the 'swap rate'.

As regards international floating balances the impression is, I think, that these have been increasing steadily but not sensationally, and that for various reasons the greater part still repose in New York. The volume of these balances, however, is now so gigantic that the movement of even a small proportion of them amounts to a large absolute figure. This is shown by the remarkable figures collected by the United States Federal Reserve Board and Department of Commerce. According to the former authority:—*

Estimates based on the published balance sheets of about thirty central banks indicate that at the end of March 1927 these banks held substantial amounts of liquid foreign assets, aggregating altogether at least $1,600,000,000. Of this amount about one half was held by banks required by law to maintain reserves and authorised to include these foreign holdings as part of their required reserves. More than $800,000,000, however, was held as a matter of policy by other foreign banks of issue either having no specified legal reserve requirements, as in the case of the Bank of France, or having no authority to count foreign assets as legal reserves, as in the case of the central banks of the Netherlands and Sweden...Of the total holdings of foreign assets by central banks, a considerable proportion is held in the United States. While there is no way to determine this proportion precisely, there is reason to believe that it is large, and that perhaps as much as $1,000,000,000 of the operating reserves of foreign central banks is in the form of dollar exchange.

This relates to central banks only. The U.S. Department of Commerce, as the result of its revised questionnaire to bankers for 1926, has arrived at the following results as to the grand total of foreign balances and other 'unfunded' items:—

Unfunded items† due from U.S. to foreigners‡

	Dec. 31, 1925	Dec. 31, 1926
Deposits (time and demand) of foreigners	$1,108,000,000	$1,443,000,000
Loans and advances from foreigners	448,000,000	384,000,000
Short-term investments made by U.S. banks for foreigners (including bills and call and time loans placed on their behalf)	288,000,000	419,000,000
Total	$1,844,000,000	$2,246,000,000

† The questionnaire totals have been increased by 10 per cent to cover many smaller banks which did not report.

‡ 'Foreigners' is interpreted to include (1) foreign governments, banks, bankers and others resident abroad, and (2) foreign branches of American banks.

* *Bulletin* for June 1927.

Unfunded items* due to U.S. from foreigners†

	Dec. 31, 1925	Dec. 31, 1926
Deposits (time and demand) with foreigners	$367,000,000	$327,000,000
Loans and advances to foreigners	592,000,000	682,000,000
Short-term investments made for U.S. banks by foreigners	87,000,000	80,000,000
Total	$1,046,000,000	$1,089,000,000

* The questionnaire totals have been increased by 10 per cent to cover many smaller banks which did not report.
† 'Foreigners' is interpreted to include (1) foreign governments, banks, bankers and others resident abroad, and (2) foreign branches of American banks.

This table exhibits the remarkable result that at the end of 1926 foreigners held liquid assets in the United States to the value of about £450,000,000, and had increased them by about £80,000,000 during the year. Further, the excess of such assets over similar assets held by American abroad had increased during the year by about £70,000,000.

If we were to include the foreign balances held in London and other international centres we should probably have at the end of 1926 an aggregate of floating international balances of the order of magnitude of £600,000,000. The existence of an aggregate so large compared with the volume of foreign trade and other international items on current, as distinct from capital, account is a very novel thing. Some considerable part of these funds is undoubtedly influenced in its location by relative money rates (taken in conjunction with the actual and prospective rates of exchange). This means that the efficiency of bank rates as an expedient for liquidating international indebtedness by short borrowing (or lending, as the case may be), without exerting a corresponding influence towards the establishment of permanent equilibrium by affecting any of the current items of international income and expenditure, is very powerful indeed, perhaps dangerously so, for a country standing in good credit. It means that it is very easy for such a country to live for a considerable time by, in effect, increasing its overdraft.

At any rate there is nothing improbable in the various factors which have been analysed above having led to a diminution of anything between £150,000,000 and £200,000,000 in Great Britain's (net) international liquid assets (exclusive of the French repayment) over the past two or three years. My conjectural balance sheet is, therefore, as follows:—

Great Britain's International Account, 1925–27

Net surplus on income account	£100,000,000	New foreign issues in London	£300,000,000
Bank of France repayment	50,000,000	Other long-term investment (net)	—
Decrease of liquid international assets (net)	150,000,000		
	£300,000,000		£300,000,000

Possibly £25,000,000 should be added to the total on both sides of the account; possibly £25,000,000 should be subtracted. It is, however, something of a scandal that it should not be possible to answer these questions for certain within a margin of error of (say) £50,000,000!

The satisfactory feature of the situation lies in the fact that we appear to have had a surplus of £100,000,000 on income account in respect of these years, which include the strike period. Our problem is, therefore, primarily, not a problem of restriction, but one of adjustment between our long-term lending and our short-term borrowing. We are comfortably solvent even on the basis of the reduced level of exports of 1925–27. So long, however, as we continue to lend abroad more than our current surplus and to balance the account by attracting foreign funds, there is, obviously, in the situation, a dangerous element of artificiality.

The picture of the international balance sheet will not be complete without a further glance at the American situation.

The U.S. Department of Commerce report on 'The Balance of International Payments of the United States in 1926'* has disclosed certain facts which will be, I think very surprising to most European readers. We have, most of us, come to regard the United States as having an almost inexhaustible surplus available for foreign lending, so that the chief problem is to keep her supplied with an adequate crop of foreign bonds suited to the tastes of her investors. It now appears that this is a delusion. America's large foreign investments of the last two or three years have been made—like Great Britain's—by no means entirely out of surplus income, but partly by incurring increased short-period indebtedness. The figures for the years 1924–26 are as follows:—

	1924	1925	1926
Net long-term investment abroad	$522,000,000	$432,000,000	$522,000,000
Net surplus on income account	310,000,000	429,000,000	13,000,000
Excess of long-term investment over surplus income	$212,000,000	$3,000,000	$509,000,000

Of the aggregate excess ($724,000,000) over the three years, $514,000,000 has been definitely traced by the questionnaires to a net increase in foreign liquid assets in the United States, the balance representing untraced 'errors and omissions'.

Thus in these three years America's surplus on income account averaged not more than about £50,000,000, whilst her net long-term foreign investment averaged about £100,000,000. Now the first figure is not quite so high as Great Britain's surplus (apart from the strike year, 1926), whilst her net foreign investment is also slightly less than Great Britain's over the same period. Thus in spite of our diminished exports, our international financial capacity is not yet markedly inferior to that of the United States. Moreover, the United States has in recent years

* By Ray Hall, with a foreword by Herbert Hoover (Trade Information Bulletin, no. 503).

been doing just the same thing that we have been doing, namely, investing long out of the proceeds of borrowing short.

In 1926 the American surplus on current account fell so low that, if it had not been for what we paid her in respect of war debts, she would have shown a deficit. This surprising state of affairs is mainly due to the terrific expenditure of American citizens travelling abroad, which is estimated for 1926 at $761,000,000 (say, £150,000,000), inclusive of the expenditure of Americans more or less permanently resident abroad.

I should add, to avoid the exaggerated conclusions from the above, that in 1926 America's merchandise export surplus was unusually low. During the first eight months of 1927 her visible trade balance was about £58,000,000 more favourable than in the same period of 1926. Thus the surpluses on income account in 1924 and 1925 are probably more representative of the present position than the surplus in 1926.

However this may be, it is unlikely that the United States can continue to absorb foreign bonds at the present rate, when foreign balances in New York cease, as they must sooner or later, to rise, or begin to decline. A prolonged continuance, therefore, of the present cheap money policy of the Federal Reserve Board may be expected to lead eventually to an export of gold; and the above figures suggest that the United States must be much nearer losing gold than has commonly been supposed. It would seem probable indeed that an outward flow of gold may be both foreseen and desired by the Federal Reserve authorities, who must presumably be alive to the true situation of the international account. In this case the monetary history of next year may largely depend on how public opinion takes it when the gold actually flows. The public has been taught for so long to regard the loss of gold as a sign of weakness that it may alarm them unduly even if the Federal Reserve authorities take measures to neutralise the effect of the loss of gold on the credit situation. If, however, the Federal Reserve Board proves strong and determined enough to go through with it, the reassuring effect on the central banks of Europe should have a marked influence in relaxing credit restrictions throughout the world, raising the international price level and stimulating trade and expansion. Let me add that I am here following through the conclusions of an argument on a limited *terrain*,—there are also other influences of a kind which lie outside the scope of this article which are capable of diverting the course of events.

It will be observed that foreign investment since 1924, both by Great Britain and by the United States, has been peculiar and abnormal in character, inasmuch as it has not translated itself, as it normally does, into a demand either for goods or for gold, but has been hoarded in liquid form in the foreign centre where the borrowing has occurred. I think that we have here a very important clue to the monetary events of recent years. The use of the proceeds of foreign borrowing by European central banks to build up liquid reserves abroad has had a strong deflationary influence. We and the United States have been continually creating purchasing power for foreigners on a very generous scale in relation to our true surpluses, but they have not been using it. It has not translated itself, as it normally would, into a demand for goods and a stimulus to trade. Sooner or later this hoarding process must come to an end. When it does, a seriously depressing influence on international trade and general economic expansion will have been removed.

The modern age, in which debits or credits between nations are settled by changes in the volumes of liquid balances held in international financial centres, instead of by movements of gold, brings with it a new type of problem for which ready solutions are not yet available. This is partly the fault of economists who have not yet forged sufficiently sharp weapons of analysis—though the task of saying just how their present weapons are deficient and how they could be improved lies beyond the scope of this article. But it is also true, at least in Great Britain, that our statistical apparatus is deplorably deficient. It is absolutely vital to a sound monetary policy that we should be accurately aware of the direction and magnitude of the movements of international balances. At present our authorities are content that the so-called 'invisible' items in the international balance-sheet should remain invisible in the literal sense. It is just as though in the old days we had not known within a wide margin of error whether gold was flowing into or out of the country or in what quantities. I do not see why questionnaires issued in London should not produce as useful results as questionnaires issued in New York, or why, when in search of facts of vital national importance, we should continue to grope in barbaric darkness.

From The Economic Journal, *March 1928*

NOTE ON THE BRITISH BALANCE OF TRADE

Since the publication of my article on 'The British Balance of Trade, 1925–27', which appeared in *The Economic Journal* for December 1927, p. 551, the definitive figures for 1927 have been published by the Board of Trade. The apparent excess of new foreign capital issues in 1927, over the net surplus on income account comes out at £43,000,000, instead of £61,000,000 as in my provisional estimate. This modification does not materially affect my argument as to what had been happening during the three years 1925–27. The final estimates of the Board of Trade are shown in detail below; it will be seen that they have increased their estimate of the net shipping income by £20,000,000.

The following table is set out (with the 1927 figures brought up to date) in the same form as in 'Britain's Industrial Future', p. 29.* The figures for the years prior to 1927 only differ from

---

* There is a slip (corrected below) in the table as there published, the Bank of France repayments being reckoned as an addition to, instead of as a subtraction from, net foreign investment.

those in my previous article in that certain small subsequent corrections by the Board of Trade for the years 1922 and 1923 are now allowed for.

	£ (million)						
	1913	1922	1923	1924	1925	1926	1927*
I. Income Account							
Estimated net income from overseas investments	210	175†	200†	220	250	270	270
Estimated net national shipping income	94	133†	133†	140	124	120	140
Estimated receipts from short interest and commissions	25	40†	50†	60	60	60	63
Estimated receipts from other services	10	12†	15†	15	15	15	15
Total	339	360†	398†	435	449	465	488
Deduct estimated excess of Government payments made overseas	—	?	25	25	11	—	—
Net non-merchandise surplus	339	360†	373†	410	438	465	488
Net merchandise deficiency (i.e. excess of imports of goods and bullion over exports)	158	171	195	324	384	477	392
Net surplus on income account	181	189	178	86	54	−12	96
II. Capital Account							
New foreign issues of capital in London	+198	+135	+136	+134	+88	+112	+139
Bank of France repayments to Bank of England‡	—	−5	−5	−5	−6	−7	−37
Assumed increase (+) or decrease (−) of other capital items required to balance the account	−17	+59	+47	−43	−28	−117	−6
Total of capital account	+181	+189	+178	+86	+54	−12	+96

* Non-merchandise surplus assumed to be the same as in 1926.

† Board of Trade original estimates (*Board of Trade Journal*, January 31, 1924, p. 152) revised to harmonise with the official revision of their original estimates for 1924 and 1925.

‡ Estimates.

Compiled from the Board of Trade Journal, January 31, 1924, p. 152, January 27, 1927, p. 93, February 2, 1928; *Midland Bank Review*.

On 14 October Keynes spoke to a new forum, the Cambridge Institute of Bankers, at its inaugural meeting. His speaking notes appear below. A fairly full report of his talk appeared in the November 1927 issue of *The Banker*.

NOTES FOR 'THE FUTURE OPPORTUNITIES OF THE BANK OFFICIAL'

Honour to preside at inaugural of Cambridge branch

Possibility of a gathering such as these lectures enormous

Change during even my experience in Cambridge

Bank clerk of today has to realise that although a member of something so stable, he belongs to a rapidly shifting institution with deep roots in the past but probably new and changed complexion in the future.

The chief topic of my address is the future

But proper on this occasion to consider for a moment the past and the great men who have gone before us.

Extreme antiquity of banking temples (smallness of Semitic influence in English banking unique; in the Scotch and the Quakers we have found their equal)

In England, records at least go back to about the time of Cromwell

Trinity

Hoares Lloyds

Bagehots private banker—reference to father

The Big Five essentially a development of last 25 years

Still a period of transition

Some have passed further (e.g. Midland Bank—memories of Sir E. Holden) from old traditions than others (e.g. Barclays). But still dependent for boards and higher personnel on men inherited from the old system

One of the great questions of today for Big Five how far they will prove capable of training up from their own staff men fit for the really big positions—whether period of too much routine and too little responsibility may last too long

For Big Five have reached the stage where they are up against problems of socialism

Bank staffs are in fact a huge civil service working on a salaried basis with great security of tenure

Shareholders more and more remote

Hardly any of the responsible people acutely affected in their own pockets by degree of profits within wide limits

Competition, it is true, between the separate great institutions but not of a kind which eliminates

The Banks—and Insurance Cies—have gone furthest along the line of evolution which probably a large part of big business will follow presently

Divorce between ownership and management and between risk and management which is the problem of state-run things

But retention of ultimate profit test and some measure of decentralisation and independence of political influences

This semi-socialism the type of the future

The old individualism, however desirable, simply impossible

Well you here are units in great machines of this most modern type. It lies with you to evolve some principles of education, selection and promotion—for these rest quite as much with the staff as with the management

Freedom from pettiness, protection of vested interest, jealousies

Spirit of public service; feeling of being servants of the public

Immense attention to education of the talented young

Every bank clerk ought to keep himself going outside his routine in a real professional interest in some semi-professional sideline

    Competent economists RES special opportunities in Cambridge

    Finance and investment

    Money markets and exchanges

    London and Cambridge

    American and Continental conditions

But not just in an amateurish way

Everyone ought to make himself a real expert in some direction or other—and one day—quite unexpectedly—his chance will come

In particular banks likely to be the great centres of statistical information in future. Combination of individual secrecy with collective publicity

Beginning of scientific age in economics and business

Immense contribution which the banks can make to this

Beginning made with Lloyds

Collaboration with economists

Great further development of smaller accounts. Abolition of or reduction of cheque stamp—chequelets

In this case necessity of economising routine

Mechanical methods (pass books)

Prudential experiment

Reduction of unnecessary routine (e.g. continental practices)

Great scope for persons of a different type of brain

Then historical hobbies

I conceive the banks of the future with bodies of wonderfully contrived mechanisation and brains which make them the centre of the scientific interpretation and control of the broad movements of business. A great civil service with high traditions of public service and wide opportunities for the development and employment of many different types of talents.

But they might develop otherwise greed at the top sloth at the bottom

It is in the next 25 years that the destiny of British banking will be settled and it will depend on the moral and intellectual qualities of the bank official what happens in the end.

In October 1927 *System: the Magazine of Business* published an article by Sir Alfred Mond, the chairman of Imperial Chemical Industries Limited. In his article entitled 'Amalgamation, Rationalisation, Imperial Arrangement: The Latest Phase in Industry', Sir Alfred set out the forces leading to rationalisation in industry and raised the question as to whether rationalisation in Britain should be linked to European or Imperial developments. At the request of the Editor Keynes commented in the next issue.

From System, *November 1927*

I agree with Sir Alfred Mond's general philosophy of what British industry should be today, so far as the basic industries are concerned, which he has set forth in *System* for October.

When an industry is a new one, and going ahead at a great pace so that plant and machinery and skilled labour have their work cut out to keep up with demand, the perplexing problems of overproduction scarcely arise. Apart from cyclical depressions, which were sharp while they lasted but were soon over, many of our greatest industries were almost continuously in this state of development through the nineteenth century.

Nowadays, the problem of adjusting output to demand in an old-established industry cannot be avoided even in the most go-ahead countries. Some of our industries have learned this lesson. Other have not learned it, or are learning it far too slowly through prolonged and bitter experience.

I have had some experience lately of an industry which has signally failed to solve the problem of potential over-production—the section of the Lancashire cotton industry which spins American cotton. Sir Alfred Mond writes as the head of an industry which has solved it as completely as it can be solved, and has built up on these foundations one of the most splendidly equipped producing organisations in the world. Units of different size are appropriate to different industries. I do not say that all industries should imitate the scale of Imperial Chemical Industries Limited, which Sir Alred Mond tells us is a combination of what were originally 113 independent firms. Indeed, I am sure that there are many important industries in which the unit of maximum efficiency falls far short of this. But, whether the right unit is a relatively large or a relatively small one, no industry today can afford to neglect altogether the adjustment of the capacity to produce to the probable scale of consumption—an adjustment to be deliberately thought out by the industry coming together as a whole.

It may be true that a great combine like Imperial Chemical Industries might, in conceivable conditions, become a dangerous monopoly. There ought to be some suitable machinery for watching it from this point of view and for securing any needful publicity. But as regards efficiency of production and control, which is after all an essential ingredient of national success in industry, it seems to me absolutely undeniable that a concern like Sir Alfred Mond's has reached a level which is a very great deal higher than the level of those industries which are still trying to carry on with innumerable small independent units mainly engaged in trying to cut one another's throats.

On 5 January 1928 a conference of University Liberal Societies meeting in Manchester passed a resolution calling for a repeal of the Safeguarding of Industry Acts of 1921 and 1926, the repeal of the McKenna duties, after due notice to the industries affected, and thus a phased return to free trade. The next day Mr W. M. R. Pringle wrote to *The Guardian* criticising the resolution as a dilution of Toryism and calling on Keynes, whose name had been used by supporters of the resolution, to repudiate it. The University Liberals protested and on 9 January Keynes also commented.

To the Editor of The Manchester Guardian, *9 January 1928*

Sir,

Mr Pringle is wrong—when is he not?—in suggesting in today's *Manchester Guardian* that I have expressed any opinion about the repeal of the safeguarding duties. To judge from the abbreviated report which I have seen, Lord Pentland was quoting me to the effect that the free trade case must be based in future, not on abstract principles of *laissez-faire*, which few now accept, but on the actual expediency and advantages of such a policy.

In his anxiety, however, to extend his heresy hunt to the ranks of the Young University Liberals Mr Pringle has overlooked one important aspect of the traditional free trade case—namely, that the extreme difficulty of removing protective duties when they have been put on is one of the weightiest of the arguments against them. When industries and employments have grown up behind a tariff it is not always practicable to undo what has been done by a stroke of the pen. Mr Pringle is unduly simplifying a difficult problem if he thinks that it is.

The existing duties, taken as a whole, constitute, in my opinion, one of the stupidest, as well as one of the highest, tariff systems in the world. Nevertheless, the right policy will probably be found in that advocated in the resolution of the University Liberal Societies—namely, in a time-schedule of reductions with a view to their eventual disappearance. The Young University Liberals have shown in this resolution a greater sense of responsibility and actuality—that is, of statesmanship—than their critic.

Mr Pringle will doubtless write you another letter to say that it is now clear that Mr Keynes is not only against economy but in favour of protection. But again—when is he not?—he will be wrong.

Yours, &c.,

J. M. KEYNES

On 22 January 1928 the University Liberals approached Keynes to see if he would stand for the University at the next general election. He refused for the present, but after some discussion said he would reconsider later in the year. The following week saw him providing Lloyd George with his view of the economic prospects for 1928 in response to a forecast made by Jules Menken, an economist on the Liberal Industrial Inquiry staff.

To DAVID LLOYD GEORGE, *31 January 1928*

Dear Mr Lloyd George,

Sylvester[2] has sent me a copy of Menken's Forecast for British Trade in 1928, and says that you would like to have my views.

[2] A. J. Sylvester was Lloyd George's private secretary.

I think that Menken's collection of facts and figures is a very excellent one, and I have nothing to criticise in it. Nor do I seriously differ from his forecast, except that he takes a rather more optimistic view than I should be ready to commit myself to. The position seems to me, indeed, to be very obscure. While there might be quite an appreciable improvement, there is really no very solid reason for expecting one.

Since he has marshalled most of the arguments for being cheerful, I might supplement this by a few points on the other side.

(1) Not only are the unemployment figures actually bad at the moment, taking everything into account, but it is so much concentrated in a few particular industries where we have no particular reason to expect a revival that one does not see where a great deal of improvement is to come from. Obviously, the high unemployment in the building trade is likely to prove seasonal and temporary. But it is difficult to see where else there is likely to be much reduction. I know that Bowley takes rather a pessimistic view judging purely on the statistical side.

(2) The position of the farmers is really quite extraordinarily bad—a good deal worse, I think, than the public generally is appreciating.

(3) Iron and steel are by no means keeping up the spurt which they made in the first half of last year, and I see nothing hopeful in the position of coal or cotton.

(4) The monetary outlook is obscure and not so satisfactory as it was when Menken wrote. Prices have now been falling heavily for three years, and it is not certain that we are yet at the end. For example, the Board of Trade wholesale index number averaged 166 for 1924, 159 for 1925, 148 for 1926, and 141 for 1927. There never has been a time when trade could hold up its head against a continuous decline of that order of magnitude. If one could feel confident that an upward turn is now in sight I would be ready to be more optimistic; but I have no such confidence. Nor have I any confident hopes for an early

reduction of Bank rate. As you know, I put more blame on the falling price level and the restriction of credit than on anything else, except the return to the gold standard, with which of course they are associated.

I have set out above all the chief unsatisfactory points. But I concur entirely with the various factors which Menken points out on the other side. On the whole, I should expect the average of 1928 to be a trifle better than the average of 1927, but am not prepared to go further than that.

Yours sincerely,
[copy initialled] J.M.K.

The major event of early 1928 in the political circles in which Keynes moved was the publication of the report of the Liberal Industrial Inquiry under the title *Britain's Industrial Future*. The inquiry, set up in the summer of 1926, was the marriage of an initiative of the Liberal Summer School Committee and the financial resources of Lloyd George, with the Summer School maintaining control of the enterprise. Keynes was a member of the Inquiry's Executive Committee chaired by Walter Layton, as were Hubert Henderson, Phillip Kerr, Ramsay Muir, B. S. Rowntree, Sir Herbert Samuel, E. D. Simon and Sir John Simon. During the eighteen months of the Inquiry's existence, if we are to judge from Keynes's appointments books and his letters to Lydia, Keynes took an active part in its proceedings, attending numerous meetings in London and working weekends at Churt, Lloyd George's country house, and in Cambridge. However, almost nothing remains in Keynes's own papers to suggest the extent of his detailed involvement beyond a clear acknowledgement of his inspiration of the proposals for preserving the countryside (pp. 303–4) and a reference in a letter to Lydia on 20 November 1927 that he was drafting the chapter on Currency and Banking (ch. XXVIII). Harrod[3] records a detailed influence and credits Keynes with drafting Book II, 'The Organisation of Business',[4] and Book V, chapters XXVIII and XXIX, 'Currency and Banking' and 'Reform of the National Accounts'.[5]

---

[3] *The Life of John Maynard Keynes* (London, 1951), p. 393.
[4] He collaborated with Sir William Beveridge on chapter X, 'An Economic General Staff'.
[5] Keynes collaborated with Hubert Henderson on chapter XXX, 'The Burden of Taxation', with Ramsay Muir on chapter XXXI, 'Rating Reform and the Rating System', and with both Muir and Henderson on the 'Summary of Conclusions'. The information for this and the previous footnote came from Hubert Phillips, economic adviser to the Inquiry's executive committee.

On publication of the report, Keynes received letters from J. L. Garvin of *The Observer* and a postcard from H. G. Wells.

From J. L. GARVIN, *20 January 1928*

Dear Keynes,

I have just received the advance copy of the Report. Thank you many times. It was just what I wanted—a fair chance for a thorough study and a well-considered opinion. You may depend upon my bringing a dispassionate mind to it; though I never believed since the war that anything but a common policy, continuously pursued by Governments of all parties can meet the nation's needs in the times before us.

Yours sincerely,

J. L. GARVIN

From J. L. GARVIN, *7 February 1928*

Dear Keynes,

I never had such a terrific job of its kind as your Report—so packed with matter and remarks that it was like a thousand pages of ordinary stiff Blue Book. Hopeless to summarise adequately. At the last moment, to find room for a little more epitome I had to cut out a chunk of praise for the masterly character of the classification and digest.

Two things.

Of course exclusive party self-praise little endurable to me when by my own side is as repellent on yours. 'Ism, 'Ism, 'Ism on every side of our short plastic life, full of sinewy contradictions. How does Schiller go? I forget perhaps the exact words but something like this:—

Leicht bei einander whonen die Gedanken

Doch hart im Raume stossen sich die Sachen.

Nearly ten years ago Edwin Montagu and I talked and talked of Reconstruction and Development. I had all sorts of ideas recommended by your Report, but thought nothing adequate except an agreed national programme laid out for twenty years and carried on by successive Governments irrespective of party.

Of course a big loan for Imperial development played a bigger part in my mind than you and your colleagues would think well.

However I only meant to write about another thing. Having a Debit and Credit mind, I am unable from your data to estimate either side. In your *Nation* articles will you please say how you suppose Budget, income-tax, exports and imports, total employment, would look five years hence supposing your Report could be applied now!

Yours sincerely,

J. L. GARVIN

To J. L. GARVIN, *9 February 1928*

Dear Garvin,

Many thanks for your letter. We are very grateful to you for taking so much trouble about the Report and giving it such valuable publicity.

I agree that it would be much better if things could be done otherwise than through the agency of Party. But I much doubt whether our Report would have received so much publicity, and even more whether other Parties would have been so likely to borrow from it, if it had appeared, for example, as the work of a little committee of economists. If one regards the existence and activities of a Liberal Party as a route to power, I agree that one is probably wasting one's time. But if one regards it as a method of bringing a sensible programme to the notice of the public and of politicians, much of which one party or another will carry out in the next ensuing years, then I think it plays a quite invaluable part. I am convinced, from the discussions which actually took place when we were compiling the Report, and from other conversations which I have heard since, that it would have been utterly impracticable to produce this document or anything like it in the environment either of the Conservative Party or of the Labour Party. In fact, as things are at present, the Liberal Party, split and divided as it is and with uncertain aims, provides an almost perfect tabernacle for independent thought which shall at the same time be not too independent but in touch with realities of politics and of political life.

You ask me how much our proposals would cost the Chancellor of the Exchequer. I don't think that they contain anything particularly expensive except rating reform and continuation schools. You must remember that a large number of things which we propose would involve only capital expenditure and that of a remunerative kind, so that they would bring no burden on to the Budget proper. Moreover, rating reform is merely a readjustment of existing burdens and means no net increase whatever to the total public expenditure, national and

733

local. Thus, our only material new expenditure is in connection with education. If you were to carry out at once a full programme of raising the school-leaving age and of continuation schools, I believe it would cost a good deal—probably not less than £20,000,000, and conceivably more. A good deal of our programme could, however, be done for much less; and since the need for accommodation in the elementary schools would have reached its peak in a very few years the rest of the programme could be carried out by means of economies arising out of its being no longer necessary to be perpetually increasing accommodation for elementary education. Our rating reform would, as stated in the report, cost about £55,000,000.

On the other side of the account I see no room for important economies, except on armaments. But with the restoration of prosperity there would undoubtedly reappear the normal elasticity of the revenue, and the yield of the existing taxes ought to rise by £15,000,000 per annum at the very least.

Yours sincerely,
[copy initialled] J.M.K.

From J. L. GARVIN, *10 February 1928*

Dear Keynes,

Thank you for a fair comment and a useful elucidation. A number of things valuably treated by the Report I think nationally essential though not exclusively Liberal. Samuel in *The Observer* next Sunday replies on the debate. I still see more financial and commercial snags than the Report does, but shall go on thinking.

Yours sincerely,
J. L. GARVIN

From H. G. WELLS, *30 January 1928*

A good report & I don't find it 'heavy' to read. I'm not writing articles in a regular way just now but I hope to get a chance of blessing it loudly before long.

Best love to you both,
H.G.

I'm publishing a little book soon 'The Open Conspiracy: Blue Prints for a World Revolution'.

Keynes also gave Lydia his view of the Report.

From a letter to LYDIA KEYNES, *5 February 1928*

> The Liberal Inquiry has had rather a bad press, I think. But daresay it deserves it. Long-winded, speaking when it has nothing to say, as well as when it has, droning at intervals 'Liberals, liberals all are we, gallant hearted liberals'. It would have been so much better at half the length speaking only what is new and interesting and important. As it is, *any* reader must be discouraged.

Keynes took to the platform to discuss the Report, speaking to the Cambridge University Liberal Club on 16 February. The notes for his remarks have not survived.

He also returned to the Inquiry when Winston Churchill unveiled the Government's scheme for the reform of local rates in his 1928 Budget.

From The Nation and Athenaeum, *28 April 1928*

MR CHURCHILL ON RATES AND THE LIBERAL INDUSTRIAL INQUIRY

Mr Churchill's scheme of rating reform has one thing in common with the proposals put forward by the Liberal Industrial Inquiry—namely, a recognition of the pernicious effects of the existing law, in respect both of the weight of the burden and of the character of the present rating areas. But—though the details of his scheme are still obscure—the similarities between the two seem to end there. Perhaps this is because Mr Churchill has not yet thought about the problem or discussed it with competent critics, as keenly as we did on the Industrial Committee. For it is interesting now to record that this Committee in fact went through a stage almost identical with Mr Churchill's present state of mind, a proposal to reduce rates on all industrial establishments by 50 per cent (as compared with Mr Churchill's 75 per cent) being before the Committee in draft in the course of their discussions. We rejected it for reasons which may be expected to receive increasing attention as the debate—which is going to occupy the rest of this year—continues.

A relief to industry is plausible at first sight because it seems to concentrate assistence where it is most needed. But this impression disappears on closer consideration. It is true that the distressed areas are industrial. But it is wholly remote from the facts to suppose that areas are distressed in proportion as they are industrial. It is notorious, for example, that the highly industrial areas of Southern England and of parts of the Midlands are amongst the least distressed. Accordingly a far greater effect is produced for a given sum of money, if relief is concentrated on those services which fall on certain areas altogether out of proportion to their average weight throughout the country—in particular the relief of the able-bodied poor. The aggregate cost of this relief is not in fact very great for the country as a whole—not more than £15,000,000 in the worst of recent years. Consequently a comparatively small burden on the National Exchequer is capable of affording very great relief where relief is necessary. Mr Churchill referred to the Liberal proposal in his speech and tried to rebut it by the cheap clap-trap, which is the usual stock-in-trade of those opposed to social reform, about hordes of officials in Whitehall and the lessening of local responsibility. So far as the officials are concerned, the criticism is ill-based, because it forgets that the new plan is to be linked up with the existing local organisations of the labour exchanges and unemployment insurance, so that there would be a consolidation, not an extension, of bureaucracy, by which one set of officials would deal with what is now handled by two. As for the lessening of local responsibility, recent experience has shown that there is no question less suited to local autonomy than the scale of relief to the able-bodied poor. It is astonishing to hear a colleague of Mr Neville Chamberlain defending Poplarism.

But this is not the only reason for rejecting the method of

a special relief to industry. A considerable part of the expenditure covered by local rates is for so-called 'beneficial' expenditure, i.e., for services rendered in the shape of lighting, streets, drainage, police, &c., which is directly incurred for the benefit of the ratepayers more or less in proportion to their rateable value. If industry is to have an all-round relief of 75 per cent, this means not only that industry (and *a fortiori* agriculture) will be freed from relief services, but that other taxpayers or ratepayers must directly subsidise expenditure incurred for services rendered to industry.

Finally, whilst we were impressed by the evils resulting from the burdens of rates on industry, we were not less impressed by the wholly disproportionate burdens on working-class houses. We showed that in the case of a working man with a large family the rates may consume nearly 10 per cent of his income, whereas in the case of the rich man they will usually amount to less than 1 per cent. We considered that it would be absolutely indefensible to relieve industry, including prosperous industries, not only of real burdens but also of payments for services rendered, whilst doing nothing to relieve the working class of what is now by far the heaviest and least defensible of the fiscal burdens upon them. When the time comes for Mr Churchill's scheme to be discussed up and down the country, this aspect of it is not likely to commend itself to the sense of justice, or to the common sense, of the electorate.

There are other features of Mr Churchill's proposals not yet adequately elucidated, which indicate that he is not at heart such a friend to the ratepayer as he would fain appear, and that he is not above taking away with one hand what he is more conspicuously giving with the other. By substituting block grants for percentage grants in the case of the health services and by giving assistance by block grants to unclassified roads, he is taking a most retrograde step. This means that any increased expenditures on these services after the block grants are fixed will fall wholly on the ratepayer, whilst the Chancellor

737

of the Exchequer will be protected a hundred per cent against the cost of the desirable consequences of normal progress. These are precisely the services on which we should spend more year by year as the position of the national Exchequer improves. It is most wrong that the development of these services should depend on the vagaries of local 'economy' campaigns appealing with inevitable force to the instincts of self-protection of the over-burdened ratepayer. Again by substituting block grants for the present percentages of the assigned revenues, Mr Churchill is depriving local authorities of any future benefit from the natural buoyancy of the taxes. Thus he is ensuring that, so far as possible, all future increases in expenditure due to progress shall fall on the ratepayer rather than on the Exchequer. His measures—so far from relieving the householder from his present excessive burdens—are, therefore, calculated to increase them in the future above what they would otherwise be. The Liberal plan, of an average all-round reduction in the rates of 33 per cent, concentrated on the areas suffering from abnormal unemployment, is designed in such a way as to promote progress in health and road developments; Mr Churchill's to retard them.

Thus Mr Churchill's plan, so far as he has vouchsafed it to us, bears the marks—to put it mildly—of haste and of reactionary bias. Incidentally he has not provided this year a single penny wherewith to relieve the rates except by raiding the reserves of the currency note issue, which is the same thing as raising a loan of an equal amount in the open market, on last year's realised surplus.

The previous month, at the request of a French publisher, Keynes collected some of his writings from previous years under the title *Reflections on the Franc and Other Things*. Below we print the table of contents, indicating the location of the various items in this edition, and the preface, which echoes *Essays in Persuasion* (*JMK*, vol. IX).

INDUSTRY, ECONOMY, CURRENCY AND TRADE

From the English draft for Réflexions sur le franc et sur quelques autres
sujets (*Paris, 1928*)

PREFACE

A writer, who is invited to reprint what he has been rash enough
to contribute to the press during these recent years of rapid
change, must turn to the task of re-reading his old articles with
some measure of trepidation. How far to one who reads to-day
will the march of events have contradicted and exposed them?
How obsolete will be their atmosphere? How faded their ideas?

A sensible author suppresses, of course, his worst efforts, and
it is not for him to express an opinion on those which have
survived his own scrutiny. But in the last ten years no one in
the world of politico-finance has been rasher than I in making
prophecies. And having offered so many pledges to fortune, I

739

am justified, perhaps, in redeeming some of them when the course of time and events allows me to do so.

On three principal occasions in these ten years I have ventured to oppose the current flow of contemporary opinion and to forecast denouements contrary to those generally anticipated. The first was after the Treaty of Versailles, when I gave estimates of the damage suffered by the Allies and of the maximum possibilities of payments by Germany which meet with more favour now than they did then. The second occasion was before the return of Great Britain to the gold standard when I predicted consequences to the internal economy of the country and to the effect on the export trades which have been—not by universal admission but on the balance of opinion—on the whole fulfilled. The third occasion was during the flight from the franc, during which I published a large number of articles maintaining that the situation was totally different from the currency collapses in Germany, Austria and Russia, and that it could undoubtedly be solved by firm treatment, provided the level at which the stabilisation of the franc was attempted did not throw too heavy a burden on the taxpayer. From this series of articles a selection is here reprinted. On 9 January 1926 I wrote that the right figure for the franc would lie between 25 francs and 30 francs to the dollar. The rate actually prevailing at the present date is 25·5 francs to the dollar. In July 1926 I argued that a stabilisation of the franc between 160 and 170 to the £ sterling would give an exchange value of the franc too low in relation to its internal value and would have inevitably involved a substantial rise of internal prices.

In chapter IV I pass from national and international finance to a few personalities—some scattered opinions on four typical figures amongst contemporary publicists.

J. M. KEYNES

30 March 1928

In his Budget statement, Mr Churchill announced that a Bill would appear shortly to carry out the amalgamation of the wartime Treasury currency note issue with that of the Bank of England. Before the Budget, Keynes, who had been in Russia during the Cambridge Easter vacation, had written to the Treasury's Comptroller of Finance on one aspect of the matter.

To SIR RICHARD HOPKINS, *19 April 1928*

Dear Hopkins,

On my way to Russia, whence I have just returned, I spent a little time in Germany and had many interesting conversations—in particular with Melchior, the German representative of the League of Nations Financial Committee, and with Schacht [the President of the Reichsbank]. In order to get indirectly a line as to what their reactions would probably be towards any method we may adopt of regulating our note issue, I asked them whether they approved of the constitutions which our financial authorities have been forcing upon the state banks of those countries which have required assistance from the League of Nations,—in particular the rule requiring that a fixed percentage of gold be maintained against the note issue in spite of the fact that gold no longer circulates, so that the old reason for a relationship between the volume of the note issue and the volume of the reserves has largely disappeared. They both separately informed me that they believed these regulations to be a great mistake and that the policy of the Bank of England in causing so many European countries to lock up their gold reserves beyond all possibility of use was both foolish and dangerous. So long, they said, as the Bank of England controls the American market through their relationships with Strong, we must acquiesce. 'But', Schacht added, 'you must not conclude from this that the policies in question secure our intellectual assent.'

It was quite clear that in their view at any rate the strength of a central bank lay in its holding large free reserves. Indeed, how any sane person can suppose that a bank strengthens itself

741

in public opinion by diminishing the amount of its available reserves it is difficult to see.

The more I think about it, the more I am impressed with the extreme rashness and folly of carrying on an international banking business in these days of large figures, when we are no longer the only international centre, with a free gold reserve not only of trifling magnitude in itself but a very small fraction of the free reserves of the rival financial centre, the United States. I believe that as soon as people turn their minds to it, this opinion will be found to prevail, not only in many quarters in this country, but very widely indeed outside it.

Yours sincerely,
[copy initialled] J.M.K.

From SIR RICHARD HOPKINS, *20 April 1928*

Dear Keynes,
I am indebted for your letter which I have read with interest.

Yours sincerely,
R. V. N. HOPKINS

When the Bill on note issue amalgamation appeared on 3 May, Keynes prepared an extended discussion of it for *The Times*. The article appeared on 12 May, unfortunately from Keynes's point of view on a remote page. Keynes reprinted the article and a supplementary letter to *The Times* (below pp. 750–2) in *The Economic Journal* for June 1928.

From The Times, *12 May 1928*

TREASURY AND BANK NOTES, CONDITIONS OF AMALGAMATION:
AN ECONOMIST'S CRITICISM

The Chancellor of the Exchequer announced in his Budget statement that the conditions to be proposed for the amalgamation of the Treasury and Bank of England note issues would provide a 'greater elasticity' than hitherto. The expectations thus raised are disappointed by the terms of the Bill now published.

At present the combined fiduciary issues of the two sets of notes is £264,685,000, and, since this total depends only on a Treasury Minute, it is capable of being revised by the Treasury without an alteration of the law. The new Bill reduces the fiduciary total to £260,000,000, and retains, in effect, the provision for increasing this by Treasury Minute, though with limitations on the length of time for which such a Minute can remain in force. The reduction of the fiduciary issue may be compensated by the return of notes from Ireland. But in any case the elasticity of the issue is not increased, as compared with the existing state of affairs. Since there has been so far almost no public discussion to elucidate the principles which ought to govern the gold reserve in modern conditions, it may be opportune to open the debate.

Formerly the gold reserve was held partly to provide for an increase in the number of sovereigns circulating within the country—namely, the 'internal drain', and partly to meet fluctuations in the balance of international payments—namely, the 'external drain'. The Act of 1844 was mainly concerned with the first. It was directed to the obviously desirable purpose of preventing a change in the composition of the internal circulation from having any tendency to change its quantity. Moreover, at a time when most payments were effected by the means of notes, an expansion in the note issue was a fairly reliable indicator of an expansion in credit. As time went on, however, cheques gradually superseded notes for most business purposes, and provision against the external drain grew steadily in importance as compared with provision against the internal drain. But up to the War no change was made in the law. Since the War we have finally abandoned the use of sovereigns in circulation, so that the internal drain is now non-existent. Thus both the conditions which the old system was designed to meet have passed away; and it would, therefore, be an extraordinary

743

coincidence if this system were, nevertheless, to need no amendment.

The active note circulation—i.e., excluding notes held by the joint stock banks as a part of their reserves, is now exclusively employed for petty cash and for the payment of weekly wages; while the Bank of England's gold reserve is exclusively required to meet the fluctuations in our international account, which depend partly on the balance of trade, but mainly on our huge international banking and investment business. In these changed circumstances it is no longer reasonable to provide that the amount of gold available for the latter purpose should depend on the amount of notes required for the former. For there is very little direct connection between the two.

The right level of Bank rate and the right volume of bank credit are highly complex questions which cannot be determined by a rigid formula laid down by Parliament years in advance. Yet a legal formula connecting the gold reserve and the note issue is in fact nothing but a crude and obsolete method of attempting to do this. A loss of gold abroad generally indicates that money rates in London are not quite high enough compared with similar rates elsewhere, or that we are investing in excess of our savings. It very seldom indicates that the internal note issue should be correspondingly curtailed. Nor indeed is it practicable for the Bank of England—since it has no power to reduce wages—to curtail the active circulation appreciably, except by inaugurating a credit policy which deliberately aims at creating unemployment as a first step towards lower wages. Indications that the Bank of England will be well advised to protect its reserves by raising the Bank rate or curtailing the volume of credit are to be found, as everyone knows, in a variety of symptoms, of which in modern conditions the volume of the note issue is one of the least important and—what is most serious in an indicator—the latest to develop in point of time. To compel the Bank of England to measure its margin of safety by the volume of the note issue is, therefore, to compel it to pay more attention to a particular symptom than the Bank, left to itself, would deem reasonable, and to do something which to its own untrammelled judgement seems unwise. In particular, when employment is reviving and the wages bill increasing, such a provision has the effect of putting pressure on the Bank of England to terminate the reviving prosperity, even though the Bank, left to itself, may see no reason in the world for doing such a thing.

What, then, is the right method, if any, of regulating the amount of the gold reserve? In a sense it is foolish to lock away any of our gold so as to prevent its being used. As a means of providing against a shortage of gold, it is analogous to the famous regulation of a German municipality to provide against a shortage of cabs—namely, that there must always be at least one cab on every rank. Nevertheless, there is much to be said in favour of holding against extreme emergencies an ultimate reserve which is not available for use in any ordinary circumstances. The rational procedure, by whatever rubric one may enforce it, is to divide a country's gold reserves into two parts, one part of prescribed amount being set on one side against extreme emergencies, and the other part, the amount of which would be left to the judgement and the discretion of the central bank, being freely available to meet daily needs. That is to say, the law governing the gold reserve could be extremely short, and might run:—'The gold reserve of the Bank of England shall not fall below £x.'

An alternative way, however, of arriving at the same result is to maintain, in deference to tradition, a formula connecting the gold reserve and the note issue, but to take care that it shall be of such a character as to be inoperative in all ordinary circumstances. Such a provision may even have value as an ultimate check against grave abuses. This is the present position in the United States, where the gold reserves actually held are three or four hundred of millions sterling above the legal minimum. We could produce the same sort of result here, without appearing to depart too seriously from tradition, by fixing the maximum of the fiduciary issue at a sufficiently high figure.

Our present stocks of gold are about £160,000,000. But this is the favourable season of the year, and a few months ago they were £8,000,000 less. The aggregate note issue varies, at the present level of employment and wages, between £370,000,000 and £380,000,000, according to the season of the year. With a fiduciary issue of £260,000,000, as proposed, and a note issue of £370,000,000, we should have £110,000,000 of gold locked up and £50,000,000 available for use. If the autumn season drew £10,000,000 of gold abroad (which might happen for the most trivial reasons) and the Christmas season drew £10,000,000 more notes into circulation, we should have £120,000,000 of our gold locked up and £30,000,000 available for use. A combination of reviving trade, good wages, and a holiday season is easily capable of raising the note issue to £400,000,000. In this case, assuming a gold stock of £160,000,000, the Bank of England's reserve would fall to £20,000,000. *Prima facie*, such an arrangement is extremely imprudent—even though there be a possible recourse to a Treasury Minute. Can we suggest a better arrangement?

In the first place, is there really any need to lock away so much as £110,000,000? I suggest that £75,000,000—which is double the total pre-war gold stock of the Bank of England—would be plenty on any reasonable criterion, having regard to the importance for the world at large of economising the amount of immobilised gold. This would leave £85,000,000 in the Bank of England's reserve—a figure which would enable it to face the world with considerable confidence.

In the second place, is it safe for the Bank of England to operate with a reserve of £50,000,000, which it would take very little to reduce to £30,000,000? This amount is surely wholly inadequate for its responsibilities. Since the Bank obviously cannot allow its free reserves to sink to the neighbourhood of zero, these figures mean that it cannot afford in practice to lose even £20,000,000 of gold without considerable anxiety. Yet it is of great importance to industry that the Bank should be free to lose fully this sum, and better if it could lose double this sum, without being necessarily compelled to upset the basis of domestic credit.

We transact a foreign trade (imports and exports together) approaching £2,000,000,000 a year. A fluctuation of 1 per cent in our imports represents £11,000,000. In addition, London is the centre of a large foreign investment market, having a vast weekly turnover with foreign countries, the magnitude of which it is impossible even to estimate. And further, we are carrying on a gigantic international banking business with liquid foreign balances, withdrawable at short notice, probably, exceeding £200,000,000, and very possibly approaching £300,000,000. (We do not even know for certain within a margin of, say, £100,000,000, how large a business it is.) The Bank of France alone is reputed to hold more than £100,000,000 in London. Now a mere breath of wind might diminish these foreign balances by 10 per cent, or, say, £20,000,000; for they have shown themselves capable of increasing by such an amount within a very short period. In short, we are conducting this business on an altogether inadequate margin, and, even as it is, it has required all the bluff, cajolery, and prestige which our authorities can command to get along as well as we have. At any moment, therefore, the expansion of production and of employment will be liable to be interfered with by mainly irrelevant considerations arising out of our international banking business. I do not doubt—let me add—the ability of the Bank of England to protect itself even with the small margin proposed. But I doubt its ability to protect itself without sometimes enforcing a contraction of credit injurious to home industry.

Nevertheless, our total gold reserves of £160,000,000, more than four times the pre-war figure, are very substantial—if only we could use them. Is it not asking for trouble to lock up more than two thirds of this outside the Bank of England's reserve, and to publish less than one third as our actually available assets? For this is not a question of how much gold we actually hold—it is solely a question of how much we publish to the world as available at call. It is an odd mentality which seeks simultaneously to enlarge our international business and to diminish both our actual and our ostensible strength to meet its inevitable fluctuations. It is also peculiar to associate any further release of gold with a public declaration of weakness on the part of the Bank of England—which is exactly what in such circumstances one would wish to avoid.

The proposed arrangement means, moreover, that London will be competing with New York for the world's banking business on very unequal terms. Our net annual surplus available for new foreign investment is still very nearly as great as theirs. The international business we do is in some respects greater, and in the holding of foreign balances perhaps one half of theirs. But our free gold reserve is only about one eighth. It means nothing to them if their international customers take away £20,000,000. Indeed, they did take away approximately that sum last April, and nearly as much last March. Apart from previously ear-marked gold, the Federal Reserve Banks have lost some £60,000,000 in recent months without turning a hair. We cannot aspire, indeed, to this degree of strength. But we need not put ourselves under unnecessary handicaps. Foreign banks will assuredly hold their balances in the long run in centres from which they can rely on removing them at short notice without questions asked.

One point of the first importance, which might easily be overlooked, remains for mention. Not the whole of the existing note issue is in active circulation. A substantial, but unknown, proportion—perhaps nearly £100,000,000—is held by the joint stock banks. Some of this is indispensable till-money; the rest is a part of their reserves, which might just as well be held in the form of deposits at the Bank of England. In the event of stringency arising, it would be easy for the banks, either on their own initiative or at the suggestion of the Bank of England, to pay in, say, £30,000,000 in notes to the credit of their deposits. This would leave the reserves of the joint stock banks unchanged, but would increase the reserves of the Bank of England by the amount paid in. The point illustrates what a farce the proposed Bill may be as a means of regulating our affairs. It removes the real discretion away from the Bank of England to the joint stock banks, who, within wide limits, can make the reserves of the Bank of England what they choose, according as they hold their own reserves in the shape of Bank of England notes or Bank of England deposits. Nevertheless, if the joint stock banks were to take this course, it would not only defeat the objects, if any, of the Bill, but would also partly meet the criticisms made above. Not completely, however. It would still be better if the Bill were simply to read:—'The gold held by the Bank of England shall not be less than £75,000,000'; or, alternatively, if the fixed fiduciary total were put at not less than £300,000,000.

The next day, Keynes wrote to the Chancellor on the Bill.

To WINSTON CHURCHILL, *13 May 1928*

Dear Chancellor of the Exchequer,

What an imbecile Currency Bill you have introduced! But the mandarins have really overdone it this time. Even their usual supporters, e.g. *Economist* and *Manchester Guardian* City Editor are flinching. I discussed the Bill in all sorts of quarters last week and was unable to discover a serious defence of it in any quarter, but on the other hand much nervousness as to its possible consequences. For the moment the increase of unemployment* is strengthening the Bank's position (for the more unemployment, the less is the wages bill, and therefore the less is the circulation

* Appreciably worse than this time last year.

and the greater the Bank's reserves under our peculiar laws). But you cannot rely on this as a permanency. It is NOT TRUE in the long run that the maximum of imbecility is wisdom.

I hope you're better.

Yours sincerely,

J. M. KEYNES

From WINSTON CHURCHILL, *28 May 1928*

My dear Keynes,

Thank you so much for your letter. I am very sorry I have not had time to acknowledge it before. I have been recovering from a very disagreeable and depressing attack of influenza; and I am not yet up to the mark, although quite fit for anything except hard work.

I will read your article enclosed and reflect carefully, as I always do, on all you say.

Yours sincerely,

WINSTON S. CHURCHILL

As the Bill moved through the House of Commons a Government statement in the course of the debate moved Keynes to write to *The Times*.

To the Editor of The Times, *18 May 1928*

Sir,

Sir L. Worthington-Evans's reply to the Labour Party's proposal to increase the fiduciary note issue by £15,000,000 brings to light an important consideration which has hitherto escaped notice. He pointed out that the effect of this amendment would be to reduce the securities held in the Banking Department by £15,000,000, and therefore to reduce the Bank's profits by (say) £600,000.

This is quite correct under the terms of the Bill; though he did not point out that the securities in question would be sold, not to the public, but to the Issue Department, with the result that the Treasury would gain an equal sum. For an increase of the fiduciary issue by £15,000,000 would involve a transfer of £15,000,000 in cash from the Issue Department to the Banking Department, and a transfer of £15,000,000 in securities from the Banking Department to the Issue Department. The former transfer would strengthen the Bank's reserve of free gold; but the latter transfer would mean that the Treasury instead of the Bank would receive the interest on the securities. Sir Laming's point could, of course, easily be met by limiting the profit of the Treasury to the interest on £260,000,000. But under the Bill as drafted the Bank has a financial interest in fixing the fiduciary issue as low as possible, because it is the amount of the fiduciary issue which fixes the Treasury's share in the profits from state banking. We now have, therefore, from Sir L. Worthington-Evans, the first rational explanation yet given of why the Bank desires a level of the fiduciary issue which so greatly weakens the strength of its international position. The larger the Bank's reserves the smaller its profits. The Bank would like to have larger reserves; but it would also like to have larger profits. The present Bill represents the point of equilibrium in the Bank's mind between these conflicting advantages.

Now this discloses a serious fault inherent in the present arrangements. It is most desirable that the Bank of England should earn adequate profits; for the Bank ought to be free to pursue the right policy regardless of the effect on its profits. But under the terms of the present Bill, to raise the Bank's reserves to a really comfortable figure would, as Sir L. Worthington-Evans justly pointed out, have a serious effect on its profits and might, if it were effected by increasing the fiduciary issue, raise the Treasury's share to an excessive figure—though at present no one, not even the Chancellor of the Exchequer, has any means of knowing whether the Bank's profits are or are not, adequate, since (unlike most other state banks) the Bank of England's true profits are kept a dead secret.

But is not all this rather absurd? Why should not the Bank of England have both adequate reserves and adequate profits? We have plenty of gold and plenty of profit from the currency. But we have tied ourselves up in such a peculiar way that we can only assign profit to the Bank of England by taking gold away from its reserve and locking it up in the Issue Department, where it cannot be used. Thus the whole question requires reconsideration, and is eminently a proper subject, as Mr Snowden argued, for inquiry and report.

The Bank of England thinks that it can burke discussion by not allowing the slightest change in outward forms, however obsolete and inconvenient. This is a great mistake. Besides, why should the Bank fear discussion? We do not want to be governed by masked men in false beards muttering 'Mumbo Jumbo'. But every wise reformer knows that the strength, prestige, and independence of the Bank of England are the corner-stones of a sound credit system in this country. Adequate profits, adequate reserves, adequate knowledge, and adequate freedom from interference by 'interests', political or financial, are the necessary conditions of successful management. But the Bank will not, in the long run, increase its prestige or secure its future or avoid suspicion by putting forward a case which will not stand ten minutes' expert cross-examination, whilst its real reasons and motive, however praiseworthy, remain, like its profits and its statistics, secret and unavowed.[6]

Yours, &c.,

J. M. KEYNES

[6] When Keynes reprinted the text of the letter in *The Economic Journal* for June 1928, he added the two following paragraphs.

The following table, lately compiled by the United States Federal Reserve Board, of the principal gold stocks held by central banks and Governments at the end of 1913 and 1927 respectively, may be useful in guiding our sense of proportions:

	1913 £ million	1927 £ million
United States	265	818
Great Britain	35	153
France	140	146
Japan	13	112
Spain	19	103
Argentine	46	95
Germany	57	91
Italy	59	49
Total for all countries	982	1,894

Thus the general withdrawal of gold from circulation has strengthened the central banks of the world about in proportion to the rise of prices and the growth of business. The risk of a future shortage of gold need not, therefore, be acute—unless we ourselves adopt, and encourage others to adopt, the short-sighted policy of locking away too much of it out of use, thus leading to brisk competition between the central banks each to secure for itself an adequate margin out of the inadequate total which remains.

Keynes sent a copy of his letter to Philip Snowden, the Shadow Chancellor. On receiving it Snowden replied.

From PHILIP SNOWDEN, *20 May 1928*

My Dear Keynes,

I am very much obliged to you for sending me the cutting of your letter in *The Times*. I had seen it, though I had prepared the notes of my speech before doing so and I was glad to find that I had followed much on the lines of your argument.

The provision in the Bill will depend for its usefulness or otherwise on the policy of the Bank, but with a Chancellor who can stand up to the Bank it may be made operative.

I was surprised at the general support we received for an enquiry into the Bank Charter and the currency policy and should we get back to office I think we can embark upon such an enquiry with general approval.

All good wishes.

Yours sincerely,
PHILIP SNOWDEN

As the Bill moved through the House of Lords, Keynes provided another, unsigned comment.

From The Nation and Athenaeum, *16 June 1928*

The second reading of the Currency and Bank Notes Bill in the House of Lords last Thursday was the occasion of a very effective speech by Lord Arnold, setting forth once more in the clearest language the objections to the new Bill. No one in the course of the debate made any serious attempt to answer him. But it was ominous that Lord Hunsdon and Lord Bradbury took the opportunity to water down the undertakings which have been given in the House of Commons about the use of the clause allowing an expansion of the fiduciary issue on application to the Treasury. Both of them declared that, while circumstances might arise in which this clause should be used, it should not come into operation in any ordinary circumstances. We fear there is little doubt that this represents the real attitude of the Bank of England, with whom discretion in this matter will lie for the future, although, equally, we do not doubt the sincerity of the spokesman of the Treasury in the House of Commons in taking the opposite view. That the Bank of England has been adamant against any inquiry into currency arrangements at the present time will prove, we believe, to have been as mistaken from its own point of view as it is, in our judgement, from that of the public interest. The effect has been to produce a widespread impression that the Bank of England is obscurantist and out of touch with instructed opinion, however modest, and that it does not feel itself strong enough to come out into the open and defend its policy under cross-examination. The Bank has had to draw on its prestige very heavily in order to force the Bill through unamended, and the debates, in which various members of the Labour Party have played an honorable and enlightened part, have not left the position where it was.

Keynes also commented anonymously on another aspect of Churchill's Budget as it passed though its later stages in the House.

From The Nation and Athenaeum, *5 May 1928*

Mr Churchill has moved slightly in the direction recommended by the Liberal Industrial Inquiry in his proposed changes in the form of the Budget. But there is one important reform which he has so far ignored—namely, the provision of an estimate as to how far the revenue collected within the year exceeded or fell short of the revenue acquired within that year. In answer to a question in the House on Tuesday, he admitted that the arrears of super-tax carried forward were £5,000,000 less than the arrears brought in—so here, on the top of all the other wangles is another very substantial one. Without this contribution from previous years' revenue, extracted under special pressure by Somerset House, last year's results would have shown, once more, a deficit. We suggest that some Liberal Member should invite him to give corresponding figures for the income tax, and also the amount of the balances of the Revenue Departments not paid over into the Exchequer—which otherwise we shall not know until the Finance Accounts appear six months hence.

On 24 June France moved from a *de facto* to a *de jure* stabilisation of the franc. Keynes commented on the stabilisation in *The Nation* for 30 June (*JMK*, vol. IX, pp. 82–5). He also examined the stabilisation legislation in the next issue of *The Economic Journal*.

From The Economic Journal, *September 1928*

THE FRENCH STABILISATION LAW

The new law fixing the French franc in terms of gold and making various other new provisions, which came into force on June 24, is set out below. The gold value fixed for the franc, which is equivalent to 124·21 francs to the £, was in accordance with expectations, being no more than a recognition of the *de facto* situation. Certain other provisions of the law, however, are unexpected. In particular, reserve provisions are laid down for the Bank of France on lines considerably different from those which have prevailed in France hitherto. The traditional French system has been to fix a maximum for the note issue from time to time, but to make no particular arrangements as to the amount or proportion of gold to be held against it—an arrangement in favour of which there is in modern conditions a great deal to be said, especially if the maximum is suitably varied from time to time. By the new law, however, the Bank of France is required to conform with the new fashion of holding a rigid percentage gold reserve. This percentage is fixed at 35 per cent and applies not only to the notes in circulation, but also to the Bank of France's current deposits and other sight liabilities. The result of this provision is to lock up irrevocably something approaching £200,000,000, the effective gold reserve of the Bank of France to meet a foreign drain or for any other purpose being such amount as the Bank may hold in excess of this figure.

755

It is interesting to note that the new law also does away with the last remnants of the traditional bimetallism of France. The old five-franc pieces are to be demonetised and melted down, and silver will play no part in the future currency arrangements of the country.

The text of the law, slightly abridged, is as follows:—

Article 1. The provisions of Article 3 of the Law of August 5, 1914, provisionally fixing the value of notes issued by the Bank of France and the Bank of Algeria, are annulled.

Article 2. The franc, the French monetary unit, consists of 65·5 milligrammes of gold, 900/1,000 fine. Payments in gold francs of the former denomination, which were arranged in earlier agreements, are not affected.

Article 3. The Bank of France undertakes to convert its notes into gold at sight and on demand. It can do this either with legal gold currency or with gold bullion at the rate of 65·5 milligrammes, 900/1,000 fine, per franc. Payments of gold may be limited to the head office of the Bank, and to minimum quantities agreed upon with the Minister of Finance. Conversion will be effected by the Bank of Algeria under similar conditions. The Bank of France will buy gold at its head or branch offices at the rate of one franc per 65·5 milligrammes of gold, 900/1,000 fine, without deducting interest, but it may deduct mint charges. Assay charges will be borne by the seller.

Article 4. The Bank of France will keep a reserve of gold bullion and coin worth at least 35 per cent of the combined total of notes in circulation payable to bearer and of the credit balances of current accounts. Existing legal limits on the note issue are abolished.

Article 5. The Mint will strike 100-franc gold coins, 900/1,000 fine, within a margin of accuracy of one thousandth by value and two thousandths by weight either way. These coins will be unlimited legal tender.

Article 6. The date and other conditions of the general issue of gold coins by the Currency Office will be fixed by Government decree. In the meanwhile, coins will be struck only by the Bank of France, and the minting charge will be 40 francs per kilogramme of gold, 900/1,000 fine.

Article 7. To take the place of the Bank of France 5-franc, 10-franc, and 20-franc notes, which will be withdrawn from circulation before December 31, 1932, and will then cease to be legal tender, the Currency Office will strike, on the account of the State, silver coins of the nominal value of 10 francs and 20 francs, 680/1,000 fine. These must not exceed a total value of three milliards of francs. (This article, which has already been amended by the Finance Committee of the Chamber, originally provided for 5-franc pieces instead of 20-franc pieces.) The types of the new coins will be fixed by special decree. No individual will be compelled to accept more than 250 francs in silver coins. One third of the proceeds of the minting of silver coins will be paid at the end of each Budget period into a fund for the upkeep of the coinage. The other two thirds will be disposed of as arranged in the new Convention between the state and the Bank of France.

Article 8. Chamber of Commerce tokens will be taken out of circulation as they come in, and coins of the same denominations will be issued by the state in their stead. Private individuals need not accept more than 50 francs worth of aluminium-bronze alloy coins, or more than 10 francs worth of nickel or bronze coins.

Article 9. All earlier gold and silver currency will cease to be legal tender on the date of promulgation of the present law.

Article 10. Stocks of gold and silver, held by banks which have been granted powers of issue in Colonies and Protectorates where the franc is legal tender, will be revalued on the new monetary basis. The Minister of Finance is authorised to settle with such banks the conditions under which the state will receive credits for the resulting surplus.

Article 11. Deposit accounts opened with the Central Treasury Fund by the Minister of Finance on December 17, 1920, are abolished. Article 104 of the Law of April 19, 1926, is withdrawn except as regards specially authorised accounts. The provisions of the present Law will come into force on July 1, 1928.

Article 12. The Law of the 17th Germinal, year XI, and subsequent laws, controlling the minting and issue of money and the export of currency are withdrawn.

Article 13 approves the new Conventions between the state, the Bank of France, and the Caisse Autonome, by which the Bank of France undertakes to revalue in francs the stocks of gold in France, gold and reserves abroad, and silver which are shown in its weekly statement. It will also revalue in francs the bills bought by it from the Treasury in virtue of previous Conventions, and the gold, silver, and bills acquired in preparation for stabilisation. The surplus created by these revaluations will be used to redeem the outstanding temporary advances of the Bank to the Treasury, which will therefore be freed from its existing debt to the Bank. Treasury bonds held by the Bank under the agreement of February 3, 1927, which represent advances to foreign governments, and are in fact composed by the Russian debt, will cease to bear interest for the Bank, and will be taken over and paid for gradually by the Caisse Autonome.

As soon as the new law is promulgated, the Bank of France will place a sum of three milliards of francs, free of interest, to the credit of the Treasury account. It will receive in return a Treasury bond of the same value, due for payment at the expiry of the new Convention on December 31, 1945. The Bank will be free to purchase short-dated bills for foreign issue banks in account with it. Its stock of silver coins will be held by it for the present and will be transferred to the state as required for conversion into the new silver coinage.

The Convention between the state and the Caisse Autonome provides for the transfer to the Treasury of the claim on Soviet Russia. If the Russian bonds are not redeemed by December 31, 1945, the outstanding balance will be paid by the state. The Convention between the Caisse Autonome and the Bank of

France also provides for the liquidation of the Russian bonds. Article 13, as amended by the Finance Committee of the Chamber, also has a clause to increase permanent advances to the state by two milliards in order to provide credits for agriculture, housing, and social services.

The first weekly return of the Bank of France (for June 25, 1928) in its new form showed in terms of sterling the following gigantic total of gold and foreign currency assets, which is more than three times the gold holdings of the Bank of England:—

	£
Gold coin and ingots	233,000,000
Cash available at sight abroad	129,000,000
Forward foreign exchange purchased	79,000,000
Negotiable securities bought abroad	87,000,000
	£528,000,000

Since June the forward foreign exchange purchased has been running off and has been mainly replaced by other forms of foreign assets and of gold, the figures of August 16, corresponding to the above, being as follows:—

	£
Gold coin and ingots	244,000,000
Cash available at sight abroad	117,000,000
Forward foreign exchange purchased	49,000,000
Negotiable securities bought abroad	125,000,000
	£535,000,000

It would seem possible that the part of the reserve held in gold has not yet reached as high a figure as the Bank would like. In any case, it is clear that the provisions of the new French law are of a kind to confirm the anxieties of those who have been anticipating that the supply of monetary gold might be inadequate to the requirements of the world after the general return to the gold standard. It is evident that if every country were to lock away 35 per cent of the sight liabilities of its state bank and then

759

hold some substantial amount in excess of this in order to
l comfortable, there would be a steady deflationary pressure
ich, failing wiser courses, might continue over a long period.
any rate the future of gold now lies in the hands of the Bank
France as well as in those of the Federal Reserve System.

Chapter 9

CAN LLOYD GEORGE DO IT?

On 17 July 1928 Keynes wrote to Lord Beaverbrook offering him an article on the causes of unemployment in the same vein as *The Economic Consequences of Mr Churchill*. Beaverbrook accepted Keynes's offer.

From The Evening Standard, *31 July 1928*

HOW TO ORGANISE A WAVE OF PROSPERITY

In the spring of every year there is a seasonal recovery of certain industries which have been held back by the winter. This comes handy for the annual speeches of the chairmen of the big banks and for the Chancellor of the Exchequer introducing his Budget. So at each of their annual celebrations the professional optimists assure us, on the strength of the spring trade, that at last the revival is at hand.

By July we always know that we have been had again. This year particularly so. It is certain that trade on the whole is bad. There are 200,000 more unemployed than at this date a year ago. Indeed, there are as many unemployed as in any July in the last six years except during the great strike.

The railway traffics confirm these figures. So does the condition of the staple industries considered separately—coal, agriculture, cotton, shipbuilding, iron and steel, motors, and (more doubtfully) building and construction. A small increase in certain classes of exports is the only favourable feature.

In short, both profits and employment are disastrously poor. Moreover, the more successful the efforts which are being made to restore the margin of profits by 'rationalisation', the greater the likelihood—at first anyhow—of increasing unemployment.

761

And the more successful the efforts of the Treasury, in the pursuit of so-called 'Economy', to damp down the forms of capital expansion which they control—telephones, roads, housing, etc., again the greater the certainty of increasing unemployment.

The post-war building programmes of local authorities will begin to peter out before long, and, unless their place is taken by something else, the building trades will join the depressed industries.

Since there can be no doubt about the explanation, it is well to remind ourselves from time to time what it is. Labour costs, measured by the wage index of eleven leading industries, are exactly what they were three years ago or four years ago.

Meanwhile wholesale prices have fallen 9 per cent compared with three years ago and 13 per cent compared with four years ago, whilst the cost of living has fallen 5 per cent. But many industries have not enough margin of profit to employ men at the same wages as before and to sell their products 5 to 10 per cent cheaper.

This situation is what I ventured to predict when I wrote in *The Evening Standard* three years ago, shortly after the return to the gold standard. We have deflated prices by raising the exchange value of sterling and by controlling the volume of credit; *but we have not deflated costs.*

The fundamental blunder of the Treasury and of the Bank of England has been due, from the beginning, to their belief that if they looked after the deflation of prices the deflation of costs would look after itself.

Regarding these two different things as though they were practically the same thing, they did not hesitate to commit us to a deflation of costs without having any idea or any plan as to how it was to be brought about. Yet, as I pointed out when they made the commitment, it is extraordinarily difficult to deflate costs. Broadly, there are three ways of doing it.

The first is a general assault on the level of money wages. The coal lock-out of 1926 represented an attempt along this line of advance, and if the employers had been allowed to press home their advantages after the defeat of the General Strike some success might have been achieved. But Mr Baldwin decided— quite rightly—that it would be socially and politically inexpedient to take advantage of the situation in this way.

The events of this period confirmed the conclusion that in modern conditions an assault on wages is not only politically impossible, but also maladroit, because the wage rates which will be most likely to yield before the assault will be those in which wages are already relatively low because of bargaining weakness.

Today, on the eve of a general election, a general assault on wages is more entirely out of the question than ever.

The second way of deflating costs is that which is now being adopted in the best-led industries—namely, the restoration of the normal margin of profit by concentration of production on the most profitable lines and the curtailment of unprofitable business. This is called rationalisation.

The reason why we are only feeling now at this late date, when there are no other clouds on the horizon, the full effects on employment of the disequilibrium set up by our monetary policy three and four years ago is because many employers have been prepared, for a time and in hopes of the turn for the better which has been promised them, to continue without profit or at a loss.

But they will not do so indefinitely. In present circumstances there is for them no alternative to pressing on with rationalisation—which is likely, moreover, to achieve some economies and increased efficiencies which were already overdue. But this is bound to aggravate, rather than cure, the problem of unemployment.

The third way of deflating costs is to take advantage of the economies of successful bold enterprise and the working of plant and productive resources to a hundred per cent of capacity.

Industry might afford the higher wages imposed on it if it could work at full steam. The wastefulness of plant employed

10 or 20 or 30 per cent below capacity is extreme. Moreover, the increased purchasing power of a working population in full employment would react quickly and cumulatively on the prosperity of numberless industries and occupations.

Probably, even so, it would be impossible to bridge the existing gap between costs and prices without the assistance of some inflation of the latter. In any case, to organise a wave of prosperity which shall sweep us out of the pool of stagnation in which we are decaying is extremely difficult, involves some risks, and might be unsuccessful. But it ought to be tried.

Unfortunately, it lies entirely outside the power of individual business men to take the initiative. The first steps can be taken only by the Bank of England and the Chancellor of the Exchequer. Yet the consequences of their policy so far has been to ensure that businesses shall be unprofitable and that the level of unemployment shall not fall below the million level.

Nevertheless, it is well to recognise squarely the nature of the risks which stand in the way of any departure from the Bank of England's present policy. Unemployment will not decline unless business men have the incentive of plentiful credit, high hopes and a slightly rising level of prices—a slight inflation of prices *but not of costs*.

The newly employed men will need increased imports of raw materials to work on, and as their earnings improve their consumption will increase. Yet owing to the length of the period of production, they will not have much to show for it for six months or a year, and, if they are producing capital goods, adjustments of the capital market will be required. In the meantime one would expect the visible balance of trade to move against us.

Thus the process of getting more men to work is calculated to cause a drain on the resources of the Bank of England, just as the depression has raised its resources to a record level.

The practical steps which ought to be taken if we really want to reduce unemployment are, I suggest, the following:—

First, as Mr McKenna has consistently maintained, the Bank of England must gradually increase the reserve resources of the joint stock banks up to (say) £10,000,000 above their present figure—an augmentation of the basis of credit which will ensure that no worthy business borrower will be turned down by his bank.

Secondly—since this would greatly reduce and perhaps avoid altogether the risks of the experiment—the Governor of the Bank must induce his colleagues throughout the world to change their tune when he changes his, instead of his encouraging a general deflationary atmosphere by insisting on every state bank in Europe locking up its gold against note issues which do not need it.

Thirdly, the Chancellor of the Exchequer must remove and reverse his pressure against public spending on capital account.

Every public department and every local authority should be encouraged and helped to go forward with all good projects for capital expansion which they have ready or can prepare—roads, bridges, ports, buildings, slum clearances, electrification, telephones, etc., etc.

When we have unemployed men and unemployed plant and more savings than we are using at home, it is utterly imbecile to say that we cannot *afford* these things. *For it is with the unemployed men and the unemployed plant, and with nothing else, that these things are done.*

To have labour and cement and steel and machinery and transport lying by, and to say that you cannot *afford* to embark on harbour works or whatever it may be is the delirium of mental confusion.

For several years past these policies have not lacked powerful advocates who have some claim to wisdom and experience—Mr McKenna, Lord Melchett, Sir Josiah Stamp, for example, amongst business authorities, Mr Lloyd George and Lord Beaverbrook amongst public men, and many economists and journalists.

I do not believe that the Chancellor of the Exchequer is naturally unsympathetic to this outlook. But he has succumbed, just as Mr Snowden did before him, to the timidities and mental confusions of the so-called 'sound' finance, which establishes as an end to be worshipped what should only be pursued so long as it is successful as a means to the creation of wealth and the useful employment of men and things.

According to the census of production, the average net output of an employed person in this country is £220. Therefore, the output of a million persons over five years is £1,100,000,000.

It is very possible, therefore, that the policy of the Bank of England over this period has reduced the wealth of the country by not less than £500,000,000.

The nature of the error committed will never be exactly understood by the public. But its consequences will have a profound effect on the general election and on the future government of this country.

Keynes's article was the subject of extensive press comment. It also received an interesting comment from Allyn Young, who had just come to the London School of Economics from Harvard.

From ALLYN YOUNG, *7 August 1928*

Dear Keynes,

You may wait upon having my address on 'Increasing Returns and Economic Progress' for the December *Journal*.[1] I shall want to append a mathematical note (which I shall *not* read at Glasgow, but which I am having privately printed for distribution to interested persons) which will occupy not more than three additional pages.

I read a contribution of yours to *The Evening Standard* with much interest. I agree altogether with what you say about public expenditures. In respect of Bank policy I go a long way with you. But, of course, one doesn't know whether the release of, say, £100,000,000 more purchasing power in the

[1] Young was giving the Presidential Address to Section F, the economics section, of the British Association for the Advancement of Science in Glasgow on 10 September. It appeared in *The Economic Journal* for December 1928.

London market would mean an increase of £50,000,000 or £100,000,000 in the demand for *British* labour. In general, of course, the best results would be got from an expansion of credit effected by other means than a marked reduction of Bank rate *relative* to the rates of other countries. On the whole, I think, it might be better to devise some sort of bonus on *new productive investments* within Great Britain. 'Rating reform' won't do it, for that mostly affects quasi-rents, and has little effect on prime costs. Radical as it may seem, I should prefer to give *new* constructions and installations an exemption from rates on a graduated (time) scale.

We really need a theory of economic *inertia*.

Yours sincerely,

ALLYN A. YOUNG

On 18 August, *The Economist* in the course of a leading article discussed Keynes's *Evening Standard* proposals critically. Keynes replied to one particular comment.

To the Editor of The Economist, *27 August 1928*

Sir,

In commenting on a recent article of mine in *The Evening Standard* you allege that I 'have failed to draw the distinction between wage costs and wage rates'. This is not correct—indeed, it is the opposite of the truth. The argument of the article was as follows:—

(1) That the decision to appreciate the currency committed us to a reduction of production costs in terms of money;

(2) That this is a very difficult thing to accomplish, and there was no plan beforehand as to how to do it;

(3) That there are three ways—(i) to reduce wage rates, (ii) to reduce costs by rationalisation often involving a contraction of employment, (iii) to reduce costs by an outburst of intensive activity based on full-time working;

(4) That (i) was politically and socially impracticable in an adequate degree, that (ii) was proceeding in the best-led industries and was in many ways desirable, but tended, at first, to aggravate unemployment, and that, therefore, (iii) deserves a trial.

Your article was based apparently on the belief that wage costs have been *already* reduced—over the average of agriculture, transport, public utilities and industry—proportionately to the increase in the value of money. Why you believe this nobody knows.

Yours, etc.,

J. M. KEYNES

On 3 August, at the Liberal Summer School in Oxford, Keynes took part in a debate with Tom Johnston, a Labour M.P., on the motion 'That the Socialist solution to the economic evils of today is to be preferred to that contained in the Liberal Industrial Report'. After the meeting he went on with Lydia to stay with Margot Asquith at The Wharf.

During the rest of 1928 Keynes was relatively inactive as a publicist, for except for a speech in the opening debate of the Cambridge Union on 16 October favouring a change of government, and a book review, he stayed out of the public prints while working on his *Treatise on Money*.[2] He did, however, enter the lists when the Editor of *The Observer* attacked 'Professor Keynes' on 28 October for certain comments that had appeared in *The Nation* on *The Observer*'s dismissal of a Liberal revival.

To J. L. GARVIN, *30 October 1928*

My dear Garvin,

On opening my *Observer* on Sunday I was rather astonished to find a leading article directed to my poor self, describing me as 'an ungovernable soda-water siphon', spuming 'in *The Nation*'. Since I have been very busy in recent weeks on a book, and have not written an article for *The Nation* for some time, I could not imagine to what it might refer. On picking up *The Nation* I was still rather at a loss, because, while I found a paragraph referring to your electoral arithmetic, I could find nothing anywhere in the paper about 'the political wisdom of Lord Beaverbrook'.

[2] *JMK*, vols. V and VI.

At any rate, I wrote nothing in last week's *Nation*, and am not and never have been a 'Professor'. May I rely on your giving equal prominence next Sunday to a withdrawal of this attack on me, and possibly, if you feel inclined, something in the nature of an apology? For it is really rather annoying to be attacked so vituperatively for something with which one has no concern. I may add that I have hardly ever written an article for *The Nation* (or for any other paper) except over my own name, and have never had any connection whatever with the column in which the offending paragraph appeared.

Yours sincerely,

[copy initialled] J.M.K.

From J. L. GARVIN, *31 October 1928*

My dear Keynes,

Your letter reaches me here. I make a practice of taking difference of opinion in politics as a matter of course and never initiate personalities. When they are initiated by others at my expense they must be dealt with. *The Nation* began the personalities a fortnight ago about a matter where I was solely concerned with examining facts. I took no notice. The second week it repeated, in a manner below its name. Then, action was required. *The Nation* is yours. 'Kaffa' is supposed to be you. You imply that this supposition is mistaken and that you had nothing to do with these paragraphs. I am glad to know this. I am very glad. To open personalities with you on a difference of mind would be the last thought in my head. *The Nation* owes amends to me, in the first case. What of that?

Yours sincerely,

J. L. GARVIN

P.S. To say *Evening Standard* is to say Lord Beaverbrook in these matters. I like realities.

To J. L. GARVIN, *1 November 1928*

My dear Garvin,

Why do you think it natural to assume that the Chairmen of Companies owning newspapers write all the contents—I all of

The Nation and Beaverbrook, apparently, *The Evening Standard*? Wouldn't Lord Astor be rather surprised if I wrote a sharp letter to him for writing an article calling me an ungovernable soda-water siphon? Shall I Try? Soda-water siphon would really be much more applicable to him, and he might take it as a compliment!

Seriously—I am horrified to think that I have ever been supposed to be 'Kaffa' of *The Nation*, as you would appreciate if you knew what I'd been in the habit of saying about him. But I must leave him and his defence to his *Editor*.

Yours sincerely,
J. M. KEYNES

Garvin closed the issue with a telegram.

From J. L. GARVIN, *1 November 1928*

Letter just received welcome explanation happy put matters right as regards yourself but is *Nation* making any amends for offensive paragraphs two weeks running on opinions of mine carefully formed and fairly expressed?

Garvin.

On 2 November, Keynes reviewed Reginald McKenna's recent collection of speeches entitled *The Post-War Banking Policy*.

From Britannia, *2 November 1928*

Mr McKenna has done a bold thing. He has dared to reprint without alteration the advice, the explanations, the prophecies which have adorned his annual addresses to the shareholders of the Midland Bank since 1920. But he emerges with remarkable success. He has said substantially the same thing, brought up-to-date, every year; he has never been listened to; and his warnings have turned out right. But the authorities of the Bank of England, against whom in polite and covert language he has been inveighing, have possessed the inestimable advantage of never explaining themselves or having to justify their policies. So Cassandra, though having a tongue, has not prevailed against them.

Yet his story is a simple one which might—one would have thought—be understood even by the dumb unless they are also deaf. It is a clear and argued exposition of the inevitable consequences of a prolonged attempt, spread over years, to deflate prices through the instrument of Bank rate and credit restriction. Business losses, curtailment of production, severe unemployment, a heavy aggravation of the burden of the national debt—this is what Mr McKenna has told us each year that we are heading for; and this, each year, is what we have got.

The argument, put very briefly, is as follows. There have often been periods of what Mr McKenna calls 'speculative inflation', in which prices have gone up out of proportion to wages with the result that exceptionally high profits have been earned, leading in their turn to over-trading. Against such developments the Bank of England's traditional weapon of high Bank rate and the restriction of traders' credit is ideally suitable, and always likely to be successful. But there is also quite a different kind of inflation, such as that which was the legacy of the War period, when wages have had time to rise just as much as prices, so that profits are no longer excessive.

Now it is vital to distinguish between these two kinds of inflation and to be quite clear, before we use the weapon of credit restriction to cure the second kind, exactly what we are in for and whether it is worth while. This is the piece of clear thinking which, time after time in the course of these addresses, Mr McKenna has demanded, yet which the Treasury and the Bank of England have never provided.

For how does the process work? Clearly prices cannot fall unless either profits fall or wages fall or efficiency increases. Over a long period we might hope a good deal from an increase in efficiency; but manufacturers could not possibly hope to increase efficiency quickly in a degree corresponding to the fall of prices. Moreover, an atmosphere of restriction is the worst possible atmosphere in which to increase efficiency in modern conditions, where much depends on full-scale production.

How then will a restriction of credit by the Bank of England bring down prices? The first effect will be to cause manufacturers to drop all their less profitable business—which means less output and less employment. The second effect will be to bring towards bankruptcy those manufacturers who happen to be working—because of foreign competition or for any other reason—with a narrow margin of profit, as, in this case, the heavy industries of coal, iron and steel and the textile industries. These industries have to choose between losing money and embarking on a struggle with their operatives to reduce wages; and they generally go in for a bit of both. By this time there is—one way or another—a large body of unemployed. When the Bank of England [has] achieved this result, one half—the easier half—of the Bank's task has been accomplished.

The next stage is to use the pressure of unemployment to bring down wages. In modern conditions this is exceedingly difficult, and the resistance to it has been tenacious and on the whole successful. That is why the phase of unemployment has been so exceedingly prolonged. When wages have come down to the necessary extent—and in so far as efficiency is increased, the extent to which wages need fall is correspondingly diminished—profits are restored at a lower price level than before. The workers will be no worse off than they were, when once the process is completed; for though their money wages will be lower, their purchasing power will be maintained. But the reasonableness of this final outcome does not make it any the easier to bring about in practice.

Many people, who did not think so at the time, now realise it would have been much wiser to have established both prices and wages at a higher level—thus avoiding business losses, unemployment and a heavier national debt. Nor are we yet out of the wood.

CAN LLOYD GEORGE DO IT?

As Bagehot wrote many years ago:—'The directors of the Bank of England were neither acquainted with right principles, nor were they protected by a judicious routine.' But, at any rate, the Chairman of our greatest joint stock bank did what he could to warn the Government and the public.

In the winter of 1928 Keynes was approached as a possible Liberal candidate for Cambridge University. Initially he had declined the approach but he subsequently weakened, partially under parental influence as he told Lydia on 6 March, and agreed to consider the issue again in the autumn. Thus on 11 October he was approached again by F. A. Potts of Trinity Hall.

From F. A. POTTS, *11 October 1928*

Dear Keynes,

Has the time now come when you can give a definite answer to an invitation to stand for the University constituency? I do hope that things have so fallen out that you do feel free to stand.

Yours sincerely,

F. A. POTTS

To F. A. POTTS, *14 October 1928*

Dear Potts,

During the vacation I have thought a great deal about the very attractive invitation to me to stand for the University constituency. From many points of view I am much tempted, and I don't know when I have vacillated more about making a decision. But on the balance of considerations I must say No. On a later occasion the balance might come down on the other side. But at present I have too much else on hand, particularly writing, which I cannot bring myself to give up.

I am very grateful for the long time which has been allowed me to make up my mind.

Yours sincerely,

J. M. KEYNES

The attempt to run Keynes as a candidate did not stop with his letter of 14 October.

From SIR HERBERT SAMUEL, *5 December 1928*

Dear Keynes,

I had heard that you had declined the invitation of the Cambridge University Liberals to stand at the next election; and this morning I have heard from Mr Potts, who writes on behalf of their Committee. I do not think I can do better than send you his letter, so that you may see precisely how the matter stands. You will realise as fully as I do the importance of a strong body of Liberal candidates at the next election, and particularly of Liberalism being well-represented in the University contests. It would be of great assistance to me, and to all of us who are working for the revival of the Party, if you would 'consider yet again'; and, in view of the circumstances which the letter describes, would agree to the urgent desire of the Cambridge University Liberals.

Yours sincerely,

HERBERT SAMUEL

To SIR HERBERT SAMUEL *10 December 1928*

Dear Sir Herbert,

It is very kind of you to have written to me in the terms of your letter of December 5th. I was very much attracted by the idea of standing for the University, and gave it the most prolonged and anxious consideration before I declined. Since getting your letter I have thought it over again. But I am sorry to say I still feel that I must not take up this commitment. It would be difficult or impossible for me to take membership for the University in the spirit of a rather light-hearted outsider, as some people might quite appropriately do. If I were to come into the House I should inevitably find myself drawn to make it the major call on my time. Indeed, it would not be satisfactory to me on any other terms. But this would mean giving up many of my present activities, and that is what at this moment of time—one cannot say how one would feel after various pieces of writing work have been finished—I am, most reluctantly, not prepared to do.

Yours sincerely,

[copy initialled] J.M.K.

P.S. I return Mr Potts's letter.

774

CAN LLOYD GEORGE DO IT?

In the New Year Keynes became more active. His first article of the year concerned the adequacy of world stocks of gold, a matter he had alluded to in discussing the Currency and Bank Notes Act of 1928 and the French stabilisation legislation (above pp. 746, 752 and 759–60). On 14 December 1928 the Council of the League of Nations on the recommendation of the Financial Committee had agreed to set up an inquiry. After serious difficulties in staffing such an inquiry in the face of central bank vetoes of key personnel, the Financial Committee delegated some of its members to join with outside experts in the summer of 1929 to form the Gold Delegation, which issued three reports between 1930 and 1932.

From The Nation and Athenaeum, *19 January 1929*

IS THERE ENOUGH GOLD?
THE LEAGUE OF NATIONS INQUIRY

From the days of the Genoa Conference in 1922 anxiety has often been expressed whether the world's stock of gold would be adequate to its needs in the event of the great majority of countries returning to the gold standard. Professor Cassel has been foremost in predicting a scarcity. I confess that for my own part I did not, until recently, rate this risk very high. For I assumed—so far correctly—that a return to the gold standard would not mean the return of gold coins into the pockets of the public; so that monetary gold would be required in future solely for the purpose of meeting temporary adverse balances on international account, pending the restoration of equilibrium by Bank rate or other expedients. Accordingly—so I supposed, and here I was wrong—the monetary laws of the world would no longer insist on locking up most of the world's gold as cover for note issues. For the contingency against which such laws had been intended traditionally to provide, namely, the public wishing to exchange their notes for gold, was a contingency which could no longer arise when gold coins no longer circulated. Moreover, to meet an adverse international balance, bills and deposits held at foreign centres would be just as good as

775

gold, whilst having the advantage of earning interest between-times.

But I was forgetting that gold is a fetish. I did not foresee that ritual observances would, therefore, be continued after they had lost their meaning. Recent events and particularly those of the last twelve months are proving Professor Cassel to have been right. A difficult, and even a dangerous, situation is developing, which is the object of this article to examine.

The point to be stated very shortly. The volume of notes in circulation depends mainly on a country's habits and on its income, and cannot be materially altered at short notice. Thus if the law provides that the central bank must keep not less than (e.g.) 30 per cent of the note issue in gold, this gold is locked up and might just as well not exist for the purposes of day-to-day policy. A bank's effective reserve to meet emergencies is, therefore, not its total reserve, but the excess over its legal reserve. It follows that if the legal reserves of the central banks of the world are fixed at a high figure, and if they prefer gold in their own vaults to liquid resources in foreign centres, then there may not be enough gold in the world to allow all the central banks to feel comfortable at the same time. In this event they will compete to get what gold there is—which means that each will force his neighbour to tighten credit in self-protection, and that a protracted deflation will restrict the world's economic activity, until, at long last, the working classes of every country have been driven down against their impassioned resistance to a lower money wage.

The rashness and want of foresight of our monetary authorities was not fully disclosed until the passing of the British and French currency laws in 1928. But by the shape in which they have allowed these laws to be drafted the responsible authorities in Great Britain and in France have given their approval and example to useless and illogical conventions which, if they are applied all round, cannot help but cause an artificial shortage of gold. Moreover, it is only within the last few months that the willingness of certain central banks to keep their reserves abroad, which lasted so long as their currency stabilisations were incomplete, has been yielding to a desire to convert more of their resources into gold situated in their own vaults.

Generally speaking, the central banks of the world are now required by law to hold in actual gold a proportion of their note issue which varies in different cases from 30 to 40 per cent. Some of them, notably France and the United States, require a fixed proportion of gold (35 per cent in these cases) to be held against their deposits. The recommendation of the Genoa Conference that the law should allow reserves to be held alternatively in gold or in liquid assets in foreign centres has been widely disregarded. Apart from certain minor countries, whose currencies were reorganised under the auspices of the League of Nations, Italy is alone in allowing a provision of this kind. Moreover, during the last few months certain important banks, which had been in the habit of holding a large part of their excess reserves as deposits in foreign centres, notably, France, Italy, and Germany, have shown an inclination gradually, as opportunity offers, to bring these resources home again in the shape of actual gold. Germany's power to take gold in this way may be almost exhausted. But Italy will probably proceed further (the Bank of Italy held 38 per cent of its total reserves in actual gold on January 10th, 1928, and 46 per cent on December 10th); and France has only just begun (on January 10th, 1929, the Bank of France still held 49 per cent of its total reserves, and 89 per cent of its excess reserves at foreign centres). Where is the gold to come from—in addition to what is wanted for the normal expansion of the world's economic life—to meet the requirements of these new laws and habits?

The dimensions of the problem can be best indicated by a few fundamental statistics. At the present time the world's stock of gold available for monetary purposes may be estimated at somewhere about £2,000 million, of which about 40 per cent is in the United States of America (not so long ago the American proportion was in the neighbourhood of 50 per cent). The annual production of gold has been in recent years at the rate of about £80,000,000, of which the industrial arts and the East absorb more than half, leaving less than £40,000,000 for monetary purposes or (say) about 2 per cent of the monetary stock. The annual rate of increase of the world's requirements due to the normal expansion of its economic life is generally estimated, assuming stable prices, at about 3 per cent. This figure is not based on any secure evidence, but, if it is correct, and if central banks maintain their reserve practices, &c., unchanged, world prices will have to fall on the average by 1 per cent per annum; or—putting it the other way—central banks will have to economise in their gold habits by 1 per cent per annum if prices (cyclical fluctuations apart) are to be kept stable. At any rate, there is no surplus to allow a lessened economy in gold held in reserves.

Now to economise the use of gold by 1 per cent per annum would present no difficulty if the central banks had not tied themselves so unfortunately with legal reserves which they are bound to hold to meet contingencies which can no longer arise. Of the total gold available for monetary purposes I calculate that something between two thirds and three quarters is locked away in legal reserves where it can never be used. Leaving out the United States, which is in a somewhat stronger position, I should say—it is difficult to make an exact estimate—that the free gold reserves of the central banks of the rest of the world do not exceed on the average about 10 per cent of the liabilities in respect of notes and deposits at call. This is the whole of their effective reserves to meet calls upon them. It is not much with which to meet all the chances and fluctuations of economic life. It follows that a very little upsets them and compels them to look for protection by restricting the supply of credit. But what helps each is not a high Bank rate but a higher rate than the others. So that a raising of rates all round helps no one until, after an interregnum during which the economic activity of the whole world has been retarded, prices and wages have been forced to a lower level.

The following was the position of the four leading banks of the world at the beginning of 1929:—

| | | £ (million) | | |
| | | | Of which | |
	Date of return	Total gold reserves	Legal reserves	Free reserves
U.S. Federal Reserve Banks	Jan. 9	541	304	237
Bank of England	Jan. 9	154	109	45
Bank of France	Jan. 10	263	232	31
Reichsbank	Jan. 7	143	66	68

But this table does not tell the whole story. The strength of the Reichsbank is probably temporary; this institution has been allowing its resources to take the form of gold, rather than foreign balances, in order that any future reduction of them may occur with ostentation. The apparent weakness of the Bank of France is altogether deceptive; for in addition to this gold the Bank of France holds abroad, mostly in London and New York, the gigantic sum of £257,000,000 in liquid reserves. More than £100,000,000 of this is believed to be in London. Thus the Bank of France holds in London, withdrawable at short notice, three or four times the total free reserves of the Bank of England, and also holds simultaneously in New York an amount equal to nearly three quarters of the free reserves of the U.S. Federal Reserve Banks. The Bank of France is in the unprecedented position of being able, if she wished it, to draw to herself practically the whole of the surplus gold of all the central banks of Europe and America.

It is evident that we all survive, and the Bank of England in particular, by favour of the Bank of France. The Bank of France has used her position so far with an extraordinary considerateness, and there is no reason to suppose that she will act otherwise in future. But it would be wholly contrary to French mentality for the Bank of France to remain content with so little free gold at home. It is certain that she will use every convenient opportunity to increase her stock of gold; and no one can prevent her. The question of the sufficiency of the world's gold supplies and the abundance or scarcity of credit in the world's business lies, therefore, for the near future in the hands of the Bank of France. But however gradually and reasonably France draws her gold, there will be a continuing pressure of incipient scarcity on everyone else. Great Britain's free gold being near to nothing, accessions to the Bank of France must necessarily come from Germany, the United States, and the current output of the mines.

It is most timely, therefore, that the League of Nations should be directing attention to the position. Last May the Economic Consultative Committee of the League passed a resolution recalling the fears entertained by the Genoa Conference of the dangers which might arise from undue fluctuations in the purchasing power of gold. In June the Finance Committee, for whom Sir Henry Strakosch had written an excellent memorandum, were authorised by the Council to consider how the League could most usefully assist in the study and solution of the problem; and at the recent meeting of the Council, they were authorised to appoint a special Committee. It is believed that some of the central banks are reluctant to allow the opening up of what might, they feel, be a dangerous discussion. But everyone will suffer alike, in the long run, from a scramble for gold leading to a general restriction of credit. The Finance Committee of the League will be doing the world a service if, within the limits of tactful diplomacy, they press on with the work.

The next month, on 13 February, Keynes lectured members of the Royal United Service Institution on National Finance in War. A full record of his remarks was circulated by the Institution.

Not even the prolegomena to the financial history of the late war have yet been written, and perhaps this history never will be written in any adequate way. Too many of the essential statistics were suppressed at the time and are still difficult or impossible to procure, while our memories of the magnitude of figures and the order of events are growing weak. Today I wish to speak mainly of general principles, but I shall, inevitably, be speaking in the light of the events of the late war, and to a considerable degree with special reference to them. Looking back on them I am struck by the inadequacy of the theoretical views which, so far as I remember, we held at the time as to what was going on. I do not recall that anyone emphasised, during the War what now seems to me the essential feature of the situation, a feature which I shall develop in a few moments.

The importance of current output

The first general principle which I would lay before you is that a country during a war must depend to a far greater degree than is commonly supposed on its current output. Delusions have always been common as to the relative degrees in which a country can depend on its accumulated wealth with which to wage war and on the current effort of its working population during the war. We spoke about mobilising the wealth of the country for the war. Now, if that meant the accumulated capital of the country I say that it was largely a delusion. There is very little of the capital wealth of a country which is capable of being used for war, perhaps fortunately. Countries cannot ruin themselves in war to the extent that they might be willing to, if they were able to, during its course. The wealth of this country, and of all countries, consists mainly of its houses, its railways, its roads, its cultivated fields, its drainage, its agriculture. None of these things can be turned into munitions of war. The liquid stocks of materials which exist in the country at the outbreak of war are of trifling quantity in relation to its needs—perhaps not more than a few weeks' supply at the very outside. So that, putting on one side for the moment something which I will come to later, namely, the possibility of realising foreign investments, what is used during the war will have to be almost wholly produced during the war and produced in the country itself. So that the problem of war economy is to develop the greatest possible surplus of output over the current consumption of the country for other than war purposes. That is the problem in terms of real things, and one will never be clear about the financial part of it unless one has that clear first, and then considers and interprets the financial difficulties that arise in their relation to the real facts behind them.

I say that the problem is to develop the greatest possible surplus of the output of a country over its consumption for ordinary purposes. Now there is always a certain surplus which in ordinary peace times represents the savings of the country *plus* what it expends on replacement, that is to say, on making good the things which have worn out and on keeping buildings and other objects which deteriorate in good condition. In this surplus, namely, the normal savings of the country, we have resources which can be diverted at once to war purposes. On an occasion such as the late war, the amount which we could obtain in that way was, of course, hopelessly inadequate to meet requirements. It has to be expanded; and it can be expanded in two directions, first of all by more work being accomplished, i.e., by greater output, and on the other side, by diminishing consumption. The problem of war finance is a problem of how to secure that the general public should simultaneously put forward more effort and yet consume less; and the study of war finance is a study of the best devices—I might almost say, the best tricks—for securing this; and no financial device which does not either cause people to make more or to consume less is of the slightest use. One or other of those tests must be the criterion of whatever is put forward.

Difficulties to the production of a surplus

Now there are three ways that offer themselves for securing this surplus—this difference between output and consumption, of which two are ordinarily considered as correct, orthodox finance, and the third as something highly undesirable. But—as I shall argue—it is the third which, on the occasion of great emergencies, is the only method which really presents itself as effective, and which, if properly used, may not be so very disadvantageous.

The orthodox methods prescribe that this surplus should be created partly by increased voluntary saving and partly by taxation; that is to say, people should reduce their consumption partly by saving more than usual, partly by being prevented from spending by having some part of their income taken from them by taxes. Voluntary saving, that is to say voluntary reduction of consumption, is obviously excellent so far as it goes. But so very great a part of the current consumption of the country, particularly in war, is by the working classes, that you will certainly not secure sufficient reduction in consumption unless they save, and that is an extraordinarily difficult thing to bring about on an adequate scale. People who have fairly large incomes and can save without depriving themselves to any severe degree may be expected to save. But I do not think it has ever yet been found that any sufficient inducement can be offered, even in wartime, to the great mass of the population voluntarily to undergo privation in order that during the war they may save more. And even if the working classes do something in that direction, they are very unlikely to do enough. They will be earning more than usual. The efforts to increase output will lead to there being no unemployment and a great deal of overtime. If they receive the same rates of wages as before they will be enjoying larger incomes, and it will be extremely difficult to prevent them from spending some part, at any rate, of these increases. No country has found that voluntary saving is a thing on which it can depend.

Theorists have always recommended that that part which cannot be realised by voluntary saving must be raised by taxation. This again is a counsel of perfection, good in so far as it is practicable. But during a war one of the great objectives is to secure an immense amount of effort and output, and it is very difficult to devise a system of taxation which will not in some way or another be a deterrent to such activity. At a moment when you want everybody to be straining themselves to the utmost it is likely to be impolitic to introduce taxes which, however sound financially, will always be liable to exert some influence in the other direction.

War revenue by taxation

But I think there is an even stronger argument against supposing that you can cover the whole of the expenses by taxation, that is to say, taxation unassisted by any other devices—because my ultimate solution is a solution by taxation. It is, to a great extent, the current expenditure of the working classes which has to be curtailed, so that it means not merely a tax on the comparatively rich. Taxation of the comparatively rich will often be, during war, largely at the expense of what they would otherwise have saved. They will probably have curtailed their unnecessary expenditure, and you will only get by taxes what could have been got by voluntary saving. If you are to get enough, therefore, you will have to tax the wages of the working classes. At a rough guess it would certainly have been necessary in the late war to have put a tax on wages of not less than 5/- in the £. It may be very good advice to tell a government to do that, but does anyone see a government in time of war landing itself in all the additional difficulties that a tax on wages would be bound to involve? Actually during the late war, in spite of our exceptional opportunities of taxation during its later phases, of a kind which I shall discuss in a moment, we only raised something like one sixth of the cost of the war by taxes. It does not seem to me serious politics to suggest that we could have kept the country together and carried on the war with taxation vastly heavier than it was. So the war finance will almost inevitably drive the Government and the Treasury back on some further expedient.

Inflation

The nature of this third expedient has been, I think, commonly somewhat misunderstood. The third expedient is the use of the instrument of inflation to bring about forced transferences from the consumer, partly to the government and partly to the *entrepreneur*, who then becomes a suitable object of further taxation. It is the expedient which every government at war has employed, and in the case of a serious war, one which every government always will employ. When a government orders munitions of war at a rate faster than that of current savings as supplemented by taxation—the inevitable effect of such measures must be to cause prices to rise faster than wages. The government secures purchasing power for itself at the expense of the consumer, who is constantly finding that the real value of his income is less than he had supposed. By that means a transference of purchasing power takes place on precisely the scale which is required, in a way which it is impossible for the consumer to avoid, and without the various resistances which would inevitably take place against any form of forced savings or compulsory taxation.

Now, perhaps this sounds very shocking and unorthodox, but in my judgement it only is so if this process is not followed up by something further. What I have to say next is something to which I would particularly invite your attention. The transference which takes place when people find that their incomes are not able to buy as much as they expected, puts some resources directly into the hands of the government. But to a very great extent the gains accrue in the first instance not to the government, but to business men, who, owing to this rise of price, are able to sell what they have produced at an unexpectedly high price which yields them a profit in excess of what they had anticipated. The selling price of their goods is rising all the time faster than their cost of production. That is to say, if this method of forced transference is adopted, the business men are made, in the first instance, the collectors—the agents, so to speak—for the government, to collect the purchasing power which has been thus forcibly diverted from the consumers. It is after this diversion into the hands of the business men has taken place that there comes, in my judgement, the real divergence between the sound finance and unsound finance. If you regard the business men not as agents, but as principals; if you regard them as entitled to these windfall profits, then you are embarking on essentially unsound finance. If you then borrow from the business man,—if you get the money from them in the shape of loans—you are allowing them to act as principals and to obtain a permanent claim against the public which they should never have had. But if, having allowed them to receive this additional sum, you then proceed to withdraw it from them through taxes, and in fact treat them as having been agents for the government, then this device is far and away the most efficient that exists for collecting purchasing power from the consumers and transferring it into the hands of the government.

Taxation of excess profits

I think it is a great tribute to the practical cleverness of this country that by the end of the War this is almost precisely the scheme which we had succeeded in evolving. We allowed prices to rise faster than wages. We did not trouble too much about keeping prices and wages down, because we knew that it would almost certainly react on effort if we were to be fighting prices and wages all the time. There is a sentence in the new volume of Mr Churchill's book in which he remarks that when he was

Minister of Munitions nearly every manifestation of discontent on the part of munition workers had in the end been met by increase of wages, and that the motto of the Government was: 'Let 'em have it, and let's get the stuff'. 'Let 'em have it and let's get the stuff' will inevitably be the motto of all departments in a hurry. But let 'em have it, and do not let 'em keep it; do not trouble too much about what is happening to prices and wages, but make certain that you secure by means of excess profits duties and other forms of direct taxation practically the whole of the excess profits which would otherwise accrue to the business man,—that is the secret of British war finance. It was not carried out with the same completeness in any other country. We found that while you can do something by voluntary saving and something by taxation, these would be inadequate by themselves. By taxation I mean taxation of the ordinary kind—as distinct from the taking away of excess profits duties, etc. We then found that you could obtain this great surplus of output over consumption by constantly allowing the consumer's income to be worth less than he had expected; and then securing for the Treasury the excess profits which thus accrued by means of specially contrived taxes.

In Germany they made the mistake of allowing the business man to keep too much of his profit and of then borrowing it from him. Other countries tried various other expedients. But I believe that the method which we pursued will necessarily be the method which will be employed in any war which involves really great expenses. The mistake which we made in this country was in not developing our method early enough—it was only in the last year of the war that the method of excess profits duty had been completed—and further in not completing the work done by the excess profits duty by means of a capital levy. There ought to have been a capital levy immediately after the end of the war, in 1919, by which the Treasury would have recovered the remaining amount which it had failed to get even by its most efficient excess profits duty. In that case business men would have been treated entirely as agents and not at all as principals, and you would have got the whole of the reduced consumption of the public inuring to the benefit of the state, which during war must be your ultimate objective.

Objections to taxation of excess profits

These methods, of course, have great practical objections to them and are often the seeds of great evils which will follow the conclusion of a war. But I am afraid that in any such event as the late war any government which adhered to orthodox finance and refused the use of any of these expedients would inevitably find that the time factor was against them, and that they could not possibly succeed soon enough in securing the surplus required for the successful conduct of the war. If that is true it is useless to complain against the use of other methods, and one's object should be to perfect these other methods so that they lead to as little ill-consequence as may be. As soon as you realise that you must somehow reduce the value of people's incomes for the purposes of consumption; as soon as you realise that the whole object is to create this surplus and that somehow or other you have to prevent people from consuming as much as they would like, it becomes a matter of secondary importance precisely what device you adopt to bring about this reduction of consumption and the evil only arises if you allow a leakage—if you allow some part of the reduction of consumption of the patient public to inure to the benefit not of the state, but of the profiteer. So that my expedient for war finance would be to permit, in a sense, such an amount of profiteering as was required for extreme activity of output and then to devise technical methods for securing to the state the profits of the entrepreneur. As I say, during the war the Treasury and the Board of Inland Revenue in effect evolved precisely this system, but they did it by methods of trial and error without fully realising in the earlier stages exactly what they were doing or exactly what the justification for it was.

Sources of revenue abroad

I have omitted so far one feature of war finance, namely, the possibility of raising resources abroad. That is a direction in which the accumulated wealth of a country has some importance. But here again, I think public opinion attaches too much importance to the relief that can be obtained from this source. In our case we were in a position of unexampled strength to benefit in that way, because we had a large volume of American securities which we sold to America and we realised a very substantial sum in that way. But even so, we were not in a position to realise substantial sums relatively to the cost of the War. If by such realisations and by borrowing abroad you could raise 10 per cent of the cost of the War you would be very successful. This is necessarily, therefore, an expedient of secondary importance.

During the whole of the War this country borrowed in neutral countries a sum of about £42,000,000 or less than 1/200th part of the cost of the War. And it was not through not trying. I think I was myself responsible for drafting all the financial agreements that related to the raising of those loans, and the limitation of the possibilities was exceedingly plain. Further, it is an expedient only open to the state which at any given moment appears to be on the winning side. What was happening in the field used to make an extraordinary difference to the possibility of borrowing in neutral countries. During the early part of 1918, for example, the possibilities of such borrowing dried up almost completely. The whole tone of the negotiations was altered. But what we borrowed from America falls, of course, into a different category. That was on a very large scale and of enormous importance. But even including what we borrowed from America we only paid something like one seventh of the expenses of the War out of foreign loans, of which the greater part came from the American Government and was offset by what we lent to our allies. We were, in fact, a conduit pipe for collecting foreign money and then distributing it to our allies. We lent to our allies during the War more than we borrowed abroad; so that so far as the war expenditure of this country was concerned, as distinct from the expenditure of our allies, we obtained no assistance from foreign borrowing. You may take it that practically the whole of our war effort came out of the current output of the country during the period of the War. This is a most extraordinary fact,—that the vast production of goods was achieved in addition to what was required to keep body and soul together during the War. It shows, as compared with the existing situation, what is possible in the way of the creation of wealth with whole-hearted organisation, when everybody's efforts are directed to the production of the maximum quantity of material things.

When one looks back on the course of events one feels, as I have just said, that the high taxation of profits should have been started sooner and should have been rounded off at the end by a capital levy, but that, subject to that, it was true, what sometimes the Treasury was disposed to deny and what other people were inclined to affirm, namely, that at home there could be no financial problem in the proper sense of the word, provided the Government could secure the goods. The question of financing them was in the nature of a contrivance rather than a fundamental factor.

The exterior financial crisis, 1916–17

But when you come to the foreign situation that is by no means the truth. Even though it was true that the purists took up too strict a view as to the home position, the spending departments were inclined to take up too lax a view as regards expenditure abroad. In my opinion, the rate at which this country was entering into foreign commitments in 1916, before the United States came into the War, was reckless in the extreme and might have involved us in exceedingly serious trouble if the United States had not come in,—which was something we were by no means banking on in the latter part of 1916. On the financial front there is no question that the worst point of the war was in the period between December, 1916, and the entry of America into the War in the Spring of 1917. Our power of meeting foreign payments at the end of 1916 had been almost exhausted. The history of those weeks has never yet been written, and the outside world by no means guessed the degree of our extremity. Indeed, now that so many war memoirs have been published, it is remarkable to discover that when the German Government were wondering whether unrestricted 'U boat' warfare would be worth while, no one in the German Government seems to have raised the point: Is it not possible that the British Treasury are getting into deep water and that the only thing that can save them will be the entry of the United States into the war? That was a point which was not mentioned, so far as I know, in any of the revelations which have been made in regard to the counsels of the German Government at that time. If it had not been for the entry of the United States into the War, nothing is more certain than that we could not have continued, at the rate at which we were buying in 1916, either our purchases of munitions from abroad or the assistance which we were giving to our allies. That was partly the result of the greatly increased rate of expenditure during 1916. I feel, in looking back, that that was our outstanding point of weakness; and the general principle which I should draw from it is this,—that whilst the home financial problem could be in a certain sense neglected, the foreign financial problem must always be one to which the most careful and meticulous calculations should be accorded from day to day.

The financing of allies

There is another aspect of war finance which played a great part in the late war, although it may not play so great a part in other wars, and that was the question of financing our allies and the methods adopted—an exceedingly difficult question. I do not feel much clearer about it now than I did at the time. I was in charge of the department of the Treasury which was concerned particularly with the business of arranging the assistance given to the allies and of endeavouring to control it. First of all there was the political side to it. A certain amount of the financial support accorded to the allies was in order to secure and retain the support of those who, at any rate in the first instance or at the moment, might be dubious allies. But whilst a certain amount of assistance was given on political grounds, it was often exceedingly difficult to distinguish between the political aspect and the purely economic aspect. Thus, there is a tendency for what would be, on economic grounds, the right sort of control to be rejected on political grounds, and for no one to be very clear-headed as to where one begins and the other ends. Apart from that, every ally not unnaturally tries to put as much of the burden on the others as he can. Naturally, it is the object of every Treasury during war to save its own resources so far as it can, and, whenever there is a plausible case for it, to obtain all the assistance it is able to obtain from outside. That means that an exceedingly meticulous check on all expenditure has to be adopted. The method of lending to allies instead of subsidising them was, in my judgement, essentially in the nature of a device. It follows that the inter-allied debts are a very objectionable feature of the post-war settlement. But psychologically it was, during the War, necessary to finance the allies in that way, because it did to a certain extent diminish the strength of the motive to throw the greatest possible burden on to us. Much more important, however, was the necessity of Treasury control over allied expenditure—which raises very ticklish questions. In the early days of the War we would lend to a certain ally a certain number of millions of pounds and leave the spending of it to them. Then it used to happen that in a few months or a few weeks they would spend that money and come for more; to which we would reply: 'You have spent it too soon, too quickly'; but there would be no means by that time of demonstrating whether it had been wisely or extravagantly spent. Therefore in 1915–16, a system was gradually evolved by which all of the allies, with the exception of France, had to obtain British Treasury sanction for every single purchase of any magnitude which they were making abroad which was to be paid for out of British money, in order that we might test the wisdom of the expenditure day-by-day as it was incurred. That was an extraordinarily difficult thing to do with wisdom, but there would unquestionably have been an immense amount of waste if this method had not been adopted.

The relations between the Treasury and the spending departments

That leads me to a general question which lies at the heart of national finance in war, and that is the right relation between the Treasury, as the controlling department, and the spending departments. So far as expenditure in this country was involved, the Treasury during the war recognised that the financial problem was secondary and Treasury control was practically suspended. But it was maintained necessarily and rightly, so far as related to expenditure outside this country and in the case of loans to our allies. That Treasury control could have been carried out much more efficiently, I think, if there had been a profounder understanding and sympathy between the Treasury and the spending departments, is manifest. I suppose it is inevitable in war that every department should exaggerate its own importance and believe that it, and it alone, is going to win the war, and that any attempt to diminish its rate of expenditure is to be regarded as cheese-paring. But if the spending departments could really understand that it is a choice between alternatives, and that anyone who misleads the Treasury as to the situation is causing the money to be spent in a wrong way instead of in a right way, a very much more efficient division of the national resources would be reached than was actually the case. There were many notorious instances of an analogous kind, when the shortage of shipping occurred. Many departments in their eagerness to obtain freight facilities would exaggerate their needs and possibly give misleading information as to stocks in order to get more than their share of the available shipping space. In the same way there would be a tendency to try and get more than their share of the available finance. That was a source of very great inefficiency—of less inefficiency, perhaps, in this country than in some others, yet I never felt that the right relations existed between the Treasury and the spending departments in this particular respect. If the spending departments had had a more profound understanding of the basic nature of war finance, a much higher degree of efficiency could have been obtained.

Finance as a preventive of war

I have been talking mainly about how finance can be made efficient for the purposes of war. I should like to conclude on a different note, namely, the possible efficiency of finance for the purpose of preventing war. A few days ago a report of the Finance Committee of the League of Nations was published which has obtained far less attention and publicity than it deserves. This Committee of the League of Nations has been working for some time on the question as to whether the financial power of the leading countries of the world could be employed as an instrument for the preservation of peace. They have now reached the point of putting forward certain pro-visional and tentative proposals. The essence of those proposals is that an arrangement should be made beforehand by which the leading powers represented on the League should definitely agree, each taking its proper quota, that they would guarantee loans to the party in a dispute which the Council of the League decided was not the aggressor—that the whole thing should be cut-and-dried beforehand, so that the loans could be floated through the agency of the Financial Committees of the League with the least possible delay. For the prevention of war, particularly between minor powers, that seems to me to be a weapon of immense effect, because of the terrific importance which I have been stressing, of the external finances of a country during a period of hostilities. For a poor country which has no foreign investments and not much credit of its own, a country which has very inferior opportunities for manufacturing its own munitions, foreign finance is absolutely vital. Suppose the League of Nations was in a position to say that the injured party, or the party which was the injured party according the decision of the League, should forthwith have financial assistance in the form of foreign currency up to, say, £50,000,000, that would be almost a decisive factor in keeping the peace among all minor nations. Take a case which might lead up to much more serious consequences—a war between two minor powers in the Balkans. I do not think the aggressor could stand up for a moment against a decision on the part of the League that financial assistance of that sort on that scale would be given instantly to the other party. It would practically settle the war before it had been begun. It is essential, however, for an arrangement of that kind that everything should be arranged beforehand—that all the great powers should be committed to follow the lead of the League in the matter so that there would be no avoidable delay. That, I understand, is the proposal of the Finance Committee. No country would have to support more than a reasonable burden. I feel it to be of the utmost importance that public attention should be concentrated on the possibilities of a development of this kind. It arms the League of Nations with a purely pacific instrument of a positive kind. I agree that for the prevention of major wars between very great powers other methods must be relied on. But the threat to the disturbance of the peace is much more likely to come in the first instance through troubles between minor powers than between major powers; and in such cases I believe that the possibilities of the methods now suggested are by no means, as yet, fully appreciated.

On 7 February, after struggling for some months to hold Bank rate at $4\frac{1}{2}$ per cent in the face of substantial outflows of funds to the United States, the Bank of England raised its rate a full percentage point. Keynes's comments appeared in the next *Nation*.

From The Nation and Athenaeum, *16 February 1929*

THE BANK RATE: FIVE-AND-A-HALF PER CENT

After remaining at $4\frac{1}{2}$ per cent for the best part of two years, the Bank rate has been raised to $5\frac{1}{2}$ per cent,—the highest figure since 1921. There is nothing in business and financial conditions at home to justify this step; it is wholly consequent on the rates which, for its own domestic reasons, the Federal Reserve Board is maintaining in the United States. Nevertheless, it is useless to blame the Bank of England for being dragged at the heels of America. Indeed the Bank has done very well—considering the rates in Berlin and New York—to maintain its rate at the lower figure for so many months. For I cannot agree with those critics who seem to suppose that, having returned to the gold standard, we can, all the same, behave as though we had not. The present episode is one of the inevitable by-products of the policy we have deliberately chosen.

Presumably the Governor of the Bank of England, who was recently in New York, has satisfied himself that there is no chance of the American rates coming down in the near future. In this case an upward movement in our Bank rate was probably inevitable. It is true that this can do no good to the prospects of British employment and may do serious harm. But there are two considerations of a more cheerful kind which we need to emphasise. In the first place the necessity to raise our Bank rate is not to be interpreted as a sign of real weakness. In the second place, it need not react disastrously on the industrial situation at home, *if the attendant measures taken by the Bank of England are of the right kind*.

So far from London having shown signs of weakness, I think

that any candid critic must reckon it as a sign of considerable underlying financial strength, that it should have been possible for the London money market to last out so long with its rates so much below those of New York. Unquestionably this continuing disparity of rates must have attracted foreign short-term borrowing to the London market on a substantial scale, partly by the withdrawal of foreign funds previously deposited here, partly by remittances of British funds to New York to take advantage of the high rates obtaining there, and most of all by the increased volume of bills, arising out of international trade, accepted and discounted in London. It is probable that we could not have supported this drain until now, if it had not been for a surprising number of financial windfalls which have come our way, out of the bounty of Wall Street, in recent months. The sale at prodigious prices by British investors to American optimists of such things as Columbia Graphophone shares, Ford of England, General Electrics, Mond Nickel, South American telephone properties, and many others may easily have brought in upwards of £50,000,000 within quite a brief period. This will have been partly offset by British investments in the United States and by an undue complaisance towards excessive Australian loans, and the like, in the shape of new overseas issues in London. But I should surmise that a fair proportion of our windfalls has been absorbed in meeting the drain from the international short-loan market under the pressure of dear money in New York and Berlin. This means that—looking a little further ahead—we have materially strengthened our real position and have liquidated a part of London's previous indebtedness. When American rates come down again and the pressure of reparation remittances once more turns the tide against Berlin—both of which events are fairly probable before the end of the year—we can expect to get our gold back again. If only we knew our *net* position in the international short-loan market, I believe we should find that it is better today, even after allowing for our loss of gold, than it was six months

797

ago. Doubtless we still owe far too much to the Bank of France—but that is another story.

The main question, however, is how best to mitigate the blow to the industrial prospects at home. I have very strong convictions on this point, for which I beg most earnestly the attention of our financial authorities. There are—broadly speaking —three sets of circumstances, in which it is necessary to raise Bank rate. First, to check a tendency to excessive expansion and speculation at home, in which case it is of the essence of the proceeding to curtail *the volume* of credit as well as to raise its price. Secondly, to bring interest rates at home into line with the real rate of interest on investment prevailing in the world at large, in which case the chief thing is to weaken the bond and investment market and to make short-money rates as effective as possible in this direction. Thirdly, to stop a drain on our short-loan position, and hence on our gold reserves due to a temporary technical position abroad. The first set of circumstances does not exist today—far from it. Nor does the second in my judgement—our trouble in this field is due to the supply of new investments at home being inadequate to permit a right distribution of our current savings between home and foreign loans, having regard to our available balance of trade. Unquestionably it is the third which character-ises the present position.

Now the international short-loan market is exceedingly sensitive to the *rate of interest*. Business, on the other hand, is far more sensitive to the *quantity* of credit than it is to a moderate change in its price. If the same or a greater quantity of credit than before is made available to business, the evils ensuing on its costing 1 per cent more may not be very great; whereas the results of a curtailment in the volume of credit would be disastrous. The problem before the Bank of England is, therefore, to make the higher rate effective in the short-loan market without curtailing the volume of credit. In the long run this might prove impracticable. But for a few months I believe that it is perfectly feasible by agreement between the Bank of

England, the Big Five, and the money market. If the rates charged by the banks for loans and particularly for loans to the call market and for bills are maintained at the higher level by agreement, then the existing volume of credit can be safely maintained and even augmented. If some existing borrowers are deterred by the higher rates, their place can be taken by new borrowers who were left unsatisfied before or by the banks facilitating the issue of long-period bonds to finance capital improvements at home. If this can be managed, the volume of employment need not suffer—and might even improve. If not, unemployment will increase as surely as night follows day.

Therefore our programme should have three heads. To keep the higher rate effective in the short-loan market by agreement. To increase the basis of credit by the Bank of England purchasing securities—at least until it is proved to be impossible to combine this with keeping the higher rate effective. To press on with capital developments at home.

On the other hand, to allow unemployment to spread would be, at this juncture, a rather dangerous thing.

So far as concerns our relations with the American Federal Reserve Board, one hopes that the Governor of the Bank of England has come to an understanding on the following points. Since we are assisting the aims of the Federal Reserve Board in raising our rate, they must not raise theirs still further; for if they do, we shall be no further forward. Secondly, they must take all the steps in their power, other than a higher rate, to remedy what they deem objectionable in the present technical position in New York, and—if they are not successful within another six months—abandon what may be a misguided attempt. For it is scarcely playing the gold-standard game for the Federal Reserve authorities to use their preponderant position to jeopardise the trading prosperity of the whole world in pursuit of a local objective which many well-instructed Americans believe to lie at the extreme edge of, and possibly outside, their proper sphere of action.

On 23 February *The Economist* published an article on Free Trade and Protection which contained a statement Keynes took exception to. In the ensuing weeks, in a series of letters he tried to draw the Editor out.

To the Editor of The Economist, *26 February 1929*

Sir,

In an article on Free Trade and Protection published in your issue of February 23 you write as follows:—'Capital exports stimulate commodity exports—a statement which will be supported by all, only with a variety of emphasis and qualification.' It will, I think, be helpful if you will develop this point a little further, explaining by what chain of causation the result follows.

Where the borrower borrows expressly for the purpose of making purchases in this country, as was often the case with the railway loans of the mid-nineteenth century, the connection is obvious. It is also arguable that any loan gives a fillip to international trade, from which we all benefit roughly in the proportion which our trade bears to the trade of the world. Let us suppose, for the sake of illustration, that 20 per cent of the sums which we lend abroad—and I should think that this proportion is higher than the truth—leads more or less directly to exports in the manner described above. But what about the remaining 80 per cent? The train of causation by which this leads to commodity exports is what I should like to see explained in detail.

Yours, etc.,
J. M. KEYNES

The Editor tried to oblige Keynes when he published Keynes's letter on 9 March. This explanation did not succeed, for the Editor published another letter the next week with further comment.

To the Editor of The Economist, *16 March 1929*

Sir,

In reply to my inquiry for an explanation as to *how* foreign investment stimulates exports, in those cases in which it does not directly lead to additional purchases of British goods by foreigners, you reply:—'The cumulative effect on the world's exchanges as a whole of such increases in the supply of sterling for sale is to make the pound cheaper, which involves the relative cheapening of goods whose price is expressed in terms of sterling; in other words, to stimulate British exports and to hinder our imports.'

This seems to me to be quite a correct account of what would happen if we were not on the gold standard. Is it that you have overlooked the fact of our return to gold? For the possible changes in the price of sterling within the gold points are insignificant in their effect on the price of goods. Moreover, it is impossible that sterling should be cheaper than it is now—so long as we remain on the gold standard.

Your argument does not make sense, therefore, unless your meaning is that foreign investment stimulates exports by driving us off the gold standard. But this, I take it, is not your meaning. So I still await an answer to my question.

Yours, etc.,

J. M. KEYNES

This explanation was also incomplete, for Keynes wrote two days later.

To the Editor of The Economist, *18 March 1929*

Sir,

I thank you for your comment on my letter, which carries the argument a step further. In answer to my question as to how foreign lending on our part indirectly stimulates British exports in those cases where it does not do so directly, you reply that (amongst other things) it causes a tendency for gold to flow abroad, which in turn leads to a rise in Bank rate, and it is this rise in Bank rate which stimulates exports. I think that exporters (who have not been as grateful as, on your theory, they should have been for the recent rise of Bank rate) would like to have it explained in what way a higher Bank rate improves their competitive position in foreign markets. For, on the face of it, it is a paradox that an increase in one of the items of their costs of production should have this effect. Since you think my method a little abstract, I suggest that you might illustrate your reply by reference to the benefits accruing from a higher Bank rate to one or another of our leading export industries—for example, textiles or coal or the iron and steel trades.

Yes; I had noticed that the Balfour Commission agree with you—which makes it all the more important that the details of the argument should be elucidated.

Yours, etc.,

J. M. KEYNES

The correspondence concluded with another letter, which appeared on 6 April.

To the Editor of The Economist, *26 March 1929*

Sir,

This time, I fear, your comment on my letter does *not* carry the argument a step further. For you only repeat what you said before—namely, that a higher Bank rate stimulates exports because it 'tends to lower sterling prices in general and thus enhances British competitive power in foreign markets'. But you do not give your readers the slightest hint as to *how* a higher Bank rate brings this about.

May I, therefore, offer a suggestion? I know of only two ways in which this effect can be produced by that cause, of which the first can be only temporary and of secondary importance. In the first place, holders of stocks of commodities may (conceivably) be induced by the higher cost of carrying them to throw their goods on the market at a loss or at less than their usual profit. But, clearly, this cannot last, and is a precarious (and unprofitable) foundation on which to base an increased export trade. May I take it that you do not merely mean that a higher Bank rate stimulates exports by compelling British manufacturers to sell their goods at a loss?

If then, we dismiss this particular effect of dear money as having no enduring value, it would seem that a higher Bank rate can only stimulate exports if it reduces, not merely prices, but *costs of production*. For here we should be on firmer ground. And here, indeed, we may find the answer to the conundrum. For a higher Bank rate, due to a loss of gold, is generally associated with a curtailment of credit, which in turns limits the opportunities of business men to provide employment. New unemployment, if it is sufficiently severe and sufficiently prolonged, may be expected in the end to bring down the rates of wages. Here at last is our goal. For if wages are reduced, 'British competitive power in foreign markets' is indubitably enhanced; and exports are increased.

Have I rightly interpreted your meaning? Have you any other explanation?

I have not ventured at any time in the course of this correspondence to deny your conclusion that, if we lend more abroad, this will stimulate our exports. For, evidently, there must be a balance between the two. I have only wanted to be clear just how this comes about; and I thank you for your collaboration in reaching the above conclusion. If next time you applaud the tendency of foreign lending to stimulate exports, you will add the explanatory words 'because it will make the maintenance of full employment impossible at the present level of wages, so that unemployment will continue until British wages are reduced, which will enhance our competitive power in foreign markets', then I will promise to write you no more letters!

Yours, &c.,

J. M. KEYNES

During the winter of 1928–9 a special committee of the Liberal party, chaired by Seebohm Rowntree, developed specific proposals for national development along the lines of the Yellow Book, *Britain's Industrial Future*. Keynes had attended many of the meetings that discussed these proposals and advised Mr Lloyd George to issue a dramatic pledge to a meeting of Liberal M.P.s and candidates on 1 March:

> If the nation entrusts the Liberal Party at the next General Election with the responsibilities of government, we are ready with schemes of work which we can put immediately into operation...The work put in hand will reduce the terrible figures of the workless in the course of a single year to normal proportions, and will, when completed, enrich the nation and equip it for competing successfully with all its rivals in the business of the world. These plans will not add one penny to national or local taxation.

The committee's proposals for putting the pledge into effect were published in a pamphlet entitled *We Can Conquer Unemployment*, soon named the Orange Book. Keynes analysed the programme on 19 March.

From The Evening Standard, *19 March 1929*

MR LLOYD GEORGE'S PLEDGE

Mr Lloyd George's pledge to reduce unemployment has been received by the other parties, and by the public, too, with mixed feelings—a suspicion that it must, surely, be a bit exaggerated, and an even stronger suspicion that there may, after all, be something in it.

The first suspicion is a curious symptom of the fatalistic state of mind into which we have fallen about unemployment. Why should we think it improbable that the disease of unemployment can be cured? For the present condition of affairs is an abnormal one, whether in the history of our own country or of any other. Why should we distrust Mr Lloyd George's very common-sense, and, indeed, obvious remedy?

'We have unemployed men and unemployed plant. It has gone on for years. There are many possible improvements in the equipment of this country which readily occur to one. Why not employ men and the plant on making the improvements?' This, in effect, is all he has said. The extraordinary thing is that it should make a sensation, or that any one should contradict him.

To hear Cabinet Ministers talk one would suppose that he was promising to make chickens out of cheese. It could not be so if we had not allowed our heads to be stuffed full of sophistries as contrary to sound logic as they are to common sense.

Let me try to answer the questions which I imagine reasonable men to be asking. First of all, are there things worth doing? Or is this country a completed proposition incapable of further development or improvement, a finished structure needing nothing more for ever than an occasional coat of paint?

The answer is obvious. For several years Royal Commissions, local authorities, and Government Departments have been putting forward all sorts of schemes as necessary and desirable and, often, as urgent, and the Treasury have been pigeonholing them. They have been pigeonholing them under the influence of what I can only describe as a mental affliction.

They have believed that, if people can be induced to save as much as possible, and if steps are then taken to prevent anything being done with these savings, the rate of interest will fall, and if the rate of interest falls the national debt will cost less.

Subject to a leakage to be mentioned in a moment, this is quite true. Indeed, if all forms of capital enterprise were to be rendered illegal, the rate of interest would sink towards zero—while the rate of unemployment would mount towards heaven.

So complete an achievement is beyond the Treasury's power. But, unfortunately, they have a voice in nearly all the forms of capital enterprise which are capable of absorbing large sums of money—housing, roads and bridges, telephones, electricity, drainage, ports, etc.

Even so, there is the leakage hinted at above. For if we save and can find no outlet for our savings at home, we lend the money abroad on a scale disproportionate to our export surplus at the present level of wages, the Bank of England loses gold and raises the Bank rate.

So in the end, the Treasury find that all their well-intentioned prudence has gone for nothing, and that they haven't even got a lower rate of interest.

Let them, then, reverse their policy and plunge a lively hand into the pigeonholes. The Liberal pamphlet, *We can Conquer Unemployment* (Cassell, 6d.), amounts to no more than this. It is mainly a recapitulation of the recommendations of Royal Commissions and other official or semi-official bodies.

I am reminded of the first time I ever set eyes on Mr Lloyd George. I was an undergraduate at the Cambridge Union shortly after the Boer War. Mr Lloyd George, not a popular figure in those days, came down to a Visitor's Debate to arraign the Government's conduct of the late war.

He delivered an attack in highly rhetorical tones suggestive of exaggeration, and finally succeeded in stimulating the opposition to cry out 'Question! Question!'

'Do honourable members question my remarks?'

'Yes.'

The tone changed. Out of his tail-coat pocket came the blue-covered Report of the Royal Commission. In a quiet voice Mr Lloyd George read out from the Commissioners' conclusions the same words *verbatim* which, having got them by heart, he had previously clothed with rhetorical fervour.

Twenty-six years and another war have passed by. Popularity and power have come and gone. But he is doing it again!

Would the demand for labour resulting from a practicable programme of capital development make an appreciable impression on the existing unemployment?

It is reasonable to suppose that an investment of £250, in types of capital production which do not require a heavy proportion of imports, will provide wages to employ the equivalent of at least one man for a year, after meeting outgoings other than wages, and that man, in spending his wages, will set further miscellaneous productive activity moving.

Thus it is a conservative estimate, in my opinion, to assume that each £1,000,000 of the kind of investment contemplated by Mr Lloyd George's programme will reduce unemployment by at least 5,000 to 6,000 men, and perhaps by more.

For, once the impulse to prosperity has been started the effect will be cumulative. Accordingly, an investment programme of £100,000,000 might be expected to break the back of the abnormal unemployment. Anyway, the problem of transferring labour will be insoluble unless we first create opportunities of employment elsewhere.

Now for the most searching question of all. Will the financing of this programme merely divert capital from other uses, and thereby cause just as much unemployment in other directions? I answer, No!

It will, I hope, divert a considerable amount of what is now being lent to foreigners, enough both to relieve the present strain on the Bank of England and to finance the additional imports which the development programme will require.

It will be necessary to offer a rate of interest which can compete with foreign borrowers. How much margin there is for borrowing without using inflationary methods cannot be safely predicted until we try. But all the indications suggest that it is large.

It will be time enough for prudence when we see prices tending to rise and the demand for labour in excess of the supply.

The orthodox theory *assumes* that everyone is employed. If this were so, a stimulus in one direction would be at the expense of production in others. But when there is a large surplus of *unused* productive resources, as at present, the case is totally different.

The notion that saving and investment are always exactly balanced—i.e., that whenever I save £100 some entrepreneur sets on foot a new capital enterprise for £100—is an unfounded delusion. So is the view that our exports will increase by £2,000,000 because last week we lent £2,000,000 to Chile.

Moreover, if the above were true, it would be just as true that the building of a new factory by Sir Herbert Austin or Mr Samuel Courtauld would add nothing to employment—which nobody believes. In short, the fatalistic belief that there can never be more employment than there is is altogether baseless.

I do not doubt that Mr Lloyd George's programme would greatly increase employment. Just how fast he could overcome inertia and get things moving no one can say until he tries. But he has promised nothing so improbable of accomplishment to the doubting mind as the munitions programme, safely delivered, of 1916.

On 14 April Sir Laming Worthington-Evans, the Secretary for War, suggested in *The Evening Standard* that Lloyd George would be able to fulfil neither his employment nor his taxation pledges and he attacked Keynes's reasoning. Keynes replied on 19 April, echoing the arguments of chapter IX of *Can Lloyd George Do It?* (*JMK*, vol. IX, pp. 115–21) which was soon to appear.

From The Evening Standard, *19 April 1929*

A CURE FOR UNEMPLOYMENT

The reply by Sir Laming Worthington-Evans, published in Friday's *Evening Standard*, to my article defending the Liberal policy of capital development as a cure for unemployment is very timely. For it discloses in a most straightforward way what is, I do not doubt, one of the main reasons which have influenced the Government in their policy—practised with disastrous results for four years—of strangling to the full extent that public opinion will allow all capital improvements in this country which are controlled or influenced by the Treasury.

Sir Laming's *credo* is as follows:—

He believes that, whatever we do, all the savings of the country, or approximately all, find their outlet in employment. Thus the housing schemes have not materially increased employment. If they had not existed something else would have taken their place.

Conversely, Mr Lloyd George's schemes will not materially diminish unemployment: they will only displace some other kind of enterprise. Equally, if Mr Courtauld builds a new factory, someone else, whose credit is not so good, will be unable to build one. For there is nothing in the reasoning to lead us to differentiate between the effects of state investment and those of private investment.

There is, therefore, little or nothing that the Government can usefully do. For Sir Laming's argument implies that the aggregate sum which can be made available for investment in this country is not enough to employ everyone. So the case is hopeless, and we must just drift along.

In his Budget speech on Monday the Chancellor of the Exchequer repeated the same thing.

'It is the orthodox Treasury dogma, steadfastly held', he told the House of Commons, 'that whatever might be the political or social advantages, very little additional employment and no permanent additional employment can, in fact, and as a general rule, be created by state borrowing and state expenditure'. Some state expenditure, he concluded is inevitable and even wise and right for his own sake,—*but not as a cure for unemployment.*

The issue is, therefore, joined on a clear and definite question. I say that the Treasury dogma is fallacious. It is neither plausible nor true. It is not supported by the leading economists of the country. Professor Pigou, Mr McKenna, Sir Josiah Stamp—to quote authorities of diverse gifts—will tell him that it is erroneous.

Certainly this dogma is not derived from common sense. On the contrary, it is a highly sophisticated theory. No ordinary man, left to himself, is able to believe that, if there had been no housing schemes in recent years, there would, nevertheless, have been just as much employment.

He is much readier to believe that if the overwhelming weight of public opinion had not, in this particular case, forced the hand of the Treasury the unemployed would probably have reached two million. And, accordingly, most ordinary men are easily persuaded by Mr Lloyd George that, if his new enterprises are set in motion, more men will be employed.

But the theory lacks truth as well as plausibility. There are three sources from which means can be found to enable new investment to provide a net addition to the amount of employment within the country.

In the first place savings—namely, the excess of the incomes of individuals over their consumption—do not necessarily materialise in investments. The amount of investment in capital improvements depends, on the one hand, on the amount of credit created by the Bank of England; and, on the other hand, on the eagerness of entrepreneurs to invest, of whom the Government itself—since the amount of expenditure on roads, electricity, telephones, ports, drainage, and also on railways and houses mainly depends on its policy—is nowadays the most important.

When the demand for investment at home is brisk, the Bank of England can safely create more credit without losing its gold, than it can when the additional credit is used to lend abroad. So far from the total of investment, as determined by these factors, being necessarily equal to the total of saving, disequilibrium between the two is at the root of many of our troubles.

When investment runs ahead of saving we have a boom, intense employment, and a tendency to inflation. When investment lags behind we have a slump and abnormal unemployment, as at present. For all the indications suggest that it would be safe today to create more credit, provided it was being absorbed by home investment and not by foreign lending.

I turn to the second source. Individual saving means that some individuals are *producing* more than they are *consuming*. This surplus may, and should, be used to increase capital equipment. But unfortunately this is not the only way in which it can be used. It can also be used to enable other individuals to *consume* more than they *produce*.

This is what happens when there is unemployment. We are using our savings to pay for unemployment, instead of using them to equip the country. The savings which Mr Lloyd George's schemes will employ will be diverted not from financing other capital equipment but largely from financing unemployment. From the unemployment fund alone we are now paying out £50,000,000 a year; and this is not the whole of the waste of savings which is now going on.

The whole of the labour of the unemployed is available to increase the national wealth. It is crazy to believe that we shall ruin ourselves financially by trying to find means for using it and that safety lies in continuing to maintain men in idleness.

It is precisely *with* our unemployed productive resources that we shall make the new investments.

The third source of funds required for the Liberal policy will be found by a reduction of foreign lending. But this will not operate, as Sir Laming supposes, by a reduction of our exports. Partly it will relieve the pressure on the Bank of England; and partly it will take the form of an increase in our imports; for the new schemes will require a certain amount of imported raw materials, and those who are now unemployed will consume more imported food when they are once again earning decent wages.

Why is it, then, that Sir Laming holds such very odd opinions? It is like asking me why he wears a top hat. He is a Conservative. The reasons are wrapped in the mists of history. But, roughly, I think I know them. He half understands an ancient theory, the premises of which he has forgotten.

This theory assumes that all the productive resources— savings, labour and the gifts of nature—which are at any time in existence are normally employed because, so the argument assumes, whenever they are unemployed they are ready to accept a lower rate of remuneration, and employment will always be forthcoming at a sufficiently low rate of wages. That is to say, the theory starts off by assuming the non-existence of the very phenomenon which is under investigation.

Sir Laming's final point is directed to my admission that we shall have to pay a rate of interest which is in due relation to the rate of interest in the world at large.

Obviously we cannot avoid inflation, if we refuse to pay the appropriate rates of interest. But, of course, this does not mean, as Sir Laming alleges, in a passage which suggests an astonishing ignorance of the principles governing the relative rates of interest on different types of bonds, that the British Government would have to pay the *same* rate that foreign borrowers are now paying.

Sir Laming Worthington-Evans replied with an article which quoted Keynes's published views over a period of years. He suggested that Keynes was speaking as a politician, not as an economist, and it was misleading the electors and cruel to the unemployed to suggest that Lloyd George had discovered a new cure for unemployment. Keynes replied in a letter to the editor.

To the Editor of The Evening Standard, *30 April 1929*

Sir,

Sir Laming Worthington-Evans has shifted the controversy from the very interesting question, 'What will cure unemployment?' to the question—moderately interesting to me, but not equally so, I should suppose to the readers of *The Evening Standard*—'Has Mr Keynes changed his mind in the course of the last five years?' Politicians, I know, always much prefer to discuss one another's pasts to the merits of an argument. But what a boring method of controversy it is!

Sir Laming's selection of isolated sentences from articles of mine scattered over five years cannot, of course, give an intelligible summary of my past opinions. But how can I confute false suggestions except by reprinting substantial portions of these articles? And who would be interested if I did? I can only say that I began advocating schemes of National Development as a cure for unemployment four years or more ago—indeed, as soon as I realised that, the effect of the return to gold having been to put our money rates of wages too high relatively to our foreign competitors we could not, for a considerable time, hope to employ as much labour as formerly in the export industries.

Right or wrong, I have been singularly consistent—indeed, obstinate. Moreover, Sir Laming is quite mistaken in supposing that he has economic orthodoxy on his side. I know no British economist of reputation who supports the proposition that schemes of National Development are incapable of curing unemployment. Sir Laming, not I, is 'the mad Mullah'.

Boiled down, Sir Laming's criticisms are directed to two admissions, which I have never hesitated to make. I have always admitted that, when everyone is employed, those prices which are determined locally and are not governed by world prices may rise slightly. If, at long last, you bring deflation to an end, some slight rise of prices is clearly probable. I have also admitted that, in order to avoid inflation, it will be necessary to maintain interest rates at a figure adjusted to world rates.

Sir Laming reckons, I suppose, that these are the phrases which—the argument apart—have the most unpopular sound. Let me say a word about each of them.

On the rate of interest I owe him an apology. I read his former article as suggesting that the British Government might have to pay as much as foreign borrowers. I am glad that I misunderstood him, and that even he does not expect that the rate payable would be much higher than the present Bank rate.

But his view, that it is better to have a million unemployed than that British rates of interest should be on a parity with world rates, seems to me, like some of his other opinions, extremely odd. Moreover, what we have at present is *both* unemployment *and* dear money. Regarded as a cheap money policy, the Government's achievements up to date are scarcely a success.

On the question of the rise of prices, I invite him to think again. He brightened up his former article by declaring in this connection that 'Mr Keynes is gambling with the people's food.' I admit that when a million families are earning full wages and are filling their bellies again they will buy more food. The effect of this on the world prices of food will be very trifling.

On the other hand, in the case of home-produced food—for example milk, which is not governed by world prices—it is idle to deny that increased demand might enable our farmers to get a slightly better price for their produce. But there is nothing in the Liberal policy to send food prices up except an increased demand for food from those who now go hungry. This is a form of 'gambling with the people's food' which I am ready to risk.

Conversely, if Sir Laming can increase unemployment to *two* million, he may have the satisfaction of seeing prices fall a little further. And if the housing subsidy is finally abolished and Mr Churchill raids again what remains of the Road Fund, it is even possible that the rate of interest might fall a trifle. For the greater the number of unemployed who have inadequate wages with which to buy food, the cheaper will food be: and the fewer the ways in which we can use our savings the lower will be the interest which they bring us in.

But I foresee that Sir Laming will disclaim such ambitious designs. Everything is just right as it is! He would—let us do him justice—be as reluctant to do anything to increase unemployment as he is to do anything to diminish it.

Yours, etc.,

J. M. KEYNES

Sir Laming returned to the charge with a letter published on 6 May asking how much Lloyd George could borrow; Keynes replied the next day.

To the Editor of The Evening Standard, *7 May 1929*

Sir,

Sir L. Worthington-Evans demands that I tell him how much could be borrowed to finance the Liberal policy without raising the rate of interest. It is obvious that any answer must be in the nature of a guess. My guess for what it is worth (Sir Laming will find some details to support it in a pamphlet *Can Lloyd George Do It?* by Mr H. D. Henderson and myself to be published on Friday) is that about three quarters of the sum required could be raised without pressing appreciably on the capital market. The remaining quarter would have a tendency to raise, or more probably maintain, gilt-edged interest rates. But I should not expect that the effect would be sufficient to raise the Bank rate above its present level or to increase charges to industry.

But whatever the exact result may turn out to be, Sir Laming's line of argument leads us well on the road to Dottyville. In a sense it is true that whenever anybody does anything—puts up a factory, builds a house, modernises the railways, even if Sir Laming smokes a cigar when he might have saved the money—it tends to put the rate of interest up. If, on the contrary, we were all dead, the rate of interest would sink to nothing. When in 1894–96, the Bank rate stood unchanged at 2 per cent for two and a half years, this was accompanied by stagnant trade and continuous unemployment on a greater scale than had ever been known before,—the result of a lack of enterprise both abroad and at home. Today we have a demand for money abroad with stagnation at home. So we get the worst of both worlds—unemployment *and* dear money.

Nor is there anything peculiar in British Government borrowing. Foreign government borrowing in London, or indeed any kind of borrowing for any kind of purpose, has just the same effect. When the Government of Roumania or Imperial Chemicals raise a large sum on the London market, does Sir Laming cry out and declare that it will ruin us? Why not?

Mr Keynes or Professor Keynes

However, there is one question perplexing him which I can hope to clear up. He keeps asking whether I am Mr Keynes or Professor Keynes. I am not, and I never have been, a Professor.

He has also twice suggested that I am somehow demeaning myself by entering into debate with a politician like himself. Not at all! The honour is mine! I welcome the opportunity.

Yours etc.,
J. M. KEYNES

By this time the nation was in the midst of an election campaign. As a part of that campaign Keynes wrote public statements supporting two Liberal candidates, Hubert Henderson who had accepted the offer Keynes had refused to contest the University of Cambridge seat, and Sir Maurice Amos who was standing in the Borough of Cambridge.

MR H. D. HENDERSON: AN APPRECIATION

Mr Hubert Henderson has strong claims to the support of all Cambridge Liberals who are interested in the two causes of international peace and disarmament, and of national development as a remedy for unemployment, which look like being the two principal issues of this Election. For Mr Henderson has played a prominent part in forming the opinion and policy of the Party on these questions. In his weekly articles in *The Nation & Athenæum*, of which he has been the Editor since 1923, he has repeatedly crystallised the best Liberal opinion about them. Indeed, so far as the unemployment policy is concerned, he may almost claim the credit of having first started it in a series of articles putting it forward so long ago as 1924, to which he persuaded Mr Lloyd George and others to contribute.

But apart from this, he was one of the Liberals most concerned, behind the scenes, with the long work of research and drafting which eventuated in the famous Yellow Book, *Britain's Industrial Future*.

Hubert Douglas Henderson was educated at Aberdeen Grammar School, Rugby School and Emmanuel College, Cambridge. In his academic career he took a First in the Economics Tripos, Part II, held a Research Studentship at Emmanuel, and, returning to Cambridge after the War, became a Fellow of Clare College and University Lecturer in Economics until 1923. During the War he was Secretary of the Cotton Control Board in Lancashire. He afterwards wrote the history of this, and has also published a volume entitled *Supply and Demand* in the series of Cambridge Economic Handbooks.

Since 1923 he has been Editor of *The Nation*, and it will be generally admitted that he has made that journal the most authoritative exponent of modern economic thought as applied to current political problems. But his influence, as I mentioned above, has also been strongly exerted on the policy of the Liberal Party through his active membership of the Summer School Committee and of the Liberal Industrial Enquiry.

When Mr Henderson was an undergraduate he was President of the Union (October Term, 1912).

He has therefore exceptional qualifications for a parliamentary career, not only because economic questions now bulk so largely in politics, but also because he has rare analytical and constructive powers of mind and formidable debating qualities. I know hardly anyone who would do more than he to strengthen the debating powers of the Liberal Party in the House of Commons, and to ensure that the Party would be in a position to make the really right, penetrating comments with the least possible delay, on all issues concerning finance, economics or international peace which may arise in Parliament.

J. M. KEYNES

A note from the Granta

When Mr Henderson became President of the Union, the *Granta* published a brief sketch which is still recognisable by those who know him.

J.M.K.

In some respects the President is a very young man. He has a habit of sleeping a great deal like the Dormouse, but when he hears an illogical argument he rises up upon his hind legs and pricks up his ears like Brer Rabbit; then he drops his glasses and destroys the argument. It is delightful to see some

817

self-confident but ill-informed person meet Mr Henderson for the first time. The President's smile is pensive and childlike on these occasions, like that of the Heathen Chinee. For a few minutes the conversation is rather one-sided; the President is gratefully receiving instruction; then a puzzled look disturbs his innocent features, and he asks an awkward question. Generally, a self-confident person shies at the question and attempts to ride off with bluster. Then Brer Rabbit rises, the glasses fall and the self-confidence rapidly changes its home. It is, indeed, an unnatural clear-headedness and a mental apparatus beyond his years that have made Mr Henderson the best debater of his generation, and have fitted him, by general consent, for the great office which he now holds.

To SIR MAURICE AMOS, *8 May 1929*

My Dear Amos,

I hope that you will obtain much support as Liberal candidate for the borough of Cambridge. Cambridge is a constituency which has been, traditionally, won by the Liberal Party whenever the tide was flowing with us; and there are unmistakable signs that the tide has turned at last in the Liberal direction.

I reckon that there are two main issues before the country—international peace and disarmament, and a remedy for unemployment. I would add safeguarding, if it were not for the extreme vagueness of Mr Baldwin's declarations on the subject. It is because of their right-mindedness on these issues that the return of Liberals to authority and influence in the state is so greatly to be desired.

No one would dispute that all three parties alike are genuinely devoted to the maintenance of peace and to the restoration of the country's economic prosperity. The difference between them lies in the efficacy of the methods which their traditions and their abilities make it practicable for them to apply. With the best will in the world, Sir Austen Chamberlain has not during his term of office forwarded the cause of peace as it should be forwarded.

Mr Hoover's recent gesture is a sign that if we show ourselves ready to trust the United States and to enter into sincere comradeship with them, extraordinary results might be accomplished, which would seem today quite utopian. For I do not doubt that of all the countries in the world it is we and the United States who are genuinely like-minded in our aspirations after peace and disarmament, and it is only through joint and united action by these two powers that results will be obtained. It is vital to have in office a Government whose natural sympathies and principles will enable them to take full advantage of the fact that the new President of the United States is a man of Quaker upbringing and genuine pacific ideals.

In the matter of unemployment I have written at greater length elsewhere about the Liberal Policy. I am convinced that it is not only practicable, but can be justified as the appropriate remedy on the basis of an analysis of the fundamentals of our economic position. The notion that it can be right to maintain a tenth of our population unemployed for eight years is crazy. The time has come for us simply to decide that we are going to put an end to it. Alone amongst the Party leaders Mr Lloyd George has pledged himself to accomplish this, and I believe that he could do it.

Yours sincerely,

J. M. KEYNES

On 10 May, after successful collaboration, Keynes and Hubert Henderson published *Can Lloyd George Do It?* (*JMK*, vol. IX, pp. 86–125). On 13 May the Government took the unusual step of issuing a White Paper, *Memoranda on Certain Proposals Relating to Unemployment*, as a counterblast to the Lloyd George scheme. Keynes reviewed it in *The Nation*.

From The Nation and Athenaeum, *18 May 1929*

THE TREASURY CONTRIBUTION TO THE WHITE PAPER

Speaking on Tuesday, Mr Winston Churchill declared that 'the only reason why the Government did not publish the exact text of the reports they received was that they did not wish to bring the officials into electioneering controversy'. This comes very oddly from a Minister who *has* published the exact text of the report he received, and over, not his own name, but the name of his officials. Moreover, the report is not of a general character, but a reasoned answer, line by line, to the pamphlet *We Can Conquer Unemployment*, and to some newspaper articles written by myself.

I am always glad to enter into debate—sometimes for my good and sometimes for theirs—with my old friends at the Treasury; and I am not sorry to do it now. But I confess that I did not expect to debate with them on, as it were, *the hustings*; and perhaps it is a pity that they should have committed themselves in public to opinions, purely scientific and technical in character, which I am sure they will find it necessary to revise in course of time.

Their document is a curious one—reasoned, intelligent, and obviously the offspring of honest conviction, but equally obviously the work of persons who are not familiar with modern economic thought. The *form* is such as to invite discussion as between one expert and another. But the *content* makes this impossible—for the mistakes and omissions are of such a character that, before getting to grips with the real questions, one would have to take them over much ground which ought to be familiar to a specialist. That they are ill acquainted with the literature of the subject is confirmed by their apparent belief that what they are talking is orthodoxy; whereas this is simply not the case. Not one of the leading economists of the country, who has published his views or with whose opinions I am otherwise familiar, would endorse the general character of their argument. All this is not surprising; for Treasury officials are naturally far too much occupied with other forms of economy to have much leisure for the political variety. But it makes it the more unfortunate that they should be dragged into the limelight to pose as 'experts'.

It is a pity, too, that they had not had an opportunity of

reading chapter IX of the pamphlet *Can Lloyd George Do It?* by the Editor of *The Nation* and myself. For they have not anticipated a single one of the possible sources of funds there indicated—with the result that their arguments and ours have failed to meet.

In the main, therefore, I need do no more than refer readers of the White Paper to this chapter IX, a copy of which is probably already in the hands of everyone who possesses a copy of the White Paper. But I will re-emphasise the main points.

The Treasury begin with the assumption that no funds, or next to no funds, can be obtained at home which are not already in use. Therefore the finance required by the Liberal Plan must come off foreign investment, if it is to be obtainable at all as a net increase to what is already in use at home. Since our investment abroad is estimated at £120,000,000 a year, they show (page 47) that home development schemes costing £125,000,000 would, therefore, reduce investment abroad to *minus* £5,000,000.

This argument really leaves one gasping! For it totally leaves out—and the omission is not repaired anywhere else in the memorandum—all the resources which are available without trenching on any part of the existing volume of investment whether it be at home or abroad. Let me mention the more important: (1) the dole and other forms of relief now paid to the unemployed, which will no longer be payable when they are employed—this alone would furnish between a quarter and a third of the total cost; (2) the gain to the Exchequer corresponding to the increase in the national income—which might be estimated at an eighth of the gross cost; (3) that part of the original capital expenditure which by going to business profits, purchases of land, &c., is likely to be saved for a time at least; and (4) similar benefits from the repercussions of the expenditure of the newly employed out of their wages in increasing employment in other industries—which, though not precisely calculable, are substantial.

Let me put the whole thing another way round. The ball is set rolling, according to the Liberal Plan, by starting capital works. The men employed on these receive standard wages, which they expend on consumption, but the goods which they themselves produce are not consumption goods. The financial or investment problem consists, expressed in terms of real things, in how to supply them with these consumption goods.

My answer to this problem under the above headings can be restated as follows: (1) not the whole of the consumption of the newly employed is *additional* consumption, for the poor fellows and their families consume *something* even when they are unemployed; (2) and (3) not the whole of the gross expenditure on the capital works eventuates in immediate consumption, for part of it finds its way to business profits, taxation and new saving; and (4) part, perhaps a large part, of the consumption of the newly employed is supplied by the indirect employment on the production of consumption goods of persons now unemployed.

I had better enlarge a little on item (4), because this gain, resulting from the *indirect* employment set up, seems to be the thing which the public find it most difficult to understand. A man newly employed on making roads spends part of his wages on buying boots. There is no problem of 'finance' or 'investment' except to supply him with the boots. But the increased demand for boots leads to more employment of boot operatives—whence the boots. Now the employment of more boot operatives, being on consumption goods, finances itself, except in respect of the small addition required to working capital; and so on, over again, when the boot operatives spend their wages. Thus to the extent that indirect employment on consumption goods is set up in trades where there is now unemployment, we get more employment (and, therefore, more relief from items (1), (2), and (3)) without any fresh investment. For example, there will be a saving on the dole not only from men, previously unemployed, who make roads; but also from men, now unemployed, who will make boots for the men who make the roads; and from men, now unemployed, who will make shirts for the newly employed boot operatives; and so on.

There remains, however, a certain balance—I have guessed, elsewhere, that it might be a quarter of the whole. Part of the cost of the capital works and part of the consumption of the newly employed can only be satisfied by increased imports or, occasionally, by diversion from other undertakings. This will have the effect of reducing correspondingly our foreign investment, because the international balance in our favour will be diminished. But there is no reason in the world why it should reduce our exports, except where men now engaged in producing for export become wanted for home purposes.

Now can it be believed that the Treasury experts totally overlook (1), (2), (3), and (4)? Yet such is the case. They argue that there is no source from which any material part of the consumption of the newly employed can come except (1) the consumption of persons previously employed, with the result of causing compensatory unemployment elsewhere, or (2) goods now exported, or (3) additional imports. Thus they overlook entirely the sources of about three-quarters of the funds required. They use an argument which would be correct *if everyone were employed already*, but is only correct *on that assumption*. The Treasury are wholly oblivious of what is the essence of the matter, namely, that it is largely *with* our unemployed factors of production that we shall make the new investments.

If I had more space and time, I would deal faithfully with their travesty (pages 51, 52) of my argument as to the way in which increased lending to foreigners (*lending* not *investment*) is capable of reacting on our exports. But this is wide of the present main issue.

I cannot refrain, however, from a comment on their final conclusion. They sum up by saying that the root of our troubles is to be found in the fact that our money costs of production are, for the time being, too high, and that unemployment is inevitable so long as this lasts. This is too much—for the Treasury to tell this to *me*. Have they forgotten how four years ago, when they were restoring the gold standard, I told them that excessive money-costs of production and consequent unemployment were the inevitable result of their policy? How they then retorted—and indeed believed—that we were already at that date, four years ago, already fully adjusted to the new parity of the exchange? They have taken four years to find out this elementary fact. But I have spend the four years trying to find the remedy for the transitional period and to persuade the country of its efficacy. I do not doubt that four years hence they will believe what I am saying now, just as they now believe what I was saying four years ago. But it is a terrible time-lag!

At the close of the campaign Keynes made two forays onto the hustings. On 28 May he spoke to a meeting in the City of London on the Liberal proposals supporting T. O. Jacobson, the first Liberal candidate in the constituency for twenty years. The next evening, election eve, after two 'doughty bourgeois' from the City came to Cambridge to ask him the previous Saturday, he spoke in Leicester. His notes for the speech survive.

Notes for a Campaign Speech in Leicester, 29 May 1929

The question before the Electors is the cure for the monstrous evil of Unemployment.

Many of you know what an evil it is in the homes of the unemployed themselves.

Let me give you a few figures to make clear and vivid the waste to the nation as a whole.

We are paying £1,000,000 a week for the dole. This has continued for eight years.

We have got literally nothing for this.

The money we have wasted in this way would have built a million houses.

We could with it have revolutionised the equipment of industry and education.

It would provide every third family in the country with a motor car.

But the waste is far greater than this.

For a British working man is worth much more than the dole he gets.

The wasted labour of the last eight years

Would build all the railways in the country twice over

It would pay our war debt to America twice over

It is more than the total sum asked from Germany for reparations.

Can we, therefore, doubt that it is a monstrous evil?

How can any British working man vote for a Government which has declared itself helpless to find a remedy.

Mr Baldwin's slogan Safety First.

Safety first—to go on having a million unemployed—That is safety for him.

But is it safety for the unemployed?

Safety is to be found nowhere but in the happiness and contentment of the country.

An honest day's work for a fair wage waiting for every honest worker—that is safety.

Mr Lloyd George speaking for the Liberal Party has declared that We Can Conquer Unemployment

Can we?

I stand here tonight to say that, if we wish to, we can.

The Liberal Plan is plain common sense

There are things to be done

There are men to do them

Why not bring the two together?

Why not put the men to work?

This country is not a finished proposition—far from it.

It is crazy to sit puffing one's pipe and telling the unemployed that it would be most unsafe to find them any work.

The Liberal Plan is not a stunt. We have been working at it for four years. During these four years I and many others have spent long hours and days with Mr Lloyd George and Sir Herbert

Samuel hearing the evidence of experts, collecting reports, discussing details.

The plan which we have produced is the result of long hours of careful work.

That is why it has stood criticism

The Government have tried to pick holes

They have set their Civil Servants and all their experts to help them. But they have failed completely. The Liberal Plan stands justified.

I stood up in the City of London yesterday afternoon before a thousand businessmen and invited questions and criticisms. The meeting was enthusiastic. There could be no doubt that those present believed that the Plan came out unshaken.

Let me try to explain in a few words how the Plan will work.

Unemployment is an infectious illness

It multiplies itself and spreads from house to house unless something is done to check it

It is obvious why this should be so:

For if a collier or a bricklayer or a steelworker falls out of work, he and his family have no wages to spend. They cannot buy boots and clothing. So the shopkeepers cannot order from the manufacturers. It is not long, therefore, before there is unemployment in the boot industry and the clothing industries. This in its turn spreads and so on.

Every man who is unemployed puts another man out of work

But the opposite is also true

Employment is infectious health

Employment and prosperity multiply themselves and spread from house to house

If men are employed on roads or on housebuilding or on modernising the railways or on any of the Liberal schemes, they will earn full wages again. They will have money to spend. They will buy once more the boots and clothing which they and their families have gone so long without.

In this way they will bring employment to others also; who in

826

their turn will have wages to spend and in their turn will employ others.

This is the basic idea of the Liberal Scheme, to start the ball rolling. To spread infectious health. To bring back optimism and cheerfulness and activity throughout the whole community. Take Leicester for example. There are important industries in Leicester such as the boot and shoes trade who manufactures [sic] articles for working class consumption. If ten per cent of the working class are out of work, ten per cent of Leicester's customers have no wages with which to buy Leicester's goods. Ten per cent of Leicester's possible output goes unsold. Ten per cent of Leicester's workers are put out of work.

Nothing can restore the full prosperity of Leicester until Leicester's customers are earning full wages again.

The Liberal policy will bring back into employment not only the men directly employed on its schemes, but as many men again indirectly who will be drawn back by the purchasing power of the men directly employed.

What a tragic farce it is!

We want more houses

The men who could make the houses stand idle.

These men need boots

But they have no wages to buy the boots

So men who could make the boots stand idle.

And so it spreads from one industry to another.

Do nothing Do nothing Do nothing are the Government's watch words

Turn from them to the men who will act, to the men who know what they want to do

End of post-war period

Restoration of prosperity only the final thing

Safety first indeed!

What is there to be afraid of?

Nothing

We are a healthy people

We have a great future before us of increasing wealth and increasing opportunities.

Let us be active and cheerful, and do the deeds which lie ready to our hands.

At the polls, Labour won 288 seats, the Conservatives 260 and the Liberals 59. In bets on the result, Keynes won £10 from Winston Churchill but lost £160 on the Stock Exchange.

The post-election period saw Keynes continuing to focus on many of the matters that had occupied him in previous months. During the last week in July he gave four lectures at the School of International Studies in Geneva. Two of the lectures concerned reparations but the other two covered 'The Theory of Foreign Investment' (including 'The Theory in Relation to the Present State of England') and recent proposals for a Bank for International Settlements. On his return to London, he found himself entering the columns of *The Times*.

To the Editor of The Times, *5 August 1929*

Sir,

Your leading article of today under the heading 'The Treasury View', seems to invite a reconsideration of the problem of financing additional employment in the atmosphere of post-election calm. In my view the resources for a development programme of, say, £100,000,000 gross outlay would come from the following sources:—

(1) An unemployed man and his family are consuming something, even when he is unemployed. In round figures, a man who spends £3 a week when he is employed probably spends nearly 30s. a week even when he is unemployed, obtaining it from the dole, from the Poor Law, from his relations, by getting into debt, or by using up his savings. Thus nearly half the wages bill is provided, taking the national economy as a whole, through this 30s. no longer having to be obtained in the above ways.

(2) Part of the additional expenditure of the newly employed

will serve to increase employment in home industries which produce consumption goods. This additional home production will be a net addition to the national resources available to meet the additional consumption of persons becoming (directly or indirectly) employed. Moreover, not only will the direct employment on development schemes create indirect employment in industries producing consumption goods, but this indirect employment will create further indirect employment, and so on.

(3) Not the whole of the gross outlay on development schemes eventuates in increased consumption. Part comes back to the Treasury in additional receipts from taxation, part takes the form of contractors' profits, with which the latter can finance themselves for the time being, and part, being spent on such things as the purchase of land, &c., is a mere transfer from one pocket to another, having no effect on the national economy as a whole.

(4) The development schemes will involve some increase in the import of raw materials, and the additional consumption of the newly employed and their families will involve some increase in the import of food, &c. Most of this must be provided either by a reduction in our foreign lending, by an export of gold, or by ourselves borrowing abroad as an offset to the gross amount of our foreign lending.

(5) In so far as the greater volume of employment and business means that wage earners carry in their pockets increased purchasing power in banknotes, and that business men keep at their banks an increased purchasing power in bank deposits, there can be an increased volume of credit of an entirely innocent and non-inflationary description.

(6) Finally, there is the expedient of an increase of credit which—being inflationary or anti-deflationary in character unless it is balanced by increased voluntary savings—has the effect of causing prices to rise, or of preventing them from falling. In so far as this expedient is used, the purchasing power obtained by the newly employed is found by reducing the

purchasing power of the money incomes of the rest of the community—i.e., it effects a certain redistribution of consuming power. But—as you point out in your article—the same result, namely a redistribution of purchasing power, can be produced by increased voluntary savings, and a quite modest increase would probably be enough.

Now, not a single one of these sources has any clear tendency to divert employment from the previously employed. Not even does the last expedient have this effect; for, although it diverts consumption, it does not divert employment. 'Diversion of employment', which is the Treasury bugbear, only occurs if the banking system refuses to allow the expansion of credit under (5), which is in all circumstances the *sine qua non* of increased industrial activity, however arising, and the expansion, if any, under (6), necessary to make good the deficiency of resources after allowing for what accrues under (1), (2), (3), (4), and (5) plus additional voluntary savings.

Now, the error of the Treasury view, as expounded in the White Paper, is that they entirely overlook all these sources except (4) and (6). They argue that it is not feasible to obtain as much as £100,000,000 from (4); nor to obtain such a sum from (6) consistently with the gold standard. I am not concerned to dispute these conclusions. The mistake is to overlook sources (1), (2), (3), and (5). The untenability of the Treasury view follows from the fact that their arguments would apply with equal force if unemployed workers were to receive a dole equal to the full rate of their wages when employed; whereas it is clear that bringing them back to work would, in such circumstances, involve no financial problem whatever.

So long as the Treasury adhere to their view that nothing is obtainable from sources (1), (2), (3), and (5), a rational discussion of the problem appears to me to be impossible. The only subject for reasonable debate is how much we can get from these sources, and whether the balance for which we have to fall back on (4) and (6), is, or is not, more than we can manage with safety.

My own guess is that—subject, perhaps, to a short time lag—sources (1), (2), (3), and (5) will furnish not less than 75 per cent of the gross outlay on development schemes of a type which do not involve exceptionally large imports of raw materials. Assuming an annual programme of £100,000,000, additional to what we have been doing hitherto, this would, therefore, leave a balance of not more than £25,000,000 to be obtained from (4) and (6). The increase of investment opportunities at home resulting from the development programme itself, coupled with an appeal to issue houses to go slowly with foreign loans and to handle domestic development loans instead, should be able to reduce our net foreign lending by this amount in the course of a year. After the preliminary period was over and results were beginning to show, a mere change of sentiment towards home investments, engendered by the sight of rising prosperity, might be sufficient by itself. Indeed, the continuance of the present bad sentiment on the part of investors towards the prospects of British industry is a far greater danger than the most ambitious development programme could be.

Unless, therefore, these quantitative estimates are very wrong, the risk is negligible of our having to resort to (6) on a scale which would endanger the stability of our currency. Merely to desist from the pressure towards deflation which has persisted for so long should be enough. The dangers of doing nothing are to be rated much higher. The execution of these ideas does not require a reduction of the Bank rate, although the task of stimulating home investment would, of course, be facilitated if international conditions were to change in such a way as to make a lower Bank rate possible, just as it will be aggravated if these conditions make a higher Bank rate unavoidable. But it does absolutely require some moderate increase in the basis of credit. For without some such increase the diversion of employment, which the Treasury fear, might quite possibly occur—at least to some extent. Moreover, while an increase of credit unaccompanied by a development programme might become dangerous by rendering the Bank rate ineffective, an increase of credit accompanied by borrowing for development purposes, and only permitted to occur in so far as it was required as an adjunct of such borrowing, need have no such effect. Provided, indeed, an appropriate (quite small) proportion of the new borrowing were to take the form of Treasury bills, the Bank of England's task of keeping Bank rate effective would be directly facilitated.

Thus the main difficulty is neither one of finance nor one of bank credit. The trouble is to devise sound development schemes and to get them moving quickly. The grave injury done to the country by the 'Treasury View' is that it makes us tardy and half-hearted in tackling the real problem—which is no easy one. The country being uncertain which view is sense and which nonsense, we are encouraged to compromise—as you suggest we should—between the two.

Yours, &c.,

J. M. KEYNES

Keynes's letter led to further correspondence, including a letter from a Mr Frank Morris, who examined his arguments in detail and suggested that they ignored the possibility of the diversion of resources from other activities and people.

To the Editor of The Times, *15 August 1929*

Sir,

It should be understood that the arguments of Mr Frank Morris in the letter which you publish today apply to *all* capital improvements made in this country. For the finance of national development schemes is exactly the same as that of private development schemes. Now (other things being equal) every increase of capital investment in this country tends to put more men into employment and at the same time slightly to raise prices; and every decrease puts men out of employment and in so doing slightly lowers prices. My letter was directed to showing that in present circumstances the effect of national development schemes in raising prices is likely to be small and innocuous compared with their effect on employment.

Because I admit that there will, or may, be a slight tendency to raise prices, Mr Morris considers the proposal to be tainted; and many people agree with him. But why does he think that the existing price–employment structure is exactly right? If he wants prices to be as low as possible, then he could get prices still lower, at the cost of increasing unemployment, by still further curtailing investment, e.g., by abolishing the housing subsidy. As Mr Morris probably knows, prices are generally at their lowest at the bottom point of a business slump, and every recovery from a slump involves some rise of prices. But if he agrees that the lowest possible prices are not always desirable, then the question arises—What is the most suitable level of investment, employment, and prices? A point would come when the effect of excessive investment on prices would be such as to throw us out of gear with the rest of our environment. But in present circumstances, though not, of course, in *all* circumstances, an increase of investment would, in my judgement, bring us into *better* equilibrium with our environment. A dislike of booms is not a good reason for maintaining permanently in a slump.

I am confident that there are only two means open to us to get our national economy into better equilibrium. One is an all-round reduction of real efficiency wages; the other is an increase of home investment. Either of these courses would tend to increase employment and to diminish business losses. I agree with those who think that the former expedient, if it were practicable, would operate with the greater efficacy and certainty. But I consider that the adequate application of it is—as I pointed out it would be when we set ourselves this problem by returning to gold at too high a parity—ruled out by political and social considerations. Therefore we have to try the only alternative. Moreover, if we can jolt ourselves out of our rut and get going full-steam, we may be able to improve our efficiency so materially as to relax in the end the pressure towards a reduction of existing wages.

The preoccupation of many authorities with a reduction of prices as such is due, I think, to a confusion between a reduction of prices resulting from a reduction of wages (or an increase of efficiency) and a reduction of prices due to other causes (such as credit deflation and under-investment), unaccompanied by any change in wages or in efficiency. The latter necessarily involves business losses, and only gets us farther into the bog.

I should add that I do not accept either of Mr Morris's detailed arguments. Indirect employment created by the expenditure of those directly employed *does* lead to an increased production of immediately consumable articles; and a decrease of foreign lending, *accompanied by an increase of imports*, has no tendency whatever to decrease exports, as Mr Morris will surely recognise on a moment's reflection.

Yours, &c.,

J. M. KEYNES

On 26 September, after supporting the exchanges through much of the summer with gold shipments and sales of foreign currency, both owned and borrowed, the Bank of England raised its rate to $6\frac{1}{2}$ per cent. Keynes commented in a broadcast the next day.

From The Listener, *4 October 1929*

THE BANK RATE

I have been set a difficult—perhaps an impossible—task in being expected to say something simple and intelligible about the consequences of the increase of Bank rate from $5\frac{1}{2}$ per cent to $6\frac{1}{2}$ per cent, which is announced in this morning's papers. For the theory of Bank rate is not like—shall we say?—astronomy, a matter where there is an ascertained true doctrine with which all experts agree. It is at present, unfortunately, much more like theology. For it is not only obscure—it is also extremely controversial. Yet I do not want this evening to bring in controversy where I can avoid it. It is my duty to try to explain to you some of the consequences of Bank rate without praising or blaming them.

Bank rate has been raised because gold has been flowing out of the Bank of England on a large scale to meet payments due to foreign countries. The Bank has lost more than £40,000,000 in a year, which is nearly a quarter of its total stock. Why has gold been flowing out? Because we owe foreign countries more than they owe us. But why on balance are we debtors to foreign countries?

On trading account foreign countries are usually debtors to us. For the sums we earn as interest on our foreign investment—for our services to the world as shipowners and business men and in payment for our exports—are greater than what we spend on our imports and our tourist expenditure and so forth—greater by between £100,000,000 and £150,000,000 a year. This means that we are in a position to lend to foreign countries on capital account an amount equal to this favourable surplus of our trading account. If we lend more than this, *we* must pay *them* the difference in gold.

Since there are innumerable transactions both ways, it is practically impossible to get any direct knowledge how much we are lending on balance. But if gold is flowing out and continues to flow out on a large scale, as it has in recent months, this proves that we are lending on capital account more than our surplus on trading account.

If this is due to temporary causes, we can afford to let the gold go for a time—that is the purpose for which we hold gold reserves; or the Bank of England could borrow abroad to balance the temporary deficiency. But if the trouble is thought to be too deep-seated for these expedients to be suitable, then there are only two remedies: either we must lend less on capital account, or we must have a larger surplus in our favour on trading account. Now, how much we lend on capital account depends on whether our terms for lending are cheap compared with those abroad. And how large our surplus is on trading account chiefly depends on whether our costs of production of the goods which enter into international trade are low compared with those abroad. That is to say—in order to right the balance—we must either lend our money dearer or sell our goods cheaper.

Now, the importance of Bank rate is that it affects the rate at which the banks lend money. The immediate reason, therefore, why it is a remedy for a loss of gold is because, by raising the terms on which we lend money to foreigners, it causes them to borrow less from us. But there is also a secondary and much more complicated reason why Bank rate is a remedy, namely, that if it is carried to its logical conclusion, it may cause us in the long run to sell more cheaply and so to increase the favourable balance on trading account which is the source of our ability to lend abroad.

That the immediate and direct effect of Bank rate is to cause us to lend less abroad there is, and can be, no doubt. The difficult thing to understand and explain is its indirect effect. How can it be that Bank rate tends to reduce our costs of production, when it starts off by doing the exact opposite—for it increases one of the costs of production, namely, the cost of interest? This is what I must try to explain. For it is entirely in the indirect effects that the troublesome consequences of Bank rate are to be found.

We have seen that when the Bank rate is raised, it costs more to borrow money, and this deters foreign borrowers. But it also deters home borrowers—particularly if the cost is raised to a figure so high that it has only been equalled in the past for short periods and in times of grave crisis—which is true of the present $6\frac{1}{2}$ per cent rate. If home borrowers are discouraged by the high rate, then fewer orders are placed, new projects are put off and consequently employment is decreased. But how does this help us to attain our goal of reducing our costs of production? This only comes about if unemployment rises to so high a figure and continues for so long a time that wages are forced down. Then, indeed, our costs of production are decreased, so that we are able to sell more abroad. Thus the effect of a high Bank rate is to discourage borrowing and to cause the postponement of new enterprises. So far as this affects borrowing by foreigners, it removes the strain on the Bank of England's gold. But in so far as it affects borrowing at home, it causes business losses and increases unemployment.

Left to itself the Bank rate inevitably produces both sets of consequences. The first thing, therefore, which our authorities have to decide is whether they desire both sets or only the first. Some people think that our wages are too high and ought to be reduced. If so, then both sets of consequences are desired; for it is difficult to see how wages can be reduced except by the pressure of increasing unemployment. In this case we must not complain if unemployment increases, for this is part of the mighty process, part of the process of restoring international equilibrium by reducing British wages. But if we decide that we desire only the first set, namely, the reduction of foreign lending, then we must accompany the increase of Bank rate with other measures intended to counteract so far as possible its effect on enterprise at home.

I think it is true to say that the intention of the authorities today is to produce the first set of consequences, namely, the reduction of foreign lending, and not the second set, namely, the reduction of enterprise and employment at home. The question is: How far is it practicable for them to do the one and not the other?

In so far as the Bank of England can increase the rate of interest without restricting the volume of credit—so that all home borrowers who are ready to pay the higher rate of interest can be accommodated—this will help somewhat. But in so far as this very willingness to be enterprising is checked by the higher rate, other remedies are necessary; for example, the diminished amount of private enterprise might be replaced by programmes of public development. But if I were to develop these ideas I should fall into controversial issues. This much, however, I can say. The more that everybody carries on as usual so far as all home business and home investment are concerned, and the less they allow themselves to be discouraged by the high Bank rate, the better it will be. One hopes, on the other hand, that the discouragement to loans to foreign countries will be as great as possible, and that investors will be reluctant, for the present, to subscribe to new loans to overseas. For the prime purpose of raising the Bank rate is, on this occasion, to diminish our foreign lending; and not as on some previous occasions, to damp down excessive optimism amongst business men at home.

I may sum up by saying that the direct consequences of a high Bank rate on foreign lending are likely to be efficacious in hindering the outward flow of gold. Nor is there any reason at all to expect immediate or sensational adverse developments in other directions. But the gradual and indirect consequences on business and other employment at home are likely to be serious—if no other measures are taken to counterbalance the discouragement of such very dear money. It lies outside my province to say why we find ourselves in these troubles—how far it is due to events outside this country over which we have no control, and how far they are the fruits of our own past policy.

Even as Keynes made his broadcast, the British and American economies were moving into recession. The problem of unemployment which had been a local difficulty of the British economy of the late 1920s was about to become a general world problem.

APPENDIX

MINUTES OF EVIDENCE

TAKEN BEFORE THE

COMMITTEE ON NATIONAL DEBT AND
TAXATION

TWENTY-FOURTH DAY
WEDNESDAY 6 MAY 1925

Present

The Right Honourable Lord Colwyn (*Chairman*)

Sir Charles Addis, K.C.M.G.	Mrs Barbara Wootton
Professor Fred Hall	Mr G. R. Hamilton (*Secretary*)
Sir William McLintock K.B.E.,	Mr G. Ismay (*Assistant*
C.V.O.	*Secretary*)

Mr J. M. Keynes, C.B., called and examined.
Evidence-in-Chief handed in by Mr Keynes

1. It would not be reasonable to introduce a new and disturbing form of taxation, such as a capital levy, except for an important and definite purpose. I am not aware that any reasons could be advanced in favour of the levy which would satisfy this criterion, except the following:—

   (1) In order to redeem the national debt more rapidly than would be possible otherwise.
   (2) In order to change the incidence of taxation as between different types of taxes.
   (3) In order to effect a redistribution of wealth as between different classes in the community.

Since different taxes generally affect different classes unequally, there is no sharp line of division between the second of these objects and the third.

2. Let me take them in order:—

(1) Circumstances might exist in which the rapid redemption of the dead-weight debt was a matter of primary importance. I see, however, no reasons for supposing that this is the case at present. Indeed, on the contrary. If the demand for new gilt-edged investments was exceeding the flow of

savings into those channels, there would be a *prima facie* reason for expediting debt redemption. But at present, in my opinion, the opposite is true. Indeed, I think it unlikely that there would be a strong argument for a more rapid redemption of debt unless (1) we were anticipating a war at an early date, or (2) the Government or other public bodies were embarking on new capital expenditure of a productive kind on a somewhat large scale.

(2) The object of changing the incidence of taxation made me in favour of a capital levy in 1920. At that time the income and super-taxes had reached what seemed to me to be the limit of what was tolerable, and perhaps to have passed it. At the same time I felt doubtful whether the Budget could be balanced without some additional taxation. I was in favour of a capital levy in order that the standard rate of income tax might be reduced. The effect of a capital levy, provided that its proceeds were used in this way, would be to throw more of the burden of taxation on the holders of wealth already existing at the date of the levy, and less on current profits and on the fruits of present effort. It would transfer some part of the burden of taxation from the brain worker and the earner of profit on to those who were rentiers and capitalists at the date of the levy. It seemed to me better to do this than to lay what was becoming a crushing burden upon salaries and profits. In existing circumstances I am no longer in favour of the levy on this ground, partly because it is now probable that the budget can be balanced without raising the income tax to an oppressive level, and partly because the arguments put forward by Sir J. Stamp have convinced me that the amount of the relief which could be obtained from a levy of given amount is appreciably less than I used to think. I can, however, conceive that circumstances might still arise in which a combination of reasons, arising out of (1) and (2) would again cause me to advocate a levy. I limit myself to saying that sufficient arguments in its favour do not, in my opinion, exist at present.

(3) As regards the third possible object of a levy, namely, to effect a redistribution of wealth, it is sufficient perhaps to say that if this measure is to be on a scale which would take it out of the category of a mere modification of the incidence of taxation, it ought to be the last, rather than the first, step in any transition from individualistic capitalism to a new order of society. If the state had taken over the main responsibility for future savings, and was at the same time involved in large capital expenditure for state-operated concerns, the case would be changed. It is not necessary, however, that I should expatiate upon a measure which would belong to a late rather than to an early phase of purely hypothetical developments.

3. The most important arguments against a levy may be summarised under the following heads:—

(1) Any new tax to which taxpayers have not adjusted themselves is a bad

tax. Unless there are strong, positive reasons for a change, it is always better to continue with the existing taxes than to introduce new ones.

(2) Exceptional disturbance is likely to be caused by a non-recurrent tax.

(3) Experience shows that taxes on capital present exceptional difficulties of valuation.

(4) It is commonly held that a non-recurrent tax on capital is essentially unjust because it upsets reasonable expectation and thus discourages future savings.

4. The first three of these arguments all have, in my opinion, some weight, but rather less weight, I think, than is often attached to them. I do not believe that a capital levy is unworkable. And, in so far as its results would be worse than those of any other new tax, I think that the ill consequences would be due to psychological rather than to economic or technical causes. I should not, therefore, regard these counter-arguments as conclusive, if a state of affairs was to recur in which the positive reasons for a levy appeared to be very strong.

5. To the last of these objections I attach only such weight as must be attached to any ground of opposition which is widely held. This argument is always adduced against an unfamiliar tax and could be urged just as strongly against the rates of income tax and super-tax to which we have already submitted, and against the existing rates of death duty, as against the capital levy. I see nothing more unjust or injurious to the saving motive in a tax on capital than in a tax on income. Indeed, a very heavy tax on income may be more injurious not only to saving, but also to earning, than a moderate tax on capital.

6. In conclusion, one point is perhaps worth mentioning, namely, the tendency to attribute any misfortune which occurs to any recent and unfamiliar innovation. The first introduction of iron ploughshares into Poland, Sir James Frazer tells us in *The Golden Bough*, having been followed by a succession of bad harvests, the farmers attributed the badness of the crops to the iron ploughshares, and discarded them for the old wooden ones. If we had had a capital levy in 1919 and had used the proceeds to reduce the income tax, it is possible that the net results might have been very good. But even though important advantages had accrued from such a measure, we certainly should not have avoided entirely, merely by that means, the slump of 1921; and if a levy in 1919 had been followed by a slump in 1920–21 all the misfortunes of that slump—from which, with no capital levy to explain it, we even still suffer—would certainly have been attributed to the operation of the levy, and the opponents of the levy would be now maintaining that all their fears and warnings had been more than justified.

APPENDIX

7551 (CHAIRMAN) *Would you like to amplify the paper you have given us?*
I assume in this evidence that minor considerations for or against can be
neglected, because no one would advocate new taxation of this kind except
for some large, clear and well-defined purpose.

7552 (SIR CHARLES ADDIS) *With regard to the objects of a capital levy
that you mention, would you mind saying a word upon the point—how far you
would consider that increased expenditure on social services would be a
justification for a capital levy?* If the expenditure of the state, under any
heading whatever, had to be unavoidably increased, I should be prepared
to consider this tax, amongst others. If the choice was between a capital levy
and raising the income tax to a materially higher level, I should prefer the
capital levy. I regard that, however, simply as part of the problem of how
to meet new unavoidable expenditure. The fact that it is for a social service
makes no difference compared with war expenditure, for example.

7553 *If there was a capital levy, say, to the extent of half the debt, as has
been proposed, you would then have a certain amount of revenue on the present
basis free for social expenditure?* I should simply regard that as the choice of
a particular form of taxation, falling upon a particular class of taxpayers, in
order to meet that expenditure. I would prefer to treat it as part of the general
Budget problem.

7554 *You would prefer that, for example, to increasing the income tax?* If
I was so much in favour of the new expenditure that I felt we must commit
ourselves to it, and if the choice was between a capital levy and a very material
increase of the income tax, I should prefer the levy.

7555 (CHAIRMAN) *Supposing you had the alternatives: an increased
income tax or a capital levy, with the dislocation which it would cause, which
would you choose today?* I should prefer a capital levy. I think that the
disadvantages of a very heavy income tax on current effort are most serious.
I think there are disadvantages in a capital levy, too—there are in any new
tax. It is a choice between two sets of disadvantages. If I was limited in my
choice between a capital levy and say, doubling the income tax, I should
prefer the capital levy. That is all I am saying.

7556 (SIR WILLIAM MCLINTOCK) *Repayment of £3,000,000,000, which
is a figure that has been taken would give a gross saving of, roughly, £150,000,000
a year?* Yes.

7557 *It has been estimated that, with the loss of death duties and income tax
and super-tax, you might probably have a net surplus of £50,000,000. Assuming
that figure to be as near as one can get, it is equal to 1s. additional income tax?*
Yes.

7558 *Would you still suggest that if a sum of £50,000,000, or thereby, is all
that is required for any additional expenditure, the disturbance of a capital levy*

would not be a much more serious matter than simply 1s. *on the income tax?*
If that is the choice, I am against the capital levy, as I have explained here.
I am very much impressed by that argument which you have just outlined,
which I think was first elaborated by Sir Josiah Stamp, that a capital levy
approximately of such magnitude as you have mentioned would have very
disappointing results. In the earlier discussions of the capital levy I do not
think anyone was quite alive to that—I certainly was not—and the force of
those figures is very great. I think it would be much better to have 1s. extra
on the income tax than to have the disturbance of a capital levy, which would
amount to £3,000,000,000 gross and yet would not be equivalent to more
relief than 1s. on the income tax.

7559 (CHAIRMAN) *Will you now go to the next paragraph in your paper?*
I might perhaps elaborate my first point a little more. It is connected with
the evidence I gave before the Committee last time I was here. Paying off
Government debt means taking money from the public at large, or from
capitalists at large, and using the proceeds to give cash to holders of gilt-edged
securities in exchange for their gilt-edged securities. Those investors will
want to invest the money which they receive in a similar manner, that is to
say, in other gilt-edged securities. Therefore a very important consideration
in my mind is how far there is a demand for capital in that particular form.
If the Government was engaged in big productive works so that they needed
the money themselves on a huge scale, and if the natural supply of the
investment market for that sort of investment was inadequate to the
demands, then I think you would have a certain argument in favour of the
levy. In the opposite case if the gilt-edged market is congested with available
funds and new opportunities for investment in gilt-edged securities are
mainly overseas, then I hold there is no object in rapidly repaying the
national debt, but the contrary. It is much better to leave the resources in
the hands of the people who are free to use them in any way, rather than
to transfer them to the hands of people who are limited to using them in
a particular way.

7560 (SIR CHARLES ADDIS) *That is on the assumption that the people who
are paid out would demand the same kind of security?* Presumably they would.
They do not hold Government debt by accident; they hold it by choice,
which means that they have some motive for preferring that particular form
of investment to others.

7561 *Have you considered, when you take account of the enormous amount
of the whole stock, whether that argument can be quite followed throughout?* I
think it holds in spite of that.

7562 *With regard to other changes, do you attach much importance to
increased expenditure by local authorities, for example?* If it involved heavy

borrowing, yes. In 1920, in the early days of the housing programme, it was involving heavy borrowing; at present it is not.

7563 *In some industrial enterprises under the Trade Facilities Act, for example, there has been another channel opened up?* They have not in fact come to much. My belief is that for the last year and a half, say, the new home trustee securities available, minus the debt paid off, are far short of the natural accumulations seeking an outlet of that kind.

7564 *Yes, that is so; but I rather thought there was a growing expansion there to which one might look in the near future?* Unless there is a change of policy, I see no reason to expect a great acceleration.

7565 *You attach a great deal of importance to the argument that it would be diverted abroad?* If we change our policy and our local authorities embark on great road schemes and port schemes and the like, the situation would be changed. I see no probability that we shall do these things in the near future; I should like to do them, but we are not doing them at present.

7566 *Nor is there much expansion of investment abroad at present?* There are certain hindrances of an artificial kind in the way of that.

7567 *To that extent the argument is weakened with regard to investment abroad?* Not in the slightest, because my argument depends on the lack of outlet at home. If you choose to put our export trade in difficulties by cutting off foreign loans and not putting home ones in their place, you are doing the maximum amount of damage in every direction.

7568 *Is there not a reactive effect on investment at home if you discourage investment abroad?* There might be. If you keep it going long enough you would affect the rate of interest, but I do not think that there is very much in the difference between $4\frac{1}{4}$ per cent and $4\frac{1}{2}$ per cent. What would happen if you kept up your artificial methods long enough would be that the people would find ways of defeating them.

7569 *In your view is there any way of testing the annual amount which we might pay off without the adverse results which you fear? Is there any criterion?* I do not think there is any criterion that you could lay down now which would hold good for the next ten years. I think it is a thing you ought to budget for in the light of the circumstances of each year. I think that at the moment there is no argument for paying off more than a small amount of debt, but that might rapidly change if we embarked upon important new schemes. When enterprise of this particular kind is dead, for whatever reason, political or economic, the argument for paying off debt is diminished. As soon as the Government or public boards, or public authorities, have a policy of productive investment, then the argument for paying off the debt rapidly is quickly increased; so that it is a thing you must think over afresh almost every year.

7570 *How far, in your view, is the argument that we ought to anticipate a renewal of war at an early date an argument for repayment?* Personally, I do not anticipate a renewal of war.

7571 *You do not think that can properly be taken as a test of the amount to be annually paid off?* I think it ought to be considered, but I think even if one did anticipate war, say, ten years hence, the extent to which one could be armed against it by an increased sinking fund is very small. If I foresaw a war ten years hence, I would rather spend the money upon the fighting services than upon the sinking fund.

7572 *As we are going now, we are paying off £50,000,000 a year. At the end of 20 years we shall only have paid off £1,000,000,000 of debt; so that at the end of 20 years we should still be in a very serious position, so far as concerns the argument from the possibility of a war in the near future?* I agree.

7573 *Therefore, you do not consider that possibility of much importance as a test of the amount that ought to be paid off?* No. I attach almost no importance to it.

7574 (PROFESSOR HALL) *I would like to ask how your view regarding repayment would be affected if deflation were taking place rather rapidly and the real burden of the debt charges were increasing in consequence?* I think that would be an additional reason, probably, against. But I do not think I should attach so much importance to that argument as to the question of the demand for capital in the form of gilt-edged securities. If deflation was proceeding, I should be more, rather than less, against paying off debt, because we should be repaying the lenders in an appreciated currency.

7575 *You would not think it desirable for that reason to get the debt cleared off quickly before the burden increased enormously?* But I do not look forward to progressive deflation lasting over years.

7576 *But I am assuming that it is taking place, and continually taking place?* Then I should say the game was up, anyhow.

7577 (SIR CHARLES ADDIS) *With regard to your change of view since 1920, concerning a capital levy, to which factor do you attach more importance—the amelioration of the existing burden of taxation or the comparatively small net amount which would result from a capital levy?* It is hard to say; at that time income tax was 6s., and I thought it quite possible that it might rise to 8s. or 9s. or 10s., and at that time I thought that a capital levy might perhaps make 3s. or 4s. difference. Now the rate of income tax is 4s., and the type of capital levy under discussion would be worth only 1s. of income tax, so the two things together entirely alter the situation, in my mind. What I wanted to avoid was an income tax in excess of 6s., and the argument for avoiding income tax in excess of 6s. is quite different from the argument for reducing income tax from 4s. to 3s.

845

7578 *But do you not consider that existing taxation is exerting a very depressing effect upon industry, in restricting enterprise particularly?* I think that it is dangerous to have a very high tax on profits, including in that term the reward of risk taking. The super-tax, together with the income tax, is a deterrent to a rich man who contemplates taking a risk, or rather taking a risk which is an isolated risk, or one not easy to average. To that extent I agree. I also think that a great part of saving is generally done by people of big fortunes who make large profits, and if you tax them very heavily you interfere with saving to a certain extent. On the other hand, the argument that income tax and super-tax are responsible for the general lethargy of trade is greatly exaggerated, in my opinion. I think that there is extremely little in it.

7579 *If the present burden of taxation were to fall once for all upon the accumulations of past efforts rather than on current income, would the result not be a very considerable incentive to enterprise and to risk taking?* If you used the proceeds for an important reduction of income tax and super-tax, yes. My difficulty is that unless you are going in for a very huge tax, which we are not discussing at the moment, the relief to enterprise is so very small. If, by a not unreasonable capital levy, I could reduce the income tax and super-tax to something like the pre-war level, I should be strongly in favour of it; but I do not believe that 1s. off the income tax would make a significant difference to enterprise.

7580 *Would you on general grounds be in favour of any kind of tax on capital, say a small annual tax, especially for debt redemption? Would there be anything to be gained by exploring in that direction?* The best way of doing that is by increasing the income tax on 'investment' income. The experience of the United States in a tax on capital is rather discouraging. It is practically impossible to have an annual valuation of capital. The result is that you tend to tax realised capital profits only, and that works out in all sorts of unequal and inconvenient ways. I believe that, if you want to relieve current effort and to tax more heavily past accumulation, the way to do it is to increase the tax on what used to be called unearned income, and is now called investment income. The objection is that you mix up the rentier with the profiteer. But the tax on capital has exactly the same effect, if it is an annual tax. There is no difference whatever in incidence that I can see between a tax on capital and an increased tax on unearned income, and the latter is much easier to collect.

7581 (SIR CHARLES ADDIS) *They both tax past accumulations?* They both tax the accumulations up to the beginning of that year.

7582 (SIR WILLIAM MCLINTOCK) *You mentioned that you would be in favour of a capital levy as compared, say, with doubling the income tax?* Yes.

7583 *Taking the figures we have already had of a levy for £3,000,000,000 (yielding a net £50,000,000) being equivalent to 1s. income tax, it would follow that a levy equivalent to a 4s. tax would produce about £12,000,000,000?* Yes.

7584 *So that that figure indicates a sum far in excess of any requirements we are ever likely to have?* Well, I do not know.

7585 *Assuming there is not another war?* Sir Charles Addis was suggesting that there might be new social expenditure of a very heavy kind. I am not in favour of a heavy increase of expenditure, but suppose I was either compelled to accept or was convinced of the necessity for heavy increased expenditure, and if I was limited to a choice between doubling the income tax and a very heavy capital levy, I should choose the capital levy. But that is all very hypothetical and contingent.

7586 *Evidence has been given to us, and the suggestion with regard to social expenditure was made, by a witness who was assuming a net saving of £150,000,000 a year from a capital levy to produce £3,000,000,000?* He was simply mistaken in his arithmetic.

7587 *He said he would spend probably £20,000,000 or £30,000,000 on social betterment schemes, and the balance would be saved. So he was assuming that he was going to have a very large fund available, something to reduce the current rates of income tax and something for social schemes at the same time?* His arithmetic was not correct.

7588 (SIR CHARLES ADDIS) *I would like to ask you one more general question. On the last occasion that you were here, I think you considered that a sinking fund of £50,000,000 in the present circumstances was enough. I just want to ask you once more, have you considered whether a non-cumulative fund of that amount is sufficient effort for us to make for the purpose of repayment of debt?* I see no object in reducing the debt as such. Your question assumes that there is something desirable in extinguishing the debt sooner or later.

7589 *Would you go so far as to say that was not desirable? On general grounds it is a desirable thing, is it not?* I think it is a matter almost of indifference.

7590 *So that you would confirm the opinion expressed before that a non-cumulative £50,000,000 a year is an adequate amount?* I think the argument for extinguishing the national debt is partly an aesthetic argument, that it looks nice to have a clean balance sheet, and I think it is partly false analogy from private account keeping; an individual likes to be out of debt, but for a nation as a whole it is merely a book-keeping transaction.

7591 (CHAIRMAN) *That is a very interesting opinion.*

(SIR CHARLES ADDIS) *I find it very difficult to follow that, partly, I dare say, from the prejudice of which you speak. It is very difficult for me to regard it as anything but a bad thing.*

7592 (SIR WILLIAM MCLINTOCK) *Do you not think the average indivi-*

dual who might be liable to a capital levy, if he could be assured of a permanent annual relief in his current taxation, would be quite ready to part with some capital? I think so. I have never seen any objection of principles to the capital levy on that ground.

7593 *One of the difficulties is that he can have no guarantee that, having made a capital contribution and got a temporary relief of the annual burden, say on income tax and super-tax, that relief will be continued to him?* I do not think he has any right to any such guarantee.

7594 *And so long as he cannot get that guarantee, he will not be in favour of a capital levy; he will not take kindly to it.* (PROFESSOR HALL): *Rightly or wrongly, a great many people are psychologically affected by the existence of the debt, and is there not among a section of the community a very strong feeling that they are being overtaxed in order that interest may be paid upon the debt? Rightly or wrongly, that feeling exists?* (WITNESS): I think that the matter is widely misunderstood.

7595 *You think it is a matter of which no notice should be taken?* I think there is no end to it if you set out in your legislative programme not to produce the best results but to get rid of unfounded misapprehensions in the mind of the ignorant.

7596 *But Parliament has to take some account of public opinion?* It takes account of nothing else.

7597 *And if public opinion demands a certain policy, Parliament may be forced along a certain line?* It will certainly be so. That does not affect the question whether it is wise.

7598 *No; but I wanted to know your view of how that position should be met?* It is a difficult question. You are assuming a state of affairs in which public opinion is pressing Parliament to do something foolish. If I knew the remedy for that, I should know the remedy for many of the evils of society.

7599 *What I am asking you to give us, really, is some argument that can be put up against that expression of opinion, to show how foolish it is. You said it is simply a question of book keeping. Well, that does not convince people when you tell them that?* I cannot, at short notice, think of a very brief platform way of putting it. I do not think it is more difficult than a great many other economic questions which have gradually been made plain to the big public. All these matters are hard at first, but there are many of them which, in the course of years, the public get to understand, so long as good sense is talked to them in a reasonably lucid way, year after year. That is the only method I think.

7600 *Do you think that this statement of yours, published in the evidence, will do anything to correct that feeling?* This was not prepared from the point of view of the platform.

7601 *No, but it may be read by thoughtful people, who may be able to interest others from the platform?* I think it would need a good deal more elaboration.

7602 *The statement that it is merely a matter of book-keeping may be acceptable to us; we may see it quite clearly; but I think the outside public would want some arguments to show that it was merely a question of book-keeping?* I should argue in some such way as this. This is not a proposal for confiscation, nor is it a proposal to increase savings; it is a proposal that the holders of the national debt should hold some other form of security; that is to say, that they should receive the same income as before. A certain proportion of the fruits of industry would go to those individuals, exactly as hitherto, but they would not first be collected from industry by the Government and then handed to the *rentier*; they would reach him by some more direct channel. Now there is a large class of investors who like to have the Government guarantee for the security of their income, and they will accept a smaller income if they have that guarantee than if they have not. So there may be some positive advantages in their income reaching those individuals through the hands of the Government out of the proceeds of taxation, and with the guarantee of the Government, rather than more directly. But whether that be so or not, it does not affect the total wealth of the country nor the total burden of anyone, whether their income reaches them direct or through the channels of the Treasury.

7603 (SIR WILLIAM MCLINTOCK) *Of course, the holders of national debt would not have the same income as before. You said that they would, from a different form of security. All those having capital above the minimum amount would have a portion of their national investment taken from them as well?* Certainly the capital levy is a form of taxation. I was answering the point whether paying off the national debt as such, apart from laying a new burden upon a particular class of taxpayers, was any relief. That was the question I was answering. If your method of paying off the national debt is by a capital levy, then you are placing a new tax upon a particular class of the community, and therefore reducing their wealth. That is quite true.

7604 (CHAIRMAN) *It is a striking statement that Mr Keynes makes today, which makes one feel more reassured and more comfortable. What Professor Hall wanted was that there should be some argument to present to the minds of the people who are looking at this debt as a very dire and oppressive calamity?* I think that a person who is in favour of repaying the national debt rapidly has two indirect reasons for it, both of which have some force. The first is that all Chancellors of the Exchequer have a natural disposition to cut their Budgets rather too fine. A substantial sinking fund, therefore, provides a margin and it is a corrective to that natural tendency of Chancellors of the Exchequer. Suppose anything goes wrong with the Estimates, the result is that we have not repaid quite as much debt as we expected, but we have not positively got into arrears, and I think it is right to wish for some margin of that sort. I have supported a moderate sinking fund for exactly that reason—that it is a good practical method of seeing that there is a margin on the Budget. The other reason is that they believe that it will increase the aggregate saving of the community, because in so far as the Government repays debt, it is taking away money from the taxpayers, not all of which will be saved, and using it to repay holders of the Government debt, who will probably save the whole of it. So that the point is not to repay the national debt, but to increase the national savings, a result which would be achieved equally well if you had used the proceeds of taxation not to repay the national debt, but for productive capital expenditure. I think it is very hard to decide how much you should favour saving. We may, sometimes, be inclined to exaggerate it. We assume too lightly that more saving is always the most desirable thing. But no doubt with an increasing population there is a powerful reason for increased savings, and therefore there is a ground for using the sinking fund as an indirect way to promote saving. I am not now disputing either of those reasons, I agree that there ought to be a margin on the Budget. I think that it ought to be a matter of anxiety for the state that the community saves an adequate sum each year. But such reasons are distinct from those for paying off the national debt as such. They can be met without paying off the national debt; and I intended to limit my remarks to the desirability of paying off the national debt as such, apart from any effect it might have in stimulating saving or in enforcing on the Chancellors of the Exchequer prudent finance.

7605 (PROFESSOR HALL) *While you feel that it is a matter of indifference whether we repay the debt rapidly or not, you do not think the existence of the debt is a good thing in itself, as some people sometimes suggest?* I am not sure that it is not a good thing that there should be a considerable volume of capital available for investment, the interest of which is guaranteed by Government. There is a large class of investors to whom that is an advantage, but it would be much better if the debt was productive debt, instead of deadweight debt. I do not believe that the national debt will ever be greatly reduced. I should be surprised if it ever stood below, say, £5,000,000,000; because, after a certain point, demands for productive capital expenditure are likely to arise. It is just possible that the debt may appear to fall below £5,000,000,000, because the new debt will be raised, not by the Treasury, but by other public bodies. But taking the public debt in a wide sense, I should anticipate that in the future there will be some reduction, but that it will not actually fall towards nothing at all. As soon as so much debt has been repaid, that there is a distinct shortage for investment purposes, there will be a strong swing of opinion against repaying it faster. The arguments which I am now advancing in an abstract way will then have practical force.

7606 *That assumes, of course, that there are not other available opportunities of investing in public securities?* If there are, I should say that there was no net reduction of the public debt, but only of the deadweight debt.

7607 (CHAIRMAN) *What do you think of the demand for a reduction in the rate of interest upon the national debt?* I think that the power of the Treasury to reduce the rate of interest on the national debt below the world rate of interest on first-class securities is very limited. In the years immediately succeeding the War, the rate of interest on the debt was probably above the true rate of interest, and prudent finance has had its reward in bringing the rate of interest down to somewhere near the true rate of interest. But once you have achieved that, you cannot achieve much more. You cannot proceed, by prudent finance, to reduce the rate of interest from $4\frac{1}{2}$ per cent to $3\frac{1}{2}$ per cent and then to $2\frac{1}{2}$ per cent, merely by paying off debt, irrespective of what the rate of interest is in the outside world. The most you can do is to get into a situation where you are an absolutely prime borrower and need never pay more than the international rate of interest for a prime borrower; and I should say that we have practically achieved that already, and that the rate of interest on the national debt in future, assuming reasonable prudence, will depend upon the general movement of the rate of interest rather than upon the particular policy of the Treasury.

7608 (PROFESSOR HALL) *I forget whether you mentioned this point in your previous evidence; do you attach any importance to hypothecating the receipts from death duties for debt reduction purposes instead of for current expenditure?* Not the slightest. I see no connection between one particular form of taxation and the sinking fund.

7609 (SIR WILLIAM MCLINTOCK) *If you come down to a mere matter of book-keeping and take the national accounts, you could quite easily find almost an equivalent amount of capital expenditure on the one side of the account as against the revenue from death duties, which is considered a tax on capital, on the other: but the public accounts are prepared in such a way that they do not bring that out clearly?* Yes, very likely that is so.

7610 *I think it could be shown every year that the capital expenditure on the one side is almost equivalent to the amount raised from death duties on the other; the difference is not material?* I think there is no more force in the argument for equating the two than there would be for equating the proceeds of the sugar duty with the cost of meals for school children, so as to be able to say that the amount you spend on meals for school children exactly equals the receipts from the sugar duty.

7611 *But if there is any point in the argument for using death duties for current expenditure there is nothing left in it when you come to analyse that current expenditure, and find that an equivalent amount of it is truly capital expenditure?* I have not worked that out myself. I am not at all surprised. Summing the whole matter up, I feel, at any rate in the present circumstances, that the sort of moderate capital levy which has been under discussion is not worth while, and that the advocate of the capital levy is probably wanting it as a first instalment of a radical redistribution of wealth. My feeling about this is that, assuming such a policy, I doubt whether this is a wise way in which to take your first instalment. If I were considering a completely different order of society in which saving was looked after by the state, so that you had not got to pay much attention to encouraging or discouraging saving by private individuals, then measures of this sort might be worthy of serious consideration. But, to begin at this end, to take steps which might interfere with the private motive to save, before you had established in operation a thoroughly efficient alternative method of saving, would be to make a mistake, from any point of view. This is the dilemma: that if the capital levy is part of a new social order it is not the thing to begin with. If it is not, if it is meant to be something which is quite compatible with our present order of society, then it is not worth while.

7612 (PROFESSOR HALL) *You differ, then, from one of our witnesses who has suggested that a capital levy of £1,000,000,000 might be desirable, and would not really be disturbing. You do not think it is worth while, and the smaller the amount the less worth while it is?* The capital levy is extraordinarily disturbing in proportion to its magnitude—far more so than any other tax. You are insulting, by it, a set of very strong irrational feelings in men.

7613 (SIR WILLIAM MCLINTOCK) *Have you considered the other aspect of it—that the payers of the levy in many cases would have to hand over an interest in their business to the Government, to hold in the form of shares?* I believe that there are ways round all these technical points. I admit that these grounds of objection are troublesome, and that therefore no one would undertake to meet them except in connection with a large and important scheme; but I do not think they are insuperable.

7614 *Then there are people who earn substantial incomes with very little capital. Would they escape?* Yes they would; but they are just the people I should wish to let off. If the object is to put more burdens upon owners of accumulated capital in order to relieve those who are earning big current incomes and making big current profits, the result you indicate is just what is sought.

7615 *The suggestion has been made that those with incomes of a certain size and very little capital should have their contribution commuted in some way. Then it comes back to an income tax?* Yes, I have heard that suggestion. If you think that, I see no object in not doing it by income tax. Of course that has constantly happened in experience. The capital levies which have been proposed in foreign countries have generally been elaborated and whittled away until they were practically additional income taxes. If all the payers of a capital levy proceeded to set up a sinking fund, out of their current income, in order to replace what the capital levy had taken from them, it would then be equivalent to an income tax on the holder of the capital at the date of the imposition. But even then it would not be a general income tax, because not all the income tax payers would be paying it.

7616 *There is no other method left to them?* Even so, you still achieve your object by transferring the burden from the income tax payers as a whole to a particular section of the income tax payers, namely, those who own capital at the date of the levy.

7617 (PROFESSOR HALL) *Should I be right in in saying that you think a capital levy is practicable, but in present circumstances undesirable?* Yes, and not worth while. That is the aspect I should emphasise.

7618 *It is practicable. The question of valuation does not trouble you at all?* It troubles me a little. I think it is quite a serious and difficult matter and an argument against the capital levy unless you are achieving a big object. But if you have a big object in view, I think that these valuation difficulties are capable of solution.

7619 *It is not an insuperable obstacle?* No. After all, if there was no income tax, it would be an objection to the income tax that you would have to set up that tremendous machinery of Somerset House

7620 (CHAIRMAN) *Have you any further point, Mr Keynes?* There is one point upon which I have not said anything, but which you emphasised in the questionnaire sent me. That was the question of the effect of a capital levy in producing inflation or deflation. My view of that is that a capital levy would set up two tendencies. There would be some people who would be so much alarmed that they would sell out securities beyond what they required for the purpose of the levy, and would keep money in their banks. The effect would be deflationary. There would be other people who would be either unable or unwilling to sell out their securities, and who would try to obtain part of the amount of the levy, partly by using their bank balances up to the hilt and partly by borrowing additionally from their bank. That would be inflationary. If we had a managed currency there need be no effect on balance because it would be easy to counteract the net effect of those two influences. If we had a currency in which we took no steps to counteract tendencies towards inflation or deflation, then it would depend upon which of those two sets of motives was the stronger. I should have supposed that the tendency to borrow would be incomparably stronger than the tendency to hoard, and that consequently the net effect would be inflationary rather than deflationary.

7621 (MRS WOOTTON) *When you say a managed currency, would that be affected by a gold standard?* You can have a gold standard that is to a great extent a managed currency. I am not assuming the absence of a gold standard; I am assuming the presence of a standard which has been worked on managed lines, although it may have a gold basis. It is too soon to predict along what lines these things will develop. Recent talk has been to lay stress upon the amount of gold reserves as governing credit policy. If we were to manage our credit by reference to the inflow and outflow of gold, then it would be impossible for us to counteract such influences as these.

7622 *Either way?* Either way. Suppose that we did not pay too much attention to gold and attended mainly to credit influences at home, then in spite of the gold standard we could do a good deal to counteract these influences.

7623 *If we had an entirely unmanaged standard?* If we had a gold standard of the kind which the orthodox gold party advocate, we could do nothing.

7624 *We could do nothing, but the gold standard would do something in time?* Yes, but what it would do would be a matter of chance.

7625 (PROFESSOR HALL) *What would you do with any repayments that come to us from France or some other of our debtor countries? Would you utilise those amounts for repayment of debt?* I think that there is a strong sentimental and psychological argument for doing that, just as there is for using reparation receipts in that way, but I do not know that there is much in it, really. I should take the money into my Budget, and, whatever I might say, the effect would be to ease the Budget situation as a whole.

7626 (SIR WILLIAM MCLINTOCK) *If they do not budget for those reparations, as has not been done the last year, they will not automatically go to the reduction of debt, if anything comes in?* The Treasury budget for a certain amount of reparation receipts this year, and I should suppose that, as soon as the reparation receipts can be accurately foreseen, they will be budgeted for. The only reason for not budgeting them is the fact that the Treasury is not quite sure how much they will be.

7627 (PROFESSOR HALL) *But since we have borrowed for the purpose of these loans, does it not seem that on grounds of public policy it would be desirable to utilise the repayments for repayment of the capital burden?* We could say we were doing that, just as we can say that we are using the death duties for this purpose; but I should not increase the sinking fund above £50,000,000 merely because we had got an extra £5,000,000 from France.

7628 (SIR WILLIAM MCLINTOCK) *The same principle has been operating every year in the sale of war stores. We are treating the proceeds from sales as current income?* Yes.

7629 (PROFESSOR HALL) *Taking the choice between reducing income tax and increasing the amount of the sinking fund above £50,000,000, would you suggest that it would be better to apply the money received in reducing the income tax?* I should bring it into the Budget as a whole and treat it very much like other receipts in deciding how I should use it.

(CHAIRMAN) *Thank you very much for your most interesting evidence.*

The witness withdrew.

DOCUMENTS REPRODUCED
IN THIS VOLUME

UNPUBLISHED LETTERS

DOCUMENTS REPRODUCED IN THIS VOLUME

MISCELLANEOUS

INDEX

INDEX

Balance of payments (*cont.*)
  effect on, of return to gold at parity, 426, 437; balanced by deflation, 555
  German, 17, 28
  gold reserves in relation to, 514
Balance of trade
  adverse: and gold reserves, 514, 744, 835; a sound currency the best corrective, 30–2; Bank discount as, 235, 376, 385, 390, 836
  daily balance, 29, 31; seasonal imbalances, 52–3
  devaluation problems, 46
  foreign loans and, 70, 432, 433, 570–1, 798, 823, 835
  in Germany, 23–4, 26–33; India, 494, 514
  visible and invisible balances, 402–3, 570–1; in U.S.A., 719–22
  articles on: 'The balance of trade (1924–6)', 570–2; 'The British Balance of Trade, 1925–1927', 703, 704–22, 739; 'Note on the British Balance of Trade' (1928), 722–3
  see also Balance of payments; Imports and exports
Baldwin, Stanley
  Chancellor of The Exchequer (1922–May 1923), 3, 101, 103; Safeguarding of Industries Bill, 3; monetary policy, 212
  Prime Minister (May 1923–January 1924): non-flationary speech (July 1923), 241, 242, 262, 266, 272; basic *laissez-faire* beliefs, 232, protectionist leanings, 147, 149, 151–6, 220, calls general election on issue, 143; speech at Manchester, 144; defeated in Speech from the Throne, resigns, 157
  leader of the Opposition, 267
  Prime Minister (October 1924–1929): Election Address, 325; return to gold standard at pre-war parity announced, 337; no cure for world depresion, 444; handling of general strike, 531, 543–5, 560, 763; supports Eight-Hour Bill, 559, 561; 'Mr Baldwin's Qualms', 559–63; his brand of Toryism, 145, 640, 648; 'Safety First', 825
  relations with JMK, 76, 267, 451, 542
  list of letters, 862
Balfour, Sir Arthur
  member, Committee on National Debt and Taxation, 1924–7, 295
  Chairman, Committee on Industry and Trade, 1924–9, 382, 383, 385, 386–7, 389–93, 394, 398–9, 404–6, 413, 415, 802

Balkans, The, 277, 795
Ball, Sidney: Sidney Ball lecture delivered by JMK at Oxford (1924), 327
Bandoeng tin pool, 550
Bank advances, 84, 97, 104, 575–7; in Lancashire cotton crisis, 601, 616; in U.S., 716, 717
Bank of Algeria, 756
Bank bills, domestic, 577
Bank Charter Act (1844), 339–40; Section IV, 362, 366, 378
Bank deposits, 12, 81–2, 187, 305–6; decrease in (1921–3), 83–5, 97–8; and Bank Charter Act of 1844, 340; purchasing power in the form of, 360–1, 829; as credit-money, 340
  in Germany, 29; in France, 179–80
  see also under Bank of England
Bank of England
  Bagehot on, 466–72, 773
  Bank Charter Act of 1844, 339–40, 366, 743, 753; under Gold Standard Act, 1925, 366
Bank notes, *see* Bank of England notes; Currency notes
Bank rate policy, 100–3, 252–4, 264–7, 334–5, 336, 390, 447, 771, 798–9, 832, 834; City Editors on, 104–5, 234–5; 'The Policy of the Bank of England' (*The Nation and Athenaeum*, 16 July 1924), 261–7; 'The Policy of the Bank of England' (*Evening Standard*, 17 July 1925), 417, 421
  credit, control of, 242, 254–5, 348, 377, 393, 569, 573–4, 585, 744–5, 771, 772, 810; more concerned with dollar exchange than flagging trade, 101, 397, 398–9, 421, 442, 445, 764, 766; deflation on Cunliffe Report model, 101, 117, 161, 261–4, 555, 765; measures to bring down internal price level, 391, 762, 771
  foreign borrowers, 71–2, 335, 376–7; embargo on foreign investment, 390–1, 426, 437
  gold: gold reserves, 165, 240, 284–5, 291, 426, 744, 751–2, 759, 779; loss of gold, 835–6; proportion of gold to note issue, 482, 483, 741, 744–50
  price for gold, 166, 284, 344, 377
  Government of, 468–71, 674–5
  Bank Court, 94, 258, 335, 340, 471
  Banking Department, 252, 467, 750–1
  Committee of Treasury, 255, 258, 468–9, 471
  Comptrollership, 468

867

Bank of England (*cont.*)
Directors, 259–60, 468–9, 471–2, 505
Discount Office, 469
Governors, 188, 264, 468–7, 674–5, 765, *see also* Norman, Montagu; Deputy-Governor, 469, 470–1
Issue Dept, 750–1
in an international agreement, 211
and joint-stock banks, 187–8, 569, 765. *See also below under* resources
Lancashire Cotton Corporation formed by, 632, 633–4
McKenna on, 770–2
resources: Bank of England stock, 94, 203; 'other deposits' (of banks), 97–8, 189–90, 748–9; share of national debt held by, 216; profits, 258, 684, 750–2; purchase of securities, 258–9, 799; credits with New York Federal Reserve Bank, 398, 426, 437, 449, 574; repayments from Bank of France, *see under* Bank of France
return to gold standard, policy on, 336, 337, 340, 341, 358, 394–5, 427
secrecy of operations, 98, 447, 597, 751, 771; mysteries of the old lady of Threadneedle Street, 446–7, 752; lack of 'clear thinking', 771
seigniorage rights, 344, 357
status: a 'Heaven-sent institution', neither private nor public, 255, 347–8, 468, 504, 675, 752; strait-laced or sensible?, 446–7
Treasury relations with, 188, 255, 257, 258–9; payment for management of national debt, 671–3
Bank of England notes
amalgamation of Treasury wartime issues (Bradburies) and Bank notes, 238, 371; Committee on, *see* Currency and Bank of England Note Issues; involvement with return to gold standard, 268–9, 343–4; JMK examined only on amalgamation of issues, 371 n
Bill for amalgamation (1928), 741, 742, 750, 753; convertibility limited to Bank of England notes, 379; article on (*The Times*, 12 May 1928), 742–9; letter to Churchill on Bill, 749–50, to *The Times*, 750–2; comment on, in *The Nation and Athenaeum*, 753–4
Bank of France
Bank of France notes, 178; note issue, 463–4, under Stabilisation Law, *see below* gold reserves
franc, refusal to peg, 57

repayments of war debt to Bank of England, (1922–27), 704, 706, 709, 711, 722 n, 723, 854; Churchill's settlement with Caillaux (1926), 566
gold reserves, 482, 759, 779–80; control of world supply, 779; available, but not used, to stabilise franc, 180–1, 455, 457–8, 459, 465, 564–6; borrows abroad instead, 233, 433, 565; liquid reserves, 710, 716, 759, 777, 779; proportion of reserves to note issues under Stabilisation Law (1928), 755, 756, 759–60, 777, 779; other terms relating to Bank of France in new law, 756, 757, 758
service of National Debt, 461
U.K. debt to (1929), 798
Bank for International Settlements, 828
Bank of Italy, 777
Bank of Japan, 291
Bank rate
articles on: 'Bank Rate at Four per Cent' (*The Nation and Athenaeum*, 14 July 1923), 100–3; 'Bank Rate and Stability of Prices:...' (*The Nation and Athenaeum*, 21 July 1923), 103–6; 'The Bank Rate' (*The Nation and Athenaeum*, 19 July 1924), 264–7; 'The Bank Rate' (*The Nation and Athenaeum*, 7 March 1925) 333–7; 'The Bank Rate: Five-and-a-Half Per Cent' (*The Nation and Athenaeum*), 16 February 1929), 796–9; 'The Bank Rate' (*The Listener*, 4 October 1929), 834–8
(1894–6), 2½ per cent, 815
(1921), 5½ per cent, 796; fall by half, 81
(1922), further fall, effect on gilt-edged securities, 81–2, 85
(July 1923), raised to 4 per cent, 100–3; discouraging effect on trade, 100, 104
(1924), 4 per cent, 334; threatened rise (June), 234–5
(March 1925), raised to 5 per cent, 333, 335; (August), 4½ per cent, 426, 433
(August 1927), still 4½ per cent, 711–12
(February 1929), raised to 5½ per cent, 796; (October), 6½ per cent, 834–5
for adjustment of monetary disequilibrium, 10; as means of controlling credit, 97–8, 103, 180, 189, 235, 242, 254, 265, 336, 447, 731, 831, or for deflating prices, 771; for restoring industrial equilibrium, 375–7, 385, 391–2, 445, 775, in theory, an automatic process, 395
JMK's ideal object, price stability, 104;

Bradbury, Sir John *(cont.)*
  criticises *Economic Consequences of Mr Churchill* in *The Financial News*, 421, 432, answered, 425–7; other differences with JMK, 337, 753
  'Bradburies' (the Bradbury £1 and 10s notes), 161, 504–5
Brailsford, H. N., editor of *The New Leader*: on 'liberalism and labour' in 1926, 472–3 list of letters, 862
Bramley, Fred, member, Committee on National Debt and Taxation, 1924–7, 295, 305, 312, 314, 315
Brand, R. H., 229, 231, 232
Brazil
  coffee valorisation scheme, 175, 550
  loans to, 277
  Revolutions, 273
Bread
  subsidy ends in Germany, 25–6
  terms of trade between manufactures and, 119
'Britain's Industrial Future', Report of the Liberal Industrial Inquiry, 1928, the 'Yellow Book', 722, 731–8, 804, 816
  see also Liberal Industrial Inquiry
Britannia: review of McKenna's *Post-War Banking Policy* (JMK, 2 November 1928), 770–3
British
  banking tradition, 468
  farmers, 93; workman, 407
  instincts of government, 348, 676
  investors abroad, 277, 707–8; and enterprise, 328–33
  rubber interests, 705
  standard consumption of articles in cost-of-living index, 407
British Association for the Advancement of Science: Liverpool, 1923, Beveridge's Presidential Address to Economics Section, 119, 120, 124, 125, 136, 138; Glasgow, 1928, 766
British Broadcasting Company (BBC), 474
  see also Broadcasts
British Commonwealth, 348
British Empire
  cost of policing, 2
  cotton growers, 156
  investment in, 279, 706; embargo on, 437
  and Liberalism, 638, 732
  output and stock of gold, 165, 167
  trade conditions, 386
British Institute of Philosophical Studies,

discussion chaired by JMK on 'State Control of Industry' (January 1927), 649
Broadbent, Henry, 162
Broadcasts, 144, 544; political broad-casting, 473–6
  JMK: 'University Men in Business', discussion (16 February 1927), 649–61
  'The Bank Rate' (26 September 1929), 834–8
Brokers, 96; Indian, 489
  bill brokers, 466, 684
  see also Stockbrokers
Budgets, 842, 854, 855
  balancing problems, 178, 257, 313; margins, 296; surplus, 354; budgeting for repayment of debt, 844; unbalanced budgets, 58, 179
  in U.K.: (1920), 840; (1922), 4, 63; (1924), article on distribution of national debt and, 215–17; (1925), Budget Speech, on return to gold standard, 337; (1926), 555; and financing of large-scale public enterprise, 696
  on broadcasting the Budget Speech (1926), 473–6
  see also under Churchill, Winston, France; Germany; Snowden, Philip
Building and construction industries, 183, 222, 435, 761–2; unemployment in, 730, 765
  building programmes, 762, 843–4
Building Societies, 695
Bulgaria, 129, 323; Bulgarian loan, 574
Bulk buying and selling, 635
Burma, silver production, 518
Business
  accounting methods, 303–4
  big business, 660, 697, ownership and management, 641–3; small business, 660; Representative Firm, 686
  business losses, 771–2, 833–4
  business world and Lancashire cotton industry, 413–14; application of 'sound business principles', 634
  cash problems in post-war Germany, 11
  definition (Sir Ernest Benn), 650, 657; distinguished from industry, 658–9
  effect on, of rise in Bank Rate, 100, 336, of changes in quantity of credit, 771–2, 798–9
  family business, 651–2, 657–8
  investment advice for business firms, 87, 92
  secretiveness, 597, 644, 697
  'University Men in Business', broadcast discussion, 649–61

Business *(cont.)*
  weighed down by timidity', 221; Liberal
    encouragement to 'launch out', 446
  see also Enterprise
Business administration, as a career, 697
  'The Organisation of Business', chapter in
    Yellow Book drafted by JMK, 731
Business cycle, 81–2, slump, 833
  see also Credit cycle
Businessmen
  addressed by JMK on Liberal Plan to end
    Unemployment (1929), 826
  Bagehot on, 466; JMK's view of, 545, of
    third generation businessmen, 585, 652;
    Tory picture of, 144; University men as,
    649–61 *passim*
  international connections, 70; earnings on
    foreign business, 835
  market preoccupation of, 642
  and rate of interest, 7–9; in a boom, 189;
    in depressions, 445, 803, 838
  return to gold at parity, effect on, 346
  the right people to run public services,
    696–7
  views on taxation, 677
  windfall profits from inflation, 785–8
Buxton, W. L., Assistant Secretary, Com-
    mittee on Industry and Trade, 1925–9,
    383

Cabinet, 347; Baldwin's Cabinet and the coal
    (general) strike of 1926, 533, 544, 560,
    562; Liberal Shadow Cabinet, 1926, 538
Cabinet Ministers, 696, 805
Ca' canny, 443, 444, 448–9
Caillaux, Joseph, French Finance Minister,
    461, 565, 566
Cambridge
  booksellers, 664
  during general strike, 544
  Liberal Summer Schools at (1923), 113,
    (1927), 695; meetings of Liberal Indus-
    trial Inquiry Committee, 731
Cambridge Borough: election campaigns:
    October 1924, speech by JMK in Corn
    Exchange, and public letter on behalf of
    Liberal candidate, 324–5; 1929, cam-
    paign for Sir Maurice Amos, 816, 818–19
Cambridge Economic Handbooks, 817
Cambridge Institute of Bankers: notes for
    inaugural address to (JMK, October
    1927), 724–6
Cambridge University
  JMK engaged at, 357 n 1, 593, 659, 824;
    as Bursar of King's College, on Colleges

and the Tithe Bill, 451–3; represented
    by JMK at celebrations in Moscow and
    Leningrad, 434
  engineering labs, 655
  Henderson's career at, 816–17
  industrial careers through Appointments
    Board, 653–4
  Union: JMK as undergraduate sees Lloyd
    George at, 806; speech at (1928), 768;
    Henderson as President of, 817
Cambridge University Liberal club, 735;
    invitation of University Liberals to JMK
    to stand for University (1928), 729,
    773–4; campaign for Henderson, 816–17
Can Lloyd George Do It?, (H. D. Henderson
    and JMK), 808, 815; publication (10
    May 1929), 819; White Paper counter-
    blast, 819, answered in *The Nation and
    Athenaeum* (18 May 1929), 819–24
Canada
  competition from Canadian coal, 399
  gold: output and reserves, 165; gold cost of
    living, 201, 365, 384
  investment: in Grand Trunk Railway,
    98–9; trustee loans, 317
  wheat, 92, 273, 274
Cannan, Professor Edwin
  takes part in League of Nations conference
    on unemployment (March 1924), 182–4,
    186–7, 188, 189; agreements and differ-
    ences with JMK on monetary theory,
    191–3
  discusses monetary reform at R.E.S. annual
    meeting (June 1924), 206, 207, 208
Capital
  accumulation of, 79, 124, 844; tax on, 840,
    846, 852, *see also* Capital levy; national,
    estimated ownership of, in U.K., 687;
    unimportant compared with national
    income, 688, 781
  capital development at home, instead of
    abroad, 237, 284, 409–10; shortage of
    capital for, 80, 321, of outlets for
    available capital, 226; state encourage-
    ment for, 221–4, 229–32, 322, 646, 832–3,
    for productive expenditure, 222, 225–6,
    367; repayment of national debt should
    be geared to, 282, 311–12, 367, 692;
    national capital already in semi-state ente-
    rprise, 696; the 'sensible' approach to,
    446; Liberal plan for, 733–4, 806–15,
    821–4; discouraged by deflation, 226,
    264, by Treasury economy campaign,
    762, 765, 805. *See also under* Foreign
    investment

INDEX

Consumption (*cont.*)
  as a source of capital expansion, 822
Consumption goods, 134–5, 235
  staple articles of consumption as monetary
  standard, 167; in cost of living indexes,
  407
  working class, 827, 829, 834; (as Class B in
  price categories), 427, 429–32, 434
Contracts, 45–7, 64, 161; loans tied to, 70;
  standard forms of, 600
Conversion Loan, 80, 81, 86, 93, 94, 105,
  189–90, 199, 203. *See also under* Loans
Convertibility
  of currencies into gold, 89, 166, 254, 292;
  in Sweden, 214; return to, in U.K.,
  343–4, 373, under Gold Standard Act,
  1925, 379
  inconvertible currencies and credit control,
  103, 339
  of notes in India, 502
Coolidge, Calvin, President of the United
  States of America, 551
Co-operative societies, 695
Copper
  imports, 155; in abundant supply, 442
  prices, 92, 363, 383, 427
  silver a by-product of, 478, 485–6; copper
  interests and price of silver, 490
Corporations, 286, 438; and taxation, 298–9;
  investment problems, 320
  Bank of England as a corporation, 347–8
Cost of living
  effect on, of exchange movements, 228,
  427–8; internal stability of, *vs* exchange
  stability, 342; results of return to gold at
  pre-war par, 386–9, 399, 400, 413, 552–4
  gold cost of living in England and other
  countries, 352–3, 364–5, 384–5, 401, 419,
  663; gold cost of production, 443, 449
  index numbers, 321, 364, 384, 395, 406–7,
  427, 430–1, 629, 663
  wages and: out of line with wage level, 66–7,
  413, 762; in sheltered industries, 394–5,
  402, 411, 428, 662; proposals for coal,
  527
Cost of production
  in coal industry, 532, 536
  in cotton spinning, 578, 585, 620; increased
  by short-time working, 582–3, 587, 608
  discrepancy between internal and external,
  413, 426, 836, due to excessive gold value
  of sterling, 405, 443, 449, 823–4
  overhead costs, 582, 583, 596, 620, 622, 669
  also mentioned, 268, 392–3, 552
Cotton Control Board, 817

Cotton industry, Lancashire, 574
  articles and speeches on: 'The Position of
  the Lancashire Cotton Trade' (13
  November 1926), 578–87; 'The Prospects of the Lancashire Cotton Trade'
  (27 November 1926), 587–92; 'The
  Cotton Yarn Association (24 December
  1926), 593–601; address to spinners of
  American cotton (4 January 1927),
  601–6; letter to *Manchester Guardian* on
  the Association (10 January 1927),
  607–9; 'The Progress of the Cotton Yarn
  Association' (27 August 1927), 610–14;
  speech on the Association in Manchester
  Town Hall (6 September 1927), 614–21;
  'The Retreat of The Cotton Yarn Asso-
  ciation' (19 November 1927), 622–7;
  letter to *Manchester Guardian Commer-
  cial* on the attempt at amalgamation (27
  November 1927), 628–9; discussion of
  'Post-war Depression in The Lancashire
  Cotton Industry', at Royal Statistical
  Society (17 January 1928), 629–31; 'The
  Lancashire Cotton Corporation' (2 February 1928), 632–6; letter to *Manchester
  Guardian* on statistical work of Cotton
  Yarn Association (25 April 1929), 637
  American branch (coarse cottons): the
  section of industry most in trouble,
  582–7, 588–91, 615–16, 624, 628; in the
  Cotton Yarn Association, 594–601, 609,
  610–13, 616–18, 624–5, 632; JMK's
  speech to, 601–6; unhelpful attitude of
  other sections, 626–7; margins, 598, 602,
  603, 609; pre- and post-war, 629–30;
  financial problems solved by formation
  of Lancashire Cotton Corporation, 634
  export trade, 627; decay of, 579–84, 587–8,
  595, 608, 612–13, 615, 618, 622, 631;
  marketing weaknesses, 621, 634; declining trade with China, 413–14, 625
  fine cotton goods, 581–2, 594, 626–7;
  advantage to, of Association, 603
  management: unorganised individualism,
  584, 590, 591, 596–7, 610, 612, 617, 619,
  626–7; need for rationalisation, 579, 584,
  592, 607, 622; for organised curtailment
  of output, 616; alternatives, bankruptcy,
  cartels, combines, 625; JMK's proposal
  for cartel, 586, 589, 591, 592, 622–3;
  Cotton Association an attempt, 593–4,
  600, 605, 608, 623
  financial unsoundness, 591–2, 597, 603,
  621; decline of profit percent on turnover, 685–6; lack of working capital,

877

INDEX

Credit *(cont.)*

to keep prices steady, 161; to tide over seasonal shortages of cash, 89; to avoid cyclical unemployment, 362

restriction of credit, 354; to deflate prices, 241–2, 243, 432–3, 445, 449–50, medicine too nasty to swallow, 426; after return to gold standard, 363, 369, subordinated to American credit system, 341–2, 344–5, 372; to reduce wages, 375, 385, 417, 803; to reverse adverse gold movement, 376–7; over-enhanced by return to parity, 390–1; result seen in 1928, 731, 771–2, prices but not costs deflated, 762

based on confidence, 35–6

cooperative credit for cotton industry, 600, 606

Exports Credits Scheme, 405

of foreign borrowers, 70; control to discourage foreign, but not home loans, 266, 377, 810

Genoa scheme for international control, 377

gold as criterion for regulation of credit, 335; legal formulas linking note issues to gold, effect on credit, 744–5, 778, 780, 854; in France, 181

gold standard party *versus* monetary reformers, credit policy, 338–42, 346; both, a managed system, 340

individual and national credit, 187–8

for industry and business, not price but volume important, 764–5, 798–9, 829–31, 837–8

Inter-Allied credits, ended in 1919, 90

Liberal (JMK) policy on, 324; 'sensible' approach, 447, 720–1, 803

as means of economising use of gold, 209

post war inflation of, 153, deflation, 97–8; in Germany, 11

in United States, 269, 289–90, 334

Credit cycle, 159, 167, 184, 207–8, 223, 243, 335, 373

Credit-money, 339–40, 348

Creditors and debtors: and changes in value of currency, 45–9, 74, in value of gold, 176; in cotton industry, 632–3; prime borrowers, 851

debtor and creditor countries, 53, 176; U.K. as debtor, 835, in wartime, borrower and lender, 789–90

see also under Allies

'Critic', writer of a letter to *The Manchester Evening Chronicle*, 636

Crook, W. M., of London, 542

Crops

as base for standard value of money in India, 496–501

movements, finance for, 89

withheld in expectation of rising market in U.S., 551–2

world wheat crops, 92–3

Crown, Czech monetary unit, 59–60

Crown Colonies, 546

Cuba: sugar restriction scheme, 550, 552

Cunliffe, Lord, formerly Governor of Bank of England

Chairman, Committee on Currency and Foreign Exchanges, 235 n 6; Report (1918), 101, 117, 235–6, 239, 243; as basis for Currency Committee of 1924, 238, 241, 244, 258, 262, 291

Currency

articles on: 'Currency Policy and Unemployment' (*The Nation and Athenaeum*, 11 August 1923), 113–18; 'The Committee on the Currency'(*Economic Journal*, June 1925), 371–8; 'Comment on the Currency and Bank Notes Bill' (*The Nation and Athenaeum*, 16 June 1928), 753–4

Notes for a speech at the National Liberal Club on 'Currency Policy and Social Reform' (13 December 1923), 158–62

demand for, not dependent on price level, 243; affected by use of cheques, 244

in Germany: shortage of (1919), 11, 13, 14–15, 21–3; foreign, used as reserves, 17, 42; suggested paper and gold as separate currencies, 41–3

international, Marshall on, 162–3

management of, 163, 248; in history, 338–40, 358, 492, debasement, 397; Indian, 493; danger of binding currency unit to gold, 341–2; proposals for Currency Bill (JMK) in 1925, 344; letters to *The Times* on, 344–9; currency not self-regulating, 493

stabilisation for European currencies: at pre-war gold parity *vs* current value, 43–60; for sterling, *see under* Sterling; for franc, *see under* Francs, foundations on which credit of a currency rests, 179; stable volume of, takes care of balance of trade, 30–1; stability of currency and prices, 831

Currency and Bank of England Note Issues, Committee on, June 1924, 238, 239, 371;

Enterprise (*cont.*)
Trade Facilities Act useless, 231–2; in coal-mines, 528; taxation and, 846
see also under Capital
Entrepreneurs
and changes in value of money, 184–5; depreciation a benefit to, 49; under regime of money-control, 159; in war finance, 785, 788
Government as, 810
see also Businessmen
Equation of exchange, 120–1
Equilibrium
in balance of trade, 31
in coal trade, between output, prices and wages, 537
with our environment, 833
of exchange, 57; disequilibrium, *see under* Exchange
fiscal, in France, 179, and in England, 460
international, and wages, 837
between population and means of existence, 833
and restoring sterling parity, 62, 65–7
of sheltered and unsheltered prices, 663–4
'Essays on Money and the Exchanges', first proposed title for *Tract on Monetary Reform*, 76
Eton College, JMK at, 162
Eugenists, 136
Europe
crops, 92–3, 129–30
economic and political instability, 65, 98, 115, 123, 153, 220; bank reserves exhausted, 167; dear money, 265; depreciation, 298, 401
overpopulation, 120, 125, 137, 139–40, 141
past catastrophes, 5; reconstruction schemes, 634
U.K. and: military commitments in, 2; loss of markets, 3, 100; flight from sterling, 269
U.S., seasonal debts to, 572
wages, 387–8
European Currency and Finance (U.S., 1925), including article by JMK 'The United States and Gold', 289 n 2, 370
Evening Standard, The, Lord Beaverbrook's paper, 416, 769–70; publishes three articles on 'Unemployment and Monetary Policy' (22, 23, 24 July 1925, expanded into *The Economic Consequences of Mr Churchill*), 416–17, 418, 421, 762
other articles and letters: 'Why Labour's

Surtax is Bad Finance' (22 November 1927), 701–3; 'How to Organise a Wave of Prosperity' (31 July 1928), 761–6, correspondence on, 766–8; 'Mr Lloyd George's Pledge' (19 March 1929), 804–8; controversy with Sir Laming Worthington-Evans (April 1929), 808–16, 'A Cure for Unemployment' (19 April), 808–12, letters to Editor (30 April), 812–14, (7 May), 814–16
Excess profits duty, 687, 787, 790; 'Objections to taxation of excess profits', 788
Exchange
articles on: 'The Foreign Exchanges and the Seasons' (*The Nation and Athenaeum*, 19 May 1923), 87–91; 'The Arithmetic of the Sterling Exchange' (*The Nation and Athenaeum*, 13 June 1925), 379–81
Bank-rate policy, centred on, 234–6, 265–6, 345
equilibrium: no automatic mechanism, 57; three remedies for disequilibrium between internal prices and exchange, 385, 397–8, 402, 408, 411–12; adjustment of exchange preferable, 356; prevented by return to gold at par, 422
exchange deterrent *versus* interest incentive, 380–2, 713–15
exchange policy for India, 508–9
fixed *versus* fluctuating: for Germany, 38–41; advantages of stabilised exchange, 37–8, 40–1, for seasonal needs, 52–7, 73, 89–91; advantages of fluctuating, 397; stabilised prices *versus* fixed exchange, *see under* Prices; pegged exchange advised for France, 56, 455, 456, 564; Allied exchanges unpegged in 1919, 55; pegged and unpegged, comparative effects on price adjustments, 75–6, 345
free foreign market in, 39
German: rate of exchange for exports and for imports, 26–7; and balance of trade, 31; plan of the four experts, no regulations, fixed exchange, 37–9; a stabilising policy, 41; of the three experts, no fixed rate, a supportive policy, 41; speculation in, *see under* Speculation
movements of sterling exchange: fluctuations between American and (1920–4), 400, 422–3; effect on, of excessive foreign payments, 236–7, 283–4, 328–9; down to its true economic level (June 1924), 236, 355, 422, below parity (July), 240; in disequilibrium (March 1925),

Gold Standard (*cont.*)
Great Britain: pre-war, 441; ten years without (1914–24), 176, 191–2, 241; Cunliffe Committee recommendation for return to, at pre-war parity (1918), 238, *see also under* Cunliffe, Lord; prospect of return to, 212, 214, 238, 290–1, 292, 336, speculative anticipation, 343, 709–10; argument against, 160, 345–6, 349–52, 356, 360, 373, 388–9, 431, 740; 'Return-to-Gold Controversy', 351, 444–5; suggested terms (March 1925), 343–4; Gold Standard party, 361
return to, at pre-war gold parity (28 April 1925), 337, 354, 357, 364–5, 382, 384, 520–1; terms, 357–8, 362, 365–6, 377; 'Bill to facilitate the return to a gold standard', 362, 365, 370; Gold Standard Act, 1925, 378–9; a year later, 508, 552–6 consequences of return, 388–400 *passim*, 420, 545, 796, 801, 824; effect on exports, 384–5, 595, 812–13, on exchange, 409, 431–2, 713, on burden of national debt, 693; disequilibrium between sheltered and unsheltered prices, 373–6, 385, 435–6, 663; falling prices, 731; three remedies, 353–4, 432–4; embargo on foreign investment, 359, 377, 573; 'correct policy' politically impossible, 427, 446, 833
versus price stability, or credit management, as U.K. policy, 106, 161, 248, 250–1, 338–9, 340–2, 344–6, 348–9
in general: general return to, 492, 507, effect on value of gold, 174–5, 290–1, on gold supplies, 759, 775; objections to, 345, 366, 371 n, 569–70, doubts on merit of gold as standard of value, 335, 389, 409, 507–8, 'a barbarous relic', 519
America: adoption of gold standard (1898), 518, and the 'gold-standard game', 799; Japan and Russia, adoption in 1897, 518; Sweden, return to, 214, 365, 384
proposed for India, 476; Memorandum on, 477–9; JMK examined on proposal (22 March 1926), 480–524; main objections to proposal, 480–1, 485–8, 490, 516; his advice, leave Indian system as it is, 491–2, 496, 501, 508, 524
also mentioned, 164, 707
Golden yoke, the, 354
Goods, *see* Commodities
Goschen, George Joachim, Viscount, 256

Government
Agenda and non-Agenda, 568
and bank rate, relation to Bank of England, 255
expenditure, 2, 402; in Government Departments, 672–4, 765; economy on, 443–4, 674, 762; productive capital expenditure, 676, 685, 809, 840, 843, 844, 850; finance and inflation, 116, 339; Finance Accounts, 671–4
governmental control in the three economic epochs, 438; present and future role in industry, 643–8, 695–8; proposed assistance to coal industry, 526–7, 529; as entrepreneurs, 810
as party to contract with bondholders, 255–6; guarantee on trustee investment securities, 282, 285–8
see also Coalition Governments; Conservative Governments; Labour Governments; *and under* State
Graham, William, Labour M.P., 701
Grain bills, 715
Granta, The, sketch of H. D. Henderson, 817–18
Grand Trunk Railway, Canada, 97, 98–9, 283
Graphic, The, 194
Great Britain
consumption of raw cotton, 580
deflation, 116
gold: reserves, 175, 291–2, 752 n 6; gold value of paper currency, 201; gold cost of living, 364–5, 384; loans not fixed in terms of gold, 176, *but see* 167
investment abroad, 275–88, in U.S., 706–8
population, 122–3, 140
prices, Great Britain and United States, 349, 430–2
wheat imports, 274–5; British wheat, 273
see also British; England; United Kingdom
Great Western Railway, 198, 203
Greece, 277, 323
Gregory, T. E., 182

Hall, Professor Fred: member, Committee on National Debt and Taxation, 1924–7, 295, 303, 310; 1925, 839, 845, 848–9, 849, 850–2, 852, 853, 854, 855; submits his own Report, 689
Hall, Ray, 719 n
Hamburg, 568; JMK in (1922), 15
Hamilton, R. G., Secretary to Committee on National Debt and Taxation, 1924–7, 294, 295, 839; his part in preparing the Report, 676

INDEX

Housing (*cont.*)

Government policy on, 810; Snowden's Budget provisions for, 216; Housing Bill (1924), 273; Treasury economy on, 762, 805; subsidy, 814, 833; in France, 759

housing schemes, 204, 283, 808; programme of 1920, 367, 844; to absorb labour, 410, 809

Liberal policy on, 324, 824, 826, 827

loans to finance foreign housing, 224

mass production of, 222, 231

new houses (1924), 683; as part of national wealth, 781

in purchasing-power-parity theory, 364, 383–4

shortage of capital for, 80, 149; abundant resources for, 684; and repayment of national debt, 296, 314

slum clearance, 765

working-class: need for, 123; an obstacle to labour mobility, 396, 404; burden of rates on, 737

Hulton, Sir Edward, 194

Hulton Press, 194

Human nature, 159, 347–8, 465, 514

humanitarianism, 441

Hungary

default on loans, 277, 323

gold, 175, 291

wheat, 92, 129

Hunsdon, Lord, 753

Hurst, Sir Hugo, of the General Electric Company, 656–7

Illustrated Sunday Herald, The, 194

Imagination, 531; power of ideas, 665; JMK's bright ideas, 688

Imperial Bank of India, 503, 505

Imperial Chemical Industries Limited, 726, 727–8, 815

Import duties, 3, 149–50, 156, 488, 547

see also Tariffs, Protection

Imports

additional, for 'development' programmes, 807, 811, 823, 829

of 'manufactured' articles, 155–6

'our income', 149

prices, response to alterations in exchange, 21–2; after return to gold, 571

wheat, 25

also mentioned, 31, 57, 705

Imports and exports, 72, 148–9, 154–5, 283–4, 329, 834, 835

effect on, of discrepancy between internal

and external prices, 67, 235, 400, 437; with pegged exchange, 75–6

German post-war, 26–7, 28; between U.K. and Germany and France, 1914, 1923, 154

gold export and import points, 380–2, 522, 712

manufactured exports and food imports, 126–8, 130–5, 137–40; ratio of real interchange for, 135, 283

visible import surplus, invisible export surplus (1922–27), 704–6, 719, 723

see also Balance of payments; Balance of trade; Exports; Imports

Inchcape, Lord, 673–4

Income tax, 3, 674, 701–2, 855

and capital levy, 852–3; effect of levy on, 688; levy preferable if tax very high, 842, as in 1920, 840, 845, but not when tax low, 688, 842–3, 845

Colwyn Report on, 677–82, 702; tables showing tax on earned and unearned incomes, 678–81

with depreciating currency, 24

on dividends, 80; double, on foreign securities, 706; influence on rate of interest, 204, 381; Savings Certificates exempt from, 206

in Germany, 17–18, 19

no effect on prices, 677; not responsible for trade lethargy, 702, 846

a deterrent to saving, 295, 298–9, 841, 846; proposal for reorganising income and supertax in interests of corporate earnings, 298–307

Income Tax Commission, 301

Incomes

current incomes and accumulated wealth, 313, 688, 852

per capita, in France and Great Britain, 456

and taxation, *see* Income tax

Independent Labour Party, JMK's address to 'The Future Balance of British Industry' (4 August 1926), 568

Index-linked securities, proposal for, 297, 319–22

Index numbers

American, 498

for internal and external prices (sheltered and unsheltered), 364, 374, 384, 395, 429–31

Statist, and cotton industry, 629

see also Bowley, A. L.; Board of Trade; Cost of living

INDEX

Loans (*cont.*)

mortgages, 332

short loans, 9–10, 101–2, 308–10, 319, 797–8; and gold points, 251–2; in foreign indebtedness, 704, 706, 709–20

tied loans, 70

for war finance, 789–91; loans to Allies, 792–3, 854. Loans to prevent war, 794–5. *See also under* Bank of France; War loans *see also* Foreign Investment; Investment; Trustee Acts

Local Loans Stock, 80, 199, 203, 226, 296, 314

Lombard Street, 234

London

bookshops, 664

clearing banks, *see under* Banks

financial editors, 455

in general strike, 530

JMK and: marriage to Lydia Lopokova (4 August 1925), 425; meets deputation from Lancashire cotton industry in, 593; address to London Liberal Candidates Association (1927), 638–48; attends meetings of Liberal Industrial Inquiry Executive Committee, 731

League of Nations Union Conference (1924), 182

newspapers, 194

prices in Germany and, 22

as seat of Government, 36

underground, 283

wages, 408

London, City of

Bagehot on, 465–6, 470, 471

foreign loans raised in, 59, 200, 202, 227, 236–7, 280, 335, 571, 704, 705–6, 747; embargo on, 359, 574; refused to Germany in 1919, 35; short-term loans, 251, 376; principal international loan market, 226–7

international banking, 483, 571–2, 742, 747–8; centre for international balances, 555, 571, 710

JMK and: City men and JMK's system, 260; the prophet Jonah speaks to them, 162; election speech to City business men (1929), 824, 826

money market, 252, 271, 477, 575; London the financial centre of the world, 466; 'freedom of finance' essence of its success, 72

and Mr Snowden's budget, 215

its sacred mysteries, 105, 273, 446; faith in

pre-war monetary and credit arrangements, 159; threatened with the doom of Nineveh, 161–2; its copy-book maxims, 230, 272

sales of gold, 173, 344, 483, 485

and newspaper finance, 197

sterling, views on return to parity, 214, 262, 264

tradition on use of reserves, 35, 467–8

see also Stock Exchange

London County Council stocks, 204

London, Midland and Scottish Railway, 198, 203

London and New York

competition in international banking, 748

and credit for India, 484–5

floating balances between, 53, 709–10, 715–17; flow of funds on capital account, 350, 370; effect of cheap money in New York, 265–6, 429

gilt-edged security prices, 82

gold reserves, 779

relative rates of interest, 101, 126–7, 226–7, 317, 390–1, 711–15; discount rates, 334–5, 379–82, 796–7 799; terms for foreign borrowers, 69–72

risks involved in linking money markets, 252, 271

sales and purchase of securities, 708

short-loan market, 102, 251–2, 370

statistics, 722

London and North-Eastern Railway, 198, 203, 204

Long-period

argument against gold standard, 160

changes in value of money, 159

criterion for devaluation, 46, 47–8

policy for home capital development, 409–10

trends, 125, 127

Lopokova, Lydia: engagement to JMK (July 1925), 420–1; marriage (4 August 1925), 425

as Mrs J. M. Keynes, 529, 698, 731, 735, 768, 773

list of letters, 862

Louis XVI, 272

Low, David, 701

Lowe, Robert, Chancellor of the Exchequer, 1868–73, 467

Lubbock, Cecil, Deputy-Governor, Bank of England, letter from, 162, 862

Lunatics, 643

Luxuries, 688

Morgan, Messrs J. P., 181; Treasury borrowing powers from, 379, 382

Morning Post, The
City Editor, 104–5; letter in response to discussions on JMK's articles on monetary policy, 419–20; one of the 'pious school', 443–4
Financial Editor, 456–7

Morris, Frank, writer of a letter to *The Times*, 832; reply to (15 August 1929), 832–4

Mortgages, 332, 601, 633

Moscow, 702
JMK lectures in, 434–42
Moscow Riots (1904–5), 169

Motor industry, 148, 151, 342, 442, 761
motor cars, 520, 825, in U.S., 221, 342; tax on, 155; car for the Prime Minister, 293–4
motor transport, 222–3, 544

Moulton, Henry, *The French Debt Problem*, 456, 461

Muir, Ramsay, member, Liberal Industrial Inquiry Executive Committee, 731

Munitions, 781–2, 785, 791, 795
Minister of Munitions (Churchill), 786–7; programme of 1916, 808

Murray, Sir Alexander Robertson, member, Royal Commission on Indian Currency and Finance, 1926, 480, 519–21

Mussolini, Benito, 58, 446

Napoleonic wars, 61, 74, 339, 368

Nation and Athenaeum, The
passes under control of Liberal group (1923), JMK as chairman, 80, 769–70; repercussions of JMK's articles in press generally, 103, 106, 732, JMK described in *Observer* as 'spuming' like a soda-water siphon in, 768–70; contributions from 'Kaffa' mistaken for JMK's, 769–70
editor, Hubert Henderson, 664, 665, 703, 770, 816, 817; letters to, other than JMK's, 588; editorial lead in discussion on book industry, 664
other contributors to, 665; Lloyd George, 218; Beveridge, 567
readers, 87, 154
also mentioned, 263, 446
articles by JMK: 11 August 1923; 'Currency Policy and Unemployment', 113–18; 6 October 1923, 'Population and Unemployment', 120–4; 17 November 1923, 'The Liberal Party', 143–6; 24 November, 1 December 1923, 'Free Trade', 147–56; 2 February 1924, 'Gold

in 1923', 164–8, 173; 16 February 1924, 'The Prospects of Gold', 173–6; 15 March 1924, 'The Franc', 177–81; 5 April 1924, 'Newspaper Finance', 193, 194–7; 24 May 1924, 'Does Unemployment Need a Drastic Remedy?', 219–23; 7 June 1924, 'A Drastic Remedy for Unemployment: Reply to Critics', 225–31; 19 July 1924, 'The Policy of the Bank of England', 261–7, 26 July, reply to critic, 272–3; 26 July 1924, 'Wheat', 273–5; 9 August 1924, 'Foreign Investment and National Advantage', 275–84; 18 October 1924, 'Defaults by Foreign Governments', 323; 8 November 1924, 'The Balance of Political Power at the Elections', 325–7; 10 January 1925, 'Inter-Allied Debts', 328 n 4; 17 January 1925, 'Some Tests for Loans to Foreign and Colonial Governments', 328–33; 7 March 1925, 'The Bank Rate', 333–7; 21 March 1925, 'The Problem of the Gold Standard', 337–44; 4, 18 April 1925, 'Is Sterling Overvalued?', 349–54, 363; 2 May 1925, 'The Gold Standard', 357–61, 365; 9 May 1925, 'The Gold Standard – A Correction', 362–5, 369; 13 June 1925, 'The Arithmetic of the Sterling Exchange', 379–82; 10, 27, 24 October 1925, 'Soviet Russia', 442; 9 January 1926, 'An Open Letter to the French Minister of Finance...', 455; 16 January 1926, 'The French Franc: A Reply to Comments on "An Open Letter"', 455–60; 30 January 1926; 'Some Facts and Last Reflections about the Franc, 460–5; 20 February 1926, 'Liberalism and Labour', 472; 24 April 1926, 'Coal: A Suggestion', 525–9; 15 May 1926, 'Back to the Coal Problem', 534–7; 12 June 1926, 'The Control of Raw Materials by Governments', 546–52; 26 June 1926, 'The First-Fruits of the Gold Standard', 552–6; 10 July 1926, 'Mr Baldwin's Qualms', 559–63; 17 July 1926, 'The Franc Once More', 563–7; 23 October 1926, 'The Autumn Prospects for Sterling', 568–74; 13 November 1926, 'The Position of the Lancashire Cotton Trade', 578–85; 27 November 1926, 'The Prospects of the Lancashire Cotton Trade', 587–92; 24 December 1926, 'The Cotton Yarn Association', 593–601; 12 February 1927, 'Mr McKenna on Monetary

Orange Book, The (*We Can Conquer Unemployment*), 804
Orthodoxy, 545
 economic, 643, 813; doctrine of foreign investment, 572–3; orthodox gold party, 854; theory of employment, 807
 financial, 783, 785–6; Treasury view of State expenditure, 809, 811
 JMK's unorthodoxy, 695, 785
Output
 average net output of an employed person, 766
 in cotton industry, 583; need to curtail, 588, 595–8, 622–3; quotas fixed by Cotton Yarn Association, 599, 611, 613, 623, 629; percentage of capacity output, 609–10, 612, 616, 624
 current, as main source of war finance, 781–2
 discouraged by deflation, 263
 Liberal policy on, 324
 limitations, to secure better price, 547
 see also Production
Overdrafts, 483, 577, 718; for Germany, 36; to help employment projects, 569
Overseas Trade, Department of, 672
Overstone, Lord, 339
Ownership, *see* Management
Oxford
 JMK and: gives Sidney Ball lecture, 'The End of *Laissez-Faire*' (6 November 1924), 327; speech at Liberal Summer School, 1924, 275–84, 285, debates at Summer School, 1928, 768
 bookshops, 664
 University: and advertising, 658; Colleges, and tithes, 451, 453
Oxford, Lord, *see* Asquith, Herbert

P. and O. (Peninsular and Oriental Steam Navigation Company), 674
Palestine, 2
Panic, 88–9, 467, 470
Paper currencies, gold value of, 201
 paper currency reserve, India, 483, 485, 494–6, 509–10, 522
 see also Currency notes
Paris, 36, 143, 702, 708
 Financial Editors, 455
 gold wages, 351; cost of living, 388, 408
 as international financial centre, 706, 708
 JMK represents International Chamber of Commerce at, 593
 newspapers, 168–72
Paris Conference, 1919, 566

Parity, *see under* Gold standard; Prices; Purchasing power
Parliament, 294, 324; Act of Parliament, 695; qualifications for parliamentary career, 817; dependence upon public opinion, 848
 parliamentary Opposition, 560
Party, 1, 144, 702–3
 broadcasts, 476
 at end of Coalition government, 146
 and the industrial problem, 647
 Labour not a 'party', 145
 Lloyd George's party funds, 539
 party struggle, 145
Peace
 industrial, 350, 360, 375, 385, 534, 649, 697
 Liberal policy for, 2, 5, 146, 325, 648, 816, 817, 818, 819
 population and, 124
 preservation of, through finance, 794–5
Peace Treaty, *see* Versailles, Treaty of
Peel, Sir Robert, 467
Pensions, 2, 402; old-age pensioners, 122–3; proposed for ex-Prime Ministers, 294; pension funds, 320
 in France, 50, 458, 461, 462
Persia, 167
Peru, 167, 323
Pethick-Lawrence, F. W. (1st Baron), M.P., 556
Picard, R., Governor of the Bank of France, 51
Pigou, A. C.: quantity theory of money, 11; opposed to Treasury dogma on unemployment, 809
 member, Committee on the Currency and Bank of England Note Issues, 1924, 238, 239, 371, 676
Pious school, the, 443–4
Pittman Act, on silver prices, 489
Poincare, Raymond, President of France (1913–20), 171–2; Premier (1922–4), 179, 181, 262; (1926–9), 456
Poland, 129, 583
Political Economy Club, 162
Politics
 abusive attacks on, 559–60
 'Balance of Political Power at the Elections' (November 1924), 325–7
 and broadcasting, 473–6
 and the Colwyn Report, 690
 emoluments of a political career, 293–4
 in Europe, effect on business confidence, 100, 115–16
 and journalism, 768–70

INDEX

Runciman, Walter, Liberal M.P. (*cont.*)
'Mr Runciman's Letter' (*The Nation and Athenaeum*, 3 July 1926), 542
Rupees: proposed change from silver to gold, 478, 485–6; JMK's advice to keep silver rupees, 501–2, 516, 518; notes in competition with silver, 503; return to cultivators in terms of, 496–7, advantages of silver over gold coins, 517; proposed 10 rupee or 20 rupee gold coins, 520
silver rupees in paper currency reserve, 494, 509, 516, 519, 523–4; total outstanding, 516, 523
value in terms of sterling, 479, 491, 505–6, 510–11, 515–16, 520, 522; quantity of, in a 'crore', 484 n1
Russia
cotton industry, 580–1
currency depreciation, 48, 178, 179, 740
French loan to, 277, 758–9; defaults on loans, 277, 323, 332
'The French Press and Russia', 168–72
gold reserves, 175, 291; adoption of gold standard (1897), 518
JMK and: visit to Lydia's parents (September 1925), 434, lectures at Bicentennial Celebrations of Academy of Sciences, 'The Economic Position of England', 434–37, 'The Economic Transition in England', 438–42; visit in 1928, 741
'Soviet Russia' (*The Nation and Athenaeum*, October 1925), published as *A Short View of Russia* (December 1925), 442
overpopulation, 140, 437
Revolution of 1917, 168, 437; in a transitional era, 438
wheat production, 92, 129
Russo-Japanese war (1904–5), 168, 169
Ryan, John, Chairman and Secretary, Committee for Cotton Yarn Association: arranges meeting with JMK in London, 592–3; initial success, 609, later failure, 626; his wisdom and diplomacy, 632
Rylands, Sir Peter, member, Committee on Industry and Trade, 1924–9, 383, 388, 393–4, 400–2, 415

'Safety First', 825, 827; for sinking funds, 849–50
St Petersburg, 170. *See also* Leningrad
Salesmanship, 659
Salter, F. R., Liberal candidate for Cambridge Borough (1924), letter in support of, 324–5

Samuel, Sir Herbert, Liberal M.P
correspondence on JMK's candidature for University of Cambridge, 774
plan for *concordat* in coal industry, 534–5, 537, 545
president, Liberal Summer School (1927), 695; member, Liberal Industrial Inquiry Executive Committee, 731, 734; his part in 'We Can Conquer Unemployment', 825–6
list of letters, 862
Sao Paulo, 550
Saturday Review, The, 105
Savings
capital saving, 303
compulsory, 302, 785; voluntary, 302, 783–4, 787, 829–30
definition, 810
depreciation of, 38, 49
hazards of, 100; need for direction, 324, 441, 645
of insurance companies, 307
and investment, 810; not automatically balanced, 807–8, 810; conservative *credo* on, 808–9; foreign investment and, 275–6, 284, 335, 376; should go into home capital development, 221–2, 223, 224, 225, 284, 409, 569, 765, 805; trustee savings drawn abroad, 280–1, 282
national savings: diminished, and import controls, 149, and interest rates, 204, 805; lack of outlet at home, 226; estimate of (1924), 683
and newspaper advertising, 197
public opinion and, 304–5; social value of saving, 305, 850
and repayment of national debt, 296, 309, 311, 367–8, 677, 839–40, 850
return to new savings (1921–23), 80–1
taxation, deterrent effect, 295, 296, 298, 301, 307, 677, 841, 846; proposal to lighten burden, 298–300, 302, 304–5, 307
of the unemployed, 828; of the newly employed, 822
see also Investment; Trustee Acts
Savings Banks, 216, 257–8
Savings Certificates, *see* National Savings Certificates
Sazonov, Sergei, Russian Foreign Minister (1912), 171–2
Scandinavia, 291, 323 n
Scarcity
epoch of, 438
scarcity value, 691
of world credit, and gold supplies, 780

913

INDEX

Schacht, Hjalmar, President of Reichsbank, 741

Schiller, Johann von, 732

School of International Studies, Geneva: four lectures given by JMK (July 1924), 828

Schuster, Felix, 269

Science, 79, 124, 160, 161, 639; and business, 659, 726

Scotland: Scotch enterprise, 276, 658, 724

Scott, C. P., editor of *The Manchester Guardian*, 472

Seasonal fluctuations
of exchange, 52–8, 67–8, 73, 75–6, 89–91, 101, 243; seasonal debts, 568, 572; of gold stocks, 746
of farm products, 113–14
of industries, 761; bookselling, 667

Securities
advice to investors on, 93–6, 329–32
American, 707–8; American profits on sterling securities, 355
bond market, 798; international securities market, 706–9
cotton debentures, 633
fixed-interest, 98, 332
in Germany, 18, 19–20; in France, 181
Government, 93, 198–9, 217, 245, 258–9, 340, 354–5, 849; national debt as, 849
held against fiduciary note issue, 247, 258–9; held in Banking Dept of Bank of England, 750, 799; Stock accounts, 673
industrial, 93, 281, 311–12, 314
long-dated, 81, 82, 83, 93–4, 105, 203–4, 281, 310, 335, 380–1, 706, 799; short-dated, 85, 93, 95–6, 203, 204–5; criterion for long- or short-in national debt, 295–6, 308, 319
possible effects on, of capital levy, 853
sterling, sales of, in India, 483, 484, 485, 490, 491, in reserves, 477, 509, 510, 522
see also Bonds, Investment, Loans, War loans

Self-interest, and *laissez-faire* principles, 149, 278

Services
as key industries, 147–8
paid for out of local rates, 737
sensitivity to external prices, 22–3, 25, 360, 364, 383–4

Shakespeare, *The Tempest*, 142–3

Shareholders
in Bank of England, 466–7
in cotton companies, 614, 616, 617, 631, 633
in large-scale business, 651, 697, 725; of the Shell Group, 653; in combines, 642

in newspapers, 195–7

Shell Oil Group, 653

Sherman Anti-Trust law, 551

Shipbuilding, 153, 269; unemployment, 219, 335, 435, 761

Shipping
as invisible exports, 403, 571, 835; net national shipping income, 722–3
sensitivity to external prices (class E3), 428–32
shipping freights, 430, 431; in wartime, 794
unemployment in shipping industry, 435

Shipping, Chamber of, 430

Short period argument against gold standard, 160

short-dated investments, *see under* Securities

Short-time, in cotton industry, 529, 578, 582–4, 586–91, 593, 596–7, 608, 610–11, 612, 616, 624, 627; abandoned by cotton spinners, 593, 596, 600, 622

Short-Time Committee of the Federation of Master Cotton Spinners 596–7, meet JMK in Manchester (22 November 1926), 585–6, 587

Siam, 269

'Siela', *nom-de-plume* used by JMK, 284–5, 293–4

Sieveking, Lance, 650

Silk, 155
artificial silk, 435, 442, 607

Silver
currency: silver-using countries, 64–5; Turkey, 30; China, 64, 488; India, 478, 501, 502, 516–18, *see also* Rupees; in France, 463, demonetisation of silver, 756
demand for, 478, 485; supplies, 478, 485, 518
effect on price of silver if India adopted gold standard, 477, 478–9, 481, 484, 485–90, 503, 513; silver market disrupted, 487, 490, 516, 517
export of, from India, 488; sales of, 487, 488, 490, 503; hoarding, 487, 503, 516, 517
silver controversies in history, 517–18; Pittman silver, 489
silver exchange, 64–5
silver interests, 486, 489, 490, 517; Indian interest in stability, 486, 503, 518

Simon, E. D., member, Liberal Industrial Inquiry Executive Committee, 731

Simon, Sir John, Liberal M.P., 531, 532, 538–9, 545; member, Liberal Industrial Inquiry Executive Committee, 731

914

INDEX

Tokyo, 568, 572, 574

Tomlinson, Fred A., 586–7

Tories, 145, 324, 327, 639; and Liberals, 144, 647, 728, Lloyd George, 540–1

Tourists, 21–3, 28, 89, 720, 835

Tract on Monetary Reform, A

work on, 76, 97; letter to Macmillan on progress (15 January 1923), 76–7; publication (11 December 1923), 158

letters of comment on, 162–4; other comments, 272, reply to Mr Hooper, 347–8; references to, by JMK, 345, 713 n

plans to develop views in a further book, 289

Trade

course of: (1912–23), 130–5; 'straining at the leash' (1922), 65, tendency towards revival (1922–3), 65, 78; 'discouraged', (July 1923), 97, 98, further discouraged by Bank rate, 100, 103–4, 237, and by occupation of Ruhr, 115; (1923–4), 392–3; (1924–5), 386–7; state of, October 1925, 442; (1927), 677, 678; (1928), 729–31, 761; course of foreign trade, (1881–1914), 128

and currency stabilisation, 49, in seasonal trades, 52–60, 68; deterring influence of sterling exchange, 64–5, 67, 73, 136, 346; effect of pegged exchange, 75–6, of price fluctuations, 104; volume of currency dependence on, 243

home investment as stimulating to, as foreign, 328; transference of resources from export to internal trade, 411–12; repayment of national debt as an aid to, 309–11; need for improved technique, 78–9; hampered by deflation and inflation, 153, 267

international, 113, 124, 514–15, 717, 797, 800; different role of, to U.K. and U.S.A., 70, 415, U.S. cheap money policy a stimulus to, 721; and the investment market, 283–4, investment in foreign trade, 275–6; foreign trade in wartime, 130–1; and control of raw materials, 546–52; volume of U.K. annual foreign trade, 747–8

and the return to gold parity, 268, 270, 360

sheltered and unsheltered trades, 364, 383–5, 402

taxation not cause of lethargy, 846

trades suitable for protection, 147–9

in U.S.A., 399–400

see also Balance of trade; Commerce;

Exports; Imports; Industry; Industry and Trade, Committee on; Manufactures

Trade associations, 613

see also under Cotton

Trade bills, 102, 104, 714–15, 797

Trade cycle, 160, 336. *See also* Booms; Business cycle; Depressions; Slumps

Trade Facilities Act, 222, 224, 226, 229, 231–2, 287, 405, 844

Trade Unions

affiliation with Labour Party, 472

in general strike, 533–4, 543, 545–6; their loyalty, 543

national debt held by, 216

power, for good or ill, 221, 639–40; rigid organisation, 228, 404

resistance to wage reductions, 183, 230–1, 360, 396, 436

in the Third economic epoch, 438, 439–40

unemployment figures, 153

also mentioned, 554, 684

Trades Union Council (T.U.C.): and general strike, 530, 532, 533, 537, 543, 544

Transfer duty, 199

forced transference, 785–6

Transitional period

of adjustment to gold parity, 555, 824; from higher to lower price, 121, 242; in U.S.A., pending return of Europe to gold standard, 290

in banking, 724; relations between Treasuries and Central banks, 505

in currency stabilisation, 24, 32–3; for sterling-dollar exchange, 61, 73

'The Economic Transition in England', 438–42; the age of transition, 638–9, 642–3, 646

Transport

canals, 287; tramways, 276

Ministry of, 672, 674

technicians, 222–3

transport charges, 620; in cost of living, 389, 394

wages, 768

see also Motors; Railways, Roads; Shipping

Transvaal, 165

Transylvania, 93

Treasury

American debt, repayments, 101, 265

cost to, of capital levy, 687–8

Financial Controller, 258; salaries and expenses, 672

investments: policy on foreign loans, 72, 331, 343, for India, 484, 574; proposed

919

THE COLLECTED WRITINGS OF JOHN MAYNARD KEYNES

Managing Editors:
Professor Sir Austin Robinson and Professor Donald Moggridge